Los Angeles County 2012A Tax Sale

Enhanced Catalog of Properties

Volume 1: Agoura Hills-Malibu

Agoura Hills, Calabasas

Apex-Austin Management, LLC

Los Angeles County 2012A Tax Sale

Enhanced Catalog of Properties

Apex-Austin Management, LLC • P.O. Box 17386 • Anaheim, CA. 92817-7386
(714) 312-6626 • www.apex-austin.com • robert.lee@apex-austin.com

Volume 1: Agoura Hills-Malibu Region

Agoura Hills, Calabasas

Contents

Volume 4: Downey-Norwalk, Long Beach-Lakewood Region

Artesia, Bellflower, Cerritos, Downey, Hawaiian Gardens, Lakewood, Long Beach, Norwalk, Paramount, Signal Hill, Wilmington

Contents   i

Volume 5: East San Gabriel Valley Region

Avacado Heights - Bassett, Azusa, Baldwin Park, Claremont, Covina, Diamond Bar, Glendora, Hacienda Heights, Industry, Irwindale, La Puente, La Verne, Pomona, Rowland Heights, San Dimas, San Jose Hills, Valinda, Walnut, West Covina, West Puente Valley

Contents   i

Volume 6: Inglewood, Los Angeles Region

Del Aire, Gardena, Hawthorne, Inglewood, Lawndale, Lennox, West Alondra Park, Westmont / West Athens

Contents   i

Volume 7: Los Angeles Region

Adams-La Brea, Bel Air, Beverly Hills, Boyle Heights, Brentwood, Crenshaw, Culver City, Downtown, Eagle Rock-Glassell

Volume 8: Los Angeles Region

El Sereno, Green Meadows, Harbor City, Highland Park

Volume 9: Los Angeles Region

Hollywood, Hollywood Hills, Ladera Heights, Lincoln Heights, Los Feliz, Mar Vista, Miracle Mile

Volume 10: Los Angeles Region

N Shoestring, Pacific Palisades, Palms, Playa Del Rey, San Pedro, Silverlake/Chinatown, South Park, South Vermont, Venice, Vermont Square, View Park - Windsor Hills, W Adms-Expo Park, Watts, West Hollywood, West LA, Westchester, Westlake, Wholesale

Contents

Volume 11: Newhall Region

Agua Dulce, Canyon Country, Castaic - Val Verde, Santa Clarita, Stevenson Ranch

Contents i

Volume 12: North Antelope Valley Region

Del Sur, Edwards, Gorman

Contents i

Volume 13: North Antelope Valley Region

Hi Vista

Contents i

Volume 14: North Antelope Valley Region

Lake Hughes, Lake Los Angeles

Contents i

Volume 15: North Antelope Valley Region

Lancaster, Leona Valley, Quartz Hill

Volume 16: Pasadena Region

Altadena, Kinneloa Mesa, La Canada Flintridge, La Crescenta - Montrose, Pasadena, San Marino, South Pasadena

Volume 17: San Fernando Valley Region

Burbank, Canoga Park, Chatsworth, Encino, Glendale, Granada Hills, Mission Hills, Newhall, North Hills, North Hollywood, Northridge, Pacoima, Panorama City, Reseda

Volume 18: San Fernando Valley Region

San Fernando, Sherman Oaks, Studio City, Sun Valley, Sunland, Sylmar, Tarzana, Tujunga, Van Nuys, Winnetka, Woodland Hills

Contents   i

Volume 19: South Antelope Valley Region

Acton, Angeles National Forest, Littlerock, Llano

Contents   i

Volume 20: South Antelope Valley Region

Palmdale, Pearblossom, South Antelope Valley, Valyermo

Volume 21: South Gate-East Los Angeles Region

Bell, Bell Gardens, Commerce, East Los Angeles, Florence-Graham, Huntington Park, Maywood, South Gate, Walnut Park

Volume 22: Southwest San Gabriel Valley, Upper San Gabriel Valley, Whittier Region

Alhambra, Arcadia, Duarte, East San Gabriel, El Monte, La Habra Heights, La Mi-rada, Monrovia, Montebello, Monterey Park, Pico Rivera, Rosemead, San Gabriel, Santa Fe Springs, Sierra Madre, South El Monte, South San Gabriel, South Whittier, Temple City, West Whittier - Los Nietos, Whittier

Volume 23: Palos Verdes, Santa Monica, South Bay Cities, Torrance Region

El Segundo, Hermosa Beach, Lomita, Rancho Palos Verdes, Redondo Beach, Rolling Hills, Santa Monica, Torrance

Volume 24: Property Cross References

Index of Properties by Auction ID and by Location

Introduction

This book covers the Agoura Hills-Malibu region of Los Angeles County. This is represented by the communities of: Agoura Hills, Calabasas.

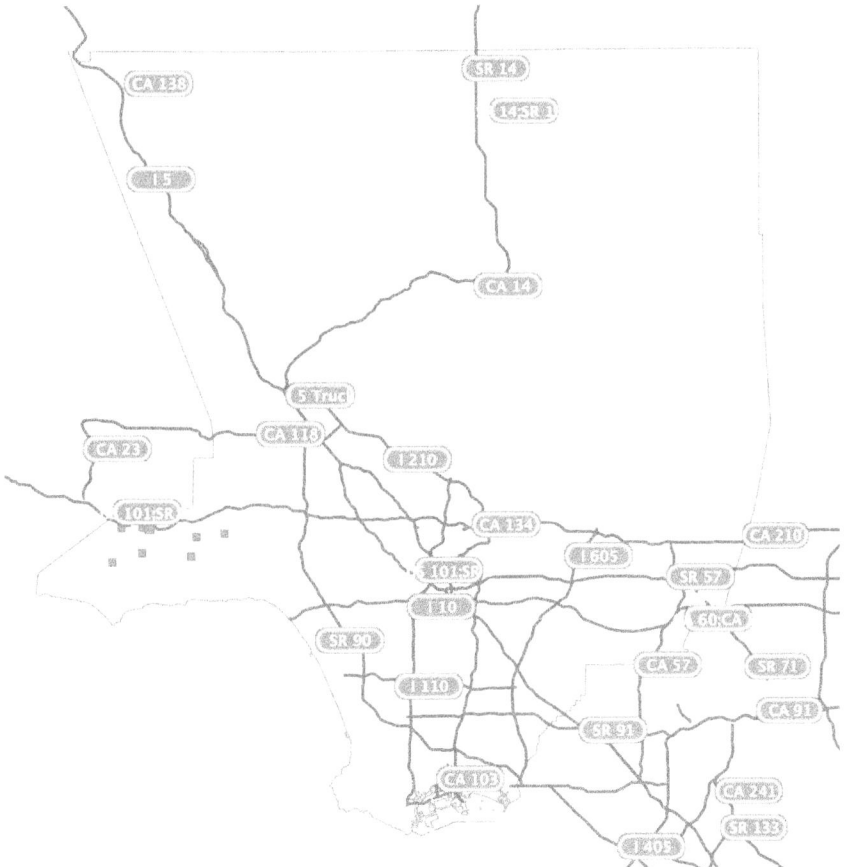

Figure 1.1: Auction properties covered in this book, Volume 1: Agoura Hills-Malibu

74 properties are to be auctioned in Agoura Hills-Malibu, as summarized in Table 1.1. The entries are ordered by starting bid price – lowest bid first.

The Agoura Hills-Malibu region has multiple properties that are assessed to possibly the same entity. Table 1.2 presents this information where it may apply. In some cases, the entity may be assessed for properties both in the Agoura Hills-Malibu region and outside of it. Table 1.2 provide cross references to those books where applicable.

Table 1.1: Properties for auction in the Agoura Hills-Malibu region

Auction ID	Community	Starting Bid	Property Details
97	Agoura Hills	$1,517	See page 300
65	Agoura Hills	$1,576	See page 187
67	Agoura Hills	$1,598	See page 193
66	Agoura Hills	$1,610	See page 190
96	Agoura Hills	$2,009	See page 296
82	Agoura Hills	$2,011	See page 240
5137	Agoura Hills	$2,621	See page 303
35	Agoura Hills	$3,097	See page 37
47	Agoura Hills	$3,245	See page 97
48	Agoura Hills	$3,254	See page 102
50	Agoura Hills	$3,254	See page 112
57	Agoura Hills	$3,254	See page 147
45	Agoura Hills	$3,303	See page 87
58	Agoura Hills	$3,303	See page 152
59	Agoura Hills	$3,334	See page 157
46	Agoura Hills	$3,343	See page 92
44	Agoura Hills	$3,354	See page 82
49	Agoura Hills	$3,361	See page 107
33	Agoura Hills	$3,471	See page 27
34	Agoura Hills	$3,481	See page 32
42	Agoura Hills	$3,805	See page 72
43	Agoura Hills	$3,835	See page 77
56	Agoura Hills	$3,844	See page 142
36	Agoura Hills	$3,894	See page 42
31	Agoura Hills	$3,963	See page 17
41	Agoura Hills	$3,972	See page 67
37	Agoura Hills	$4,002	See page 47
38	Agoura Hills	$4,032	See page 52
32	Agoura Hills	$4,071	See page 22
39	Agoura Hills	$4,799	See page 57
40	Agoura Hills	$4,838	See page 62
77	Agoura Hills	$4,880	See page 220
76	Agoura Hills	$5,823	See page 216
62	Agoura Hills	$6,038	See page 172
2410	Calabasas	$6,149	See page 314
61	Agoura Hills	$7,093	See page 167
51	Agoura Hills	$7,145	See page 117
60	Agoura Hills	$7,151	See page 162
63	Agoura Hills	$7,347	See page 177
26	Agoura Hills	$7,500	See page 13
64	Agoura Hills	$7,643	See page 182
55	Agoura Hills	$7,903	See page 137
52	Agoura Hills	$8,201	See page 122
111	Calabasas	$8,238	See page 306
53	Agoura Hills	$8,315	See page 127
54	Agoura Hills	$8,704	See page 132
74	Agoura Hills	$8,776	See page 208
75	Agoura Hills	$9,554	See page 212
84	Agoura Hills	$9,633	See page 248
91	Agoura Hills	$10,455	See page 276

Table 1.1: Properties for auction in the Agoura Hills-Malibu region (continued)

Auction ID	Community	Starting Bid	Property Details
90	Agoura Hills	$10,954	See page 272
2407	Calabasas	$11,150	See page 312
85	Agoura Hills	$11,922	See page 252
89	Agoura Hills	$11,976	See page 268
92	Agoura Hills	$12,267	See page 280
78	Agoura Hills	$12,734	See page 224
88	Agoura Hills	$13,074	See page 264
87	Agoura Hills	$13,076	See page 260
72	Agoura Hills	$13,352	See page 200
73	Agoura Hills	$13,827	See page 204
86	Agoura Hills	$14,744	See page 256
79	Agoura Hills	$15,113	See page 228
69	Agoura Hills	$15,490	See page 198
68	Agoura Hills	$15,936	See page 196
93	Agoura Hills	$18,584	See page 284
80	Agoura Hills	$19,601	See page 232
83	Agoura Hills	$22,279	See page 244
81	Agoura Hills	$23,022	See page 236
23	Agoura Hills	$23,873	See page 11
94	Agoura Hills	$25,244	See page 288
95	Agoura Hills	$29,901	See page 292
2382	Calabasas	$85,016	See page 310
2380	Calabasas	$88,818	See page 308
29	Agoura Hills	$119,872	See page 15

Table 1.2: Possible same-entities with multiple properties in this auction (Agoura Hills-Malibu region and elsewhere in Los Angeles County)

ID	Possible Assessed Entity	Property Details
72	AGOURA CORNELL ROADS LP	Agoura Hills, page 200
73	AGOURA CORNELL ROADS LP	Agoura Hills, page 204
74	AGOURA CORNELL ROADS LP	Agoura Hills, page 208
75	AGOURA CORNELL ROADS LP	Agoura Hills, page 212
76	AGOURA CORNELL ROADS LP	Agoura Hills, page 216
77	AGOURA CORNELL ROADS LP	Agoura Hills, page 220
78	AGOURA CORNELL ROADS LP	Agoura Hills, page 224
79	AGOURA CORNELL ROADS LP	Agoura Hills, page 228
80	AGOURA CORNELL ROADS LP	Agoura Hills, page 232
81	AGOURA CORNELL ROADS LP	Agoura Hills, page 236
82	AGOURA CORNELL ROADS LP	Agoura Hills, page 240
83	AGOURA CORNELL ROADS LP	Agoura Hills, page 244
84	AGOURA CORNELL ROADS LP	Agoura Hills, page 248
85	AGOURA CORNELL ROADS LP	Agoura Hills, page 252
86	AGOURA CORNELL ROADS LP	Agoura Hills, page 256
87	AGOURA CORNELL ROADS LP	Agoura Hills, page 260
88	AGOURA CORNELL ROADS LP	Agoura Hills, page 264

Table 1.2: Possible same-entities with multiple properties in this auction (Agoura Hills-Malibu region and elsewhere in Los Angeles County) (continued)

ID	POSSIBLE ASSESSED ENTITY	PROPERTY DETAILS
89	AGOURA CORNELL ROADS LP	Agoura Hills, page 268
90	AGOURA CORNELL ROADS LP	Agoura Hills, page 272
91	AGOURA CORNELL ROADS LP	Agoura Hills, page 276
92	AGOURA CORNELL ROADS LP	Agoura Hills, page 280
93	AGOURA CORNELL ROADS LP	Agoura Hills, page 284
94	AGOURA CORNELL ROADS LP	Agoura Hills, page 288
95	AGOURA CORNELL ROADS LP	Agoura Hills, page 292
96	AGOURA CORNELL ROADS LP	Agoura Hills, page 296
68	DAVID PICK FAMILY PARTNERSHIP ...	Agoura Hills, page 196
69	DAVID PICK FAMILY PARTNERSHIP ...	Agoura Hills, page 198
31	SHEA ESTATES DEVELOPMENT CORP	Agoura Hills, page 17
32	SHEA ESTATES DEVELOPMENT CORP	Agoura Hills, page 22
33	SHEA ESTATES DEVELOPMENT CORP	Agoura Hills, page 27
34	SHEA ESTATES DEVELOPMENT CORP	Agoura Hills, page 32
35	SHEA ESTATES DEVELOPMENT CORP	Agoura Hills, page 37
36	SHEA ESTATES DEVELOPMENT CORP	Agoura Hills, page 42
37	SHEA ESTATES DEVELOPMENT CORP	Agoura Hills, page 47
38	SHEA ESTATES DEVELOPMENT CORP	Agoura Hills, page 52
39	SHEA ESTATES DEVELOPMENT CORP	Agoura Hills, page 57
40	SHEA ESTATES DEVELOPMENT CORP	Agoura Hills, page 62
41	SHEA ESTATES DEVELOPMENT CORP	Agoura Hills, page 67
42	SHEA ESTATES DEVELOPMENT CORP	Agoura Hills, page 72
43	SHEA ESTATES DEVELOPMENT CORP	Agoura Hills, page 77
44	SHEA ESTATES DEVELOPMENT CORP	Agoura Hills, page 82
45	SHEA ESTATES DEVELOPMENT CORP	Agoura Hills, page 87
46	SHEA ESTATES DEVELOPMENT CORP	Agoura Hills, page 92
47	SHEA ESTATES DEVELOPMENT CORP	Agoura Hills, page 97
48	SHEA ESTATES DEVELOPMENT CORP	Agoura Hills, page 102
49	SHEA ESTATES DEVELOPMENT CORP	Agoura Hills, page 107
50	SHEA ESTATES DEVELOPMENT CORP	Agoura Hills, page 112
51	SHEA ESTATES DEVELOPMENT CORP	Agoura Hills, page 117
52	SHEA ESTATES DEVELOPMENT CORP	Agoura Hills, page 122
53	SHEA ESTATES DEVELOPMENT CORP	Agoura Hills, page 127
54	SHEA ESTATES DEVELOPMENT CORP	Agoura Hills, page 132
55	SHEA ESTATES DEVELOPMENT CORP	Agoura Hills, page 137
56	SHEA ESTATES DEVELOPMENT CORP	Agoura Hills, page 142
57	SHEA ESTATES DEVELOPMENT CORP	Agoura Hills, page 147
58	SHEA ESTATES DEVELOPMENT CORP	Agoura Hills, page 152
59	SHEA ESTATES DEVELOPMENT CORP	Agoura Hills, page 157
60	SHEA ESTATES DEVELOPMENT CORP	Agoura Hills, page 162
61	SHEA ESTATES DEVELOPMENT CORP	Agoura Hills, page 167
62	SHEA ESTATES DEVELOPMENT CORP	Agoura Hills, page 172
63	SHEA ESTATES DEVELOPMENT CORP	Agoura Hills, page 177
64	SHEA ESTATES DEVELOPMENT CORP	Agoura Hills, page 182
65	STROUD ROBERT C CO TR ET AL ST ...	Agoura Hills, page 187
66	STROUD ROBERT C CO TR ET AL ST ...	Agoura Hills, page 190
67	STROUD ROBERT C CO TR ET AL ST ...	Agoura Hills, page 193

Table 1.2: Possible same-entities with multiple properties in this auction (Agoura Hills-Malibu region and elsewhere in Los Angeles County) (continued)

ID	POSSIBLE ASSESSED ENTITY	PROPERTY DETAILS
97	STROUD ROBERT C CO TR ET AL ST ...	Agoura Hills, page 300

Agoura Hills

A total of 69 properties are listed for auction in the Agoura Hills community. Table 2.1 lists the improved properties by lowest starting bid; Table 2.2 show the non-improved properties in the same fashion. In both cases, estimated comparable pricing is indicated as well.

Table 2.3 presents the properties in Agoura Hills ordered by auction ID.

Table 2.1: Improved properties for auction in Agoura Hills sorted by starting bid price

PROPERTY ID	AIN	STARTING BID	COMPARABLE FINISHED $/SQFT	COMPARABLE LOT $/SQFT	PROPERTY DETAILS
23	2054020114	$23,873	$262	$136	See page 11

Table 2.2: Non-improved properties for auction in Agoura Hills sorted by starting bid price

PROPERTY ID	AIN	STARTING BID	COMPARABLE FINISHED $/SQFT	COMPARABLE LOT $/SQFT	PROPERTY DETAILS
97	2061030019	$1,517	$298	$60	See page 300
65	2061024005	$1,576	$297	$45	See page 187
67	2061028040	$1,598	$297	$48	See page 193
66	2061027013	$1,610	$295	$49	See page 190
96	2061030017	$2,009	$292	$63	See page 296
82	2061029023	$2,011	$292	$63	See page 240
5137	2061025045	$2,621	$297	$45	See page 303
35	2061020005	$3,097	$294	$49	See page 37
47	2061020027	$3,245	$294	$49	See page 97
48	2061020028	$3,254	$294	$49	See page 102
50	2061020030	$3,254	$294	$49	See page 112
57	2061021015	$3,254	$294	$49	See page 147
45	2061020025	$3,303	$294	$49	See page 87
58	2061021016	$3,303	$294	$49	See page 152
59	2061021017	$3,334	$294	$49	See page 157
46	2061020026	$3,343	$294	$49	See page 92
44	2061020024	$3,354	$294	$49	See page 82
49	2061020029	$3,361	$294	$49	See page 107

Table 2.2: Non-improved properties for auction in Agoura Hills
sorted by starting bid price (continued)

Property ID	AIN	Starting Bid	Comparable Finished $/sqft	Comparable Lot $/sqft	Property Details
33	2061020003	$3,471	$294	$49	See page 27
34	2061020004	$3,481	$294	$49	See page 32
42	2061020022	$3,805	$294	$49	See page 72
43	2061020023	$3,835	$294	$49	See page 77
56	2061021014	$3,844	$294	$49	See page 142
36	2061020006	$3,894	$294	$49	See page 42
31	2061020001	$3,963	$294	$49	See page 17
41	2061020021	$3,972	$294	$49	See page 67
37	2061020007	$4,002	$294	$49	See page 47
38	2061020008	$4,032	$294	$49	See page 52
32	2061020002	$4,071	$294	$49	See page 22
39	2061020009	$4,799	$297	$49	See page 57
40	2061020010	$4,838	$297	$49	See page 62
77	2061029013	$4,880	$296	$64	See page 220
76	2061029012	$5,823	$296	$64	See page 216
62	2061021020	$6,038	$294	$49	See page 172
61	2061021019	$7,093	$294	$49	See page 167
51	2061021009	$7,145	$297	$48	See page 117
60	2061021018	$7,151	$294	$49	See page 162
63	2061021021	$7,347	$294	$49	See page 177
26	2055019027	$7,500	$292	$56	See page 13
64	2061021022	$7,643	$294	$49	See page 182
55	2061021013	$7,903	$294	$49	See page 137
52	2061021010	$8,201	$294	$49	See page 122
53	2061021011	$8,315	$294	$49	See page 127
54	2061021012	$8,704	$294	$49	See page 132
74	2061029010	$8,776	$292	$63	See page 208
75	2061029011	$9,554	$296	$64	See page 212
84	2061030002	$9,633	$289	$74	See page 248
91	2061030009	$10,455	$295	$64	See page 276
90	2061030008	$10,954	$296	$64	See page 272
85	2061030003	$11,922	$289	$74	See page 252
89	2061030007	$11,976	$298	$65	See page 268
92	2061030010	$12,267	$295	$64	See page 280
78	2061029014	$12,734	$295	$64	See page 224
88	2061030006	$13,074	$298	$65	See page 264
87	2061030005	$13,076	$300	$66	See page 260
72	2061029008	$13,352	$292	$62	See page 200
73	2061029009	$13,827	$292	$62	See page 204
86	2061030004	$14,744	$291	$71	See page 256
79	2061029015	$15,113	$295	$64	See page 228
69	2061029004	$15,490	$299	$54	See page 198
68	2061029003	$15,936	$299	$54	See page 196
93	2061030011	$18,584	$296	$65	See page 284
80	2061029016	$19,601	$295	$64	See page 232
83	2061030001	$22,279	$289	$74	See page 244

Table 2.2: Non-improved properties for auction in Agoura Hills sorted by starting bid price (continued)

Property ID	AIN	Starting Bid	Comparable Finished $/sqft	Comparable Lot $/sqft	Property Details
81	2061029017	$23,022	$296	$65	See page 236
94	2061030012	$25,244	$296	$65	See page 288
95	2061030013	$29,901	$295	$68	See page 292
29	2061001007	$119,872	$279	$108	See page 15

Table 2.3: Properties for auction in Agoura Hills sorted by auction property ID

Auction ID	AIN	Starting Bid	Property Details
23	2054020114	$23,873	See page 11
26	2055019027	$7,500	See page 13
29	2061001007	$119,872	See page 15
31	2061020001	$3,963	See page 17
32	2061020002	$4,071	See page 22
33	2061020003	$3,471	See page 27
34	2061020004	$3,481	See page 32
35	2061020005	$3,097	See page 37
36	2061020006	$3,894	See page 42
37	2061020007	$4,002	See page 47
38	2061020008	$4,032	See page 52
39	2061020009	$4,799	See page 57
40	2061020010	$4,838	See page 62
41	2061020021	$3,972	See page 67
42	2061020022	$3,805	See page 72
43	2061020023	$3,835	See page 77
44	2061020024	$3,354	See page 82
45	2061020025	$3,303	See page 87
46	2061020026	$3,343	See page 92
47	2061020027	$3,245	See page 97
48	2061020028	$3,254	See page 102
49	2061020029	$3,361	See page 107
50	2061020030	$3,254	See page 112
51	2061021009	$7,145	See page 117
52	2061021010	$8,201	See page 122
53	2061021011	$8,315	See page 127
54	2061021012	$8,704	Scc page 132
55	2061021013	$7,903	See page 137
56	2061021014	$3,844	See page 142
57	2061021015	$3,254	See page 147
58	2061021016	$3,303	See page 152
59	2061021017	$3,334	See page 157
60	2061021018	$7,151	See page 162
61	2061021019	$7,093	See page 167
62	2061021020	$6,038	See page 172

Table 2.3: Properties for auction in Agoura Hills sorted by auction property ID (continued)

Auction ID	AIN	Starting Bid	Property Details
63	2061021021	$7,347	See page 177
64	2061021022	$7,643	See page 182
65	2061024005	$1,576	See page 187
66	2061027013	$1,610	See page 190
67	2061028040	$1,598	See page 193
68	2061029003	$15,936	See page 196
69	2061029004	$15,490	See page 198
72	2061029008	$13,352	See page 200
73	2061029009	$13,827	See page 204
74	2061029010	$8,776	See page 208
75	2061029011	$9,554	See page 212
76	2061029012	$5,823	See page 216
77	2061029013	$4,880	See page 220
78	2061029014	$12,734	See page 224
79	2061029015	$15,113	See page 228
80	2061029016	$19,601	See page 232
81	2061029017	$23,022	See page 236
82	2061029023	$2,011	See page 240
83	2061030001	$22,279	See page 244
84	2061030002	$9,633	See page 248
85	2061030003	$11,922	See page 252
86	2061030004	$14,744	See page 256
87	2061030005	$13,076	See page 260
88	2061030006	$13,074	See page 264
89	2061030007	$11,976	See page 268
90	2061030008	$10,954	See page 272
91	2061030009	$10,455	See page 276
92	2061030010	$12,267	See page 280
93	2061030011	$18,584	See page 284
94	2061030012	$25,244	See page 288
95	2061030013	$29,901	See page 292
96	2061030017	$2,009	See page 296
97	2061030019	$1,517	See page 300
5137	2061025045	$2,621	See page 303

2.1 Auction ID 23

The Los Angeles County Auction Book describes the property as follows.

```
PM 155-17-18 LOT 1 CONDO UNITS 299 THRU 306 0 ASSESSED TO IWANOFF,JAMES
AND SANDRA AND LAWNOFF,STOJAN AND SIGRID LOCATION CITY-AGOURA HILL
PROPERTY ADDRESS: 30423 CANWOOD ST NO 225 AGOURA HILLS CA 91301-4367
```

The property is located in the general vicinity of Figure 2.1. It is identified by Assessor's Identification Number (AIN) 2054020114. The starting bid is $23,873. Comparable improved properties in this area is about $262/sqft. Comparable unimproved lots in this area is about $136/sqft. This parcel is approximately 134639 sqft. Note, however, that the parcel may be larger than the property under consideration. In case of condominiums, for example, the parcel may encompass other units of the development - those unrelated to the property to be auctioned.

The property is in a parcel zoned Commercial Retail/Service in Agoura Hills, for 0 to 0 dwelling units.

Figures 2.2 and 2.3 show street map and corresponding detailed aerial view, respectively. In both cases, the map is centered on the property with the containing parcel marked in heavy blue. If surrounding nearby properties are also part of this auction, the street and aerial maps highlights these in heavy, dashed blue outline.

A parcel may encompass multiple street addresses. The following address(es) are at this parcel:

- 30423 CANWOOD STREET UNIT225, 91301

Figure 2.1: Property 23, AIN 2054020114, overview map

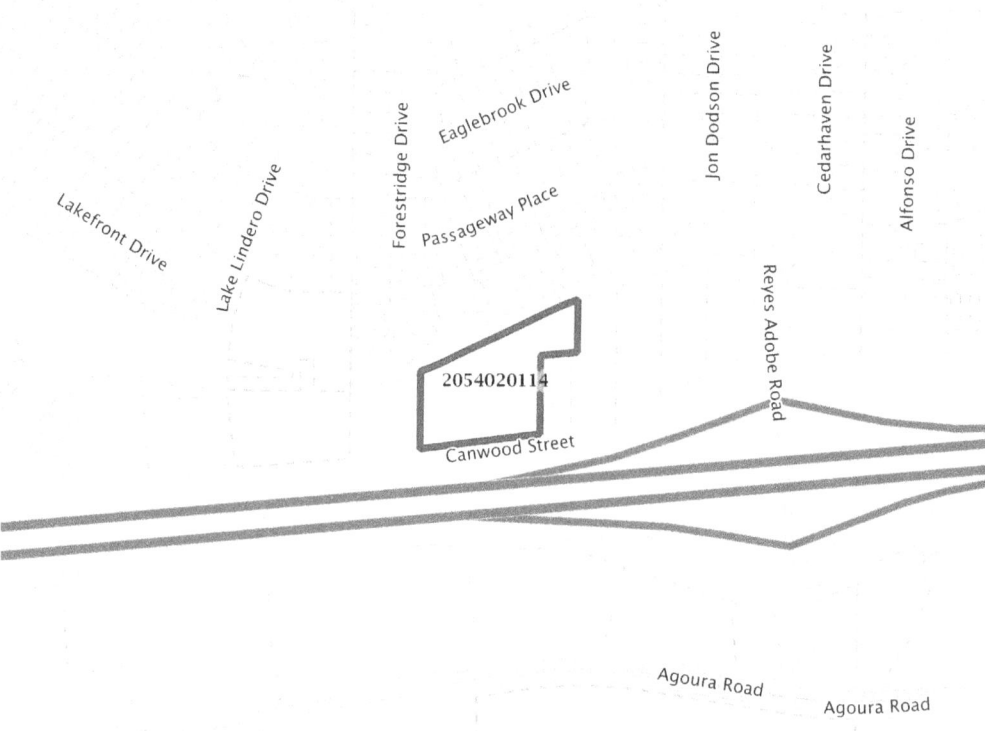

Figure 2.2: Property 23, AIN 2054020114, neighborhood view

Figure 2.3: Property 23, AIN 2054020114, detailed view

2.2 Auction ID 26

The Los Angeles County Auction Book describes the property as follows.

```
TRACT NO 8451 LOT 4 BLK 7 ASSESSED TO SLEZAK, MARCELLA O LOCATION
CITY-AGOURA HILL PROPERTY ADDRESS: VACANT LOT
```

The property is located in the general vicinity of Figure 2.4. It is identified by Assessor's Identification Number (AIN) 2055019027. The starting bid is $7,500. Comparable improved properties in this area is about $292/sqft. Comparable unimproved lots in this area is about $56/sqft. This parcel is approximately 43542 sqft. Note, however, that the parcel may be larger than the property under consideration. In case of condominiums, for example, the parcel may encompass other units of the development - those unrelated to the property to be auctioned.

The property is in a parcel zoned Very Low-Residential in Agoura Hills, for 0 to 1 dwelling units.

Figures 2.5 and 2.6 show street map and corresponding detailed aerial view, respectively. In both cases, the map is centered on the property with the containing parcel marked in heavy blue. If surrounding nearby properties are also part of this auction, the street and aerial maps highlights these in heavy, dashed blue outline.

Figure 2.4: Property 26, AIN 2055019027, overview map

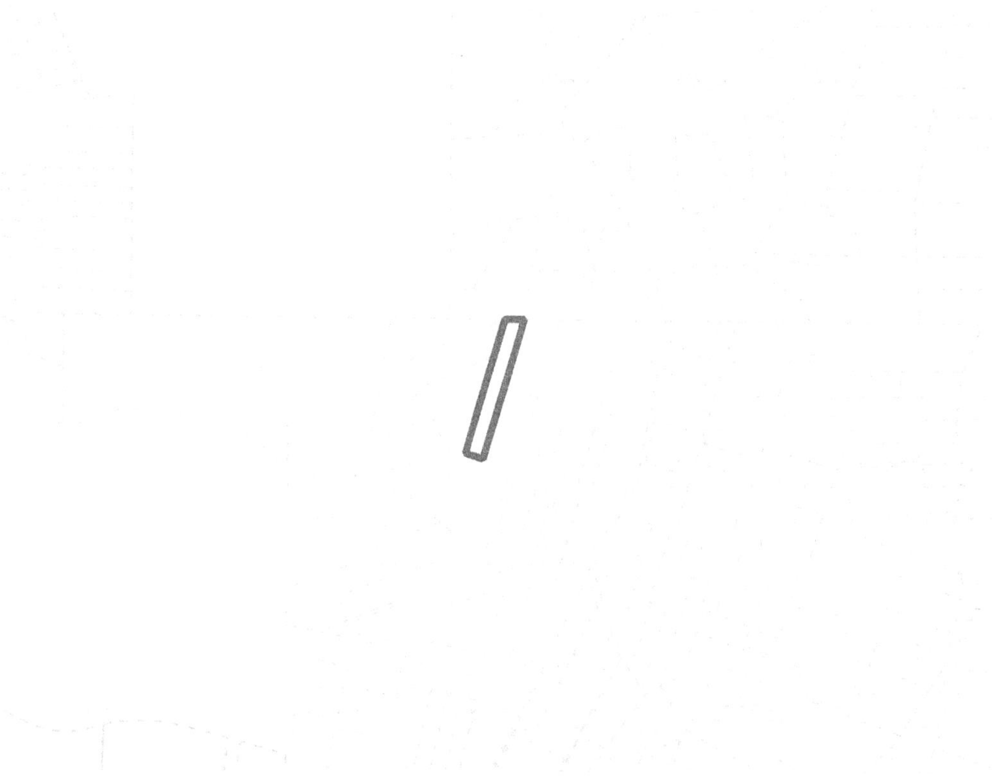

Figure 2.5: Property 26, AIN 2055019027, neighborhood view

Figure 2.6: Property 26, AIN 2055019027, detailed view

2.3   Auction ID 29

The Los Angeles County Auction Book describes the property as follows.

```
SCC 2898 CF138*FOR DESC SEE ASSESSOR' S MAPS POR OF 0 MINNIE RUMP
IN LOT D ASSESSED TO EDISON,REUBEN AND SHAVALIAN,PARVIZ LOCATION CITY-AGOURA
HILL PROPERTY ADDRESS: VACANT LOT
```

The property is located in the general vicinity of Figure 2.7. It is identified by Assessor's Identification Number (AIN) 2061001007. The starting bid is $119,872. Comparable improved properties in this area is about $279/sqft. Comparable unimproved lots in this area is about $108/sqft. This parcel is approximately 3241943 sqft. Note, however, that the parcel may be larger than the property under consideration. In case of condominiums, for example, the parcel may encompass other units of the development - those unrelated to the property to be auctioned.

The property is in a parcel zoned Specific Plan in Agoura Hills, for 0 to 0 dwelling units.

Figures 2.8 and 2.9 show street map and corresponding detailed aerial view, respectively. In both cases, the map is centered on the property with the containing parcel marked in heavy blue. If surrounding nearby properties are also part of this auction, the street and aerial maps highlights these in heavy, dashed blue outline.

Figure 2.7: Property 29, AIN 2061001007, overview map

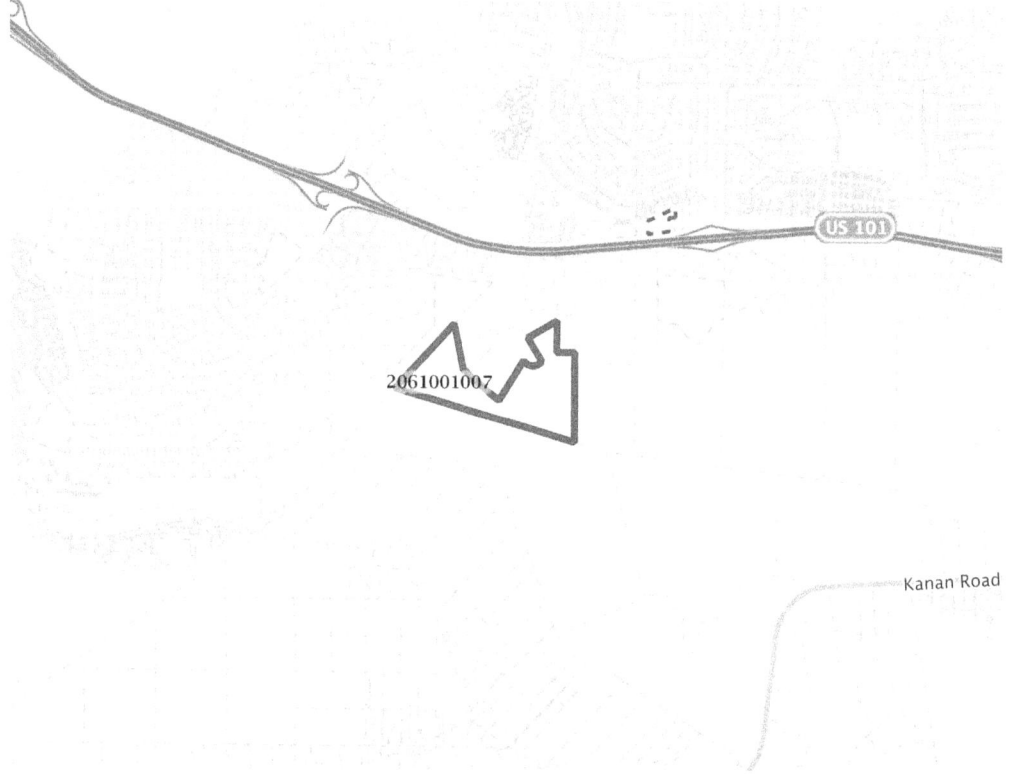

Figure 2.8: Property 29, AIN 2061001007, neighborhood view

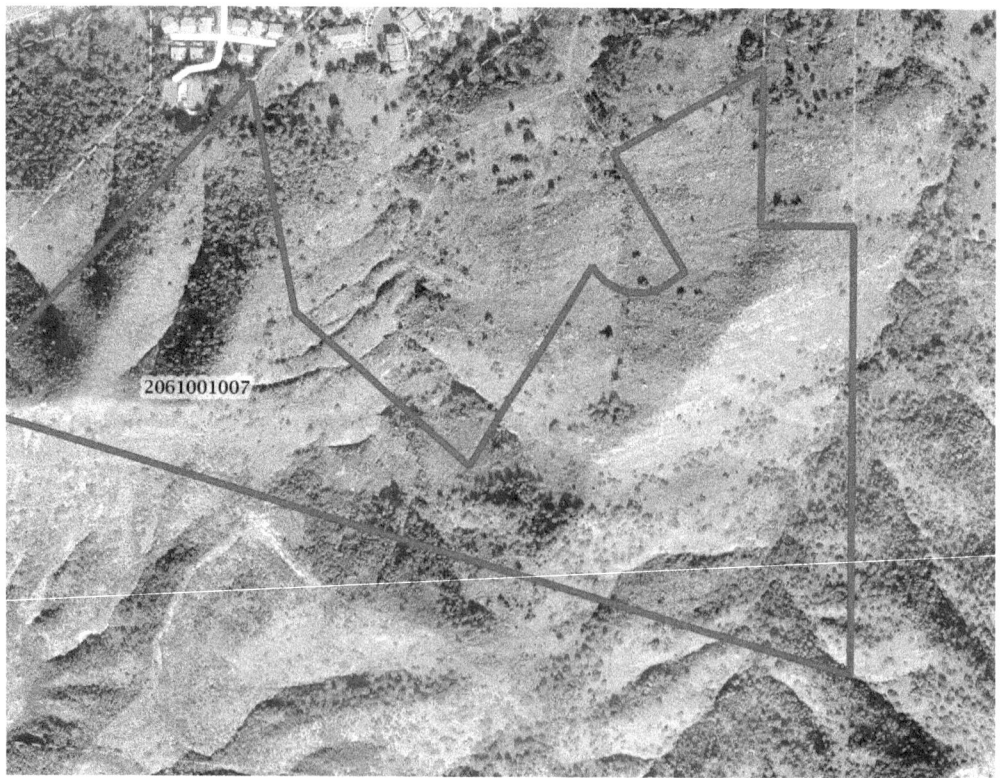

Figure 2.9: Property 29, AIN 2061001007, detailed view

2.4   Auction ID 31

The Los Angeles County Auction Book describes the property as follows.

```
TRACT NO 8793 LOT 16 BLK 4 ASSESSED TO SHEA ESTATES 0 DEVELOPMENT
CORP LOCATION CITY-AGOURA HILL PROPERTY ADDRESS: VACANT LOT
```

The property is located in the general vicinity of Figure 2.10. It is identified by Assessor's Identification Number (AIN) 2061020001. The starting bid is $3,963. Comparable improved properties in this area is about $294/sqft. Comparable unimproved lots in this area is about $49/sqft. This parcel is approximately 8903 sqft. Note, however, that the parcel may be larger than the property under consideration. In case of condominiums, for example, the parcel may encompass other units of the development - those unrelated to the property to be auctioned.

The property is in a parcel zoned Restricted Open Space in Agoura Hills, for 0 to 0 dwelling units.

Figures 2.11 and 2.12 show street map and corresponding detailed aerial view, respectively. In both cases, the map is centered on the property with the containing parcel marked in heavy blue. If surrounding nearby properties are also part of this auction, the street and aerial maps highlights these in heavy, dashed blue outline.

This assessed entity may have other properties that are also in this auction:

1. AIN 2061020002 (auction ID 32): TRACT NO 8793 LOT 17 BLK 4 ... ASSESSED TO SHEA ESTATES 0 DEVELOPMENT CORP LOCATION CITY-AGOURA HILL PROPERTY ADDRESS: VACANT LOT. See page 22.

2. AIN 2061020003 (auction ID 33): TRACT NO 8793 LOT 18 BLK 4 ... ASSESSED TO SHEA ESTATES 0 DEVELOPMENT CORP LOCATION CITY-AGOURA HILL PROPERTY ADDRESS: VACANT LOT. See page 27.

3. AIN 2061020004 (auction ID 34): TRACT NO 8793 LOT 19 BLK 4 ... ASSESSED TO SHEA ESTATES 0 DEVELOPMENT CORP LOCATION CITY-AGOURA HILL PROPERTY ADDRESS: VACANT LOT. See page 32.

4. AIN 2061020005 (auction ID 35): TRACT NO 8793 LOT 20 BLK 4 ... ASSESSED TO SHEA ESTATES 0 DEVELOPMENT CORP LOCATION CITY-AGOURA HILL PROPERTY ADDRESS: VACANT LOT. See page 37.

5. AIN 2061020006 (auction ID 36): TRACT NO 8793 LOT 21 BLK 4 ... ASSESSED TO SHEA ESTATES 0 DEVELOPMENT CORP LOCATION CITY-AGOURA HILL PROPERTY ADDRESS: VACANT LOT. See page 42.

6. AIN 2061020007 (auction ID 37): TRACT NO 8793 LOT 22 BLK 4 ... ASSESSED TO SHEA ESTATES 0 DEVELOPMENT CORP LOCATION CITY-AGOURA HILL PROPERTY ADDRESS: VACANT LOT. See page 47.

7. AIN 2061020008 (auction ID 38): TRACT NO 8793 LOT 23 BLK 4 ... ASSESSED TO SHEA ESTATES 0 DEVELOPMENT CORP LOCATION CITY-AGOURA HILL PROPERTY ADDRESS: VACANT LOT. See page 52.

8. AIN 2061020009 (auction ID 39): TRACT NO 8793 LOT 24 BLK 4 ... ASSESSED TO SHEA ESTATES 0 DEVELOPMENT CORP LOCATION CITY-AGOURA HILL PROPERTY ADDRESS: VACANT LOT. See page 57.

9. AIN 2061020010 (auction ID 40): TRACT NO 8793 LOT 25 BLK 4 ... ASSESSED TO SHEA ESTATES 0 DEVELOPMENT CORP LOCATION CITY-AGOURA HILL PROPERTY ADDRESS: VACANT LOT. See page 62.

10. AIN 2061020021 (auction ID 41): TRACT NO 8793 LOT 62 BLK 4 ... ASSESSED TO SHEA ESTATES 0 DEVELOPMENT CORP LOCATION CITY-AGOURA HILL PROPERTY ADDRESS: VACANT LOT. See page 67.

11. AIN 2061020022 (auction ID 42): TRACT NO 8793 LOT 63 BLK 4 ... ASSESSED TO SHEA ESTATES 0 DEVELOPMENT CORP LOCATION CITY-AGOURA HILL PROPERTY ADDRESS: VACANT LOT. See page 72.

12. AIN 2061020023 (auction ID 43): TRACT NO 8793 LOT 64 BLK 4 ... ASSESSED TO SHEA ESTATES 0 DEVELOPMENT CORP LOCATION CITY-AGOURA HILL PROPERTY ADDRESS: VACANT LOT. See page 77.

13. AIN 2061020024 (auction ID 44): TRACT NO 8793 LOT 65 BLK 4 ... ASSESSED TO SHEA ESTATES 0 DEVELOPMENT CORP LOCATION CITY-AGOURA HILL PROPERTY ADDRESS: VACANT LOT. See page 82.

14. AIN 2061020025 (auction ID 45): TRACT NO 8793 LOT 66 BLK 4 ... ASSESSED TO SHEA ESTATES 0 DEVELOPMENT CORP LOCATION CITY-AGOURA HILL PROPERTY ADDRESS: VACANT LOT. See page 87.

15. AIN 2061020026 (auction ID 46): TRACT NO 8793 LOT 67 BLK 4 ... ASSESSED TO SHEA ESTATES 0 DEVELOPMENT CORP LOCATION CITY-AGOURA HILL PROPERTY ADDRESS: VACANT LOT. See page 92.

16. AIN 2061020027 (auction ID 47): TRACT NO 8793 LOT 68 BLK 4 ... ASSESSED TO SHEA ESTATES 0 DEVELOPMENT CORP LOCATION CITY-AGOURA HILL PROPERTY ADDRESS: VACANT LOT. See page 97.

17. AIN 2061020028 (auction ID 48): TRACT NO 8793 LOT 69 BLK 4 ... ASSESSED TO SHEA ESTATES 0 DEVELOPMENT CORP LOCATION CITY-AGOURA HILL - PROPERTY ADDRESS: VACANT LOT. See page 102.

18. AIN 2061020029 (auction ID 49): TRACT NO 8793 LOT 70 BLK 4 ... ASSESSED TO SHEA ESTATES 0 DEVELOPMENT CORP LOCATION CITY-AGOURA HILL PROPERTY ADDRESS: VACANT LOT. See page 107.

19. AIN 2061020030 (auction ID 50): TRACT NO 8793 LOT 71 BLK 4 ... ASSESSED TO SHEA ESTATES 0 DEVELOPMENT CORP LOCATION CITY-AGOURA HILL PROPERTY ADDRESS: VACANT LOT. See page 112.

20. AIN 2061021009 (auction ID 51): TRACT NO 8793 LOT 10 BLK 4 ... ASSESSED TO SHEA ESTATES 0 DEVELOPMENT CORP LOCATION CITY-AGOURA HILL PROPERTY ADDRESS: VACANT LOT. See page 117.

21. AIN 2061021010 (auction ID 52): TRACT NO 8793 LOT 11 BLK 4 ... ASSESSED TO SHEA ESTATES 0 DEVELOPMENT CORP LOCATION CITY-AGOURA HILL PROPERTY ADDRESS: VACANT LOT. See page 122.

22. AIN 2061021011 (auction ID 53): TRACT NO 8793 LOT 12 BLK 4 ... ASSESSED TO SHEA ESTATES 0 DEVELOPMENT CORP LOCATION CITY-AGOURA IIILL PROPERTY ADDRESS: VACANT LOT. See page 127.

23. AIN 2061021012 (auction ID 54): TRACT NO 8793 LOT 13 BLK 4 ... ASSESSED TO SHEA ESTATES 0 DEVELOPMENT CORP LOCATION CITY-AGOURA HILL PROPERTY ADDRESS: VACANT LOT. See page 132.

24. AIN 2061021013 (auction ID 55): TRACT NO 8793 LOT 14 BLK 4 ... ASSESSED TO SHEA ESTATES 0 DEVELOPMENT CORP LOCATION CITY-AGOURA HILL PROPERTY ADDRESS: VACANT LOT. See page 137.

25. AIN 2061021014 (auction ID 56): TRACT NO 8793 LOT 15 BLK 4 . . . ASSESSED TO SHEA ESTATES 0 DEVELOPMENT CORP LOCATION CITY-AGOURA HILL PROPERTY ADDRESS: VACANT LOT. See page 142.

26. AIN 2061021015 (auction ID 57): TRACT NO 8793 LOT 72 BLK 4 . . . ASSESSED TO SHEA ESTATES 0 DEVELOPMENT CORP LOCATION CITY-AGOURA HILL PROPERTY ADDRESS: VACANT LOT. See page 147.

27. AIN 2061021016 (auction ID 58): TRACT NO 8793 LOT 73 BLK 4 . . . ASSESSED TO SHEA ESTATES 0 DEVELOPMENT CORP LOCATION CITY-AGOURA HILL PROPERTY ADDRESS: VACANT LOT. See page 152.

28. AIN 2061021017 (auction ID 59): TRACT NO 8793 LOT 74 BLK 4 . . . ASSESSED TO SHEA ESTATES 0 DEVELOPMENT CORP LOCATION CITY-AGOURA HILL PROPERTY ADDRESS: VACANT LOT. See page 157.

29. AIN 2061021018 (auction ID 60): TRACT NO 8793 LOT 75 BLK 4 . . . ASSESSED TO SHEA ESTATES 0 DEVELOPMENT CORP LOCATION CITY-AGOURA HILL PROPERTY ADDRESS: VACANT LOT. See page 162.

30. AIN 2061021019 (auction ID 61): TRACT NO 8793 LOT 76 BLK 4 . . . ASSESSED TO SHEA ESTATES 0 DEVELOPMENT CORP LOCATION CITY-AGOURA HILL PROPERTY ADDRESS: VACANT LOT. See page 167.

31. AIN 2061021020 (auction ID 62): TRACT NO 8793 LOT 77 BLK 4 . . . ASSESSED TO SHEA ESTATES 0 DEVELOPMENT CORP LOCATION CITY-AGOURA HILL PROPERTY ADDRESS: VACANT LOT. See page 172.

32. AIN 2061021021 (auction ID 63): TRACT NO 8793 LOT 78 BLK 4 . . . ASSESSED TO SHEA ESTATES 0 DEVELOPMENT CORP LOCATION CITY-AGOURA HILL PROPERTY ADDRESS: VACANT LOT. See page 177.

33. AIN 2061021022 (auction ID 64): TRACT NO 8793 LOT 79 BLK 4 . . . ASSESSED TO SHEA ESTATES 0 DEVELOPMENT CORP LOCATION CITY-AGOURA HILL PROPERTY ADDRESS: VACANT LOT. See page 182.

Figure 2.10: Property 64, AIN 2061020001, overview map

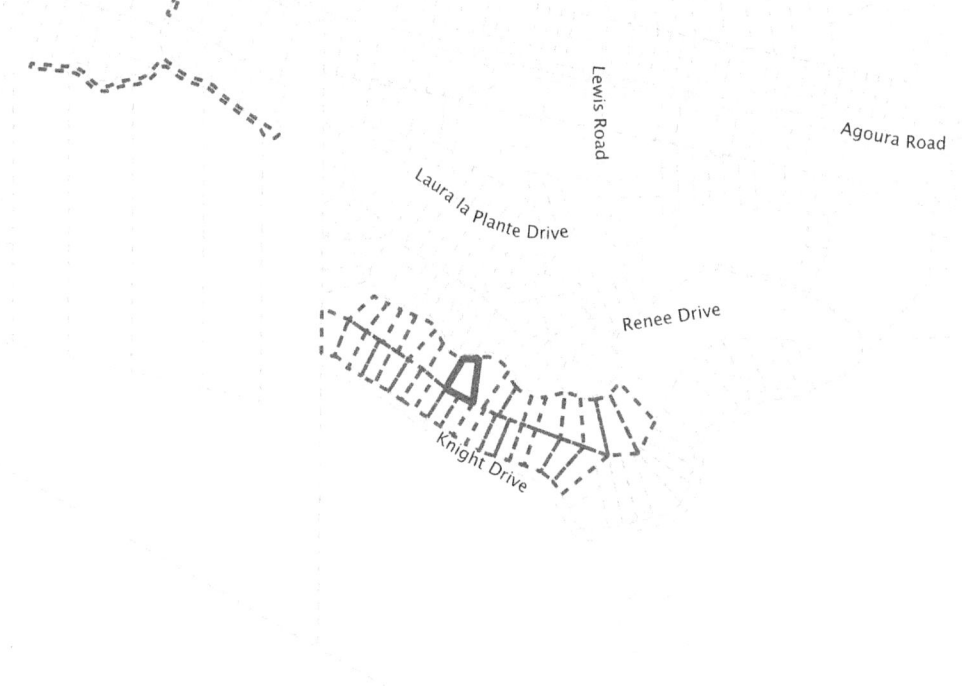

Figure 2.11: Property 64, AIN 2061020001, neighborhood view

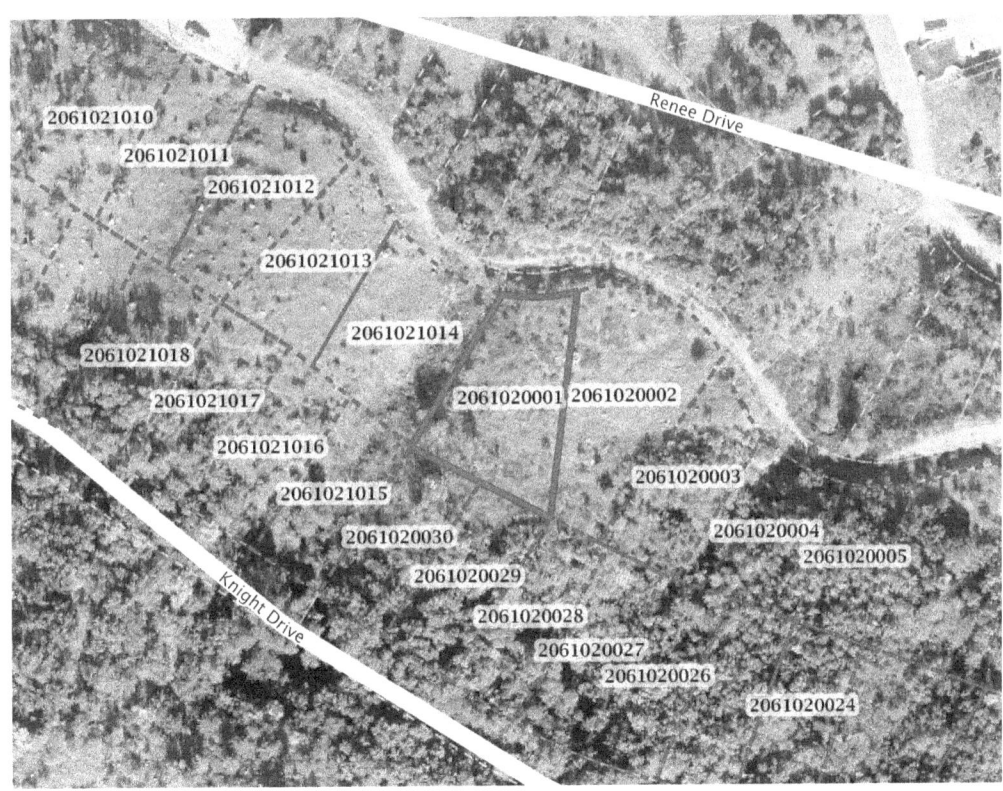

Figure 2.12: Property 64, AIN 2061020001, detailed view

2.5   Auction ID 32

The Los Angeles County Auction Book describes the property as follows.

```
TRACT NO 8793 LOT 17 BLK 4 ASSESSED TO SHEA ESTATES 0 DEVELOPMENT
CORP LOCATION CITY-AGOURA HILL PROPERTY ADDRESS: VACANT LOT
```

The property is located in the general vicinity of Figure 2.13. It is identified by Assessor's Identification Number (AIN) 2061020002. The starting bid is \$4,071. Comparable improved properties in this area is about \$294/sqft. Comparable unimproved lots in this area is about \$49/sqft. This parcel is approximately 10805 sqft. Note, however, that the parcel may be larger than the property under consideration. In case of condominiums, for example, the parcel may encompass other units of the development - those unrelated to the property to be auctioned.

The property is in a parcel zoned Restricted Open Space in Agoura Hills, for 0 to 0 dwelling units.

Figures 2.14 and 2.15 show street map and corresponding detailed aerial view, respectively. In both cases, the map is centered on the property with the containing parcel marked in heavy blue. If surrounding nearby properties are also part of this auction, the street and aerial maps highlights these in heavy, dashed blue outline.

This assessed entity may have other properties that are also in this auction:

1. AIN 2061020001 (auction ID 31): TRACT NO 8793 LOT 16 BLK 4 ... ASSESSED TO SHEA ESTATES 0 DEVELOPMENT CORP LOCATION CITY-AGOURA HILL PROPERTY ADDRESS: VACANT LOT. See page 17.

2. AIN 2061020003 (auction ID 33): TRACT NO 8793 LOT 18 BLK 4 ... ASSESSED TO SHEA ESTATES 0 DEVELOPMENT CORP LOCATION CITY-AGOURA HILL PROPERTY ADDRESS: VACANT LOT. See page 27.

3. AIN 2061020004 (auction ID 34): TRACT NO 8793 LOT 19 BLK 4 ... ASSESSED TO SHEA ESTATES 0 DEVELOPMENT CORP LOCATION CITY-AGOURA HILL PROPERTY ADDRESS: VACANT LOT. See page 32.

4. AIN 2061020005 (auction ID 35): TRACT NO 8793 LOT 20 BLK 4 ... ASSESSED TO SHEA ESTATES 0 DEVELOPMENT CORP LOCATION CITY-AGOURA HILL PROPERTY ADDRESS: VACANT LOT. See page 37.

5. AIN 2061020006 (auction ID 36): TRACT NO 8793 LOT 21 BLK 4 ... ASSESSED TO SHEA ESTATES 0 DEVELOPMENT CORP LOCATION CITY-AGOURA HILL PROPERTY ADDRESS: VACANT LOT. See page 42.

6. AIN 2061020007 (auction ID 37): TRACT NO 8793 LOT 22 BLK 4 ... ASSESSED TO SHEA ESTATES 0 DEVELOPMENT CORP LOCATION CITY-AGOURA HILL PROPERTY ADDRESS: VACANT LOT. See page 47.

7. AIN 2061020008 (auction ID 38): TRACT NO 8793 LOT 23 BLK 4 ... ASSESSED TO SHEA ESTATES 0 DEVELOPMENT CORP LOCATION CITY-AGOURA HILL PROPERTY ADDRESS: VACANT LOT. See page 52.

8. AIN 2061020009 (auction ID 39): TRACT NO 8793 LOT 24 BLK 4 ... ASSESSED TO SHEA ESTATES 0 DEVELOPMENT CORP LOCATION CITY-AGOURA HILL PROPERTY ADDRESS: VACANT LOT. See page 57.

9. AIN 2061020010 (auction ID 40): TRACT NO 8793 LOT 25 BLK 4 ... ASSESSED TO SHEA ESTATES 0 DEVELOPMENT CORP LOCATION CITY-AGOURA HILL PROPERTY ADDRESS: VACANT LOT. See page 62.

10. AIN 2061020021 (auction ID 41): TRACT NO 8793 LOT 62 BLK 4 ... ASSESSED TO SHEA ESTATES 0 DEVELOPMENT CORP LOCATION CITY-AGOURA HILL PROPERTY ADDRESS: VACANT LOT. See page 67.

11. AIN 2061020022 (auction ID 42): TRACT NO 8793 LOT 63 BLK 4 ... ASSESSED TO SHEA ESTATES 0 DEVELOPMENT CORP LOCATION CITY-AGOURA HILL PROPERTY ADDRESS: VACANT LOT. See page 72.

12. AIN 2061020023 (auction ID 43): TRACT NO 8793 LOT 64 BLK 4 ... ASSESSED TO SHEA ESTATES 0 DEVELOPMENT CORP LOCATION CITY-AGOURA HILL PROPERTY ADDRESS: VACANT LOT. See page 77.

13. AIN 2061020024 (auction ID 44): TRACT NO 8793 LOT 65 BLK 4 ... ASSESSED TO SHEA ESTATES 0 DEVELOPMENT CORP LOCATION CITY-AGOURA HILL PROPERTY ADDRESS: VACANT LOT. See page 82.

14. AIN 2061020025 (auction ID 45): TRACT NO 8793 LOT 66 BLK 4 ... ASSESSED TO SHEA ESTATES 0 DEVELOPMENT CORP LOCATION CITY-AGOURA HILL PROPERTY ADDRESS: VACANT LOT. See page 87.

15. AIN 2061020026 (auction ID 46): TRACT NO 8793 LOT 67 BLK 4 ... ASSESSED TO SHEA ESTATES 0 DEVELOPMENT CORP LOCATION CITY-AGOURA HILL PROPERTY ADDRESS: VACANT LOT. See page 92.

16. AIN 2061020027 (auction ID 47): TRACT NO 8793 LOT 68 BLK 4 ... ASSESSED TO SHEA ESTATES 0 DEVELOPMENT CORP LOCATION CITY-AGOURA HILL PROPERTY ADDRESS: VACANT LOT. See page 97.

17. AIN 2061020028 (auction ID 48): TRACT NO 8793 LOT 69 BLK 4 ... ASSESSED TO SHEA ESTATES 0 DEVELOPMENT CORP LOCATION CITY-AGOURA HILL - PROPERTY ADDRESS: VACANT LOT. See page 102.

18. AIN 2061020029 (auction ID 49): TRACT NO 8793 LOT 70 BLK 4 ... ASSESSED TO SHEA ESTATES 0 DEVELOPMENT CORP LOCATION CITY-AGOURA HILL PROPERTY ADDRESS: VACANT LOT. See page 107.

19. AIN 2061020030 (auction ID 50): TRACT NO 8793 LOT 71 BLK 4 ... ASSESSED TO SHEA ESTATES 0 DEVELOPMENT CORP LOCATION CITY-AGOURA HILL PROPERTY ADDRESS: VACANT LOT. See page 112.

20. AIN 2061021009 (auction ID 51): TRACT NO 8793 LOT 10 BLK 4 ... ASSESSED TO SHEA ESTATES 0 DEVELOPMENT CORP LOCATION CITY-AGOURA HILL PROPERTY ADDRESS: VACANT LOT. See page 117.

21. AIN 2061021010 (auction ID 52): TRACT NO 8793 LOT 11 BLK 4 ... ASSESSED TO SHEA ESTATES 0 DEVELOPMENT CORP LOCATION CITY-AGOURA HILL PROPERTY ADDRESS: VACANT LOT. See page 122.

22. AIN 2061021011 (auction ID 53): TRACT NO 8793 LOT 12 BLK 4 ... ASSESSED TO SHEA ESTATES 0 DEVELOPMENT CORP LOCATION CITY-AGOURA HILL PROPERTY ADDRESS: VACANT LOT. See page 127.

23. AIN 2061021012 (auction ID 54): TRACT NO 8793 LOT 13 BLK 4 ... ASSESSED TO SHEA ESTATES 0 DEVELOPMENT CORP LOCATION CITY-AGOURA HILL PROPERTY ADDRESS: VACANT LOT. See page 132.

24. AIN 2061021013 (auction ID 55): TRACT NO 8793 LOT 14 BLK 4 ... ASSESSED TO SHEA ESTATES 0 DEVELOPMENT CORP LOCATION CITY-AGOURA HILL PROPERTY ADDRESS: VACANT LOT. See page 137.

25. AIN 2061021014 (auction ID 56): TRACT NO 8793 LOT 15 BLK 4 ... ASSESSED TO SHEA ESTATES 0 DEVELOPMENT CORP LOCATION CITY-AGOURA HILL PROPERTY ADDRESS: VACANT LOT. See page 142.

26. AIN 2061021015 (auction ID 57): TRACT NO 8793 LOT 72 BLK 4 ... ASSESSED TO SHEA ESTATES 0 DEVELOPMENT CORP LOCATION CITY-AGOURA HILL PROPERTY ADDRESS: VACANT LOT. See page 147.

27. AIN 2061021016 (auction ID 58): TRACT NO 8793 LOT 73 BLK 4 ... ASSESSED TO SHEA ESTATES 0 DEVELOPMENT CORP LOCATION CITY-AGOURA HILL PROPERTY ADDRESS: VACANT LOT. See page 152.

28. AIN 2061021017 (auction ID 59): TRACT NO 8793 LOT 74 BLK 4 ... ASSESSED TO SHEA ESTATES 0 DEVELOPMENT CORP LOCATION CITY-AGOURA HILL PROPERTY ADDRESS: VACANT LOT. See page 157.

29. AIN 2061021018 (auction ID 60): TRACT NO 8793 LOT 75 BLK 4 ... ASSESSED TO SHEA ESTATES 0 DEVELOPMENT CORP LOCATION CITY-AGOURA HILL PROPERTY ADDRESS: VACANT LOT. See page 162.

30. AIN 2061021019 (auction ID 61): TRACT NO 8793 LOT 76 BLK 4 ... ASSESSED TO SHEA ESTATES 0 DEVELOPMENT CORP LOCATION CITY-AGOURA HILL PROPERTY ADDRESS: VACANT LOT. See page 167.

31. AIN 2061021020 (auction ID 62): TRACT NO 8793 LOT 77 BLK 4 ... ASSESSED TO SHEA ESTATES 0 DEVELOPMENT CORP LOCATION CITY-AGOURA HILL PROPERTY ADDRESS: VACANT LOT. See page 172.

32. AIN 2061021021 (auction ID 63): TRACT NO 8793 LOT 78 BLK 4 ... ASSESSED TO SHEA ESTATES 0 DEVELOPMENT CORP LOCATION CITY-AGOURA HILL PROPERTY ADDRESS: VACANT LOT. See page 177.

33. AIN 2061021022 (auction ID 64): TRACT NO 8793 LOT 79 BLK 4 ... ASSESSED TO SHEA ESTATES 0 DEVELOPMENT CORP LOCATION CITY-AGOURA HILL PROPERTY ADDRESS: VACANT LOT. See page 182.

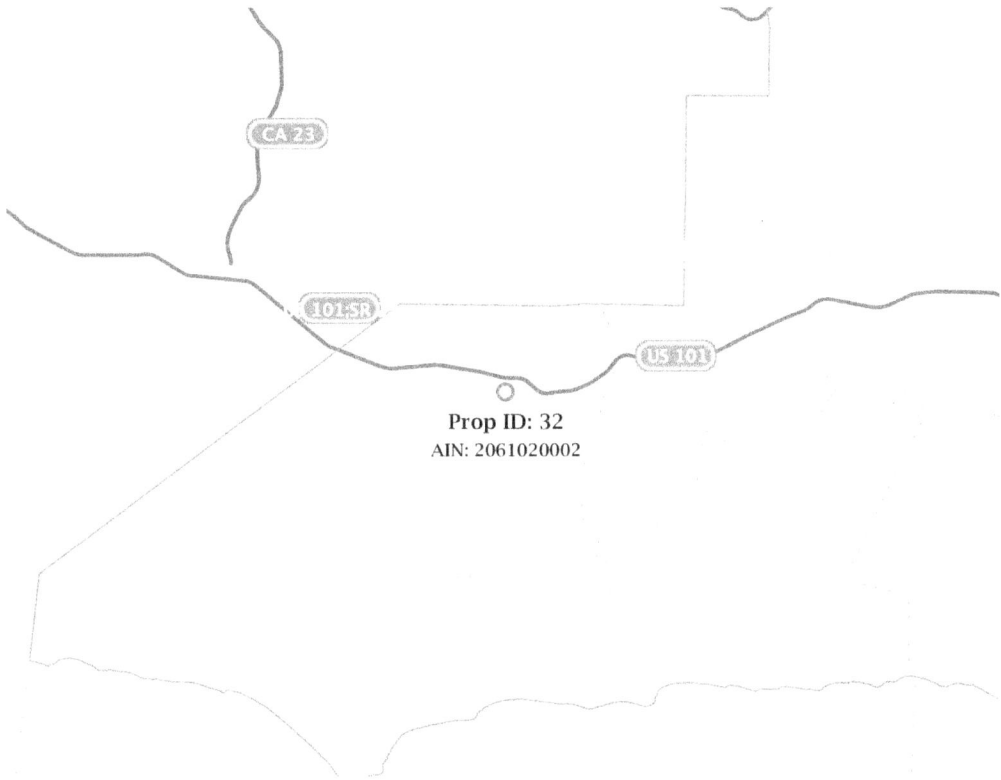

Figure 2.13: Property 64, AIN 2061020002, overview map

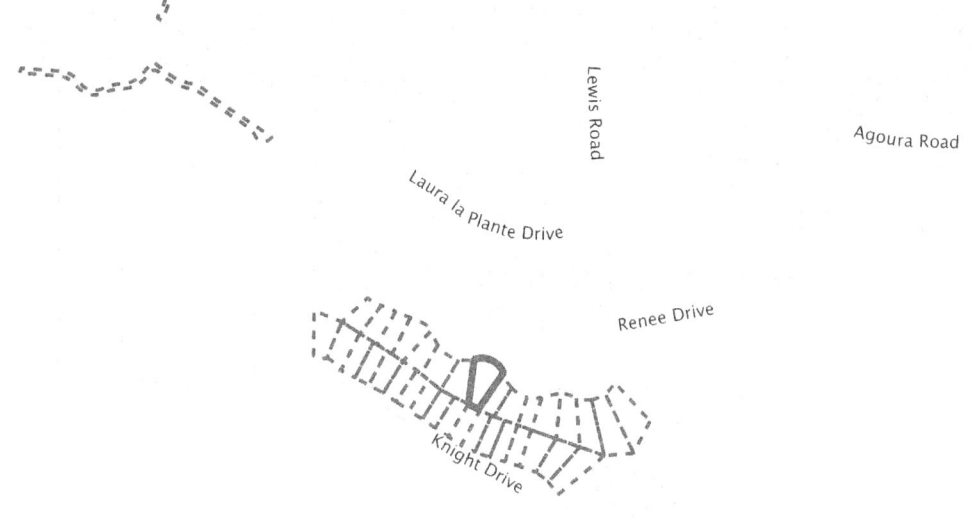

Figure 2.14: Property 64, AIN 2061020002, neighborhood view

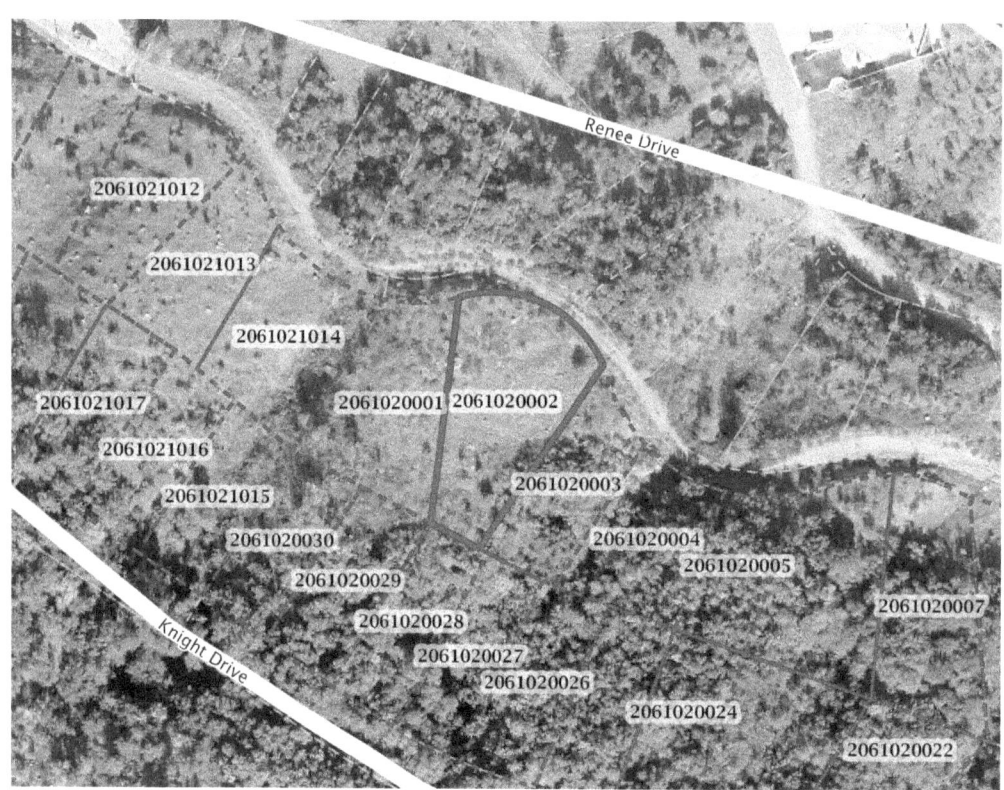

Figure 2.15: Property 64, AIN 2061020002, detailed view

2.6 Auction ID 33

The Los Angeles County Auction Book describes the property as follows.

```
TRACT NO 8793 LOT 18 BLK 4 ASSESSED TO SHEA ESTATES 0 DEVELOPMENT
CORP LOCATION CITY-AGOURA HILL PROPERTY ADDRESS: VACANT LOT
```

The property is located in the general vicinity of Figure 2.16. It is identified by Assessor's Identification Number (AIN) 2061020003. The starting bid is $3,471. Comparable improved properties in this area is about $294/sqft. Comparable unimproved lots in this area is about $49/sqft. This parcel is approximately 6258 sqft. Note, however, that the parcel may be larger than the property under consideration. In case of condominiums, for example, the parcel may encompass other units of the development - those unrelated to the property to be auctioned.

The property is in a parcel zoned Restricted Open Space in Agoura Hills, for 0 to 0 dwelling units.

Figures 2.17 and 2.18 show street map and corresponding detailed aerial view, respectively. In both cases, the map is centered on the property with the containing parcel marked in heavy blue. If surrounding nearby properties are also part of this auction, the street and aerial maps highlights these in heavy, dashed blue outline.

This assessed entity may have other properties that are also in this auction:

1. AIN 2061020001 (auction ID 31): TRACT NO 8793 LOT 16 BLK 4 . . . ASSESSED TO SHEA ESTATES 0 DEVELOPMENT CORP LOCATION CITY-AGOURA HILL PROPERTY ADDRESS: VACANT LOT. See page 17.

2. AIN 2061020002 (auction ID 32): TRACT NO 8793 LOT 17 BLK 4 . . . ASSESSED TO SHEA ESTATES 0 DEVELOPMENT CORP LOCATION CITY-AGOURA HILL PROPERTY ADDRESS: VACANT LOT. See page 22.

3. AIN 2061020004 (auction ID 34): TRACT NO 8793 LOT 19 BLK 4 . . . ASSESSED TO SHEA ESTATES 0 DEVELOPMENT CORP LOCATION CITY-AGOURA HILL PROPERTY ADDRESS: VACANT LOT. See page 32.

4. AIN 2061020005 (auction ID 35): TRACT NO 8793 LOT 20 BLK 4 . . . ASSESSED TO SHEA ESTATES 0 DEVELOPMENT CORP LOCATION CITY-AGOURA HILL PROPERTY ADDRESS: VACANT LOT. See page 37.

5. AIN 2061020006 (auction ID 36): TRACT NO 8793 LOT 21 BLK 4 . . . ASSESSED TO SHEA ESTATES 0 DEVELOPMENT CORP LOCATION CITY-AGOURA HILL PROPERTY ADDRESS: VACANT LOT. See page 42.

6. AIN 2061020007 (auction ID 37): TRACT NO 8793 LOT 22 BLK 4 . . . ASSESSED TO SHEA ESTATES 0 DEVELOPMENT CORP LOCATION CITY-AGOURA HILL PROPERTY ADDRESS: VACANT LOT. See page 47.

7. AIN 2061020008 (auction ID 38): TRACT NO 8793 LOT 23 BLK 4 . . . ASSESSED TO SHEA ESTATES 0 DEVELOPMENT CORP LOCATION CITY-AGOURA HILL PROPERTY ADDRESS: VACANT LOT. See page 52.

8. AIN 2061020009 (auction ID 39): TRACT NO 8793 LOT 24 BLK 4 . . . ASSESSED TO SHEA ESTATES 0 DEVELOPMENT CORP LOCATION CITY-AGOURA HILL PROPERTY ADDRESS: VACANT LOT. See page 57.

9. AIN 2061020010 (auction ID 40): TRACT NO 8793 LOT 25 BLK 4 . . . ASSESSED TO SHEA ESTATES 0 DEVELOPMENT CORP LOCATION CITY-AGOURA HILL PROPERTY ADDRESS: VACANT LOT. See page 62.

10. AIN 2061020021 (auction ID 41): TRACT NO 8793 LOT 62 BLK 4 . . . ASSESSED TO SHEA ESTATES 0 DEVELOPMENT CORP LOCATION CITY-AGOURA HILL PROPERTY ADDRESS: VACANT LOT. See page 67.

11. AIN 2061020022 (auction ID 42): TRACT NO 8793 LOT 63 BLK 4 . . . ASSESSED TO SHEA ESTATES 0 DEVELOPMENT CORP LOCATION CITY-AGOURA HILL PROPERTY ADDRESS: VACANT LOT. See page 72.

12. AIN 2061020023 (auction ID 43): TRACT NO 8793 LOT 64 BLK 4 . . . ASSESSED TO SHEA ESTATES 0 DEVELOPMENT CORP LOCATION CITY-AGOURA HILL PROPERTY ADDRESS: VACANT LOT. See page 77.

13. AIN 2061020024 (auction ID 44): TRACT NO 8793 LOT 65 BLK 4 . . . ASSESSED TO SHEA ESTATES 0 DEVELOPMENT CORP LOCATION CITY-AGOURA HILL PROPERTY ADDRESS: VACANT LOT. See page 82.

14. AIN 2061020025 (auction ID 45): TRACT NO 8793 LOT 66 BLK 4 . . . ASSESSED TO SHEA ESTATES 0 DEVELOPMENT CORP LOCATION CITY-AGOURA HILL PROPERTY ADDRESS: VACANT LOT. See page 87.

15. AIN 2061020026 (auction ID 46): TRACT NO 8793 LOT 67 BLK 4 . . . ASSESSED TO SHEA ESTATES 0 DEVELOPMENT CORP LOCATION CITY-AGOURA HILL PROPERTY ADDRESS: VACANT LOT. See page 92.

16. AIN 2061020027 (auction ID 47): TRACT NO 8793 LOT 68 BLK 4 . . . ASSESSED TO SHEA ESTATES 0 DEVELOPMENT CORP LOCATION CITY-AGOURA HILL PROPERTY ADDRESS: VACANT LOT. See page 97.

17. AIN 2061020028 (auction ID 48): TRACT NO 8793 LOT 69 BLK 4 . . . ASSESSED TO SHEA ESTATES 0 DEVELOPMENT CORP LOCATION CITY-AGOURA HILL - PROPERTY ADDRESS: VACANT LOT. See page 102.

18. AIN 2061020029 (auction ID 49): TRACT NO 8793 LOT 70 BLK 4 . . . ASSESSED TO SHEA ESTATES 0 DEVELOPMENT CORP LOCATION CITY-AGOURA HILL PROPERTY ADDRESS: VACANT LOT. See page 107.

19. AIN 2061020030 (auction ID 50): TRACT NO 8793 LOT 71 BLK 4 . . . ASSESSED TO SHEA ESTATES 0 DEVELOPMENT CORP LOCATION CITY-AGOURA HILL PROPERTY ADDRESS: VACANT LOT. See page 112.

20. AIN 2061021009 (auction ID 51): TRACT NO 8793 LOT 10 BLK 4 . . . ASSESSED TO SHEA ESTATES 0 DEVELOPMENT CORP LOCATION CITY-AGOURA HILL PROPERTY ADDRESS: VACANT LOT. See page 117.

21. AIN 2061021010 (auction ID 52): TRACT NO 8793 LOT 11 BLK 4 . . . ASSESSED TO SHEA ESTATES 0 DEVELOPMENT CORP LOCATION CITY-AGOURA HILL PROPERTY ADDRESS: VACANT LOT. See page 122.

22. AIN 2061021011 (auction ID 53): TRACT NO 8793 LOT 12 BLK 4 . . . ASSESSED TO SHEA ESTATES 0 DEVELOPMENT CORP LOCATION CITY-AGOURA HILL PROPERTY ADDRESS: VACANT LOT. See page 127.

23. AIN 2061021012 (auction ID 54): TRACT NO 8793 LOT 13 BLK 4 . . . ASSESSED TO SHEA ESTATES 0 DEVELOPMENT CORP LOCATION CITY-AGOURA HILL PROPERTY ADDRESS: VACANT LOT. See page 132.

24. AIN 2061021013 (auction ID 55): TRACT NO 8793 LOT 14 BLK 4 . . . ASSESSED TO SHEA ESTATES 0 DEVELOPMENT CORP LOCATION CITY-AGOURA HILL PROPERTY ADDRESS: VACANT LOT. See page 137.

25. AIN 2061021014 (auction ID 56): TRACT NO 8793 LOT 15 BLK 4 . . . ASSESSED TO SHEA ESTATES 0 DEVELOPMENT CORP LOCATION CITY-AGOURA HILL PROPERTY ADDRESS: VACANT LOT. See page 142.

26. AIN 2061021015 (auction ID 57): TRACT NO 8793 LOT 72 BLK 4 . . . ASSESSED TO SHEA ESTATES 0 DEVELOPMENT CORP LOCATION CITY-AGOURA HILL PROPERTY ADDRESS: VACANT LOT. See page 147.

27. AIN 2061021016 (auction ID 58): TRACT NO 8793 LOT 73 BLK 4 . . . ASSESSED TO SHEA ESTATES 0 DEVELOPMENT CORP LOCATION CITY-AGOURA HILL PROPERTY ADDRESS: VACANT LOT. See page 152.

28. AIN 2061021017 (auction ID 59): TRACT NO 8793 LOT 74 BLK 4 . . . ASSESSED TO SHEA ESTATES 0 DEVELOPMENT CORP LOCATION CITY-AGOURA HILL PROPERTY ADDRESS: VACANT LOT. See page 157.

29. AIN 2061021018 (auction ID 60): TRACT NO 8793 LOT 75 BLK 4 . . . ASSESSED TO SHEA ESTATES 0 DEVELOPMENT CORP LOCATION CITY-AGOURA HILL PROPERTY ADDRESS: VACANT LOT. See page 162.

30. AIN 2061021019 (auction ID 61): TRACT NO 8793 LOT 76 BLK 4 . . . ASSESSED TO SHEA ESTATES 0 DEVELOPMENT CORP LOCATION CITY-AGOURA HILL PROPERTY ADDRESS: VACANT LOT. See page 167.

31. AIN 2061021020 (auction ID 62): TRACT NO 8793 LOT 77 BLK 4 . . . ASSESSED TO SHEA ESTATES 0 DEVELOPMENT CORP LOCATION CITY-AGOURA HILL PROPERTY ADDRESS: VACANT LOT. See page 172.

32. AIN 2061021021 (auction ID 63): TRACT NO 8793 LOT 78 BLK 4 . . . ASSESSED TO SHEA ESTATES 0 DEVELOPMENT CORP LOCATION CITY-AGOURA HILL PROPERTY ADDRESS: VACANT LOT. See page 177.

33. AIN 2061021022 (auction ID 64): TRACT NO 8793 LOT 79 BLK 4 . . . ASSESSED TO SHEA ESTATES 0 DEVELOPMENT CORP LOCATION CITY-AGOURA HILL PROPERTY ADDRESS: VACANT LOT. See page 182.

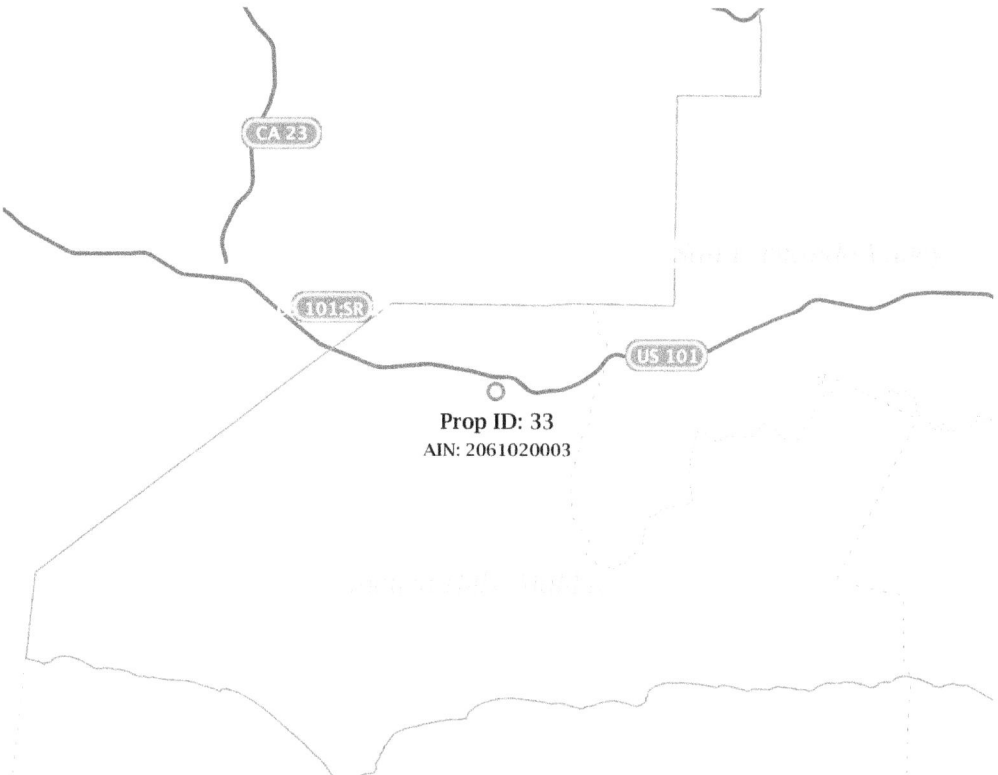

Figure 2.16: Property 64, AIN 2061020003, overview map

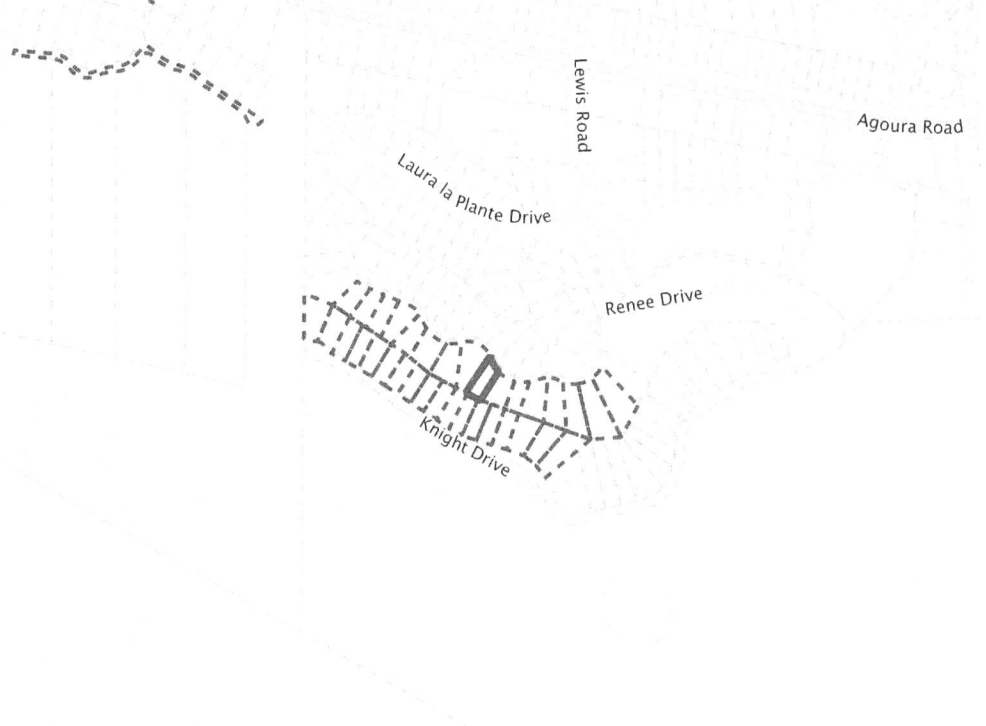

Figure 2.17: Property 64, AIN 2061020003, neighborhood view

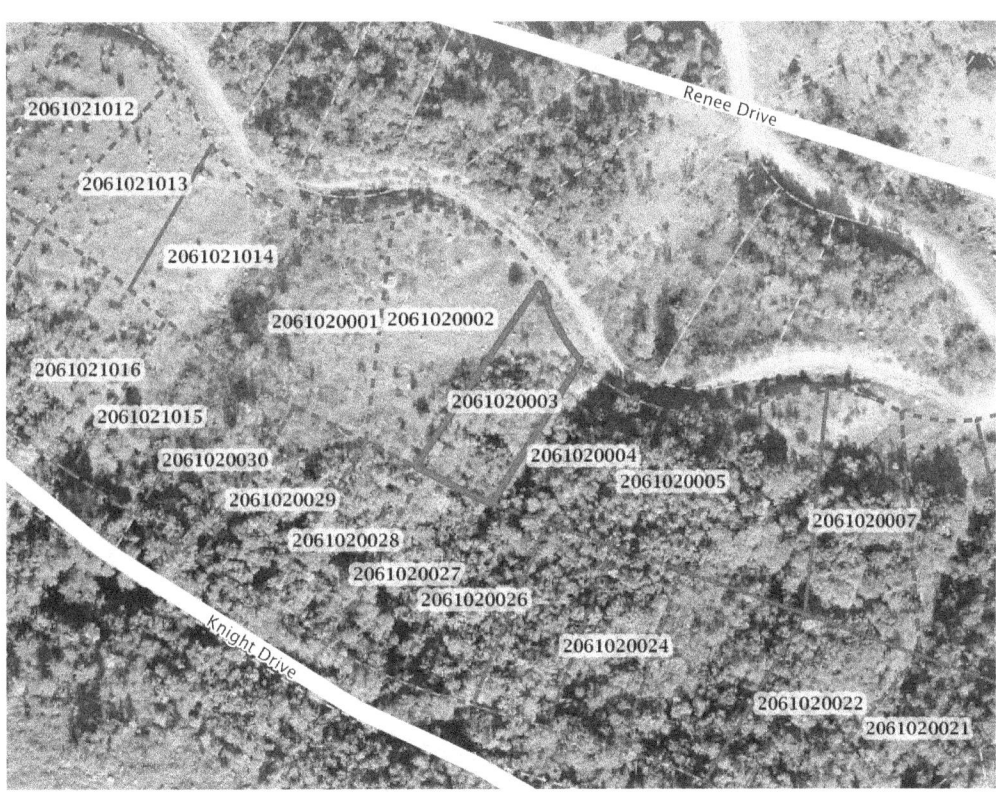

Figure 2.18: Property 64, AIN 2061020003, detailed view

2.7   Auction ID 34

The Los Angeles County Auction Book describes the property as follows.

```
TRACT NO 8793 LOT 19 BLK 4 ASSESSED TO SHEA ESTATES 0 DEVELOPMENT
CORP LOCATION CITY-AGOURA HILL PROPERTY ADDRESS: VACANT LOT
```

The property is located in the general vicinity of Figure 2.19. It is identified by Assessor's Identification Number (AIN) 2061020004. The starting bid is $3,481. Comparable improved properties in this area is about $294/sqft. Comparable unimproved lots in this area is about $49/sqft. This parcel is approximately 6700 sqft. Note, however, that the parcel may be larger than the property under consideration. In case of condominiums, for example, the parcel may encompass other units of the development - those unrelated to the property to be auctioned.

The property is in a parcel zoned Restricted Open Space in Agoura Hills, for 0 to 0 dwelling units.

Figures 2.20 and 2.21 show street map and corresponding detailed aerial view, respectively. In both cases, the map is centered on the property with the containing parcel marked in heavy blue. If surrounding nearby properties are also part of this auction, the street and aerial maps highlights these in heavy, dashed blue outline.

This assessed entity may have other properties that are also in this auction:

1. AIN 2061020001 (auction ID 31): TRACT NO 8793 LOT 16 BLK 4 . . . ASSESSED TO SHEA ESTATES 0 DEVELOPMENT CORP LOCATION CITY-AGOURA HILL PROPERTY ADDRESS: VACANT LOT. See page 17.

2. AIN 2061020002 (auction ID 32): TRACT NO 8793 LOT 17 BLK 4 . . . ASSESSED TO SHEA ESTATES 0 DEVELOPMENT CORP LOCATION CITY-AGOURA HILL PROPERTY ADDRESS: VACANT LOT. See page 22.

3. AIN 2061020003 (auction ID 33): TRACT NO 8793 LOT 18 BLK 4 . . . ASSESSED TO SHEA ESTATES 0 DEVELOPMENT CORP LOCATION CITY-AGOURA HILL PROPERTY ADDRESS: VACANT LOT. See page 27.

4. AIN 2061020005 (auction ID 35): TRACT NO 8793 LOT 20 BLK 4 . . . ASSESSED TO SHEA ESTATES 0 DEVELOPMENT CORP LOCATION CITY-AGOURA HILL PROPERTY ADDRESS: VACANT LOT. See page 37.

5. AIN 2061020006 (auction ID 36): TRACT NO 8793 LOT 21 BLK 4 . . . ASSESSED TO SHEA ESTATES 0 DEVELOPMENT CORP LOCATION CITY-AGOURA HILL PROPERTY ADDRESS: VACANT LOT. See page 42.

6. AIN 2061020007 (auction ID 37): TRACT NO 8793 LOT 22 BLK 4 . . . ASSESSED TO SHEA ESTATES 0 DEVELOPMENT CORP LOCATION CITY-AGOURA HILL PROPERTY ADDRESS: VACANT LOT. See page 47.

7. AIN 2061020008 (auction ID 38): TRACT NO 8793 LOT 23 BLK 4 . . . ASSESSED TO SHEA ESTATES 0 DEVELOPMENT CORP LOCATION CITY-AGOURA HILL PROPERTY ADDRESS: VACANT LOT. See page 52.

8. AIN 2061020009 (auction ID 39): TRACT NO 8793 LOT 24 BLK 4 . . . ASSESSED TO SHEA ESTATES 0 DEVELOPMENT CORP LOCATION CITY-AGOURA HILL PROPERTY ADDRESS: VACANT LOT. See page 57.

9. AIN 2061020010 (auction ID 40): TRACT NO 8793 LOT 25 BLK 4 . . . ASSESSED TO SHEA ESTATES 0 DEVELOPMENT CORP LOCATION CITY-AGOURA HILL PROPERTY ADDRESS: VACANT LOT. See page 62.

10. AIN 2061020021 (auction ID 41): TRACT NO 8793 LOT 62 BLK 4 . . . ASSESSED TO SHEA ESTATES 0 DEVELOPMENT CORP LOCATION CITY-AGOURA HILL PROPERTY ADDRESS: VACANT LOT. See page 67.

11. AIN 2061020022 (auction ID 42): TRACT NO 8793 LOT 63 BLK 4 . . . ASSESSED TO SHEA ESTATES 0 DEVELOPMENT CORP LOCATION CITY-AGOURA HILL PROPERTY ADDRESS: VACANT LOT. See page 72.

12. AIN 2061020023 (auction ID 43): TRACT NO 8793 LOT 64 BLK 4 . . . ASSESSED TO SHEA ESTATES 0 DEVELOPMENT CORP LOCATION CITY-AGOURA HILL PROPERTY ADDRESS: VACANT LOT. See page 77.

13. AIN 2061020024 (auction ID 44): TRACT NO 8793 LOT 65 BLK 4 . . . ASSESSED TO SHEA ESTATES 0 DEVELOPMENT CORP LOCATION CITY-AGOURA HILL PROPERTY ADDRESS: VACANT LOT. See page 82.

14. AIN 2061020025 (auction ID 45): TRACT NO 8793 LOT 66 BLK 4 . . . ASSESSED TO SHEA ESTATES 0 DEVELOPMENT CORP LOCATION CITY-AGOURA HILL PROPERTY ADDRESS: VACANT LOT. See page 87.

15. AIN 2061020026 (auction ID 46): TRACT NO 8793 LOT 67 BLK 4 . . . ASSESSED TO SHEA ESTATES 0 DEVELOPMENT CORP LOCATION CITY-AGOURA HILL PROPERTY ADDRESS: VACANT LOT. See page 92.

16. AIN 2061020027 (auction ID 47): TRACT NO 8793 LOT 68 BLK 4 . . . ASSESSED TO SHEA ESTATES 0 DEVELOPMENT CORP LOCATION CITY-AGOURA HILL PROPERTY ADDRESS: VACANT LOT. See page 97.

17. AIN 2061020028 (auction ID 48): TRACT NO 8793 LOT 69 BLK 4 . . . ASSESSED TO SHEA ESTATES 0 DEVELOPMENT CORP LOCATION CITY-AGOURA HILL - PROPERTY ADDRESS: VACANT LOT. See page 102.

18. AIN 2061020029 (auction ID 49): TRACT NO 8793 LOT 70 BLK 4 . . . ASSESSED TO SHEA ESTATES 0 DEVELOPMENT CORP LOCATION CITY-AGOURA HILL PROPERTY ADDRESS: VACANT LOT. See page 107.

19. AIN 2061020030 (auction ID 50): TRACT NO 8793 LOT 71 BLK 4 . . . ASSESSED TO SHEA ESTATES 0 DEVELOPMENT CORP LOCATION CITY-AGOURA HILL PROPERTY ADDRESS: VACANT LOT. See page 112.

20. AIN 2061021009 (auction ID 51): TRACT NO 8793 LOT 10 BLK 4 . . . ASSESSED TO SHEA ESTATES 0 DEVELOPMENT CORP LOCATION CITY-AGOURA HILL PROPERTY ADDRESS: VACANT LOT. See page 117.

21. AIN 2061021010 (auction ID 52): TRACT NO 8793 LOT 11 BLK 4 . . . ASSESSED TO SHEA ESTATES 0 DEVELOPMENT CORP LOCATION CITY-AGOURA HILL PROPERTY ADDRESS: VACANT LOT. See page 122.

22. AIN 2061021011 (auction ID 53): TRACT NO 8793 LOT 12 BLK 4 . . . ASSESSED TO SHEA ESTATES 0 DEVELOPMENT CORP LOCATION CITY-AGOURA HILL PROPERTY ADDRESS: VACANT LOT. See page 127.

23. AIN 2061021012 (auction ID 54): TRACT NO 8793 LOT 13 BLK 4 . . . ASSESSED TO SHEA ESTATES 0 DEVELOPMENT CORP LOCATION CITY-AGOURA HILL PROPERTY ADDRESS: VACANT LOT. See page 132.

24. AIN 2061021013 (auction ID 55): TRACT NO 8793 LOT 14 BLK 4 . . . ASSESSED TO SHEA ESTATES 0 DEVELOPMENT CORP LOCATION CITY-AGOURA HILL PROPERTY ADDRESS: VACANT LOT. See page 137.

25. AIN 2061021014 (auction ID 56): TRACT NO 8793 LOT 15 BLK 4 ... ASSESSED TO SHEA ESTATES 0 DEVELOPMENT CORP LOCATION CITY-AGOURA HILL PROPERTY ADDRESS: VACANT LOT. See page 142.

26. AIN 2061021015 (auction ID 57): TRACT NO 8793 LOT 72 BLK 4 ... ASSESSED TO SHEA ESTATES 0 DEVELOPMENT CORP LOCATION CITY-AGOURA HILL PROPERTY ADDRESS: VACANT LOT. See page 147.

27. AIN 2061021016 (auction ID 58): TRACT NO 8793 LOT 73 BLK 4 ... ASSESSED TO SHEA ESTATES 0 DEVELOPMENT CORP LOCATION CITY-AGOURA HILL PROPERTY ADDRESS: VACANT LOT. See page 152.

28. AIN 2061021017 (auction ID 59): TRACT NO 8793 LOT 74 BLK 4 ... ASSESSED TO SHEA ESTATES 0 DEVELOPMENT CORP LOCATION CITY-AGOURA HILL PROPERTY ADDRESS: VACANT LOT. See page 157.

29. AIN 2061021018 (auction ID 60): TRACT NO 8793 LOT 75 BLK 4 ... ASSESSED TO SHEA ESTATES 0 DEVELOPMENT CORP LOCATION CITY-AGOURA HILL PROPERTY ADDRESS: VACANT LOT. See page 162.

30. AIN 2061021019 (auction ID 61): TRACT NO 8793 LOT 76 BLK 4 ... ASSESSED TO SHEA ESTATES 0 DEVELOPMENT CORP LOCATION CITY-AGOURA HILL PROPERTY ADDRESS: VACANT LOT. See page 167.

31. AIN 2061021020 (auction ID 62): TRACT NO 8793 LOT 77 BLK 4 ... ASSESSED TO SHEA ESTATES 0 DEVELOPMENT CORP LOCATION CITY-AGOURA HILL PROPERTY ADDRESS: VACANT LOT. See page 172.

32. AIN 2061021021 (auction ID 63): TRACT NO 8793 LOT 78 BLK 4 ... ASSESSED TO SHEA ESTATES 0 DEVELOPMENT CORP LOCATION CITY-AGOURA HILL PROPERTY ADDRESS: VACANT LOT. See page 177.

33. AIN 2061021022 (auction ID 64): TRACT NO 8793 LOT 79 BLK 4 ... ASSESSED TO SHEA ESTATES 0 DEVELOPMENT CORP LOCATION CITY-AGOURA HILL PROPERTY ADDRESS: VACANT LOT. See page 182.

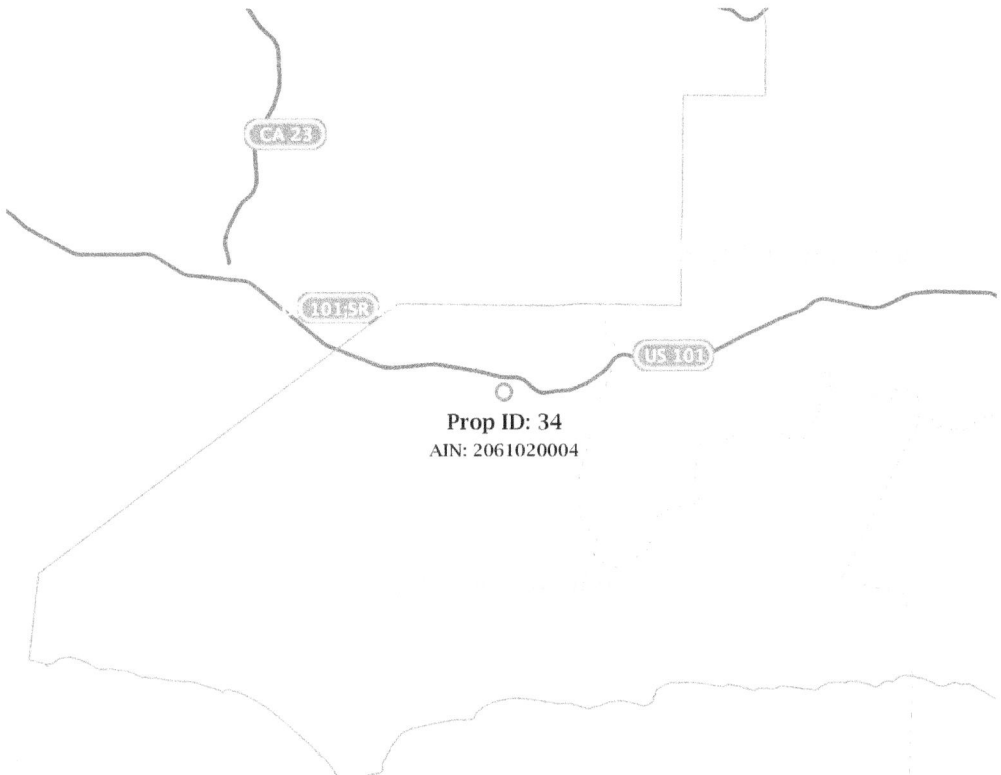

Figure 2.19: Property 64, AIN 2061020004, overview map

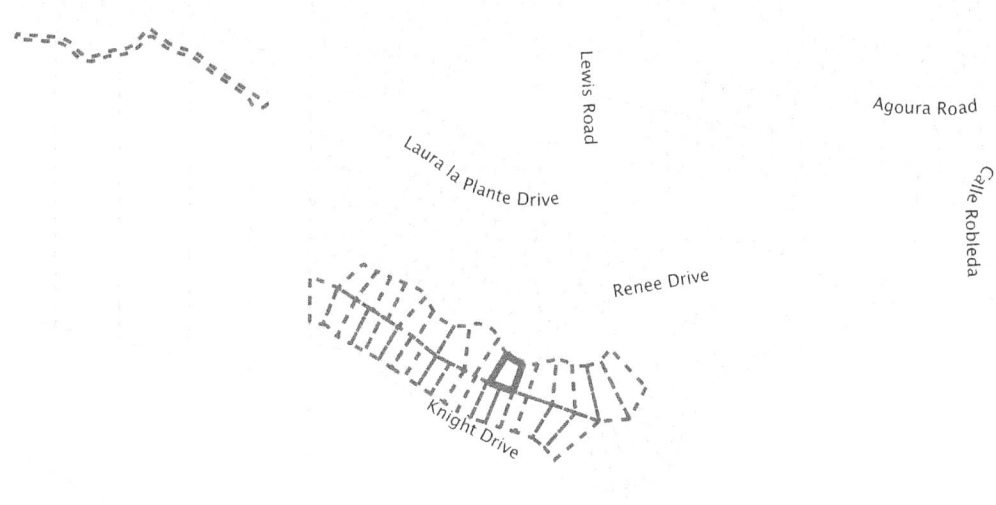

Figure 2.20: Property 64, AIN 2061020004, neighborhood view

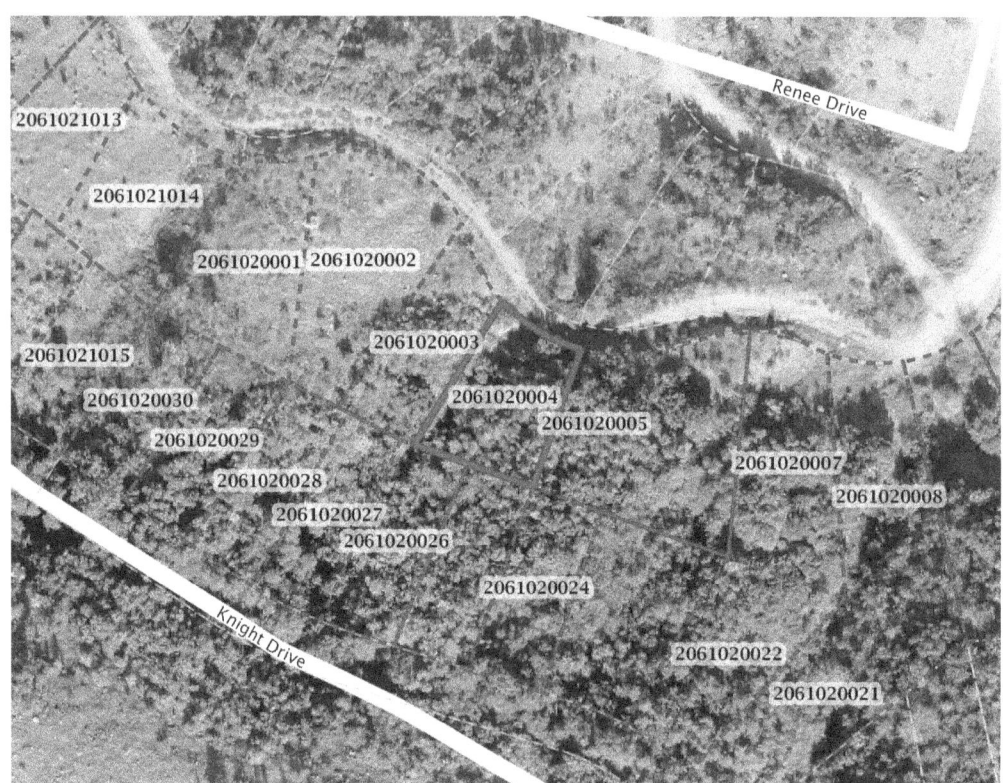

Figure 2.21: Property 64, AIN 2061020004, detailed view

2.8 Auction ID 35

The Los Angeles County Auction Book describes the property as follows.

```
TRACT NO 8793 LOT 20 BLK 4 ASSESSED TO SHEA ESTATES 0 DEVELOPMENT
CORP LOCATION CITY-AGOURA HILL PROPERTY ADDRESS: VACANT LOT
```

The property is located in the general vicinity of Figure 2.22. It is identified by Assessor's Identification Number (AIN) 2061020005. The starting bid is $3,097. Comparable improved properties in this area is about $294/sqft. Comparable unimproved lots in this area is about $49/sqft. This parcel is approximately 4524 sqft. Note, however, that the parcel may be larger than the property under consideration. In case of condominiums, for example, the parcel may encompass other units of the development - those unrelated to the property to be auctioned.

The property is in a parcel zoned Restricted Open Space in Agoura Hills, for 0 to 0 dwelling units.

Figures 2.23 and 2.24 show street map and corresponding detailed aerial view, respectively. In both cases, the map is centered on the property with the containing parcel marked in heavy blue. If surrounding nearby properties are also part of this auction, the street and aerial maps highlights these in heavy, dashed blue outline.

This assessed entity may have other properties that are also in this auction:

1. AIN 2061020001 (auction ID 31): TRACT NO 8793 LOT 16 BLK 4 ... ASSESSED TO SHEA ESTATES 0 DEVELOPMENT CORP LOCATION CITY-AGOURA HILL PROPERTY ADDRESS: VACANT LOT. See page 17.

2. AIN 2061020002 (auction ID 32): TRACT NO 8793 LOT 17 BLK 4 ... ASSESSED TO SHEA ESTATES 0 DEVELOPMENT CORP LOCATION CITY-AGOURA HILL PROPERTY ADDRESS: VACANT LOT. See page 22.

3. AIN 2061020003 (auction ID 33): TRACT NO 8793 LOT 18 BLK 4 ... ASSESSED TO SHEA ESTATES 0 DEVELOPMENT CORP LOCATION CITY-AGOURA HILL PROPERTY ADDRESS: VACANT LOT. See page 27.

4. AIN 2061020004 (auction ID 34): TRACT NO 8793 LOT 19 BLK 4 ... ASSESSED TO SHEA ESTATES 0 DEVELOPMENT CORP LOCATION CITY-AGOURA HILL PROPERTY ADDRESS: VACANT LOT. See page 32.

5. AIN 2061020006 (auction ID 36): TRACT NO 8793 LOT 21 BLK 4 ... ASSESSED TO SHEA ESTATES 0 DEVELOPMENT CORP LOCATION CITY-AGOURA HILL PROPERTY ADDRESS: VACANT LOT. See page 42.

6. AIN 2061020007 (auction ID 37): TRACT NO 8793 LOT 22 BLK 4 ... ASSESSED TO SHEA ESTATES 0 DEVELOPMENT CORP LOCATION CITY-AGOURA HILL PROPERTY ADDRESS: VACANT LOT. See page 47.

7. AIN 2061020008 (auction ID 38): TRACT NO 8793 LOT 23 BLK 4 ... ASSESSED TO SHEA ESTATES 0 DEVELOPMENT CORP LOCATION CITY-AGOURA HILL PROPERTY ADDRESS: VACANT LOT. See page 52.

8. AIN 2061020009 (auction ID 39): TRACT NO 8793 LOT 24 BLK 4 ... ASSESSED TO SHEA ESTATES 0 DEVELOPMENT CORP LOCATION CITY-AGOURA HILL PROPERTY ADDRESS: VACANT LOT. See page 57.

9. AIN 2061020010 (auction ID 40): TRACT NO 8793 LOT 25 BLK 4 ... ASSESSED TO SHEA ESTATES 0 DEVELOPMENT CORP LOCATION CITY-AGOURA HILL PROPERTY ADDRESS: VACANT LOT. See page 62.

10. AIN 2061020021 (auction ID 41): TRACT NO 8793 LOT 62 BLK 4 ... ASSESSED TO SHEA ESTATES 0 DEVELOPMENT CORP LOCATION CITY-AGOURA HILL PROPERTY ADDRESS: VACANT LOT. See page 67.

11. AIN 2061020022 (auction ID 42): TRACT NO 8793 LOT 63 BLK 4 ... ASSESSED TO SHEA ESTATES 0 DEVELOPMENT CORP LOCATION CITY-AGOURA HILL PROPERTY ADDRESS: VACANT LOT. See page 72.

12. AIN 2061020023 (auction ID 43): TRACT NO 8793 LOT 64 BLK 4 ... ASSESSED TO SHEA ESTATES 0 DEVELOPMENT CORP LOCATION CITY-AGOURA HILL PROPERTY ADDRESS: VACANT LOT. See page 77.

13. AIN 2061020024 (auction ID 44): TRACT NO 8793 LOT 65 BLK 4 ... ASSESSED TO SHEA ESTATES 0 DEVELOPMENT CORP LOCATION CITY-AGOURA HILL PROPERTY ADDRESS: VACANT LOT. See page 82.

14. AIN 2061020025 (auction ID 45): TRACT NO 8793 LOT 66 BLK 4 ... ASSESSED TO SHEA ESTATES 0 DEVELOPMENT CORP LOCATION CITY-AGOURA HILL PROPERTY ADDRESS: VACANT LOT. See page 87.

15. AIN 2061020026 (auction ID 46): TRACT NO 8793 LOT 67 BLK 4 ... ASSESSED TO SHEA ESTATES 0 DEVELOPMENT CORP LOCATION CITY-AGOURA HILL PROPERTY ADDRESS: VACANT LOT. See page 92.

16. AIN 2061020027 (auction ID 47): TRACT NO 8793 LOT 68 BLK 4 ... ASSESSED TO SHEA ESTATES 0 DEVELOPMENT CORP LOCATION CITY-AGOURA HILL PROPERTY ADDRESS: VACANT LOT. See page 97.

17. AIN 2061020028 (auction ID 48): TRACT NO 8793 LOT 69 BLK 4 ... ASSESSED TO SHEA ESTATES 0 DEVELOPMENT CORP LOCATION CITY-AGOURA HILL - PROPERTY ADDRESS: VACANT LOT. See page 102.

18. AIN 2061020029 (auction ID 49): TRACT NO 8793 LOT 70 BLK 4 ... ASSESSED TO SHEA ESTATES 0 DEVELOPMENT CORP LOCATION CITY-AGOURA HILL PROPERTY ADDRESS: VACANT LOT. See page 107.

19. AIN 2061020030 (auction ID 50): TRACT NO 8793 LOT 71 BLK 4 ... ASSESSED TO SHEA ESTATES 0 DEVELOPMENT CORP LOCATION CITY-AGOURA HILL PROPERTY ADDRESS: VACANT LOT. See page 112.

20. AIN 2061021009 (auction ID 51): TRACT NO 8793 LOT 10 BLK 4 ... ASSESSED TO SHEA ESTATES 0 DEVELOPMENT CORP LOCATION CITY-AGOURA HILL PROPERTY ADDRESS: VACANT LOT. See page 117.

21. AIN 2061021010 (auction ID 52): TRACT NO 8793 LOT 11 BLK 4 ... ASSESSED TO SHEA ESTATES 0 DEVELOPMENT CORP LOCATION CITY-AGOURA HILL PROPERTY ADDRESS: VACANT LOT. See page 122.

22. AIN 2061021011 (auction ID 53): TRACT NO 8793 LOT 12 BLK 4 ... ASSESSED TO SHEA ESTATES 0 DEVELOPMENT CORP LOCATION CITY-AGOURA HILL PROPERTY ADDRESS: VACANT LOT. See page 127.

23. AIN 2061021012 (auction ID 54): TRACT NO 8793 LOT 13 BLK 4 ... ASSESSED TO SHEA ESTATES 0 DEVELOPMENT CORP LOCATION CITY-AGOURA HILL PROPERTY ADDRESS: VACANT LOT. See page 132.

24. AIN 2061021013 (auction ID 55): TRACT NO 8793 LOT 14 BLK 4 ... ASSESSED TO SHEA ESTATES 0 DEVELOPMENT CORP LOCATION CITY-AGOURA HILL PROPERTY ADDRESS: VACANT LOT. See page 137.

25. AIN 2061021014 (auction ID 56): TRACT NO 8793 LOT 15 BLK 4 . . . ASSESSED TO SHEA ESTATES 0 DEVELOPMENT CORP LOCATION CITY-AGOURA HILL PROPERTY ADDRESS: VACANT LOT. See page 142.

26. AIN 2061021015 (auction ID 57): TRACT NO 8793 LOT 72 BLK 4 . . . ASSESSED TO SHEA ESTATES 0 DEVELOPMENT CORP LOCATION CITY-AGOURA HILL PROPERTY ADDRESS: VACANT LOT. See page 147.

27. AIN 2061021016 (auction ID 58): TRACT NO 8793 LOT 73 BLK 4 . . . ASSESSED TO SHEA ESTATES 0 DEVELOPMENT CORP LOCATION CITY-AGOURA HILL PROPERTY ADDRESS: VACANT LOT. See page 152.

28. AIN 2061021017 (auction ID 59): TRACT NO 8793 LOT 74 BLK 4 . . . ASSESSED TO SHEA ESTATES 0 DEVELOPMENT CORP LOCATION CITY-AGOURA HILL PROPERTY ADDRESS: VACANT LOT. See page 157.

29. AIN 2061021018 (auction ID 60): TRACT NO 8793 LOT 75 BLK 4 . . . ASSESSED TO SHEA ESTATES 0 DEVELOPMENT CORP LOCATION CITY-AGOURA HILL PROPERTY ADDRESS: VACANT LOT. See page 162.

30. AIN 2061021019 (auction ID 61): TRACT NO 8793 LOT 76 BLK 4 . . . ASSESSED TO SHEA ESTATES 0 DEVELOPMENT CORP LOCATION CITY-AGOURA HILL PROPERTY ADDRESS: VACANT LOT. See page 167.

31. AIN 2061021020 (auction ID 62): TRACT NO 8793 LOT 77 BLK 4 . . . ASSESSED TO SHEA ESTATES 0 DEVELOPMENT CORP LOCATION CITY-AGOURA HILL PROPERTY ADDRESS: VACANT LOT. See page 172.

32. AIN 2061021021 (auction ID 63): TRACT NO 8793 LOT 78 BLK 4 . . . ASSESSED TO SHEA ESTATES 0 DEVELOPMENT CORP LOCATION CITY-AGOURA HILL PROPERTY ADDRESS: VACANT LOT. See page 177.

33. AIN 2061021022 (auction ID 64): TRACT NO 8793 LOT 79 BLK 4 . . . ASSESSED TO SHEA ESTATES 0 DEVELOPMENT CORP LOCATION CITY-AGOURA HILL PROPERTY ADDRESS: VACANT LOT. See page 182.

Figure 2.22: Property 64, AIN 2061020005, overview map

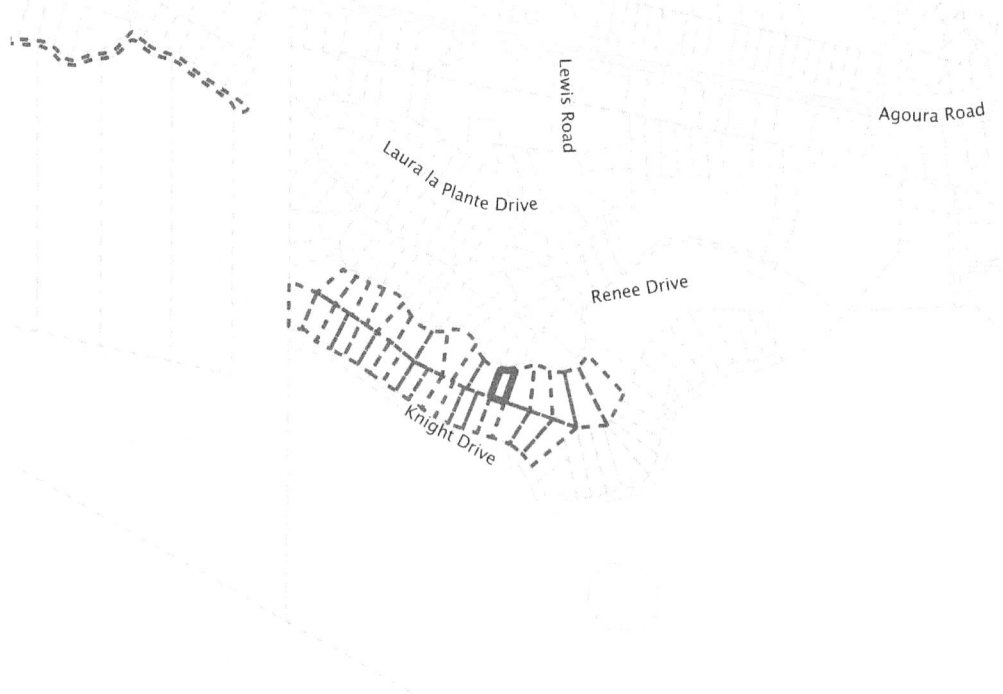

Figure 2.23: Property 64, AIN 2061020005, neighborhood view

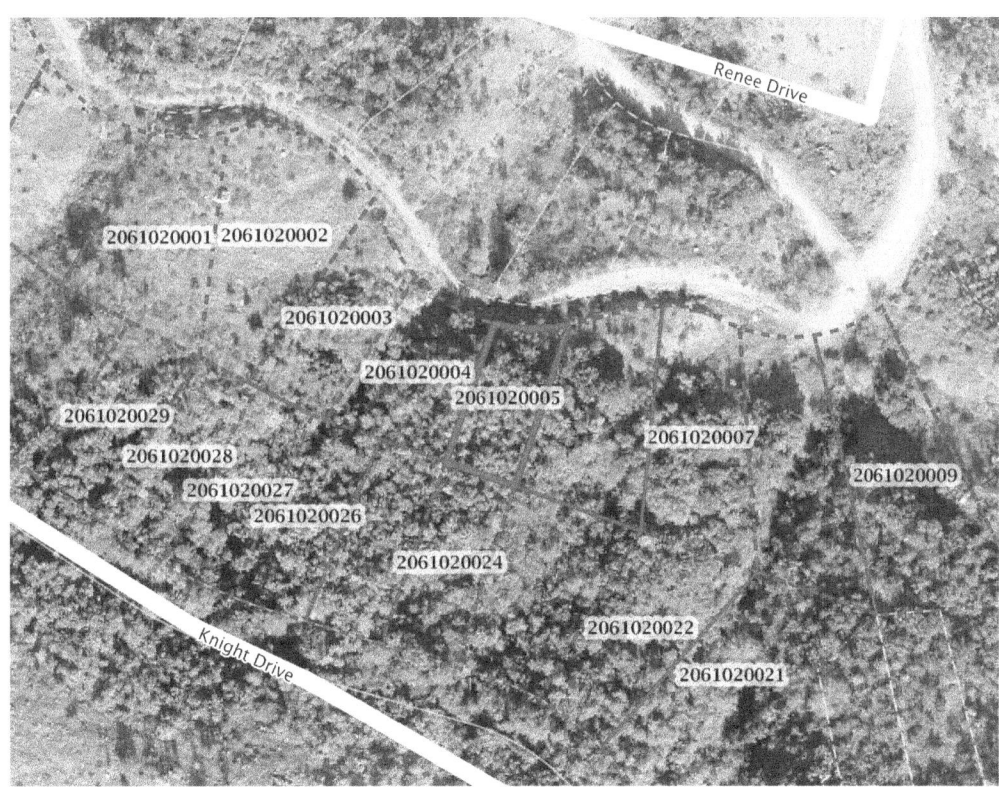

Figure 2.24: Property 64, AIN 2061020005, detailed view

2.9　Auction ID 36

The Los Angeles County Auction Book describes the property as follows.

```
TRACT NO 8793 LOT 21 BLK 4 ASSESSED TO SHEA ESTATES 0 DEVELOPMENT
CORP LOCATION CITY-AGOURA HILL PROPERTY ADDRESS: VACANT LOT
```

The property is located in the general vicinity of Figure 2.25. It is identified by Assessor's Identification Number (AIN) 2061020006. The starting bid is $3,894. Comparable improved properties in this area is about $294/sqft. Comparable unimproved lots in this area is about $49/sqft. This parcel is approximately 8760 sqft. Note, however, that the parcel may be larger than the property under consideration. In case of condominiums, for example, the parcel may encompass other units of the development - those unrelated to the property to be auctioned.

The property is in a parcel zoned Restricted Open Space in Agoura Hills, for 0 to 0 dwelling units.

Figures 2.26 and 2.27 show street map and corresponding detailed aerial view, respectively. In both cases, the map is centered on the property with the containing parcel marked in heavy blue. If surrounding nearby properties are also part of this auction, the street and aerial maps highlights these in heavy, dashed blue outline.

This assessed entity may have other properties that are also in this auction:

1. AIN 2061020001 (auction ID 31): TRACT NO 8793 LOT 16 BLK 4 . . . ASSESSED TO SHEA ESTATES 0 DEVELOPMENT CORP LOCATION CITY-AGOURA HILL PROPERTY ADDRESS: VACANT LOT. See page 17.

2. AIN 2061020002 (auction ID 32): TRACT NO 8793 LOT 17 BLK 4 . . . ASSESSED TO SHEA ESTATES 0 DEVELOPMENT CORP LOCATION CITY-AGOURA HILL PROPERTY ADDRESS: VACANT LOT. See page 22.

3. AIN 2061020003 (auction ID 33): TRACT NO 8793 LOT 18 BLK 4 . . . ASSESSED TO SHEA ESTATES 0 DEVELOPMENT CORP LOCATION CITY-AGOURA HILL PROPERTY ADDRESS: VACANT LOT. See page 27.

4. AIN 2061020004 (auction ID 34): TRACT NO 8793 LOT 19 BLK 4 . . . ASSESSED TO SHEA ESTATES 0 DEVELOPMENT CORP LOCATION CITY-AGOURA HILL PROPERTY ADDRESS: VACANT LOT. See page 32.

5. AIN 2061020005 (auction ID 35): TRACT NO 8793 LOT 20 BLK 4 . . . ASSESSED TO SHEA ESTATES 0 DEVELOPMENT CORP LOCATION CITY-AGOURA HILL PROPERTY ADDRESS: VACANT LOT. See page 37.

6. AIN 2061020007 (auction ID 37): TRACT NO 8793 LOT 22 BLK 4 . . . ASSESSED TO SHEA ESTATES 0 DEVELOPMENT CORP LOCATION CITY-AGOURA HILL PROPERTY ADDRESS: VACANT LOT. See page 47.

7. AIN 2061020008 (auction ID 38): TRACT NO 8793 LOT 23 BLK 4 . . . ASSESSED TO SHEA ESTATES 0 DEVELOPMENT CORP LOCATION CITY-AGOURA HILL PROPERTY ADDRESS: VACANT LOT. See page 52.

8. AIN 2061020009 (auction ID 39): TRACT NO 8793 LOT 24 BLK 4 . . . ASSESSED TO SHEA ESTATES 0 DEVELOPMENT CORP LOCATION CITY-AGOURA HILL PROPERTY ADDRESS: VACANT LOT. See page 57.

9. AIN 2061020010 (auction ID 40): TRACT NO 8793 LOT 25 BLK 4 . . . ASSESSED TO SHEA ESTATES 0 DEVELOPMENT CORP LOCATION CITY-AGOURA HILL PROPERTY ADDRESS: VACANT LOT. See page 62.

10. AIN 2061020021 (auction ID 41): TRACT NO 8793 LOT 62 BLK 4 ... ASSESSED TO SHEA ESTATES 0 DEVELOPMENT CORP LOCATION CITY-AGOURA HILL PROPERTY ADDRESS: VACANT LOT. See page 67.

11. AIN 2061020022 (auction ID 42): TRACT NO 8793 LOT 63 BLK 4 ... ASSESSED TO SHEA ESTATES 0 DEVELOPMENT CORP LOCATION CITY-AGOURA HILL PROPERTY ADDRESS: VACANT LOT. See page 72.

12. AIN 2061020023 (auction ID 43): TRACT NO 8793 LOT 64 BLK 4 ... ASSESSED TO SHEA ESTATES 0 DEVELOPMENT CORP LOCATION CITY-AGOURA HILL PROPERTY ADDRESS: VACANT LOT. See page 77.

13. AIN 2061020024 (auction ID 44): TRACT NO 8793 LOT 65 BLK 4 ... ASSESSED TO SHEA ESTATES 0 DEVELOPMENT CORP LOCATION CITY-AGOURA HILL PROPERTY ADDRESS: VACANT LOT. See page 82.

14. AIN 2061020025 (auction ID 45): TRACT NO 8793 LOT 66 BLK 4 ... ASSESSED TO SHEA ESTATES 0 DEVELOPMENT CORP LOCATION CITY-AGOURA HILL PROPERTY ADDRESS: VACANT LOT. See page 87.

15. AIN 2061020026 (auction ID 46): TRACT NO 8793 LOT 67 BLK 4 ... ASSESSED TO SHEA ESTATES 0 DEVELOPMENT CORP LOCATION CITY-AGOURA HILL PROPERTY ADDRESS: VACANT LOT. See page 92.

16. AIN 2061020027 (auction ID 47): TRACT NO 8793 LOT 68 BLK 4 ... ASSESSED TO SHEA ESTATES 0 DEVELOPMENT CORP LOCATION CITY-AGOURA HILL PROPERTY ADDRESS: VACANT LOT. See page 97.

17. AIN 2061020028 (auction ID 48): TRACT NO 8793 LOT 69 BLK 4 ... ASSESSED TO SHEA ESTATES 0 DEVELOPMENT CORP LOCATION CITY-AGOURA HILL - PROPERTY ADDRESS: VACANT LOT. See page 102.

18. AIN 2061020029 (auction ID 49): TRACT NO 8793 LOT 70 BLK 4 ... ASSESSED TO SHEA ESTATES 0 DEVELOPMENT CORP LOCATION CITY-AGOURA HILL PROPERTY ADDRESS: VACANT LOT. See page 107.

19. AIN 2061020030 (auction ID 50): TRACT NO 8793 LOT 71 BLK 4 ... ASSESSED TO SHEA ESTATES 0 DEVELOPMENT CORP LOCATION CITY-AGOURA HILL PROPERTY ADDRESS: VACANT LOT. See page 112.

20. AIN 2061021009 (auction ID 51): TRACT NO 8793 LOT 10 BLK 4 ... ASSESSED TO SHEA ESTATES 0 DEVELOPMENT CORP LOCATION CITY-AGOURA HILL PROPERTY ADDRESS: VACANT LOT. See page 117.

21. AIN 2061021010 (auction ID 52): TRACT NO 8793 LOT 11 BLK 4 ... ASSESSED TO SHEA ESTATES 0 DEVELOPMENT CORP LOCATION CITY-AGOURA HILL PROPERTY ADDRESS: VACANT LOT. See page 122.

22. AIN 2061021011 (auction ID 53): TRACT NO 8793 LOT 12 BLK 4 ... ASSESSED TO SHEA ESTATES 0 DEVELOPMENT CORP LOCATION CITY-AGOURA HILL PROPERTY ADDRESS: VACANT LOT. See page 127.

23. AIN 2061021012 (auction ID 54): TRACT NO 8793 LOT 13 BLK 4 ... ASSESSED TO SHEA ESTATES 0 DEVELOPMENT CORP LOCATION CITY-AGOURA HILL PROPERTY ADDRESS: VACANT LOT. See page 132.

24. AIN 2061021013 (auction ID 55): TRACT NO 8793 LOT 14 BLK 4 ... ASSESSED TO SHEA ESTATES 0 DEVELOPMENT CORP LOCATION CITY-AGOURA HILL PROPERTY ADDRESS: VACANT LOT. See page 137.

25. AIN 2061021014 (auction ID 56): TRACT NO 8793 LOT 15 BLK 4 . . . ASSESSED TO SHEA ESTATES 0 DEVELOPMENT CORP LOCATION CITY-AGOURA HILL PROPERTY ADDRESS: VACANT LOT. See page 142.

26. AIN 2061021015 (auction ID 57): TRACT NO 8793 LOT 72 BLK 4 . . . ASSESSED TO SHEA ESTATES 0 DEVELOPMENT CORP LOCATION CITY-AGOURA HILL PROPERTY ADDRESS: VACANT LOT. See page 147.

27. AIN 2061021016 (auction ID 58): TRACT NO 8793 LOT 73 BLK 4 . . . ASSESSED TO SHEA ESTATES 0 DEVELOPMENT CORP LOCATION CITY-AGOURA HILL PROPERTY ADDRESS: VACANT LOT. See page 152.

28. AIN 2061021017 (auction ID 59): TRACT NO 8793 LOT 74 BLK 4 . . . ASSESSED TO SHEA ESTATES 0 DEVELOPMENT CORP LOCATION CITY-AGOURA HILL PROPERTY ADDRESS: VACANT LOT. See page 157.

29. AIN 2061021018 (auction ID 60): TRACT NO 8793 LOT 75 BLK 4 . . . ASSESSED TO SHEA ESTATES 0 DEVELOPMENT CORP LOCATION CITY-AGOURA HILL PROPERTY ADDRESS: VACANT LOT. See page 162.

30. AIN 2061021019 (auction ID 61): TRACT NO 8793 LOT 76 BLK 4 . . . ASSESSED TO SHEA ESTATES 0 DEVELOPMENT CORP LOCATION CITY-AGOURA HILL PROPERTY ADDRESS: VACANT LOT. See page 167.

31. AIN 2061021020 (auction ID 62): TRACT NO 8793 LOT 77 BLK 4 . . . ASSESSED TO SHEA ESTATES 0 DEVELOPMENT CORP LOCATION CITY-AGOURA HILL PROPERTY ADDRESS: VACANT LOT. See page 172.

32. AIN 2061021021 (auction ID 63): TRACT NO 8793 LOT 78 BLK 4 . . . ASSESSED TO SHEA ESTATES 0 DEVELOPMENT CORP LOCATION CITY-AGOURA HILL PROPERTY ADDRESS: VACANT LOT. See page 177.

33. AIN 2061021022 (auction ID 64): TRACT NO 8793 LOT 79 BLK 4 . . . ASSESSED TO SHEA ESTATES 0 DEVELOPMENT CORP LOCATION CITY-AGOURA HILL PROPERTY ADDRESS: VACANT LOT. See page 182.

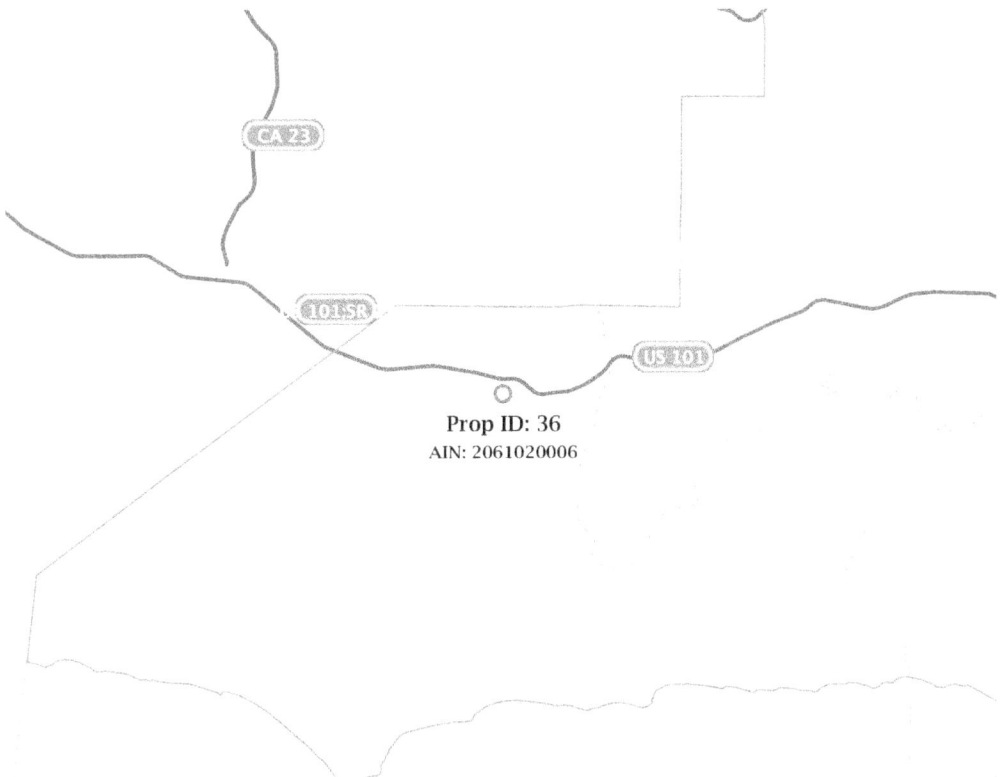

Figure 2.25: Property 64, AIN 2061020006, overview map

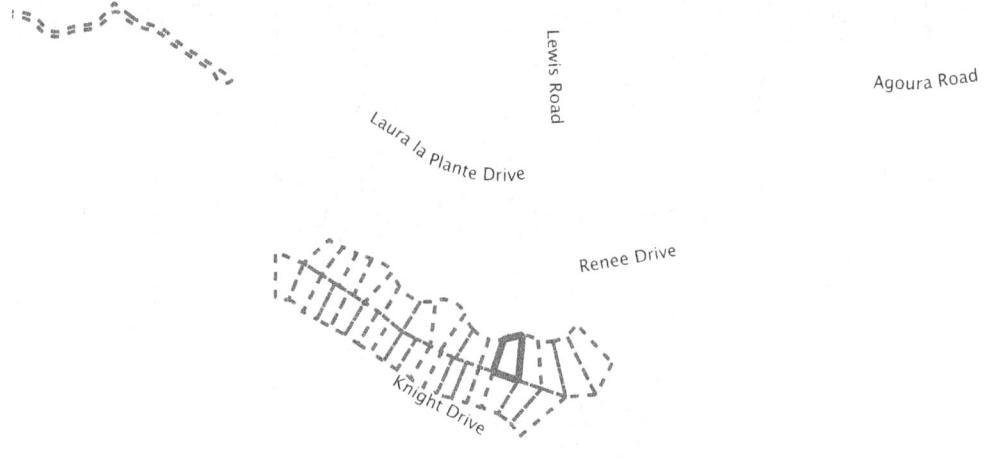

Figure 2.26: Property 64, AIN 2061020006, neighborhood view

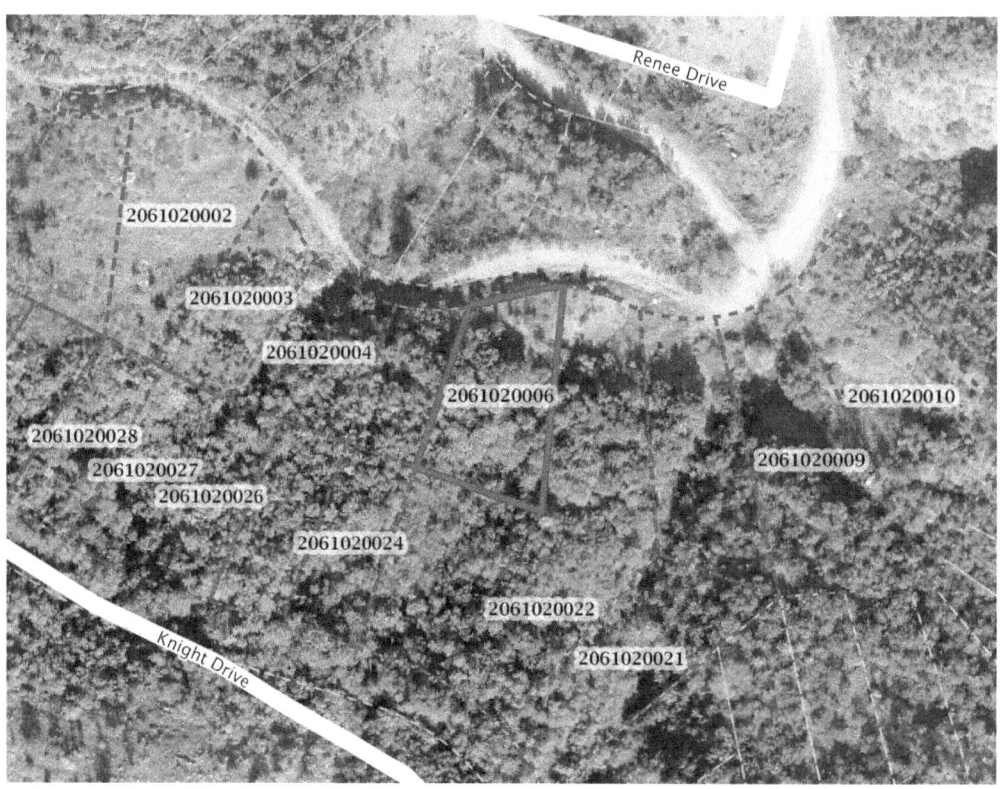

Figure 2.27: Property 64, AIN 2061020006, detailed view

2.10 Auction ID 37

The Los Angeles County Auction Book describes the property as follows.

```
TRACT NO 8793 LOT 22 BLK 4 ASSESSED TO SHEA ESTATES 0 DEVELOPMENT
CORP LOCATION CITY-AGOURA HILL PROPERTY ADDRESS: VACANT LOT
```

The property is located in the general vicinity of Figure 2.28. It is identified by Assessor's Identification Number (AIN) 2061020007. The starting bid is \$4,002. Comparable improved properties in this area is about \$294/sqft. Comparable unimproved lots in this area is about \$49/sqft. This parcel is approximately 9275 sqft. Note, however, that the parcel may be larger than the property under consideration. In case of condominiums, for example, the parcel may encompass other units of the development - those unrelated to the property to be auctioned.

The property is in a parcel zoned Restricted Open Space in Agoura Hills, for 0 to 0 dwelling units.

Figures 2.29 and 2.30 show street map and corresponding detailed aerial view, respectively. In both cases, the map is centered on the property with the containing parcel marked in heavy blue. If surrounding nearby properties are also part of this auction, the street and aerial maps highlights these in heavy, dashed blue outline.

This assessed entity may have other properties that are also in this auction:

1. AIN 2061020001 (auction ID 31): TRACT NO 8793 LOT 16 BLK 4 . . . ASSESSED TO SHEA ESTATES 0 DEVELOPMENT CORP LOCATION CITY-AGOURA HILL PROPERTY ADDRESS: VACANT LOT. See page 17.

2. AIN 2061020002 (auction ID 32): TRACT NO 8793 LOT 17 BLK 4 . . . ASSESSED TO SHEA ESTATES 0 DEVELOPMENT CORP LOCATION CITY-AGOURA HILL PROPERTY ADDRESS: VACANT LOT. See page 22.

3. AIN 2061020003 (auction ID 33): TRACT NO 8793 LOT 18 BLK 4 . . . ASSESSED TO SHEA ESTATES 0 DEVELOPMENT CORP LOCATION CITY-AGOURA HILL PROPERTY ADDRESS: VACANT LOT. See page 27.

4. AIN 2061020004 (auction ID 34): TRACT NO 8793 LOT 19 BLK 4 . . . ASSESSED TO SHEA ESTATES 0 DEVELOPMENT CORP LOCATION CITY-AGOURA HILL PROPERTY ADDRESS: VACANT LOT. See page 32.

5. AIN 2061020005 (auction ID 35): TRACT NO 8793 LOT 20 BLK 4 . . . ASSESSED TO SHEA ESTATES 0 DEVELOPMENT CORP LOCATION CITY-AGOURA HILL PROPERTY ADDRESS: VACANT LOT. See page 37.

6. AIN 2061020006 (auction ID 36): TRACT NO 8793 LOT 21 BLK 4 . . . ASSESSED TO SHEA ESTATES 0 DEVELOPMENT CORP LOCATION CITY-AGOURA HILL PROPERTY ADDRESS: VACANT LOT. See page 42.

7. AIN 2061020008 (auction ID 38): TRACT NO 8793 LOT 23 BLK 4 . . . ASSESSED TO SHEA ESTATES 0 DEVELOPMENT CORP LOCATION CITY-AGOURA HILL PROPERTY ADDRESS: VACANT LOT. See page 52.

8. AIN 2061020009 (auction ID 39): TRACT NO 8793 LOT 24 BLK 4 . . . ASSESSED TO SHEA ESTATES 0 DEVELOPMENT CORP LOCATION CITY-AGOURA HILL PROPERTY ADDRESS: VACANT LOT. See page 57.

9. AIN 2061020010 (auction ID 40): TRACT NO 8793 LOT 25 BLK 4 . . . ASSESSED TO SHEA ESTATES 0 DEVELOPMENT CORP LOCATION CITY-AGOURA HILL PROPERTY ADDRESS: VACANT LOT. See page 62.

10. AIN 2061020021 (auction ID 41): TRACT NO 8793 LOT 62 BLK 4 . . . ASSESSED TO SHEA ESTATES 0 DEVELOPMENT CORP LOCATION CITY-AGOURA HILL PROPERTY ADDRESS: VACANT LOT. See page 67.

11. AIN 2061020022 (auction ID 42): TRACT NO 8793 LOT 63 BLK 4 . . . ASSESSED TO SHEA ESTATES 0 DEVELOPMENT CORP LOCATION CITY-AGOURA HILL PROPERTY ADDRESS: VACANT LOT. See page 72.

12. AIN 2061020023 (auction ID 43): TRACT NO 8793 LOT 64 BLK 4 . . . ASSESSED TO SHEA ESTATES 0 DEVELOPMENT CORP LOCATION CITY-AGOURA HILL PROPERTY ADDRESS: VACANT LOT. See page 77.

13. AIN 2061020024 (auction ID 44): TRACT NO 8793 LOT 65 BLK 4 . . . ASSESSED TO SHEA ESTATES 0 DEVELOPMENT CORP LOCATION CITY-AGOURA HILL PROPERTY ADDRESS: VACANT LOT. See page 82.

14. AIN 2061020025 (auction ID 45): TRACT NO 8793 LOT 66 BLK 4 . . . ASSESSED TO SHEA ESTATES 0 DEVELOPMENT CORP LOCATION CITY-AGOURA HILL PROPERTY ADDRESS: VACANT LOT. See page 87.

15. AIN 2061020026 (auction ID 46): TRACT NO 8793 LOT 67 BLK 4 . . . ASSESSED TO SHEA ESTATES 0 DEVELOPMENT CORP LOCATION CITY-AGOURA HILL PROPERTY ADDRESS: VACANT LOT. See page 92.

16. AIN 2061020027 (auction ID 47): TRACT NO 8793 LOT 68 BLK 4 . . . ASSESSED TO SHEA ESTATES 0 DEVELOPMENT CORP LOCATION CITY-AGOURA HILL PROPERTY ADDRESS: VACANT LOT. See page 97.

17. AIN 2061020028 (auction ID 48): TRACT NO 8793 LOT 69 BLK 4 . . . ASSESSED TO SHEA ESTATES 0 DEVELOPMENT CORP LOCATION CITY-AGOURA HILL - PROPERTY ADDRESS: VACANT LOT. See page 102.

18. AIN 2061020029 (auction ID 49): TRACT NO 8793 LOT 70 BLK 4 . . . ASSESSED TO SHEA ESTATES 0 DEVELOPMENT CORP LOCATION CITY-AGOURA HILL PROPERTY ADDRESS: VACANT LOT. See page 107.

19. AIN 2061020030 (auction ID 50): TRACT NO 8793 LOT 71 BLK 4 . . . ASSESSED TO SHEA ESTATES 0 DEVELOPMENT CORP LOCATION CITY-AGOURA HILL PROPERTY ADDRESS: VACANT LOT. See page 112.

20. AIN 2061021009 (auction ID 51): TRACT NO 8793 LOT 10 BLK 4 . . . ASSESSED TO SHEA ESTATES 0 DEVELOPMENT CORP LOCATION CITY-AGOURA HILL PROPERTY ADDRESS: VACANT LOT. See page 117.

21. AIN 2061021010 (auction ID 52): TRACT NO 8793 LOT 11 BLK 4 . . . ASSESSED TO SHEA ESTATES 0 DEVELOPMENT CORP LOCATION CITY-AGOURA HILL PROPERTY ADDRESS: VACANT LOT. See page 122.

22. AIN 2061021011 (auction ID 53): TRACT NO 8793 LOT 12 BLK 4 . . . ASSESSED TO SHEA ESTATES 0 DEVELOPMENT CORP LOCATION CITY-AGOURA HILL PROPERTY ADDRESS: VACANT LOT. See page 127.

23. AIN 2061021012 (auction ID 54): TRACT NO 8793 LOT 13 BLK 4 . . . ASSESSED TO SHEA ESTATES 0 DEVELOPMENT CORP LOCATION CITY-AGOURA HILL PROPERTY ADDRESS: VACANT LOT. See page 132.

24. AIN 2061021013 (auction ID 55): TRACT NO 8793 LOT 14 BLK 4 . . . ASSESSED TO SHEA ESTATES 0 DEVELOPMENT CORP LOCATION CITY-AGOURA HILL PROPERTY ADDRESS: VACANT LOT. See page 137.

25. AIN 2061021014 (auction ID 56): TRACT NO 8793 LOT 15 BLK 4 ... ASSESSED TO SHEA ESTATES 0 DEVELOPMENT CORP LOCATION CITY-AGOURA HILL PROPERTY ADDRESS: VACANT LOT. See page 142.

26. AIN 2061021015 (auction ID 57): TRACT NO 8793 LOT 72 BLK 4 ... ASSESSED TO SHEA ESTATES 0 DEVELOPMENT CORP LOCATION CITY-AGOURA HILL PROPERTY ADDRESS: VACANT LOT. See page 147.

27. AIN 2061021016 (auction ID 58): TRACT NO 8793 LOT 73 BLK 4 ... ASSESSED TO SHEA ESTATES 0 DEVELOPMENT CORP LOCATION CITY-AGOURA HILL PROPERTY ADDRESS: VACANT LOT. See page 152.

28. AIN 2061021017 (auction ID 59): TRACT NO 8793 LOT 74 BLK 4 ... ASSESSED TO SHEA ESTATES 0 DEVELOPMENT CORP LOCATION CITY-AGOURA HILL PROPERTY ADDRESS: VACANT LOT. See page 157.

29. AIN 2061021018 (auction ID 60): TRACT NO 8793 LOT 75 BLK 4 ... ASSESSED TO SHEA ESTATES 0 DEVELOPMENT CORP LOCATION CITY-AGOURA HILL PROPERTY ADDRESS: VACANT LOT. See page 162.

30. AIN 2061021019 (auction ID 61): TRACT NO 8793 LOT 76 BLK 4 ... ASSESSED TO SHEA ESTATES 0 DEVELOPMENT CORP LOCATION CITY-AGOURA HILL PROPERTY ADDRESS: VACANT LOT. See page 167.

31. AIN 2061021020 (auction ID 62): TRACT NO 8793 LOT 77 BLK 4 ... ASSESSED TO SHEA ESTATES 0 DEVELOPMENT CORP LOCATION CITY-AGOURA HILL PROPERTY ADDRESS: VACANT LOT. See page 172.

32. AIN 2061021021 (auction ID 63): TRACT NO 8793 LOT 78 BLK 4 ... ASSESSED TO SHEA ESTATES 0 DEVELOPMENT CORP LOCATION CITY-AGOURA HILL PROPERTY ADDRESS: VACANT LOT. See page 177.

33. AIN 2061021022 (auction ID 64): TRACT NO 8793 LOT 79 BLK 4 ... ASSESSED TO SHEA ESTATES 0 DEVELOPMENT CORP LOCATION CITY-AGOURA HILL PROPERTY ADDRESS: VACANT LOT. See page 182.

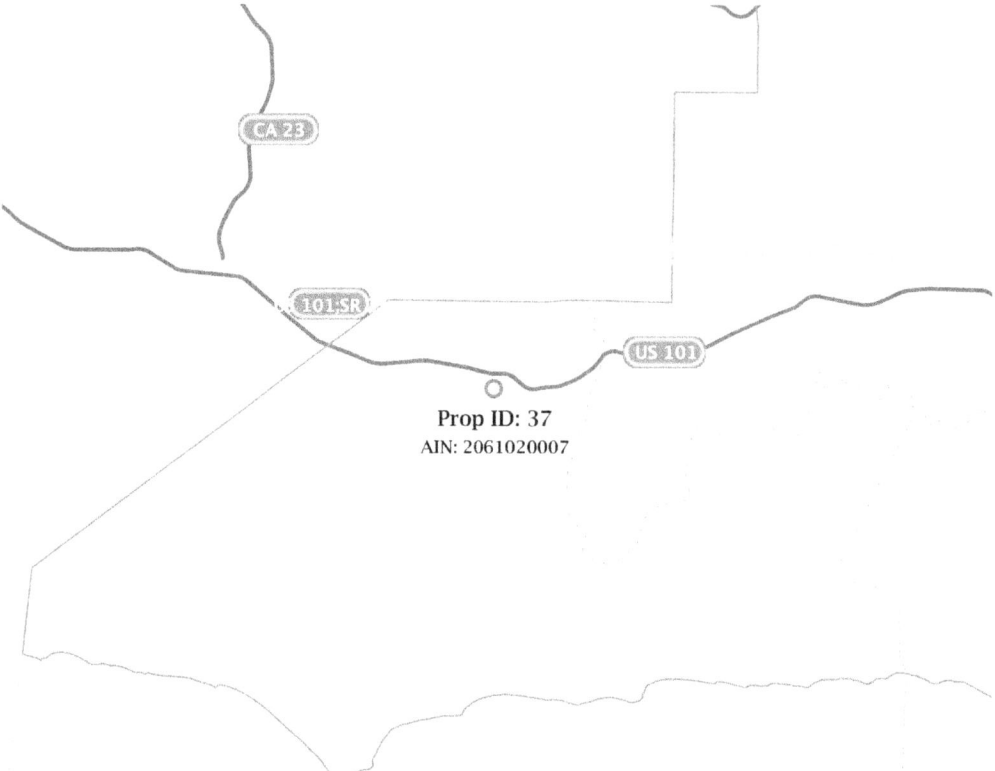

Figure 2.28: Property 64, AIN 2061020007, overview map

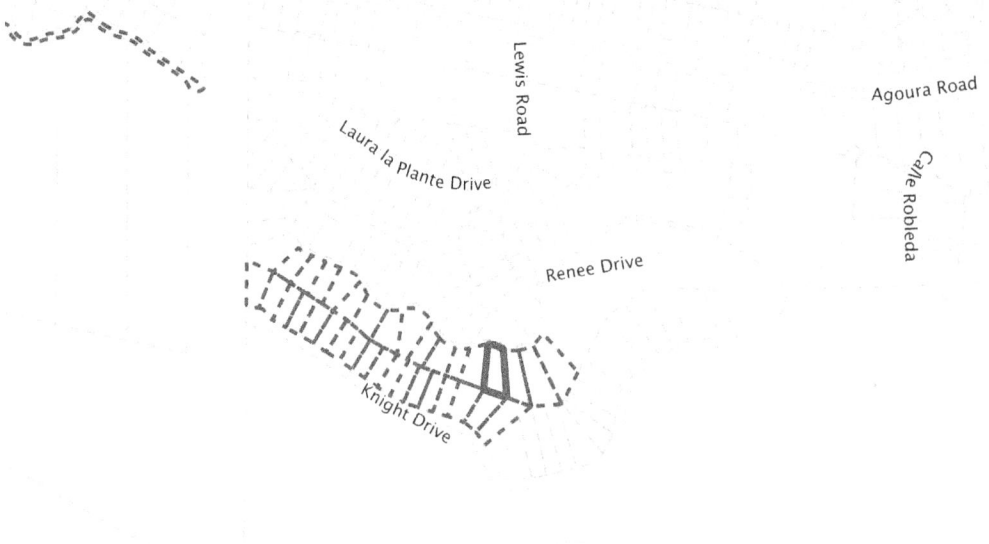

Figure 2.29: Property 64, AIN 2061020007, neighborhood view

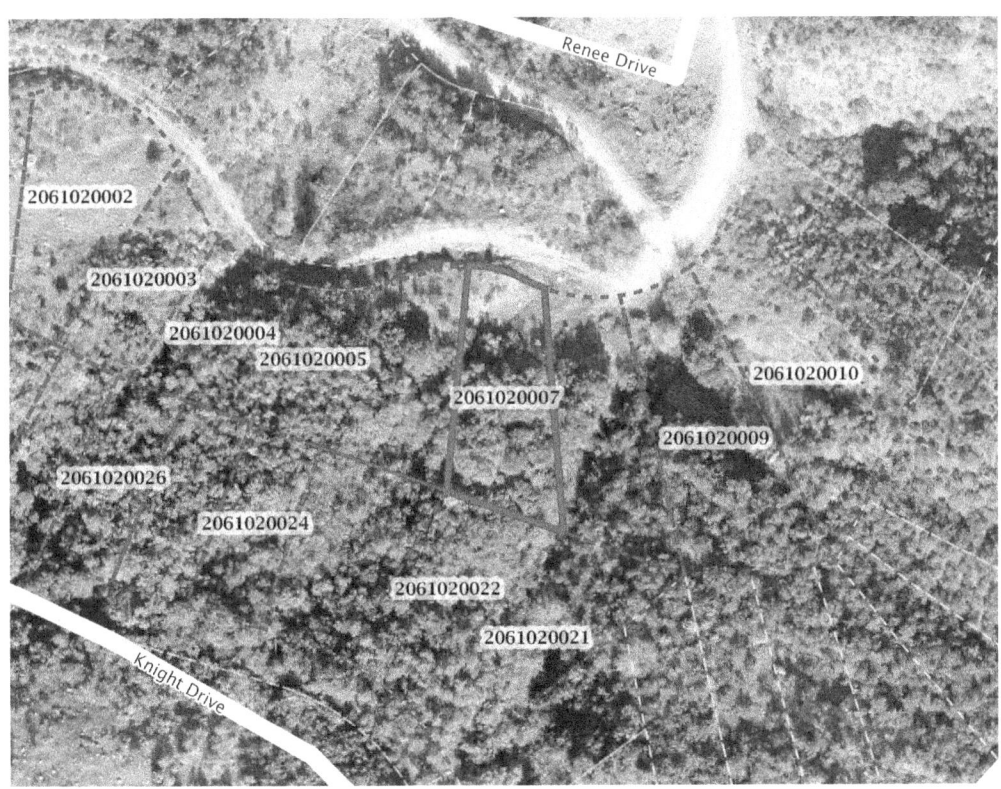

Figure 2.30: Property 64, AIN 2061020007, detailed view

2.11   Auction ID 38

The Los Angeles County Auction Book describes the property as follows.

```
TRACT NO 8793 LOT 23 BLK 4 ASSESSED TO SHEA ESTATES 0 DEVELOPMENT
CORP LOCATION CITY-AGOURA HILL PROPERTY ADDRESS: VACANT LOT
```

The property is located in the general vicinity of Figure 2.31. It is identified by Assessor's Identification Number (AIN) 2061020008. The starting bid is \$4,032. Comparable improved properties in this area is about \$294/sqft. Comparable unimproved lots in this area is about \$49/sqft. This parcel is approximately 9851 sqft. Note, however, that the parcel may be larger than the property under consideration. In case of condominiums, for example, the parcel may encompass other units of the development - those unrelated to the property to be auctioned.

The property is in a parcel zoned Restricted Open Space in Agoura Hills, for 0 to 0 dwelling units.

Figures 2.32 and 2.33 show street map and corresponding detailed aerial view, respectively. In both cases, the map is centered on the property with the containing parcel marked in heavy blue. If surrounding nearby properties are also part of this auction, the street and aerial maps highlights these in heavy, dashed blue outline.

This assessed entity may have other properties that are also in this auction:

1. AIN 2061020001 (auction ID 31): TRACT NO 8793 LOT 16 BLK 4 ... ASSESSED TO SHEA ESTATES 0 DEVELOPMENT CORP LOCATION CITY-AGOURA HILL PROPERTY ADDRESS: VACANT LOT. See page 17.

2. AIN 2061020002 (auction ID 32): TRACT NO 8793 LOT 17 BLK 4 ... ASSESSED TO SHEA ESTATES 0 DEVELOPMENT CORP LOCATION CITY-AGOURA HILL PROPERTY ADDRESS: VACANT LOT. See page 22.

3. AIN 2061020003 (auction ID 33): TRACT NO 8793 LOT 18 BLK 4 ... ASSESSED TO SHEA ESTATES 0 DEVELOPMENT CORP LOCATION CITY-AGOURA HILL PROPERTY ADDRESS: VACANT LOT. See page 27.

4. AIN 2061020004 (auction ID 34): TRACT NO 8793 LOT 19 BLK 4 ... ASSESSED TO SHEA ESTATES 0 DEVELOPMENT CORP LOCATION CITY-AGOURA HILL PROPERTY ADDRESS: VACANT LOT. See page 32.

5. AIN 2061020005 (auction ID 35): TRACT NO 8793 LOT 20 BLK 4 ... ASSESSED TO SHEA ESTATES 0 DEVELOPMENT CORP LOCATION CITY-AGOURA HILL PROPERTY ADDRESS: VACANT LOT. See page 37.

6. AIN 2061020006 (auction ID 36): TRACT NO 8793 LOT 21 BLK 4 ... ASSESSED TO SHEA ESTATES 0 DEVELOPMENT CORP LOCATION CITY-AGOURA HILL PROPERTY ADDRESS: VACANT LOT. See page 42.

7. AIN 2061020007 (auction ID 37): TRACT NO 8793 LOT 22 BLK 4 ... ASSESSED TO SHEA ESTATES 0 DEVELOPMENT CORP LOCATION CITY-AGOURA HILL PROPERTY ADDRESS: VACANT LOT. See page 47.

8. AIN 2061020009 (auction ID 39): TRACT NO 8793 LOT 24 BLK 4 ... ASSESSED TO SHEA ESTATES 0 DEVELOPMENT CORP LOCATION CITY-AGOURA HILL PROPERTY ADDRESS: VACANT LOT. See page 57.

9. AIN 2061020010 (auction ID 40): TRACT NO 8793 LOT 25 BLK 4 ... ASSESSED TO SHEA ESTATES 0 DEVELOPMENT CORP LOCATION CITY-AGOURA HILL PROPERTY ADDRESS: VACANT LOT. See page 62.

10. AIN 2061020021 (auction ID 41): TRACT NO 8793 LOT 62 BLK 4 ... ASSESSED TO SHEA ESTATES 0 DEVELOPMENT CORP LOCATION CITY-AGOURA HILL PROPERTY ADDRESS: VACANT LOT. See page 67.

11. AIN 2061020022 (auction ID 42): TRACT NO 8793 LOT 63 BLK 4 ... ASSESSED TO SHEA ESTATES 0 DEVELOPMENT CORP LOCATION CITY-AGOURA HILL PROPERTY ADDRESS: VACANT LOT. See page 72.

12. AIN 2061020023 (auction ID 43): TRACT NO 8793 LOT 64 BLK 4 ... ASSESSED TO SHEA ESTATES 0 DEVELOPMENT CORP LOCATION CITY-AGOURA HILL PROPERTY ADDRESS: VACANT LOT. See page 77.

13. AIN 2061020024 (auction ID 44): TRACT NO 8793 LOT 65 BLK 4 ... ASSESSED TO SHEA ESTATES 0 DEVELOPMENT CORP LOCATION CITY-AGOURA HILL PROPERTY ADDRESS: VACANT LOT. See page 82.

14. AIN 2061020025 (auction ID 45): TRACT NO 8793 LOT 66 BLK 4 ... ASSESSED TO SHEA ESTATES 0 DEVELOPMENT CORP LOCATION CITY-AGOURA HILL PROPERTY ADDRESS: VACANT LOT. See page 87.

15. AIN 2061020026 (auction ID 46): TRACT NO 8793 LOT 67 BLK 4 ... ASSESSED TO SHEA ESTATES 0 DEVELOPMENT CORP LOCATION CITY-AGOURA HILL PROPERTY ADDRESS: VACANT LOT. See page 92.

16. AIN 2061020027 (auction ID 47): TRACT NO 8793 LOT 68 BLK 4 ... ASSESSED TO SHEA ESTATES 0 DEVELOPMENT CORP LOCATION CITY-AGOURA HILL PROPERTY ADDRESS: VACANT LOT. See page 97.

17. AIN 2061020028 (auction ID 48): TRACT NO 8793 LOT 69 BLK 4 ... ASSESSED TO SHEA ESTATES 0 DEVELOPMENT CORP LOCATION CITY-AGOURA HILL - PROPERTY ADDRESS: VACANT LOT. See page 102.

18. AIN 2061020029 (auction ID 49): TRACT NO 8793 LOT 70 BLK 4 ... ASSESSED TO SHEA ESTATES 0 DEVELOPMENT CORP LOCATION CITY-AGOURA HILL PROPERTY ADDRESS: VACANT LOT. See page 107.

19. AIN 2061020030 (auction ID 50): TRACT NO 8793 LOT 71 BLK 4 ... ASSESSED TO SHEA ESTATES 0 DEVELOPMENT CORP LOCATION CITY-AGOURA HILL PROPERTY ADDRESS: VACANT LOT. See page 112.

20. AIN 2061021009 (auction ID 51): TRACT NO 8793 LOT 10 BLK 4 ... ASSESSED TO SHEA ESTATES 0 DEVELOPMENT CORP LOCATION CITY-AGOURA HILL PROPERTY ADDRESS: VACANT LOT. See page 117.

21. AIN 2061021010 (auction ID 52): TRACT NO 8793 LOT 11 BLK 4 ... ASSESSED TO SHEA ESTATES 0 DEVELOPMENT CORP LOCATION CITY-AGOURA HILL PROPERTY ADDRESS: VACANT LOT. See page 122.

22. AIN 2061021011 (auction ID 53): TRACT NO 8793 LOT 12 BLK 4 ... ASSESSED TO SHEA ESTATES 0 DEVELOPMENT CORP LOCATION CITY-AGOURA HILL PROPERTY ADDRESS: VACANT LOT. See page 127.

23. AIN 2061021012 (auction ID 54): TRACT NO 8793 LOT 13 BLK 4 ... ASSESSED TO SHEA ESTATES 0 DEVELOPMENT CORP LOCATION CITY-AGOURA HILL PROPERTY ADDRESS: VACANT LOT. See page 132.

24. AIN 2061021013 (auction ID 55): TRACT NO 8793 LOT 14 BLK 4 ... ASSESSED TO SHEA ESTATES 0 DEVELOPMENT CORP LOCATION CITY-AGOURA HILL PROPERTY ADDRESS: VACANT LOT. See page 137.

25. AIN 2061021014 (auction ID 56): TRACT NO 8793 LOT 15 BLK 4 ... ASSESSED TO SHEA ESTATES
    0 DEVELOPMENT CORP LOCATION CITY-AGOURA HILL PROPERTY ADDRESS: VACANT LOT.
    See page 142.

26. AIN 2061021015 (auction ID 57): TRACT NO 8793 LOT 72 BLK 4 ... ASSESSED TO SHEA ESTATES
    0 DEVELOPMENT CORP LOCATION CITY-AGOURA HILL PROPERTY ADDRESS: VACANT LOT.
    See page 147.

27. AIN 2061021016 (auction ID 58): TRACT NO 8793 LOT 73 BLK 4 ... ASSESSED TO SHEA ESTATES
    0 DEVELOPMENT CORP LOCATION CITY-AGOURA HILL PROPERTY ADDRESS: VACANT LOT.
    See page 152.

28. AIN 2061021017 (auction ID 59): TRACT NO 8793 LOT 74 BLK 4 ... ASSESSED TO SHEA ESTATES
    0 DEVELOPMENT CORP LOCATION CITY-AGOURA HILL PROPERTY ADDRESS: VACANT LOT.
    See page 157.

29. AIN 2061021018 (auction ID 60): TRACT NO 8793 LOT 75 BLK 4 ... ASSESSED TO SHEA ESTATES
    0 DEVELOPMENT CORP LOCATION CITY-AGOURA HILL PROPERTY ADDRESS: VACANT LOT.
    See page 162.

30. AIN 2061021019 (auction ID 61): TRACT NO 8793 LOT 76 BLK 4 ... ASSESSED TO SHEA ESTATES
    0 DEVELOPMENT CORP LOCATION CITY-AGOURA HILL PROPERTY ADDRESS: VACANT LOT.
    See page 167.

31. AIN 2061021020 (auction ID 62): TRACT NO 8793 LOT 77 BLK 4 ... ASSESSED TO SHEA ESTATES
    0 DEVELOPMENT CORP LOCATION CITY-AGOURA HILL PROPERTY ADDRESS: VACANT LOT.
    See page 172.

32. AIN 2061021021 (auction ID 63): TRACT NO 8793 LOT 78 BLK 4 ... ASSESSED TO SHEA ESTATES
    0 DEVELOPMENT CORP LOCATION CITY-AGOURA HILL PROPERTY ADDRESS: VACANT LOT.
    See page 177.

33. AIN 2061021022 (auction ID 64): TRACT NO 8793 LOT 79 BLK 4 ... ASSESSED TO SHEA ESTATES
    0 DEVELOPMENT CORP LOCATION CITY-AGOURA HILL PROPERTY ADDRESS: VACANT LOT.
    See page 182.

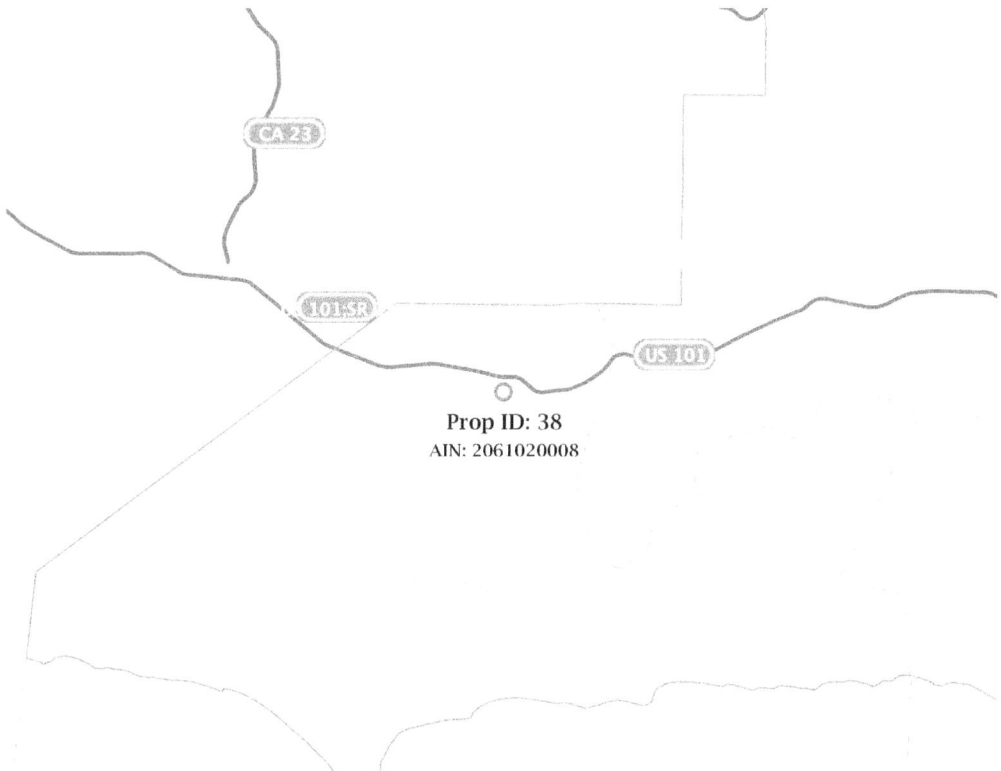

Figure 2.31: Property 64, AIN 2061020008, overview map

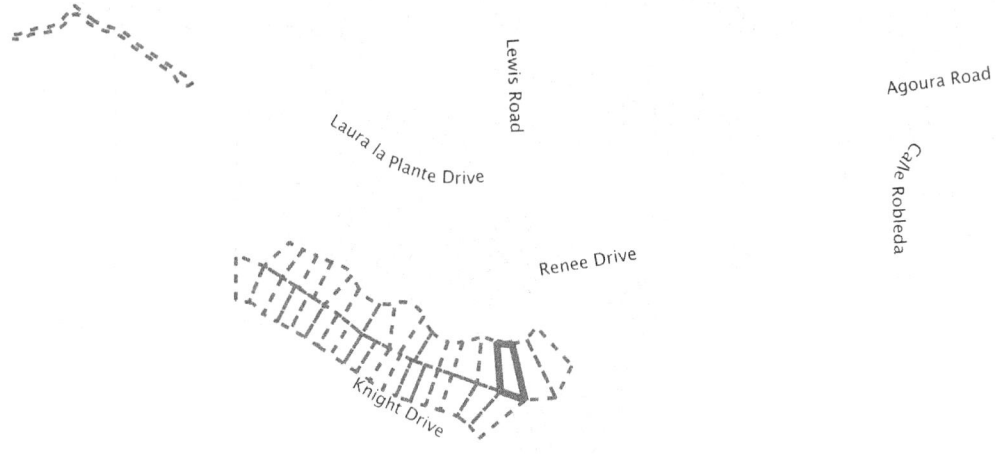

Figure 2.32: Property 64, AIN 2061020008, neighborhood view

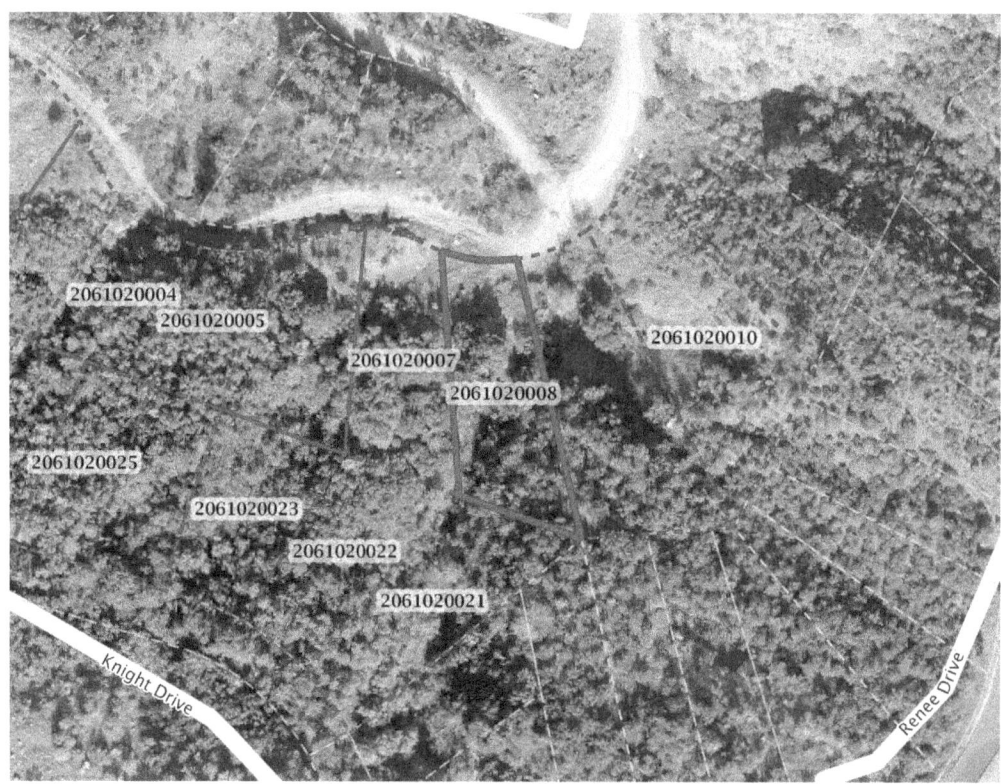

Figure 2.33: Property 64, AIN 2061020008, detailed view

2.12 Auction ID 39

The Los Angeles County Auction Book describes the property as follows.

```
TRACT NO 8793 LOT 24 BLK 4 ASSESSED TO SHEA ESTATES 0 DEVELOPMENT
CORP LOCATION CITY-AGOURA HILL PROPERTY ADDRESS: VACANT LOT
```

The property is located in the general vicinity of Figure 2.34. It is identified by Assessor's Identification Number (AIN) 2061020009. The starting bid is $4,799. Comparable improved properties in this area is about $297/sqft. Comparable unimproved lots in this area is about $49/sqft. This parcel is approximately 13610 sqft. Note, however, that the parcel may be larger than the property under consideration. In case of condominiums, for example, the parcel may encompass other units of the development - those unrelated to the property to be auctioned.

The property is in a parcel zoned Restricted Open Space in Agoura Hills, for 0 to 0 dwelling units.

Figures 2.35 and 2.36 show street map and corresponding detailed aerial view, respectively. In both cases, the map is centered on the property with the containing parcel marked in heavy blue. If surrounding nearby properties are also part of this auction, the street and aerial maps highlights these in heavy, dashed blue outline.

This assessed entity may have other properties that are also in this auction:

1. AIN 2061020001 (auction ID 31): TRACT NO 8793 LOT 16 BLK 4 ... ASSESSED TO SHEA ESTATES 0 DEVELOPMENT CORP LOCATION CITY-AGOURA HILL PROPERTY ADDRESS: VACANT LOT. See page 17.

2. AIN 2061020002 (auction ID 32): TRACT NO 8793 LOT 17 BLK 4 ... ASSESSED TO SHEA ESTATES 0 DEVELOPMENT CORP LOCATION CITY-AGOURA HILL PROPERTY ADDRESS: VACANT LOT. See page 22.

3. AIN 2061020003 (auction ID 33): TRACT NO 8793 LOT 18 BLK 4 ... ASSESSED TO SHEA ESTATES 0 DEVELOPMENT CORP LOCATION CITY-AGOURA HILL PROPERTY ADDRESS: VACANT LOT. See page 27.

4. AIN 2061020004 (auction ID 34): TRACT NO 8793 LOT 19 BLK 4 ... ASSESSED TO SHEA ESTATES 0 DEVELOPMENT CORP LOCATION CITY-AGOURA HILL PROPERTY ADDRESS: VACANT LOT. See page 32.

5. AIN 2061020005 (auction ID 35): TRACT NO 8793 LOT 20 BLK 4 ... ASSESSED TO SHEA ESTATES 0 DEVELOPMENT CORP LOCATION CITY-AGOURA HILL PROPERTY ADDRESS: VACANT LOT. See page 37.

6. AIN 2061020006 (auction ID 36): TRACT NO 8793 LOT 21 BLK 4 ... ASSESSED TO SHEA ESTATES 0 DEVELOPMENT CORP LOCATION CITY-AGOURA HILL PROPERTY ADDRESS: VACANT LOT. See page 42.

7. AIN 2061020007 (auction ID 37): TRACT NO 8793 LOT 22 BLK 4 ... ASSESSED TO SHEA ESTATES 0 DEVELOPMENT CORP LOCATION CITY-AGOURA HILL PROPERTY ADDRESS: VACANT LOT. See page 47.

8. AIN 2061020008 (auction ID 38): TRACT NO 8793 LOT 23 BLK 4 ... ASSESSED TO SHEA ESTATES 0 DEVELOPMENT CORP LOCATION CITY-AGOURA HILL PROPERTY ADDRESS: VACANT LOT. See page 52.

9. AIN 2061020010 (auction ID 40): TRACT NO 8793 LOT 25 BLK 4 ... ASSESSED TO SHEA ESTATES 0 DEVELOPMENT CORP LOCATION CITY-AGOURA HILL PROPERTY ADDRESS: VACANT LOT. See page 62.

10. AIN 2061020021 (auction ID 41): TRACT NO 8793 LOT 62 BLK 4 ... ASSESSED TO SHEA ESTATES 0 DEVELOPMENT CORP LOCATION CITY-AGOURA HILL PROPERTY ADDRESS: VACANT LOT. See page 67.

11. AIN 2061020022 (auction ID 42): TRACT NO 8793 LOT 63 BLK 4 ... ASSESSED TO SHEA ESTATES 0 DEVELOPMENT CORP LOCATION CITY-AGOURA HILL PROPERTY ADDRESS: VACANT LOT. See page 72.

12. AIN 2061020023 (auction ID 43): TRACT NO 8793 LOT 64 BLK 4 ... ASSESSED TO SHEA ESTATES 0 DEVELOPMENT CORP LOCATION CITY-AGOURA HILL PROPERTY ADDRESS: VACANT LOT. See page 77.

13. AIN 2061020024 (auction ID 44): TRACT NO 8793 LOT 65 BLK 4 ... ASSESSED TO SHEA ESTATES 0 DEVELOPMENT CORP LOCATION CITY-AGOURA HILL PROPERTY ADDRESS: VACANT LOT. See page 82.

14. AIN 2061020025 (auction ID 45): TRACT NO 8793 LOT 66 BLK 4 ... ASSESSED TO SHEA ESTATES 0 DEVELOPMENT CORP LOCATION CITY-AGOURA HILL PROPERTY ADDRESS: VACANT LOT. See page 87.

15. AIN 2061020026 (auction ID 46): TRACT NO 8793 LOT 67 BLK 4 ... ASSESSED TO SHEA ESTATES 0 DEVELOPMENT CORP LOCATION CITY-AGOURA HILL PROPERTY ADDRESS: VACANT LOT. See page 92.

16. AIN 2061020027 (auction ID 47): TRACT NO 8793 LOT 68 BLK 4 ... ASSESSED TO SHEA ESTATES 0 DEVELOPMENT CORP LOCATION CITY-AGOURA HILL PROPERTY ADDRESS: VACANT LOT. See page 97.

17. AIN 2061020028 (auction ID 48): TRACT NO 8793 LOT 69 BLK 4 ... ASSESSED TO SHEA ESTATES 0 DEVELOPMENT CORP LOCATION CITY-AGOURA HILL - PROPERTY ADDRESS: VACANT LOT. See page 102.

18. AIN 2061020029 (auction ID 49): TRACT NO 8793 LOT 70 BLK 4 ... ASSESSED TO SHEA ESTATES 0 DEVELOPMENT CORP LOCATION CITY-AGOURA HILL PROPERTY ADDRESS: VACANT LOT. See page 107.

19. AIN 2061020030 (auction ID 50): TRACT NO 8793 LOT 71 BLK 4 ... ASSESSED TO SHEA ESTATES 0 DEVELOPMENT CORP LOCATION CITY-AGOURA HILL PROPERTY ADDRESS: VACANT LOT. See page 112.

20. AIN 2061021009 (auction ID 51): TRACT NO 8793 LOT 10 BLK 4 ... ASSESSED TO SHEA ESTATES 0 DEVELOPMENT CORP LOCATION CITY-AGOURA HILL PROPERTY ADDRESS: VACANT LOT. See page 117.

21. AIN 2061021010 (auction ID 52): TRACT NO 8793 LOT 11 BLK 4 ... ASSESSED TO SHEA ESTATES 0 DEVELOPMENT CORP LOCATION CITY-AGOURA HILL PROPERTY ADDRESS: VACANT LOT. See page 122.

22. AIN 2061021011 (auction ID 53): TRACT NO 8793 LOT 12 BLK 4 ... ASSESSED TO SHEA ESTATES 0 DEVELOPMENT CORP LOCATION CITY-AGOURA HILL PROPERTY ADDRESS: VACANT LOT. See page 127.

23. AIN 2061021012 (auction ID 54): TRACT NO 8793 LOT 13 BLK 4 ... ASSESSED TO SHEA ESTATES 0 DEVELOPMENT CORP LOCATION CITY-AGOURA HILL PROPERTY ADDRESS: VACANT LOT. See page 132.

24. AIN 2061021013 (auction ID 55): TRACT NO 8793 LOT 14 BLK 4 ... ASSESSED TO SHEA ESTATES 0 DEVELOPMENT CORP LOCATION CITY-AGOURA HILL PROPERTY ADDRESS: VACANT LOT. See page 137.

25. AIN 2061021014 (auction ID 56): TRACT NO 8793 LOT 15 BLK 4 ... ASSESSED TO SHEA ESTATES 0 DEVELOPMENT CORP LOCATION CITY-AGOURA HILL PROPERTY ADDRESS: VACANT LOT. See page 142.

26. AIN 2061021015 (auction ID 57): TRACT NO 8793 LOT 72 BLK 4 ... ASSESSED TO SHEA ESTATES 0 DEVELOPMENT CORP LOCATION CITY-AGOURA HILL PROPERTY ADDRESS: VACANT LOT. See page 147.

27. AIN 2061021016 (auction ID 58): TRACT NO 8793 LOT 73 BLK 4 ... ASSESSED TO SHEA ESTATES 0 DEVELOPMENT CORP LOCATION CITY-AGOURA HILL PROPERTY ADDRESS: VACANT LOT. See page 152.

28. AIN 2061021017 (auction ID 59): TRACT NO 8793 LOT 74 BLK 4 ... ASSESSED TO SHEA ESTATES 0 DEVELOPMENT CORP LOCATION CITY-AGOURA HILL PROPERTY ADDRESS: VACANT LOT. See page 157.

29. AIN 2061021018 (auction ID 60): TRACT NO 8793 LOT 75 BLK 4 ... ASSESSED TO SHEA ESTATES 0 DEVELOPMENT CORP LOCATION CITY-AGOURA HILL PROPERTY ADDRESS: VACANT LOT. See page 162.

30. AIN 2061021019 (auction ID 61): TRACT NO 8793 LOT 76 BLK 4 ... ASSESSED TO SHEA ESTATES 0 DEVELOPMENT CORP LOCATION CITY-AGOURA HILL PROPERTY ADDRESS: VACANT LOT. See page 167.

31. AIN 2061021020 (auction ID 62): TRACT NO 8793 LOT 77 BLK 4 ... ASSESSED TO SHEA ESTATES 0 DEVELOPMENT CORP LOCATION CITY-AGOURA HILL PROPERTY ADDRESS: VACANT LOT. See page 172.

32. AIN 2061021021 (auction ID 63): TRACT NO 8793 LOT 78 BLK 4 ... ASSESSED TO SHEA ESTATES 0 DEVELOPMENT CORP LOCATION CITY-AGOURA HILL PROPERTY ADDRESS: VACANT LOT. See page 177.

33. AIN 2061021022 (auction ID 64): TRACT NO 8793 LOT 79 BLK 4 ... ASSESSED TO SHEA ESTATES 0 DEVELOPMENT CORP LOCATION CITY-AGOURA HILL PROPERTY ADDRESS: VACANT LOT. See page 182.

Figure 2.34: Property 64, AIN 2061020009, overview map

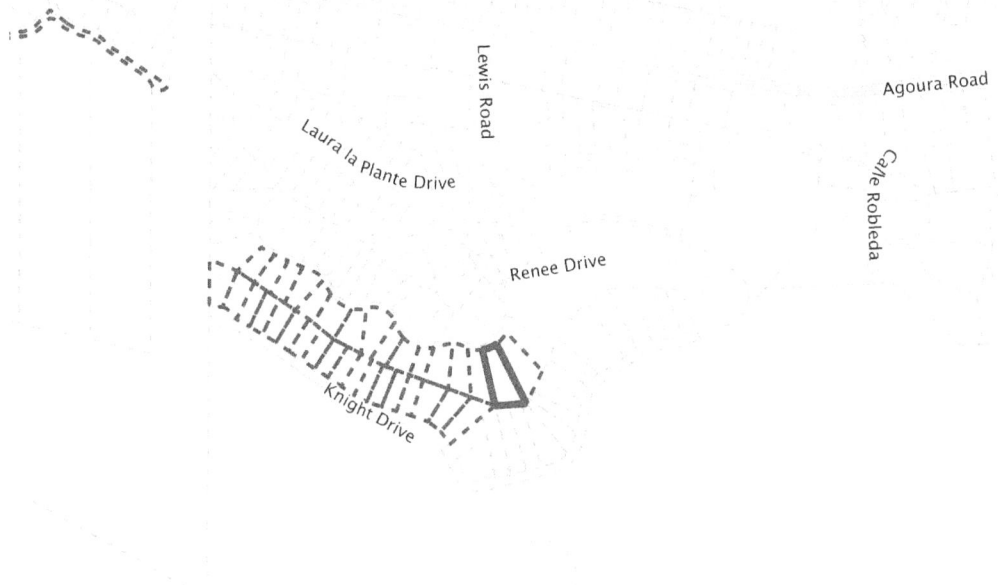

Figure 2.35: Property 64, AIN 2061020009, neighborhood view

Figure 2.36: Property 64, AIN 2061020009, detailed view

2.13   Auction ID 40

The Los Angeles County Auction Book describes the property as follows.

```
TRACT NO 8793 LOT 25 BLK 4 ASSESSED TO SHEA ESTATES 0 DEVELOPMENT
CORP LOCATION CITY-AGOURA HILL PROPERTY ADDRESS: VACANT LOT
```

The property is located in the general vicinity of Figure 2.37. It is identified by Assessor's Identification Number (AIN) 2061020010. The starting bid is $4,838. Comparable improved properties in this area is about $297/sqft. Comparable unimproved lots in this area is about $49/sqft. This parcel is approximately 13474 sqft. Note, however, that the parcel may be larger than the property under consideration. In case of condominiums, for example, the parcel may encompass other units of the development - those unrelated to the property to be auctioned.

The property is in a parcel zoned Restricted Open Space in Agoura Hills, for 0 to 0 dwelling units.

Figures 2.38 and 2.39 show street map and corresponding detailed aerial view, respectively. In both cases, the map is centered on the property with the containing parcel marked in heavy blue. If surrounding nearby properties are also part of this auction, the street and aerial maps highlights these in heavy, dashed blue outline.

This assessed entity may have other properties that are also in this auction:

1. AIN 2061020001 (auction ID 31): TRACT NO 8793 LOT 16 BLK 4 ... ASSESSED TO SHEA ESTATES 0 DEVELOPMENT CORP LOCATION CITY-AGOURA HILL PROPERTY ADDRESS: VACANT LOT. See page 17.

2. AIN 2061020002 (auction ID 32): TRACT NO 8793 LOT 17 BLK 4 ... ASSESSED TO SHEA ESTATES 0 DEVELOPMENT CORP LOCATION CITY-AGOURA HILL PROPERTY ADDRESS: VACANT LOT. See page 22.

3. AIN 2061020003 (auction ID 33): TRACT NO 8793 LOT 18 BLK 4 ... ASSESSED TO SHEA ESTATES 0 DEVELOPMENT CORP LOCATION CITY-AGOURA HILL PROPERTY ADDRESS: VACANT LOT. See page 27.

4. AIN 2061020004 (auction ID 34): TRACT NO 8793 LOT 19 BLK 4 ... ASSESSED TO SHEA ESTATES 0 DEVELOPMENT CORP LOCATION CITY-AGOURA HILL PROPERTY ADDRESS: VACANT LOT. See page 32.

5. AIN 2061020005 (auction ID 35): TRACT NO 8793 LOT 20 BLK 4 ... ASSESSED TO SHEA ESTATES 0 DEVELOPMENT CORP LOCATION CITY-AGOURA HILL PROPERTY ADDRESS: VACANT LOT. See page 37.

6. AIN 2061020006 (auction ID 36): TRACT NO 8793 LOT 21 BLK 4 ... ASSESSED TO SHEA ESTATES 0 DEVELOPMENT CORP LOCATION CITY-AGOURA HILL PROPERTY ADDRESS: VACANT LOT. See page 42.

7. AIN 2061020007 (auction ID 37): TRACT NO 8793 LOT 22 BLK 4 ... ASSESSED TO SHEA ESTATES 0 DEVELOPMENT CORP LOCATION CITY-AGOURA HILL PROPERTY ADDRESS: VACANT LOT. See page 47.

8. AIN 2061020008 (auction ID 38): TRACT NO 8793 LOT 23 BLK 4 ... ASSESSED TO SHEA ESTATES 0 DEVELOPMENT CORP LOCATION CITY-AGOURA HILL PROPERTY ADDRESS: VACANT LOT. See page 52.

9. AIN 2061020009 (auction ID 39): TRACT NO 8793 LOT 24 BLK 4 ... ASSESSED TO SHEA ESTATES 0 DEVELOPMENT CORP LOCATION CITY-AGOURA HILL PROPERTY ADDRESS: VACANT LOT. See page 57.

10. AIN 2061020021 (auction ID 41): TRACT NO 8793 LOT 62 BLK 4 . . . ASSESSED TO SHEA ESTATES 0 DEVELOPMENT CORP LOCATION CITY-AGOURA HILL PROPERTY ADDRESS: VACANT LOT. See page 67.

11. AIN 2061020022 (auction ID 42): TRACT NO 8793 LOT 63 BLK 4 . . . ASSESSED TO SHEA ESTATES 0 DEVELOPMENT CORP LOCATION CITY-AGOURA HILL PROPERTY ADDRESS: VACANT LOT. See page 72.

12. AIN 2061020023 (auction ID 43): TRACT NO 8793 LOT 64 BLK 4 . . . ASSESSED TO SHEA ESTATES 0 DEVELOPMENT CORP LOCATION CITY-AGOURA HILL PROPERTY ADDRESS: VACANT LOT. See page 77.

13. AIN 2061020024 (auction ID 44): TRACT NO 8793 LOT 65 BLK 4 . . . ASSESSED TO SHEA ESTATES 0 DEVELOPMENT CORP LOCATION CITY-AGOURA HILL PROPERTY ADDRESS: VACANT LOT. See page 82.

14. AIN 2061020025 (auction ID 45): TRACT NO 8793 LOT 66 BLK 4 . . . ASSESSED TO SHEA ESTATES 0 DEVELOPMENT CORP LOCATION CITY-AGOURA HILL PROPERTY ADDRESS: VACANT LOT. See page 87.

15. AIN 2061020026 (auction ID 46): TRACT NO 8793 LOT 67 BLK 4 . . . ASSESSED TO SHEA ESTATES 0 DEVELOPMENT CORP LOCATION CITY-AGOURA HILL PROPERTY ADDRESS: VACANT LOT. See page 92.

16. AIN 2061020027 (auction ID 47): TRACT NO 8793 LOT 68 BLK 4 . . . ASSESSED TO SHEA ESTATES 0 DEVELOPMENT CORP LOCATION CITY-AGOURA HILL PROPERTY ADDRESS: VACANT LOT. See page 97.

17. AIN 2061020028 (auction ID 48): TRACT NO 8793 LOT 69 BLK 4 . . . ASSESSED TO SHEA ESTATES 0 DEVELOPMENT CORP LOCATION CITY-AGOURA HILL - PROPERTY ADDRESS: VACANT LOT. See page 102.

18. AIN 2061020029 (auction ID 49): TRACT NO 8793 LOT 70 BLK 4 . . . ASSESSED TO SHEA ESTATES 0 DEVELOPMENT CORP LOCATION CITY-AGOURA HILL PROPERTY ADDRESS: VACANT LOT. See page 107.

19. AIN 2061020030 (auction ID 50): TRACT NO 8793 LOT 71 BLK 4 . . . ASSESSED TO SHEA ESTATES 0 DEVELOPMENT CORP LOCATION CITY-AGOURA HILL PROPERTY ADDRESS: VACANT LOT. See page 112.

20. AIN 2061021009 (auction ID 51): TRACT NO 8793 LOT 10 BLK 4 . . . ASSESSED TO SHEA ESTATES 0 DEVELOPMENT CORP LOCATION CITY-AGOURA HILL PROPERTY ADDRESS: VACANT LOT. See page 117.

21. AIN 2061021010 (auction ID 52): TRACT NO 8793 LOT 11 BLK 4 . . . ASSESSED TO SHEA ESTATES 0 DEVELOPMENT CORP LOCATION CITY-AGOURA HILL PROPERTY ADDRESS: VACANT LOT. See page 122.

22. AIN 2061021011 (auction ID 53): TRACT NO 8793 LOT 12 BLK 4 . . . ASSESSED TO SHEA ESTATES 0 DEVELOPMENT CORP LOCATION CITY-AGOURA HILL PROPERTY ADDRESS: VACANT LOT. See page 127.

23. AIN 2061021012 (auction ID 54): TRACT NO 8793 LOT 13 BLK 4 . . . ASSESSED TO SHEA ESTATES 0 DEVELOPMENT CORP LOCATION CITY-AGOURA HILL PROPERTY ADDRESS: VACANT LOT. See page 132.

24. AIN 2061021013 (auction ID 55): TRACT NO 8793 LOT 14 BLK 4 . . . ASSESSED TO SHEA ESTATES 0 DEVELOPMENT CORP LOCATION CITY-AGOURA HILL PROPERTY ADDRESS: VACANT LOT. See page 137.

25. AIN 2061021014 (auction ID 56): TRACT NO 8793 LOT 15 BLK 4 . . . ASSESSED TO SHEA ESTATES 0 DEVELOPMENT CORP LOCATION CITY-AGOURA HILL PROPERTY ADDRESS: VACANT LOT. See page 142.

26. AIN 2061021015 (auction ID 57): TRACT NO 8793 LOT 72 BLK 4 . . . ASSESSED TO SHEA ESTATES 0 DEVELOPMENT CORP LOCATION CITY-AGOURA HILL PROPERTY ADDRESS: VACANT LOT. See page 147.

27. AIN 2061021016 (auction ID 58): TRACT NO 8793 LOT 73 BLK 4 . . . ASSESSED TO SHEA ESTATES 0 DEVELOPMENT CORP LOCATION CITY-AGOURA HILL PROPERTY ADDRESS: VACANT LOT. See page 152.

28. AIN 2061021017 (auction ID 59): TRACT NO 8793 LOT 74 BLK 4 . . . ASSESSED TO SHEA ESTATES 0 DEVELOPMENT CORP LOCATION CITY-AGOURA HILL PROPERTY ADDRESS: VACANT LOT. See page 157.

29. AIN 2061021018 (auction ID 60): TRACT NO 8793 LOT 75 BLK 4 . . . ASSESSED TO SHEA ESTATES 0 DEVELOPMENT CORP LOCATION CITY-AGOURA HILL PROPERTY ADDRESS: VACANT LOT. See page 162.

30. AIN 2061021019 (auction ID 61): TRACT NO 8793 LOT 76 BLK 4 . . . ASSESSED TO SHEA ESTATES 0 DEVELOPMENT CORP LOCATION CITY-AGOURA HILL PROPERTY ADDRESS: VACANT LOT. See page 167.

31. AIN 2061021020 (auction ID 62): TRACT NO 8793 LOT 77 BLK 4 . . . ASSESSED TO SHEA ESTATES 0 DEVELOPMENT CORP LOCATION CITY-AGOURA HILL PROPERTY ADDRESS: VACANT LOT. See page 172.

32. AIN 2061021021 (auction ID 63): TRACT NO 8793 LOT 78 BLK 4 . . . ASSESSED TO SHEA ESTATES 0 DEVELOPMENT CORP LOCATION CITY-AGOURA HILL PROPERTY ADDRESS: VACANT LOT. See page 177.

33. AIN 2061021022 (auction ID 64): TRACT NO 8793 LOT 79 BLK 4 . . . ASSESSED TO SHEA ESTATES 0 DEVELOPMENT CORP LOCATION CITY-AGOURA HILL PROPERTY ADDRESS: VACANT LOT. See page 182.

Figure 2.37: Property 64, AIN 2061020010, overview map

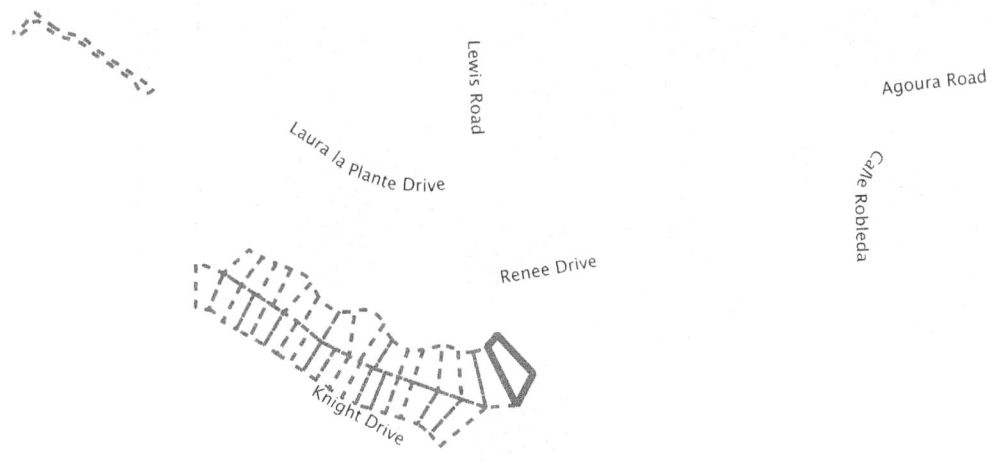

Figure 2.38: Property 64, AIN 2061020010, neighborhood view

Figure 2.39: Property 64, AIN 2061020010, detailed view

2.14 Auction ID 41

The Los Angeles County Auction Book describes the property as follows.

```
TRACT NO 8793 LOT 62 BLK 4 ASSESSED TO SHEA ESTATES 0 DEVELOPMENT
CORP LOCATION CITY-AGOURA HILL PROPERTY ADDRESS: VACANT LOT
```

The property is located in the general vicinity of Figure 2.40. It is identified by Assessor's Identification Number (AIN) 2061020021. The starting bid is \$3,972. Comparable improved properties in this area is about \$294/sqft. Comparable unimproved lots in this area is about \$49/sqft. This parcel is approximately 10326 sqft. Note, however, that the parcel may be larger than the property under consideration. In case of condominiums, for example, the parcel may encompass other units of the development - those unrelated to the property to be auctioned.

The property is in a parcel zoned Restricted Open Space in Agoura Hills, for 0 to 0 dwelling units.

Figures 2.41 and 2.42 show street map and corresponding detailed aerial view, respectively. In both cases, the map is centered on the property with the containing parcel marked in heavy blue. If surrounding nearby properties are also part of this auction, the street and aerial maps highlights these in heavy, dashed blue outline.

This assessed entity may have other properties that are also in this auction:

1. AIN 2061020001 (auction ID 31): TRACT NO 8793 LOT 16 BLK 4 . . . ASSESSED TO SHEA ESTATES 0 DEVELOPMENT CORP LOCATION CITY-AGOURA HILL PROPERTY ADDRESS: VACANT LOT. See page 17.

2. AIN 2061020002 (auction ID 32): TRACT NO 8793 LOT 17 BLK 4 . . . ASSESSED TO SHEA ESTATES 0 DEVELOPMENT CORP LOCATION CITY-AGOURA HILL PROPERTY ADDRESS: VACANT LOT. See page 22.

3. AIN 2061020003 (auction ID 33): TRACT NO 8793 LOT 18 BLK 4 . . . ASSESSED TO SHEA ESTATES 0 DEVELOPMENT CORP LOCATION CITY-AGOURA HILL PROPERTY ADDRESS: VACANT LOT. See page 27.

4. AIN 2061020004 (auction ID 34): TRACT NO 8793 LOT 19 BLK 4 . . . ASSESSED TO SHEA ESTATES 0 DEVELOPMENT CORP LOCATION CITY-AGOURA HILL PROPERTY ADDRESS: VACANT LOT. See page 32.

5. AIN 2061020005 (auction ID 35): TRACT NO 8793 LOT 20 BLK 4 . . . ASSESSED TO SHEA ESTATES 0 DEVELOPMENT CORP LOCATION CITY-AGOURA HILL PROPERTY ADDRESS: VACANT LOT. See page 37.

6. AIN 2061020006 (auction ID 36): TRACT NO 8793 LOT 21 BLK 4 . . . ASSESSED TO SHEA ESTATES 0 DEVELOPMENT CORP LOCATION CITY-AGOURA HILL PROPERTY ADDRESS: VACANT LOT. See page 42.

7. AIN 2061020007 (auction ID 37): TRACT NO 8793 LOT 22 BLK 4 . . . ASSESSED TO SHEA ESTATES 0 DEVELOPMENT CORP LOCATION CITY-AGOURA HILL PROPERTY ADDRESS: VACANT LOT. See page 47.

8. AIN 2061020008 (auction ID 38): TRACT NO 8793 LOT 23 BLK 4 . . . ASSESSED TO SHEA ESTATES 0 DEVELOPMENT CORP LOCATION CITY-AGOURA HILL PROPERTY ADDRESS: VACANT LOT. See page 52.

9. AIN 2061020009 (auction ID 39): TRACT NO 8793 LOT 24 BLK 4 . . . ASSESSED TO SHEA ESTATES 0 DEVELOPMENT CORP LOCATION CITY-AGOURA HILL PROPERTY ADDRESS: VACANT LOT. See page 57.

10. AIN 2061020010 (auction ID 40): TRACT NO 8793 LOT 25 BLK 4 . . . ASSESSED TO SHEA ESTATES 0 DEVELOPMENT CORP LOCATION CITY-AGOURA HILL PROPERTY ADDRESS: VACANT LOT. See page 62.

11. AIN 2061020022 (auction ID 42): TRACT NO 8793 LOT 63 BLK 4 . . . ASSESSED TO SHEA ESTATES 0 DEVELOPMENT CORP LOCATION CITY-AGOURA HILL PROPERTY ADDRESS: VACANT LOT. See page 72.

12. AIN 2061020023 (auction ID 43): TRACT NO 8793 LOT 64 BLK 4 . . . ASSESSED TO SHEA ESTATES 0 DEVELOPMENT CORP LOCATION CITY-AGOURA HILL PROPERTY ADDRESS: VACANT LOT. See page 77.

13. AIN 2061020024 (auction ID 44): TRACT NO 8793 LOT 65 BLK 4 . . . ASSESSED TO SHEA ESTATES 0 DEVELOPMENT CORP LOCATION CITY-AGOURA HILL PROPERTY ADDRESS: VACANT LOT. See page 82.

14. AIN 2061020025 (auction ID 45): TRACT NO 8793 LOT 66 BLK 4 . . . ASSESSED TO SHEA ESTATES 0 DEVELOPMENT CORP LOCATION CITY-AGOURA HILL PROPERTY ADDRESS: VACANT LOT. See page 87.

15. AIN 2061020026 (auction ID 46): TRACT NO 8793 LOT 67 BLK 4 . . . ASSESSED TO SHEA ESTATES 0 DEVELOPMENT CORP LOCATION CITY-AGOURA HILL PROPERTY ADDRESS: VACANT LOT. See page 92.

16. AIN 2061020027 (auction ID 47): TRACT NO 8793 LOT 68 BLK 4 . . . ASSESSED TO SHEA ESTATES 0 DEVELOPMENT CORP LOCATION CITY-AGOURA HILL PROPERTY ADDRESS: VACANT LOT. See page 97.

17. AIN 2061020028 (auction ID 48): TRACT NO 8793 LOT 69 BLK 4 . . . ASSESSED TO SHEA ESTATES 0 DEVELOPMENT CORP LOCATION CITY-AGOURA HILL - PROPERTY ADDRESS: VACANT LOT. See page 102.

18. AIN 2061020029 (auction ID 49): TRACT NO 8793 LOT 70 BLK 4 . . . ASSESSED TO SHEA ESTATES 0 DEVELOPMENT CORP LOCATION CITY-AGOURA HILL PROPERTY ADDRESS: VACANT LOT. See page 107.

19. AIN 2061020030 (auction ID 50): TRACT NO 8793 LOT 71 BLK 4 . . . ASSESSED TO SHEA ESTATES 0 DEVELOPMENT CORP LOCATION CITY-AGOURA HILL PROPERTY ADDRESS: VACANT LOT. See page 112.

20. AIN 2061021009 (auction ID 51): TRACT NO 8793 LOT 10 BLK 4 . . . ASSESSED TO SHEA ESTATES 0 DEVELOPMENT CORP LOCATION CITY-AGOURA HILL PROPERTY ADDRESS: VACANT LOT. See page 117.

21. AIN 2061021010 (auction ID 52): TRACT NO 8793 LOT 11 BLK 4 . . . ASSESSED TO SHEA ESTATES 0 DEVELOPMENT CORP LOCATION CITY-AGOURA HILL PROPERTY ADDRESS: VACANT LOT. See page 122.

22. AIN 2061021011 (auction ID 53): TRACT NO 8793 LOT 12 BLK 4 . . . ASSESSED TO SHEA ESTATES 0 DEVELOPMENT CORP LOCATION CITY-AGOURA HILL PROPERTY ADDRESS: VACANT LOT. See page 127.

23. AIN 2061021012 (auction ID 54): TRACT NO 8793 LOT 13 BLK 4 . . . ASSESSED TO SHEA ESTATES 0 DEVELOPMENT CORP LOCATION CITY-AGOURA HILL PROPERTY ADDRESS: VACANT LOT. See page 132.

24. AIN 2061021013 (auction ID 55): TRACT NO 8793 LOT 14 BLK 4 . . . ASSESSED TO SHEA ESTATES 0 DEVELOPMENT CORP LOCATION CITY-AGOURA HILL PROPERTY ADDRESS: VACANT LOT. See page 137.

25. AIN 2061021014 (auction ID 56): TRACT NO 8793 LOT 15 BLK 4 . . . ASSESSED TO SHEA ESTATES 0 DEVELOPMENT CORP LOCATION CITY-AGOURA HILL PROPERTY ADDRESS: VACANT LOT. See page 142.

26. AIN 2061021015 (auction ID 57): TRACT NO 8793 LOT 72 BLK 4 . . . ASSESSED TO SHEA ESTATES 0 DEVELOPMENT CORP LOCATION CITY-AGOURA HILL PROPERTY ADDRESS: VACANT LOT. See page 147.

27. AIN 2061021016 (auction ID 58): TRACT NO 8793 LOT 73 BLK 4 . . . ASSESSED TO SHEA ESTATES 0 DEVELOPMENT CORP LOCATION CITY-AGOURA HILL PROPERTY ADDRESS: VACANT LOT. See page 152.

28. AIN 2061021017 (auction ID 59): TRACT NO 8793 LOT 74 BLK 4 . . . ASSESSED TO SHEA ESTATES 0 DEVELOPMENT CORP LOCATION CITY-AGOURA HILL PROPERTY ADDRESS: VACANT LOT. See page 157.

29. AIN 2061021018 (auction ID 60): TRACT NO 8793 LOT 75 BLK 4 . . . ASSESSED TO SHEA ESTATES 0 DEVELOPMENT CORP LOCATION CITY-AGOURA HILL PROPERTY ADDRESS: VACANT LOT. See page 162.

30. AIN 2061021019 (auction ID 61): TRACT NO 8793 LOT 76 BLK 4 . . . ASSESSED TO SHEA ESTATES 0 DEVELOPMENT CORP LOCATION CITY-AGOURA HILL PROPERTY ADDRESS: VACANT LOT. See page 167.

31. AIN 2061021020 (auction ID 62): TRACT NO 8793 LOT 77 BLK 4 . . . ASSESSED TO SHEA ESTATES 0 DEVELOPMENT CORP LOCATION CITY-AGOURA HILL PROPERTY ADDRESS: VACANT LOT. See page 172.

32. AIN 2061021021 (auction ID 63): TRACT NO 8793 LOT 78 BLK 4 . . . ASSESSED TO SHEA ESTATES 0 DEVELOPMENT CORP LOCATION CITY-AGOURA HILL PROPERTY ADDRESS: VACANT LOT. See page 177.

33. AIN 2061021022 (auction ID 64): TRACT NO 8793 LOT 79 BLK 4 . . . ASSESSED TO SHEA ESTATES 0 DEVELOPMENT CORP LOCATION CITY-AGOURA HILL PROPERTY ADDRESS: VACANT LOT. See page 182.

Figure 2.40: Property 64, AIN 2061020021, overview map

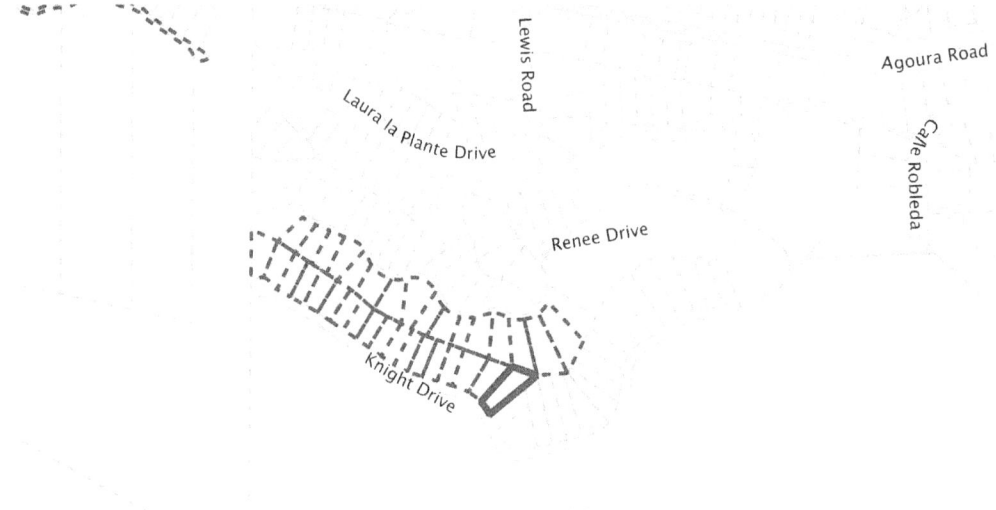

Figure 2.41: Property 64, AIN 2061020021, neighborhood view

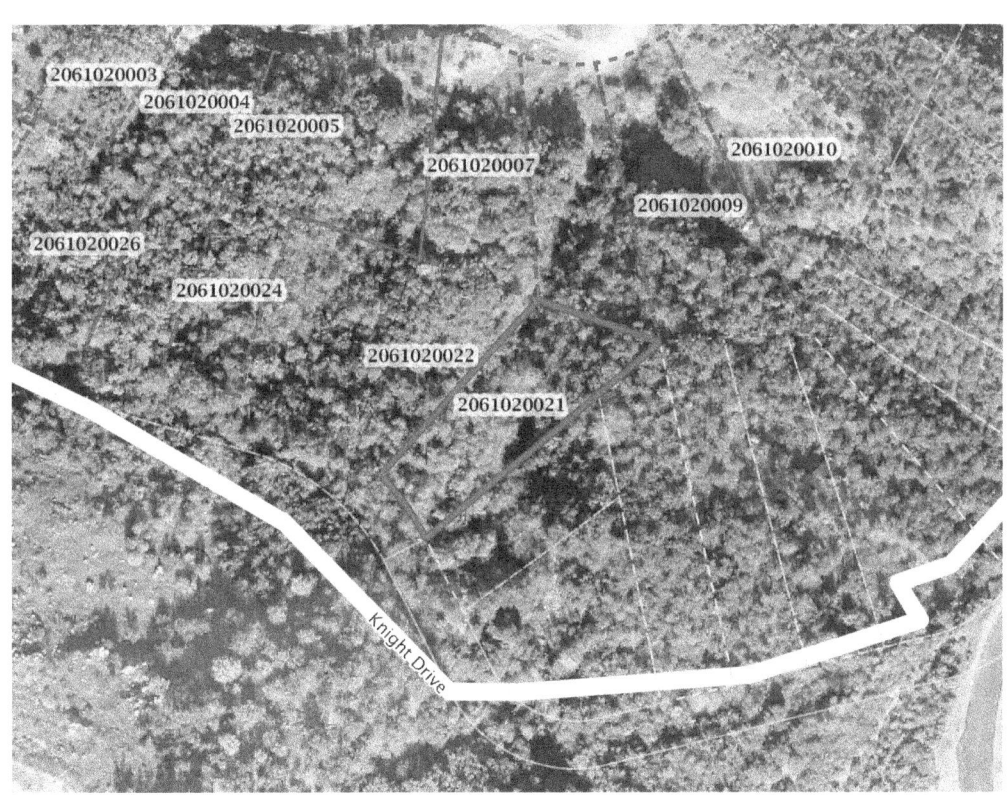

Figure 2.42: Property 64, AIN 2061020021, detailed view

2.15 Auction ID 42

The Los Angeles County Auction Book describes the property as follows.

```
TRACT NO 8793 LOT 63 BLK 4 ASSESSED TO SHEA ESTATES 0 DEVELOPMENT
CORP LOCATION CITY-AGOURA HILL PROPERTY ADDRESS: VACANT LOT
```

The property is located in the general vicinity of Figure 2.43. It is identified by Assessor's Identification Number (AIN) 2061020022. The starting bid is $3,805. Comparable improved properties in this area is about $294/sqft. Comparable unimproved lots in this area is about $49/sqft. This parcel is approximately 8475 sqft. Note, however, that the parcel may be larger than the property under consideration. In case of condominiums, for example, the parcel may encompass other units of the development - those unrelated to the property to be auctioned.

The property is in a parcel zoned Restricted Open Space in Agoura Hills, for 0 to 0 dwelling units.

Figures 2.44 and 2.45 show street map and corresponding detailed aerial view, respectively. In both cases, the map is centered on the property with the containing parcel marked in heavy blue. If surrounding nearby properties are also part of this auction, the street and aerial maps highlights these in heavy, dashed blue outline.

This assessed entity may have other properties that are also in this auction:

1. AIN 2061020001 (auction ID 31): TRACT NO 8793 LOT 16 BLK 4 ... ASSESSED TO SHEA ESTATES 0 DEVELOPMENT CORP LOCATION CITY-AGOURA HILL PROPERTY ADDRESS: VACANT LOT. See page 17.

2. AIN 2061020002 (auction ID 32): TRACT NO 8793 LOT 17 BLK 4 ... ASSESSED TO SHEA ESTATES 0 DEVELOPMENT CORP LOCATION CITY-AGOURA HILL PROPERTY ADDRESS: VACANT LOT. See page 22.

3. AIN 2061020003 (auction ID 33): TRACT NO 8793 LOT 18 BLK 4 ... ASSESSED TO SHEA ESTATES 0 DEVELOPMENT CORP LOCATION CITY-AGOURA HILL PROPERTY ADDRESS: VACANT LOT. See page 27.

4. AIN 2061020004 (auction ID 34): TRACT NO 8793 LOT 19 BLK 4 ... ASSESSED TO SHEA ESTATES 0 DEVELOPMENT CORP LOCATION CITY-AGOURA HILL PROPERTY ADDRESS: VACANT LOT. See page 32.

5. AIN 2061020005 (auction ID 35): TRACT NO 8793 LOT 20 BLK 4 ... ASSESSED TO SHEA ESTATES 0 DEVELOPMENT CORP LOCATION CITY-AGOURA HILL PROPERTY ADDRESS: VACANT LOT. See page 37.

6. AIN 2061020006 (auction ID 36): TRACT NO 8793 LOT 21 BLK 4 ... ASSESSED TO SHEA ESTATES 0 DEVELOPMENT CORP LOCATION CITY-AGOURA HILL PROPERTY ADDRESS: VACANT LOT. See page 42.

7. AIN 2061020007 (auction ID 37): TRACT NO 8793 LOT 22 BLK 4 ... ASSESSED TO SHEA ESTATES 0 DEVELOPMENT CORP LOCATION CITY-AGOURA HILL PROPERTY ADDRESS: VACANT LOT. See page 47.

8. AIN 2061020008 (auction ID 38): TRACT NO 8793 LOT 23 BLK 4 ... ASSESSED TO SHEA ESTATES 0 DEVELOPMENT CORP LOCATION CITY-AGOURA HILL PROPERTY ADDRESS: VACANT LOT. See page 52.

9. AIN 2061020009 (auction ID 39): TRACT NO 8793 LOT 24 BLK 4 ... ASSESSED TO SHEA ESTATES 0 DEVELOPMENT CORP LOCATION CITY-AGOURA HILL PROPERTY ADDRESS: VACANT LOT. See page 57.

10. AIN 2061020010 (auction ID 40): TRACT NO 8793 LOT 25 BLK 4 . . . ASSESSED TO SHEA ESTATES 0 DEVELOPMENT CORP LOCATION CITY-AGOURA HILL PROPERTY ADDRESS: VACANT LOT. See page 62.

11. AIN 2061020021 (auction ID 41): TRACT NO 8793 LOT 62 BLK 4 . . . ASSESSED TO SHEA ESTATES 0 DEVELOPMENT CORP LOCATION CITY-AGOURA HILL PROPERTY ADDRESS: VACANT LOT. See page 67.

12. AIN 2061020023 (auction ID 43): TRACT NO 8793 LOT 64 BLK 4 . . . ASSESSED TO SHEA ESTATES 0 DEVELOPMENT CORP LOCATION CITY-AGOURA HILL PROPERTY ADDRESS: VACANT LOT. See page 77.

13. AIN 2061020024 (auction ID 44): TRACT NO 8793 LOT 65 BLK 4 . . . ASSESSED TO SHEA ESTATES 0 DEVELOPMENT CORP LOCATION CITY-AGOURA HILL PROPERTY ADDRESS: VACANT LOT. See page 82.

14. AIN 2061020025 (auction ID 45): TRACT NO 8793 LOT 66 BLK 4 . . . ASSESSED TO SHEA ESTATES 0 DEVELOPMENT CORP LOCATION CITY-AGOURA HILL PROPERTY ADDRESS: VACANT LOT. See page 87.

15. AIN 2061020026 (auction ID 46): TRACT NO 8793 LOT 67 BLK 4 . . . ASSESSED TO SHEA ESTATES 0 DEVELOPMENT CORP LOCATION CITY-AGOURA HILL PROPERTY ADDRESS: VACANT LOT. See page 92.

16. AIN 2061020027 (auction ID 47): TRACT NO 8793 LOT 68 BLK 4 . . . ASSESSED TO SHEA ESTATES 0 DEVELOPMENT CORP LOCATION CITY-AGOURA HILL PROPERTY ADDRESS: VACANT LOT. See page 97.

17. AIN 2061020028 (auction ID 48): TRACT NO 8793 LOT 69 BLK 4 . . . ASSESSED TO SHEA ESTATES 0 DEVELOPMENT CORP LOCATION CITY-AGOURA HILL - PROPERTY ADDRESS: VACANT LOT. See page 102.

18. AIN 2061020029 (auction ID 49): TRACT NO 8793 LOT 70 BLK 4 . . . ASSESSED TO SHEA ESTATES 0 DEVELOPMENT CORP LOCATION CITY-AGOURA HILL PROPERTY ADDRESS: VACANT LOT. See page 107.

19. AIN 2061020030 (auction ID 50): TRACT NO 8793 LOT 71 BLK 4 . . . ASSESSED TO SHEA ESTATES 0 DEVELOPMENT CORP LOCATION CITY-AGOURA HILL PROPERTY ADDRESS: VACANT LOT. See page 112.

20. AIN 2061021009 (auction ID 51): TRACT NO 8793 LOT 10 BLK 4 . . . ASSESSED TO SHEA ESTATES 0 DEVELOPMENT CORP LOCATION CITY-AGOURA HILL PROPERTY ADDRESS: VACANT LOT. See page 117.

21. AIN 2061021010 (auction ID 52): TRACT NO 8793 LOT 11 BLK 4 . . . ASSESSED TO SHEA ESTATES 0 DEVELOPMENT CORP LOCATION CITY-AGOURA HILL PROPERTY ADDRESS: VACANT LOT. See page 122.

22. AIN 2061021011 (auction ID 53): TRACT NO 8793 LOT 12 BLK 4 . . . ASSESSED TO SHEA ESTATES 0 DEVELOPMENT CORP LOCATION CITY-AGOURA HILL PROPERTY ADDRESS: VACANT LOT. See page 127.

23. AIN 2061021012 (auction ID 54): TRACT NO 8793 LOT 13 BLK 4 . . . ASSESSED TO SHEA ESTATES 0 DEVELOPMENT CORP LOCATION CITY-AGOURA HILL PROPERTY ADDRESS: VACANT LOT. See page 132.

24. AIN 2061021013 (auction ID 55): TRACT NO 8793 LOT 14 BLK 4 . . . ASSESSED TO SHEA ESTATES 0 DEVELOPMENT CORP LOCATION CITY-AGOURA HILL PROPERTY ADDRESS: VACANT LOT. See page 137.

25. AIN 2061021014 (auction ID 56): TRACT NO 8793 LOT 15 BLK 4 ... ASSESSED TO SHEA ESTATES 0 DEVELOPMENT CORP LOCATION CITY-AGOURA HILL PROPERTY ADDRESS: VACANT LOT. See page 142.

26. AIN 2061021015 (auction ID 57): TRACT NO 8793 LOT 72 BLK 4 ... ASSESSED TO SHEA ESTATES 0 DEVELOPMENT CORP LOCATION CITY-AGOURA HILL PROPERTY ADDRESS: VACANT LOT. See page 147.

27. AIN 2061021016 (auction ID 58): TRACT NO 8793 LOT 73 BLK 4 ... ASSESSED TO SHEA ESTATES 0 DEVELOPMENT CORP LOCATION CITY-AGOURA HILL PROPERTY ADDRESS: VACANT LOT. See page 152.

28. AIN 2061021017 (auction ID 59): TRACT NO 8793 LOT 74 BLK 4 ... ASSESSED TO SHEA ESTATES 0 DEVELOPMENT CORP LOCATION CITY-AGOURA HILL PROPERTY ADDRESS: VACANT LOT. See page 157.

29. AIN 2061021018 (auction ID 60): TRACT NO 8793 LOT 75 BLK 4 ... ASSESSED TO SHEA ESTATES 0 DEVELOPMENT CORP LOCATION CITY-AGOURA HILL PROPERTY ADDRESS: VACANT LOT. See page 162.

30. AIN 2061021019 (auction ID 61): TRACT NO 8793 LOT 76 BLK 4 ... ASSESSED TO SHEA ESTATES 0 DEVELOPMENT CORP LOCATION CITY-AGOURA HILL PROPERTY ADDRESS: VACANT LOT. See page 167.

31. AIN 2061021020 (auction ID 62): TRACT NO 8793 LOT 77 BLK 4 ... ASSESSED TO SHEA ESTATES 0 DEVELOPMENT CORP LOCATION CITY-AGOURA HILL PROPERTY ADDRESS: VACANT LOT. See page 172.

32. AIN 2061021021 (auction ID 63): TRACT NO 8793 LOT 78 BLK 4 ... ASSESSED TO SHEA ESTATES 0 DEVELOPMENT CORP LOCATION CITY-AGOURA HILL PROPERTY ADDRESS: VACANT LOT. See page 177.

33. AIN 2061021022 (auction ID 64): TRACT NO 8793 LOT 79 BLK 4 ... ASSESSED TO SHEA ESTATES 0 DEVELOPMENT CORP LOCATION CITY-AGOURA HILL PROPERTY ADDRESS: VACANT LOT. See page 182.

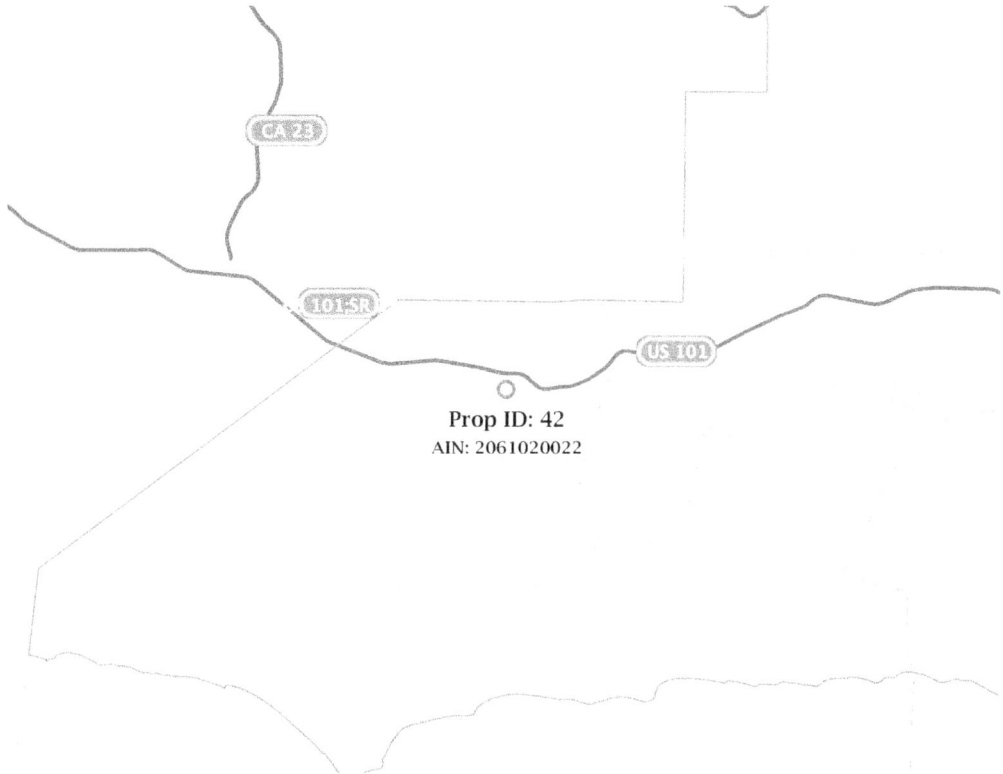

Figure 2.43: Property 64, AIN 2061020022, overview map

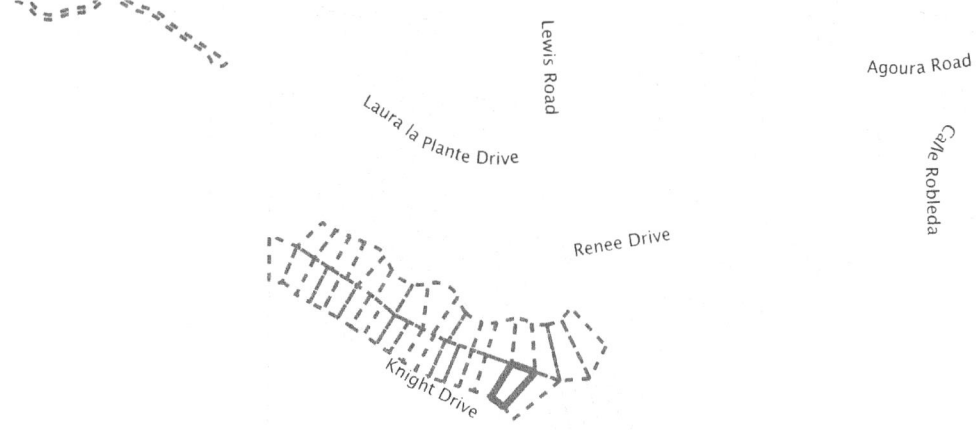

Figure 2.44: Property 64, AIN 2061020022, neighborhood view

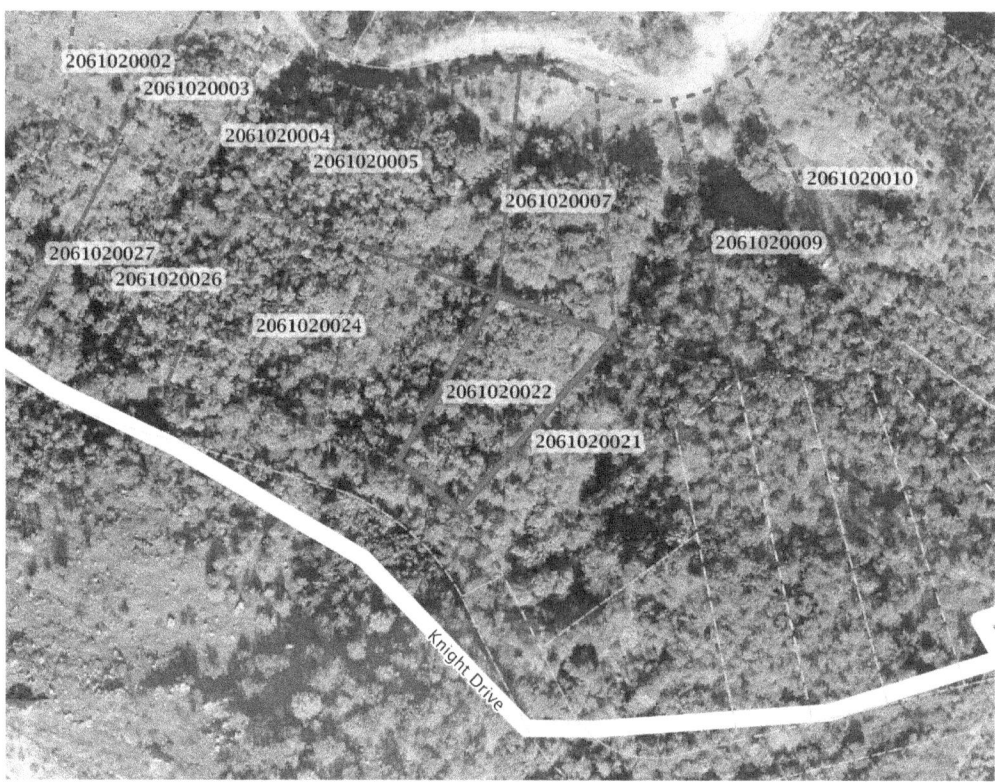

Figure 2.45: Property 64, AIN 2061020022, detailed view

2.16 Auction ID 43

The Los Angeles County Auction Book describes the property as follows.

```
TRACT NO 8793 LOT 64 BLK 4 ASSESSED TO SHEA ESTATES 0 DEVELOPMENT
CORP LOCATION CITY-AGOURA HILL PROPERTY ADDRESS: VACANT LOT
```

The property is located in the general vicinity of Figure 2.46. It is identified by Assessor's Identification Number (AIN) 2061020023. The starting bid is $3,835. Comparable improved properties in this area is about $294/sqft. Comparable unimproved lots in this area is about $49/sqft. This parcel is approximately 8503 sqft. Note, however, that the parcel may be larger than the property under consideration. In case of condominiums, for example, the parcel may encompass other units of the development - those unrelated to the property to be auctioned.

The property is in a parcel zoned Restricted Open Space in Agoura Hills, for 0 to 0 dwelling units.

Figures 2.47 and 2.48 show street map and corresponding detailed aerial view, respectively. In both cases, the map is centered on the property with the containing parcel marked in heavy blue. If surrounding nearby properties are also part of this auction, the street and aerial maps highlights these in heavy, dashed blue outline.

This assessed entity may have other properties that are also in this auction:

1. AIN 2061020001 (auction ID 31): TRACT NO 8793 LOT 16 BLK 4 ... ASSESSED TO SHEA ESTATES 0 DEVELOPMENT CORP LOCATION CITY-AGOURA HILL PROPERTY ADDRESS: VACANT LOT. See page 17.

2. AIN 2061020002 (auction ID 32): TRACT NO 8793 LOT 17 BLK 4 ... ASSESSED TO SHEA ESTATES 0 DEVELOPMENT CORP LOCATION CITY-AGOURA HILL PROPERTY ADDRESS: VACANT LOT. See page 22.

3. AIN 2061020003 (auction ID 33): TRACT NO 8793 LOT 18 BLK 4 ... ASSESSED TO SHEA ESTATES 0 DEVELOPMENT CORP LOCATION CITY-AGOURA HILL PROPERTY ADDRESS: VACANT LOT. See page 27.

4. AIN 2061020004 (auction ID 34): TRACT NO 8793 LOT 19 BLK 4 ... ASSESSED TO SHEA ESTATES 0 DEVELOPMENT CORP LOCATION CITY-AGOURA HILL PROPERTY ADDRESS: VACANT LOT. See page 32.

5. AIN 2061020005 (auction ID 35): TRACT NO 8793 LOT 20 BLK 4 ... ASSESSED TO SHEA ESTATES 0 DEVELOPMENT CORP LOCATION CITY-AGOURA HILL PROPERTY ADDRESS: VACANT LOT. See page 37.

6. AIN 2061020006 (auction ID 36): TRACT NO 8793 LOT 21 BLK 4 ... ASSESSED TO SHEA ESTATES 0 DEVELOPMENT CORP LOCATION CITY-AGOURA HILL PROPERTY ADDRESS: VACANT LOT. See page 42.

7. AIN 2061020007 (auction ID 37): TRACT NO 8793 LOT 22 BLK 4 ... ASSESSED TO SHEA ESTATES 0 DEVELOPMENT CORP LOCATION CITY-AGOURA HILL PROPERTY ADDRESS: VACANT LOT. See page 47.

8. AIN 2061020008 (auction ID 38): TRACT NO 8793 LOT 23 BLK 4 ... ASSESSED TO SHEA ESTATES 0 DEVELOPMENT CORP LOCATION CITY-AGOURA HILL PROPERTY ADDRESS: VACANT LOT. See page 52.

9. AIN 2061020009 (auction ID 39): TRACT NO 8793 LOT 24 BLK 4 ... ASSESSED TO SHEA ESTATES 0 DEVELOPMENT CORP LOCATION CITY-AGOURA HILL PROPERTY ADDRESS: VACANT LOT. See page 57.

10. AIN 2061020010 (auction ID 40): TRACT NO 8793 LOT 25 BLK 4 . . . ASSESSED TO SHEA ESTATES 0 DEVELOPMENT CORP LOCATION CITY-AGOURA HILL PROPERTY ADDRESS: VACANT LOT. See page 62.

11. AIN 2061020021 (auction ID 41): TRACT NO 8793 LOT 62 BLK 4 . . . ASSESSED TO SHEA ESTATES 0 DEVELOPMENT CORP LOCATION CITY-AGOURA HILL PROPERTY ADDRESS: VACANT LOT. See page 67.

12. AIN 2061020022 (auction ID 42): TRACT NO 8793 LOT 63 BLK 4 . . . ASSESSED TO SHEA ESTATES 0 DEVELOPMENT CORP LOCATION CITY-AGOURA HILL PROPERTY ADDRESS: VACANT LOT. See page 72.

13. AIN 2061020024 (auction ID 44): TRACT NO 8793 LOT 65 BLK 4 . . . ASSESSED TO SHEA ESTATES 0 DEVELOPMENT CORP LOCATION CITY-AGOURA HILL PROPERTY ADDRESS: VACANT LOT. See page 82.

14. AIN 2061020025 (auction ID 45): TRACT NO 8793 LOT 66 BLK 4 . . . ASSESSED TO SHEA ESTATES 0 DEVELOPMENT CORP LOCATION CITY-AGOURA HILL PROPERTY ADDRESS: VACANT LOT. See page 87.

15. AIN 2061020026 (auction ID 46): TRACT NO 8793 LOT 67 BLK 4 . . . ASSESSED TO SHEA ESTATES 0 DEVELOPMENT CORP LOCATION CITY-AGOURA HILL PROPERTY ADDRESS: VACANT LOT. See page 92.

16. AIN 2061020027 (auction ID 47): TRACT NO 8793 LOT 68 BLK 4 . . . ASSESSED TO SHEA ESTATES 0 DEVELOPMENT CORP LOCATION CITY-AGOURA HILL PROPERTY ADDRESS: VACANT LOT. See page 97.

17. AIN 2061020028 (auction ID 48): TRACT NO 8793 LOT 69 BLK 4 . . . ASSESSED TO SHEA ESTATES 0 DEVELOPMENT CORP LOCATION CITY-AGOURA HILL - PROPERTY ADDRESS: VACANT LOT. See page 102.

18. AIN 2061020029 (auction ID 49): TRACT NO 8793 LOT 70 BLK 4 . . . ASSESSED TO SHEA ESTATES 0 DEVELOPMENT CORP LOCATION CITY-AGOURA HILL PROPERTY ADDRESS: VACANT LOT. See page 107.

19. AIN 2061020030 (auction ID 50): TRACT NO 8793 LOT 71 BLK 4 . . . ASSESSED TO SHEA ESTATES 0 DEVELOPMENT CORP LOCATION CITY-AGOURA HILL PROPERTY ADDRESS: VACANT LOT. See page 112.

20. AIN 2061021009 (auction ID 51): TRACT NO 8793 LOT 10 BLK 4 . . . ASSESSED TO SHEA ESTATES 0 DEVELOPMENT CORP LOCATION CITY-AGOURA HILL PROPERTY ADDRESS: VACANT LOT. See page 117.

21. AIN 2061021010 (auction ID 52): TRACT NO 8793 LOT 11 BLK 4 . . . ASSESSED TO SHEA ESTATES 0 DEVELOPMENT CORP LOCATION CITY-AGOURA HILL PROPERTY ADDRESS: VACANT LOT. See page 122.

22. AIN 2061021011 (auction ID 53): TRACT NO 8793 LOT 12 BLK 4 . . . ASSESSED TO SHEA ESTATES 0 DEVELOPMENT CORP LOCATION CITY-AGOURA HILL PROPERTY ADDRESS: VACANT LOT. See page 127.

23. AIN 2061021012 (auction ID 54): TRACT NO 8793 LOT 13 BLK 4 . . . ASSESSED TO SHEA ESTATES 0 DEVELOPMENT CORP LOCATION CITY-AGOURA HILL PROPERTY ADDRESS: VACANT LOT. See page 132.

24. AIN 2061021013 (auction ID 55): TRACT NO 8793 LOT 14 BLK 4 . . . ASSESSED TO SHEA ESTATES 0 DEVELOPMENT CORP LOCATION CITY-AGOURA HILL PROPERTY ADDRESS: VACANT LOT. See page 137.

25. AIN 2061021014 (auction ID 56): TRACT NO 8793 LOT 15 BLK 4 ... ASSESSED TO SHEA ESTATES 0 DEVELOPMENT CORP LOCATION CITY-AGOURA HILL PROPERTY ADDRESS: VACANT LOT. See page 142.

26. AIN 2061021015 (auction ID 57): TRACT NO 8793 LOT 72 BLK 4 ... ASSESSED TO SHEA ESTATES 0 DEVELOPMENT CORP LOCATION CITY-AGOURA HILL PROPERTY ADDRESS: VACANT LOT. See page 147.

27. AIN 2061021016 (auction ID 58): TRACT NO 8793 LOT 73 BLK 4 ... ASSESSED TO SHEA ESTATES 0 DEVELOPMENT CORP LOCATION CITY-AGOURA HILL PROPERTY ADDRESS: VACANT LOT. See page 152.

28. AIN 2061021017 (auction ID 59): TRACT NO 8793 LOT 74 BLK 4 ... ASSESSED TO SHEA ESTATES 0 DEVELOPMENT CORP LOCATION CITY-AGOURA HILL PROPERTY ADDRESS: VACANT LOT. See page 157.

29. AIN 2061021018 (auction ID 60): TRACT NO 8793 LOT 75 BLK 4 ... ASSESSED TO SHEA ESTATES 0 DEVELOPMENT CORP LOCATION CITY-AGOURA HILL PROPERTY ADDRESS: VACANT LOT. See page 162.

30. AIN 2061021019 (auction ID 61): TRACT NO 8793 LOT 76 BLK 4 ... ASSESSED TO SHEA ESTATES 0 DEVELOPMENT CORP LOCATION CITY-AGOURA HILL PROPERTY ADDRESS: VACANT LOT. See page 167.

31. AIN 2061021020 (auction ID 62): TRACT NO 8793 LOT 77 BLK 4 ... ASSESSED TO SHEA ESTATES 0 DEVELOPMENT CORP LOCATION CITY-AGOURA HILL PROPERTY ADDRESS: VACANT LOT. See page 172.

32. AIN 2061021021 (auction ID 63): TRACT NO 8793 LOT 78 BLK 4 ... ASSESSED TO SHEA ESTATES 0 DEVELOPMENT CORP LOCATION CITY-AGOURA HILL PROPERTY ADDRESS: VACANT LOT. See page 177.

33. AIN 2061021022 (auction ID 64): TRACT NO 8793 LOT 79 BLK 4 ... ASSESSED TO SHEA ESTATES 0 DEVELOPMENT CORP LOCATION CITY-AGOURA HILL PROPERTY ADDRESS: VACANT LOT. See page 182.

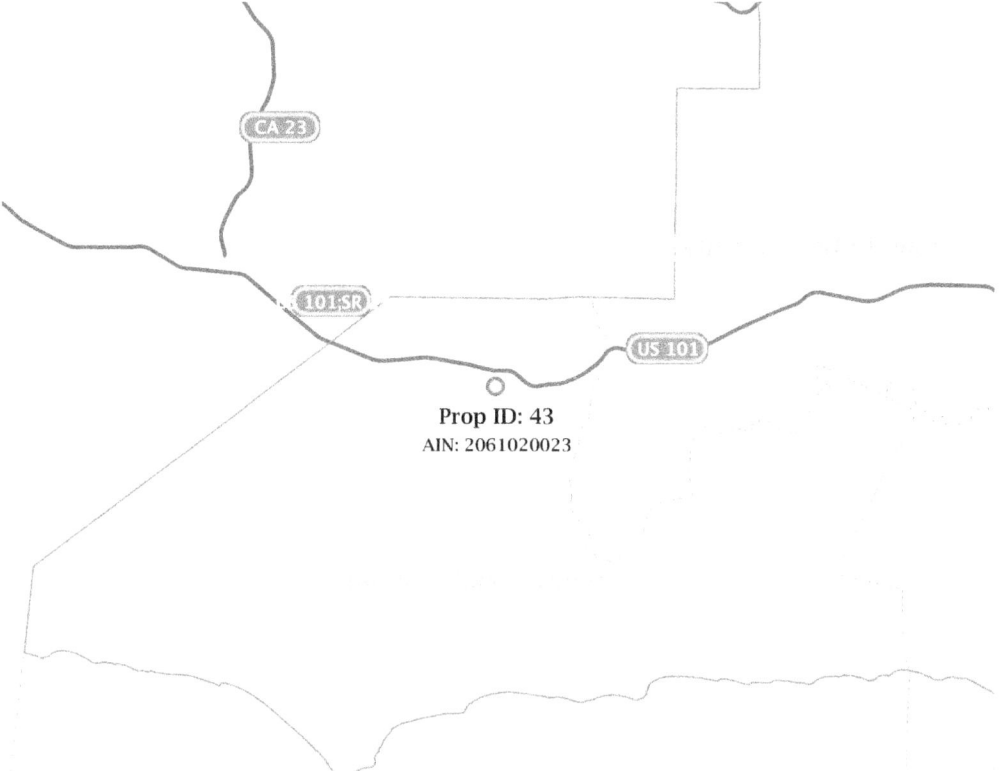

Figure 2.46: Property 64, AIN 2061020023, overview map

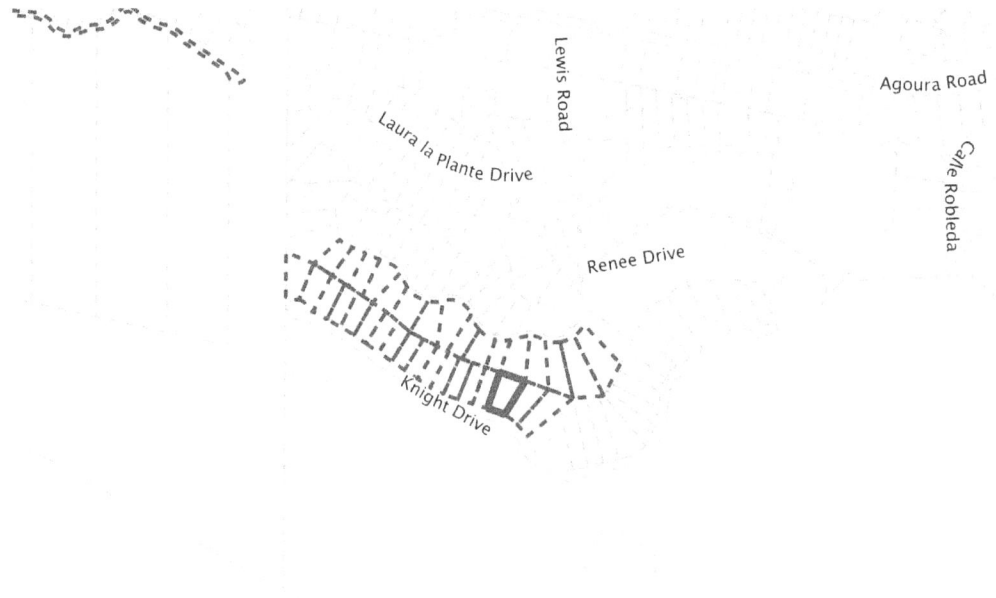

Figure 2.47: Property 64, AIN 2061020023, neighborhood view

Figure 2.48: Property 64, AIN 2061020023, detailed view

2.17   Auction ID 44

The Los Angeles County Auction Book describes the property as follows.

```
TRACT NO 8793 LOT 65 BLK 4 ASSESSED TO SHEA ESTATES 0 DEVELOPMENT
CORP LOCATION CITY-AGOURA HILL PROPERTY ADDRESS: VACANT LOT
```

The property is located in the general vicinity of Figure 2.49. It is identified by Assessor's Identification Number (AIN) 2061020024. The starting bid is $3,354. Comparable improved properties in this area is about $294/sqft. Comparable unimproved lots in this area is about $49/sqft. This parcel is approximately 5836 sqft. Note, however, that the parcel may be larger than the property under consideration. In case of condominiums, for example, the parcel may encompass other units of the development - those unrelated to the property to be auctioned.

The property is in a parcel zoned Restricted Open Space in Agoura Hills, for 0 to 0 dwelling units.

Figures 2.50 and 2.51 show street map and corresponding detailed aerial view, respectively. In both cases, the map is centered on the property with the containing parcel marked in heavy blue. If surrounding nearby properties are also part of this auction, the street and aerial maps highlights these in heavy, dashed blue outline.

This assessed entity may have other properties that are also in this auction:

1. AIN 2061020001 (auction ID 31): TRACT NO 8793 LOT 16 BLK 4 ... ASSESSED TO SHEA ESTATES 0 DEVELOPMENT CORP LOCATION CITY-AGOURA HILL PROPERTY ADDRESS: VACANT LOT. See page 17.

2. AIN 2061020002 (auction ID 32): TRACT NO 8793 LOT 17 BLK 4 ... ASSESSED TO SHEA ESTATES 0 DEVELOPMENT CORP LOCATION CITY-AGOURA HILL PROPERTY ADDRESS: VACANT LOT. See page 22.

3. AIN 2061020003 (auction ID 33): TRACT NO 8793 LOT 18 BLK 4 ... ASSESSED TO SHEA ESTATES 0 DEVELOPMENT CORP LOCATION CITY-AGOURA HILL PROPERTY ADDRESS: VACANT LOT. See page 27.

4. AIN 2061020004 (auction ID 34): TRACT NO 8793 LOT 19 BLK 4 ... ASSESSED TO SHEA ESTATES 0 DEVELOPMENT CORP LOCATION CITY-AGOURA HILL PROPERTY ADDRESS: VACANT LOT. See page 32.

5. AIN 2061020005 (auction ID 35): TRACT NO 8793 LOT 20 BLK 4 ... ASSESSED TO SHEA ESTATES 0 DEVELOPMENT CORP LOCATION CITY-AGOURA HILL PROPERTY ADDRESS: VACANT LOT. See page 37.

6. AIN 2061020006 (auction ID 36): TRACT NO 8793 LOT 21 BLK 4 ... ASSESSED TO SHEA ESTATES 0 DEVELOPMENT CORP LOCATION CITY-AGOURA HILL PROPERTY ADDRESS: VACANT LOT. See page 42.

7. AIN 2061020007 (auction ID 37): TRACT NO 8793 LOT 22 BLK 4 ... ASSESSED TO SHEA ESTATES 0 DEVELOPMENT CORP LOCATION CITY-AGOURA HILL PROPERTY ADDRESS: VACANT LOT. See page 47.

8. AIN 2061020008 (auction ID 38): TRACT NO 8793 LOT 23 BLK 4 ... ASSESSED TO SHEA ESTATES 0 DEVELOPMENT CORP LOCATION CITY-AGOURA HILL PROPERTY ADDRESS: VACANT LOT. See page 52.

9. AIN 2061020009 (auction ID 39): TRACT NO 8793 LOT 24 BLK 4 ... ASSESSED TO SHEA ESTATES 0 DEVELOPMENT CORP LOCATION CITY-AGOURA HILL PROPERTY ADDRESS: VACANT LOT. See page 57.

10. AIN 2061020010 (auction ID 40): TRACT NO 8793 LOT 25 BLK 4 ... ASSESSED TO SHEA ESTATES
0 DEVELOPMENT CORP LOCATION CITY-AGOURA HILL PROPERTY ADDRESS: VACANT LOT.
See page 62.

11. AIN 2061020021 (auction ID 41): TRACT NO 8793 LOT 62 BLK 4 ... ASSESSED TO SHEA ESTATES
0 DEVELOPMENT CORP LOCATION CITY-AGOURA HILL PROPERTY ADDRESS: VACANT LOT.
See page 67.

12. AIN 2061020022 (auction ID 42): TRACT NO 8793 LOT 63 BLK 4 ... ASSESSED TO SHEA ESTATES
0 DEVELOPMENT CORP LOCATION CITY-AGOURA HILL PROPERTY ADDRESS: VACANT LOT.
See page 72.

13. AIN 2061020023 (auction ID 43): TRACT NO 8793 LOT 64 BLK 4 ... ASSESSED TO SHEA ESTATES
0 DEVELOPMENT CORP LOCATION CITY-AGOURA HILL PROPERTY ADDRESS: VACANT LOT.
See page 77.

14. AIN 2061020025 (auction ID 45): TRACT NO 8793 LOT 66 BLK 4 ... ASSESSED TO SHEA ESTATES
0 DEVELOPMENT CORP LOCATION CITY-AGOURA HILL PROPERTY ADDRESS: VACANT LOT.
See page 87.

15. AIN 2061020026 (auction ID 46): TRACT NO 8793 LOT 67 BLK 4 ... ASSESSED TO SHEA ESTATES
0 DEVELOPMENT CORP LOCATION CITY-AGOURA HILL PROPERTY ADDRESS: VACANT LOT.
See page 92.

16. AIN 2061020027 (auction ID 47): TRACT NO 8793 LOT 68 BLK 4 ... ASSESSED TO SHEA ESTATES
0 DEVELOPMENT CORP LOCATION CITY-AGOURA HILL PROPERTY ADDRESS: VACANT LOT.
See page 97.

17. AIN 2061020028 (auction ID 48): TRACT NO 8793 LOT 69 BLK 4 ... ASSESSED TO SHEA ESTATES
0 DEVELOPMENT CORP LOCATION CITY-AGOURA HILL - PROPERTY ADDRESS: VACANT LOT.
See page 102.

18. AIN 2061020029 (auction ID 49): TRACT NO 8793 LOT 70 BLK 4 ... ASSESSED TO SHEA ESTATES
0 DEVELOPMENT CORP LOCATION CITY-AGOURA HILL PROPERTY ADDRESS: VACANT LOT.
See page 107.

19. AIN 2061020030 (auction ID 50): TRACT NO 8793 LOT 71 BLK 4 ... ASSESSED TO SHEA ESTATES
0 DEVELOPMENT CORP LOCATION CITY-AGOURA HILL PROPERTY ADDRESS: VACANT LOT.
See page 112.

20. AIN 2061021009 (auction ID 51): TRACT NO 8793 LOT 10 BLK 4 ... ASSESSED TO SHEA ESTATES
0 DEVELOPMENT CORP LOCATION CITY-AGOURA HILL PROPERTY ADDRESS: VACANT LOT.
See page 117.

21. AIN 2061021010 (auction ID 52): TRACT NO 8793 LOT 11 BLK 4 ... ASSESSED TO SHEA ESTATES
0 DEVELOPMENT CORP LOCATION CITY-AGOURA HILL PROPERTY ADDRESS: VACANT LOT.
See page 122.

22. AIN 2061021011 (auction ID 53): TRACT NO 8793 LOT 12 BLK 4 ... ASSESSED TO SHEA ESTATES
0 DEVELOPMENT CORP LOCATION CITY-AGOURA HILL PROPERTY ADDRESS: VACANT LOT.
See page 127.

23. AIN 2061021012 (auction ID 54): TRACT NO 8793 LOT 13 BLK 4 ... ASSESSED TO SHEA ESTATES
0 DEVELOPMENT CORP LOCATION CITY-AGOURA HILL PROPERTY ADDRESS: VACANT LOT.
See page 132.

24. AIN 2061021013 (auction ID 55): TRACT NO 8793 LOT 14 BLK 4 ... ASSESSED TO SHEA ESTATES
0 DEVELOPMENT CORP LOCATION CITY-AGOURA HILL PROPERTY ADDRESS: VACANT LOT.
See page 137.

25. AIN 2061021014 (auction ID 56): TRACT NO 8793 LOT 15 BLK 4 ... ASSESSED TO SHEA ESTATES 0 DEVELOPMENT CORP LOCATION CITY-AGOURA HILL PROPERTY ADDRESS: VACANT LOT. See page 142.

26. AIN 2061021015 (auction ID 57): TRACT NO 8793 LOT 72 BLK 4 ... ASSESSED TO SHEA ESTATES 0 DEVELOPMENT CORP LOCATION CITY-AGOURA HILL PROPERTY ADDRESS: VACANT LOT. See page 147.

27. AIN 2061021016 (auction ID 58): TRACT NO 8793 LOT 73 BLK 4 ... ASSESSED TO SHEA ESTATES 0 DEVELOPMENT CORP LOCATION CITY-AGOURA HILL PROPERTY ADDRESS: VACANT LOT. See page 152.

28. AIN 2061021017 (auction ID 59): TRACT NO 8793 LOT 74 BLK 4 ... ASSESSED TO SHEA ESTATES 0 DEVELOPMENT CORP LOCATION CITY-AGOURA HILL PROPERTY ADDRESS: VACANT LOT. See page 157.

29. AIN 2061021018 (auction ID 60): TRACT NO 8793 LOT 75 BLK 4 ... ASSESSED TO SHEA ESTATES 0 DEVELOPMENT CORP LOCATION CITY-AGOURA HILL PROPERTY ADDRESS: VACANT LOT. See page 162.

30. AIN 2061021019 (auction ID 61): TRACT NO 8793 LOT 76 BLK 4 ... ASSESSED TO SHEA ESTATES 0 DEVELOPMENT CORP LOCATION CITY-AGOURA HILL PROPERTY ADDRESS: VACANT LOT. See page 167.

31. AIN 2061021020 (auction ID 62): TRACT NO 8793 LOT 77 BLK 4 ... ASSESSED TO SHEA ESTATES 0 DEVELOPMENT CORP LOCATION CITY-AGOURA HILL PROPERTY ADDRESS: VACANT LOT. See page 172.

32. AIN 2061021021 (auction ID 63): TRACT NO 8793 LOT 78 BLK 4 ... ASSESSED TO SHEA ESTATES 0 DEVELOPMENT CORP LOCATION CITY-AGOURA HILL PROPERTY ADDRESS: VACANT LOT. See page 177.

33. AIN 2061021022 (auction ID 64): TRACT NO 8793 LOT 79 BLK 4 ... ASSESSED TO SHEA ESTATES 0 DEVELOPMENT CORP LOCATION CITY-AGOURA HILL PROPERTY ADDRESS: VACANT LOT. See page 182.

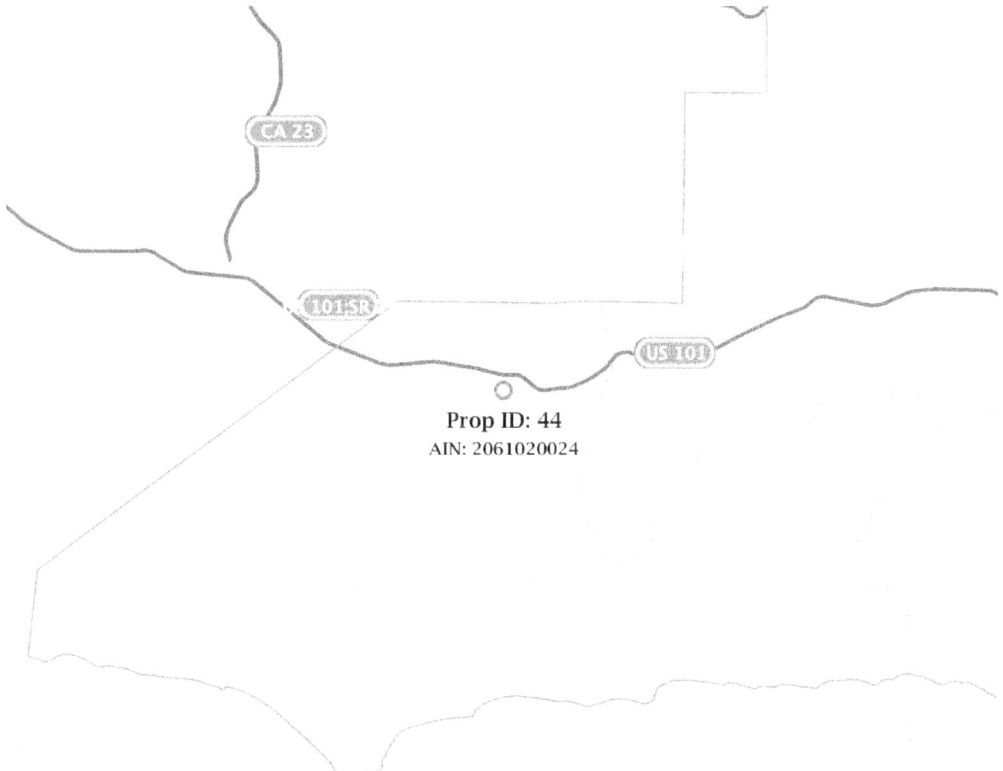

Figure 2.49: Property 64, AIN 2061020024, overview map

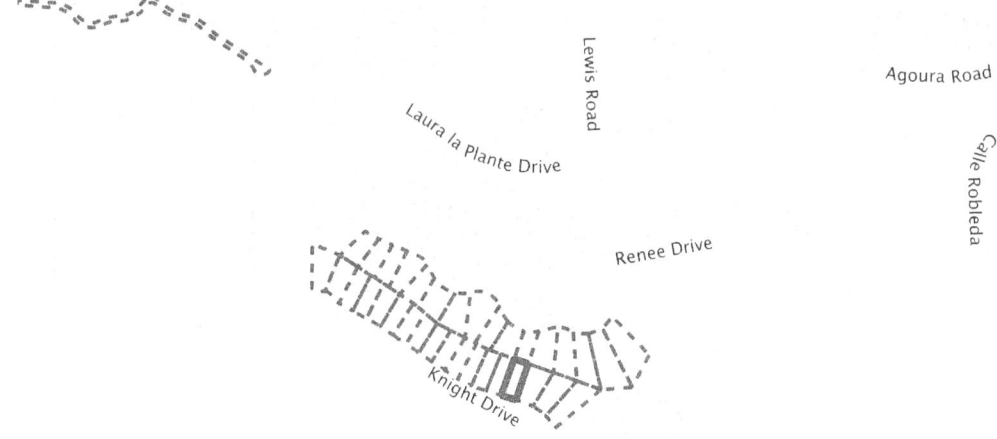

Figure 2.50: Property 64, AIN 2061020024, neighborhood view

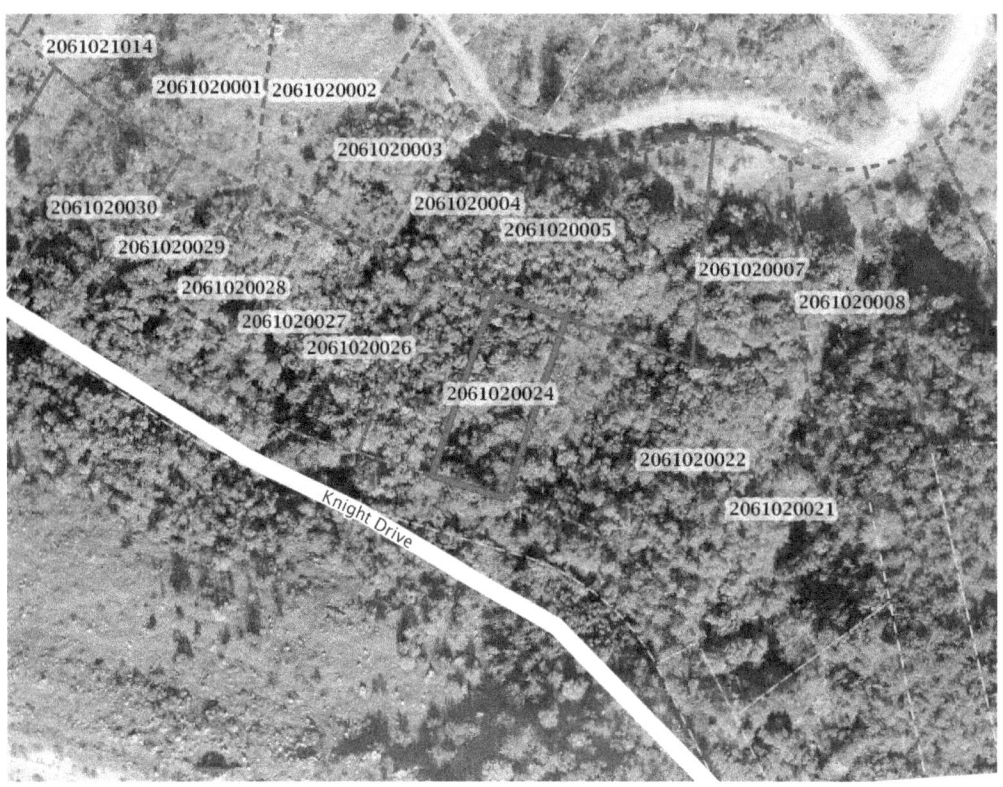

Figure 2.51: Property 64, AIN 2061020024, detailed view

2.18 Auction ID 45

The Los Angeles County Auction Book describes the property as follows.

```
TRACT NO 8793 LOT 66 BLK 4 ASSESSED TO SHEA ESTATES 0 DEVELOPMENT
CORP LOCATION CITY-AGOURA HILL PROPERTY ADDRESS: VACANT LOT
```

The property is located in the general vicinity of Figure 2.52. It is identified by Assessor's Identification Number (AIN) 2061020025. The starting bid is $3,303. Comparable improved properties in this area is about $294/sqft. Comparable unimproved lots in this area is about $49/sqft. This parcel is approximately 5775 sqft. Note, however, that the parcel may be larger than the property under consideration. In case of condominiums, for example, the parcel may encompass other units of the development - those unrelated to the property to be auctioned.

The property is in a parcel zoned Restricted Open Space in Agoura Hills, for 0 to 0 dwelling units.

Figures 2.53 and 2.54 show street map and corresponding detailed aerial view, respectively. In both cases, the map is centered on the property with the containing parcel marked in heavy blue. If surrounding nearby properties are also part of this auction, the street and aerial maps highlights these in heavy, dashed blue outline.

This assessed entity may have other properties that are also in this auction:

1. AIN 2061020001 (auction ID 31): TRACT NO 8793 LOT 16 BLK 4 . . . ASSESSED TO SHEA ESTATES 0 DEVELOPMENT CORP LOCATION CITY-AGOURA HILL PROPERTY ADDRESS: VACANT LOT. See page 17.

2. AIN 2061020002 (auction ID 32): TRACT NO 8793 LOT 17 BLK 4 . . . ASSESSED TO SHEA ESTATES 0 DEVELOPMENT CORP LOCATION CITY-AGOURA HILL PROPERTY ADDRESS: VACANT LOT. See page 22.

3. AIN 2061020003 (auction ID 33): TRACT NO 8793 LOT 18 BLK 4 . . . ASSESSED TO SHEA ESTATES 0 DEVELOPMENT CORP LOCATION CITY-AGOURA HILL PROPERTY ADDRESS: VACANT LOT. See page 27.

4. AIN 2061020004 (auction ID 34): TRACT NO 8793 LOT 19 BLK 4 . . . ASSESSED TO SHEA ESTATES 0 DEVELOPMENT CORP LOCATION CITY-AGOURA HILL PROPERTY ADDRESS: VACANT LOT. See page 32.

5. AIN 2061020005 (auction ID 35): TRACT NO 8793 LOT 20 BLK 4 . . . ASSESSED TO SHEA ESTATES 0 DEVELOPMENT CORP LOCATION CITY-AGOURA HILL PROPERTY ADDRESS: VACANT LOT. See page 37.

6. AIN 2061020006 (auction ID 36): TRACT NO 8793 LOT 21 BLK 4 . . . ASSESSED TO SHEA ESTATES 0 DEVELOPMENT CORP LOCATION CITY-AGOURA HILL PROPERTY ADDRESS: VACANT LOT. See page 42.

7. AIN 2061020007 (auction ID 37): TRACT NO 8793 LOT 22 BLK 4 . . . ASSESSED TO SHEA ESTATES 0 DEVELOPMENT CORP LOCATION CITY-AGOURA HILL PROPERTY ADDRESS: VACANT LOT. See page 47.

8. AIN 2061020008 (auction ID 38): TRACT NO 8793 LOT 23 BLK 4 . . . ASSESSED TO SHEA ESTATES 0 DEVELOPMENT CORP LOCATION CITY-AGOURA HILL PROPERTY ADDRESS: VACANT LOT. See page 52.

9. AIN 2061020009 (auction ID 39): TRACT NO 8793 LOT 24 BLK 4 . . . ASSESSED TO SHEA ESTATES 0 DEVELOPMENT CORP LOCATION CITY-AGOURA HILL PROPERTY ADDRESS: VACANT LOT. See page 57.

10. AIN 2061020010 (auction ID 40): TRACT NO 8793 LOT 25 BLK 4 . . . ASSESSED TO SHEA ESTATES 0 DEVELOPMENT CORP LOCATION CITY-AGOURA HILL PROPERTY ADDRESS: VACANT LOT. See page 62.

11. AIN 2061020021 (auction ID 41): TRACT NO 8793 LOT 62 BLK 4 . . . ASSESSED TO SHEA ESTATES 0 DEVELOPMENT CORP LOCATION CITY-AGOURA HILL PROPERTY ADDRESS: VACANT LOT. See page 67.

12. AIN 2061020022 (auction ID 42): TRACT NO 8793 LOT 63 BLK 4 . . . ASSESSED TO SHEA ESTATES 0 DEVELOPMENT CORP LOCATION CITY-AGOURA HILL PROPERTY ADDRESS: VACANT LOT. See page 72.

13. AIN 2061020023 (auction ID 43): TRACT NO 8793 LOT 64 BLK 4 . . . ASSESSED TO SHEA ESTATES 0 DEVELOPMENT CORP LOCATION CITY-AGOURA HILL PROPERTY ADDRESS: VACANT LOT. See page 77.

14. AIN 2061020024 (auction ID 44): TRACT NO 8793 LOT 65 BLK 4 . . . ASSESSED TO SHEA ESTATES 0 DEVELOPMENT CORP LOCATION CITY-AGOURA HILL PROPERTY ADDRESS: VACANT LOT. See page 82.

15. AIN 2061020026 (auction ID 46): TRACT NO 8793 LOT 67 BLK 4 . . . ASSESSED TO SHEA ESTATES 0 DEVELOPMENT CORP LOCATION CITY-AGOURA HILL PROPERTY ADDRESS: VACANT LOT. See page 92.

16. AIN 2061020027 (auction ID 47): TRACT NO 8793 LOT 68 BLK 4 . . . ASSESSED TO SHEA ESTATES 0 DEVELOPMENT CORP LOCATION CITY-AGOURA HILL PROPERTY ADDRESS: VACANT LOT. See page 97.

17. AIN 2061020028 (auction ID 48): TRACT NO 8793 LOT 69 BLK 4 . . . ASSESSED TO SHEA ESTATES 0 DEVELOPMENT CORP LOCATION CITY-AGOURA HILL - PROPERTY ADDRESS: VACANT LOT. See page 102.

18. AIN 2061020029 (auction ID 49): TRACT NO 8793 LOT 70 BLK 4 . . . ASSESSED TO SHEA ESTATES 0 DEVELOPMENT CORP LOCATION CITY-AGOURA HILL PROPERTY ADDRESS: VACANT LOT. See page 107.

19. AIN 2061020030 (auction ID 50): TRACT NO 8793 LOT 71 BLK 4 . . . ASSESSED TO SHEA ESTATES 0 DEVELOPMENT CORP LOCATION CITY-AGOURA HILL PROPERTY ADDRESS: VACANT LOT. See page 112.

20. AIN 2061021009 (auction ID 51): TRACT NO 8793 LOT 10 BLK 4 . . . ASSESSED TO SHEA ESTATES 0 DEVELOPMENT CORP LOCATION CITY-AGOURA HILL PROPERTY ADDRESS: VACANT LOT. See page 117.

21. AIN 2061021010 (auction ID 52): TRACT NO 8793 LOT 11 BLK 4 . . . ASSESSED TO SHEA ESTATES 0 DEVELOPMENT CORP LOCATION CITY-AGOURA HILL PROPERTY ADDRESS: VACANT LOT. See page 122.

22. AIN 2061021011 (auction ID 53): TRACT NO 8793 LOT 12 BLK 4 . . . ASSESSED TO SHEA ESTATES 0 DEVELOPMENT CORP LOCATION CITY-AGOURA HILL PROPERTY ADDRESS: VACANT LOT. See page 127.

23. AIN 2061021012 (auction ID 54): TRACT NO 8793 LOT 13 BLK 4 . . . ASSESSED TO SHEA ESTATES 0 DEVELOPMENT CORP LOCATION CITY-AGOURA HILL PROPERTY ADDRESS: VACANT LOT. See page 132.

24. AIN 2061021013 (auction ID 55): TRACT NO 8793 LOT 14 BLK 4 . . . ASSESSED TO SHEA ESTATES 0 DEVELOPMENT CORP LOCATION CITY-AGOURA HILL PROPERTY ADDRESS: VACANT LOT. See page 137.

25. AIN 2061021014 (auction ID 56): TRACT NO 8793 LOT 15 BLK 4 . . . ASSESSED TO SHEA ESTATES 0 DEVELOPMENT CORP LOCATION CITY-AGOURA HILL PROPERTY ADDRESS: VACANT LOT. See page 142.

26. AIN 2061021015 (auction ID 57): TRACT NO 8793 LOT 72 BLK 4 . . . ASSESSED TO SHEA ESTATES 0 DEVELOPMENT CORP LOCATION CITY-AGOURA HILL PROPERTY ADDRESS: VACANT LOT. See page 147.

27. AIN 2061021016 (auction ID 58): TRACT NO 8793 LOT 73 BLK 4 . . . ASSESSED TO SHEA ESTATES 0 DEVELOPMENT CORP LOCATION CITY-AGOURA HILL PROPERTY ADDRESS: VACANT LOT. See page 152.

28. AIN 2061021017 (auction ID 59): TRACT NO 8793 LOT 74 BLK 4 . . . ASSESSED TO SHEA ESTATES 0 DEVELOPMENT CORP LOCATION CITY-AGOURA HILL PROPERTY ADDRESS: VACANT LOT. See page 157.

29. AIN 2061021018 (auction ID 60): TRACT NO 8793 LOT 75 BLK 4 . . . ASSESSED TO SHEA ESTATES 0 DEVELOPMENT CORP LOCATION CITY-AGOURA HILL PROPERTY ADDRESS: VACANT LOT. See page 162.

30. AIN 2061021019 (auction ID 61): TRACT NO 8793 LOT 76 BLK 4 . . . ASSESSED TO SHEA ESTATES 0 DEVELOPMENT CORP LOCATION CITY-AGOURA HILL PROPERTY ADDRESS: VACANT LOT. See page 167.

31. AIN 2061021020 (auction ID 62): TRACT NO 8793 LOT 77 BLK 4 . . . ASSESSED TO SHEA ESTATES 0 DEVELOPMENT CORP LOCATION CITY-AGOURA HILL PROPERTY ADDRESS: VACANT LOT. See page 172.

32. AIN 2061021021 (auction ID 63): TRACT NO 8793 LOT 78 BLK 4 . . . ASSESSED TO SHEA ESTATES 0 DEVELOPMENT CORP LOCATION CITY-AGOURA HILL PROPERTY ADDRESS: VACANT LOT. See page 177.

33. AIN 2061021022 (auction ID 64): TRACT NO 8793 LOT 79 BLK 4 . . . ASSESSED TO SHEA ESTATES 0 DEVELOPMENT CORP LOCATION CITY-AGOURA HILL PROPERTY ADDRESS: VACANT LOT. See page 182.

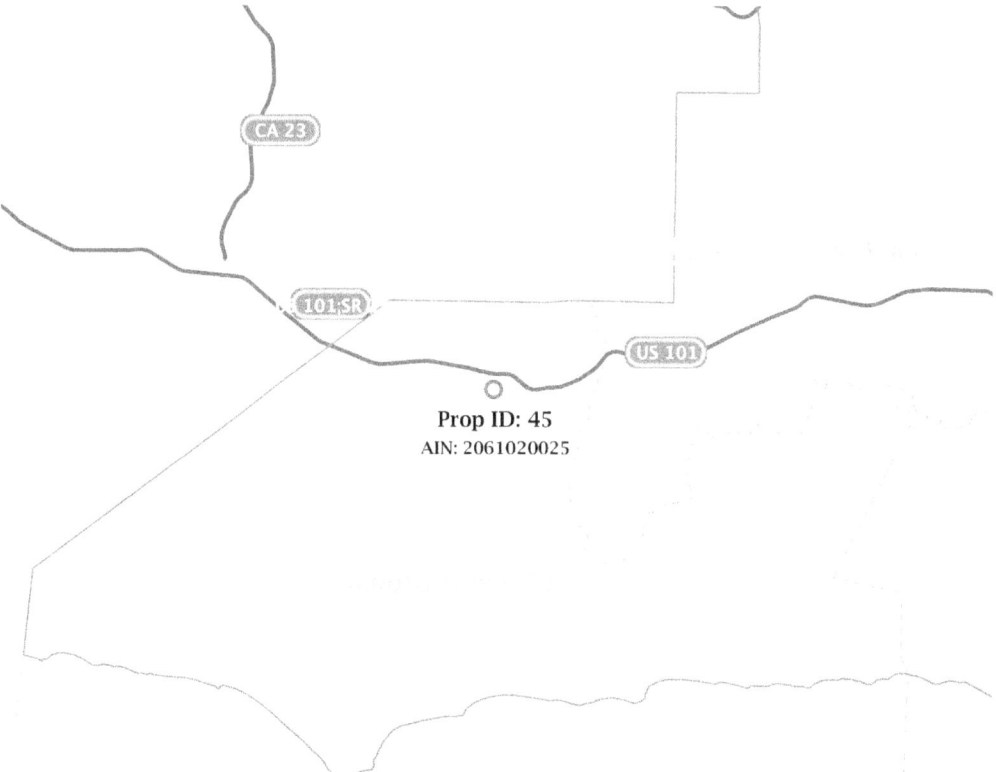

Figure 2.52: Property 64, AIN 2061020025, overview map

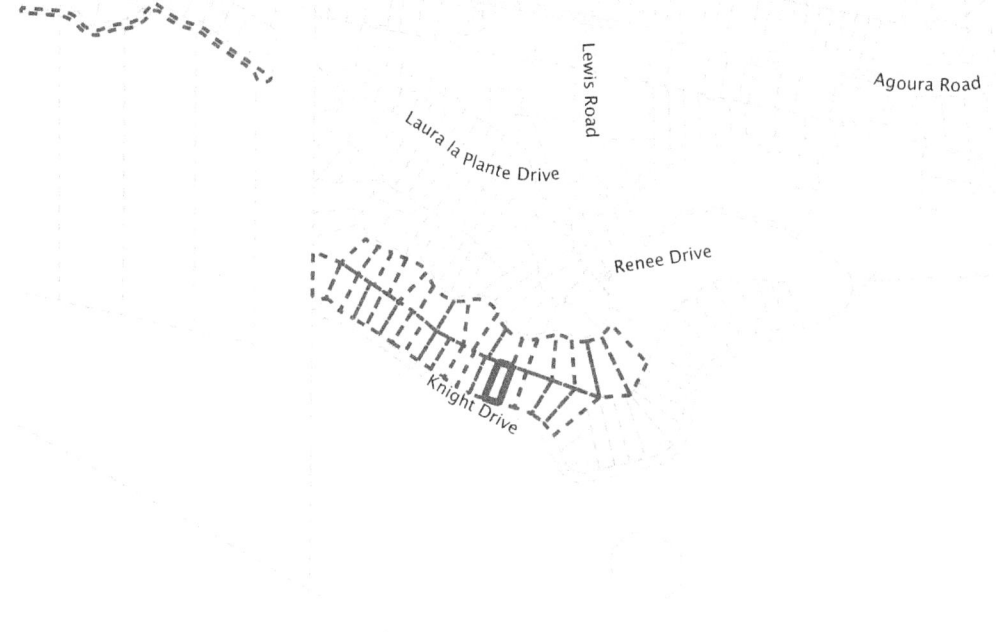

Figure 2.53: Property 64, AIN 2061020025, neighborhood view

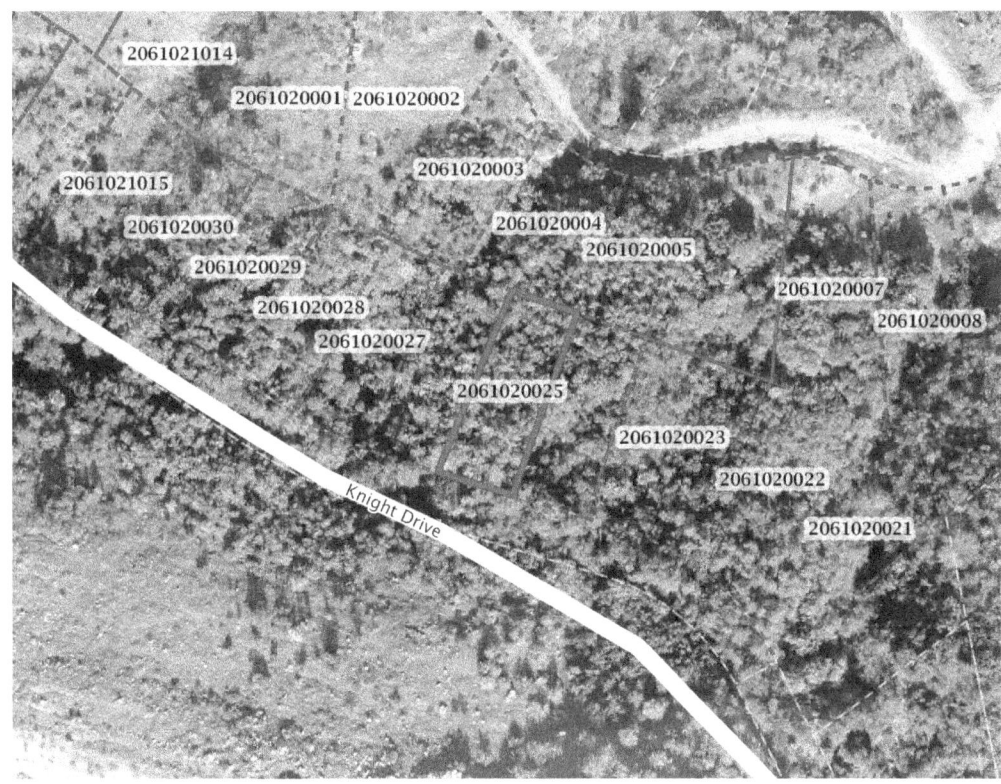

Figure 2.54: Property 64, AIN 2061020025, detailed view

2.19   Auction ID 46

The Los Angeles County Auction Book describes the property as follows.

```
TRACT NO 8793 LOT 67 BLK 4 ASSESSED TO SHEA ESTATES 0 DEVELOPMENT
CORP LOCATION CITY-AGOURA HILL PROPERTY ADDRESS: VACANT LOT
```

The property is located in the general vicinity of Figure 2.55. It is identified by Assessor's Identification Number (AIN) 2061020026. The starting bid is $3,343. Comparable improved properties in this area is about $294/sqft. Comparable unimproved lots in this area is about $49/sqft. This parcel is approximately 5948 sqft. Note, however, that the parcel may be larger than the property under consideration. In case of condominiums, for example, the parcel may encompass other units of the development - those unrelated to the property to be auctioned.

The property is in a parcel zoned Restricted Open Space in Agoura Hills, for 0 to 0 dwelling units.

Figures 2.56 and 2.57 show street map and corresponding detailed aerial view, respectively. In both cases, the map is centered on the property with the containing parcel marked in heavy blue. If surrounding nearby properties are also part of this auction, the street and aerial maps highlights these in heavy, dashed blue outline.

This assessed entity may have other properties that are also in this auction:

1. AIN 2061020001 (auction ID 31): TRACT NO 8793 LOT 16 BLK 4 . . . ASSESSED TO SHEA ESTATES 0 DEVELOPMENT CORP LOCATION CITY-AGOURA HILL PROPERTY ADDRESS: VACANT LOT. See page 17.

2. AIN 2061020002 (auction ID 32): TRACT NO 8793 LOT 17 BLK 4 . . . ASSESSED TO SHEA ESTATES 0 DEVELOPMENT CORP LOCATION CITY-AGOURA HILL PROPERTY ADDRESS: VACANT LOT. See page 22.

3. AIN 2061020003 (auction ID 33): TRACT NO 8793 LOT 18 BLK 4 . . . ASSESSED TO SHEA ESTATES 0 DEVELOPMENT CORP LOCATION CITY-AGOURA HILL PROPERTY ADDRESS: VACANT LOT. See page 27.

4. AIN 2061020004 (auction ID 34): TRACT NO 8793 LOT 19 BLK 4 . . . ASSESSED TO SHEA ESTATES 0 DEVELOPMENT CORP LOCATION CITY-AGOURA HILL PROPERTY ADDRESS: VACANT LOT. See page 32.

5. AIN 2061020005 (auction ID 35): TRACT NO 8793 LOT 20 BLK 4 . . . ASSESSED TO SHEA ESTATES 0 DEVELOPMENT CORP LOCATION CITY-AGOURA HILL PROPERTY ADDRESS: VACANT LOT. See page 37.

6. AIN 2061020006 (auction ID 36): TRACT NO 8793 LOT 21 BLK 4 . . . ASSESSED TO SHEA ESTATES 0 DEVELOPMENT CORP LOCATION CITY-AGOURA HILL PROPERTY ADDRESS: VACANT LOT. See page 42.

7. AIN 2061020007 (auction ID 37): TRACT NO 8793 LOT 22 BLK 4 . . . ASSESSED TO SHEA ESTATES 0 DEVELOPMENT CORP LOCATION CITY-AGOURA HILL PROPERTY ADDRESS: VACANT LOT. See page 47.

8. AIN 2061020008 (auction ID 38): TRACT NO 8793 LOT 23 BLK 4 . . . ASSESSED TO SHEA ESTATES 0 DEVELOPMENT CORP LOCATION CITY-AGOURA HILL PROPERTY ADDRESS: VACANT LOT. See page 52.

9. AIN 2061020009 (auction ID 39): TRACT NO 8793 LOT 24 BLK 4 . . . ASSESSED TO SHEA ESTATES 0 DEVELOPMENT CORP LOCATION CITY-AGOURA HILL PROPERTY ADDRESS: VACANT LOT. See page 57.

10. AIN 2061020010 (auction ID 40): TRACT NO 8793 LOT 25 BLK 4 . . . ASSESSED TO SHEA ESTATES 0 DEVELOPMENT CORP LOCATION CITY-AGOURA HILL PROPERTY ADDRESS: VACANT LOT. See page 62.

11. AIN 2061020021 (auction ID 41): TRACT NO 8793 LOT 62 BLK 4 . . . ASSESSED TO SHEA ESTATES 0 DEVELOPMENT CORP LOCATION CITY-AGOURA HILL PROPERTY ADDRESS: VACANT LOT. See page 67.

12. AIN 2061020022 (auction ID 42): TRACT NO 8793 LOT 63 BLK 4 . . . ASSESSED TO SHEA ESTATES 0 DEVELOPMENT CORP LOCATION CITY-AGOURA HILL PROPERTY ADDRESS: VACANT LOT. See page 72.

13. AIN 2061020023 (auction ID 43): TRACT NO 8793 LOT 64 BLK 4 . . . ASSESSED TO SHEA ESTATES 0 DEVELOPMENT CORP LOCATION CITY-AGOURA HILL PROPERTY ADDRESS: VACANT LOT. See page 77.

14. AIN 2061020024 (auction ID 44): TRACT NO 8793 LOT 65 BLK 4 . . . ASSESSED TO SHEA ESTATES 0 DEVELOPMENT CORP LOCATION CITY-AGOURA HILL PROPERTY ADDRESS: VACANT LOT. See page 82.

15. AIN 2061020025 (auction ID 45): TRACT NO 8793 LOT 66 BLK 4 . . . ASSESSED TO SHEA ESTATES 0 DEVELOPMENT CORP LOCATION CITY-AGOURA HILL PROPERTY ADDRESS: VACANT LOT. See page 87.

16. AIN 2061020027 (auction ID 47): TRACT NO 8793 LOT 68 BLK 4 . . . ASSESSED TO SHEA ESTATES 0 DEVELOPMENT CORP LOCATION CITY-AGOURA HILL PROPERTY ADDRESS: VACANT LOT. See page 97.

17. AIN 2061020028 (auction ID 48): TRACT NO 8793 LOT 69 BLK 4 . . . ASSESSED TO SHEA ESTATES 0 DEVELOPMENT CORP LOCATION CITY-AGOURA HILL - PROPERTY ADDRESS: VACANT LOT. See page 102.

18. AIN 2061020029 (auction ID 49): TRACT NO 8793 LOT 70 BLK 4 . . . ASSESSED TO SHEA ESTATES 0 DEVELOPMENT CORP LOCATION CITY-AGOURA HILL PROPERTY ADDRESS: VACANT LOT. See page 107.

19. AIN 2061020030 (auction ID 50): TRACT NO 8793 LOT 71 BLK 4 . . . ASSESSED TO SHEA ESTATES 0 DEVELOPMENT CORP LOCATION CITY-AGOURA HILL PROPERTY ADDRESS: VACANT LOT. See page 112.

20. AIN 2061021009 (auction ID 51): TRACT NO 8793 LOT 10 BLK 4 . . . ASSESSED TO SHEA ESTATES 0 DEVELOPMENT CORP LOCATION CITY-AGOURA HILL PROPERTY ADDRESS: VACANT LOT. See page 117.

21. AIN 2061021010 (auction ID 52): TRACT NO 8793 LOT 11 BLK 4 . . . ASSESSED TO SHEA ESTATES 0 DEVELOPMENT CORP LOCATION CITY-AGOURA HILL PROPERTY ADDRESS: VACANT LOT. See page 122.

22. AIN 2061021011 (auction ID 53): TRACT NO 8793 LOT 12 BLK 4 . . . ASSESSED TO SHEA ESTATES 0 DEVELOPMENT CORP LOCATION CITY-AGOURA HILL PROPERTY ADDRESS: VACANT LOT. See page 127.

23. AIN 2061021012 (auction ID 54): TRACT NO 8793 LOT 13 BLK 4 . . . ASSESSED TO SHEA ESTATES 0 DEVELOPMENT CORP LOCATION CITY-AGOURA HILL PROPERTY ADDRESS: VACANT LOT. See page 132.

24. AIN 2061021013 (auction ID 55): TRACT NO 8793 LOT 14 BLK 4 . . . ASSESSED TO SHEA ESTATES 0 DEVELOPMENT CORP LOCATION CITY-AGOURA HILL PROPERTY ADDRESS: VACANT LOT. See page 137.

25. AIN 2061021014 (auction ID 56): TRACT NO 8793 LOT 15 BLK 4 ... ASSESSED TO SHEA ESTATES 0 DEVELOPMENT CORP LOCATION CITY-AGOURA HILL PROPERTY ADDRESS: VACANT LOT. See page 142.

26. AIN 2061021015 (auction ID 57): TRACT NO 8793 LOT 72 BLK 4 ... ASSESSED TO SHEA ESTATES 0 DEVELOPMENT CORP LOCATION CITY-AGOURA HILL PROPERTY ADDRESS: VACANT LOT. See page 147.

27. AIN 2061021016 (auction ID 58): TRACT NO 8793 LOT 73 BLK 4 ... ASSESSED TO SHEA ESTATES 0 DEVELOPMENT CORP LOCATION CITY-AGOURA HILL PROPERTY ADDRESS: VACANT LOT. See page 152.

28. AIN 2061021017 (auction ID 59): TRACT NO 8793 LOT 74 BLK 4 ... ASSESSED TO SHEA ESTATES 0 DEVELOPMENT CORP LOCATION CITY-AGOURA HILL PROPERTY ADDRESS: VACANT LOT. See page 157.

29. AIN 2061021018 (auction ID 60): TRACT NO 8793 LOT 75 BLK 4 ... ASSESSED TO SHEA ESTATES 0 DEVELOPMENT CORP LOCATION CITY-AGOURA HILL PROPERTY ADDRESS: VACANT LOT. See page 162.

30. AIN 2061021019 (auction ID 61): TRACT NO 8793 LOT 76 BLK 4 ... ASSESSED TO SHEA ESTATES 0 DEVELOPMENT CORP LOCATION CITY-AGOURA HILL PROPERTY ADDRESS: VACANT LOT. See page 167.

31. AIN 2061021020 (auction ID 62): TRACT NO 8793 LOT 77 BLK 4 ... ASSESSED TO SHEA ESTATES 0 DEVELOPMENT CORP LOCATION CITY-AGOURA HILL PROPERTY ADDRESS: VACANT LOT. See page 172.

32. AIN 2061021021 (auction ID 63): TRACT NO 8793 LOT 78 BLK 4 ... ASSESSED TO SHEA ESTATES 0 DEVELOPMENT CORP LOCATION CITY-AGOURA HILL PROPERTY ADDRESS: VACANT LOT. See page 177.

33. AIN 2061021022 (auction ID 64): TRACT NO 8793 LOT 79 BLK 4 ... ASSESSED TO SHEA ESTATES 0 DEVELOPMENT CORP LOCATION CITY-AGOURA HILL PROPERTY ADDRESS: VACANT LOT. See page 182.

Figure 2.55: Property 64, AIN 2061020026, overview map

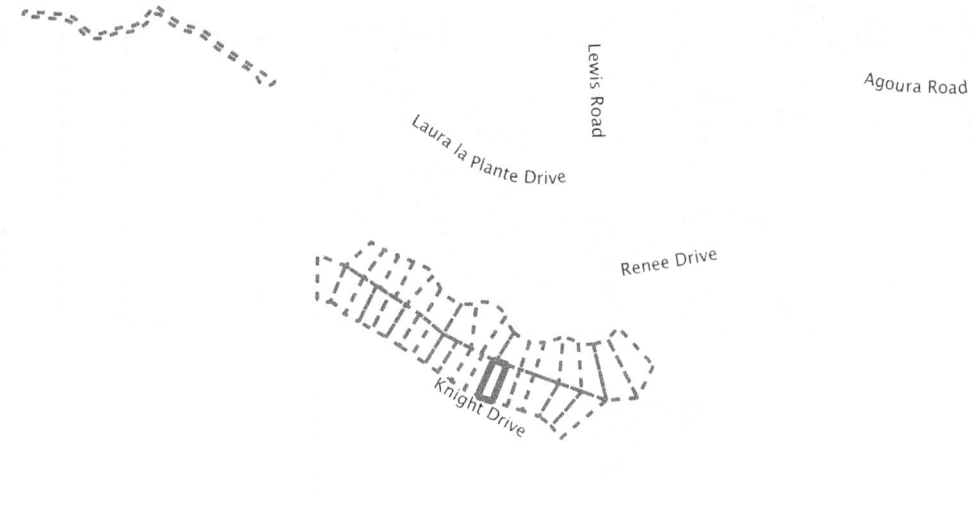

Figure 2.56: Property 64, AIN 2061020026, neighborhood view

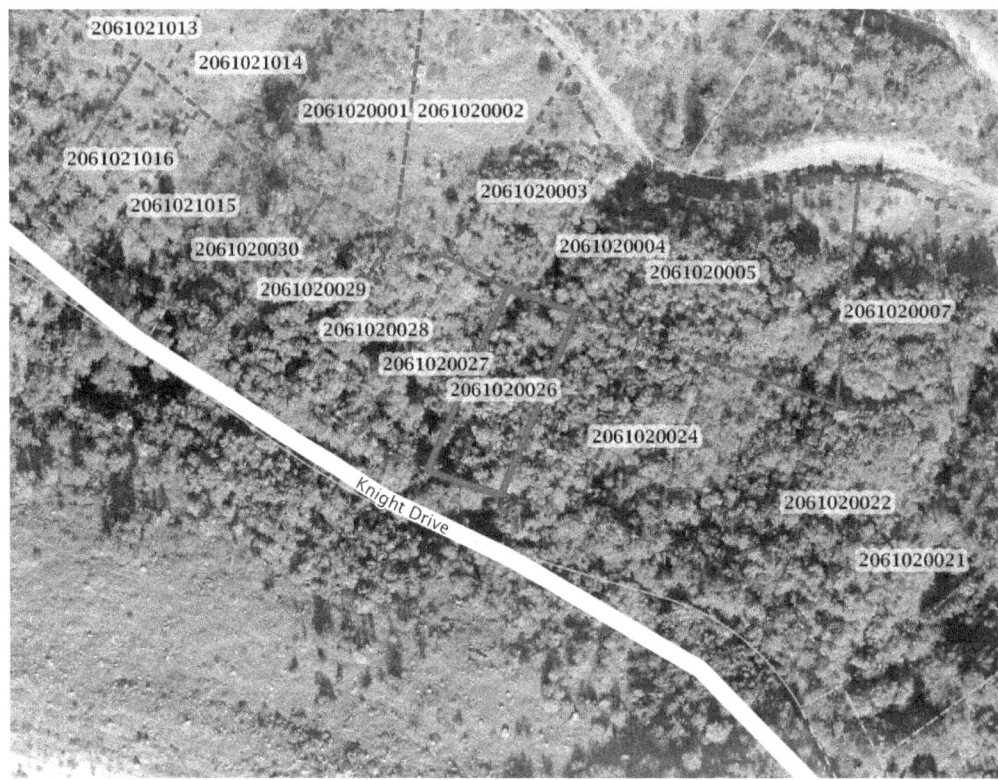

Figure 2.57: Property 64, AIN 2061020026, detailed view

2.20 Auction ID 47

The Los Angeles County Auction Book describes the property as follows.

```
TRACT NO 8793 LOT 68 BLK 4 ASSESSED TO SHEA ESTATES 0 DEVELOPMENT
CORP LOCATION CITY-AGOURA HILL PROPERTY ADDRESS: VACANT LOT
```

The property is located in the general vicinity of Figure 2.58. It is identified by Assessor's Identification Number (AIN) 2061020027. The starting bid is \$3,245. Comparable improved properties in this area is about \$294/sqft. Comparable unimproved lots in this area is about \$49/sqft. This parcel is approximately 5498 sqft. Note, however, that the parcel may be larger than the property under consideration. In case of condominiums, for example, the parcel may encompass other units of the development - those unrelated to the property to be auctioned.

The property is in a parcel zoned Restricted Open Space in Agoura Hills, for 0 to 0 dwelling units.

Figures 2.59 and 2.60 show street map and corresponding detailed aerial view, respectively. In both cases, the map is centered on the property with the containing parcel marked in heavy blue. If surrounding nearby properties are also part of this auction, the street and aerial maps highlights these in heavy, dashed blue outline.

This assessed entity may have other properties that are also in this auction:

1. AIN 2061020001 (auction ID 31): TRACT NO 8793 LOT 16 BLK 4 . . . ASSESSED TO SHEA ESTATES 0 DEVELOPMENT CORP LOCATION CITY-AGOURA HILL PROPERTY ADDRESS: VACANT LOT. See page 17.

2. AIN 2061020002 (auction ID 32): TRACT NO 8793 LOT 17 BLK 4 . . . ASSESSED TO SHEA ESTATES 0 DEVELOPMENT CORP LOCATION CITY-AGOURA HILL PROPERTY ADDRESS: VACANT LOT. See page 22.

3. AIN 2061020003 (auction ID 33): TRACT NO 8793 LOT 18 BLK 4 . . . ASSESSED TO SHEA ESTATES 0 DEVELOPMENT CORP LOCATION CITY-AGOURA HILL PROPERTY ADDRESS: VACANT LOT. See page 27.

4. AIN 2061020004 (auction ID 34): TRACT NO 8793 LOT 19 BLK 4 . . . ASSESSED TO SHEA ESTATES 0 DEVELOPMENT CORP LOCATION CITY-AGOURA HILL PROPERTY ADDRESS: VACANT LOT. See page 32.

5. AIN 2061020005 (auction ID 35): TRACT NO 8793 LOT 20 BLK 4 . . . ASSESSED TO SHEA ESTATES 0 DEVELOPMENT CORP LOCATION CITY-AGOURA HILL PROPERTY ADDRESS: VACANT LOT. See page 37.

6. AIN 2061020006 (auction ID 36): TRACT NO 8793 LOT 21 BLK 4 . . . ASSESSED TO SHEA ESTATES 0 DEVELOPMENT CORP LOCATION CITY-AGOURA HILL PROPERTY ADDRESS: VACANT LOT. See page 42.

7. AIN 2061020007 (auction ID 37): TRACT NO 8793 LOT 22 BLK 4 . . . ASSESSED TO SHEA ESTATES 0 DEVELOPMENT CORP LOCATION CITY-AGOURA HILL PROPERTY ADDRESS: VACANT LOT. See page 47.

8. AIN 2061020008 (auction ID 38): TRACT NO 8793 LOT 23 BLK 4 . . . ASSESSED TO SHEA ESTATES 0 DEVELOPMENT CORP LOCATION CITY-AGOURA HILL PROPERTY ADDRESS: VACANT LOT. See page 52.

9. AIN 2061020009 (auction ID 39): TRACT NO 8793 LOT 24 BLK 4 . . . ASSESSED TO SHEA ESTATES 0 DEVELOPMENT CORP LOCATION CITY-AGOURA HILL PROPERTY ADDRESS: VACANT LOT. See page 57.

10. AIN 2061020010 (auction ID 40): TRACT NO 8793 LOT 25 BLK 4 . . . ASSESSED TO SHEA ESTATES 0 DEVELOPMENT CORP LOCATION CITY-AGOURA HILL PROPERTY ADDRESS: VACANT LOT. See page 62.

11. AIN 2061020021 (auction ID 41): TRACT NO 8793 LOT 62 BLK 4 . . . ASSESSED TO SHEA ESTATES 0 DEVELOPMENT CORP LOCATION CITY-AGOURA HILL PROPERTY ADDRESS: VACANT LOT. See page 67.

12. AIN 2061020022 (auction ID 42): TRACT NO 8793 LOT 63 BLK 4 . . . ASSESSED TO SHEA ESTATES 0 DEVELOPMENT CORP LOCATION CITY-AGOURA HILL PROPERTY ADDRESS: VACANT LOT. See page 72.

13. AIN 2061020023 (auction ID 43): TRACT NO 8793 LOT 64 BLK 4 . . . ASSESSED TO SHEA ESTATES 0 DEVELOPMENT CORP LOCATION CITY-AGOURA HILL PROPERTY ADDRESS: VACANT LOT. See page 77.

14. AIN 2061020024 (auction ID 44): TRACT NO 8793 LOT 65 BLK 4 . . . ASSESSED TO SHEA ESTATES 0 DEVELOPMENT CORP LOCATION CITY-AGOURA HILL PROPERTY ADDRESS: VACANT LOT. See page 82.

15. AIN 2061020025 (auction ID 45): TRACT NO 8793 LOT 66 BLK 4 . . . ASSESSED TO SHEA ESTATES 0 DEVELOPMENT CORP LOCATION CITY-AGOURA HILL PROPERTY ADDRESS: VACANT LOT. See page 87.

16. AIN 2061020026 (auction ID 46): TRACT NO 8793 LOT 67 BLK 4 . . . ASSESSED TO SHEA ESTATES 0 DEVELOPMENT CORP LOCATION CITY-AGOURA HILL PROPERTY ADDRESS: VACANT LOT. See page 92.

17. AIN 2061020028 (auction ID 48): TRACT NO 8793 LOT 69 BLK 4 . . . ASSESSED TO SHEA ESTATES 0 DEVELOPMENT CORP LOCATION CITY-AGOURA HILL - PROPERTY ADDRESS: VACANT LOT. See page 102.

18. AIN 2061020029 (auction ID 49): TRACT NO 8793 LOT 70 BLK 4 . . . ASSESSED TO SHEA ESTATES 0 DEVELOPMENT CORP LOCATION CITY-AGOURA HILL PROPERTY ADDRESS: VACANT LOT. See page 107.

19. AIN 2061020030 (auction ID 50): TRACT NO 8793 LOT 71 BLK 4 . . . ASSESSED TO SHEA ESTATES 0 DEVELOPMENT CORP LOCATION CITY-AGOURA HILL PROPERTY ADDRESS: VACANT LOT. See page 112.

20. AIN 2061021009 (auction ID 51): TRACT NO 8793 LOT 10 BLK 4 . . . ASSESSED TO SHEA ESTATES 0 DEVELOPMENT CORP LOCATION CITY-AGOURA HILL PROPERTY ADDRESS: VACANT LOT. See page 117.

21. AIN 2061021010 (auction ID 52): TRACT NO 8793 LOT 11 BLK 4 . . . ASSESSED TO SHEA ESTATES 0 DEVELOPMENT CORP LOCATION CITY-AGOURA HILL PROPERTY ADDRESS: VACANT LOT. See page 122.

22. AIN 2061021011 (auction ID 53): TRACT NO 8793 LOT 12 BLK 4 . . . ASSESSED TO SHEA ESTATES 0 DEVELOPMENT CORP LOCATION CITY-AGOURA HILL PROPERTY ADDRESS: VACANT LOT. See page 127.

23. AIN 2061021012 (auction ID 54): TRACT NO 8793 LOT 13 BLK 4 . . . ASSESSED TO SHEA ESTATES 0 DEVELOPMENT CORP LOCATION CITY-AGOURA HILL PROPERTY ADDRESS: VACANT LOT. See page 132.

24. AIN 2061021013 (auction ID 55): TRACT NO 8793 LOT 14 BLK 4 . . . ASSESSED TO SHEA ESTATES 0 DEVELOPMENT CORP LOCATION CITY-AGOURA HILL PROPERTY ADDRESS: VACANT LOT. See page 137.

25. AIN 2061021014 (auction ID 56): TRACT NO 8793 LOT 15 BLK 4 . . . ASSESSED TO SHEA ESTATES 0 DEVELOPMENT CORP LOCATION CITY-AGOURA HILL PROPERTY ADDRESS: VACANT LOT. See page 142.

26. AIN 2061021015 (auction ID 57): TRACT NO 8793 LOT 72 BLK 4 . . . ASSESSED TO SHEA ESTATES 0 DEVELOPMENT CORP LOCATION CITY-AGOURA HILL PROPERTY ADDRESS: VACANT LOT. See page 147.

27. AIN 2061021016 (auction ID 58): TRACT NO 8793 LOT 73 BLK 4 . . . ASSESSED TO SHEA ESTATES 0 DEVELOPMENT CORP LOCATION CITY-AGOURA HILL PROPERTY ADDRESS: VACANT LOT. See page 152.

28. AIN 2061021017 (auction ID 59): TRACT NO 8793 LOT 74 BLK 4 . . . ASSESSED TO SHEA ESTATES 0 DEVELOPMENT CORP LOCATION CITY-AGOURA HILL PROPERTY ADDRESS: VACANT LOT. See page 157.

29. AIN 2061021018 (auction ID 60): TRACT NO 8793 LOT 75 BLK 4 . . . ASSESSED TO SHEA ESTATES 0 DEVELOPMENT CORP LOCATION CITY-AGOURA HILL PROPERTY ADDRESS: VACANT LOT. See page 162.

30. AIN 2061021019 (auction ID 61): TRACT NO 8793 LOT 76 BLK 4 . . . ASSESSED TO SHEA ESTATES 0 DEVELOPMENT CORP LOCATION CITY-AGOURA HILL PROPERTY ADDRESS: VACANT LOT. See page 167.

31. AIN 2061021020 (auction ID 62): TRACT NO 8793 LOT 77 BLK 4 . . . ASSESSED TO SHEA ESTATES 0 DEVELOPMENT CORP LOCATION CITY-AGOURA HILL PROPERTY ADDRESS: VACANT LOT. See page 172.

32. AIN 2061021021 (auction ID 63): TRACT NO 8793 LOT 78 BLK 4 . . . ASSESSED TO SHEA ESTATES 0 DEVELOPMENT CORP LOCATION CITY-AGOURA HILL PROPERTY ADDRESS: VACANT LOT. See page 177.

33. AIN 2061021022 (auction ID 64): TRACT NO 8793 LOT 79 BLK 4 . . . ASSESSED TO SHEA ESTATES 0 DEVELOPMENT CORP LOCATION CITY-AGOURA HILL PROPERTY ADDRESS: VACANT LOT. See page 182.

Figure 2.58: Property 64, AIN 2061020027, overview map

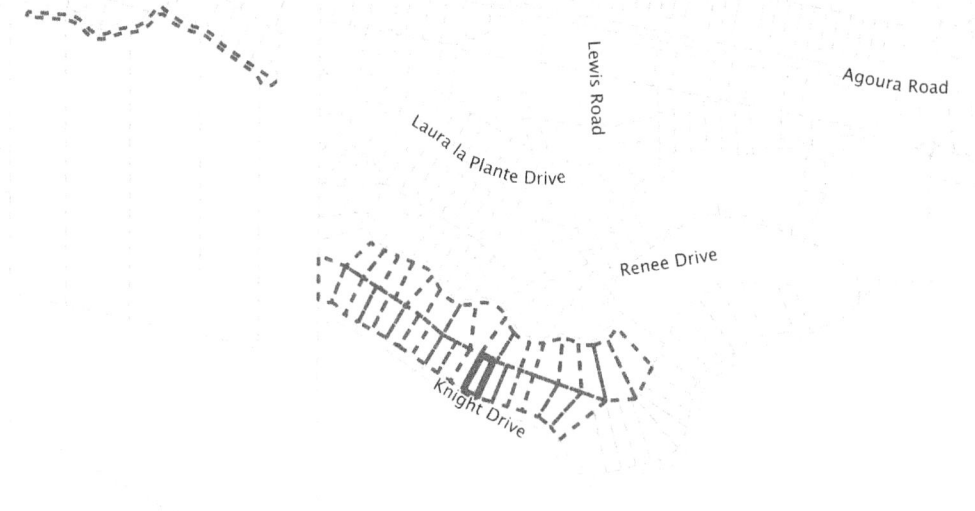

Figure 2.59: Property 64, AIN 2061020027, neighborhood view

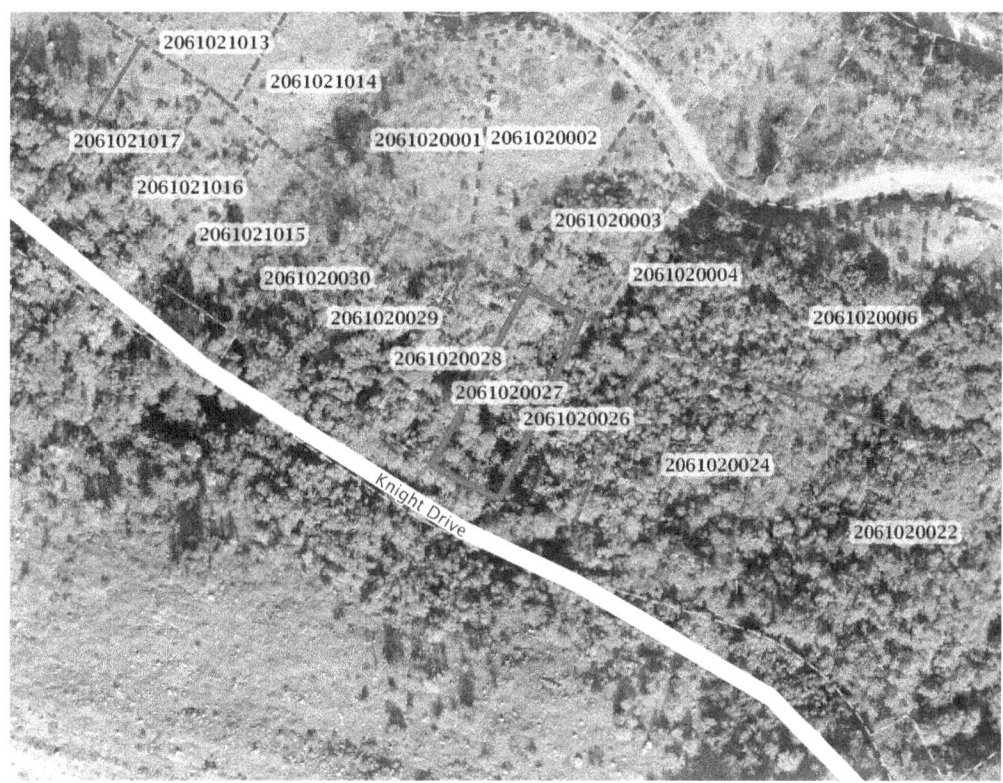

Figure 2.60: Property 64, AIN 2061020027, detailed view

2.21 Auction ID 48

The Los Angeles County Auction Book describes the property as follows.

```
TRACT NO 8793 LOT 69 BLK 4 ASSESSED TO SHEA ESTATES 0 DEVELOPMENT
CORP LOCATION CITY-AGOURA HILL - PROPERTY ADDRESS: VACANT LOT
```

The property is located in the general vicinity of Figure 2.61. It is identified by Assessor's Identification Number (AIN) 2061020028. The starting bid is $3,254. Comparable improved properties in this area is about $294/sqft. Comparable unimproved lots in this area is about $49/sqft. This parcel is approximately 5573 sqft. Note, however, that the parcel may be larger than the property under consideration. In case of condominiums, for example, the parcel may encompass other units of the development - those unrelated to the property to be auctioned.

The property is in a parcel zoned Restricted Open Space in Agoura Hills, for 0 to 0 dwelling units.

Figures 2.62 and 2.63 show street map and corresponding detailed aerial view, respectively. In both cases, the map is centered on the property with the containing parcel marked in heavy blue. If surrounding nearby properties are also part of this auction, the street and aerial maps highlights these in heavy, dashed blue outline.

This assessed entity may have other properties that are also in this auction:

1. AIN 2061020001 (auction ID 31): TRACT NO 8793 LOT 16 BLK 4 ... ASSESSED TO SHEA ESTATES 0 DEVELOPMENT CORP LOCATION CITY-AGOURA HILL PROPERTY ADDRESS: VACANT LOT. See page 17.

2. AIN 2061020002 (auction ID 32): TRACT NO 8793 LOT 17 BLK 4 ... ASSESSED TO SHEA ESTATES 0 DEVELOPMENT CORP LOCATION CITY-AGOURA HILL PROPERTY ADDRESS: VACANT LOT. See page 22.

3. AIN 2061020003 (auction ID 33): TRACT NO 8793 LOT 18 BLK 4 ... ASSESSED TO SHEA ESTATES 0 DEVELOPMENT CORP LOCATION CITY-AGOURA HILL PROPERTY ADDRESS: VACANT LOT. See page 27.

4. AIN 2061020004 (auction ID 34): TRACT NO 8793 LOT 19 BLK 4 ... ASSESSED TO SHEA ESTATES 0 DEVELOPMENT CORP LOCATION CITY-AGOURA HILL PROPERTY ADDRESS: VACANT LOT. See page 32.

5. AIN 2061020005 (auction ID 35): TRACT NO 8793 LOT 20 BLK 4 ... ASSESSED TO SHEA ESTATES 0 DEVELOPMENT CORP LOCATION CITY-AGOURA HILL PROPERTY ADDRESS: VACANT LOT. See page 37.

6. AIN 2061020006 (auction ID 36): TRACT NO 8793 LOT 21 BLK 4 ... ASSESSED TO SHEA ESTATES 0 DEVELOPMENT CORP LOCATION CITY-AGOURA HILL PROPERTY ADDRESS: VACANT LOT. See page 42.

7. AIN 2061020007 (auction ID 37): TRACT NO 8793 LOT 22 BLK 4 ... ASSESSED TO SHEA ESTATES 0 DEVELOPMENT CORP LOCATION CITY-AGOURA HILL PROPERTY ADDRESS: VACANT LOT. See page 47.

8. AIN 2061020008 (auction ID 38): TRACT NO 8793 LOT 23 BLK 4 ... ASSESSED TO SHEA ESTATES 0 DEVELOPMENT CORP LOCATION CITY-AGOURA HILL PROPERTY ADDRESS: VACANT LOT. See page 52.

9. AIN 2061020009 (auction ID 39): TRACT NO 8793 LOT 24 BLK 4 ... ASSESSED TO SHEA ESTATES 0 DEVELOPMENT CORP LOCATION CITY-AGOURA HILL PROPERTY ADDRESS: VACANT LOT. See page 57.

10. AIN 2061020010 (auction ID 40): TRACT NO 8793 LOT 25 BLK 4 . . . ASSESSED TO SHEA ESTATES 0 DEVELOPMENT CORP LOCATION CITY-AGOURA HILL PROPERTY ADDRESS: VACANT LOT. See page 62.

11. AIN 2061020021 (auction ID 41): TRACT NO 8793 LOT 62 BLK 4 . . . ASSESSED TO SHEA ESTATES 0 DEVELOPMENT CORP LOCATION CITY-AGOURA HILL PROPERTY ADDRESS: VACANT LOT. See page 67.

12. AIN 2061020022 (auction ID 42): TRACT NO 8793 LOT 63 BLK 4 . . . ASSESSED TO SHEA ESTATES 0 DEVELOPMENT CORP LOCATION CITY-AGOURA HILL PROPERTY ADDRESS: VACANT LOT. See page 72.

13. AIN 2061020023 (auction ID 43): TRACT NO 8793 LOT 64 BLK 4 . . . ASSESSED TO SHEA ESTATES 0 DEVELOPMENT CORP LOCATION CITY-AGOURA HILL PROPERTY ADDRESS: VACANT LOT. See page 77.

14. AIN 2061020024 (auction ID 44): TRACT NO 8793 LOT 65 BLK 4 . . . ASSESSED TO SHEA ESTATES 0 DEVELOPMENT CORP LOCATION CITY-AGOURA HILL PROPERTY ADDRESS: VACANT LOT. See page 82.

15. AIN 2061020025 (auction ID 45): TRACT NO 8793 LOT 66 BLK 4 . . . ASSESSED TO SHEA ESTATES 0 DEVELOPMENT CORP LOCATION CITY-AGOURA HILL PROPERTY ADDRESS: VACANT LOT. See page 87.

16. AIN 2061020026 (auction ID 46): TRACT NO 8793 LOT 67 BLK 4 . . . ASSESSED TO SHEA ESTATES 0 DEVELOPMENT CORP LOCATION CITY-AGOURA HILL PROPERTY ADDRESS: VACANT LOT. See page 92.

17. AIN 2061020027 (auction ID 47): TRACT NO 8793 LOT 68 BLK 4 . . . ASSESSED TO SHEA ESTATES 0 DEVELOPMENT CORP LOCATION CITY-AGOURA HILL PROPERTY ADDRESS: VACANT LOT. See page 97.

18. AIN 2061020029 (auction ID 49): TRACT NO 8793 LOT 70 BLK 4 . . . ASSESSED TO SHEA ESTATES 0 DEVELOPMENT CORP LOCATION CITY-AGOURA HILL PROPERTY ADDRESS: VACANT LOT. See page 107.

19. AIN 2061020030 (auction ID 50): TRACT NO 8793 LOT 71 BLK 4 . . . ASSESSED TO SHEA ESTATES 0 DEVELOPMENT CORP LOCATION CITY-AGOURA HILL PROPERTY ADDRESS: VACANT LOT. See page 112.

20. AIN 2061021009 (auction ID 51): TRACT NO 8793 LOT 10 BLK 4 . . . ASSESSED TO SHEA ESTATES 0 DEVELOPMENT CORP LOCATION CITY-AGOURA HILL PROPERTY ADDRESS: VACANT LOT. See page 117.

21. AIN 2061021010 (auction ID 52): TRACT NO 8793 LOT 11 BLK 4 . . . ASSESSED TO SHEA ESTATES 0 DEVELOPMENT CORP LOCATION CITY-AGOURA HILL PROPERTY ADDRESS: VACANT LOT. See page 122.

22. AIN 2061021011 (auction ID 53): TRACT NO 8793 LOT 12 BLK 4 . . . ASSESSED TO SHEA ESTATES 0 DEVELOPMENT CORP LOCATION CITY-AGOURA HILL PROPERTY ADDRESS: VACANT LOT. See page 127.

23. AIN 2061021012 (auction ID 54): TRACT NO 8793 LOT 13 BLK 4 . . . ASSESSED TO SHEA ESTATES 0 DEVELOPMENT CORP LOCATION CITY-AGOURA HILL PROPERTY ADDRESS: VACANT LOT. See page 132.

24. AIN 2061021013 (auction ID 55): TRACT NO 8793 LOT 14 BLK 4 . . . ASSESSED TO SHEA ESTATES 0 DEVELOPMENT CORP LOCATION CITY-AGOURA HILL PROPERTY ADDRESS: VACANT LOT. See page 137.

25. AIN 2061021014 (auction ID 56): TRACT NO 8793 LOT 15 BLK 4 ... ASSESSED TO SHEA ESTATES 0 DEVELOPMENT CORP LOCATION CITY-AGOURA HILL PROPERTY ADDRESS: VACANT LOT. See page 142.

26. AIN 2061021015 (auction ID 57): TRACT NO 8793 LOT 72 BLK 4 ... ASSESSED TO SHEA ESTATES 0 DEVELOPMENT CORP LOCATION CITY-AGOURA HILL PROPERTY ADDRESS: VACANT LOT. See page 147.

27. AIN 2061021016 (auction ID 58): TRACT NO 8793 LOT 73 BLK 4 ... ASSESSED TO SHEA ESTATES 0 DEVELOPMENT CORP LOCATION CITY-AGOURA HILL PROPERTY ADDRESS: VACANT LOT. See page 152.

28. AIN 2061021017 (auction ID 59): TRACT NO 8793 LOT 74 BLK 4 ... ASSESSED TO SHEA ESTATES 0 DEVELOPMENT CORP LOCATION CITY-AGOURA HILL PROPERTY ADDRESS: VACANT LOT. See page 157.

29. AIN 2061021018 (auction ID 60): TRACT NO 8793 LOT 75 BLK 4 ... ASSESSED TO SHEA ESTATES 0 DEVELOPMENT CORP LOCATION CITY-AGOURA HILL PROPERTY ADDRESS: VACANT LOT. See page 162.

30. AIN 2061021019 (auction ID 61): TRACT NO 8793 LOT 76 BLK 4 ... ASSESSED TO SHEA ESTATES 0 DEVELOPMENT CORP LOCATION CITY-AGOURA HILL PROPERTY ADDRESS: VACANT LOT. See page 167.

31. AIN 2061021020 (auction ID 62): TRACT NO 8793 LOT 77 BLK 4 ... ASSESSED TO SHEA ESTATES 0 DEVELOPMENT CORP LOCATION CITY-AGOURA HILL PROPERTY ADDRESS: VACANT LOT. See page 172.

32. AIN 2061021021 (auction ID 63): TRACT NO 8793 LOT 78 BLK 4 ... ASSESSED TO SHEA ESTATES 0 DEVELOPMENT CORP LOCATION CITY-AGOURA HILL PROPERTY ADDRESS: VACANT LOT. See page 177.

33. AIN 2061021022 (auction ID 64): TRACT NO 8793 LOT 79 BLK 4 ... ASSESSED TO SHEA ESTATES 0 DEVELOPMENT CORP LOCATION CITY-AGOURA HILL PROPERTY ADDRESS: VACANT LOT. See page 182.

Figure 2.61: Property 64, AIN 2061020028, overview map

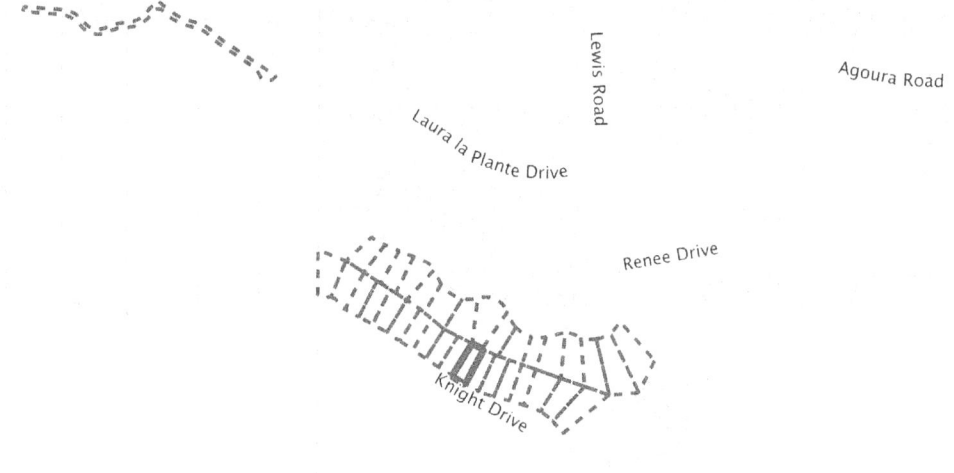

Figure 2.62: Property 64, AIN 2061020028, neighborhood view

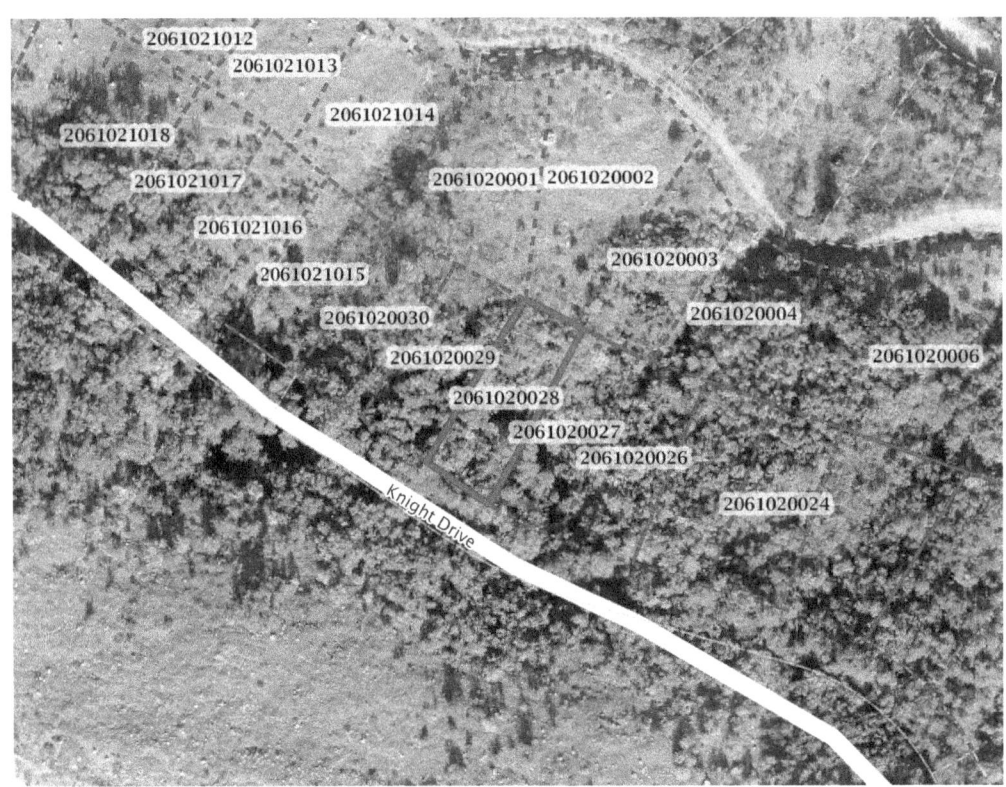

Figure 2.63: Property 64, AIN 2061020028, detailed view

2.22 Auction ID 49

The Los Angeles County Auction Book describes the property as follows.

```
TRACT NO 8793 LOT 70 BLK 4 ASSESSED TO SHEA ESTATES 0 DEVELOPMENT
CORP LOCATION CITY-AGOURA HILL PROPERTY ADDRESS: VACANT LOT
```

The property is located in the general vicinity of Figure 2.64. It is identified by Assessor's Identification Number (AIN) 2061020029. The starting bid is \$3,361. Comparable improved properties in this area is about \$294/sqft. Comparable unimproved lots in this area is about \$49/sqft. This parcel is approximately 5895 sqft. Note, however, that the parcel may be larger than the property under consideration. In case of condominiums, for example, the parcel may encompass other units of the development - those unrelated to the property to be auctioned.

The property is in a parcel zoned Restricted Open Space in Agoura Hills, for 0 to 0 dwelling units.

Figures 2.65 and 2.66 show street map and corresponding detailed aerial view, respectively. In both cases, the map is centered on the property with the containing parcel marked in heavy blue. If surrounding nearby properties are also part of this auction, the street and aerial maps highlights these in heavy, dashed blue outline.

This assessed entity may have other properties that are also in this auction:

1. AIN 2061020001 (auction ID 31): TRACT NO 8793 LOT 16 BLK 4 ... ASSESSED TO SHEA ESTATES 0 DEVELOPMENT CORP LOCATION CITY-AGOURA HILL PROPERTY ADDRESS: VACANT LOT. See page 17.

2. AIN 2061020002 (auction ID 32): TRACT NO 8793 LOT 17 BLK 4 ... ASSESSED TO SHEA ESTATES 0 DEVELOPMENT CORP LOCATION CITY-AGOURA HILL PROPERTY ADDRESS: VACANT LOT. See page 22.

3. AIN 2061020003 (auction ID 33): TRACT NO 8793 LOT 18 BLK 4 ... ASSESSED TO SHEA ESTATES 0 DEVELOPMENT CORP LOCATION CITY-AGOURA HILL PROPERTY ADDRESS: VACANT LOT. See page 27.

4. AIN 2061020004 (auction ID 34): TRACT NO 8793 LOT 19 BLK 4 ... ASSESSED TO SHEA ESTATES 0 DEVELOPMENT CORP LOCATION CITY-AGOURA HILL PROPERTY ADDRESS: VACANT LOT. See page 32.

5. AIN 2061020005 (auction ID 35): TRACT NO 8793 LOT 20 BLK 4 ... ASSESSED TO SHEA ESTATES 0 DEVELOPMENT CORP LOCATION CITY-AGOURA HILL PROPERTY ADDRESS: VACANT LOT. See page 37.

6. AIN 2061020006 (auction ID 36): TRACT NO 8793 LOT 21 BLK 4 ... ASSESSED TO SHEA ESTATES 0 DEVELOPMENT CORP LOCATION CITY-AGOURA HILL PROPERTY ADDRESS: VACANT LOT. See page 42.

7. AIN 2061020007 (auction ID 37): TRACT NO 8793 LOT 22 BLK 4 ... ASSESSED TO SHEA ESTATES 0 DEVELOPMENT CORP LOCATION CITY-AGOURA HILL PROPERTY ADDRESS: VACANT LOT. See page 47.

8. AIN 2061020008 (auction ID 38): TRACT NO 8793 LOT 23 BLK 4 ... ASSESSED TO SHEA ESTATES 0 DEVELOPMENT CORP LOCATION CITY-AGOURA HILL PROPERTY ADDRESS: VACANT LOT. See page 52.

9. AIN 2061020009 (auction ID 39): TRACT NO 8793 LOT 24 BLK 4 ... ASSESSED TO SHEA ESTATES 0 DEVELOPMENT CORP LOCATION CITY-AGOURA HILL PROPERTY ADDRESS: VACANT LOT. See page 57.

10. AIN 2061020010 (auction ID 40): TRACT NO 8793 LOT 25 BLK 4 . . . ASSESSED TO SHEA ESTATES 0 DEVELOPMENT CORP LOCATION CITY-AGOURA HILL PROPERTY ADDRESS: VACANT LOT. See page 62.

11. AIN 2061020021 (auction ID 41): TRACT NO 8793 LOT 62 BLK 4 . . . ASSESSED TO SHEA ESTATES 0 DEVELOPMENT CORP LOCATION CITY-AGOURA HILL PROPERTY ADDRESS: VACANT LOT. See page 67.

12. AIN 2061020022 (auction ID 42): TRACT NO 8793 LOT 63 BLK 4 . . . ASSESSED TO SHEA ESTATES 0 DEVELOPMENT CORP LOCATION CITY-AGOURA HILL PROPERTY ADDRESS: VACANT LOT. See page 72.

13. AIN 2061020023 (auction ID 43): TRACT NO 8793 LOT 64 BLK 4 . . . ASSESSED TO SHEA ESTATES 0 DEVELOPMENT CORP LOCATION CITY-AGOURA HILL PROPERTY ADDRESS: VACANT LOT. See page 77.

14. AIN 2061020024 (auction ID 44): TRACT NO 8793 LOT 65 BLK 4 . . . ASSESSED TO SHEA ESTATES 0 DEVELOPMENT CORP LOCATION CITY-AGOURA HILL PROPERTY ADDRESS: VACANT LOT. See page 82.

15. AIN 2061020025 (auction ID 45): TRACT NO 8793 LOT 66 BLK 4 . . . ASSESSED TO SHEA ESTATES 0 DEVELOPMENT CORP LOCATION CITY-AGOURA HILL PROPERTY ADDRESS: VACANT LOT. See page 87.

16. AIN 2061020026 (auction ID 46): TRACT NO 8793 LOT 67 BLK 4 . . . ASSESSED TO SHEA ESTATES 0 DEVELOPMENT CORP LOCATION CITY-AGOURA HILL PROPERTY ADDRESS: VACANT LOT. See page 92.

17. AIN 2061020027 (auction ID 47): TRACT NO 8793 LOT 68 BLK 4 . . . ASSESSED TO SHEA ESTATES 0 DEVELOPMENT CORP LOCATION CITY-AGOURA HILL PROPERTY ADDRESS: VACANT LOT. See page 97.

18. AIN 2061020028 (auction ID 48): TRACT NO 8793 LOT 69 BLK 4 . . . ASSESSED TO SHEA ESTATES 0 DEVELOPMENT CORP LOCATION CITY-AGOURA HILL - PROPERTY ADDRESS: VACANT LOT. See page 102.

19. AIN 2061020030 (auction ID 50): TRACT NO 8793 LOT 71 BLK 4 . . . ASSESSED TO SHEA ESTATES 0 DEVELOPMENT CORP LOCATION CITY-AGOURA HILL PROPERTY ADDRESS: VACANT LOT. See page 112.

20. AIN 2061021009 (auction ID 51): TRACT NO 8793 LOT 10 BLK 4 . . . ASSESSED TO SHEA ESTATES 0 DEVELOPMENT CORP LOCATION CITY-AGOURA HILL PROPERTY ADDRESS: VACANT LOT. See page 117.

21. AIN 2061021010 (auction ID 52): TRACT NO 8793 LOT 11 BLK 4 . . . ASSESSED TO SHEA ESTATES 0 DEVELOPMENT CORP LOCATION CITY-AGOURA HILL PROPERTY ADDRESS: VACANT LOT. See page 122.

22. AIN 2061021011 (auction ID 53): TRACT NO 8793 LOT 12 BLK 4 . . . ASSESSED TO SHEA ESTATES 0 DEVELOPMENT CORP LOCATION CITY-AGOURA HILL PROPERTY ADDRESS: VACANT LOT. See page 127.

23. AIN 2061021012 (auction ID 54): TRACT NO 8793 LOT 13 BLK 4 . . . ASSESSED TO SHEA ESTATES 0 DEVELOPMENT CORP LOCATION CITY-AGOURA HILL PROPERTY ADDRESS: VACANT LOT. See page 132.

24. AIN 2061021013 (auction ID 55): TRACT NO 8793 LOT 14 BLK 4 . . . ASSESSED TO SHEA ESTATES 0 DEVELOPMENT CORP LOCATION CITY-AGOURA HILL PROPERTY ADDRESS: VACANT LOT. See page 137.

25. AIN 2061021014 (auction ID 56): TRACT NO 8793 LOT 15 BLK 4 ... ASSESSED TO SHEA ESTATES 0 DEVELOPMENT CORP LOCATION CITY-AGOURA HILL PROPERTY ADDRESS: VACANT LOT. See page 142.

26. AIN 2061021015 (auction ID 57): TRACT NO 8793 LOT 72 BLK 4 ... ASSESSED TO SHEA ESTATES 0 DEVELOPMENT CORP LOCATION CITY-AGOURA HILL PROPERTY ADDRESS: VACANT LOT. See page 147.

27. AIN 2061021016 (auction ID 58): TRACT NO 8793 LOT 73 BLK 4 ... ASSESSED TO SHEA ESTATES 0 DEVELOPMENT CORP LOCATION CITY-AGOURA HILL PROPERTY ADDRESS: VACANT LOT. See page 152.

28. AIN 2061021017 (auction ID 59): TRACT NO 8793 LOT 74 BLK 4 ... ASSESSED TO SHEA ESTATES 0 DEVELOPMENT CORP LOCATION CITY-AGOURA HILL PROPERTY ADDRESS: VACANT LOT. See page 157.

29. AIN 2061021018 (auction ID 60): TRACT NO 8793 LOT 75 BLK 4 ... ASSESSED TO SHEA ESTATES 0 DEVELOPMENT CORP LOCATION CITY-AGOURA HILL PROPERTY ADDRESS: VACANT LOT. See page 162.

30. AIN 2061021019 (auction ID 61): TRACT NO 8793 LOT 76 BLK 4 ... ASSESSED TO SHEA ESTATES 0 DEVELOPMENT CORP LOCATION CITY-AGOURA HILL PROPERTY ADDRESS: VACANT LOT. See page 167.

31. AIN 2061021020 (auction ID 62): TRACT NO 8793 LOT 77 BLK 4 ... ASSESSED TO SHEA ESTATES 0 DEVELOPMENT CORP LOCATION CITY-AGOURA HILL PROPERTY ADDRESS: VACANT LOT. See page 172.

32. AIN 2061021021 (auction ID 63): TRACT NO 8793 LOT 78 BLK 4 ... ASSESSED TO SHEA ESTATES 0 DEVELOPMENT CORP LOCATION CITY-AGOURA HILL PROPERTY ADDRESS: VACANT LOT. See page 177.

33. AIN 2061021022 (auction ID 64): TRACT NO 8793 LOT 79 BLK 4 ... ASSESSED TO SHEA ESTATES 0 DEVELOPMENT CORP LOCATION CITY-AGOURA HILL PROPERTY ADDRESS: VACANT LOT. See page 182.

Figure 2.64: Property 64, AIN 2061020029, overview map

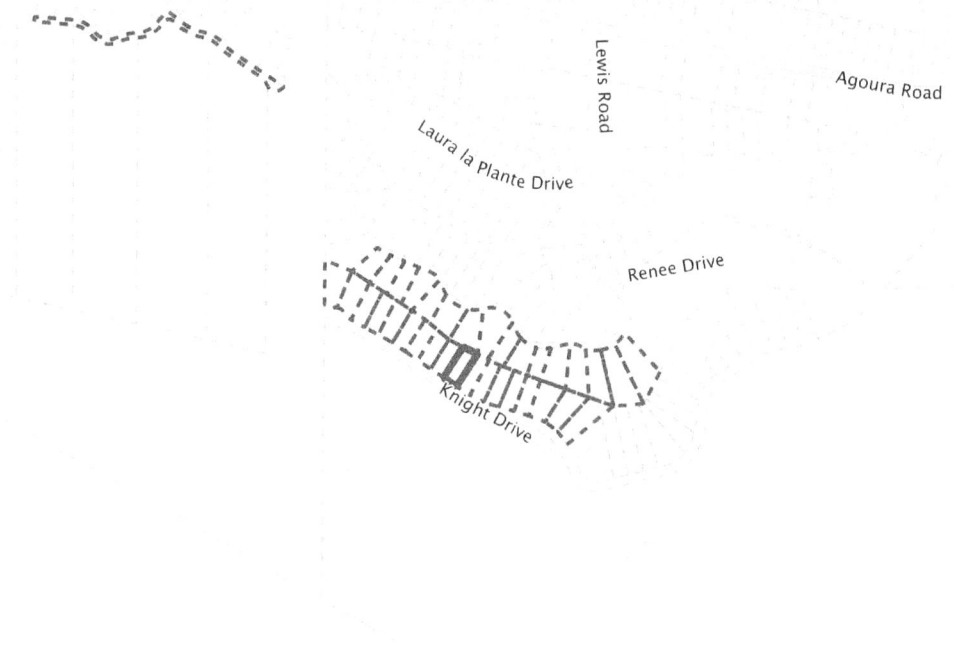

Figure 2.65: Property 64, AIN 2061020029, neighborhood view

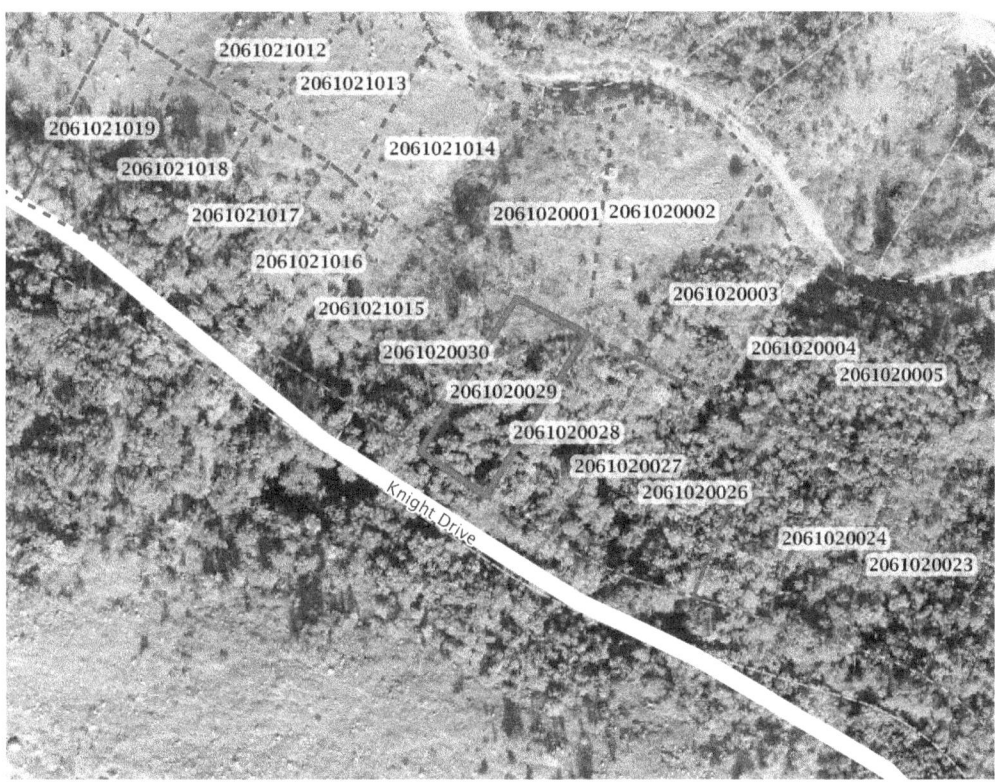

Figure 2.66: Property 64, AIN 2061020029, detailed view

2.23   Auction ID 50

The Los Angeles County Auction Book describes the property as follows.

```
TRACT NO 8793 LOT 71 BLK 4 ASSESSED TO SHEA ESTATES 0 DEVELOPMENT
CORP LOCATION CITY-AGOURA HILL PROPERTY ADDRESS: VACANT LOT
```

The property is located in the general vicinity of Figure 2.67. It is identified by Assessor's Identification Number (AIN) 2061020030. The starting bid is $3,254. Comparable improved properties in this area is about \$294/sqft. Comparable unimproved lots in this area is about \$49/sqft. This parcel is approximately 5516 sqft. Note, however, that the parcel may be larger than the property under consideration. In case of condominiums, for example, the parcel may encompass other units of the development - those unrelated to the property to be auctioned.

The property is in a parcel zoned Restricted Open Space in Agoura Hills, for 0 to 0 dwelling units.

Figures 2.68 and 2.69 show street map and corresponding detailed aerial view, respectively. In both cases, the map is centered on the property with the containing parcel marked in heavy blue. If surrounding nearby properties are also part of this auction, the street and aerial maps highlights these in heavy, dashed blue outline.

This assessed entity may have other properties that are also in this auction:

1. AIN 2061020001 (auction ID 31): TRACT NO 8793 LOT 16 BLK 4 . . . ASSESSED TO SHEA ESTATES 0 DEVELOPMENT CORP LOCATION CITY-AGOURA HILL PROPERTY ADDRESS: VACANT LOT. See page 17.

2. AIN 2061020002 (auction ID 32): TRACT NO 8793 LOT 17 BLK 4 . . . ASSESSED TO SHEA ESTATES 0 DEVELOPMENT CORP LOCATION CITY-AGOURA HILL PROPERTY ADDRESS: VACANT LOT. See page 22.

3. AIN 2061020003 (auction ID 33): TRACT NO 8793 LOT 18 BLK 4 . . . ASSESSED TO SHEA ESTATES 0 DEVELOPMENT CORP LOCATION CITY-AGOURA HILL PROPERTY ADDRESS: VACANT LOT. See page 27.

4. AIN 2061020004 (auction ID 34): TRACT NO 8793 LOT 19 BLK 4 . . . ASSESSED TO SHEA ESTATES 0 DEVELOPMENT CORP LOCATION CITY-AGOURA HILL PROPERTY ADDRESS: VACANT LOT. See page 32.

5. AIN 2061020005 (auction ID 35): TRACT NO 8793 LOT 20 BLK 4 . . . ASSESSED TO SHEA ESTATES 0 DEVELOPMENT CORP LOCATION CITY-AGOURA HILL PROPERTY ADDRESS: VACANT LOT. See page 37.

6. AIN 2061020006 (auction ID 36): TRACT NO 8793 LOT 21 BLK 4 . . . ASSESSED TO SHEA ESTATES 0 DEVELOPMENT CORP LOCATION CITY-AGOURA HILL PROPERTY ADDRESS: VACANT LOT. See page 42.

7. AIN 2061020007 (auction ID 37): TRACT NO 8793 LOT 22 BLK 4 . . . ASSESSED TO SHEA ESTATES 0 DEVELOPMENT CORP LOCATION CITY-AGOURA HILL PROPERTY ADDRESS: VACANT LOT. See page 47.

8. AIN 2061020008 (auction ID 38): TRACT NO 8793 LOT 23 BLK 4 . . . ASSESSED TO SHEA ESTATES 0 DEVELOPMENT CORP LOCATION CITY-AGOURA HILL PROPERTY ADDRESS: VACANT LOT. See page 52.

9. AIN 2061020009 (auction ID 39): TRACT NO 8793 LOT 24 BLK 4 . . . ASSESSED TO SHEA ESTATES 0 DEVELOPMENT CORP LOCATION CITY-AGOURA HILL PROPERTY ADDRESS: VACANT LOT. See page 57.

10. AIN 2061020010 (auction ID 40): TRACT NO 8793 LOT 25 BLK 4 . . . ASSESSED TO SHEA ESTATES 0 DEVELOPMENT CORP LOCATION CITY-AGOURA HILL PROPERTY ADDRESS: VACANT LOT. See page 62.

11. AIN 2061020021 (auction ID 41): TRACT NO 8793 LOT 62 BLK 4 . . . ASSESSED TO SHEA ESTATES 0 DEVELOPMENT CORP LOCATION CITY-AGOURA HILL PROPERTY ADDRESS: VACANT LOT. See page 67.

12. AIN 2061020022 (auction ID 42): TRACT NO 8793 LOT 63 BLK 4 . . . ASSESSED TO SHEA ESTATES 0 DEVELOPMENT CORP LOCATION CITY-AGOURA HILL PROPERTY ADDRESS: VACANT LOT. See page 72.

13. AIN 2061020023 (auction ID 43): TRACT NO 8793 LOT 64 BLK 4 . . . ASSESSED TO SHEA ESTATES 0 DEVELOPMENT CORP LOCATION CITY-AGOURA HILL PROPERTY ADDRESS: VACANT LOT. See page 77.

14. AIN 2061020024 (auction ID 44): TRACT NO 8793 LOT 65 BLK 4 . . . ASSESSED TO SHEA ESTATES 0 DEVELOPMENT CORP LOCATION CITY-AGOURA HILL PROPERTY ADDRESS: VACANT LOT. See page 82.

15. AIN 2061020025 (auction ID 45): TRACT NO 8793 LOT 66 BLK 4 . . . ASSESSED TO SHEA ESTATES 0 DEVELOPMENT CORP LOCATION CITY-AGOURA HILL PROPERTY ADDRESS: VACANT LOT. See page 87.

16. AIN 2061020026 (auction ID 46): TRACT NO 8793 LOT 67 BLK 4 . . . ASSESSED TO SHEA ESTATES 0 DEVELOPMENT CORP LOCATION CITY-AGOURA HILL PROPERTY ADDRESS: VACANT LOT. See page 92.

17. AIN 2061020027 (auction ID 47): TRACT NO 8793 LOT 68 BLK 4 . . . ASSESSED TO SHEA ESTATES 0 DEVELOPMENT CORP LOCATION CITY-AGOURA HILL PROPERTY ADDRESS: VACANT LOT. See page 97.

18. AIN 2061020028 (auction ID 48): TRACT NO 8793 LOT 69 BLK 4 . . . ASSESSED TO SHEA ESTATES 0 DEVELOPMENT CORP LOCATION CITY-AGOURA HILL - PROPERTY ADDRESS: VACANT LOT. See page 102.

19. AIN 2061020029 (auction ID 49): TRACT NO 8793 LOT 70 BLK 4 . . . ASSESSED TO SHEA ESTATES 0 DEVELOPMENT CORP LOCATION CITY-AGOURA HILL PROPERTY ADDRESS: VACANT LOT. See page 107.

20. AIN 2061021009 (auction ID 51): TRACT NO 8793 LOT 10 BLK 4 . . . ASSESSED TO SHEA ESTATES 0 DEVELOPMENT CORP LOCATION CITY-AGOURA HILL PROPERTY ADDRESS: VACANT LOT. See page 117.

21. AIN 2061021010 (auction ID 52): TRACT NO 8793 LOT 11 BLK 4 . . . ASSESSED TO SHEA ESTATES 0 DEVELOPMENT CORP LOCATION CITY-AGOURA HILL PROPERTY ADDRESS: VACANT LOT. See page 122.

22. AIN 2061021011 (auction ID 53): TRACT NO 8793 LOT 12 BLK 4 . . . ASSESSED TO SHEA ESTATES 0 DEVELOPMENT CORP LOCATION CITY-AGOURA HILL PROPERTY ADDRESS: VACANT LOT. See page 127.

23. AIN 2061021012 (auction ID 54): TRACT NO 8793 LOT 13 BLK 4 . . . ASSESSED TO SHEA ESTATES 0 DEVELOPMENT CORP LOCATION CITY-AGOURA HILL PROPERTY ADDRESS: VACANT LOT. See page 132.

24. AIN 2061021013 (auction ID 55): TRACT NO 8793 LOT 14 BLK 4 . . . ASSESSED TO SHEA ESTATES 0 DEVELOPMENT CORP LOCATION CITY-AGOURA HILL PROPERTY ADDRESS: VACANT LOT. See page 137.

25. AIN 2061021014 (auction ID 56): TRACT NO 8793 LOT 15 BLK 4 . . . ASSESSED TO SHEA ESTATES 0 DEVELOPMENT CORP LOCATION CITY-AGOURA HILL PROPERTY ADDRESS: VACANT LOT. See page 142.

26. AIN 2061021015 (auction ID 57): TRACT NO 8793 LOT 72 BLK 4 . . . ASSESSED TO SHEA ESTATES 0 DEVELOPMENT CORP LOCATION CITY-AGOURA HILL PROPERTY ADDRESS: VACANT LOT. See page 147.

27. AIN 2061021016 (auction ID 58): TRACT NO 8793 LOT 73 BLK 4 . . . ASSESSED TO SHEA ESTATES 0 DEVELOPMENT CORP LOCATION CITY-AGOURA HILL PROPERTY ADDRESS: VACANT LOT. See page 152.

28. AIN 2061021017 (auction ID 59): TRACT NO 8793 LOT 74 BLK 4 . . . ASSESSED TO SHEA ESTATES 0 DEVELOPMENT CORP LOCATION CITY-AGOURA HILL PROPERTY ADDRESS: VACANT LOT. See page 157.

29. AIN 2061021018 (auction ID 60): TRACT NO 8793 LOT 75 BLK 4 . . . ASSESSED TO SHEA ESTATES 0 DEVELOPMENT CORP LOCATION CITY-AGOURA HILL PROPERTY ADDRESS: VACANT LOT. See page 162.

30. AIN 2061021019 (auction ID 61): TRACT NO 8793 LOT 76 BLK 4 . . . ASSESSED TO SHEA ESTATES 0 DEVELOPMENT CORP LOCATION CITY-AGOURA HILL PROPERTY ADDRESS: VACANT LOT. See page 167.

31. AIN 2061021020 (auction ID 62): TRACT NO 8793 LOT 77 BLK 4 . . . ASSESSED TO SHEA ESTATES 0 DEVELOPMENT CORP LOCATION CITY-AGOURA HILL PROPERTY ADDRESS: VACANT LOT. See page 172.

32. AIN 2061021021 (auction ID 63): TRACT NO 8793 LOT 78 BLK 4 . . . ASSESSED TO SHEA ESTATES 0 DEVELOPMENT CORP LOCATION CITY-AGOURA HILL PROPERTY ADDRESS: VACANT LOT. See page 177.

33. AIN 2061021022 (auction ID 64): TRACT NO 8793 LOT 79 BLK 4 . . . ASSESSED TO SHEA ESTATES 0 DEVELOPMENT CORP LOCATION CITY-AGOURA HILL PROPERTY ADDRESS: VACANT LOT. See page 182.

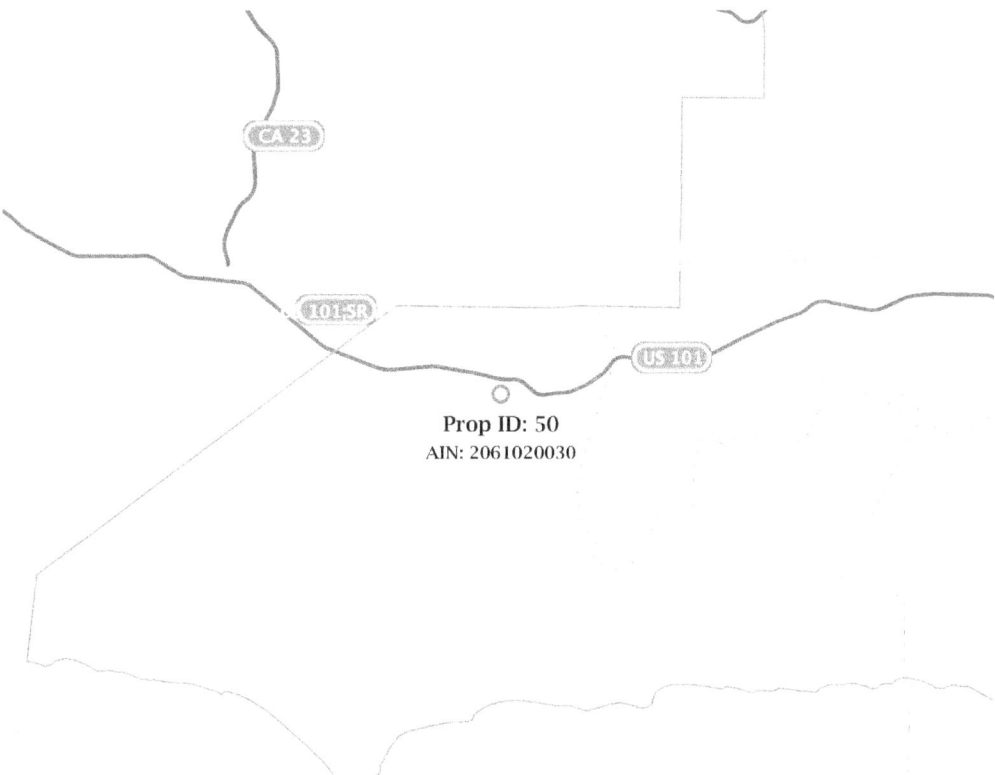

Figure 2.67: Property 64, AIN 2061020030, overview map

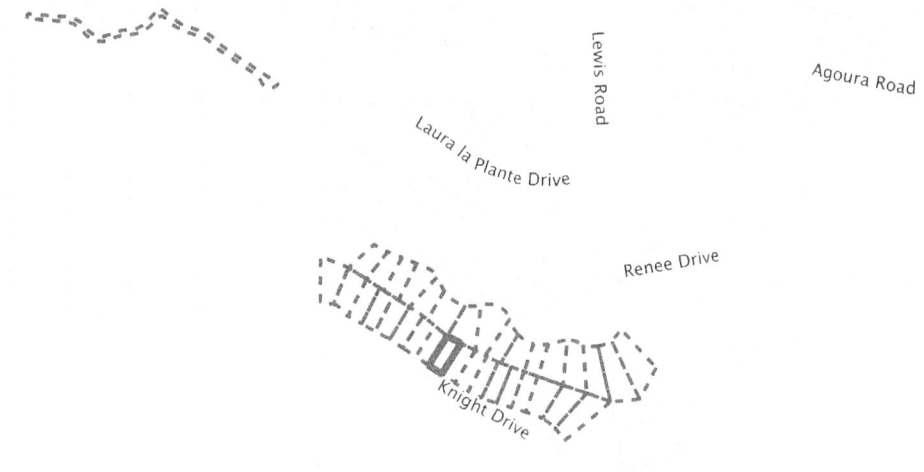

Figure 2.68: Property 64, AIN 2061020030, neighborhood view

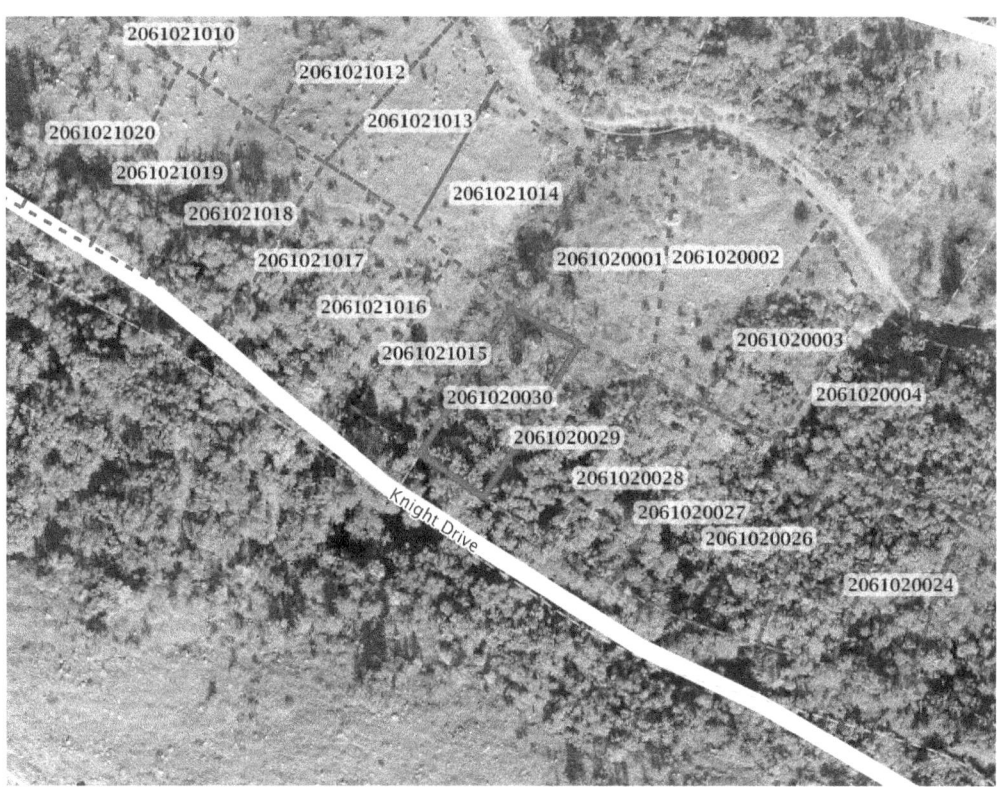

Figure 2.69: Property 64, AIN 2061020030, detailed view

2.24 Auction ID 51

The Los Angeles County Auction Book describes the property as follows.

```
TRACT NO 8793 LOT 10 BLK 4 ASSESSED TO SHEA ESTATES 0 DEVELOPMENT
CORP LOCATION CITY-AGOURA HILL PROPERTY ADDRESS: VACANT LOT
```

The property is located in the general vicinity of Figure 2.70. It is identified by Assessor's Identification Number (AIN) 2061021009. The starting bid is \$7,145. Comparable improved properties in this area is about \$297/sqft. Comparable unimproved lots in this area is about \$48/sqft. This parcel is approximately 6234 sqft. Note, however, that the parcel may be larger than the property under consideration. In case of condominiums, for example, the parcel may encompass other units of the development - those unrelated to the property to be auctioned.

The property is in a parcel zoned Restricted Open Space in Agoura Hills, for 0 to 0 dwelling units.

Figures 2.71 and 2.72 show street map and corresponding detailed aerial view, respectively. In both cases, the map is centered on the property with the containing parcel marked in heavy blue. If surrounding nearby properties are also part of this auction, the street and aerial maps highlights these in heavy, dashed blue outline.

This assessed entity may have other properties that are also in this auction:

1. AIN 2061020001 (auction ID 31): TRACT NO 8793 LOT 16 BLK 4 ... ASSESSED TO SHEA ESTATES 0 DEVELOPMENT CORP LOCATION CITY-AGOURA HILL PROPERTY ADDRESS: VACANT LOT. See page 17.

2. AIN 2061020002 (auction ID 32): TRACT NO 8793 LOT 17 BLK 4 ... ASSESSED TO SHEA ESTATES 0 DEVELOPMENT CORP LOCATION CITY-AGOURA HILL PROPERTY ADDRESS: VACANT LOT. See page 22.

3. AIN 2061020003 (auction ID 33): TRACT NO 8793 LOT 18 BLK 4 ... ASSESSED TO SHEA ESTATES 0 DEVELOPMENT CORP LOCATION CITY-AGOURA HILL PROPERTY ADDRESS: VACANT LOT. See page 27.

4. AIN 2061020004 (auction ID 34): TRACT NO 8793 LOT 19 BLK 4 ... ASSESSED TO SHEA ESTATES 0 DEVELOPMENT CORP LOCATION CITY-AGOURA HILL PROPERTY ADDRESS: VACANT LOT. See page 32.

5. AIN 2061020005 (auction ID 35): TRACT NO 8793 LOT 20 BLK 4 ... ASSESSED TO SHEA ESTATES 0 DEVELOPMENT CORP LOCATION CITY-AGOURA HILL PROPERTY ADDRESS: VACANT LOT. See page 37.

6. AIN 2061020006 (auction ID 36): TRACT NO 8793 LOT 21 BLK 4 ... ASSESSED TO SHEA ESTATES 0 DEVELOPMENT CORP LOCATION CITY-AGOURA HILL PROPERTY ADDRESS: VACANT LOT. See page 42.

7. AIN 2061020007 (auction ID 37): TRACT NO 8793 LOT 22 BLK 4 ... ASSESSED TO SHEA ESTATES 0 DEVELOPMENT CORP LOCATION CITY-AGOURA HILL PROPERTY ADDRESS: VACANT LOT. See page 47.

8. AIN 2061020008 (auction ID 38): TRACT NO 8793 LOT 23 BLK 4 ... ASSESSED TO SHEA ESTATES 0 DEVELOPMENT CORP LOCATION CITY-AGOURA HILL PROPERTY ADDRESS: VACANT LOT. See page 52.

9. AIN 2061020009 (auction ID 39): TRACT NO 8793 LOT 24 BLK 4 ... ASSESSED TO SHEA ESTATES 0 DEVELOPMENT CORP LOCATION CITY-AGOURA HILL PROPERTY ADDRESS: VACANT LOT. See page 57.

10. AIN 2061020010 (auction ID 40): TRACT NO 8793 LOT 25 BLK 4 . . . ASSESSED TO SHEA ESTATES 0 DEVELOPMENT CORP LOCATION CITY-AGOURA HILL PROPERTY ADDRESS: VACANT LOT. See page 62.

11. AIN 2061020021 (auction ID 41): TRACT NO 8793 LOT 62 BLK 4 . . . ASSESSED TO SHEA ESTATES 0 DEVELOPMENT CORP LOCATION CITY-AGOURA HILL PROPERTY ADDRESS: VACANT LOT. See page 67.

12. AIN 2061020022 (auction ID 42): TRACT NO 8793 LOT 63 BLK 4 . . . ASSESSED TO SHEA ESTATES 0 DEVELOPMENT CORP LOCATION CITY-AGOURA HILL PROPERTY ADDRESS: VACANT LOT. See page 72.

13. AIN 2061020023 (auction ID 43): TRACT NO 8793 LOT 64 BLK 4 . . . ASSESSED TO SHEA ESTATES 0 DEVELOPMENT CORP LOCATION CITY-AGOURA HILL PROPERTY ADDRESS: VACANT LOT. See page 77.

14. AIN 2061020024 (auction ID 44): TRACT NO 8793 LOT 65 BLK 4 . . . ASSESSED TO SHEA ESTATES 0 DEVELOPMENT CORP LOCATION CITY-AGOURA HILL PROPERTY ADDRESS: VACANT LOT. See page 82.

15. AIN 2061020025 (auction ID 45): TRACT NO 8793 LOT 66 BLK 4 . . . ASSESSED TO SHEA ESTATES 0 DEVELOPMENT CORP LOCATION CITY-AGOURA HILL PROPERTY ADDRESS: VACANT LOT. See page 87.

16. AIN 2061020026 (auction ID 46): TRACT NO 8793 LOT 67 BLK 4 . . . ASSESSED TO SHEA ESTATES 0 DEVELOPMENT CORP LOCATION CITY-AGOURA HILL PROPERTY ADDRESS: VACANT LOT. See page 92.

17. AIN 2061020027 (auction ID 47): TRACT NO 8793 LOT 68 BLK 4 . . . ASSESSED TO SHEA ESTATES 0 DEVELOPMENT CORP LOCATION CITY-AGOURA HILL PROPERTY ADDRESS: VACANT LOT. See page 97.

18. AIN 2061020028 (auction ID 48): TRACT NO 8793 LOT 69 BLK 4 . . . ASSESSED TO SHEA ESTATES 0 DEVELOPMENT CORP LOCATION CITY-AGOURA HILL - PROPERTY ADDRESS: VACANT LOT. See page 102.

19. AIN 2061020029 (auction ID 49): TRACT NO 8793 LOT 70 BLK 4 . . . ASSESSED TO SHEA ESTATES 0 DEVELOPMENT CORP LOCATION CITY-AGOURA HILL PROPERTY ADDRESS: VACANT LOT. See page 107.

20. AIN 2061020030 (auction ID 50): TRACT NO 8793 LOT 71 BLK 4 . . . ASSESSED TO SHEA ESTATES 0 DEVELOPMENT CORP LOCATION CITY-AGOURA HILL PROPERTY ADDRESS: VACANT LOT. See page 112.

21. AIN 2061021010 (auction ID 52): TRACT NO 8793 LOT 11 BLK 4 . . . ASSESSED TO SHEA ESTATES 0 DEVELOPMENT CORP LOCATION CITY-AGOURA HILL PROPERTY ADDRESS: VACANT LOT. See page 122.

22. AIN 2061021011 (auction ID 53): TRACT NO 8793 LOT 12 BLK 4 . . . ASSESSED TO SHEA ESTATES 0 DEVELOPMENT CORP LOCATION CITY-AGOURA HILL PROPERTY ADDRESS: VACANT LOT. See page 127.

23. AIN 2061021012 (auction ID 54): TRACT NO 8793 LOT 13 BLK 4 . . . ASSESSED TO SHEA ESTATES 0 DEVELOPMENT CORP LOCATION CITY-AGOURA HILL PROPERTY ADDRESS: VACANT LOT. See page 132.

24. AIN 2061021013 (auction ID 55): TRACT NO 8793 LOT 14 BLK 4 . . . ASSESSED TO SHEA ESTATES 0 DEVELOPMENT CORP LOCATION CITY-AGOURA HILL PROPERTY ADDRESS: VACANT LOT. See page 137.

25. AIN 2061021014 (auction ID 56): TRACT NO 8793 LOT 15 BLK 4 ... ASSESSED TO SHEA ESTATES 0 DEVELOPMENT CORP LOCATION CITY-AGOURA HILL PROPERTY ADDRESS: VACANT LOT. See page 142.

26. AIN 2061021015 (auction ID 57): TRACT NO 8793 LOT 72 BLK 4 ... ASSESSED TO SHEA ESTATES 0 DEVELOPMENT CORP LOCATION CITY-AGOURA HILL PROPERTY ADDRESS: VACANT LOT. See page 147.

27. AIN 2061021016 (auction ID 58): TRACT NO 8793 LOT 73 BLK 4 ... ASSESSED TO SHEA ESTATES 0 DEVELOPMENT CORP LOCATION CITY-AGOURA HILL PROPERTY ADDRESS: VACANT LOT. See page 152.

28. AIN 2061021017 (auction ID 59): TRACT NO 8793 LOT 74 BLK 4 ... ASSESSED TO SHEA ESTATES 0 DEVELOPMENT CORP LOCATION CITY-AGOURA HILL PROPERTY ADDRESS: VACANT LOT. See page 157.

29. AIN 2061021018 (auction ID 60): TRACT NO 8793 LOT 75 BLK 4 ... ASSESSED TO SHEA ESTATES 0 DEVELOPMENT CORP LOCATION CITY-AGOURA HILL PROPERTY ADDRESS: VACANT LOT. See page 162.

30. AIN 2061021019 (auction ID 61): TRACT NO 8793 LOT 76 BLK 4 ... ASSESSED TO SHEA ESTATES 0 DEVELOPMENT CORP LOCATION CITY-AGOURA HILL PROPERTY ADDRESS: VACANT LOT. See page 167.

31. AIN 2061021020 (auction ID 62): TRACT NO 8793 LOT 77 BLK 4 ... ASSESSED TO SHEA ESTATES 0 DEVELOPMENT CORP LOCATION CITY-AGOURA HILL PROPERTY ADDRESS: VACANT LOT. See page 172.

32. AIN 2061021021 (auction ID 63): TRACT NO 8793 LOT 78 BLK 4 ... ASSESSED TO SHEA ESTATES 0 DEVELOPMENT CORP LOCATION CITY-AGOURA HILL PROPERTY ADDRESS: VACANT LOT. See page 177.

33. AIN 2061021022 (auction ID 64): TRACT NO 8793 LOT 79 BLK 4 ... ASSESSED TO SHEA ESTATES 0 DEVELOPMENT CORP LOCATION CITY-AGOURA HILL PROPERTY ADDRESS: VACANT LOT. See page 182.

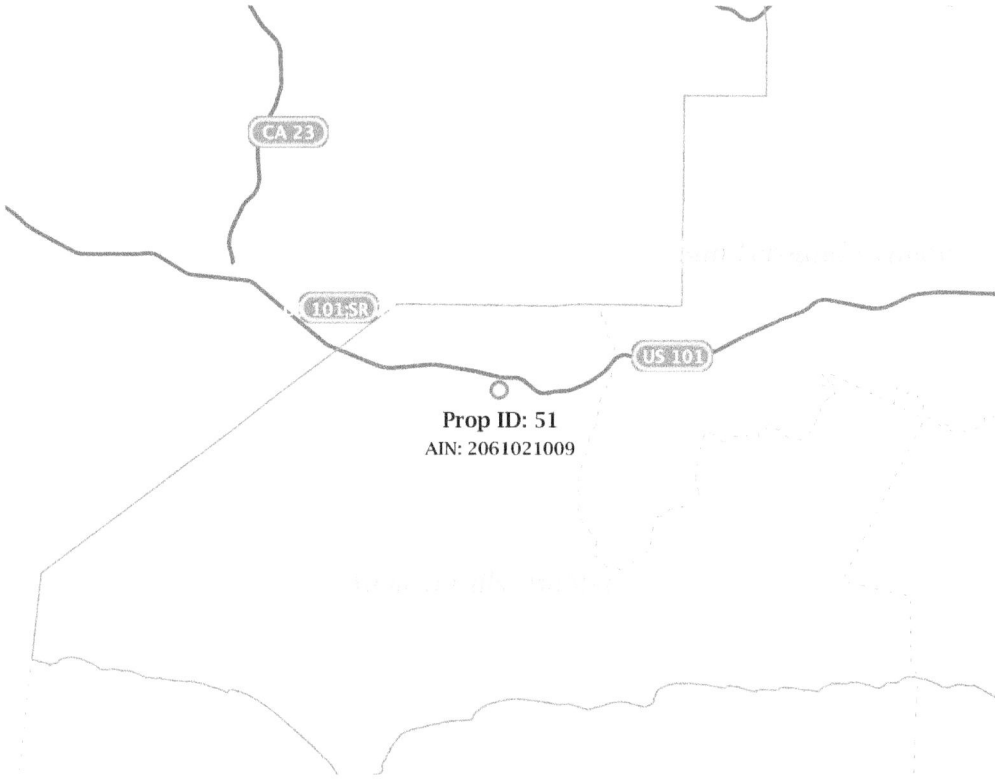

Figure 2.70: Property 64, AIN 2061021009, overview map

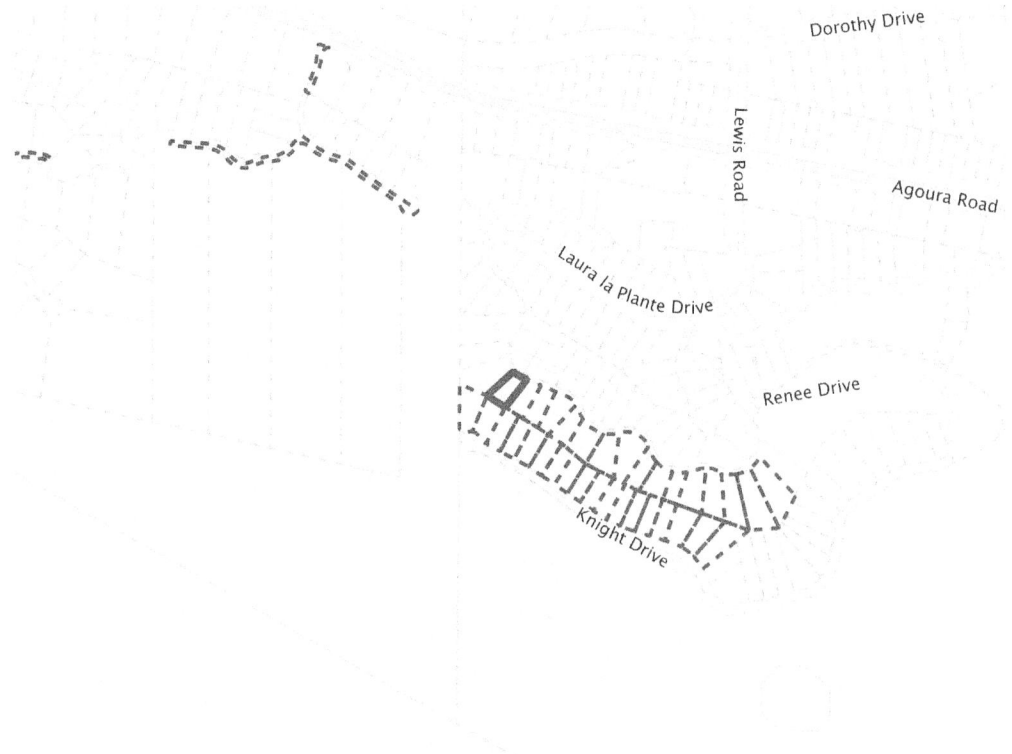

Figure 2.71: Property 64, AIN 2061021009, neighborhood view

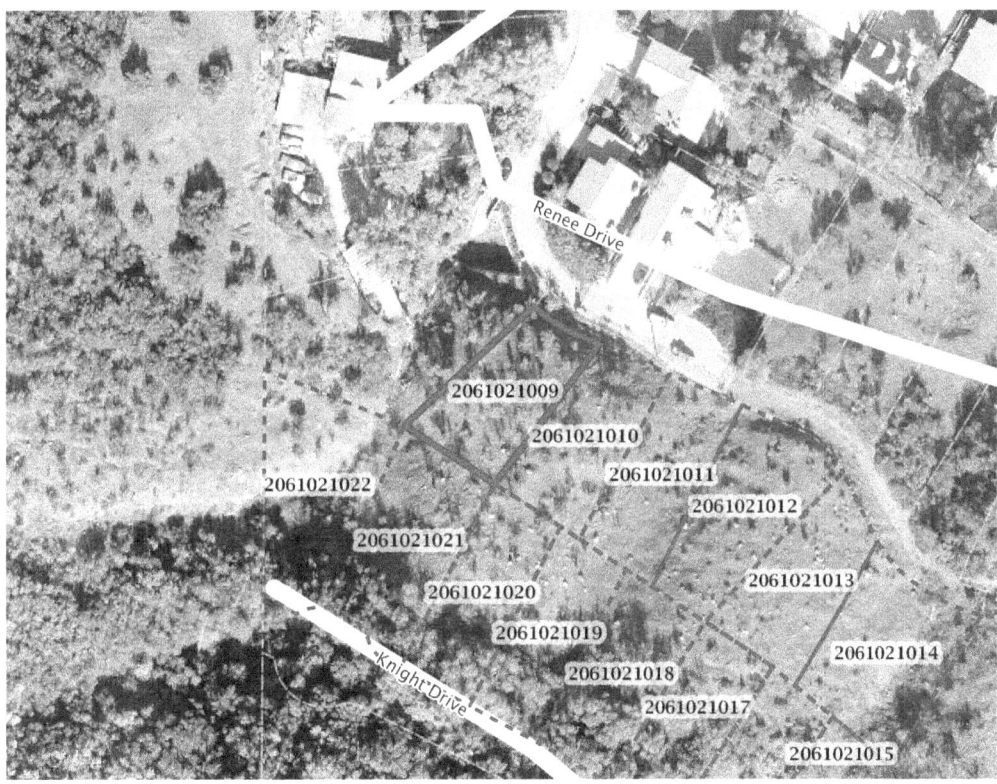

Figure 2.72: Property 64, AIN 2061021009, detailed view

2.25   Auction ID 52

The Los Angeles County Auction Book describes the property as follows.

```
TRACT NO 8793 LOT 11 BLK 4 ASSESSED TO SHEA ESTATES 0 DEVELOPMENT
CORP LOCATION CITY-AGOURA HILL PROPERTY ADDRESS: VACANT LOT
```

The property is located in the general vicinity of Figure 2.73. It is identified by Assessor's Identification Number (AIN) 2061021010. The starting bid is \$8,201. Comparable improved properties in this area is about \$294/sqft. Comparable unimproved lots in this area is about \$49/sqft. This parcel is approximately 6408 sqft. Note, however, that the parcel may be larger than the property under consideration. In case of condominiums, for example, the parcel may encompass other units of the development - those unrelated to the property to be auctioned.

The property is in a parcel zoned Restricted Open Space in Agoura Hills, for 0 to 0 dwelling units.

Figures 2.74 and 2.75 show street map and corresponding detailed aerial view, respectively. In both cases, the map is centered on the property with the containing parcel marked in heavy blue. If surrounding nearby properties are also part of this auction, the street and aerial maps highlights these in heavy, dashed blue outline.

This assessed entity may have other properties that are also in this auction:

1. AIN 2061020001 (auction ID 31): TRACT NO 8793 LOT 16 BLK 4 . . . ASSESSED TO SHEA ESTATES 0 DEVELOPMENT CORP LOCATION CITY-AGOURA HILL PROPERTY ADDRESS: VACANT LOT. See page 17.

2. AIN 2061020002 (auction ID 32): TRACT NO 8793 LOT 17 BLK 4 . . . ASSESSED TO SHEA ESTATES 0 DEVELOPMENT CORP LOCATION CITY-AGOURA HILL PROPERTY ADDRESS: VACANT LOT. See page 22.

3. AIN 2061020003 (auction ID 33): TRACT NO 8793 LOT 18 BLK 4 . . . ASSESSED TO SHEA ESTATES 0 DEVELOPMENT CORP LOCATION CITY-AGOURA HILL PROPERTY ADDRESS: VACANT LOT. See page 27.

4. AIN 2061020004 (auction ID 34): TRACT NO 8793 LOT 19 BLK 4 . . . ASSESSED TO SHEA ESTATES 0 DEVELOPMENT CORP LOCATION CITY-AGOURA HILL PROPERTY ADDRESS: VACANT LOT. See page 32.

5. AIN 2061020005 (auction ID 35): TRACT NO 8793 LOT 20 BLK 4 . . . ASSESSED TO SHEA ESTATES 0 DEVELOPMENT CORP LOCATION CITY-AGOURA HILL PROPERTY ADDRESS: VACANT LOT. See page 37.

6. AIN 2061020006 (auction ID 36): TRACT NO 8793 LOT 21 BLK 4 . . . ASSESSED TO SHEA ESTATES 0 DEVELOPMENT CORP LOCATION CITY-AGOURA HILL PROPERTY ADDRESS: VACANT LOT. See page 42.

7. AIN 2061020007 (auction ID 37): TRACT NO 8793 LOT 22 BLK 4 . . . ASSESSED TO SHEA ESTATES 0 DEVELOPMENT CORP LOCATION CITY-AGOURA HILL PROPERTY ADDRESS: VACANT LOT. See page 47.

8. AIN 2061020008 (auction ID 38): TRACT NO 8793 LOT 23 BLK 4 . . . ASSESSED TO SHEA ESTATES 0 DEVELOPMENT CORP LOCATION CITY-AGOURA HILL PROPERTY ADDRESS: VACANT LOT. See page 52.

9. AIN 2061020009 (auction ID 39): TRACT NO 8793 LOT 24 BLK 4 . . . ASSESSED TO SHEA ESTATES 0 DEVELOPMENT CORP LOCATION CITY-AGOURA HILL PROPERTY ADDRESS: VACANT LOT. See page 57.

10. AIN 2061020010 (auction ID 40): TRACT NO 8793 LOT 25 BLK 4 . . . ASSESSED TO SHEA ESTATES 0 DEVELOPMENT CORP LOCATION CITY-AGOURA HILL PROPERTY ADDRESS: VACANT LOT. See page 62.

11. AIN 2061020021 (auction ID 41): TRACT NO 8793 LOT 62 BLK 4 . . . ASSESSED TO SHEA ESTATES 0 DEVELOPMENT CORP LOCATION CITY-AGOURA HILL PROPERTY ADDRESS: VACANT LOT. See page 67.

12. AIN 2061020022 (auction ID 42): TRACT NO 8793 LOT 63 BLK 4 . . . ASSESSED TO SHEA ESTATES 0 DEVELOPMENT CORP LOCATION CITY-AGOURA HILL PROPERTY ADDRESS: VACANT LOT. See page 72.

13. AIN 2061020023 (auction ID 43): TRACT NO 8793 LOT 64 BLK 4 . . . ASSESSED TO SHEA ESTATES 0 DEVELOPMENT CORP LOCATION CITY-AGOURA HILL PROPERTY ADDRESS: VACANT LOT. See page 77.

14. AIN 2061020024 (auction ID 44): TRACT NO 8793 LOT 65 BLK 4 . . . ASSESSED TO SHEA ESTATES 0 DEVELOPMENT CORP LOCATION CITY-AGOURA HILL PROPERTY ADDRESS: VACANT LOT. See page 82.

15. AIN 2061020025 (auction ID 45): TRACT NO 8793 LOT 66 BLK 4 . . . ASSESSED TO SHEA ESTATES 0 DEVELOPMENT CORP LOCATION CITY-AGOURA HILL PROPERTY ADDRESS: VACANT LOT. See page 87.

16. AIN 2061020026 (auction ID 46): TRACT NO 8793 LOT 67 BLK 4 . . . ASSESSED TO SHEA ESTATES 0 DEVELOPMENT CORP LOCATION CITY-AGOURA HILL PROPERTY ADDRESS: VACANT LOT. See page 92.

17. AIN 2061020027 (auction ID 47): TRACT NO 8793 LOT 68 BLK 4 . . . ASSESSED TO SHEA ESTATES 0 DEVELOPMENT CORP LOCATION CITY-AGOURA HILL PROPERTY ADDRESS: VACANT LOT. See page 97.

18. AIN 2061020028 (auction ID 48): TRACT NO 8793 LOT 69 BLK 4 . . . ASSESSED TO SHEA ESTATES 0 DEVELOPMENT CORP LOCATION CITY-AGOURA HILL - PROPERTY ADDRESS: VACANT LOT. See page 102.

19. AIN 2061020029 (auction ID 49): TRACT NO 8793 LOT 70 BLK 4 . . . ASSESSED TO SHEA ESTATES 0 DEVELOPMENT CORP LOCATION CITY-AGOURA HILL PROPERTY ADDRESS: VACANT LOT. See page 107.

20. AIN 2061020030 (auction ID 50): TRACT NO 8793 LOT 71 BLK 4 . . . ASSESSED TO SHEA ESTATES 0 DEVELOPMENT CORP LOCATION CITY-AGOURA HILL PROPERTY ADDRESS: VACANT LOT. See page 112.

21. AIN 2061021009 (auction ID 51): TRACT NO 8793 LOT 10 BLK 4 . . . ASSESSED TO SHEA ESTATES 0 DEVELOPMENT CORP LOCATION CITY-AGOURA HILL PROPERTY ADDRESS: VACANT LOT. See page 117.

22. AIN 2061021011 (auction ID 53): TRACT NO 8793 LOT 12 BLK 4 . . . ASSESSED TO SHEA ESTATES 0 DEVELOPMENT CORP LOCATION CITY-AGOURA HILL PROPERTY ADDRESS: VACANT LOT. See page 127.

23. AIN 2061021012 (auction ID 54): TRACT NO 8793 LOT 13 BLK 4 . . . ASSESSED TO SHEA ESTATES 0 DEVELOPMENT CORP LOCATION CITY-AGOURA HILL PROPERTY ADDRESS: VACANT LOT. See page 132.

24. AIN 2061021013 (auction ID 55): TRACT NO 8793 LOT 14 BLK 4 . . . ASSESSED TO SHEA ESTATES 0 DEVELOPMENT CORP LOCATION CITY-AGOURA HILL PROPERTY ADDRESS: VACANT LOT. See page 137.

25. AIN 2061021014 (auction ID 56): TRACT NO 8793 LOT 15 BLK 4 . . . ASSESSED TO SHEA ESTATES 0 DEVELOPMENT CORP LOCATION CITY-AGOURA HILL PROPERTY ADDRESS: VACANT LOT. See page 142.

26. AIN 2061021015 (auction ID 57): TRACT NO 8793 LOT 72 BLK 4 . . . ASSESSED TO SHEA ESTATES 0 DEVELOPMENT CORP LOCATION CITY-AGOURA HILL PROPERTY ADDRESS: VACANT LOT. See page 147.

27. AIN 2061021016 (auction ID 58): TRACT NO 8793 LOT 73 BLK 4 . . . ASSESSED TO SHEA ESTATES 0 DEVELOPMENT CORP LOCATION CITY-AGOURA HILL PROPERTY ADDRESS: VACANT LOT. See page 152.

28. AIN 2061021017 (auction ID 59): TRACT NO 8793 LOT 74 BLK 4 . . . ASSESSED TO SHEA ESTATES 0 DEVELOPMENT CORP LOCATION CITY-AGOURA HILL PROPERTY ADDRESS: VACANT LOT. See page 157.

29. AIN 2061021018 (auction ID 60): TRACT NO 8793 LOT 75 BLK 4 . . . ASSESSED TO SHEA ESTATES 0 DEVELOPMENT CORP LOCATION CITY-AGOURA HILL PROPERTY ADDRESS: VACANT LOT. See page 162.

30. AIN 2061021019 (auction ID 61): TRACT NO 8793 LOT 76 BLK 4 . . . ASSESSED TO SHEA ESTATES 0 DEVELOPMENT CORP LOCATION CITY-AGOURA HILL PROPERTY ADDRESS: VACANT LOT. See page 167.

31. AIN 2061021020 (auction ID 62): TRACT NO 8793 LOT 77 BLK 4 . . . ASSESSED TO SHEA ESTATES 0 DEVELOPMENT CORP LOCATION CITY-AGOURA HILL PROPERTY ADDRESS: VACANT LOT. See page 172.

32. AIN 2061021021 (auction ID 63): TRACT NO 8793 LOT 78 BLK 4 . . . ASSESSED TO SHEA ESTATES 0 DEVELOPMENT CORP LOCATION CITY-AGOURA HILL PROPERTY ADDRESS: VACANT LOT. See page 177.

33. AIN 2061021022 (auction ID 64): TRACT NO 8793 LOT 79 BLK 4 . . . ASSESSED TO SHEA ESTATES 0 DEVELOPMENT CORP LOCATION CITY-AGOURA HILL PROPERTY ADDRESS: VACANT LOT. See page 182.

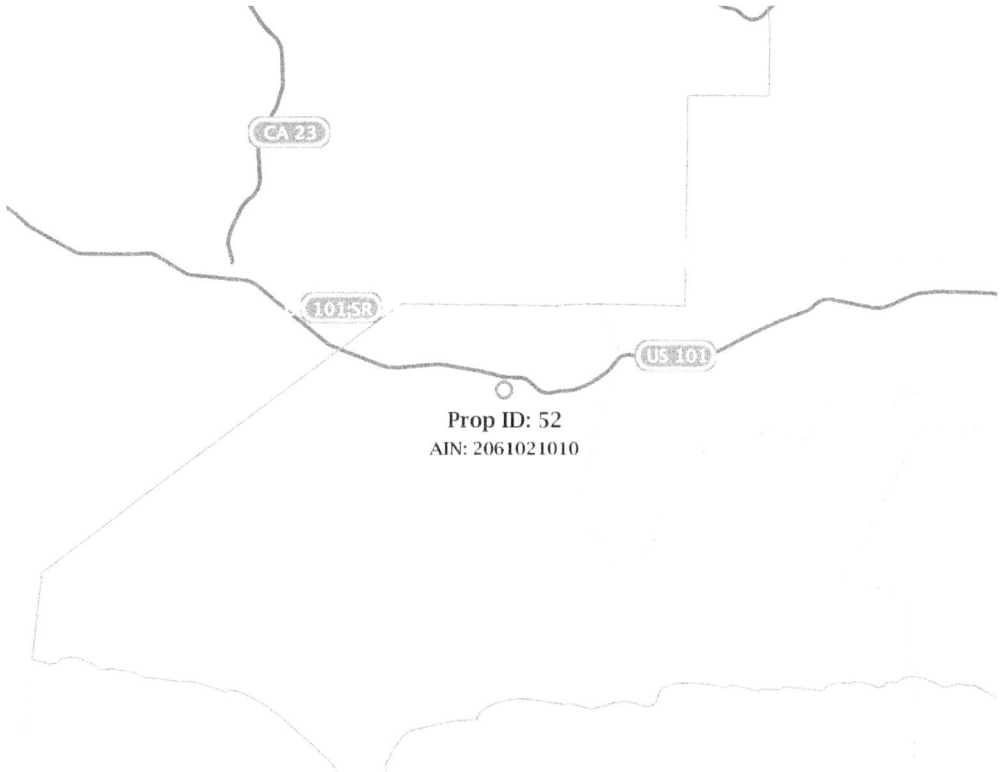

Figure 2.73: Property 64, AIN 2061021010, overview map

Figure 2.74: Property 64, AIN 2061021010, neighborhood view

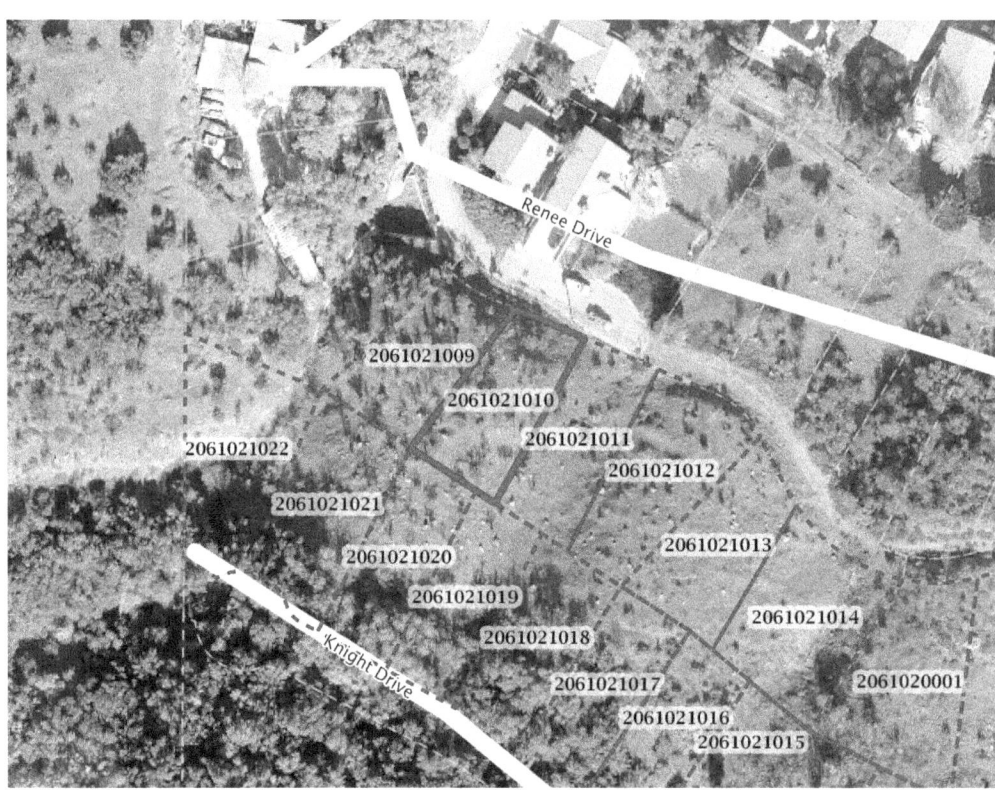

Figure 2.75: Property 64, AIN 2061021010, detailed view

2.26   Auction ID 53

The Los Angeles County Auction Book describes the property as follows.

```
TRACT NO 8793 LOT 12 BLK 4 ASSESSED TO SHEA ESTATES 0 DEVELOPMENT
CORP LOCATION CITY-AGOURA HILL PROPERTY ADDRESS: VACANT LOT
```

The property is located in the general vicinity of Figure 2.76. It is identified by Assessor's Identification Number (AIN) 2061021011. The starting bid is $8,315. Comparable improved properties in this area is about $294/sqft. Comparable unimproved lots in this area is about $49/sqft. This parcel is approximately 6521 sqft. Note, however, that the parcel may be larger than the property under consideration. In case of condominiums, for example, the parcel may encompass other units of the development - those unrelated to the property to be auctioned.

The property is in a parcel zoned Restricted Open Space in Agoura Hills, for 0 to 0 dwelling units.

Figures 2.77 and 2.78 show street map and corresponding detailed aerial view, respectively. In both cases, the map is centered on the property with the containing parcel marked in heavy blue. If surrounding nearby properties are also part of this auction, the street and aerial maps highlights these in heavy, dashed blue outline.

This assessed entity may have other properties that are also in this auction:

1. AIN 2061020001 (auction ID 31): TRACT NO 8793 LOT 16 BLK 4 ... ASSESSED TO SHEA ESTATES 0 DEVELOPMENT CORP LOCATION CITY-AGOURA HILL PROPERTY ADDRESS: VACANT LOT. See page 17.

2. AIN 2061020002 (auction ID 32): TRACT NO 8793 LOT 17 BLK 4 ... ASSESSED TO SHEA ESTATES 0 DEVELOPMENT CORP LOCATION CITY-AGOURA HILL PROPERTY ADDRESS: VACANT LOT. See page 22.

3. AIN 2061020003 (auction ID 33): TRACT NO 8793 LOT 18 BLK 4 ... ASSESSED TO SHEA ESTATES 0 DEVELOPMENT CORP LOCATION CITY-AGOURA HILL PROPERTY ADDRESS: VACANT LOT. See page 27.

4. AIN 2061020004 (auction ID 34): TRACT NO 8793 LOT 19 BLK 4 ... ASSESSED TO SHEA ESTATES 0 DEVELOPMENT CORP LOCATION CITY-AGOURA HILL PROPERTY ADDRESS: VACANT LOT. See page 32.

5. AIN 2061020005 (auction ID 35): TRACT NO 8793 LOT 20 BLK 4 ... ASSESSED TO SHEA ESTATES 0 DEVELOPMENT CORP LOCATION CITY-AGOURA HILL PROPERTY ADDRESS: VACANT LOT. See page 37.

6. AIN 2061020006 (auction ID 36): TRACT NO 8793 LOT 21 BLK 4 ... ASSESSED TO SHEA ESTATES 0 DEVELOPMENT CORP LOCATION CITY-AGOURA HILL PROPERTY ADDRESS: VACANT LOT. See page 42.

7. AIN 2061020007 (auction ID 37): TRACT NO 8793 LOT 22 BLK 4 ... ASSESSED TO SHEA ESTATES 0 DEVELOPMENT CORP LOCATION CITY-AGOURA HILL PROPERTY ADDRESS: VACANT LOT. See page 47.

8. AIN 2061020008 (auction ID 38): TRACT NO 8793 LOT 23 BLK 4 ... ASSESSED TO SHEA ESTATES 0 DEVELOPMENT CORP LOCATION CITY-AGOURA HILL PROPERTY ADDRESS: VACANT LOT. See page 52.

9. AIN 2061020009 (auction ID 39): TRACT NO 8793 LOT 24 BLK 4 ... ASSESSED TO SHEA ESTATES 0 DEVELOPMENT CORP LOCATION CITY-AGOURA HILL PROPERTY ADDRESS: VACANT LOT. See page 57.

10. AIN 2061020010 (auction ID 40): TRACT NO 8793 LOT 25 BLK 4 ... ASSESSED TO SHEA ESTATES 0 DEVELOPMENT CORP LOCATION CITY-AGOURA HILL PROPERTY ADDRESS: VACANT LOT. See page 62.

11. AIN 2061020021 (auction ID 41): TRACT NO 8793 LOT 62 BLK 4 ... ASSESSED TO SHEA ESTATES 0 DEVELOPMENT CORP LOCATION CITY-AGOURA HILL PROPERTY ADDRESS: VACANT LOT. See page 67.

12. AIN 2061020022 (auction ID 42): TRACT NO 8793 LOT 63 BLK 4 ... ASSESSED TO SHEA ESTATES 0 DEVELOPMENT CORP LOCATION CITY-AGOURA HILL PROPERTY ADDRESS: VACANT LOT. See page 72.

13. AIN 2061020023 (auction ID 43): TRACT NO 8793 LOT 64 BLK 4 ... ASSESSED TO SHEA ESTATES 0 DEVELOPMENT CORP LOCATION CITY-AGOURA HILL PROPERTY ADDRESS: VACANT LOT. See page 77.

14. AIN 2061020024 (auction ID 44): TRACT NO 8793 LOT 65 BLK 4 ... ASSESSED TO SHEA ESTATES 0 DEVELOPMENT CORP LOCATION CITY-AGOURA HILL PROPERTY ADDRESS: VACANT LOT. See page 82.

15. AIN 2061020025 (auction ID 45): TRACT NO 8793 LOT 66 BLK 4 ... ASSESSED TO SHEA ESTATES 0 DEVELOPMENT CORP LOCATION CITY-AGOURA HILL PROPERTY ADDRESS: VACANT LOT. See page 87.

16. AIN 2061020026 (auction ID 46): TRACT NO 8793 LOT 67 BLK 4 ... ASSESSED TO SHEA ESTATES 0 DEVELOPMENT CORP LOCATION CITY-AGOURA HILL PROPERTY ADDRESS: VACANT LOT. See page 92.

17. AIN 2061020027 (auction ID 47): TRACT NO 8793 LOT 68 BLK 4 ... ASSESSED TO SHEA ESTATES 0 DEVELOPMENT CORP LOCATION CITY-AGOURA HILL PROPERTY ADDRESS: VACANT LOT. See page 97.

18. AIN 2061020028 (auction ID 48): TRACT NO 8793 LOT 69 BLK 4 ... ASSESSED TO SHEA ESTATES 0 DEVELOPMENT CORP LOCATION CITY-AGOURA HILL - PROPERTY ADDRESS: VACANT LOT. See page 102.

19. AIN 2061020029 (auction ID 49): TRACT NO 8793 LOT 70 BLK 4 ... ASSESSED TO SHEA ESTATES 0 DEVELOPMENT CORP LOCATION CITY-AGOURA HILL PROPERTY ADDRESS: VACANT LOT. See page 107.

20. AIN 2061020030 (auction ID 50): TRACT NO 8793 LOT 71 BLK 4 ... ASSESSED TO SHEA ESTATES 0 DEVELOPMENT CORP LOCATION CITY-AGOURA HILL PROPERTY ADDRESS: VACANT LOT. See page 112.

21. AIN 2061021009 (auction ID 51): TRACT NO 8793 LOT 10 BLK 4 ... ASSESSED TO SHEA ESTATES 0 DEVELOPMENT CORP LOCATION CITY-AGOURA HILL PROPERTY ADDRESS: VACANT LOT. See page 117.

22. AIN 2061021010 (auction ID 52): TRACT NO 8793 LOT 11 BLK 4 ... ASSESSED TO SHEA ESTATES 0 DEVELOPMENT CORP LOCATION CITY-AGOURA HILL PROPERTY ADDRESS: VACANT LOT. See page 122.

23. AIN 2061021012 (auction ID 54): TRACT NO 8793 LOT 13 BLK 4 ... ASSESSED TO SHEA ESTATES 0 DEVELOPMENT CORP LOCATION CITY-AGOURA HILL PROPERTY ADDRESS: VACANT LOT. See page 132.

24. AIN 2061021013 (auction ID 55): TRACT NO 8793 LOT 14 BLK 4 ... ASSESSED TO SHEA ESTATES 0 DEVELOPMENT CORP LOCATION CITY-AGOURA HILL PROPERTY ADDRESS: VACANT LOT. See page 137.

25. AIN 2061021014 (auction ID 56): TRACT NO 8793 LOT 15 BLK 4 . . . ASSESSED TO SHEA ESTATES 0 DEVELOPMENT CORP LOCATION CITY-AGOURA HILL PROPERTY ADDRESS: VACANT LOT. See page 142.

26. AIN 2061021015 (auction ID 57): TRACT NO 8793 LOT 72 BLK 4 . . . ASSESSED TO SHEA ESTATES 0 DEVELOPMENT CORP LOCATION CITY-AGOURA HILL PROPERTY ADDRESS: VACANT LOT. See page 147.

27. AIN 2061021016 (auction ID 58): TRACT NO 8793 LOT 73 BLK 4 . . . ASSESSED TO SHEA ESTATES 0 DEVELOPMENT CORP LOCATION CITY-AGOURA HILL PROPERTY ADDRESS: VACANT LOT. See page 152.

28. AIN 2061021017 (auction ID 59): TRACT NO 8793 LOT 74 BLK 4 . . . ASSESSED TO SHEA ESTATES 0 DEVELOPMENT CORP LOCATION CITY-AGOURA HILL PROPERTY ADDRESS: VACANT LOT. See page 157.

29. AIN 2061021018 (auction ID 60): TRACT NO 8793 LOT 75 BLK 4 . . . ASSESSED TO SHEA ESTATES 0 DEVELOPMENT CORP LOCATION CITY-AGOURA HILL PROPERTY ADDRESS: VACANT LOT. See page 162.

30. AIN 2061021019 (auction ID 61): TRACT NO 8793 LOT 76 BLK 4 . . . ASSESSED TO SHEA ESTATES 0 DEVELOPMENT CORP LOCATION CITY-AGOURA HILL PROPERTY ADDRESS: VACANT LOT. See page 167.

31. AIN 2061021020 (auction ID 62): TRACT NO 8793 LOT 77 BLK 4 . . . ASSESSED TO SHEA ESTATES 0 DEVELOPMENT CORP LOCATION CITY-AGOURA HILL PROPERTY ADDRESS: VACANT LOT. See page 172.

32. AIN 2061021021 (auction ID 63): TRACT NO 8793 LOT 78 BLK 4 . . . ASSESSED TO SHEA ESTATES 0 DEVELOPMENT CORP LOCATION CITY-AGOURA HILL PROPERTY ADDRESS: VACANT LOT. See page 177.

33. AIN 2061021022 (auction ID 64): TRACT NO 8793 LOT 79 BLK 4 . . . ASSESSED TO SHEA ESTATES 0 DEVELOPMENT CORP LOCATION CITY-AGOURA HILL PROPERTY ADDRESS: VACANT LOT. See page 182.

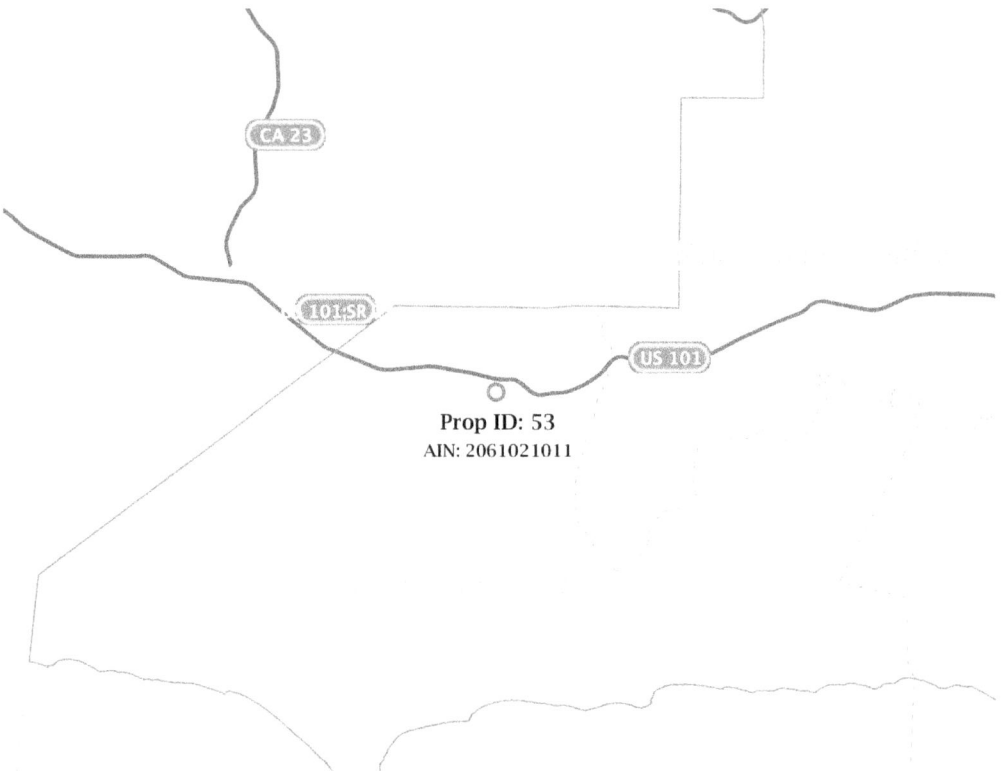

Figure 2.76: Property 64, AIN 2061021011, overview map

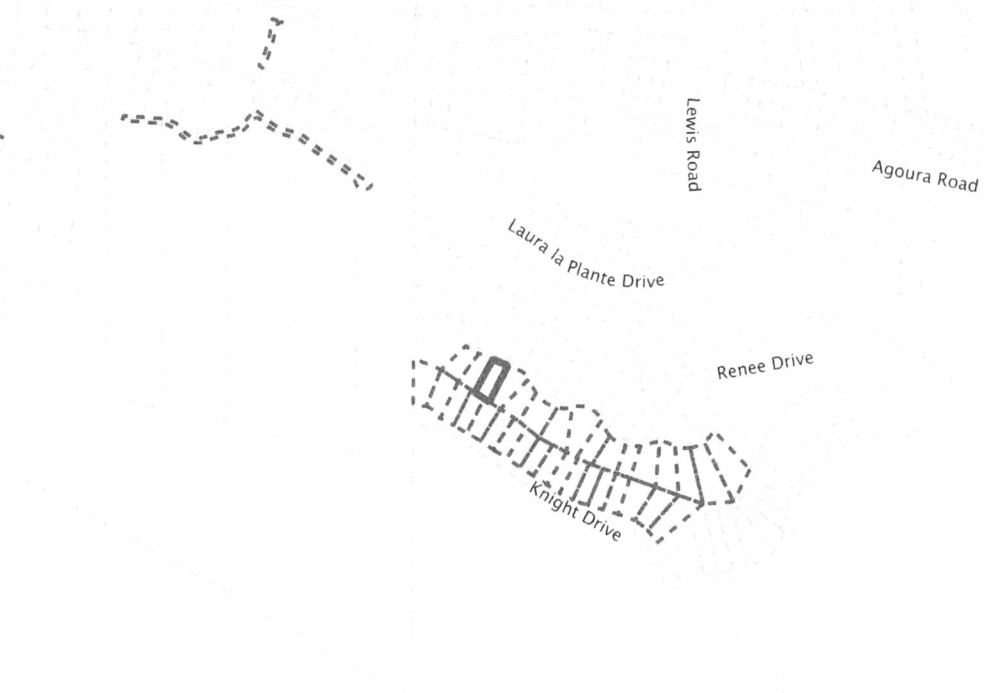

Figure 2.77: Property 64, AIN 2061021011, neighborhood view

Figure 2.78: Property 64, AIN 2061021011, detailed view

2.27 Auction ID 54

The Los Angeles County Auction Book describes the property as follows.

```
TRACT NO 8793 LOT 13 BLK 4 ASSESSED TO SHEA ESTATES 0 DEVELOPMENT
CORP LOCATION CITY-AGOURA HILL PROPERTY ADDRESS: VACANT LOT
```

The property is located in the general vicinity of Figure 2.79. It is identified by Assessor's Identification Number (AIN) 2061021012. The starting bid is $8,704. Comparable improved properties in this area is about $294/sqft. Comparable unimproved lots in this area is about $49/sqft. This parcel is approximately 7889 sqft. Note, however, that the parcel may be larger than the property under consideration. In case of condominiums, for example, the parcel may encompass other units of the development - those unrelated to the property to be auctioned.

The property is in a parcel zoned Restricted Open Space in Agoura Hills, for 0 to 0 dwelling units.

Figures 2.80 and 2.81 show street map and corresponding detailed aerial view, respectively. In both cases, the map is centered on the property with the containing parcel marked in heavy blue. If surrounding nearby properties are also part of this auction, the street and aerial maps highlights these in heavy, dashed blue outline.

This assessed entity may have other properties that are also in this auction:

1. AIN 2061020001 (auction ID 31): TRACT NO 8793 LOT 16 BLK 4 ... ASSESSED TO SHEA ESTATES 0 DEVELOPMENT CORP LOCATION CITY-AGOURA HILL PROPERTY ADDRESS: VACANT LOT. See page 17.

2. AIN 2061020002 (auction ID 32): TRACT NO 8793 LOT 17 BLK 4 ... ASSESSED TO SHEA ESTATES 0 DEVELOPMENT CORP LOCATION CITY-AGOURA HILL PROPERTY ADDRESS: VACANT LOT. See page 22.

3. AIN 2061020003 (auction ID 33): TRACT NO 8793 LOT 18 BLK 4 ... ASSESSED TO SHEA ESTATES 0 DEVELOPMENT CORP LOCATION CITY-AGOURA HILL PROPERTY ADDRESS: VACANT LOT. See page 27.

4. AIN 2061020004 (auction ID 34): TRACT NO 8793 LOT 19 BLK 4 ... ASSESSED TO SHEA ESTATES 0 DEVELOPMENT CORP LOCATION CITY-AGOURA HILL PROPERTY ADDRESS: VACANT LOT. See page 32.

5. AIN 2061020005 (auction ID 35): TRACT NO 8793 LOT 20 BLK 4 ... ASSESSED TO SHEA ESTATES 0 DEVELOPMENT CORP LOCATION CITY-AGOURA HILL PROPERTY ADDRESS: VACANT LOT. See page 37.

6. AIN 2061020006 (auction ID 36): TRACT NO 8793 LOT 21 BLK 4 ... ASSESSED TO SHEA ESTATES 0 DEVELOPMENT CORP LOCATION CITY-AGOURA HILL PROPERTY ADDRESS: VACANT LOT. See page 42.

7. AIN 2061020007 (auction ID 37): TRACT NO 8793 LOT 22 BLK 4 ... ASSESSED TO SHEA ESTATES 0 DEVELOPMENT CORP LOCATION CITY-AGOURA HILL PROPERTY ADDRESS: VACANT LOT. See page 47.

8. AIN 2061020008 (auction ID 38): TRACT NO 8793 LOT 23 BLK 4 ... ASSESSED TO SHEA ESTATES 0 DEVELOPMENT CORP LOCATION CITY-AGOURA HILL PROPERTY ADDRESS: VACANT LOT. See page 52.

9. AIN 2061020009 (auction ID 39): TRACT NO 8793 LOT 24 BLK 4 ... ASSESSED TO SHEA ESTATES 0 DEVELOPMENT CORP LOCATION CITY-AGOURA HILL PROPERTY ADDRESS: VACANT LOT. See page 57.

10. AIN 2061020010 (auction ID 40): TRACT NO 8793 LOT 25 BLK 4 ... ASSESSED TO SHEA ESTATES 0 DEVELOPMENT CORP LOCATION CITY-AGOURA HILL PROPERTY ADDRESS: VACANT LOT. See page 62.

11. AIN 2061020021 (auction ID 41): TRACT NO 8793 LOT 62 BLK 4 ... ASSESSED TO SHEA ESTATES 0 DEVELOPMENT CORP LOCATION CITY-AGOURA HILL PROPERTY ADDRESS: VACANT LOT. See page 67.

12. AIN 2061020022 (auction ID 42): TRACT NO 8793 LOT 63 BLK 4 ... ASSESSED TO SHEA ESTATES 0 DEVELOPMENT CORP LOCATION CITY-AGOURA HILL PROPERTY ADDRESS: VACANT LOT. See page 72.

13. AIN 2061020023 (auction ID 43): TRACT NO 8793 LOT 64 BLK 4 ... ASSESSED TO SHEA ESTATES 0 DEVELOPMENT CORP LOCATION CITY-AGOURA HILL PROPERTY ADDRESS: VACANT LOT. See page 77.

14. AIN 2061020024 (auction ID 44): TRACT NO 8793 LOT 65 BLK 4 ... ASSESSED TO SHEA ESTATES 0 DEVELOPMENT CORP LOCATION CITY-AGOURA HILL PROPERTY ADDRESS: VACANT LOT. See page 82.

15. AIN 2061020025 (auction ID 45): TRACT NO 8793 LOT 66 BLK 4 ... ASSESSED TO SHEA ESTATES 0 DEVELOPMENT CORP LOCATION CITY-AGOURA HILL PROPERTY ADDRESS: VACANT LOT. See page 87.

16. AIN 2061020026 (auction ID 46): TRACT NO 8793 LOT 67 BLK 4 ... ASSESSED TO SHEA ESTATES 0 DEVELOPMENT CORP LOCATION CITY-AGOURA HILL PROPERTY ADDRESS: VACANT LOT. See page 92.

17. AIN 2061020027 (auction ID 47): TRACT NO 8793 LOT 68 BLK 4 ... ASSESSED TO SHEA ESTATES 0 DEVELOPMENT CORP LOCATION CITY-AGOURA HILL PROPERTY ADDRESS: VACANT LOT. See page 97.

18. AIN 2061020028 (auction ID 48): TRACT NO 8793 LOT 69 BLK 4 ... ASSESSED TO SHEA ESTATES 0 DEVELOPMENT CORP LOCATION CITY-AGOURA HILL - PROPERTY ADDRESS: VACANT LOT. See page 102.

19. AIN 2061020029 (auction ID 49): TRACT NO 8793 LOT 70 BLK 4 ... ASSESSED TO SHEA ESTATES 0 DEVELOPMENT CORP LOCATION CITY-AGOURA HILL PROPERTY ADDRESS: VACANT LOT. See page 107.

20. AIN 2061020030 (auction ID 50): TRACT NO 8793 LOT 71 BLK 4 ... ASSESSED TO SHEA ESTATES 0 DEVELOPMENT CORP LOCATION CITY-AGOURA HILL PROPERTY ADDRESS: VACANT LOT. See page 112.

21. AIN 2061021009 (auction ID 51): TRACT NO 8793 LOT 10 BLK 4 ... ASSESSED TO SHEA ESTATES 0 DEVELOPMENT CORP LOCATION CITY-AGOURA HILL PROPERTY ADDRESS: VACANT LOT. See page 117.

22. AIN 2061021010 (auction ID 52): TRACT NO 8793 LOT 11 BLK 4 ... ASSESSED TO SHEA ESTATES 0 DEVELOPMENT CORP LOCATION CITY-AGOURA HILL PROPERTY ADDRESS: VACANT LOT. See page 122.

23. AIN 2061021011 (auction ID 53): TRACT NO 8793 LOT 12 BLK 4 ... ASSESSED TO SHEA ESTATES 0 DEVELOPMENT CORP LOCATION CITY-AGOURA HILL PROPERTY ADDRESS: VACANT LOT. See page 127.

24. AIN 2061021013 (auction ID 55): TRACT NO 8793 LOT 14 BLK 4 ... ASSESSED TO SHEA ESTATES 0 DEVELOPMENT CORP LOCATION CITY-AGOURA HILL PROPERTY ADDRESS: VACANT LOT. See page 137.

25. AIN 2061021014 (auction ID 56): TRACT NO 8793 LOT 15 BLK 4 . . . ASSESSED TO SHEA ESTATES 0 DEVELOPMENT CORP LOCATION CITY-AGOURA HILL PROPERTY ADDRESS: VACANT LOT. See page 142.

26. AIN 2061021015 (auction ID 57): TRACT NO 8793 LOT 72 BLK 4 . . . ASSESSED TO SHEA ESTATES 0 DEVELOPMENT CORP LOCATION CITY-AGOURA HILL PROPERTY ADDRESS: VACANT LOT. See page 147.

27. AIN 2061021016 (auction ID 58): TRACT NO 8793 LOT 73 BLK 4 . . . ASSESSED TO SHEA ESTATES 0 DEVELOPMENT CORP LOCATION CITY-AGOURA HILL PROPERTY ADDRESS: VACANT LOT. See page 152.

28. AIN 2061021017 (auction ID 59): TRACT NO 8793 LOT 74 BLK 4 . . . ASSESSED TO SHEA ESTATES 0 DEVELOPMENT CORP LOCATION CITY-AGOURA HILL PROPERTY ADDRESS: VACANT LOT. See page 157.

29. AIN 2061021018 (auction ID 60): TRACT NO 8793 LOT 75 BLK 4 . . . ASSESSED TO SHEA ESTATES 0 DEVELOPMENT CORP LOCATION CITY-AGOURA HILL PROPERTY ADDRESS: VACANT LOT. See page 162.

30. AIN 2061021019 (auction ID 61): TRACT NO 8793 LOT 76 BLK 4 . . . ASSESSED TO SHEA ESTATES 0 DEVELOPMENT CORP LOCATION CITY-AGOURA HILL PROPERTY ADDRESS: VACANT LOT. See page 167.

31. AIN 2061021020 (auction ID 62): TRACT NO 8793 LOT 77 BLK 4 . . . ASSESSED TO SHEA ESTATES 0 DEVELOPMENT CORP LOCATION CITY-AGOURA HILL PROPERTY ADDRESS: VACANT LOT. See page 172.

32. AIN 2061021021 (auction ID 63): TRACT NO 8793 LOT 78 BLK 4 . . . ASSESSED TO SHEA ESTATES 0 DEVELOPMENT CORP LOCATION CITY-AGOURA HILL PROPERTY ADDRESS: VACANT LOT. See page 177.

33. AIN 2061021022 (auction ID 64): TRACT NO 8793 LOT 79 BLK 4 . . . ASSESSED TO SHEA ESTATES 0 DEVELOPMENT CORP LOCATION CITY-AGOURA HILL PROPERTY ADDRESS: VACANT LOT. See page 182.

Figure 2.79: Property 64, AIN 2061021012, overview map

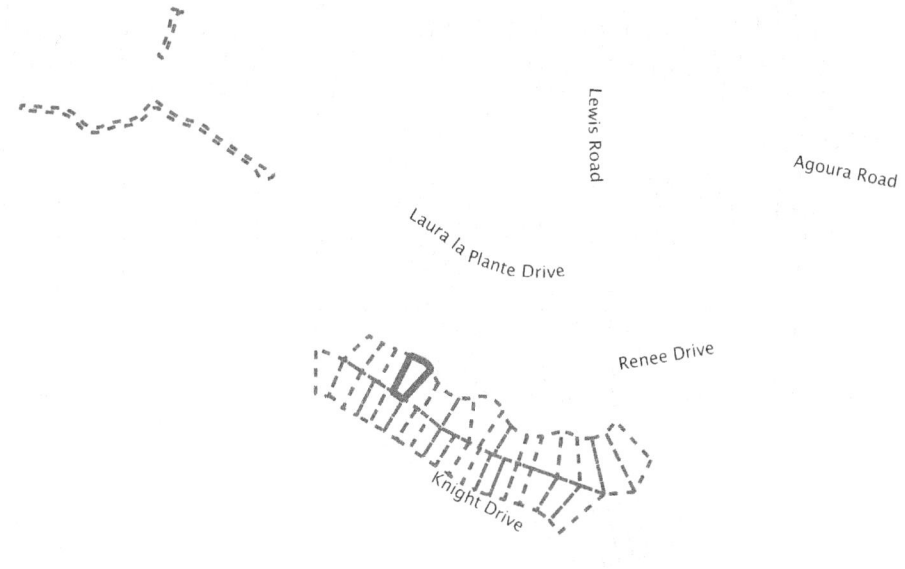

Figure 2.80: Property 64, AIN 2061021012, neighborhood view

Figure 2.81: Property 64, AIN 2061021012, detailed view

2.28 Auction ID 55

The Los Angeles County Auction Book describes the property as follows.

```
TRACT NO 8793 LOT 14 BLK 4 ASSESSED TO SHEA ESTATES 0 DEVELOPMENT
CORP LOCATION CITY-AGOURA HILL PROPERTY ADDRESS: VACANT LOT
```

The property is located in the general vicinity of Figure 2.82. It is identified by Assessor's Identification Number (AIN) 2061021013. The starting bid is $7,903. Comparable improved properties in this area is about $294/sqft. Comparable unimproved lots in this area is about $49/sqft. This parcel is approximately 6632 sqft. Note, however, that the parcel may be larger than the property under consideration. In case of condominiums, for example, the parcel may encompass other units of the development - those unrelated to the property to be auctioned.

The property is in a parcel zoned Restricted Open Space in Agoura Hills, for 0 to 0 dwelling units.

Figures 2.83 and 2.84 show street map and corresponding detailed aerial view, respectively. In both cases, the map is centered on the property with the containing parcel marked in heavy blue. If surrounding nearby properties are also part of this auction, the street and aerial maps highlights these in heavy, dashed blue outline.

This assessed entity may have other properties that are also in this auction:

1. AIN 2061020001 (auction ID 31): TRACT NO 8793 LOT 16 BLK 4 . . . ASSESSED TO SHEA ESTATES 0 DEVELOPMENT CORP LOCATION CITY-AGOURA HILL PROPERTY ADDRESS: VACANT LOT. See page 17.

2. AIN 2061020002 (auction ID 32): TRACT NO 8793 LOT 17 BLK 4 . . . ASSESSED TO SHEA ESTATES 0 DEVELOPMENT CORP LOCATION CITY-AGOURA HILL PROPERTY ADDRESS: VACANT LOT. See page 22.

3. AIN 2061020003 (auction ID 33): TRACT NO 8793 LOT 18 BLK 4 . . . ASSESSED TO SHEA ESTATES 0 DEVELOPMENT CORP LOCATION CITY-AGOURA HILL PROPERTY ADDRESS: VACANT LOT. See page 27.

4. AIN 2061020004 (auction ID 34): TRACT NO 8793 LOT 19 BLK 4 . . . ASSESSED TO SHEA ESTATES 0 DEVELOPMENT CORP LOCATION CITY-AGOURA HILL PROPERTY ADDRESS: VACANT LOT. See page 32.

5. AIN 2061020005 (auction ID 35): TRACT NO 8793 LOT 20 BLK 4 . . . ASSESSED TO SHEA ESTATES 0 DEVELOPMENT CORP LOCATION CITY-AGOURA HILL PROPERTY ADDRESS: VACANT LOT. See page 37.

6. AIN 2061020006 (auction ID 36): TRACT NO 8793 LOT 21 BLK 4 . . . ASSESSED TO SHEA ESTATES 0 DEVELOPMENT CORP LOCATION CITY-AGOURA HILL PROPERTY ADDRESS: VACANT LOT. See page 42.

7. AIN 2061020007 (auction ID 37): TRACT NO 8793 LOT 22 BLK 4 . . . ASSESSED TO SHEA ESTATES 0 DEVELOPMENT CORP LOCATION CITY-AGOURA HILL PROPERTY ADDRESS: VACANT LOT. See page 47.

8. AIN 2061020008 (auction ID 38): TRACT NO 8793 LOT 23 BLK 4 . . . ASSESSED TO SHEA ESTATES 0 DEVELOPMENT CORP LOCATION CITY-AGOURA HILL PROPERTY ADDRESS: VACANT LOT. See page 52.

9. AIN 2061020009 (auction ID 39): TRACT NO 8793 LOT 24 BLK 4 . . . ASSESSED TO SHEA ESTATES 0 DEVELOPMENT CORP LOCATION CITY-AGOURA HILL PROPERTY ADDRESS: VACANT LOT. See page 57.

10. AIN 2061020010 (auction ID 40): TRACT NO 8793 LOT 25 BLK 4 . . . ASSESSED TO SHEA ESTATES 0 DEVELOPMENT CORP LOCATION CITY-AGOURA HILL PROPERTY ADDRESS: VACANT LOT. See page 62.

11. AIN 2061020021 (auction ID 41): TRACT NO 8793 LOT 62 BLK 4 . . . ASSESSED TO SHEA ESTATES 0 DEVELOPMENT CORP LOCATION CITY-AGOURA HILL PROPERTY ADDRESS: VACANT LOT. See page 67.

12. AIN 2061020022 (auction ID 42): TRACT NO 8793 LOT 63 BLK 4 . . . ASSESSED TO SHEA ESTATES 0 DEVELOPMENT CORP LOCATION CITY-AGOURA HILL PROPERTY ADDRESS: VACANT LOT. See page 72.

13. AIN 2061020023 (auction ID 43): TRACT NO 8793 LOT 64 BLK 4 . . . ASSESSED TO SHEA ESTATES 0 DEVELOPMENT CORP LOCATION CITY-AGOURA HILL PROPERTY ADDRESS: VACANT LOT. See page 77.

14. AIN 2061020024 (auction ID 44): TRACT NO 8793 LOT 65 BLK 4 . . . ASSESSED TO SHEA ESTATES 0 DEVELOPMENT CORP LOCATION CITY-AGOURA HILL PROPERTY ADDRESS: VACANT LOT. See page 82.

15. AIN 2061020025 (auction ID 45): TRACT NO 8793 LOT 66 BLK 4 . . . ASSESSED TO SHEA ESTATES 0 DEVELOPMENT CORP LOCATION CITY-AGOURA HILL PROPERTY ADDRESS: VACANT LOT. See page 87.

16. AIN 2061020026 (auction ID 46): TRACT NO 8793 LOT 67 BLK 4 . . . ASSESSED TO SHEA ESTATES 0 DEVELOPMENT CORP LOCATION CITY-AGOURA HILL PROPERTY ADDRESS: VACANT LOT. See page 92.

17. AIN 2061020027 (auction ID 47): TRACT NO 8793 LOT 68 BLK 4 . . . ASSESSED TO SHEA ESTATES 0 DEVELOPMENT CORP LOCATION CITY-AGOURA HILL PROPERTY ADDRESS: VACANT LOT. See page 97.

18. AIN 2061020028 (auction ID 48): TRACT NO 8793 LOT 69 BLK 4 . . . ASSESSED TO SHEA ESTATES 0 DEVELOPMENT CORP LOCATION CITY-AGOURA HILL - PROPERTY ADDRESS: VACANT LOT. See page 102.

19. AIN 2061020029 (auction ID 49): TRACT NO 8793 LOT 70 BLK 4 . . . ASSESSED TO SHEA ESTATES 0 DEVELOPMENT CORP LOCATION CITY-AGOURA HILL PROPERTY ADDRESS: VACANT LOT. See page 107.

20. AIN 2061020030 (auction ID 50): TRACT NO 8793 LOT 71 BLK 4 . . . ASSESSED TO SHEA ESTATES 0 DEVELOPMENT CORP LOCATION CITY-AGOURA HILL PROPERTY ADDRESS: VACANT LOT. See page 112.

21. AIN 2061021009 (auction ID 51): TRACT NO 8793 LOT 10 BLK 4 . . . ASSESSED TO SHEA ESTATES 0 DEVELOPMENT CORP LOCATION CITY-AGOURA HILL PROPERTY ADDRESS: VACANT LOT. See page 117.

22. AIN 2061021010 (auction ID 52): TRACT NO 8793 LOT 11 BLK 4 . . . ASSESSED TO SHEA ESTATES 0 DEVELOPMENT CORP LOCATION CITY-AGOURA HILL PROPERTY ADDRESS: VACANT LOT. See page 122.

23. AIN 2061021011 (auction ID 53): TRACT NO 8793 LOT 12 BLK 4 . . . ASSESSED TO SHEA ESTATES 0 DEVELOPMENT CORP LOCATION CITY-AGOURA HILL PROPERTY ADDRESS: VACANT LOT. See page 127.

24. AIN 2061021012 (auction ID 54): TRACT NO 8793 LOT 13 BLK 4 . . . ASSESSED TO SHEA ESTATES 0 DEVELOPMENT CORP LOCATION CITY-AGOURA HILL PROPERTY ADDRESS: VACANT LOT. See page 132.

25. AIN 2061021014 (auction ID 56): TRACT NO 8793 LOT 15 BLK 4 ... ASSESSED TO SHEA ESTATES 0 DEVELOPMENT CORP LOCATION CITY-AGOURA HILL PROPERTY ADDRESS: VACANT LOT. See page 142.

26. AIN 2061021015 (auction ID 57): TRACT NO 8793 LOT 72 BLK 4 ... ASSESSED TO SHEA ESTATES 0 DEVELOPMENT CORP LOCATION CITY-AGOURA HILL PROPERTY ADDRESS: VACANT LOT. See page 147.

27. AIN 2061021016 (auction ID 58): TRACT NO 8793 LOT 73 BLK 4 ... ASSESSED TO SHEA ESTATES 0 DEVELOPMENT CORP LOCATION CITY-AGOURA HILL PROPERTY ADDRESS: VACANT LOT. See page 152.

28. AIN 2061021017 (auction ID 59): TRACT NO 8793 LOT 74 BLK 4 ... ASSESSED TO SHEA ESTATES 0 DEVELOPMENT CORP LOCATION CITY-AGOURA HILL PROPERTY ADDRESS: VACANT LOT. See page 157.

29. AIN 2061021018 (auction ID 60): TRACT NO 8793 LOT 75 BLK 4 ... ASSESSED TO SHEA ESTATES 0 DEVELOPMENT CORP LOCATION CITY-AGOURA HILL PROPERTY ADDRESS: VACANT LOT. See page 162.

30. AIN 2061021019 (auction ID 61): TRACT NO 8793 LOT 76 BLK 4 ... ASSESSED TO SHEA ESTATES 0 DEVELOPMENT CORP LOCATION CITY-AGOURA HILL PROPERTY ADDRESS: VACANT LOT. See page 167.

31. AIN 2061021020 (auction ID 62): TRACT NO 8793 LOT 77 BLK 4 ... ASSESSED TO SHEA ESTATES 0 DEVELOPMENT CORP LOCATION CITY-AGOURA HILL PROPERTY ADDRESS: VACANT LOT. See page 172.

32. AIN 2061021021 (auction ID 63): TRACT NO 8793 LOT 78 BLK 4 ... ASSESSED TO SHEA ESTATES 0 DEVELOPMENT CORP LOCATION CITY-AGOURA HILL PROPERTY ADDRESS: VACANT LOT. See page 177.

33. AIN 2061021022 (auction ID 64): TRACT NO 8793 LOT 79 BLK 4 ... ASSESSED TO SHEA ESTATES 0 DEVELOPMENT CORP LOCATION CITY-AGOURA HILL PROPERTY ADDRESS: VACANT LOT. See page 182.

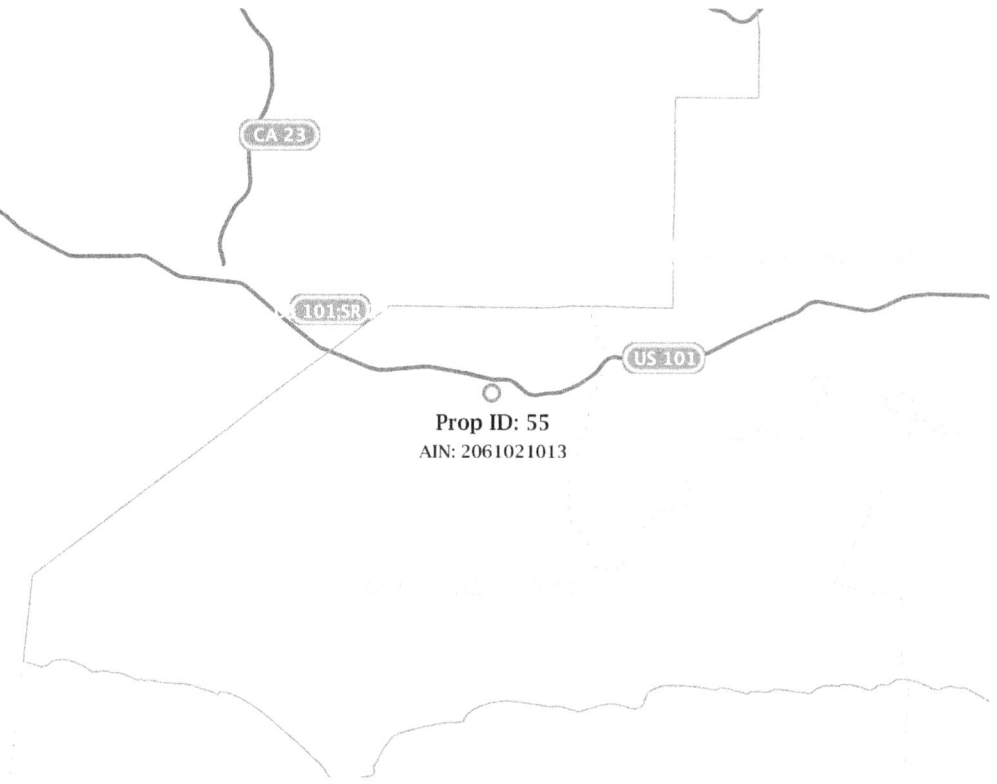

Figure 2.82: Property 64, AIN 2061021013, overview map

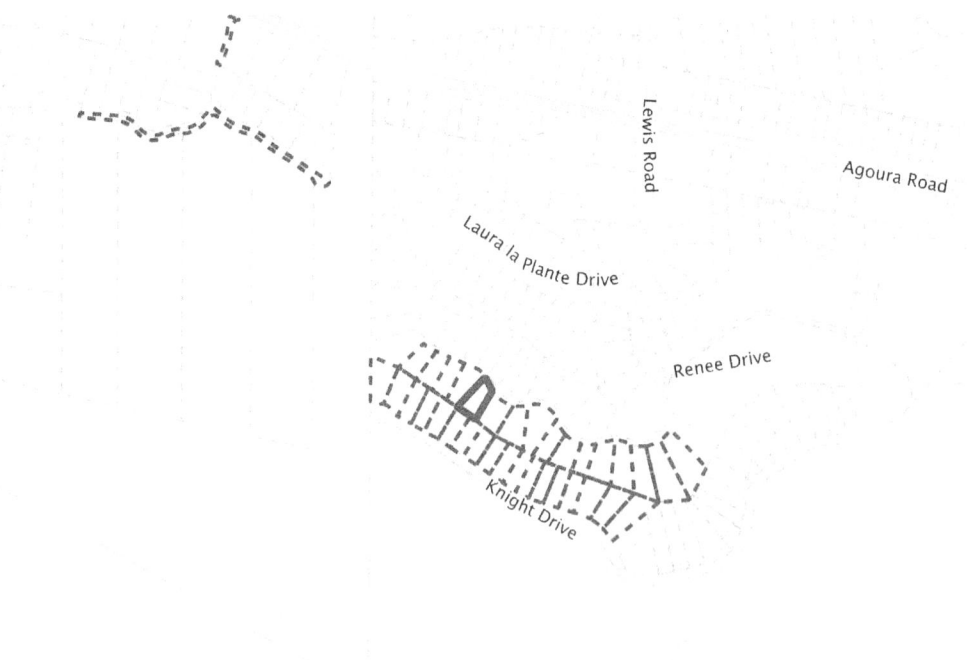

Figure 2.83: Property 64, AIN 2061021013, neighborhood view

Figure 2.84: Property 64, AIN 2061021013, detailed view

2.29   Auction ID 56

The Los Angeles County Auction Book describes the property as follows.

```
TRACT NO 8793 LOT 15 BLK 4 ASSESSED TO SHEA ESTATES 0 DEVELOPMENT
CORP LOCATION CITY-AGOURA HILL PROPERTY ADDRESS: VACANT LOT
```

The property is located in the general vicinity of Figure 2.85. It is identified by Assessor's Identification Number (AIN) 2061021014. The starting bid is \$3,844. Comparable improved properties in this area is about \$294/sqft. Comparable unimproved lots in this area is about \$49/sqft. This parcel is approximately 8323 sqft. Note, however, that the parcel may be larger than the property under consideration. In case of condominiums, for example, the parcel may encompass other units of the development - those unrelated to the property to be auctioned.

The property is in a parcel zoned Restricted Open Space in Agoura Hills, for 0 to 0 dwelling units.

Figures 2.86 and 2.87 show street map and corresponding detailed aerial view, respectively. In both cases, the map is centered on the property with the containing parcel marked in heavy blue. If surrounding nearby properties are also part of this auction, the street and aerial maps highlights these in heavy, dashed blue outline.

This assessed entity may have other properties that are also in this auction:

1. AIN 2061020001 (auction ID 31): TRACT NO 8793 LOT 16 BLK 4 . . . ASSESSED TO SHEA ESTATES 0 DEVELOPMENT CORP LOCATION CITY-AGOURA HILL PROPERTY ADDRESS: VACANT LOT. See page 17.

2. AIN 2061020002 (auction ID 32): TRACT NO 8793 LOT 17 BLK 4 . . . ASSESSED TO SHEA ESTATES 0 DEVELOPMENT CORP LOCATION CITY-AGOURA HILL PROPERTY ADDRESS: VACANT LOT. See page 22.

3. AIN 2061020003 (auction ID 33): TRACT NO 8793 LOT 18 BLK 4 . . . ASSESSED TO SHEA ESTATES 0 DEVELOPMENT CORP LOCATION CITY-AGOURA HILL PROPERTY ADDRESS: VACANT LOT. See page 27.

4. AIN 2061020004 (auction ID 34): TRACT NO 8793 LOT 19 BLK 4 . . . ASSESSED TO SHEA ESTATES 0 DEVELOPMENT CORP LOCATION CITY-AGOURA HILL PROPERTY ADDRESS: VACANT LOT. See page 32.

5. AIN 2061020005 (auction ID 35): TRACT NO 8793 LOT 20 BLK 4 . . . ASSESSED TO SHEA ESTATES 0 DEVELOPMENT CORP LOCATION CITY-AGOURA HILL PROPERTY ADDRESS: VACANT LOT. See page 37.

6. AIN 2061020006 (auction ID 36): TRACT NO 8793 LOT 21 BLK 4 . . . ASSESSED TO SHEA ESTATES 0 DEVELOPMENT CORP LOCATION CITY-AGOURA HILL PROPERTY ADDRESS: VACANT LOT. See page 42.

7. AIN 2061020007 (auction ID 37): TRACT NO 8793 LOT 22 BLK 4 . . . ASSESSED TO SHEA ESTATES 0 DEVELOPMENT CORP LOCATION CITY-AGOURA HILL PROPERTY ADDRESS: VACANT LOT. See page 47.

8. AIN 2061020008 (auction ID 38): TRACT NO 8793 LOT 23 BLK 4 . . . ASSESSED TO SHEA ESTATES 0 DEVELOPMENT CORP LOCATION CITY-AGOURA HILL PROPERTY ADDRESS: VACANT LOT. See page 52.

9. AIN 2061020009 (auction ID 39): TRACT NO 8793 LOT 24 BLK 4 . . . ASSESSED TO SHEA ESTATES 0 DEVELOPMENT CORP LOCATION CITY-AGOURA HILL PROPERTY ADDRESS: VACANT LOT. See page 57.

10. AIN 2061020010 (auction ID 40): TRACT NO 8793 LOT 25 BLK 4 . . . ASSESSED TO SHEA ESTATES 0 DEVELOPMENT CORP LOCATION CITY-AGOURA HILL PROPERTY ADDRESS: VACANT LOT. See page 62.

11. AIN 2061020021 (auction ID 41): TRACT NO 8793 LOT 62 BLK 4 . . . ASSESSED TO SHEA ESTATES 0 DEVELOPMENT CORP LOCATION CITY-AGOURA HILL PROPERTY ADDRESS: VACANT LOT. See page 67.

12. AIN 2061020022 (auction ID 42): TRACT NO 8793 LOT 63 BLK 4 . . . ASSESSED TO SHEA ESTATES 0 DEVELOPMENT CORP LOCATION CITY-AGOURA HILL PROPERTY ADDRESS: VACANT LOT. See page 72.

13. AIN 2061020023 (auction ID 43): TRACT NO 8793 LOT 64 BLK 4 . . . ASSESSED TO SHEA ESTATES 0 DEVELOPMENT CORP LOCATION CITY-AGOURA HILL PROPERTY ADDRESS: VACANT LOT. See page 77.

14. AIN 2061020024 (auction ID 44): TRACT NO 8793 LOT 65 BLK 4 . . . ASSESSED TO SHEA ESTATES 0 DEVELOPMENT CORP LOCATION CITY-AGOURA HILL PROPERTY ADDRESS: VACANT LOT. See page 82.

15. AIN 2061020025 (auction ID 45): TRACT NO 8793 LOT 66 BLK 4 . . . ASSESSED TO SHEA ESTATES 0 DEVELOPMENT CORP LOCATION CITY-AGOURA HILL PROPERTY ADDRESS: VACANT LOT. See page 87.

16. AIN 2061020026 (auction ID 46): TRACT NO 8793 LOT 67 BLK 4 . . . ASSESSED TO SHEA ESTATES 0 DEVELOPMENT CORP LOCATION CITY-AGOURA HILL PROPERTY ADDRESS: VACANT LOT. See page 92.

17. AIN 2061020027 (auction ID 47): TRACT NO 8793 LOT 68 BLK 4 . . . ASSESSED TO SHEA ESTATES 0 DEVELOPMENT CORP LOCATION CITY-AGOURA HILL PROPERTY ADDRESS: VACANT LOT. See page 97.

18. AIN 2061020028 (auction ID 48): TRACT NO 8793 LOT 69 BLK 4 . . . ASSESSED TO SHEA ESTATES 0 DEVELOPMENT CORP LOCATION CITY-AGOURA HILL - PROPERTY ADDRESS: VACANT LOT. See page 102.

19. AIN 2061020029 (auction ID 49): TRACT NO 8793 LOT 70 BLK 4 . . . ASSESSED TO SHEA ESTATES 0 DEVELOPMENT CORP LOCATION CITY-AGOURA HILL PROPERTY ADDRESS: VACANT LOT. See page 107.

20. AIN 2061020030 (auction ID 50): TRACT NO 8793 LOT 71 BLK 4 . . . ASSESSED TO SHEA ESTATES 0 DEVELOPMENT CORP LOCATION CITY-AGOURA HILL PROPERTY ADDRESS: VACANT LOT. See page 112.

21. AIN 2061021009 (auction ID 51): TRACT NO 8793 LOT 10 BLK 4 . . . ASSESSED TO SHEA ESTATES 0 DEVELOPMENT CORP LOCATION CITY-AGOURA HILL PROPERTY ADDRESS: VACANT LOT. See page 117.

22. AIN 2061021010 (auction ID 52): TRACT NO 8793 LOT 11 BLK 4 . . . ASSESSED TO SHEA ESTATES 0 DEVELOPMENT CORP LOCATION CITY-AGOURA HILL PROPERTY ADDRESS: VACANT LOT. See page 122.

23. AIN 2061021011 (auction ID 53): TRACT NO 8793 LOT 12 BLK 4 . . . ASSESSED TO SHEA ESTATES 0 DEVELOPMENT CORP LOCATION CITY-AGOURA HILL PROPERTY ADDRESS: VACANT LOT. See page 127.

24. AIN 2061021012 (auction ID 54): TRACT NO 8793 LOT 13 BLK 4 . . . ASSESSED TO SHEA ESTATES 0 DEVELOPMENT CORP LOCATION CITY-AGOURA HILL PROPERTY ADDRESS: VACANT LOT. See page 132.

25. AIN 2061021013 (auction ID 55): TRACT NO 8793 LOT 14 BLK 4 . . . ASSESSED TO SHEA ESTATES 0 DEVELOPMENT CORP LOCATION CITY-AGOURA HILL PROPERTY ADDRESS: VACANT LOT. See page 137.

26. AIN 2061021015 (auction ID 57): TRACT NO 8793 LOT 72 BLK 4 . . . ASSESSED TO SHEA ESTATES 0 DEVELOPMENT CORP LOCATION CITY-AGOURA HILL PROPERTY ADDRESS: VACANT LOT. See page 147.

27. AIN 2061021016 (auction ID 58): TRACT NO 8793 LOT 73 BLK 4 . . . ASSESSED TO SHEA ESTATES 0 DEVELOPMENT CORP LOCATION CITY-AGOURA HILL PROPERTY ADDRESS: VACANT LOT. See page 152.

28. AIN 2061021017 (auction ID 59): TRACT NO 8793 LOT 74 BLK 4 . . . ASSESSED TO SHEA ESTATES 0 DEVELOPMENT CORP LOCATION CITY-AGOURA HILL PROPERTY ADDRESS: VACANT LOT. See page 157.

29. AIN 2061021018 (auction ID 60): TRACT NO 8793 LOT 75 BLK 4 . . . ASSESSED TO SHEA ESTATES 0 DEVELOPMENT CORP LOCATION CITY-AGOURA HILL PROPERTY ADDRESS: VACANT LOT. See page 162.

30. AIN 2061021019 (auction ID 61): TRACT NO 8793 LOT 76 BLK 4 . . . ASSESSED TO SHEA ESTATES 0 DEVELOPMENT CORP LOCATION CITY-AGOURA HILL PROPERTY ADDRESS: VACANT LOT. See page 167.

31. AIN 2061021020 (auction ID 62): TRACT NO 8793 LOT 77 BLK 4 . . . ASSESSED TO SHEA ESTATES 0 DEVELOPMENT CORP LOCATION CITY-AGOURA HILL PROPERTY ADDRESS: VACANT LOT. See page 172.

32. AIN 2061021021 (auction ID 63): TRACT NO 8793 LOT 78 BLK 4 . . . ASSESSED TO SHEA ESTATES 0 DEVELOPMENT CORP LOCATION CITY-AGOURA HILL PROPERTY ADDRESS: VACANT LOT. See page 177.

33. AIN 2061021022 (auction ID 64): TRACT NO 8793 LOT 79 BLK 4 . . . ASSESSED TO SHEA ESTATES 0 DEVELOPMENT CORP LOCATION CITY-AGOURA HILL PROPERTY ADDRESS: VACANT LOT. See page 182.

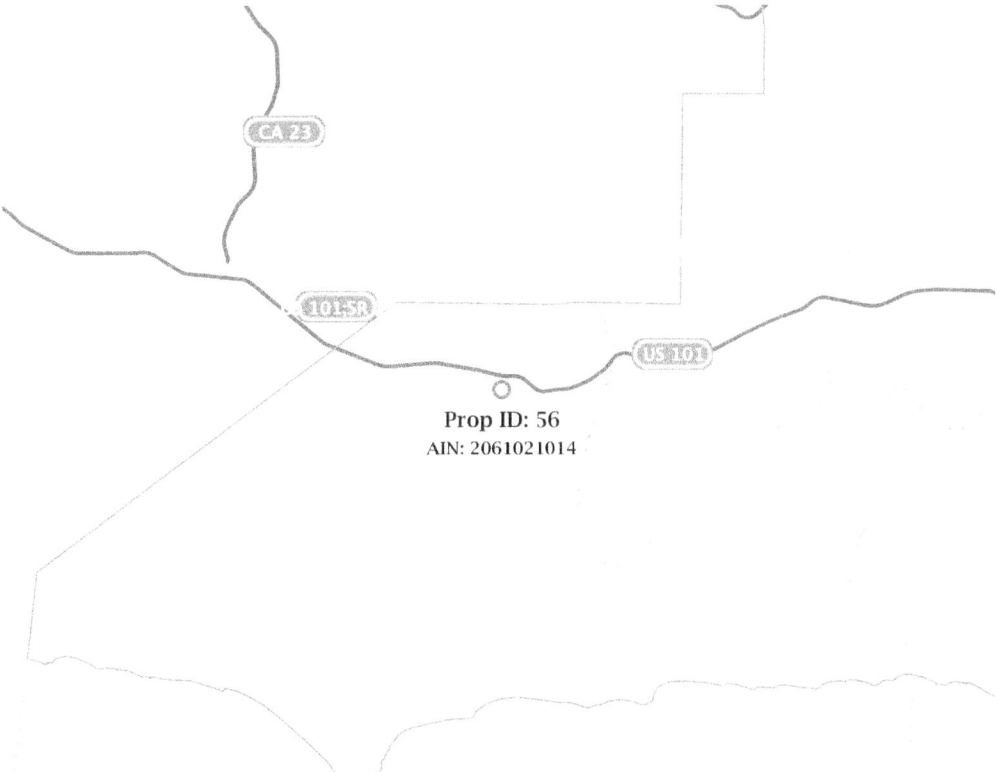

Prop ID: 56
AIN: 2061021014

Figure 2.85: Property 64, AIN 2061021014, overview map

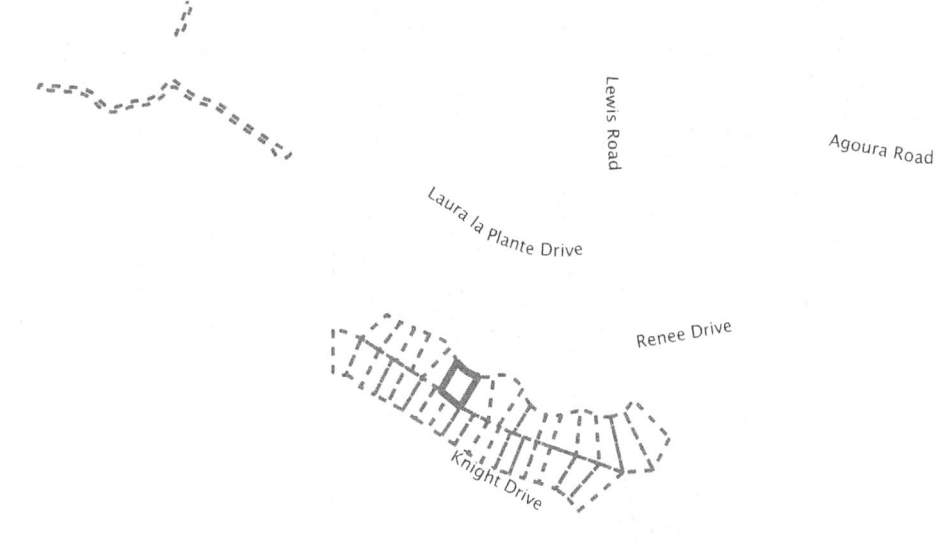

Figure 2.86: Property 64, AIN 2061021014, neighborhood view

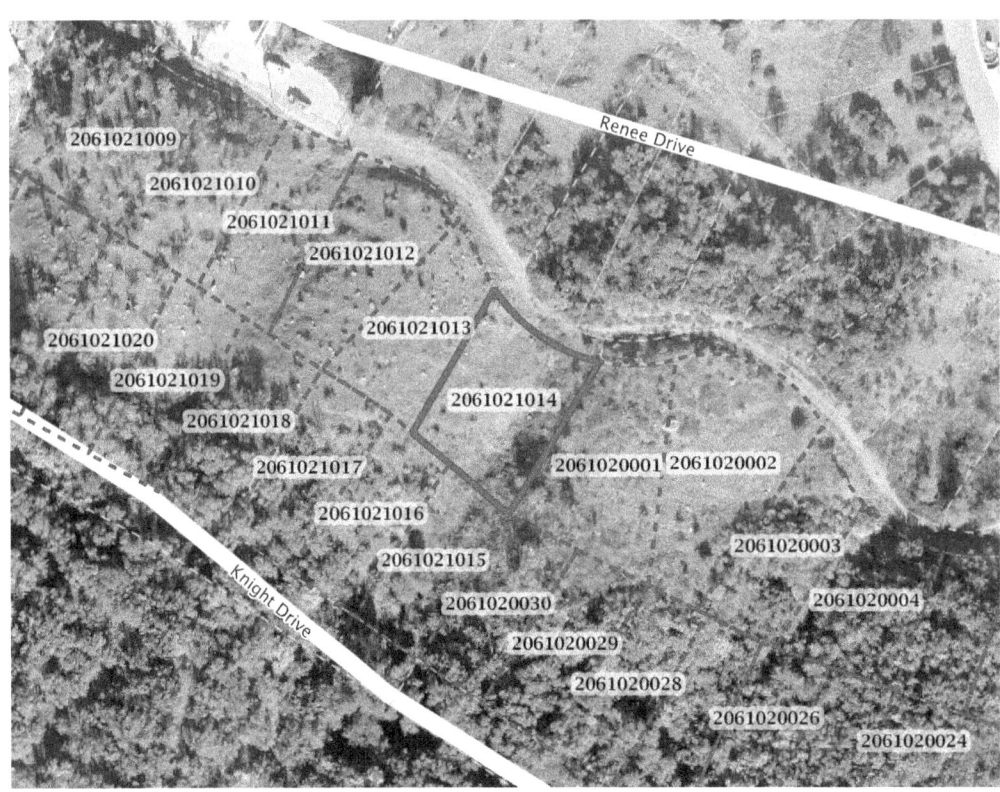

Figure 2.87: Property 64, AIN 2061021014, detailed view

2.30 Auction ID 57

The Los Angeles County Auction Book describes the property as follows.

```
TRACT NO 8793 LOT 72 BLK 4 ASSESSED TO SHEA ESTATES 0 DEVELOPMENT
CORP LOCATION CITY-AGOURA HILL PROPERTY ADDRESS: VACANT LOT
```

The property is located in the general vicinity of Figure 2.88. It is identified by Assessor's Identification Number (AIN) 2061021015. The starting bid is $3,254. Comparable improved properties in this area is about $294/sqft. Comparable unimproved lots in this area is about $49/sqft. This parcel is approximately 5543 sqft. Note, however, that the parcel may be larger than the property under consideration. In case of condominiums, for example, the parcel may encompass other units of the development - those unrelated to the property to be auctioned.

The property is in a parcel zoned Restricted Open Space in Agoura Hills, for 0 to 0 dwelling units.

Figures 2.89 and 2.90 show street map and corresponding detailed aerial view, respectively. In both cases, the map is centered on the property with the containing parcel marked in heavy blue. If surrounding nearby properties are also part of this auction, the street and aerial maps highlights these in heavy, dashed blue outline.

This assessed entity may have other properties that are also in this auction:

1. AIN 2061020001 (auction ID 31): TRACT NO 8793 LOT 16 BLK 4 . . . ASSESSED TO SHEA ESTATES 0 DEVELOPMENT CORP LOCATION CITY-AGOURA HILL PROPERTY ADDRESS: VACANT LOT. See page 17.

2. AIN 2061020002 (auction ID 32): TRACT NO 8793 LOT 17 BLK 4 . . . ASSESSED TO SHEA ESTATES 0 DEVELOPMENT CORP LOCATION CITY-AGOURA HILL PROPERTY ADDRESS: VACANT LOT. See page 22.

3. AIN 2061020003 (auction ID 33): TRACT NO 8793 LOT 18 BLK 4 . . . ASSESSED TO SHEA ESTATES 0 DEVELOPMENT CORP LOCATION CITY-AGOURA HILL PROPERTY ADDRESS: VACANT LOT. See page 27.

4. AIN 2061020004 (auction ID 34): TRACT NO 8793 LOT 19 BLK 4 . . . ASSESSED TO SHEA ESTATES 0 DEVELOPMENT CORP LOCATION CITY-AGOURA HILL PROPERTY ADDRESS: VACANT LOT. See page 32.

5. AIN 2061020005 (auction ID 35): TRACT NO 8793 LOT 20 BLK 4 . . . ASSESSED TO SHEA ESTATES 0 DEVELOPMENT CORP LOCATION CITY-AGOURA HILL PROPERTY ADDRESS: VACANT LOT. See page 37.

6. AIN 2061020006 (auction ID 36): TRACT NO 8793 LOT 21 BLK 4 . . . ASSESSED TO SHEA ESTATES 0 DEVELOPMENT CORP LOCATION CITY-AGOURA HILL PROPERTY ADDRESS: VACANT LOT. See page 42.

7. AIN 2061020007 (auction ID 37): TRACT NO 8793 LOT 22 BLK 4 . . . ASSESSED TO SHEA ESTATES 0 DEVELOPMENT CORP LOCATION CITY-AGOURA HILL PROPERTY ADDRESS: VACANT LOT. See page 47.

8. AIN 2061020008 (auction ID 38): TRACT NO 8793 LOT 23 BLK 4 . . . ASSESSED TO SHEA ESTATES 0 DEVELOPMENT CORP LOCATION CITY-AGOURA HILL PROPERTY ADDRESS: VACANT LOT. See page 52.

9. AIN 2061020009 (auction ID 39): TRACT NO 8793 LOT 24 BLK 4 . . . ASSESSED TO SHEA ESTATES 0 DEVELOPMENT CORP LOCATION CITY-AGOURA HILL PROPERTY ADDRESS: VACANT LOT. See page 57.

10. AIN 2061020010 (auction ID 40): TRACT NO 8793 LOT 25 BLK 4 . . . ASSESSED TO SHEA ESTATES 0 DEVELOPMENT CORP LOCATION CITY-AGOURA HILL PROPERTY ADDRESS: VACANT LOT. See page 62.

11. AIN 2061020021 (auction ID 41): TRACT NO 8793 LOT 62 BLK 4 . . . ASSESSED TO SHEA ESTATES 0 DEVELOPMENT CORP LOCATION CITY-AGOURA HILL PROPERTY ADDRESS: VACANT LOT. See page 67.

12. AIN 2061020022 (auction ID 42): TRACT NO 8793 LOT 63 BLK 4 . . . ASSESSED TO SHEA ESTATES 0 DEVELOPMENT CORP LOCATION CITY-AGOURA HILL PROPERTY ADDRESS: VACANT LOT. See page 72.

13. AIN 2061020023 (auction ID 43): TRACT NO 8793 LOT 64 BLK 4 . . . ASSESSED TO SHEA ESTATES 0 DEVELOPMENT CORP LOCATION CITY-AGOURA HILL PROPERTY ADDRESS: VACANT LOT. See page 77.

14. AIN 2061020024 (auction ID 44): TRACT NO 8793 LOT 65 BLK 4 . . . ASSESSED TO SHEA ESTATES 0 DEVELOPMENT CORP LOCATION CITY-AGOURA HILL PROPERTY ADDRESS: VACANT LOT. See page 82.

15. AIN 2061020025 (auction ID 45): TRACT NO 8793 LOT 66 BLK 4 . . . ASSESSED TO SHEA ESTATES 0 DEVELOPMENT CORP LOCATION CITY-AGOURA HILL PROPERTY ADDRESS: VACANT LOT. See page 87.

16. AIN 2061020026 (auction ID 46): TRACT NO 8793 LOT 67 BLK 4 . . . ASSESSED TO SHEA ESTATES 0 DEVELOPMENT CORP LOCATION CITY-AGOURA HILL PROPERTY ADDRESS: VACANT LOT. See page 92.

17. AIN 2061020027 (auction ID 47): TRACT NO 8793 LOT 68 BLK 4 . . . ASSESSED TO SHEA ESTATES 0 DEVELOPMENT CORP LOCATION CITY-AGOURA HILL PROPERTY ADDRESS: VACANT LOT. See page 97.

18. AIN 2061020028 (auction ID 48): TRACT NO 8793 LOT 69 BLK 4 . . . ASSESSED TO SHEA ESTATES 0 DEVELOPMENT CORP LOCATION CITY-AGOURA HILL - PROPERTY ADDRESS: VACANT LOT. See page 102.

19. AIN 2061020029 (auction ID 49): TRACT NO 8793 LOT 70 BLK 4 . . . ASSESSED TO SHEA ESTATES 0 DEVELOPMENT CORP LOCATION CITY-AGOURA HILL PROPERTY ADDRESS: VACANT LOT. See page 107.

20. AIN 2061020030 (auction ID 50): TRACT NO 8793 LOT 71 BLK 4 . . . ASSESSED TO SHEA ESTATES 0 DEVELOPMENT CORP LOCATION CITY-AGOURA HILL PROPERTY ADDRESS: VACANT LOT. See page 112.

21. AIN 2061021009 (auction ID 51): TRACT NO 8793 LOT 10 BLK 4 . . . ASSESSED TO SHEA ESTATES 0 DEVELOPMENT CORP LOCATION CITY-AGOURA HILL PROPERTY ADDRESS: VACANT LOT. See page 117.

22. AIN 2061021010 (auction ID 52): TRACT NO 8793 LOT 11 BLK 4 . . . ASSESSED TO SHEA ESTATES 0 DEVELOPMENT CORP LOCATION CITY-AGOURA HILL PROPERTY ADDRESS: VACANT LOT. See page 122.

23. AIN 2061021011 (auction ID 53): TRACT NO 8793 LOT 12 BLK 4 . . . ASSESSED TO SHEA ESTATES 0 DEVELOPMENT CORP LOCATION CITY-AGOURA HILL PROPERTY ADDRESS: VACANT LOT. See page 127.

24. AIN 2061021012 (auction ID 54): TRACT NO 8793 LOT 13 BLK 4 . . . ASSESSED TO SHEA ESTATES 0 DEVELOPMENT CORP LOCATION CITY-AGOURA HILL PROPERTY ADDRESS: VACANT LOT. See page 132.

25. AIN 2061021013 (auction ID 55): TRACT NO 8793 LOT 14 BLK 4 ... ASSESSED TO SHEA ESTATES 0 DEVELOPMENT CORP LOCATION CITY-AGOURA HILL PROPERTY ADDRESS: VACANT LOT. See page 137.

26. AIN 2061021014 (auction ID 56): TRACT NO 8793 LOT 15 BLK 4 ... ASSESSED TO SHEA ESTATES 0 DEVELOPMENT CORP LOCATION CITY-AGOURA HILL PROPERTY ADDRESS: VACANT LOT. See page 142.

27. AIN 2061021016 (auction ID 58): TRACT NO 8793 LOT 73 BLK 4 ... ASSESSED TO SHEA ESTATES 0 DEVELOPMENT CORP LOCATION CITY-AGOURA HILL PROPERTY ADDRESS: VACANT LOT. See page 152.

28. AIN 2061021017 (auction ID 59): TRACT NO 8793 LOT 74 BLK 4 ... ASSESSED TO SHEA ESTATES 0 DEVELOPMENT CORP LOCATION CITY-AGOURA HILL PROPERTY ADDRESS: VACANT LOT. See page 157.

29. AIN 2061021018 (auction ID 60): TRACT NO 8793 LOT 75 BLK 4 ... ASSESSED TO SHEA ESTATES 0 DEVELOPMENT CORP LOCATION CITY-AGOURA HILL PROPERTY ADDRESS: VACANT LOT. See page 162.

30. AIN 2061021019 (auction ID 61): TRACT NO 8793 LOT 76 BLK 4 ... ASSESSED TO SHEA ESTATES 0 DEVELOPMENT CORP LOCATION CITY-AGOURA HILL PROPERTY ADDRESS: VACANT LOT. See page 167.

31. AIN 2061021020 (auction ID 62): TRACT NO 8793 LOT 77 BLK 4 ... ASSESSED TO SHEA ESTATES 0 DEVELOPMENT CORP LOCATION CITY-AGOURA HILL PROPERTY ADDRESS: VACANT LOT. See page 172.

32. AIN 2061021021 (auction ID 63): TRACT NO 8793 LOT 78 BLK 4 ... ASSESSED TO SHEA ESTATES 0 DEVELOPMENT CORP LOCATION CITY-AGOURA HILL PROPERTY ADDRESS: VACANT LOT. See page 177.

33. AIN 2061021022 (auction ID 64): TRACT NO 8793 LOT 79 BLK 4 ... ASSESSED TO SHEA ESTATES 0 DEVELOPMENT CORP LOCATION CITY-AGOURA HILL PROPERTY ADDRESS: VACANT LOT. See page 182.

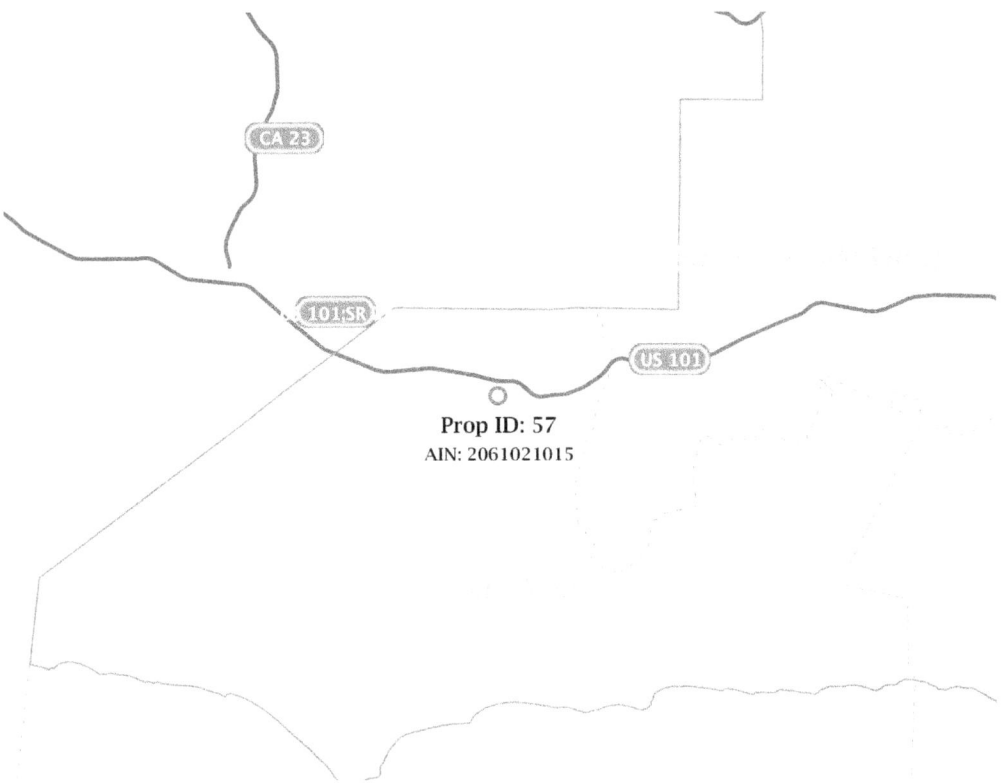

Figure 2.88: Property 64, AIN 2061021015, overview map

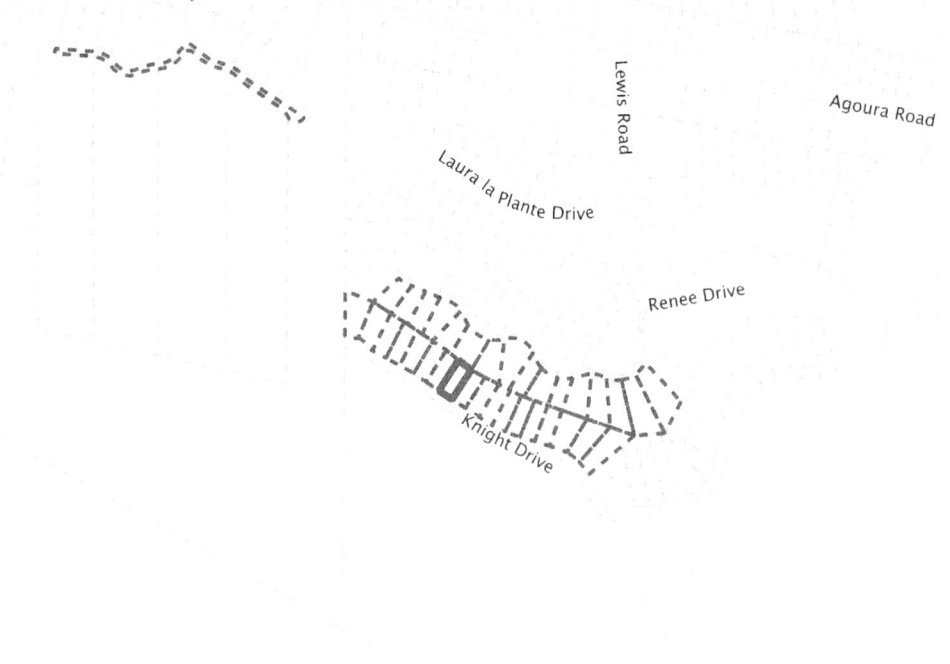

Figure 2.89: Property 64, AIN 2061021015, neighborhood view

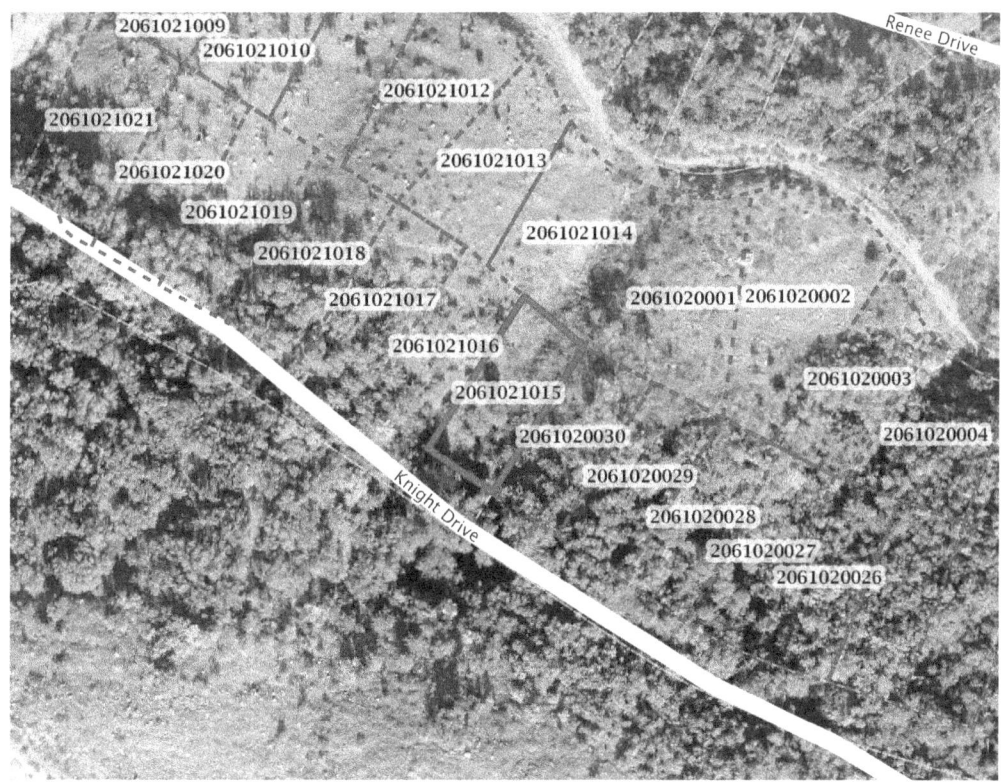

Figure 2.90: Property 64, AIN 2061021015, detailed view

2.31 Auction ID 58

The Los Angeles County Auction Book describes the property as follows.

```
TRACT NO 8793 LOT 73 BLK 4 ASSESSED TO SHEA ESTATES 0 DEVELOPMENT
CORP LOCATION CITY-AGOURA HILL PROPERTY ADDRESS: VACANT LOT
```

The property is located in the general vicinity of Figure 2.91. It is identified by Assessor's Identification Number (AIN) 2061021016. The starting bid is $3,303. Comparable improved properties in this area is about $294/sqft. Comparable unimproved lots in this area is about $49/sqft. This parcel is approximately 5753 sqft. Note, however, that the parcel may be larger than the property under consideration. In case of condominiums, for example, the parcel may encompass other units of the development - those unrelated to the property to be auctioned.

The property is in a parcel zoned Restricted Open Space in Agoura Hills, for 0 to 0 dwelling units.

Figures 2.92 and 2.93 show street map and corresponding detailed aerial view, respectively. In both cases, the map is centered on the property with the containing parcel marked in heavy blue. If surrounding nearby properties are also part of this auction, the street and aerial maps highlights these in heavy, dashed blue outline.

This assessed entity may have other properties that are also in this auction:

1. AIN 2061020001 (auction ID 31): TRACT NO 8793 LOT 16 BLK 4 ... ASSESSED TO SHEA ESTATES 0 DEVELOPMENT CORP LOCATION CITY-AGOURA HILL PROPERTY ADDRESS: VACANT LOT. See page 17.

2. AIN 2061020002 (auction ID 32): TRACT NO 8793 LOT 17 BLK 4 ... ASSESSED TO SHEA ESTATES 0 DEVELOPMENT CORP LOCATION CITY-AGOURA HILL PROPERTY ADDRESS: VACANT LOT. See page 22.

3. AIN 2061020003 (auction ID 33): TRACT NO 8793 LOT 18 BLK 4 ... ASSESSED TO SHEA ESTATES 0 DEVELOPMENT CORP LOCATION CITY-AGOURA HILL PROPERTY ADDRESS: VACANT LOT. See page 27.

4. AIN 2061020004 (auction ID 34): TRACT NO 8793 LOT 19 BLK 4 ... ASSESSED TO SHEA ESTATES 0 DEVELOPMENT CORP LOCATION CITY-AGOURA HILL PROPERTY ADDRESS: VACANT LOT. See page 32.

5. AIN 2061020005 (auction ID 35): TRACT NO 8793 LOT 20 BLK 4 ... ASSESSED TO SHEA ESTATES 0 DEVELOPMENT CORP LOCATION CITY-AGOURA HILL PROPERTY ADDRESS: VACANT LOT. See page 37.

6. AIN 2061020006 (auction ID 36): TRACT NO 8793 LOT 21 BLK 4 ... ASSESSED TO SHEA ESTATES 0 DEVELOPMENT CORP LOCATION CITY-AGOURA HILL PROPERTY ADDRESS: VACANT LOT. See page 42.

7. AIN 2061020007 (auction ID 37): TRACT NO 8793 LOT 22 BLK 4 ... ASSESSED TO SHEA ESTATES 0 DEVELOPMENT CORP LOCATION CITY-AGOURA HILL PROPERTY ADDRESS: VACANT LOT. See page 47.

8. AIN 2061020008 (auction ID 38): TRACT NO 8793 LOT 23 BLK 4 ... ASSESSED TO SHEA ESTATES 0 DEVELOPMENT CORP LOCATION CITY-AGOURA HILL PROPERTY ADDRESS: VACANT LOT. See page 52.

9. AIN 2061020009 (auction ID 39): TRACT NO 8793 LOT 24 BLK 4 ... ASSESSED TO SHEA ESTATES 0 DEVELOPMENT CORP LOCATION CITY-AGOURA HILL PROPERTY ADDRESS: VACANT LOT. See page 57.

10. AIN 2061020010 (auction ID 40): TRACT NO 8793 LOT 25 BLK 4 . . . ASSESSED TO SHEA ESTATES 0 DEVELOPMENT CORP LOCATION CITY-AGOURA HILL PROPERTY ADDRESS: VACANT LOT. See page 62.

11. AIN 2061020021 (auction ID 41): TRACT NO 8793 LOT 62 BLK 4 . . . ASSESSED TO SHEA ESTATES 0 DEVELOPMENT CORP LOCATION CITY-AGOURA HILL PROPERTY ADDRESS: VACANT LOT. See page 67.

12. AIN 2061020022 (auction ID 42): TRACT NO 8793 LOT 63 BLK 4 . . . ASSESSED TO SHEA ESTATES 0 DEVELOPMENT CORP LOCATION CITY-AGOURA HILL PROPERTY ADDRESS: VACANT LOT. See page 72.

13. AIN 2061020023 (auction ID 43): TRACT NO 8793 LOT 64 BLK 4 . . . ASSESSED TO SHEA ESTATES 0 DEVELOPMENT CORP LOCATION CITY-AGOURA HILL PROPERTY ADDRESS: VACANT LOT. See page 77.

14. AIN 2061020024 (auction ID 44): TRACT NO 8793 LOT 65 BLK 4 . . . ASSESSED TO SHEA ESTATES 0 DEVELOPMENT CORP LOCATION CITY-AGOURA HILL PROPERTY ADDRESS: VACANT LOT. See page 82.

15. AIN 2061020025 (auction ID 45): TRACT NO 8793 LOT 66 BLK 4 . . . ASSESSED TO SHEA ESTATES 0 DEVELOPMENT CORP LOCATION CITY-AGOURA HILL PROPERTY ADDRESS: VACANT LOT. See page 87.

16. AIN 2061020026 (auction ID 46): TRACT NO 8793 LOT 67 BLK 4 . . . ASSESSED TO SHEA ESTATES 0 DEVELOPMENT CORP LOCATION CITY-AGOURA HILL PROPERTY ADDRESS: VACANT LOT. See page 92.

17. AIN 2061020027 (auction ID 47): TRACT NO 8793 LOT 68 BLK 4 . . . ASSESSED TO SHEA ESTATES 0 DEVELOPMENT CORP LOCATION CITY-AGOURA HILL PROPERTY ADDRESS: VACANT LOT. See page 97.

18. AIN 2061020028 (auction ID 48): TRACT NO 8793 LOT 69 BLK 4 . . . ASSESSED TO SHEA ESTATES 0 DEVELOPMENT CORP LOCATION CITY-AGOURA HILL - PROPERTY ADDRESS: VACANT LOT. See page 102.

19. AIN 2061020029 (auction ID 49): TRACT NO 8793 LOT 70 BLK 4 . . . ASSESSED TO SHEA ESTATES 0 DEVELOPMENT CORP LOCATION CITY-AGOURA HILL PROPERTY ADDRESS: VACANT LOT. See page 107.

20. AIN 2061020030 (auction ID 50): TRACT NO 8793 LOT 71 BLK 4 . . . ASSESSED TO SHEA ESTATES 0 DEVELOPMENT CORP LOCATION CITY-AGOURA HILL PROPERTY ADDRESS: VACANT LOT. See page 112.

21. AIN 2061021009 (auction ID 51): TRACT NO 8793 LOT 10 BLK 4 . . . ASSESSED TO SHEA ESTATES 0 DEVELOPMENT CORP LOCATION CITY-AGOURA HILL PROPERTY ADDRESS: VACANT LOT. See page 117.

22. AIN 2061021010 (auction ID 52): TRACT NO 8793 LOT 11 BLK 4 . . . ASSESSED TO SHEA ESTATES 0 DEVELOPMENT CORP LOCATION CITY-AGOURA HILL PROPERTY ADDRESS: VACANT LOT. See page 122.

23. AIN 2061021011 (auction ID 53): TRACT NO 8793 LOT 12 BLK 4 . . . ASSESSED TO SHEA ESTATES 0 DEVELOPMENT CORP LOCATION CITY-AGOURA HILL PROPERTY ADDRESS: VACANT LOT. See page 127.

24. AIN 2061021012 (auction ID 54): TRACT NO 8793 LOT 13 BLK 4 . . . ASSESSED TO SHEA ESTATES 0 DEVELOPMENT CORP LOCATION CITY-AGOURA HILL PROPERTY ADDRESS: VACANT LOT. See page 132.

25. AIN 2061021013 (auction ID 55): TRACT NO 8793 LOT 14 BLK 4 ... ASSESSED TO SHEA ESTATES 0 DEVELOPMENT CORP LOCATION CITY-AGOURA HILL PROPERTY ADDRESS: VACANT LOT. See page 137.

26. AIN 2061021014 (auction ID 56): TRACT NO 8793 LOT 15 BLK 4 ... ASSESSED TO SHEA ESTATES 0 DEVELOPMENT CORP LOCATION CITY-AGOURA HILL PROPERTY ADDRESS: VACANT LOT. See page 142.

27. AIN 2061021015 (auction ID 57): TRACT NO 8793 LOT 72 BLK 4 ... ASSESSED TO SHEA ESTATES 0 DEVELOPMENT CORP LOCATION CITY-AGOURA HILL PROPERTY ADDRESS: VACANT LOT. See page 147.

28. AIN 2061021017 (auction ID 59): TRACT NO 8793 LOT 74 BLK 4 ... ASSESSED TO SHEA ESTATES 0 DEVELOPMENT CORP LOCATION CITY-AGOURA HILL PROPERTY ADDRESS: VACANT LOT. See page 157.

29. AIN 2061021018 (auction ID 60): TRACT NO 8793 LOT 75 BLK 4 ... ASSESSED TO SHEA ESTATES 0 DEVELOPMENT CORP LOCATION CITY-AGOURA HILL PROPERTY ADDRESS: VACANT LOT. See page 162.

30. AIN 2061021019 (auction ID 61): TRACT NO 8793 LOT 76 BLK 4 ... ASSESSED TO SHEA ESTATES 0 DEVELOPMENT CORP LOCATION CITY-AGOURA HILL PROPERTY ADDRESS: VACANT LOT. See page 167.

31. AIN 2061021020 (auction ID 62): TRACT NO 8793 LOT 77 BLK 4 ... ASSESSED TO SHEA ESTATES 0 DEVELOPMENT CORP LOCATION CITY-AGOURA HILL PROPERTY ADDRESS: VACANT LOT. See page 172.

32. AIN 2061021021 (auction ID 63): TRACT NO 8793 LOT 78 BLK 4 ... ASSESSED TO SHEA ESTATES 0 DEVELOPMENT CORP LOCATION CITY-AGOURA HILL PROPERTY ADDRESS: VACANT LOT. See page 177.

33. AIN 2061021022 (auction ID 64): TRACT NO 8793 LOT 79 BLK 4 ... ASSESSED TO SHEA ESTATES 0 DEVELOPMENT CORP LOCATION CITY-AGOURA HILL PROPERTY ADDRESS: VACANT LOT. See page 182.

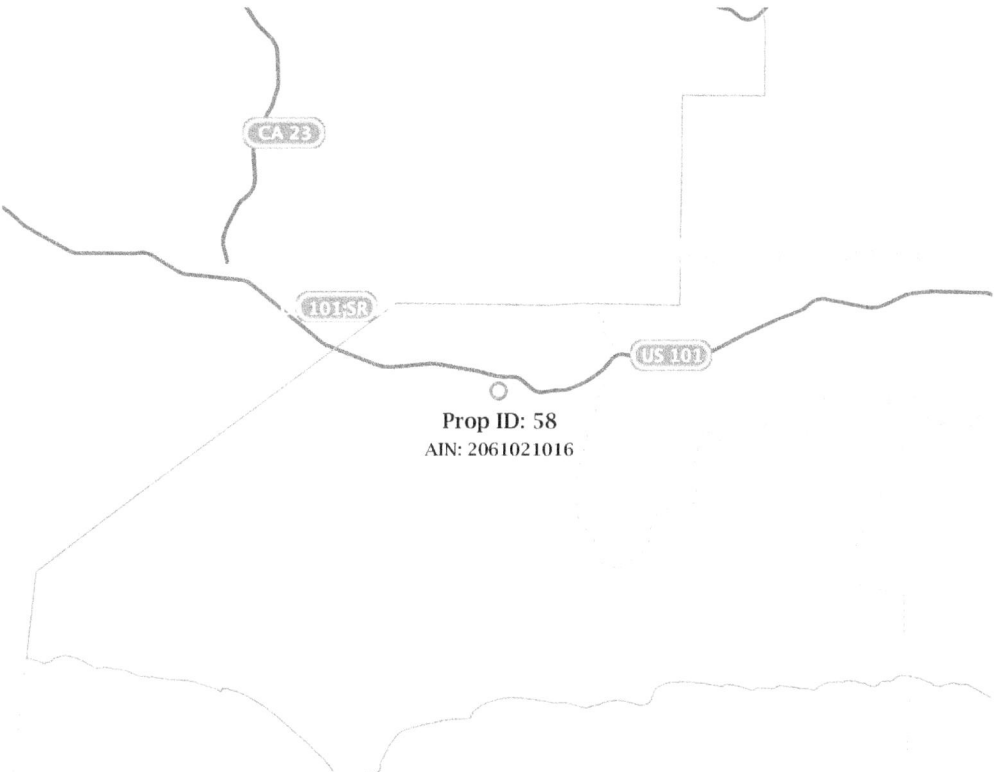

Figure 2.91: Property 64, AIN 2061021016, overview map

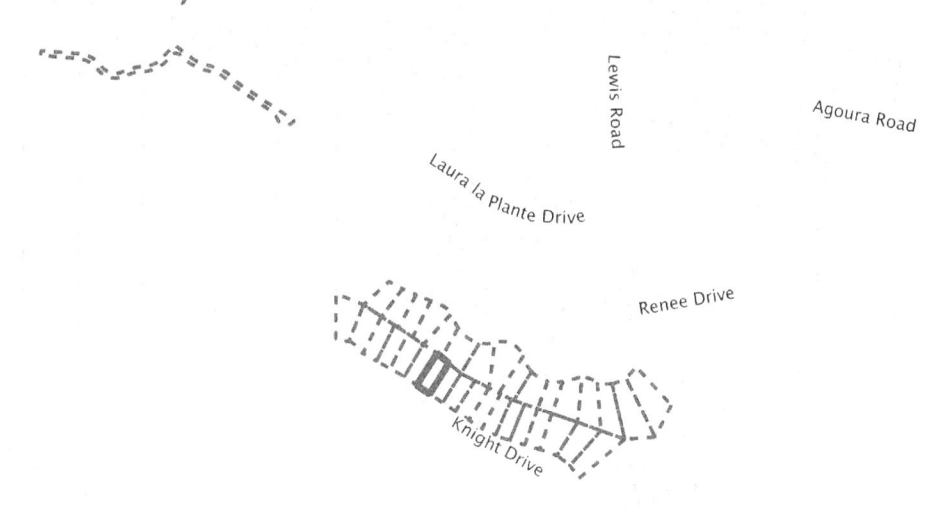

Figure 2.92: Property 64, AIN 2061021016, neighborhood view

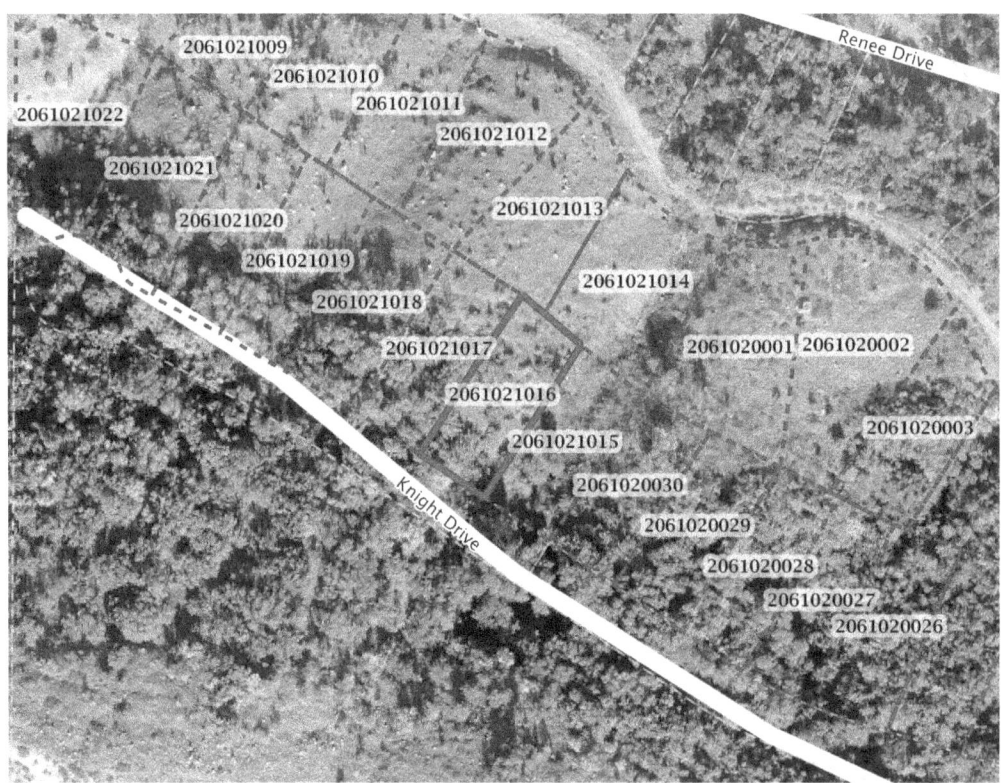

Figure 2.93: Property 64, AIN 2061021016, detailed view

2.32 Auction ID 59

The Los Angeles County Auction Book describes the property as follows.

```
TRACT NO 8793 LOT 74 BLK 4 ASSESSED TO SHEA ESTATES 0 DEVELOPMENT
CORP LOCATION CITY-AGOURA HILL PROPERTY ADDRESS: VACANT LOT
```

The property is located in the general vicinity of Figure 2.94. It is identified by Assessor's Identification Number (AIN) 2061021017. The starting bid is \$3,334. Comparable improved properties in this area is about \$294/sqft. Comparable unimproved lots in this area is about \$49/sqft. This parcel is approximately 6005 sqft. Note, however, that the parcel may be larger than the property under consideration. In case of condominiums, for example, the parcel may encompass other units of the development - those unrelated to the property to be auctioned.

The property is in a parcel zoned Restricted Open Space in Agoura Hills, for 0 to 0 dwelling units.

Figures 2.95 and 2.96 show street map and corresponding detailed aerial view, respectively. In both cases, the map is centered on the property with the containing parcel marked in heavy blue. If surrounding nearby properties are also part of this auction, the street and aerial maps highlights these in heavy, dashed blue outline.

This assessed entity may have other properties that are also in this auction:

1. AIN 2061020001 (auction ID 31): TRACT NO 8793 LOT 16 BLK 4 . . . ASSESSED TO SHEA ESTATES 0 DEVELOPMENT CORP LOCATION CITY-AGOURA HILL PROPERTY ADDRESS: VACANT LOT. See page 17.

2. AIN 2061020002 (auction ID 32): TRACT NO 8793 LOT 17 BLK 4 . . . ASSESSED TO SHEA ESTATES 0 DEVELOPMENT CORP LOCATION CITY-AGOURA HILL PROPERTY ADDRESS: VACANT LOT. See page 22.

3. AIN 2061020003 (auction ID 33): TRACT NO 8793 LOT 18 BLK 4 . . . ASSESSED TO SHEA ESTATES 0 DEVELOPMENT CORP LOCATION CITY-AGOURA HILL PROPERTY ADDRESS: VACANT LOT. See page 27.

4. AIN 2061020004 (auction ID 34): TRACT NO 8793 LOT 19 BLK 4 . . . ASSESSED TO SHEA ESTATES 0 DEVELOPMENT CORP LOCATION CITY-AGOURA HILL PROPERTY ADDRESS: VACANT LOT. See page 32.

5. AIN 2061020005 (auction ID 35): TRACT NO 8793 LOT 20 BLK 4 . . . ASSESSED TO SHEA ESTATES 0 DEVELOPMENT CORP LOCATION CITY-AGOURA HILL PROPERTY ADDRESS: VACANT LOT. See page 37.

6. AIN 2061020006 (auction ID 36): TRACT NO 8793 LOT 21 BLK 4 . . . ASSESSED TO SHEA ESTATES 0 DEVELOPMENT CORP LOCATION CITY-AGOURA HILL PROPERTY ADDRESS: VACANT LOT. See page 42.

7. AIN 2061020007 (auction ID 37): TRACT NO 8793 LOT 22 BLK 4 . . . ASSESSED TO SHEA ESTATES 0 DEVELOPMENT CORP LOCATION CITY-AGOURA HILL PROPERTY ADDRESS: VACANT LOT. See page 47.

8. AIN 2061020008 (auction ID 38): TRACT NO 8793 LOT 23 BLK 4 . . . ASSESSED TO SHEA ESTATES 0 DEVELOPMENT CORP LOCATION CITY-AGOURA HILL PROPERTY ADDRESS: VACANT LOT. See page 52.

9. AIN 2061020009 (auction ID 39): TRACT NO 8793 LOT 24 BLK 4 . . . ASSESSED TO SHEA ESTATES 0 DEVELOPMENT CORP LOCATION CITY-AGOURA HILL PROPERTY ADDRESS: VACANT LOT. See page 57.

10. AIN 2061020010 (auction ID 40): TRACT NO 8793 LOT 25 BLK 4 . . . ASSESSED TO SHEA ESTATES 0 DEVELOPMENT CORP LOCATION CITY-AGOURA HILL PROPERTY ADDRESS: VACANT LOT. See page 62.

11. AIN 2061020021 (auction ID 41): TRACT NO 8793 LOT 62 BLK 4 . . . ASSESSED TO SHEA ESTATES 0 DEVELOPMENT CORP LOCATION CITY-AGOURA HILL PROPERTY ADDRESS: VACANT LOT. See page 67.

12. AIN 2061020022 (auction ID 42): TRACT NO 8793 LOT 63 BLK 4 . . . ASSESSED TO SHEA ESTATES 0 DEVELOPMENT CORP LOCATION CITY-AGOURA HILL PROPERTY ADDRESS: VACANT LOT. See page 72.

13. AIN 2061020023 (auction ID 43): TRACT NO 8793 LOT 64 BLK 4 . . . ASSESSED TO SHEA ESTATES 0 DEVELOPMENT CORP LOCATION CITY-AGOURA HILL PROPERTY ADDRESS: VACANT LOT. See page 77.

14. AIN 2061020024 (auction ID 44): TRACT NO 8793 LOT 65 BLK 4 . . . ASSESSED TO SHEA ESTATES 0 DEVELOPMENT CORP LOCATION CITY-AGOURA HILL PROPERTY ADDRESS: VACANT LOT. See page 82.

15. AIN 2061020025 (auction ID 45): TRACT NO 8793 LOT 66 BLK 4 . . . ASSESSED TO SHEA ESTATES 0 DEVELOPMENT CORP LOCATION CITY-AGOURA HILL PROPERTY ADDRESS: VACANT LOT. See page 87.

16. AIN 2061020026 (auction ID 46): TRACT NO 8793 LOT 67 BLK 4 . . . ASSESSED TO SHEA ESTATES 0 DEVELOPMENT CORP LOCATION CITY-AGOURA HILL PROPERTY ADDRESS: VACANT LOT. See page 92.

17. AIN 2061020027 (auction ID 47): TRACT NO 8793 LOT 68 BLK 4 . . . ASSESSED TO SHEA ESTATES 0 DEVELOPMENT CORP LOCATION CITY-AGOURA HILL PROPERTY ADDRESS: VACANT LOT. See page 97.

18. AIN 2061020028 (auction ID 48): TRACT NO 8793 LOT 69 BLK 4 . . . ASSESSED TO SHEA ESTATES 0 DEVELOPMENT CORP LOCATION CITY-AGOURA HILL - PROPERTY ADDRESS: VACANT LOT. See page 102.

19. AIN 2061020029 (auction ID 49): TRACT NO 8793 LOT 70 BLK 4 . . . ASSESSED TO SHEA ESTATES 0 DEVELOPMENT CORP LOCATION CITY-AGOURA HILL PROPERTY ADDRESS: VACANT LOT. See page 107.

20. AIN 2061020030 (auction ID 50): TRACT NO 8793 LOT 71 BLK 4 . . . ASSESSED TO SHEA ESTATES 0 DEVELOPMENT CORP LOCATION CITY-AGOURA HILL PROPERTY ADDRESS: VACANT LOT. See page 112.

21. AIN 2061021009 (auction ID 51): TRACT NO 8793 LOT 10 BLK 4 . . . ASSESSED TO SHEA ESTATES 0 DEVELOPMENT CORP LOCATION CITY-AGOURA HILL PROPERTY ADDRESS: VACANT LOT. See page 117.

22. AIN 2061021010 (auction ID 52): TRACT NO 8793 LOT 11 BLK 4 . . . ASSESSED TO SHEA ESTATES 0 DEVELOPMENT CORP LOCATION CITY-AGOURA HILL PROPERTY ADDRESS: VACANT LOT. See page 122.

23. AIN 2061021011 (auction ID 53): TRACT NO 8793 LOT 12 BLK 4 . . . ASSESSED TO SHEA ESTATES 0 DEVELOPMENT CORP LOCATION CITY-AGOURA HILL PROPERTY ADDRESS: VACANT LOT. See page 127.

24. AIN 2061021012 (auction ID 54): TRACT NO 8793 LOT 13 BLK 4 . . . ASSESSED TO SHEA ESTATES 0 DEVELOPMENT CORP LOCATION CITY-AGOURA HILL PROPERTY ADDRESS: VACANT LOT. See page 132.

25. AIN 2061021013 (auction ID 55): TRACT NO 8793 LOT 14 BLK 4 ... ASSESSED TO SHEA ESTATES 0 DEVELOPMENT CORP LOCATION CITY-AGOURA HILL PROPERTY ADDRESS: VACANT LOT. See page 137.

26. AIN 2061021014 (auction ID 56): TRACT NO 8793 LOT 15 BLK 4 ... ASSESSED TO SHEA ESTATES 0 DEVELOPMENT CORP LOCATION CITY-AGOURA HILL PROPERTY ADDRESS: VACANT LOT. See page 142.

27. AIN 2061021015 (auction ID 57): TRACT NO 8793 LOT 72 BLK 4 ... ASSESSED TO SHEA ESTATES 0 DEVELOPMENT CORP LOCATION CITY-AGOURA HILL PROPERTY ADDRESS: VACANT LOT. See page 147.

28. AIN 2061021016 (auction ID 58): TRACT NO 8793 LOT 73 BLK 4 ... ASSESSED TO SHEA ESTATES 0 DEVELOPMENT CORP LOCATION CITY-AGOURA HILL PROPERTY ADDRESS: VACANT LOT. See page 152.

29. AIN 2061021018 (auction ID 60): TRACT NO 8793 LOT 75 BLK 4 ... ASSESSED TO SHEA ESTATES 0 DEVELOPMENT CORP LOCATION CITY-AGOURA HILL PROPERTY ADDRESS: VACANT LOT. See page 162.

30. AIN 2061021019 (auction ID 61): TRACT NO 8793 LOT 76 BLK 4 ... ASSESSED TO SHEA ESTATES 0 DEVELOPMENT CORP LOCATION CITY-AGOURA HILL PROPERTY ADDRESS: VACANT LOT. See page 167.

31. AIN 2061021020 (auction ID 62): TRACT NO 8793 LOT 77 BLK 4 ... ASSESSED TO SHEA ESTATES 0 DEVELOPMENT CORP LOCATION CITY-AGOURA HILL PROPERTY ADDRESS: VACANT LOT. See page 172.

32. AIN 2061021021 (auction ID 63): TRACT NO 8793 LOT 78 BLK 4 ... ASSESSED TO SHEA ESTATES 0 DEVELOPMENT CORP LOCATION CITY-AGOURA HILL PROPERTY ADDRESS: VACANT LOT. See page 177.

33. AIN 2061021022 (auction ID 64): TRACT NO 8793 LOT 79 BLK 4 ... ASSESSED TO SHEA ESTATES 0 DEVELOPMENT CORP LOCATION CITY-AGOURA HILL PROPERTY ADDRESS: VACANT LOT. See page 182.

Figure 2.94: Property 64, AIN 2061021017, overview map

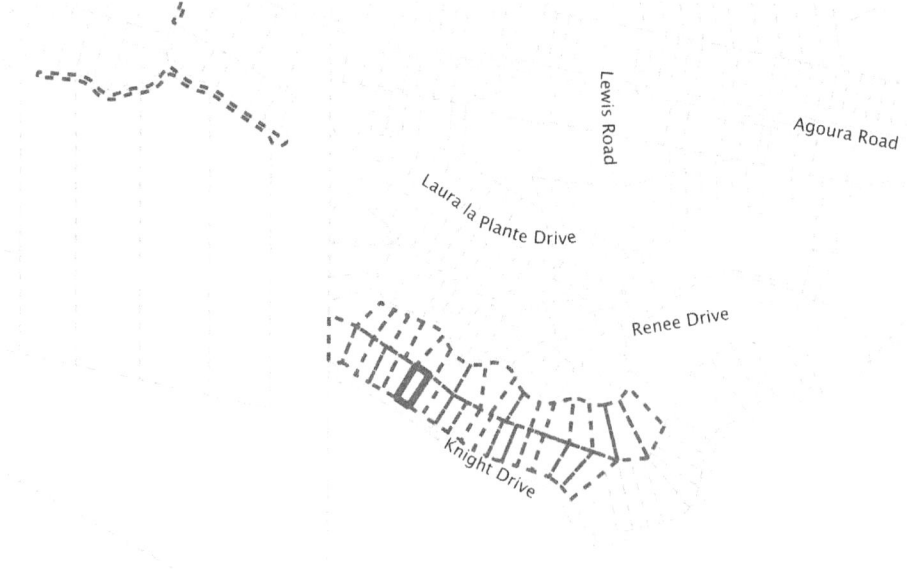

Figure 2.95: Property 64, AIN 2061021017, neighborhood view

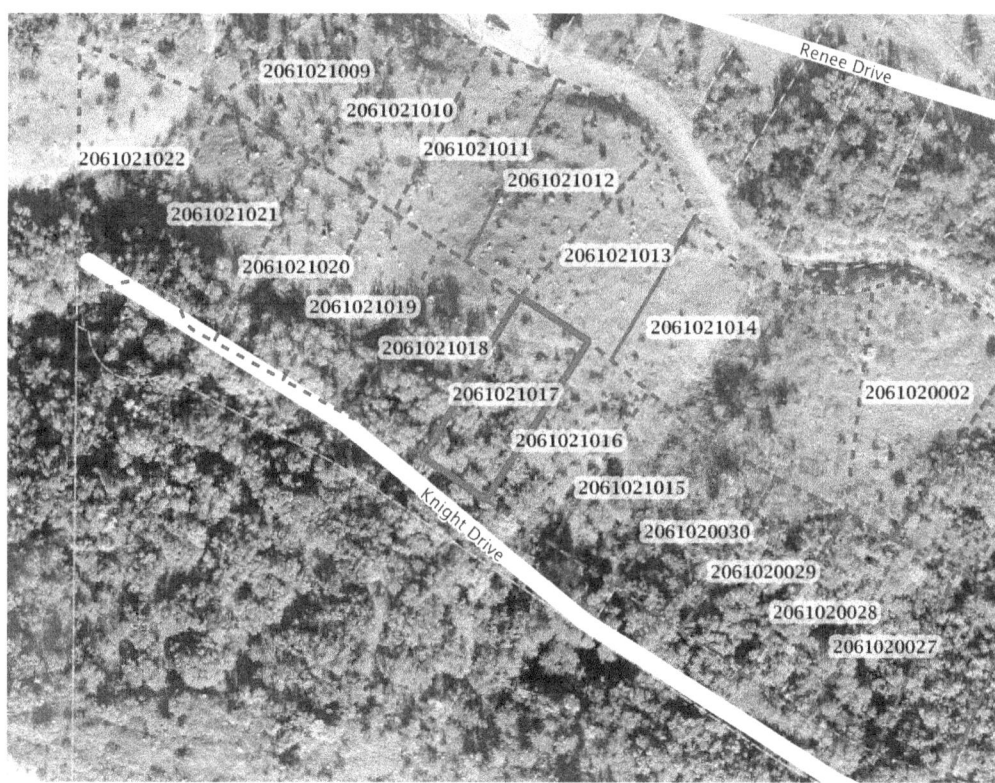

Figure 2.96: Property 64, AIN 2061021017, detailed view

2.33   Auction ID 60

The Los Angeles County Auction Book describes the property as follows.

```
TRACT NO 8793 LOT 75 BLK 4 ASSESSED TO SHEA ESTATES 0 DEVELOPMENT
CORP LOCATION CITY-AGOURA HILL PROPERTY ADDRESS: VACANT LOT
```

The property is located in the general vicinity of Figure 2.97. It is identified by Assessor's Identification Number (AIN) 2061021018. The starting bid is $7,151. Comparable improved properties in this area is about $294/sqft. Comparable unimproved lots in this area is about $49/sqft. This parcel is approximately 6792 sqft. Note, however, that the parcel may be larger than the property under consideration. In case of condominiums, for example, the parcel may encompass other units of the development - those unrelated to the property to be auctioned.

The property is in a parcel zoned Restricted Open Space in Agoura Hills, for 0 to 0 dwelling units.

Figures 2.98 and 2.99 show street map and corresponding detailed aerial view, respectively. In both cases, the map is centered on the property with the containing parcel marked in heavy blue. If surrounding nearby properties are also part of this auction, the street and aerial maps highlights these in heavy, dashed blue outline.

This assessed entity may have other properties that are also in this auction:

1. AIN 2061020001 (auction ID 31): TRACT NO 8793 LOT 16 BLK 4 ... ASSESSED TO SHEA ESTATES 0 DEVELOPMENT CORP LOCATION CITY-AGOURA HILL PROPERTY ADDRESS: VACANT LOT. See page 17.

2. AIN 2061020002 (auction ID 32): TRACT NO 8793 LOT 17 BLK 4 ... ASSESSED TO SHEA ESTATES 0 DEVELOPMENT CORP LOCATION CITY-AGOURA HILL PROPERTY ADDRESS: VACANT LOT. See page 22.

3. AIN 2061020003 (auction ID 33): TRACT NO 8793 LOT 18 BLK 4 ... ASSESSED TO SHEA ESTATES 0 DEVELOPMENT CORP LOCATION CITY-AGOURA HILL PROPERTY ADDRESS: VACANT LOT. See page 27.

4. AIN 2061020004 (auction ID 34): TRACT NO 8793 LOT 19 BLK 4 ... ASSESSED TO SHEA ESTATES 0 DEVELOPMENT CORP LOCATION CITY-AGOURA HILL PROPERTY ADDRESS: VACANT LOT. See page 32.

5. AIN 2061020005 (auction ID 35): TRACT NO 8793 LOT 20 BLK 4 ... ASSESSED TO SHEA ESTATES 0 DEVELOPMENT CORP LOCATION CITY-AGOURA HILL PROPERTY ADDRESS: VACANT LOT. See page 37.

6. AIN 2061020006 (auction ID 36): TRACT NO 8793 LOT 21 BLK 4 ... ASSESSED TO SHEA ESTATES 0 DEVELOPMENT CORP LOCATION CITY-AGOURA HILL PROPERTY ADDRESS: VACANT LOT. See page 42.

7. AIN 2061020007 (auction ID 37): TRACT NO 8793 LOT 22 BLK 4 ... ASSESSED TO SHEA ESTATES 0 DEVELOPMENT CORP LOCATION CITY-AGOURA HILL PROPERTY ADDRESS: VACANT LOT. See page 47.

8. AIN 2061020008 (auction ID 38): TRACT NO 8793 LOT 23 BLK 4 ... ASSESSED TO SHEA ESTATES 0 DEVELOPMENT CORP LOCATION CITY-AGOURA HILL PROPERTY ADDRESS: VACANT LOT. See page 52.

9. AIN 2061020009 (auction ID 39): TRACT NO 8793 LOT 24 BLK 4 ... ASSESSED TO SHEA ESTATES 0 DEVELOPMENT CORP LOCATION CITY-AGOURA HILL PROPERTY ADDRESS: VACANT LOT. See page 57.

10. AIN 2061020010 (auction ID 40): TRACT NO 8793 LOT 25 BLK 4 ... ASSESSED TO SHEA ESTATES 0 DEVELOPMENT CORP LOCATION CITY-AGOURA HILL PROPERTY ADDRESS: VACANT LOT. See page 62.

11. AIN 2061020021 (auction ID 41): TRACT NO 8793 LOT 62 BLK 4 ... ASSESSED TO SHEA ESTATES 0 DEVELOPMENT CORP LOCATION CITY-AGOURA HILL PROPERTY ADDRESS: VACANT LOT. See page 67.

12. AIN 2061020022 (auction ID 42): TRACT NO 8793 LOT 63 BLK 4 ... ASSESSED TO SHEA ESTATES 0 DEVELOPMENT CORP LOCATION CITY-AGOURA HILL PROPERTY ADDRESS: VACANT LOT. See page 72.

13. AIN 2061020023 (auction ID 43): TRACT NO 8793 LOT 64 BLK 4 ... ASSESSED TO SHEA ESTATES 0 DEVELOPMENT CORP LOCATION CITY-AGOURA HILL PROPERTY ADDRESS: VACANT LOT. See page 77.

14. AIN 2061020024 (auction ID 44): TRACT NO 8793 LOT 65 BLK 4 ... ASSESSED TO SHEA ESTATES 0 DEVELOPMENT CORP LOCATION CITY-AGOURA HILL PROPERTY ADDRESS: VACANT LOT. See page 82.

15. AIN 2061020025 (auction ID 45): TRACT NO 8793 LOT 66 BLK 4 ... ASSESSED TO SHEA ESTATES 0 DEVELOPMENT CORP LOCATION CITY-AGOURA HILL PROPERTY ADDRESS: VACANT LOT. See page 87.

16. AIN 2061020026 (auction ID 46): TRACT NO 8793 LOT 67 BLK 4 ... ASSESSED TO SHEA ESTATES 0 DEVELOPMENT CORP LOCATION CITY-AGOURA HILL PROPERTY ADDRESS: VACANT LOT. See page 92.

17. AIN 2061020027 (auction ID 47): TRACT NO 8793 LOT 68 BLK 4 ... ASSESSED TO SHEA ESTATES 0 DEVELOPMENT CORP LOCATION CITY-AGOURA HILL PROPERTY ADDRESS: VACANT LOT. See page 97.

18. AIN 2061020028 (auction ID 48): TRACT NO 8793 LOT 69 BLK 4 ... ASSESSED TO SHEA ESTATES 0 DEVELOPMENT CORP LOCATION CITY-AGOURA HILL - PROPERTY ADDRESS: VACANT LOT. See page 102.

19. AIN 2061020029 (auction ID 49): TRACT NO 8793 LOT 70 BLK 4 ... ASSESSED TO SHEA ESTATES 0 DEVELOPMENT CORP LOCATION CITY-AGOURA HILL PROPERTY ADDRESS: VACANT LOT. See page 107.

20. AIN 2061020030 (auction ID 50): TRACT NO 8793 LOT 71 BLK 4 ... ASSESSED TO SHEA ESTATES 0 DEVELOPMENT CORP LOCATION CITY-AGOURA HILL PROPERTY ADDRESS: VACANT LOT. See page 112.

21. AIN 2061021009 (auction ID 51): TRACT NO 8793 LOT 10 BLK 4 ... ASSESSED TO SHEA ESTATES 0 DEVELOPMENT CORP LOCATION CITY-AGOURA HILL PROPERTY ADDRESS: VACANT LOT. See page 117.

22. AIN 2061021010 (auction ID 52): TRACT NO 8793 LOT 11 BLK 4 ... ASSESSED TO SHEA ESTATES 0 DEVELOPMENT CORP LOCATION CITY-AGOURA HILL PROPERTY ADDRESS: VACANT LOT. See page 122.

23. AIN 2061021011 (auction ID 53): TRACT NO 8793 LOT 12 BLK 4 ... ASSESSED TO SHEA ESTATES 0 DEVELOPMENT CORP LOCATION CITY-AGOURA HILL PROPERTY ADDRESS: VACANT LOT. See page 127.

24. AIN 2061021012 (auction ID 54): TRACT NO 8793 LOT 13 BLK 4 ... ASSESSED TO SHEA ESTATES 0 DEVELOPMENT CORP LOCATION CITY-AGOURA HILL PROPERTY ADDRESS: VACANT LOT. See page 132.

25. AIN 2061021013 (auction ID 55): TRACT NO 8793 LOT 14 BLK 4 . . . ASSESSED TO SHEA ESTATES 0 DEVELOPMENT CORP LOCATION CITY-AGOURA HILL PROPERTY ADDRESS: VACANT LOT. See page 137.

26. AIN 2061021014 (auction ID 56): TRACT NO 8793 LOT 15 BLK 4 . . . ASSESSED TO SHEA ESTATES 0 DEVELOPMENT CORP LOCATION CITY-AGOURA HILL PROPERTY ADDRESS: VACANT LOT. See page 142.

27. AIN 2061021015 (auction ID 57): TRACT NO 8793 LOT 72 BLK 4 . . . ASSESSED TO SHEA ESTATES 0 DEVELOPMENT CORP LOCATION CITY-AGOURA HILL PROPERTY ADDRESS: VACANT LOT. See page 147.

28. AIN 2061021016 (auction ID 58): TRACT NO 8793 LOT 73 BLK 4 . . . ASSESSED TO SHEA ESTATES 0 DEVELOPMENT CORP LOCATION CITY-AGOURA HILL PROPERTY ADDRESS: VACANT LOT. See page 152.

29. AIN 2061021017 (auction ID 59): TRACT NO 8793 LOT 74 BLK 4 . . . ASSESSED TO SHEA ESTATES 0 DEVELOPMENT CORP LOCATION CITY-AGOURA HILL PROPERTY ADDRESS: VACANT LOT. See page 157.

30. AIN 2061021019 (auction ID 61): TRACT NO 8793 LOT 76 BLK 4 . . . ASSESSED TO SHEA ESTATES 0 DEVELOPMENT CORP LOCATION CITY-AGOURA HILL PROPERTY ADDRESS: VACANT LOT. See page 167.

31. AIN 2061021020 (auction ID 62): TRACT NO 8793 LOT 77 BLK 4 . . . ASSESSED TO SHEA ESTATES 0 DEVELOPMENT CORP LOCATION CITY-AGOURA HILL PROPERTY ADDRESS: VACANT LOT. See page 172.

32. AIN 2061021021 (auction ID 63): TRACT NO 8793 LOT 78 BLK 4 . . . ASSESSED TO SHEA ESTATES 0 DEVELOPMENT CORP LOCATION CITY-AGOURA HILL PROPERTY ADDRESS: VACANT LOT. See page 177.

33. AIN 2061021022 (auction ID 64): TRACT NO 8793 LOT 79 BLK 4 . . . ASSESSED TO SHEA ESTATES 0 DEVELOPMENT CORP LOCATION CITY-AGOURA HILL PROPERTY ADDRESS: VACANT LOT. See page 182.

Figure 2.97: Property 64, AIN 2061021018, overview map

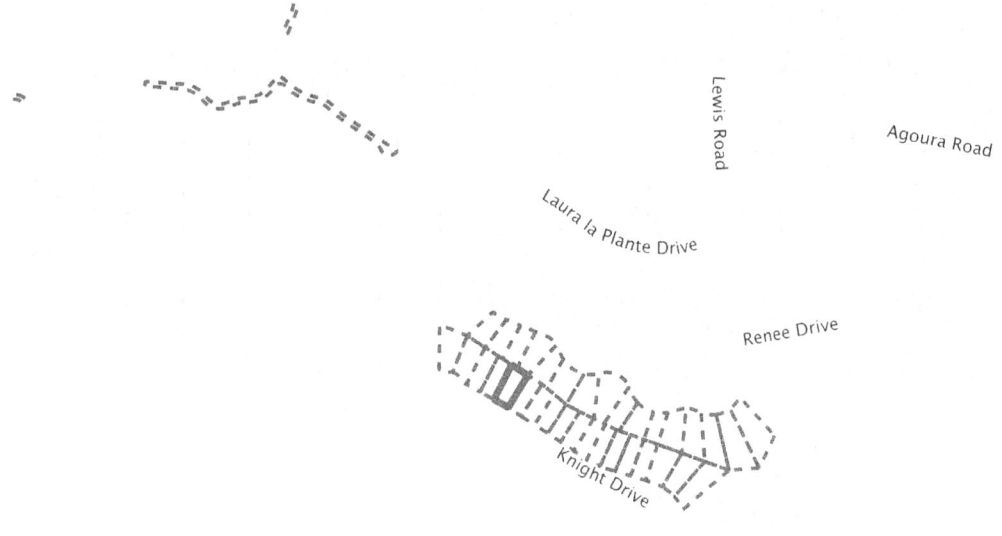

Figure 2.98: Property 64, AIN 2061021018, neighborhood view

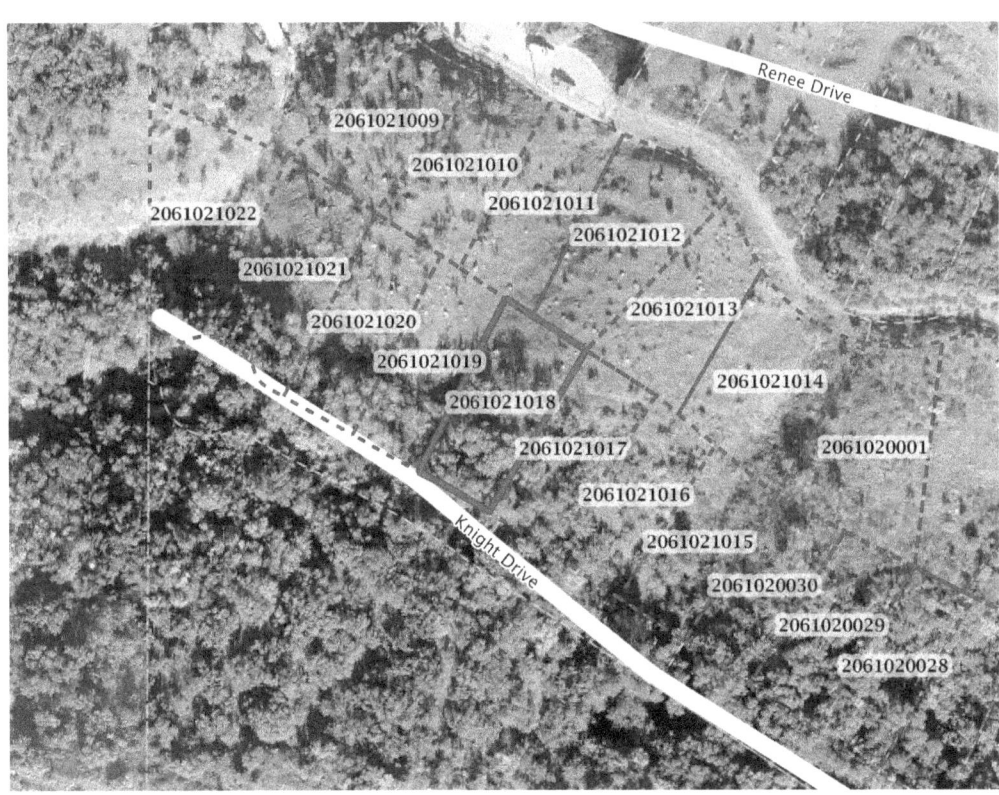

Figure 2.99: Property 64, AIN 2061021018, detailed view

2.34 Auction ID 61

The Los Angeles County Auction Book describes the property as follows.

```
TRACT NO 8793 LOT 76 BLK 4 ASSESSED TO SHEA ESTATES 0 DEVELOPMENT
CORP LOCATION CITY-AGOURA HILL PROPERTY ADDRESS: VACANT LOT
```

The property is located in the general vicinity of Figure 2.100. It is identified by Assessor's Identification Number (AIN) 2061021019. The starting bid is $7,093. Comparable improved properties in this area is about $294/sqft. Comparable unimproved lots in this area is about $49/sqft. This parcel is approximately 6191 sqft. Note, however, that the parcel may be larger than the property under consideration. In case of condominiums, for example, the parcel may encompass other units of the development - those unrelated to the property to be auctioned.

The property is in a parcel zoned Restricted Open Space in Agoura Hills, for 0 to 0 dwelling units.

Figures 2.101 and 2.102 show street map and corresponding detailed aerial view, respectively. In both cases, the map is centered on the property with the containing parcel marked in heavy blue. If surrounding nearby properties are also part of this auction, the street and aerial maps highlights these in heavy, dashed blue outline.

This assessed entity may have other properties that are also in this auction:

1. AIN 2061020001 (auction ID 31): TRACT NO 8793 LOT 16 BLK 4 . . . ASSESSED TO SHEA ESTATES 0 DEVELOPMENT CORP LOCATION CITY-AGOURA HILL PROPERTY ADDRESS: VACANT LOT. See page 17.

2. AIN 2061020002 (auction ID 32): TRACT NO 8793 LOT 17 BLK 4 . . . ASSESSED TO SHEA ESTATES 0 DEVELOPMENT CORP LOCATION CITY-AGOURA HILL PROPERTY ADDRESS: VACANT LOT. See page 22.

3. AIN 2061020003 (auction ID 33): TRACT NO 8793 LOT 18 BLK 4 . . . ASSESSED TO SHEA ESTATES 0 DEVELOPMENT CORP LOCATION CITY-AGOURA HILL PROPERTY ADDRESS: VACANT LOT. See page 27.

4. AIN 2061020004 (auction ID 34): TRACT NO 8793 LOT 19 BLK 4 . . . ASSESSED TO SHEA ESTATES 0 DEVELOPMENT CORP LOCATION CITY-AGOURA HILL PROPERTY ADDRESS: VACANT LOT. See page 32.

5. AIN 2061020005 (auction ID 35): TRACT NO 8793 LOT 20 BLK 4 . . . ASSESSED TO SHEA ESTATES 0 DEVELOPMENT CORP LOCATION CITY-AGOURA HILL PROPERTY ADDRESS: VACANT LOT. See page 37.

6. AIN 2061020006 (auction ID 36): TRACT NO 8793 LOT 21 BLK 4 . . . ASSESSED TO SHEA ESTATES 0 DEVELOPMENT CORP LOCATION CITY-AGOURA HILL PROPERTY ADDRESS: VACANT LOT. See page 42.

7. AIN 2061020007 (auction ID 37): TRACT NO 8793 LOT 22 BLK 4 . . . ASSESSED TO SHEA ESTATES 0 DEVELOPMENT CORP LOCATION CITY-AGOURA HILL PROPERTY ADDRESS: VACANT LOT. See page 47.

8. AIN 2061020008 (auction ID 38): TRACT NO 8793 LOT 23 BLK 4 . . . ASSESSED TO SHEA ESTATES 0 DEVELOPMENT CORP LOCATION CITY-AGOURA HILL PROPERTY ADDRESS: VACANT LOT. See page 52.

9. AIN 2061020009 (auction ID 39): TRACT NO 8793 LOT 24 BLK 4 . . . ASSESSED TO SHEA ESTATES 0 DEVELOPMENT CORP LOCATION CITY-AGOURA HILL PROPERTY ADDRESS: VACANT LOT. See page 57.

10. AIN 2061020010 (auction ID 40): TRACT NO 8793 LOT 25 BLK 4 ... ASSESSED TO SHEA ESTATES 0 DEVELOPMENT CORP LOCATION CITY-AGOURA HILL PROPERTY ADDRESS: VACANT LOT. See page 62.

11. AIN 2061020021 (auction ID 41): TRACT NO 8793 LOT 62 BLK 4 ... ASSESSED TO SHEA ESTATES 0 DEVELOPMENT CORP LOCATION CITY-AGOURA HILL PROPERTY ADDRESS: VACANT LOT. See page 67.

12. AIN 2061020022 (auction ID 42): TRACT NO 8793 LOT 63 BLK 4 ... ASSESSED TO SHEA ESTATES 0 DEVELOPMENT CORP LOCATION CITY-AGOURA HILL PROPERTY ADDRESS: VACANT LOT. See page 72.

13. AIN 2061020023 (auction ID 43): TRACT NO 8793 LOT 64 BLK 4 ... ASSESSED TO SHEA ESTATES 0 DEVELOPMENT CORP LOCATION CITY-AGOURA HILL PROPERTY ADDRESS: VACANT LOT. See page 77.

14. AIN 2061020024 (auction ID 44): TRACT NO 8793 LOT 65 BLK 4 ... ASSESSED TO SHEA ESTATES 0 DEVELOPMENT CORP LOCATION CITY-AGOURA HILL PROPERTY ADDRESS: VACANT LOT. See page 82.

15. AIN 2061020025 (auction ID 45): TRACT NO 8793 LOT 66 BLK 4 ... ASSESSED TO SHEA ESTATES 0 DEVELOPMENT CORP LOCATION CITY-AGOURA HILL PROPERTY ADDRESS: VACANT LOT. See page 87.

16. AIN 2061020026 (auction ID 46): TRACT NO 8793 LOT 67 BLK 4 ... ASSESSED TO SHEA ESTATES 0 DEVELOPMENT CORP LOCATION CITY-AGOURA HILL PROPERTY ADDRESS: VACANT LOT. See page 92.

17. AIN 2061020027 (auction ID 47): TRACT NO 8793 LOT 68 BLK 4 ... ASSESSED TO SHEA ESTATES 0 DEVELOPMENT CORP LOCATION CITY-AGOURA HILL PROPERTY ADDRESS: VACANT LOT. See page 97.

18. AIN 2061020028 (auction ID 48): TRACT NO 8793 LOT 69 BLK 4 ... ASSESSED TO SHEA ESTATES 0 DEVELOPMENT CORP LOCATION CITY-AGOURA HILL - PROPERTY ADDRESS: VACANT LOT. See page 102.

19. AIN 2061020029 (auction ID 49): TRACT NO 8793 LOT 70 BLK 4 ... ASSESSED TO SHEA ESTATES 0 DEVELOPMENT CORP LOCATION CITY-AGOURA HILL PROPERTY ADDRESS: VACANT LOT. See page 107.

20. AIN 2061020030 (auction ID 50): TRACT NO 8793 LOT 71 BLK 4 ... ASSESSED TO SHEA ESTATES 0 DEVELOPMENT CORP LOCATION CITY-AGOURA HILL PROPERTY ADDRESS: VACANT LOT. See page 112.

21. AIN 2061021009 (auction ID 51): TRACT NO 8793 LOT 10 BLK 4 ... ASSESSED TO SHEA ESTATES 0 DEVELOPMENT CORP LOCATION CITY-AGOURA HILL PROPERTY ADDRESS: VACANT LOT. See page 117.

22. AIN 2061021010 (auction ID 52): TRACT NO 8793 LOT 11 BLK 4 ... ASSESSED TO SHEA ESTATES 0 DEVELOPMENT CORP LOCATION CITY-AGOURA HILL PROPERTY ADDRESS: VACANT LOT. See page 122.

23. AIN 2061021011 (auction ID 53): TRACT NO 8793 LOT 12 BLK 4 ... ASSESSED TO SHEA ESTATES 0 DEVELOPMENT CORP LOCATION CITY-AGOURA HILL PROPERTY ADDRESS: VACANT LOT. See page 127.

24. AIN 2061021012 (auction ID 54): TRACT NO 8793 LOT 13 BLK 4 ... ASSESSED TO SHEA ESTATES 0 DEVELOPMENT CORP LOCATION CITY-AGOURA HILL PROPERTY ADDRESS: VACANT LOT. See page 132.

25. AIN 2061021013 (auction ID 55): TRACT NO 8793 LOT 14 BLK 4 . . . ASSESSED TO SHEA ESTATES 0 DEVELOPMENT CORP LOCATION CITY-AGOURA HILL PROPERTY ADDRESS: VACANT LOT. See page 137.

26. AIN 2061021014 (auction ID 56): TRACT NO 8793 LOT 15 BLK 4 . . . ASSESSED TO SHEA ESTATES 0 DEVELOPMENT CORP LOCATION CITY-AGOURA HILL PROPERTY ADDRESS: VACANT LOT. See page 142.

27. AIN 2061021015 (auction ID 57): TRACT NO 8793 LOT 72 BLK 4 . . . ASSESSED TO SHEA ESTATES 0 DEVELOPMENT CORP LOCATION CITY-AGOURA HILL PROPERTY ADDRESS: VACANT LOT. See page 147.

28. AIN 2061021016 (auction ID 58): TRACT NO 8793 LOT 73 BLK 4 . . . ASSESSED TO SHEA ESTATES 0 DEVELOPMENT CORP LOCATION CITY-AGOURA HILL PROPERTY ADDRESS: VACANT LOT. See page 152.

29. AIN 2061021017 (auction ID 59): TRACT NO 8793 LOT 74 BLK 4 . . . ASSESSED TO SHEA ESTATES 0 DEVELOPMENT CORP LOCATION CITY-AGOURA HILL PROPERTY ADDRESS: VACANT LOT. See page 157.

30. AIN 2061021018 (auction ID 60): TRACT NO 8793 LOT 75 BLK 4 . . . ASSESSED TO SHEA ESTATES 0 DEVELOPMENT CORP LOCATION CITY-AGOURA HILL PROPERTY ADDRESS: VACANT LOT. See page 162.

31. AIN 2061021020 (auction ID 62): TRACT NO 8793 LOT 77 BLK 4 . . . ASSESSED TO SHEA ESTATES 0 DEVELOPMENT CORP LOCATION CITY-AGOURA HILL PROPERTY ADDRESS: VACANT LOT. See page 172.

32. AIN 2061021021 (auction ID 63): TRACT NO 8793 LOT 78 BLK 4 . . . ASSESSED TO SHEA ESTATES 0 DEVELOPMENT CORP LOCATION CITY-AGOURA HILL PROPERTY ADDRESS: VACANT LOT. See page 177.

33. AIN 2061021022 (auction ID 64): TRACT NO 8793 LOT 79 BLK 4 . . . ASSESSED TO SHEA ESTATES 0 DEVELOPMENT CORP LOCATION CITY-AGOURA HILL PROPERTY ADDRESS: VACANT LOT. See page 182.

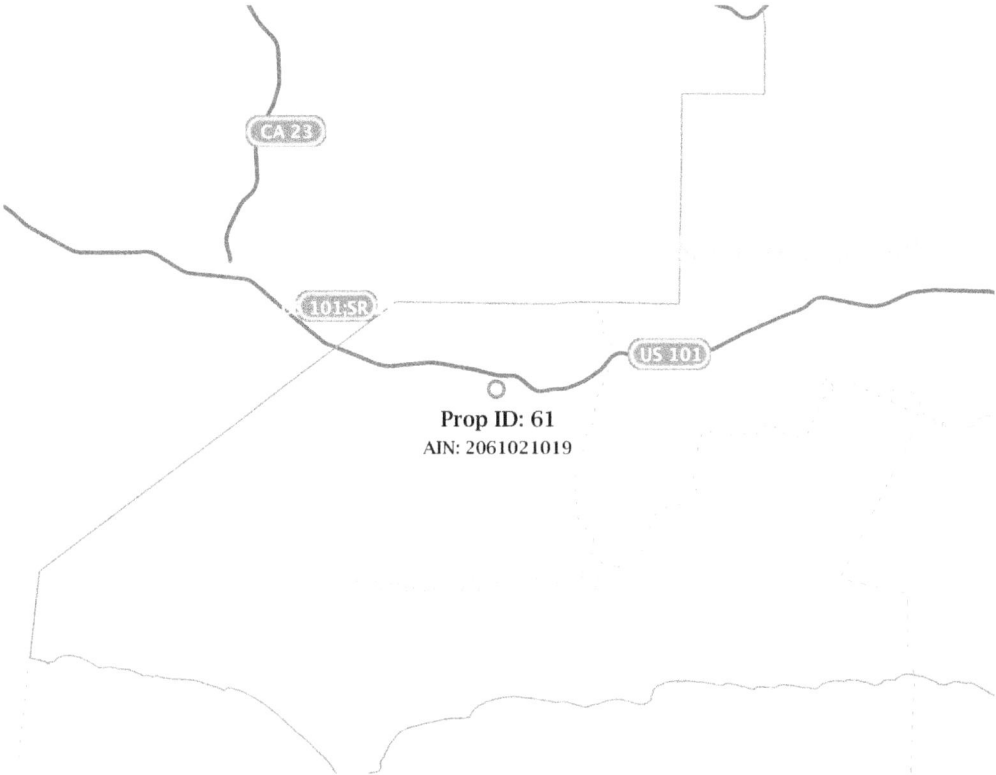

Figure 2.100: Property 64, AIN 2061021019, overview map

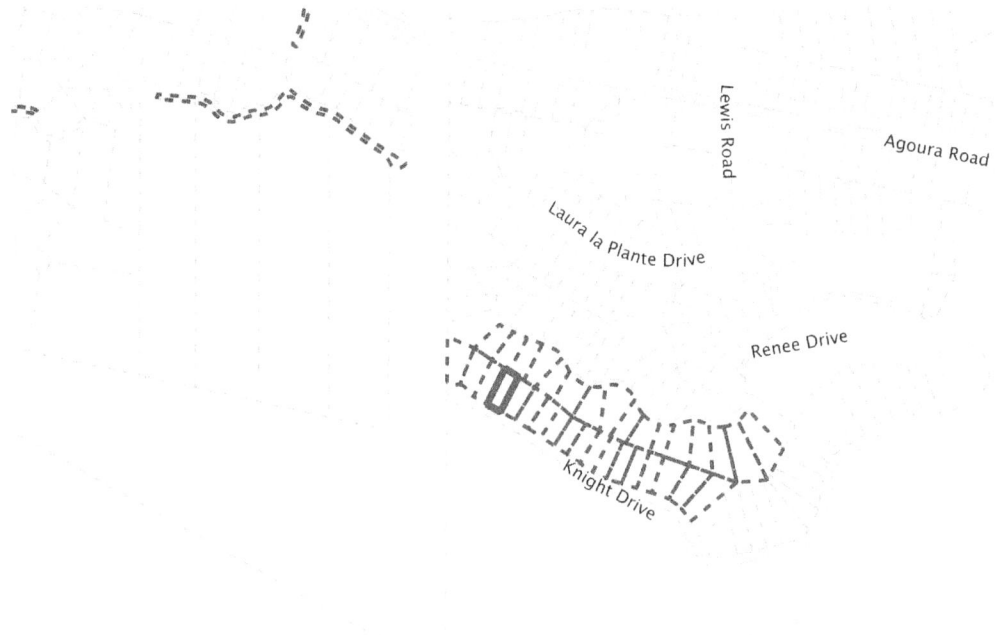

Figure 2.101: Property 64, AIN 2061021019, neighborhood view

Figure 2.102: Property 64, AIN 2061021019, detailed view

2.35   Auction ID 62

The Los Angeles County Auction Book describes the property as follows.

```
TRACT NO 8793 LOT 77 BLK 4 ASSESSED TO SHEA ESTATES 0 DEVELOPMENT
CORP LOCATION CITY-AGOURA HILL PROPERTY ADDRESS: VACANT LOT
```

The property is located in the general vicinity of Figure 2.103. It is identified by Assessor's Identification Number (AIN) 2061021020. The starting bid is \$6,038. Comparable improved properties in this area is about \$294/sqft. Comparable unimproved lots in this area is about \$49/sqft. This parcel is approximately 6385 sqft. Note, however, that the parcel may be larger than the property under consideration. In case of condominiums, for example, the parcel may encompass other units of the development - those unrelated to the property to be auctioned.

The property is in a parcel zoned Restricted Open Space in Agoura Hills, for 0 to 0 dwelling units.

Figures 2.104 and 2.105 show street map and corresponding detailed aerial view, respectively. In both cases, the map is centered on the property with the containing parcel marked in heavy blue. If surrounding nearby properties are also part of this auction, the street and aerial maps highlights these in heavy, dashed blue outline.

This assessed entity may have other properties that are also in this auction:

1. AIN 2061020001 (auction ID 31): TRACT NO 8793 LOT 16 BLK 4 . . . ASSESSED TO SHEA ESTATES 0 DEVELOPMENT CORP LOCATION CITY-AGOURA HILL PROPERTY ADDRESS: VACANT LOT. See page 17.

2. AIN 2061020002 (auction ID 32): TRACT NO 8793 LOT 17 BLK 4 . . . ASSESSED TO SHEA ESTATES 0 DEVELOPMENT CORP LOCATION CITY-AGOURA HILL PROPERTY ADDRESS: VACANT LOT. See page 22.

3. AIN 2061020003 (auction ID 33): TRACT NO 8793 LOT 18 BLK 4 . . . ASSESSED TO SHEA ESTATES 0 DEVELOPMENT CORP LOCATION CITY-AGOURA HILL PROPERTY ADDRESS: VACANT LOT. See page 27.

4. AIN 2061020004 (auction ID 34): TRACT NO 8793 LOT 19 BLK 4 . . . ASSESSED TO SHEA ESTATES 0 DEVELOPMENT CORP LOCATION CITY-AGOURA HILL PROPERTY ADDRESS: VACANT LOT. See page 32.

5. AIN 2061020005 (auction ID 35): TRACT NO 8793 LOT 20 BLK 4 . . . ASSESSED TO SHEA ESTATES 0 DEVELOPMENT CORP LOCATION CITY-AGOURA HILL PROPERTY ADDRESS: VACANT LOT. See page 37.

6. AIN 2061020006 (auction ID 36): TRACT NO 8793 LOT 21 BLK 4 . . . ASSESSED TO SHEA ESTATES 0 DEVELOPMENT CORP LOCATION CITY-AGOURA HILL PROPERTY ADDRESS: VACANT LOT. See page 42.

7. AIN 2061020007 (auction ID 37): TRACT NO 8793 LOT 22 BLK 4 . . . ASSESSED TO SHEA ESTATES 0 DEVELOPMENT CORP LOCATION CITY-AGOURA HILL PROPERTY ADDRESS: VACANT LOT. See page 47.

8. AIN 2061020008 (auction ID 38): TRACT NO 8793 LOT 23 BLK 4 . . . ASSESSED TO SHEA ESTATES 0 DEVELOPMENT CORP LOCATION CITY-AGOURA HILL PROPERTY ADDRESS: VACANT LOT. See page 52.

9. AIN 2061020009 (auction ID 39): TRACT NO 8793 LOT 24 BLK 4 . . . ASSESSED TO SHEA ESTATES 0 DEVELOPMENT CORP LOCATION CITY-AGOURA HILL PROPERTY ADDRESS: VACANT LOT. See page 57.

10. AIN 2061020010 (auction ID 40): TRACT NO 8793 LOT 25 BLK 4 . . . ASSESSED TO SHEA ESTATES 0 DEVELOPMENT CORP LOCATION CITY-AGOURA HILL PROPERTY ADDRESS: VACANT LOT. See page 62.

11. AIN 2061020021 (auction ID 41): TRACT NO 8793 LOT 62 BLK 4 . . . ASSESSED TO SHEA ESTATES 0 DEVELOPMENT CORP LOCATION CITY-AGOURA HILL PROPERTY ADDRESS: VACANT LOT. See page 67.

12. AIN 2061020022 (auction ID 42): TRACT NO 8793 LOT 63 BLK 4 . . . ASSESSED TO SHEA ESTATES 0 DEVELOPMENT CORP LOCATION CITY-AGOURA HILL PROPERTY ADDRESS: VACANT LOT. See page 72.

13. AIN 2061020023 (auction ID 43): TRACT NO 8793 LOT 64 BLK 4 . . . ASSESSED TO SHEA ESTATES 0 DEVELOPMENT CORP LOCATION CITY-AGOURA HILL PROPERTY ADDRESS: VACANT LOT. See page 77.

14. AIN 2061020024 (auction ID 44): TRACT NO 8793 LOT 65 BLK 4 . . . ASSESSED TO SHEA ESTATES 0 DEVELOPMENT CORP LOCATION CITY-AGOURA HILL PROPERTY ADDRESS: VACANT LOT. See page 82.

15. AIN 2061020025 (auction ID 45): TRACT NO 8793 LOT 66 BLK 4 . . . ASSESSED TO SHEA ESTATES 0 DEVELOPMENT CORP LOCATION CITY-AGOURA HILL PROPERTY ADDRESS: VACANT LOT. See page 87.

16. AIN 2061020026 (auction ID 46): TRACT NO 8793 LOT 67 BLK 4 . . . ASSESSED TO SHEA ESTATES 0 DEVELOPMENT CORP LOCATION CITY-AGOURA HILL PROPERTY ADDRESS: VACANT LOT. See page 92.

17. AIN 2061020027 (auction ID 47): TRACT NO 8793 LOT 68 BLK 4 . . . ASSESSED TO SHEA ESTATES 0 DEVELOPMENT CORP LOCATION CITY-AGOURA HILL PROPERTY ADDRESS: VACANT LOT. See page 97.

18. AIN 2061020028 (auction ID 48): TRACT NO 8793 LOT 69 BLK 4 . . . ASSESSED TO SHEA ESTATES 0 DEVELOPMENT CORP LOCATION CITY-AGOURA HILL - PROPERTY ADDRESS: VACANT LOT. See page 102.

19. AIN 2061020029 (auction ID 49): TRACT NO 8793 LOT 70 BLK 4 . . . ASSESSED TO SHEA ESTATES 0 DEVELOPMENT CORP LOCATION CITY-AGOURA HILL PROPERTY ADDRESS: VACANT LOT. See page 107.

20. AIN 2061020030 (auction ID 50): TRACT NO 8793 LOT 71 BLK 4 . . . ASSESSED TO SHEA ESTATES 0 DEVELOPMENT CORP LOCATION CITY-AGOURA HILL PROPERTY ADDRESS: VACANT LOT. See page 112.

21. AIN 2061021009 (auction ID 51): TRACT NO 8793 LOT 10 BLK 4 . . . ASSESSED TO SHEA ESTATES 0 DEVELOPMENT CORP LOCATION CITY-AGOURA HILL PROPERTY ADDRESS: VACANT LOT. See page 117.

22. AIN 2061021010 (auction ID 52): TRACT NO 8793 LOT 11 BLK 4 . . . ASSESSED TO SHEA ESTATES 0 DEVELOPMENT CORP LOCATION CITY-AGOURA HILL PROPERTY ADDRESS: VACANT LOT. See page 122.

23. AIN 2061021011 (auction ID 53): TRACT NO 8793 LOT 12 BLK 4 . . . ASSESSED TO SHEA ESTATES 0 DEVELOPMENT CORP LOCATION CITY-AGOURA HILL PROPERTY ADDRESS: VACANT LOT. See page 127.

24. AIN 2061021012 (auction ID 54): TRACT NO 8793 LOT 13 BLK 4 . . . ASSESSED TO SHEA ESTATES 0 DEVELOPMENT CORP LOCATION CITY-AGOURA HILL PROPERTY ADDRESS: VACANT LOT. See page 132.

25. AIN 2061021013 (auction ID 55): TRACT NO 8793 LOT 14 BLK 4 ... ASSESSED TO SHEA ESTATES 0 DEVELOPMENT CORP LOCATION CITY-AGOURA HILL PROPERTY ADDRESS: VACANT LOT. See page 137.

26. AIN 2061021014 (auction ID 56): TRACT NO 8793 LOT 15 BLK 4 ... ASSESSED TO SHEA ESTATES 0 DEVELOPMENT CORP LOCATION CITY-AGOURA HILL PROPERTY ADDRESS: VACANT LOT. See page 142.

27. AIN 2061021015 (auction ID 57): TRACT NO 8793 LOT 72 BLK 4 ... ASSESSED TO SHEA ESTATES 0 DEVELOPMENT CORP LOCATION CITY-AGOURA HILL PROPERTY ADDRESS: VACANT LOT. See page 147.

28. AIN 2061021016 (auction ID 58): TRACT NO 8793 LOT 73 BLK 4 ... ASSESSED TO SHEA ESTATES 0 DEVELOPMENT CORP LOCATION CITY-AGOURA HILL PROPERTY ADDRESS: VACANT LOT. See page 152.

29. AIN 2061021017 (auction ID 59): TRACT NO 8793 LOT 74 BLK 4 ... ASSESSED TO SHEA ESTATES 0 DEVELOPMENT CORP LOCATION CITY-AGOURA HILL PROPERTY ADDRESS: VACANT LOT. See page 157.

30. AIN 2061021018 (auction ID 60): TRACT NO 8793 LOT 75 BLK 4 ... ASSESSED TO SHEA ESTATES 0 DEVELOPMENT CORP LOCATION CITY-AGOURA HILL PROPERTY ADDRESS: VACANT LOT. See page 162.

31. AIN 2061021019 (auction ID 61): TRACT NO 8793 LOT 76 BLK 4 ... ASSESSED TO SHEA ESTATES 0 DEVELOPMENT CORP LOCATION CITY-AGOURA HILL PROPERTY ADDRESS: VACANT LOT. See page 167.

32. AIN 2061021021 (auction ID 63): TRACT NO 8793 LOT 78 BLK 4 ... ASSESSED TO SHEA ESTATES 0 DEVELOPMENT CORP LOCATION CITY-AGOURA HILL PROPERTY ADDRESS: VACANT LOT. See page 177.

33. AIN 2061021022 (auction ID 64): TRACT NO 8793 LOT 79 BLK 4 ... ASSESSED TO SHEA ESTATES 0 DEVELOPMENT CORP LOCATION CITY-AGOURA HILL PROPERTY ADDRESS: VACANT LOT. See page 182.

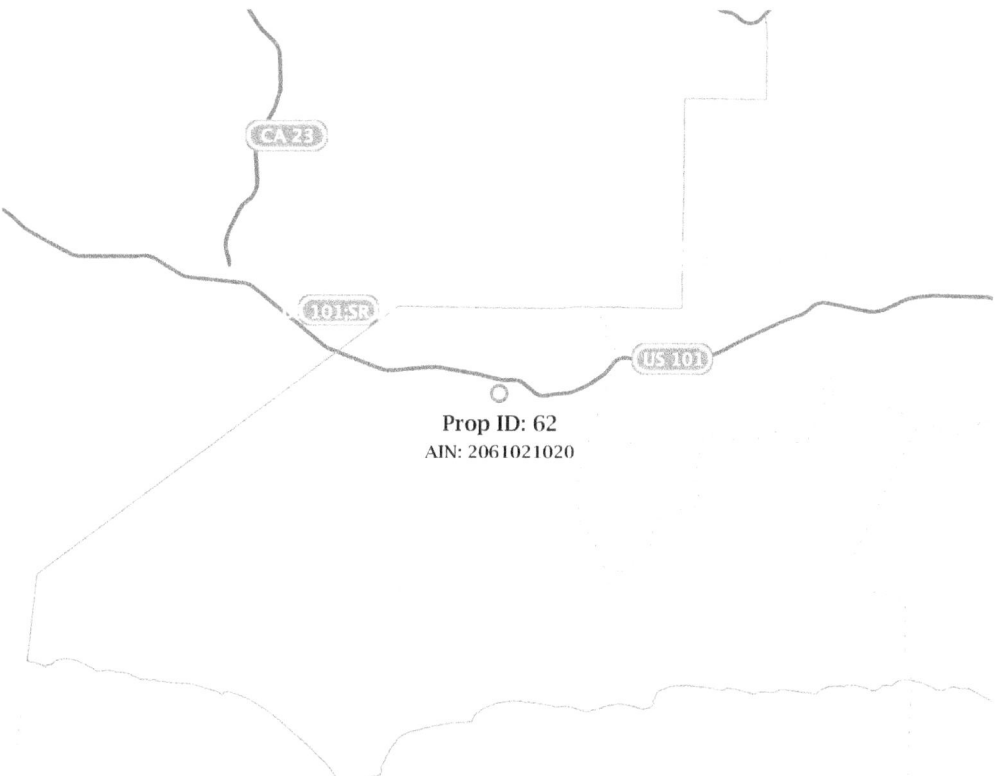

Figure 2.103: Property 64, AIN 2061021020, overview map

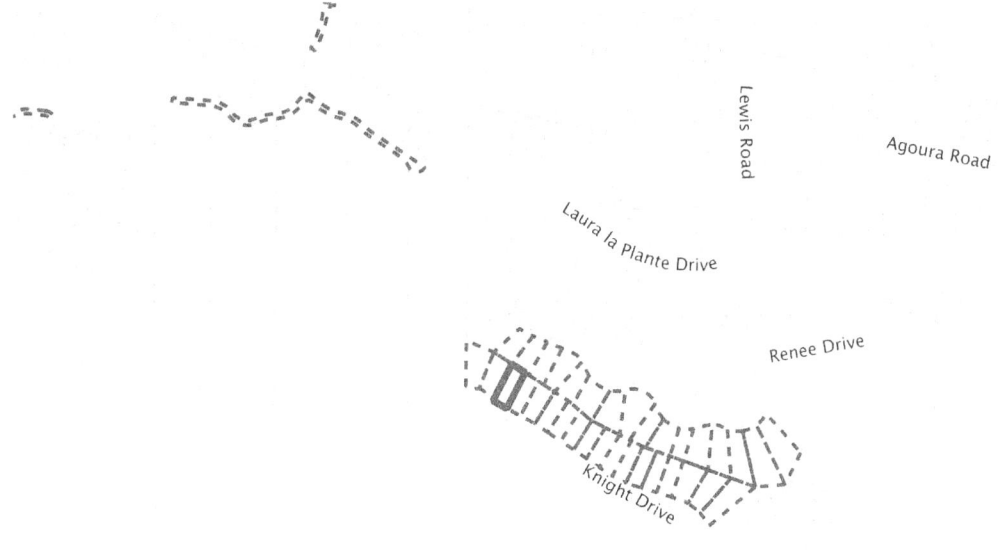

Figure 2.104: Property 64, AIN 2061021020, neighborhood view

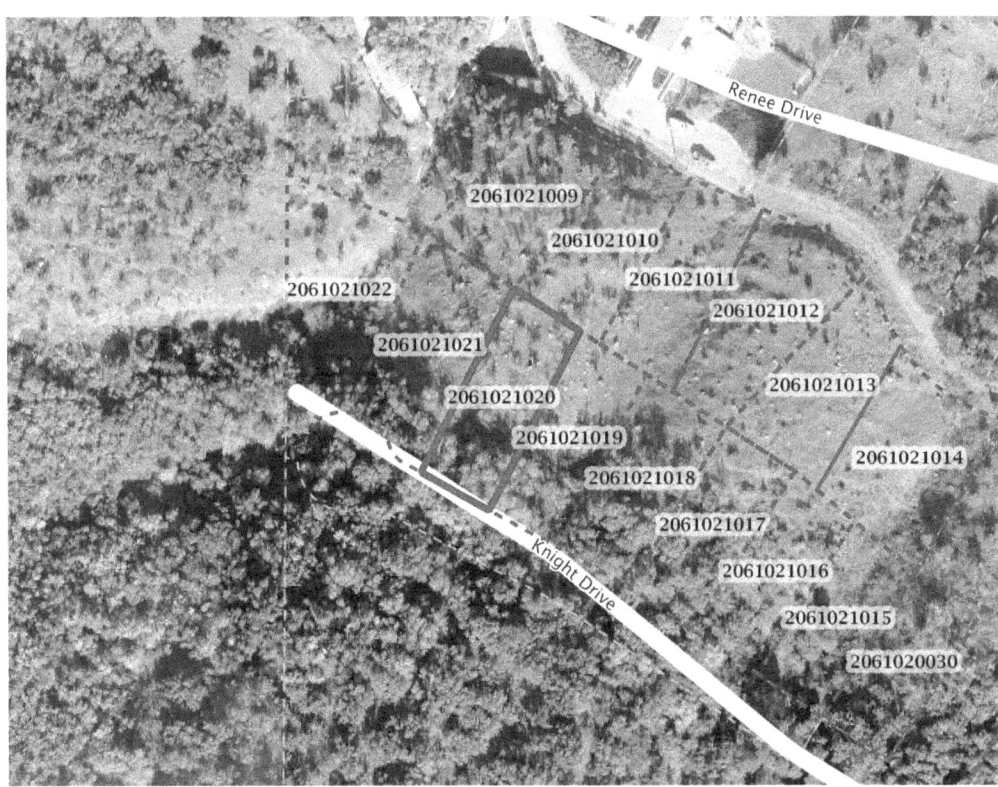

Figure 2.105: Property 64, AIN 2061021020, detailed view

2.36 Auction ID 63

The Los Angeles County Auction Book describes the property as follows.

```
TRACT NO 8793 LOT 78 BLK 4 ASSESSED TO SHEA ESTATES 0 DEVELOPMENT
CORP LOCATION CITY-AGOURA HILL PROPERTY ADDRESS: VACANT LOT
```

The property is located in the general vicinity of Figure 2.106. It is identified by Assessor's Identification Number (AIN) 2061021021. The starting bid is $7,347. Comparable improved properties in this area is about $294/sqft. Comparable unimproved lots in this area is about $49/sqft. This parcel is approximately 7842 sqft. Note, however, that the parcel may be larger than the property under consideration. In case of condominiums, for example, the parcel may encompass other units of the development - those unrelated to the property to be auctioned.

The property is in a parcel zoned Restricted Open Space in Agoura Hills, for 0 to 0 dwelling units.

Figures 2.107 and 2.108 show street map and corresponding detailed aerial view, respectively. In both cases, the map is centered on the property with the containing parcel marked in heavy blue. If surrounding nearby properties are also part of this auction, the street and aerial maps highlights these in heavy, dashed blue outline.

This assessed entity may have other properties that are also in this auction:

1. AIN 2061020001 (auction ID 31): TRACT NO 8793 LOT 16 BLK 4 ... ASSESSED TO SHEA ESTATES 0 DEVELOPMENT CORP LOCATION CITY-AGOURA HILL PROPERTY ADDRESS: VACANT LOT. See page 17.

2. AIN 2061020002 (auction ID 32): TRACT NO 8793 LOT 17 BLK 4 ... ASSESSED TO SHEA ESTATES 0 DEVELOPMENT CORP LOCATION CITY-AGOURA HILL PROPERTY ADDRESS: VACANT LOT. See page 22.

3. AIN 2061020003 (auction ID 33): TRACT NO 8793 LOT 18 BLK 4 ... ASSESSED TO SHEA ESTATES 0 DEVELOPMENT CORP LOCATION CITY-AGOURA HILL PROPERTY ADDRESS: VACANT LOT. See page 27.

4. AIN 2061020004 (auction ID 34): TRACT NO 8793 LOT 19 BLK 4 ... ASSESSED TO SHEA ESTATES 0 DEVELOPMENT CORP LOCATION CITY-AGOURA HILL PROPERTY ADDRESS: VACANT LOT. See page 32.

5. AIN 2061020005 (auction ID 35): TRACT NO 8793 LOT 20 BLK 4 ... ASSESSED TO SHEA ESTATES 0 DEVELOPMENT CORP LOCATION CITY-AGOURA HILL PROPERTY ADDRESS: VACANT LOT. See page 37.

6. AIN 2061020006 (auction ID 36): TRACT NO 8793 LOT 21 BLK 4 ... ASSESSED TO SHEA ESTATES 0 DEVELOPMENT CORP LOCATION CITY-AGOURA HILL PROPERTY ADDRESS: VACANT LOT. See page 42.

7. AIN 2061020007 (auction ID 37): TRACT NO 8793 LOT 22 BLK 4 ... ASSESSED TO SHEA ESTATES 0 DEVELOPMENT CORP LOCATION CITY-AGOURA HILL PROPERTY ADDRESS: VACANT LOT. See page 47.

8. AIN 2061020008 (auction ID 38): TRACT NO 8793 LOT 23 BLK 4 ... ASSESSED TO SHEA ESTATES 0 DEVELOPMENT CORP LOCATION CITY-AGOURA HILL PROPERTY ADDRESS: VACANT LOT. See page 52.

9. AIN 2061020009 (auction ID 39): TRACT NO 8793 LOT 24 BLK 4 ... ASSESSED TO SHEA ESTATES 0 DEVELOPMENT CORP LOCATION CITY-AGOURA HILL PROPERTY ADDRESS: VACANT LOT. See page 57.

10. AIN 2061020010 (auction ID 40): TRACT NO 8793 LOT 25 BLK 4 . . . ASSESSED TO SHEA ESTATES 0 DEVELOPMENT CORP LOCATION CITY-AGOURA HILL PROPERTY ADDRESS: VACANT LOT. See page 62.

11. AIN 2061020021 (auction ID 41): TRACT NO 8793 LOT 62 BLK 4 . . . ASSESSED TO SHEA ESTATES 0 DEVELOPMENT CORP LOCATION CITY-AGOURA HILL PROPERTY ADDRESS: VACANT LOT. See page 67.

12. AIN 2061020022 (auction ID 42): TRACT NO 8793 LOT 63 BLK 4 . . . ASSESSED TO SHEA ESTATES 0 DEVELOPMENT CORP LOCATION CITY-AGOURA HILL PROPERTY ADDRESS: VACANT LOT. See page 72.

13. AIN 2061020023 (auction ID 43): TRACT NO 8793 LOT 64 BLK 4 . . . ASSESSED TO SHEA ESTATES 0 DEVELOPMENT CORP LOCATION CITY-AGOURA HILL PROPERTY ADDRESS: VACANT LOT. See page 77.

14. AIN 2061020024 (auction ID 44): TRACT NO 8793 LOT 65 BLK 4 . . . ASSESSED TO SHEA ESTATES 0 DEVELOPMENT CORP LOCATION CITY-AGOURA HILL PROPERTY ADDRESS: VACANT LOT. See page 82.

15. AIN 2061020025 (auction ID 45): TRACT NO 8793 LOT 66 BLK 4 . . . ASSESSED TO SHEA ESTATES 0 DEVELOPMENT CORP LOCATION CITY-AGOURA HILL PROPERTY ADDRESS: VACANT LOT. See page 87.

16. AIN 2061020026 (auction ID 46): TRACT NO 8793 LOT 67 BLK 4 . . . ASSESSED TO SHEA ESTATES 0 DEVELOPMENT CORP LOCATION CITY-AGOURA HILL PROPERTY ADDRESS: VACANT LOT. See page 92.

17. AIN 2061020027 (auction ID 47): TRACT NO 8793 LOT 68 BLK 4 . . . ASSESSED TO SHEA ESTATES 0 DEVELOPMENT CORP LOCATION CITY-AGOURA HILL PROPERTY ADDRESS: VACANT LOT. See page 97.

18. AIN 2061020028 (auction ID 48): TRACT NO 8793 LOT 69 BLK 4 . . . ASSESSED TO SHEA ESTATES 0 DEVELOPMENT CORP LOCATION CITY-AGOURA HILL - PROPERTY ADDRESS: VACANT LOT. See page 102.

19. AIN 2061020029 (auction ID 49): TRACT NO 8793 LOT 70 BLK 4 . . . ASSESSED TO SHEA ESTATES 0 DEVELOPMENT CORP LOCATION CITY-AGOURA HILL PROPERTY ADDRESS: VACANT LOT. See page 107.

20. AIN 2061020030 (auction ID 50): TRACT NO 8793 LOT 71 BLK 4 . . . ASSESSED TO SHEA ESTATES 0 DEVELOPMENT CORP LOCATION CITY-AGOURA HILL PROPERTY ADDRESS: VACANT LOT. See page 112.

21. AIN 2061021009 (auction ID 51): TRACT NO 8793 LOT 10 BLK 4 . . . ASSESSED TO SHEA ESTATES 0 DEVELOPMENT CORP LOCATION CITY-AGOURA HILL PROPERTY ADDRESS: VACANT LOT. See page 117.

22. AIN 2061021010 (auction ID 52): TRACT NO 8793 LOT 11 BLK 4 . . . ASSESSED TO SHEA ESTATES 0 DEVELOPMENT CORP LOCATION CITY-AGOURA HILL PROPERTY ADDRESS: VACANT LOT. See page 122.

23. AIN 2061021011 (auction ID 53): TRACT NO 8793 LOT 12 BLK 4 . . . ASSESSED TO SHEA ESTATES 0 DEVELOPMENT CORP LOCATION CITY-AGOURA HILL PROPERTY ADDRESS: VACANT LOT. See page 127.

24. AIN 2061021012 (auction ID 54): TRACT NO 8793 LOT 13 BLK 4 . . . ASSESSED TO SHEA ESTATES 0 DEVELOPMENT CORP LOCATION CITY-AGOURA HILL PROPERTY ADDRESS: VACANT LOT. See page 132.

25. AIN 2061021013 (auction ID 55): TRACT NO 8793 LOT 14 BLK 4 ... ASSESSED TO SHEA ESTATES 0 DEVELOPMENT CORP LOCATION CITY-AGOURA HILL PROPERTY ADDRESS: VACANT LOT. See page 137.

26. AIN 2061021014 (auction ID 56): TRACT NO 8793 LOT 15 BLK 4 ... ASSESSED TO SHEA ESTATES 0 DEVELOPMENT CORP LOCATION CITY-AGOURA HILL PROPERTY ADDRESS: VACANT LOT. See page 142.

27. AIN 2061021015 (auction ID 57): TRACT NO 8793 LOT 72 BLK 4 ... ASSESSED TO SHEA ESTATES 0 DEVELOPMENT CORP LOCATION CITY-AGOURA HILL PROPERTY ADDRESS: VACANT LOT. See page 147.

28. AIN 2061021016 (auction ID 58): TRACT NO 8793 LOT 73 BLK 4 ... ASSESSED TO SHEA ESTATES 0 DEVELOPMENT CORP LOCATION CITY-AGOURA HILL PROPERTY ADDRESS: VACANT LOT. See page 152.

29. AIN 2061021017 (auction ID 59): TRACT NO 8793 LOT 74 BLK 4 ... ASSESSED TO SHEA ESTATES 0 DEVELOPMENT CORP LOCATION CITY-AGOURA HILL PROPERTY ADDRESS: VACANT LOT. See page 157.

30. AIN 2061021018 (auction ID 60): TRACT NO 8793 LOT 75 BLK 4 ... ASSESSED TO SHEA ESTATES 0 DEVELOPMENT CORP LOCATION CITY-AGOURA HILL PROPERTY ADDRESS: VACANT LOT. See page 162.

31. AIN 2061021019 (auction ID 61): TRACT NO 8793 LOT 76 BLK 4 ... ASSESSED TO SHEA ESTATES 0 DEVELOPMENT CORP LOCATION CITY-AGOURA HILL PROPERTY ADDRESS: VACANT LOT. See page 167.

32. AIN 2061021020 (auction ID 62): TRACT NO 8793 LOT 77 BLK 4 ... ASSESSED TO SHEA ESTATES 0 DEVELOPMENT CORP LOCATION CITY-AGOURA HILL PROPERTY ADDRESS: VACANT LOT. See page 172.

33. AIN 2061021022 (auction ID 64): TRACT NO 8793 LOT 79 BLK 4 ... ASSESSED TO SHEA ESTATES 0 DEVELOPMENT CORP LOCATION CITY-AGOURA HILL PROPERTY ADDRESS: VACANT LOT. See page 182.

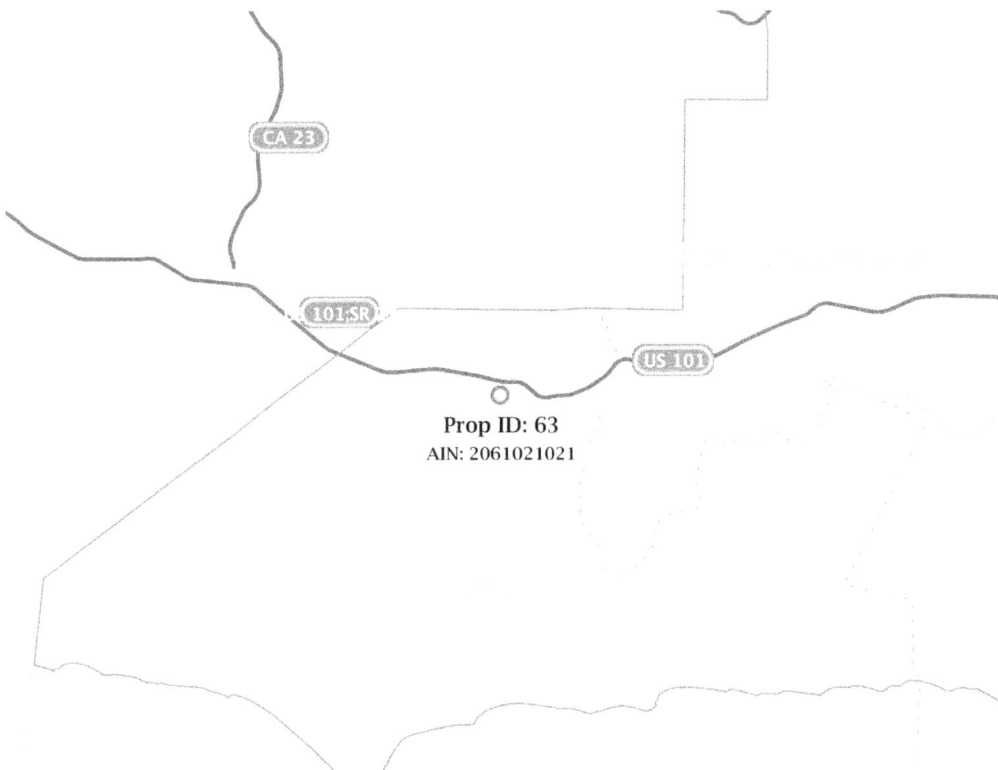

Figure 2.106: Property 64, AIN 2061021021, overview map

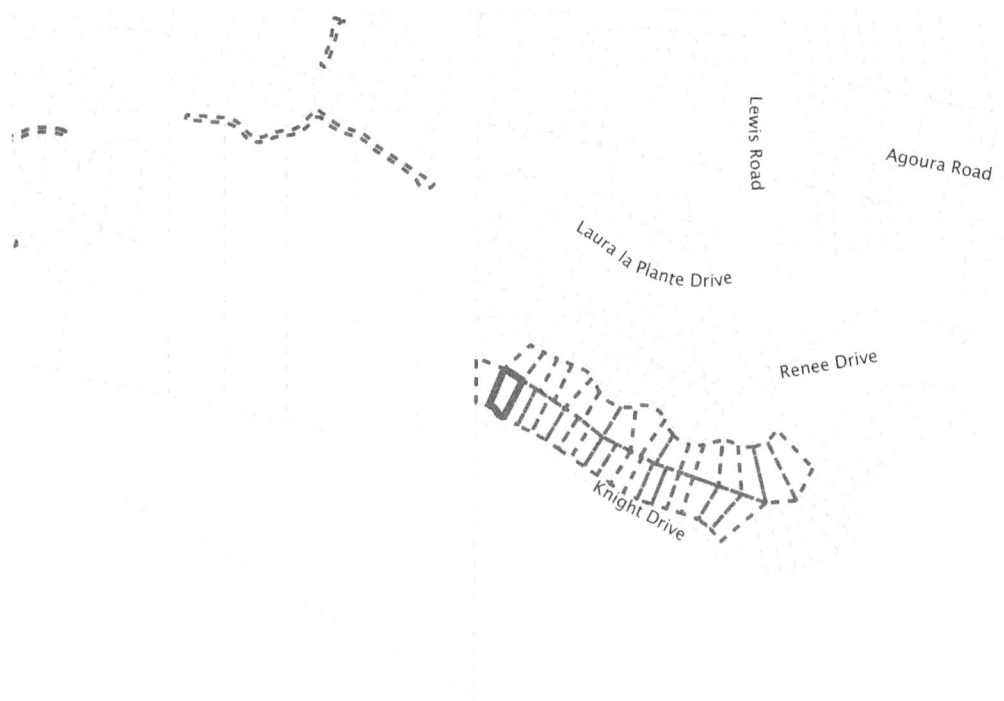

Figure 2.107: Property 64, AIN 2061021021, neighborhood view

Figure 2.108: Property 64, AIN 2061021021, detailed view

2.37 Auction ID 64

The Los Angeles County Auction Book describes the property as follows.

```
TRACT NO 8793 LOT 79 BLK 4 ASSESSED TO SHEA ESTATES 0 DEVELOPMENT
CORP LOCATION CITY-AGOURA HILL PROPERTY ADDRESS: VACANT LOT
```

The property is located in the general vicinity of Figure 2.109. It is identified by Assessor's Identification Number (AIN) 2061021022. The starting bid is $7,643. Comparable improved properties in this area is about $294/sqft. Comparable unimproved lots in this area is about $49/sqft. This parcel is approximately 9027 sqft. Note, however, that the parcel may be larger than the property under consideration. In case of condominiums, for example, the parcel may encompass other units of the development - those unrelated to the property to be auctioned.

The property is in a parcel zoned Restricted Open Space in Agoura Hills, for 0 to 0 dwelling units.

Figures 2.110 and 2.111 show street map and corresponding detailed aerial view, respectively. In both cases, the map is centered on the property with the containing parcel marked in heavy blue. If surrounding nearby properties are also part of this auction, the street and aerial maps highlights these in heavy, dashed blue outline.

This assessed entity may have other properties that are also in this auction:

1. AIN 2061020001 (auction ID 31): TRACT NO 8793 LOT 16 BLK 4 . . . ASSESSED TO SHEA ESTATES 0 DEVELOPMENT CORP LOCATION CITY-AGOURA HILL PROPERTY ADDRESS: VACANT LOT. See page 17.

2. AIN 2061020002 (auction ID 32): TRACT NO 8793 LOT 17 BLK 4 . . . ASSESSED TO SHEA ESTATES 0 DEVELOPMENT CORP LOCATION CITY-AGOURA HILL PROPERTY ADDRESS: VACANT LOT. See page 22.

3. AIN 2061020003 (auction ID 33): TRACT NO 8793 LOT 18 BLK 4 . . . ASSESSED TO SHEA ESTATES 0 DEVELOPMENT CORP LOCATION CITY-AGOURA HILL PROPERTY ADDRESS: VACANT LOT. See page 27.

4. AIN 2061020004 (auction ID 34): TRACT NO 8793 LOT 19 BLK 4 . . . ASSESSED TO SHEA ESTATES 0 DEVELOPMENT CORP LOCATION CITY-AGOURA HILL PROPERTY ADDRESS: VACANT LOT. See page 32.

5. AIN 2061020005 (auction ID 35): TRACT NO 8793 LOT 20 BLK 4 . . . ASSESSED TO SHEA ESTATES 0 DEVELOPMENT CORP LOCATION CITY-AGOURA HILL PROPERTY ADDRESS: VACANT LOT. See page 37.

6. AIN 2061020006 (auction ID 36): TRACT NO 8793 LOT 21 BLK 4 . . . ASSESSED TO SHEA ESTATES 0 DEVELOPMENT CORP LOCATION CITY-AGOURA HILL PROPERTY ADDRESS: VACANT LOT. See page 42.

7. AIN 2061020007 (auction ID 37): TRACT NO 8793 LOT 22 BLK 4 . . . ASSESSED TO SHEA ESTATES 0 DEVELOPMENT CORP LOCATION CITY-AGOURA HILL PROPERTY ADDRESS: VACANT LOT. See page 47.

8. AIN 2061020008 (auction ID 38): TRACT NO 8793 LOT 23 BLK 4 . . . ASSESSED TO SHEA ESTATES 0 DEVELOPMENT CORP LOCATION CITY-AGOURA HILL PROPERTY ADDRESS: VACANT LOT. See page 52.

9. AIN 2061020009 (auction ID 39): TRACT NO 8793 LOT 24 BLK 4 . . . ASSESSED TO SHEA ESTATES 0 DEVELOPMENT CORP LOCATION CITY-AGOURA HILL PROPERTY ADDRESS: VACANT LOT. See page 57.

10. AIN 2061020010 (auction ID 40): TRACT NO 8793 LOT 25 BLK 4 . . . ASSESSED TO SHEA ESTATES 0 DEVELOPMENT CORP LOCATION CITY-AGOURA HILL PROPERTY ADDRESS: VACANT LOT. See page 62.

11. AIN 2061020021 (auction ID 41): TRACT NO 8793 LOT 62 BLK 4 . . . ASSESSED TO SHEA ESTATES 0 DEVELOPMENT CORP LOCATION CITY-AGOURA HILL PROPERTY ADDRESS: VACANT LOT. See page 67.

12. AIN 2061020022 (auction ID 42): TRACT NO 8793 LOT 63 BLK 4 . . . ASSESSED TO SHEA ESTATES 0 DEVELOPMENT CORP LOCATION CITY-AGOURA HILL PROPERTY ADDRESS: VACANT LOT. See page 72.

13. AIN 2061020023 (auction ID 43): TRACT NO 8793 LOT 64 BLK 4 . . . ASSESSED TO SHEA ESTATES 0 DEVELOPMENT CORP LOCATION CITY-AGOURA HILL PROPERTY ADDRESS: VACANT LOT. See page 77.

14. AIN 2061020024 (auction ID 44): TRACT NO 8793 LOT 65 BLK 4 . . . ASSESSED TO SHEA ESTATES 0 DEVELOPMENT CORP LOCATION CITY-AGOURA HILL PROPERTY ADDRESS: VACANT LOT. See page 82.

15. AIN 2061020025 (auction ID 45): TRACT NO 8793 LOT 66 BLK 4 . . . ASSESSED TO SHEA ESTATES 0 DEVELOPMENT CORP LOCATION CITY-AGOURA HILL PROPERTY ADDRESS: VACANT LOT. See page 87.

16. AIN 2061020026 (auction ID 46): TRACT NO 8793 LOT 67 BLK 4 . . . ASSESSED TO SHEA ESTATES 0 DEVELOPMENT CORP LOCATION CITY-AGOURA HILL PROPERTY ADDRESS: VACANT LOT. See page 92.

17. AIN 2061020027 (auction ID 47): TRACT NO 8793 LOT 68 BLK 4 . . . ASSESSED TO SHEA ESTATES 0 DEVELOPMENT CORP LOCATION CITY-AGOURA HILL PROPERTY ADDRESS: VACANT LOT. See page 97.

18. AIN 2061020028 (auction ID 48): TRACT NO 8793 LOT 69 BLK 4 . . . ASSESSED TO SHEA ESTATES 0 DEVELOPMENT CORP LOCATION CITY-AGOURA HILL - PROPERTY ADDRESS: VACANT LOT. See page 102.

19. AIN 2061020029 (auction ID 49): TRACT NO 8793 LOT 70 BLK 4 . . . ASSESSED TO SHEA ESTATES 0 DEVELOPMENT CORP LOCATION CITY-AGOURA HILL PROPERTY ADDRESS: VACANT LOT. See page 107.

20. AIN 2061020030 (auction ID 50): TRACT NO 8793 LOT 71 BLK 4 . . . ASSESSED TO SHEA ESTATES 0 DEVELOPMENT CORP LOCATION CITY-AGOURA HILL PROPERTY ADDRESS: VACANT LOT. See page 112.

21. AIN 2061021009 (auction ID 51): TRACT NO 8793 LOT 10 BLK 4 . . . ASSESSED TO SHEA ESTATES 0 DEVELOPMENT CORP LOCATION CITY-AGOURA HILL PROPERTY ADDRESS: VACANT LOT. See page 117.

22. AIN 2061021010 (auction ID 52): TRACT NO 8793 LOT 11 BLK 4 . . . ASSESSED TO SHEA ESTATES 0 DEVELOPMENT CORP LOCATION CITY-AGOURA HILL PROPERTY ADDRESS: VACANT LOT. See page 122.

23. AIN 2061021011 (auction ID 53): TRACT NO 8793 LOT 12 BLK 4 . . . ASSESSED TO SHEA ESTATES 0 DEVELOPMENT CORP LOCATION CITY-AGOURA HILL PROPERTY ADDRESS: VACANT LOT. See page 127.

24. AIN 2061021012 (auction ID 54): TRACT NO 8793 LOT 13 BLK 4 . . . ASSESSED TO SHEA ESTATES 0 DEVELOPMENT CORP LOCATION CITY-AGOURA HILL PROPERTY ADDRESS: VACANT LOT. See page 132.

25. AIN 2061021013 (auction ID 55): TRACT NO 8793 LOT 14 BLK 4 . . . ASSESSED TO SHEA ESTATES 0 DEVELOPMENT CORP LOCATION CITY-AGOURA HILL PROPERTY ADDRESS: VACANT LOT. See page 137.

26. AIN 2061021014 (auction ID 56): TRACT NO 8793 LOT 15 BLK 4 . . . ASSESSED TO SHEA ESTATES 0 DEVELOPMENT CORP LOCATION CITY-AGOURA HILL PROPERTY ADDRESS: VACANT LOT. See page 142.

27. AIN 2061021015 (auction ID 57): TRACT NO 8793 LOT 72 BLK 4 . . . ASSESSED TO SHEA ESTATES 0 DEVELOPMENT CORP LOCATION CITY-AGOURA HILL PROPERTY ADDRESS: VACANT LOT. See page 147.

28. AIN 2061021016 (auction ID 58): TRACT NO 8793 LOT 73 BLK 4 . . . ASSESSED TO SHEA ESTATES 0 DEVELOPMENT CORP LOCATION CITY-AGOURA HILL PROPERTY ADDRESS: VACANT LOT. See page 152.

29. AIN 2061021017 (auction ID 59): TRACT NO 8793 LOT 74 BLK 4 . . . ASSESSED TO SHEA ESTATES 0 DEVELOPMENT CORP LOCATION CITY-AGOURA HILL PROPERTY ADDRESS: VACANT LOT. See page 157.

30. AIN 2061021018 (auction ID 60): TRACT NO 8793 LOT 75 BLK 4 . . . ASSESSED TO SHEA ESTATES 0 DEVELOPMENT CORP LOCATION CITY-AGOURA HILL PROPERTY ADDRESS: VACANT LOT. See page 162.

31. AIN 2061021019 (auction ID 61): TRACT NO 8793 LOT 76 BLK 4 . . . ASSESSED TO SHEA ESTATES 0 DEVELOPMENT CORP LOCATION CITY-AGOURA HILL PROPERTY ADDRESS: VACANT LOT. See page 167.

32. AIN 2061021020 (auction ID 62): TRACT NO 8793 LOT 77 BLK 4 . . . ASSESSED TO SHEA ESTATES 0 DEVELOPMENT CORP LOCATION CITY-AGOURA HILL PROPERTY ADDRESS: VACANT LOT. See page 172.

33. AIN 2061021021 (auction ID 63): TRACT NO 8793 LOT 78 BLK 4 . . . ASSESSED TO SHEA ESTATES 0 DEVELOPMENT CORP LOCATION CITY-AGOURA HILL PROPERTY ADDRESS: VACANT LOT. See page 177.

Figure 2.109: Property 63, AIN 2061021022, overview map

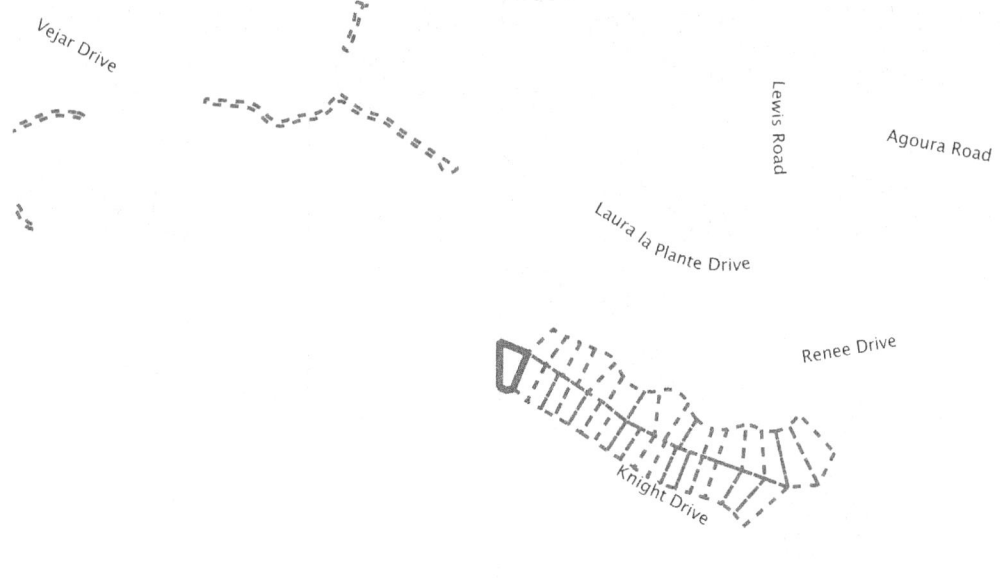

Figure 2.110: Property 63, AIN 2061021022, neighborhood view

Figure 2.111: Property 63, AIN 2061021022, detailed view

2.38 Auction ID 65

The Los Angeles County Auction Book describes the property as follows.

```
VAC ST ADJ LOTS 146,147,148 AND 149 TRACT NO 0 7661 ON N ASSESSED
TO STROUD,ROBERT C CO TR ET AL STROUD FAMILY TRUST AND GERTLER,CO
TR GERTLER TRUST LOCATION CITY-AGOURA HILL PROPERTY ADDRESS: VACANT
LOT
```

The property is located in the general vicinity of Figure 2.112. It is identified by Assessor's Identification Number (AIN) 2061024005. The starting bid is $1,576. Comparable improved properties in this area is about $297/sqft. Comparable unimproved lots in this area is about $45/sqft. This parcel is approximately 14983 sqft. Note, however, that the parcel may be larger than the property under consideration. In case of condominiums, for example, the parcel may encompass other units of the development - those unrelated to the property to be auctioned.

The property is in a parcel zoned Restricted Open Space in Agoura Hills, for 0 to 0 dwelling units.

Figures 2.113 and 2.114 show street map and corresponding detailed aerial view, respectively. In both cases, the map is centered on the property with the containing parcel marked in heavy blue. If surrounding nearby properties are also part of this auction, the street and aerial maps highlights these in heavy, dashed blue outline.

This assessed entity may have other properties that are also in this auction:

1. AIN 2061027013 (auction ID 66): VAC STS ADJ LOTS119 THRU 130 TR NO 7661 ON NE AND NW 0 ... ASSESSED TO STROUD, ROBERT C CO TR ET AL STROUD FAMILY TRUST AND .... See page 190.

2. AIN 2061028040 (auction ID 67): VAC ST ADJ LOTS 63 THRU 73 TR NO 7661 ON SW AND SE 0 ... ASSESSED TO STROUD, ROBERT C CO TR ET AL STROUD FAMILY TRUST .... See page 193.

3. AIN 2061030019 (auction ID 97): VAC ST ADJ LOTS 116, 117 AND 118 TR NO 7661 ON NE 0 ... ASSESSED TO STROUD, ROBERT C CO TR ET AL STROUD FAMILY TRUST AND .... See page 300.

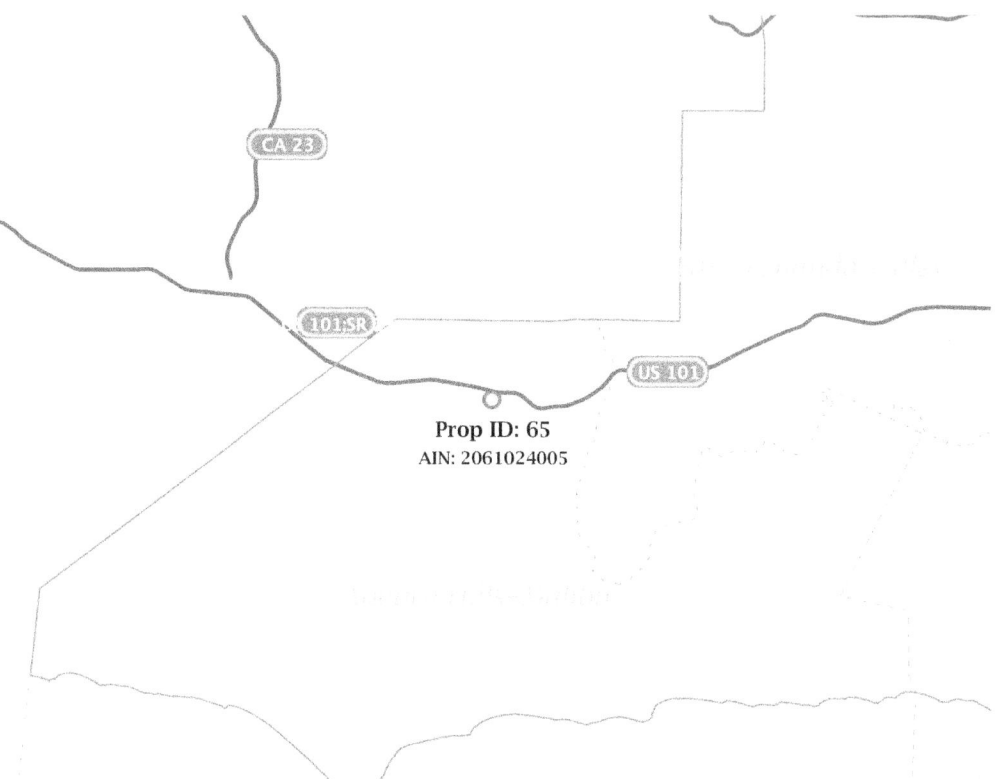

Prop ID: 65
AIN: 2061024005

Figure 2.112: Property 97, AIN 2061024005, overview map

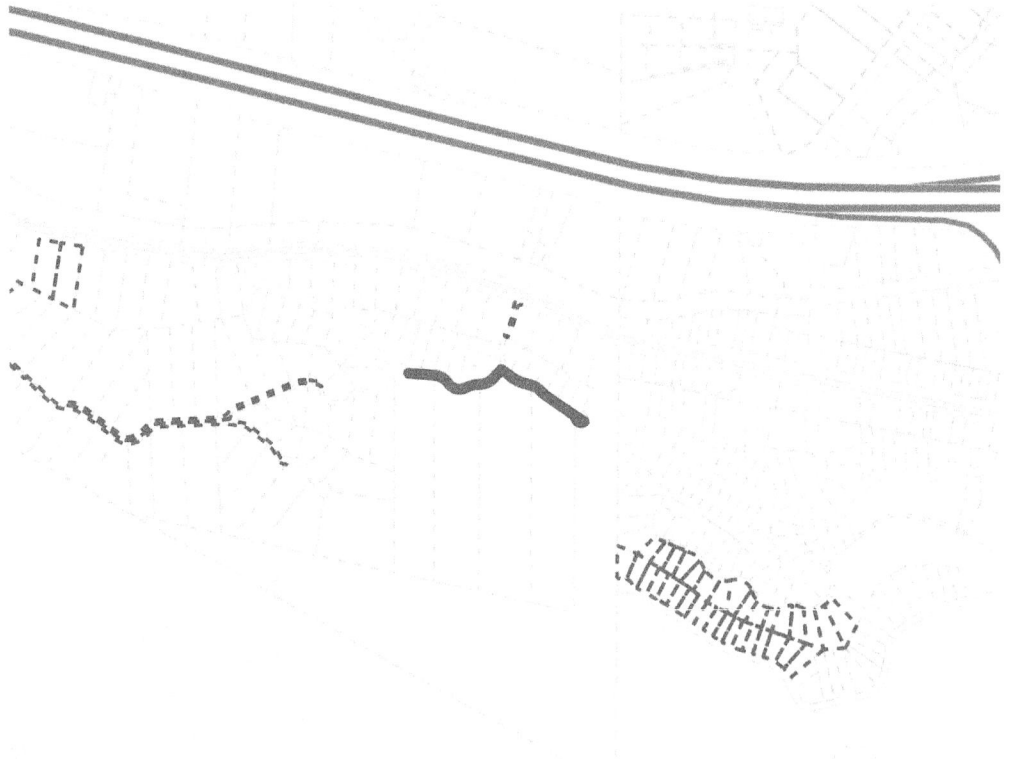

Figure 2.113: Property 97, AIN 2061024005, neighborhood view

Figure 2.114: Property 97, AIN 2061024005, detailed view

2.39 Auction ID 66

The Los Angeles County Auction Book describes the property as follows.

```
VAC STS ADJ LOTS119 THRU 130 TR NO 7661 ON NE AND NW 0 ASSESSED TO
STROUD,ROBERT C CO TR ET AL STROUD FAMILY TRUST AND GERTLER,CO TR
GERTLER TRUST LOCATION CITY-AGOURA HILL PROPERTY ADDRESS: VACANT LOT
```

The property is located in the general vicinity of Figure 2.115. It is identified by Assessor's Identification Number (AIN) 2061027013. The starting bid is $1,610. Comparable improved properties in this area is about $295/sqft. Comparable unimproved lots in this area is about $49/sqft. This parcel is approximately 21531 sqft. Note, however, that the parcel may be larger than the property under consideration. In case of condominiums, for example, the parcel may encompass other units of the development - those unrelated to the property to be auctioned.

The property is in a parcel zoned Restricted Open Space in Agoura Hills, for 0 to 0 dwelling units.

Figures 2.116 and 2.117 show street map and corresponding detailed aerial view, respectively. In both cases, the map is centered on the property with the containing parcel marked in heavy blue. If surrounding nearby properties are also part of this auction, the street and aerial maps highlights these in heavy, dashed blue outline.

This assessed entity may have other properties that are also in this auction:

1. AIN 2061024005 (auction ID 65): VAC ST ADJ LOTS 146, 147, 148 AND 149 TRACT NO 0 7661 ON N ... ASSESSED TO STROUD, ROBERT C CO TR ET AL STROUD FAMILY TRUST .... See page 187.

2. AIN 2061028040 (auction ID 67): VAC ST ADJ LOTS 63 THRU 73 TR NO 7661 ON SW AND SE 0 ... ASSESSED TO STROUD, ROBERT C CO TR ET AL STROUD FAMILY TRUST .... See page 193.

3. AIN 2061030019 (auction ID 97): VAC ST ADJ LOTS 116, 117 AND 118 TR NO 7661 ON NE 0 ... ASSESSED TO STROUD, ROBERT C CO TR ET AL STROUD FAMILY TRUST AND .... See page 300.

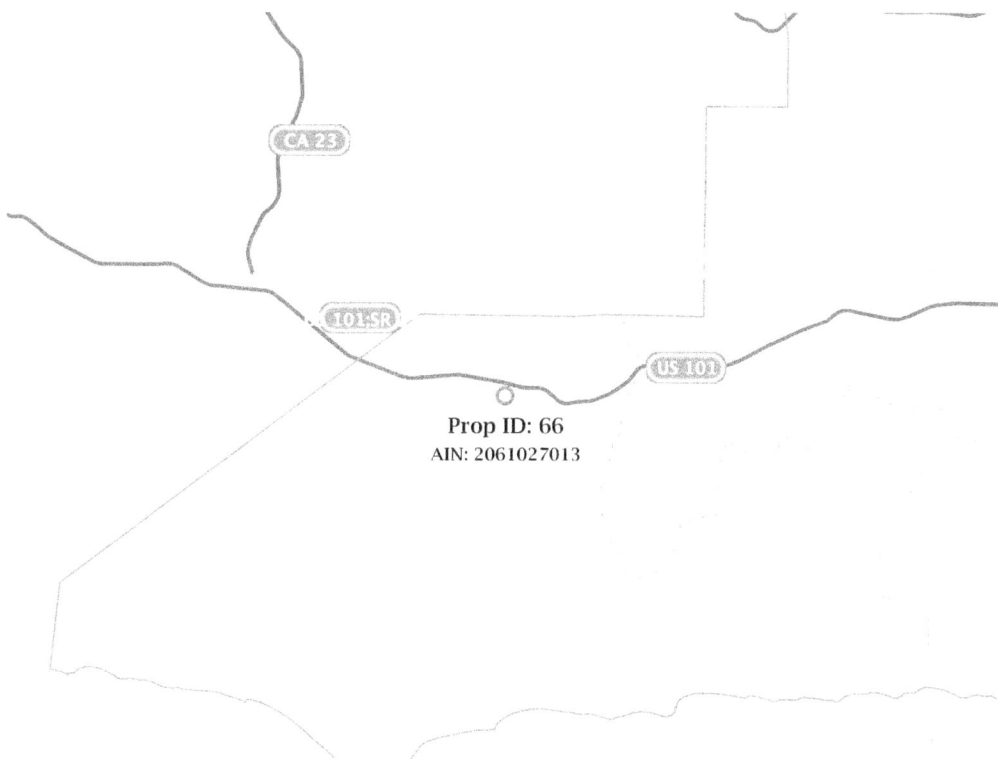

Figure 2.115: Property 97, AIN 2061027013, overview map

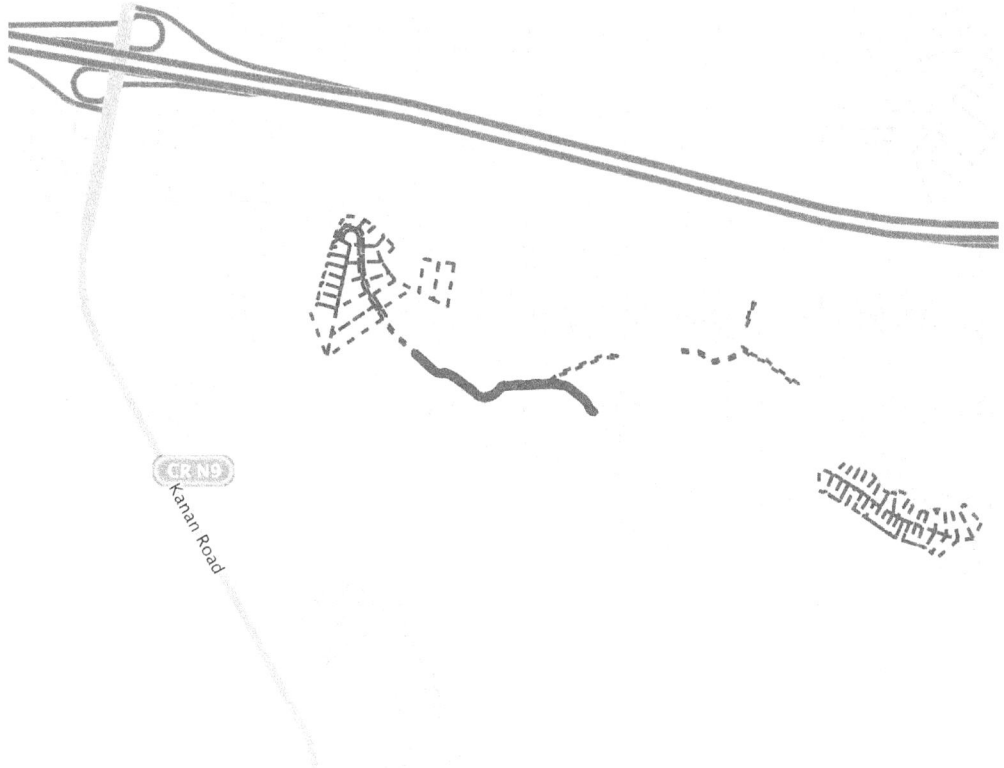

Figure 2.116: Property 97, AIN 2061027013, neighborhood view

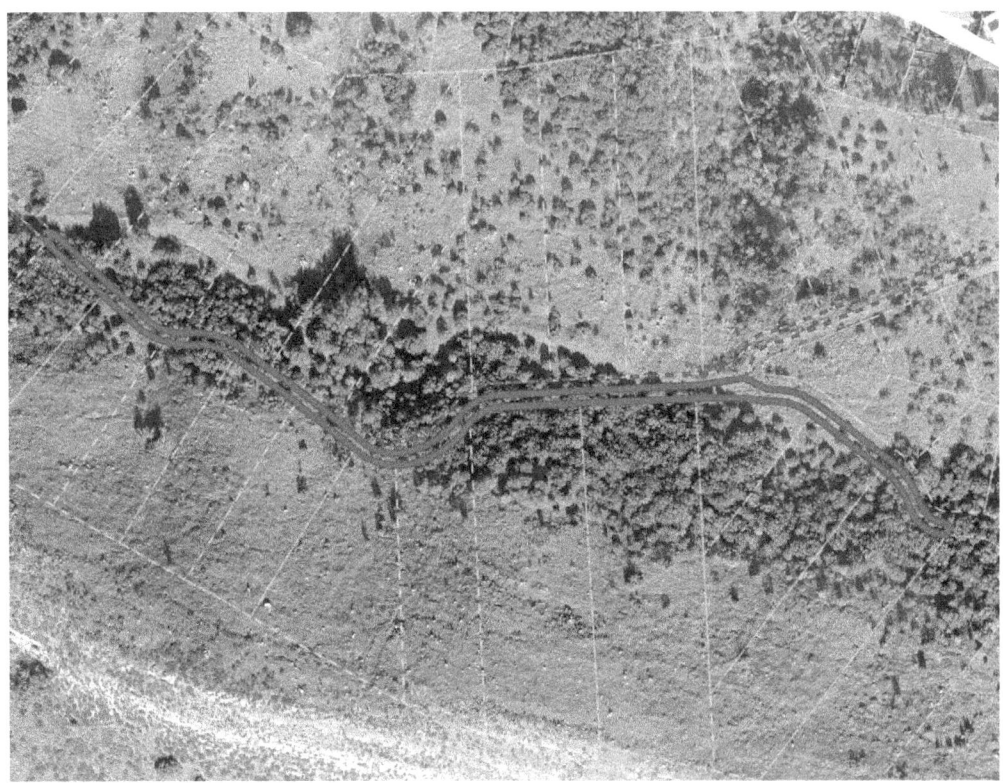

Figure 2.117: Property 97, AIN 2061027013, detailed view

2.40   Auction ID 67

The Los Angeles County Auction Book describes the property as follows.

```
VAC ST ADJ LOTS 63 THRU 73 TR NO 7661 ON SW AND SE 0 ASSESSED TO STROUD,ROBERT
C CO TR ET AL STROUD FAMILY TRUST AND GERTLER,CO TR GERTLER TRUST
LOCATION CITY-AGOURA HILL PROPERTY ADDRESS: VACANT LOT
```

The property is located in the general vicinity of Figure 2.118. It is identified by Assessor's Identification Number (AIN) 2061028040. The starting bid is $1,598. Comparable improved properties in this area is about $297/sqft. Comparable unimproved lots in this area is about $48/sqft. This parcel is approximately 19269 sqft. Note, however, that the parcel may be larger than the property under consideration. In case of condominiums, for example, the parcel may encompass other units of the development - those unrelated to the property to be auctioned.

The property is in a parcel zoned Restricted Open Space in Agoura Hills, for 0 to 0 dwelling units.

Figures 2.119 and 2.120 show street map and corresponding detailed aerial view, respectively. In both cases, the map is centered on the property with the containing parcel marked in heavy blue. If surrounding nearby properties are also part of this auction, the street and aerial maps highlights these in heavy, dashed blue outline.

This assessed entity may have other properties that are also in this auction:

1. AIN 2061024005 (auction ID 65): VAC ST ADJ LOTS 146, 147, 148 AND 149 TRACT NO 0 7661 ON N . . . ASSESSED TO STROUD, ROBERT C CO TR ET AL STROUD FAMILY TRUST . . . . See page 187.

2. AIN 2061027013 (auction ID 66): VAC STS ADJ LOTS119 THRU 130 TR NO 7661 ON NE AND NW 0 . . . ASSESSED TO STROUD, ROBERT C CO TR ET AL STROUD FAMILY TRUST AND . . . . See page 190.

3. AIN 2061030019 (auction ID 97): VAC ST ADJ LOTS 116, 117 AND 118 TR NO 7661 ON NE 0 . . . ASSESSED TO STROUD, ROBERT C CO TR ET AL STROUD FAMILY TRUST AND . . . . See page 300.

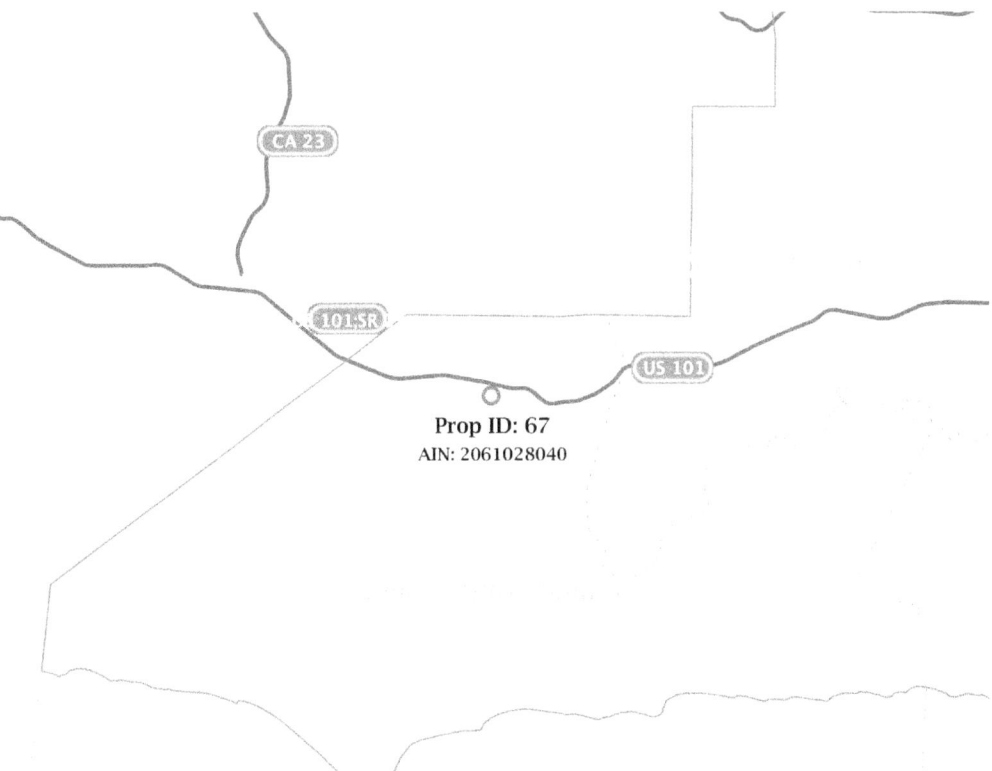

Figure 2.118: Property 97, AIN 2061028040, overview map

Figure 2.119: Property 97, AIN 2061028040, neighborhood view

Figure 2.120: Property 97, AIN 2061028040, detailed view

2.41   Auction ID 68

The Los Angeles County Auction Book describes the property as follows.

```
TRACT NO 7661 LOT 44 ASSESSED TO DAVID PICK FAMILY 0 PARTNERSHIP LP
LOCATION CITY-AGOURA HILL PROPERTY ADDRESS: VACANT LOT
```

The property is located in the general vicinity of Figure 2.121. It is identified by Assessor's Identification Number (AIN) 2061029003. The starting bid is \$15,936. Comparable improved properties in this area is about \$299/sqft. Comparable unimproved lots in this area is about \$54/sqft. This parcel is approximately 26317 sqft. Note, however, that the parcel may be larger than the property under consideration. In case of condominiums, for example, the parcel may encompass other units of the development - those unrelated to the property to be auctioned.

The property is in a parcel zoned Specific Plan in Agoura Hills, for 0 to 15 dwelling units.

Figures 2.122 and 2.123 show street map and corresponding detailed aerial view, respectively. In both cases, the map is centered on the property with the containing parcel marked in heavy blue. If surrounding nearby properties are also part of this auction, the street and aerial maps highlights these in heavy, dashed blue outline.

This assessed entity may have other properties that are also in this auction:

1. AIN 2061029004 (auction ID 69): TRACT NO 7661 LOT 45 ... ASSESSED TO DAVID PICK FAMILY 0 PARTNERSHIP LP LOCATION CITY-AGOURA HILL PROPERTY ADDRESS: VACANT LOT. See page 198.

Figure 2.121: Property 69, AIN 2061029003, overview map

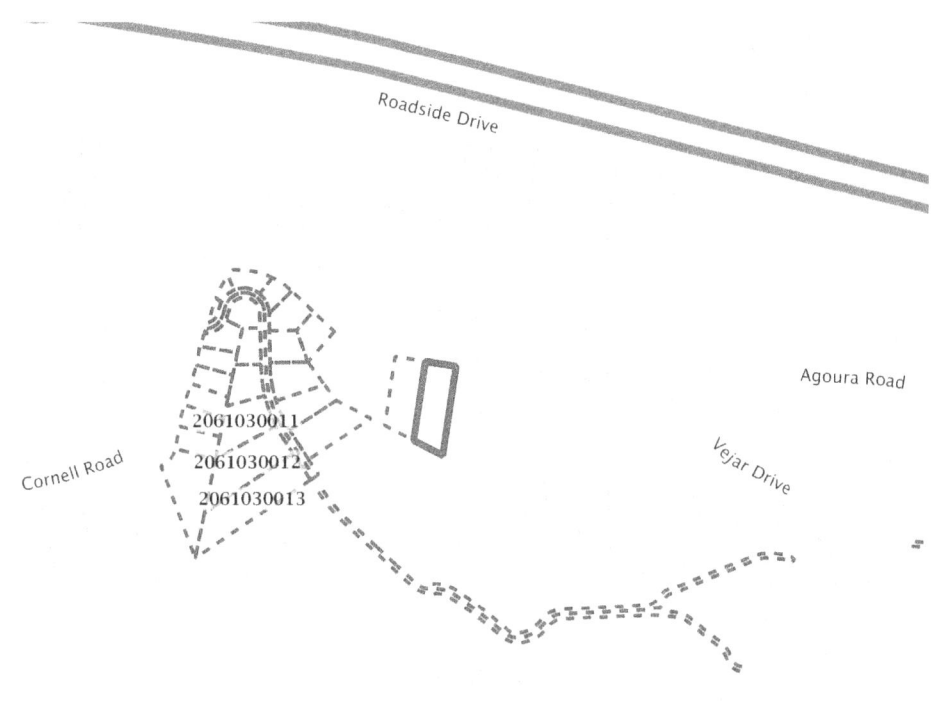

Figure 2.122: Property 69, AIN 2061029003, neighborhood view

Figure 2.123: Property 69, AIN 2061029003, detailed view

2.42   Auction ID 69

The Los Angeles County Auction Book describes the property as follows.

```
TRACT NO 7661 LOT 45 ASSESSED TO DAVID PICK FAMILY O PARTNERSHIP LP
LOCATION CITY-AGOURA HILL PROPERTY ADDRESS: VACANT LOT
```

The property is located in the general vicinity of Figure 2.124. It is identified by Assessor's Identification Number (AIN) 2061029004. The starting bid is $15,490. Comparable improved properties in this area is about $299/sqft. Comparable unimproved lots in this area is about $54/sqft. This parcel is approximately 23075 sqft. Note, however, that the parcel may be larger than the property under consideration. In case of condominiums, for example, the parcel may encompass other units of the development - those unrelated to the property to be auctioned.

The property is in a parcel zoned Specific Plan in Agoura Hills, for 0 to 15 dwelling units.

Figures 2.125 and 2.126 show street map and corresponding detailed aerial view, respectively. In both cases, the map is centered on the property with the containing parcel marked in heavy blue. If surrounding nearby properties are also part of this auction, the street and aerial maps highlights these in heavy, dashed blue outline.

This assessed entity may have other properties that are also in this auction:

1. AIN 2061029003 (auction ID 68): TRACT NO 7661 LOT 44 ... ASSESSED TO DAVID PICK FAMILY 0 PARTNERSHIP LP LOCATION CITY-AGOURA HILL PROPERTY ADDRESS: VACANT LOT. See page 196.

Figure 2.124: Property 68, AIN 2061029004, overview map

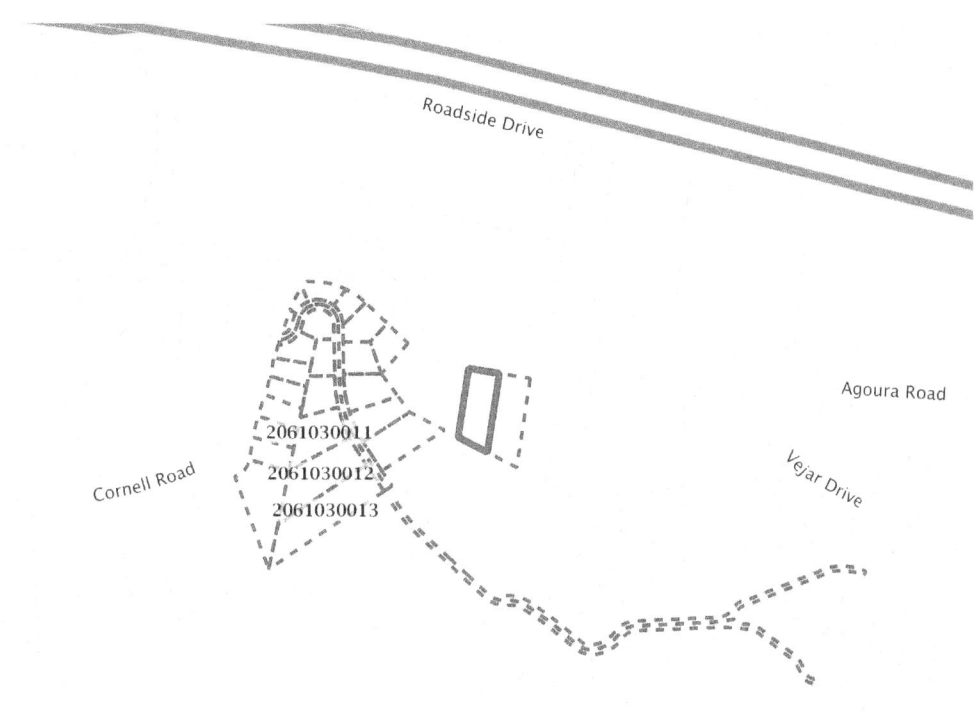

Figure 2.125: Property 68, AIN 2061029004, neighborhood view

Figure 2.126: Property 68, AIN 2061029004, detailed view

2.43 Auction ID 72

The Los Angeles County Auction Book describes the property as follows.

```
TRACT NO 7661 LOT 48 ASSESSED TO AGOURA AND CORNELL 0 ROADS LP LOCATION
CITY-AGOURA HILL PROPERTY ADDRESS: VACANT LOT
```

The property is located in the general vicinity of Figure 2.127. It is identified by Assessor's Identification Number (AIN) 2061029008. The starting bid is $13,352. Comparable improved properties in this area is about $292/sqft. Comparable unimproved lots in this area is about $62/sqft. This parcel is approximately 9600 sqft. Note, however, that the parcel may be larger than the property under consideration. In case of condominiums, for example, the parcel may encompass other units of the development - those unrelated to the property to be auctioned.

The property is in a parcel zoned Specific Plan in Agoura Hills, for 0 to 15 dwelling units.

Figures 2.128 and 2.129 show street map and corresponding detailed aerial view, respectively. In both cases, the map is centered on the property with the containing parcel marked in heavy blue. If surrounding nearby properties are also part of this auction, the street and aerial maps highlights these in heavy, dashed blue outline.

This assessed entity may have other properties that are also in this auction:

1. AIN 2061029009 (auction ID 73): TRACT NO 7661 LOT 49 ... ASSESSED TO AGOURA AND CORNELL 0 ROADS LP LOCATION CITY-AGOURA HILL PROPERTY ADDRESS: VACANT LOT. See page 204.

2. AIN 2061029010 (auction ID 74): TRACT NO 7661 LOT 50 ... ASSESSED TO AGOURA AND CORNELL 0 ROADS LP LOCATION CITY-AGOURA HILL PROPERTY ADDRESS: VACANT LOT. See page 208.

3. AIN 2061029011 (auction ID 75): TRACT NO 7661 EX OF ST LOT 51 ... ASSESSED TO AGOURA AND 0 CORNELL ROADS LP LOCATION CITY-AGOURA HILL PROPERTY ADDRESS: VACANT LOT. See page 212.

4. AIN 2061029012 (auction ID 76): TRACT NO 7661 EX OF ST LOT 52 ... ASSESSED TO AGOURA AND 0 CORNELL ROADS LP LOCATION CITY-AGOURA HILL PROPERTY ADDRESS: VACANT LOT. See page 216.

5. AIN 2061029013 (auction ID 77): TRACT NO 7661 EX OF ST LOT 53 ... ASSESSED TO AGOURA AND 0 CORNELL ROADS LP LOCATION CITY-AGOURA HILL PROPERTY ADDRESS: VACANT LOT. See page 220.

6. AIN 2061029014 (auction ID 78): TRACT NO 7661 LOT 54 ... ASSESSED TO AGOURA AND CORNELL 0 ROADS LP LOCATION CITY-AGOURA HILL PROPERTY ADDRESS: VACANT LOT. See page 224.

7. AIN 2061029015 (auction ID 79): TRACT NO 7661 LOT 55 ... ASSESSED TO AGOURA AND CORNELL 0 ROADS LP LOCATION CITY-AGOURA HILL PROPERTY ADDRESS: VACANT LOT. See page 228.

8. AIN 2061029016 (auction ID 80): TRACT NO 7661 LOT 56 ... ASSESSED TO AGOURA AND CORNELL 0 ROADS LP LOCATION CITY-AGOURA HILL PROPERTY ADDRESS: VACANT LOT. See page 232.

9. AIN 2061029017 (auction ID 81): TRACT NO 7661 LOT 57 ... ASSESSED TO AGOURA AND CORNELL 0 ROADS LP LOCATION CITY-AGOURA HILL PROPERTY ADDRESS: VACANT LOT. See page 236.

10. AIN 2061029023 (auction ID 82): VAC ST ADJ LOTS 49 THRU 58 TR NO 7661 ON SW 0 . . . ASSESSED TO AGOURA AND CORNELL ROADS LP LOCATION CITY-AGOURA HILL PROPERTY ADDRESS: VACANT LOT. See page 240.

11. AIN 2061030001 (auction ID 83): TRACT NO 7661 LOT 103 . . . ASSESSED TO AGOURA AND CORNELL 0 ROADS LP LOCATION CITY-AGOURA HILL PROPERTY ADDRESS: VACANT LOT. See page 244.

12. AIN 2061030002 (auction ID 84): TRACT NO 7661 LOT 104 . . . ASSESSED TO AGOURA AND CORNELL - 0 ROADS LP LOCATION CITY-AGOURA HILL PROPERTY ADDRESS: VACANT LOT. See page 248.

13. AIN 2061030003 (auction ID 85): TRACT NO 7661 LOT 105 . . . ASSESSED TO AGOURA AND CORNELL 0 ROADS LP LOCATION CITY-AGOURA HILL PROPERTY ADDRESS: VACANT LOT. See page 252.

14. AIN 2061030004 (auction ID 86): TRACT NO 7661 LOT 106 . . . ASSESSED TO AGOURA AND CORNELL 0 ROADS LP LOCATION CITY-AGOURA HILL PROPERTY ADDRESS: VACANT LOT. See page 256.

15. AIN 2061030005 (auction ID 87): TRACT NO 7661 LOT 107 . . . ASSESSED TO AGOURA AND CORNELL 0 ROADS LP LOCATION CITY-AGOURA HILL PROPERTY ADDRESS: VACANT LOT. See page 260.

16. AIN 2061030006 (auction ID 88): TRACT NO 7661 EX OF ST LOT 108 . . . ASSESSED TO AGOURA AND 0 CORNELL ROADS LP LOCATION CITY-AGOURA HILL PROPERTY ADDRESS: VACANT LOT. See page 264.

17. AIN 2061030007 (auction ID 89): TRACT NO 7661 EX OF ST LOT 109 . . . ASSESSED TO AGOURA AND 0 CORNELL ROADS LP LOCATION CITY-AGOURA HILL PROPERTY ADDRESS: VACANT LOT. See page 268.

18. AIN 2061030008 (auction ID 90): TRACT NO 7661 LOT 110 . . . ASSESSED TO AGOURA AND CORNELL 0 ROADS LP LOCATION CITY-AGOURA HILL PROPERTY ADDRESS: VACANT LOT. See page 272.

19. AIN 2061030009 (auction ID 91): TRACT NO 7661 LOT 111 . . . ASSESSED TO AGOURA AND CORNELL 0 ROADS LP LOCATION CITY-AGOURA HILL PROPERTY ADDRESS: VACANT LOT. See page 276.

20. AIN 2061030010 (auction ID 92): TRACT NO 7661 LOT 112 . . . ASSESSED TO AGOURA AND CORNELL 0 ROADS LP LOCATION CITY-AGOURA HILL PROPERTY ADDRESS: VACANT LOT. See page 280.

21. AIN 2061030011 (auction ID 93): TRACT NO 7661 LOT 113 . . . ASSESSED TO AGOURA AND CORNELL 0 ROADS LP LOCATION CITY-AGOURA HILL PROPERTY ADDRESS: VACANT LOT. See page 284.

22. AIN 2061030012 (auction ID 94): TRACT NO 7661 LOT 114 . . . ASSESSED TO AGOURA AND CORNELL 0 ROADS LP LOCATION CITY-AGOURA HILL PROPERTY ADDRESS: VACANT LOT. See page 288.

23. AIN 2061030013 (auction ID 95): TRACT NO 7661 LOT 115 . . . ASSESSED TO AGOURA AND CORNELL 0 ROADS LP LOCATION CITY-AGOURA HILL PROPERTY ADDRESS: VACANT LOT. See page 292.

24. AIN 2061030017 (auction ID 96): VAC ST ADJ LOTS 109 THRU 115 TR NO 7661 ON NW AND NE 0 . . . ASSESSED TO AGOURA AND CORNELL ROADS LP LOCATION CITY-AGOURA HILL PROPERTY ADDRESS: . . . . See page 296.

Figure 2.127: Property 96, AIN 2061029008, overview map

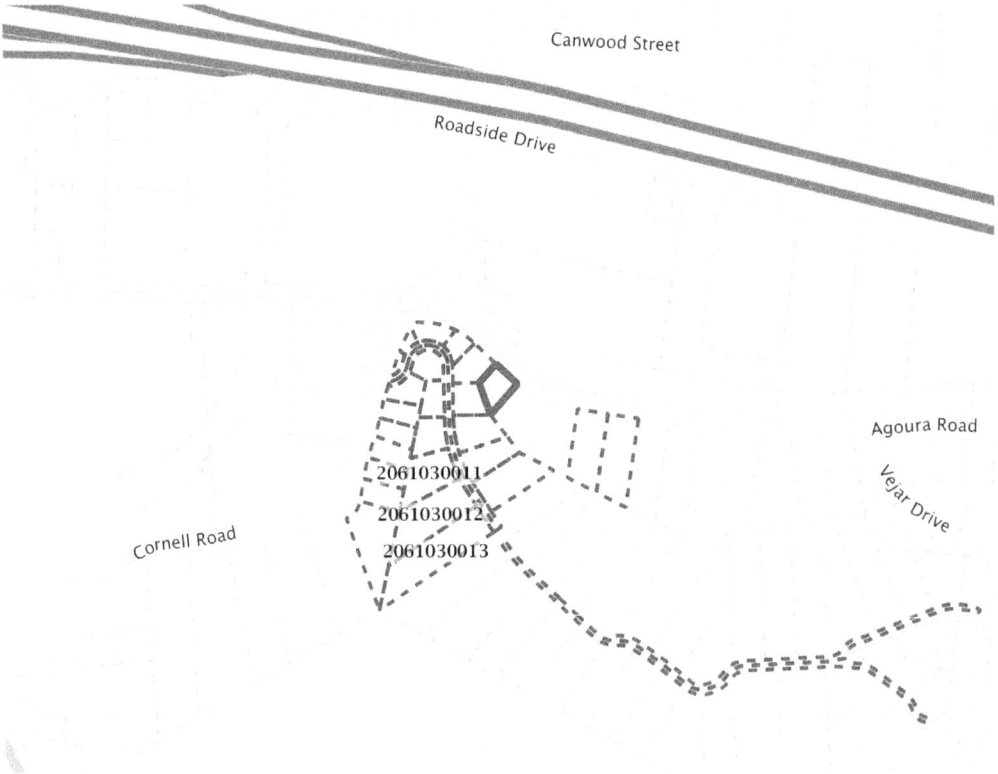

Figure 2.128: Property 96, AIN 2061029008, neighborhood view

Figure 2.129: Property 96, AIN 2061029008, detailed view

2.44   Auction ID 73

The Los Angeles County Auction Book describes the property as follows.

> TRACT NO 7661 LOT 49 ASSESSED TO AGOURA AND CORNELL 0 ROADS LP LOCATION
> CITY-AGOURA HILL PROPERTY ADDRESS: VACANT LOT

The property is located in the general vicinity of Figure 2.130. It is identified by Assessor's Identification Number (AIN) 2061029009. The starting bid is $13,827. Comparable improved properties in this area is about $292/sqft. Comparable unimproved lots in this area is about $62/sqft. This parcel is approximately 11090 sqft. Note, however, that the parcel may be larger than the property under consideration. In case of condominiums, for example, the parcel may encompass other units of the development - those unrelated to the property to be auctioned.

The property is in a parcel zoned Specific Plan in Agoura Hills, for 0 to 15 dwelling units.

Figures 2.131 and 2.132 show street map and corresponding detailed aerial view, respectively. In both cases, the map is centered on the property with the containing parcel marked in heavy blue. If surrounding nearby properties are also part of this auction, the street and aerial maps highlights these in heavy, dashed blue outline.

This assessed entity may have other properties that are also in this auction:

1. AIN 2061029008 (auction ID 72): TRACT NO 7661 LOT 48 . . . ASSESSED TO AGOURA AND CORNELL 0 ROADS LP LOCATION CITY-AGOURA HILL PROPERTY ADDRESS: VACANT LOT. See page 200.

2. AIN 2061029010 (auction ID 74): TRACT NO 7661 LOT 50 . . . ASSESSED TO AGOURA AND CORNELL 0 ROADS LP LOCATION CITY-AGOURA HILL PROPERTY ADDRESS: VACANT LOT. See page 208.

3. AIN 2061029011 (auction ID 75): TRACT NO 7661 EX OF ST LOT 51 . . . ASSESSED TO AGOURA AND 0 CORNELL ROADS LP LOCATION CITY-AGOURA HILL PROPERTY ADDRESS: VACANT LOT. See page 212.

4. AIN 2061029012 (auction ID 76): TRACT NO 7661 EX OF ST LOT 52 . . . ASSESSED TO AGOURA AND 0 CORNELL ROADS LP LOCATION CITY-AGOURA HILL PROPERTY ADDRESS: VACANT LOT. See page 216.

5. AIN 2061029013 (auction ID 77): TRACT NO 7661 EX OF ST LOT 53 . . . ASSESSED TO AGOURA AND 0 CORNELL ROADS LP LOCATION CITY-AGOURA HILL PROPERTY ADDRESS: VACANT LOT. See page 220.

6. AIN 2061029014 (auction ID 78): TRACT NO 7661 LOT 54 . . . ASSESSED TO AGOURA AND CORNELL 0 ROADS LP LOCATION CITY-AGOURA HILL PROPERTY ADDRESS: VACANT LOT. See page 224.

7. AIN 2061029015 (auction ID 79): TRACT NO 7661 LOT 55 . . . ASSESSED TO AGOURA AND CORNELL 0 ROADS LP LOCATION CITY-AGOURA HILL PROPERTY ADDRESS: VACANT LOT. See page 228.

8. AIN 2061029016 (auction ID 80): TRACT NO 7661 LOT 56 . . . ASSESSED TO AGOURA AND CORNELL 0 ROADS LP LOCATION CITY-AGOURA HILL PROPERTY ADDRESS: VACANT LOT. See page 232.

9. AIN 2061029017 (auction ID 81): TRACT NO 7661 LOT 57 . . . ASSESSED TO AGOURA AND CORNELL 0 ROADS LP LOCATION CITY-AGOURA HILL PROPERTY ADDRESS: VACANT LOT. See page 236.

10. AIN 2061029023 (auction ID 82): VAC ST ADJ LOTS 49 THRU 58 TR NO 7661 ON SW 0 . . . ASSESSED TO AGOURA AND CORNELL ROADS LP LOCATION CITY-AGOURA HILL PROPERTY ADDRESS: VACANT LOT. See page 240.

11. AIN 2061030001 (auction ID 83): TRACT NO 7661 LOT 103 . . . ASSESSED TO AGOURA AND CORNELL 0 ROADS LP LOCATION CITY-AGOURA HILL PROPERTY ADDRESS: VACANT LOT. See page 244.

12. AIN 2061030002 (auction ID 84): TRACT NO 7661 LOT 104 . . . ASSESSED TO AGOURA AND CORNELL - 0 ROADS LP LOCATION CITY-AGOURA HILL PROPERTY ADDRESS: VACANT LOT. See page 248.

13. AIN 2061030003 (auction ID 85): TRACT NO 7661 LOT 105 . . . ASSESSED TO AGOURA AND CORNELL 0 ROADS LP LOCATION CITY-AGOURA HILL PROPERTY ADDRESS: VACANT LOT. See page 252.

14. AIN 2061030004 (auction ID 86): TRACT NO 7661 LOT 106 . . . ASSESSED TO AGOURA AND CORNELL 0 ROADS LP LOCATION CITY-AGOURA HILL PROPERTY ADDRESS: VACANT LOT. See page 256.

15. AIN 2061030005 (auction ID 87): TRACT NO 7661 LOT 107 . . . ASSESSED TO AGOURA AND CORNELL 0 ROADS LP LOCATION CITY-AGOURA HILL PROPERTY ADDRESS: VACANT LOT. See page 260.

16. AIN 2061030006 (auction ID 88): TRACT NO 7661 EX OF ST LOT 108 . . . ASSESSED TO AGOURA AND 0 CORNELL ROADS LP LOCATION CITY-AGOURA HILL PROPERTY ADDRESS: VACANT LOT. See page 264.

17. AIN 2061030007 (auction ID 89): TRACT NO 7661 EX OF ST LOT 109 . . . ASSESSED TO AGOURA AND 0 CORNELL ROADS LP LOCATION CITY-AGOURA HILL PROPERTY ADDRESS: VACANT LOT. See page 268.

18. AIN 2061030008 (auction ID 90): TRACT NO 7661 LOT 110 . . . ASSESSED TO AGOURA AND CORNELL 0 ROADS LP LOCATION CITY-AGOURA HILL PROPERTY ADDRESS: VACANT LOT. See page 272.

19. AIN 2061030009 (auction ID 91): TRACT NO 7661 LOT 111 . . . ASSESSED TO AGOURA AND CORNELL 0 ROADS LP LOCATION CITY-AGOURA HILL PROPERTY ADDRESS: VACANT LOT. See page 276.

20. AIN 2061030010 (auction ID 92): TRACT NO 7661 LOT 112 . . . ASSESSED TO AGOURA AND CORNELL 0 ROADS LP LOCATION CITY-AGOURA HILL PROPERTY ADDRESS: VACANT LOT. See page 280.

21. AIN 2061030011 (auction ID 93): TRACT NO 7661 LOT 113 . . . ASSESSED TO AGOURA AND CORNELL 0 ROADS LP LOCATION CITY-AGOURA HILL PROPERTY ADDRESS: VACANT LOT. See page 284.

22. AIN 2061030012 (auction ID 94): TRACT NO 7661 LOT 114 . . . ASSESSED TO AGOURA AND CORNELL 0 ROADS LP LOCATION CITY-AGOURA HILL PROPERTY ADDRESS: VACANT LOT. See page 288.

23. AIN 2061030013 (auction ID 95): TRACT NO 7661 LOT 115 . . . ASSESSED TO AGOURA AND CORNELL 0 ROADS LP LOCATION CITY-AGOURA HILL PROPERTY ADDRESS: VACANT LOT. See page 292.

24. AIN 2061030017 (auction ID 96): VAC ST ADJ LOTS 109 THRU 115 TR NO 7661 ON NW AND NE 0 . . . ASSESSED TO AGOURA AND CORNELL ROADS LP LOCATION CITY-AGOURA HILL PROPERTY ADDRESS: . . . . See page 296.

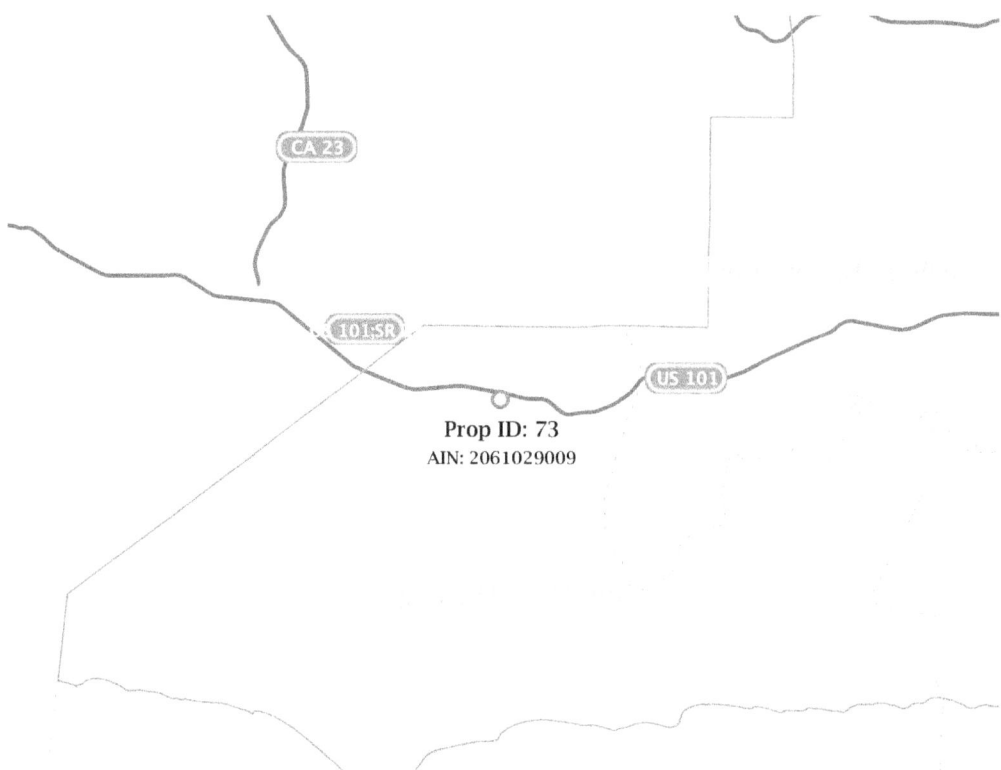

Figure 2.130: Property 96, AIN 2061029009, overview map

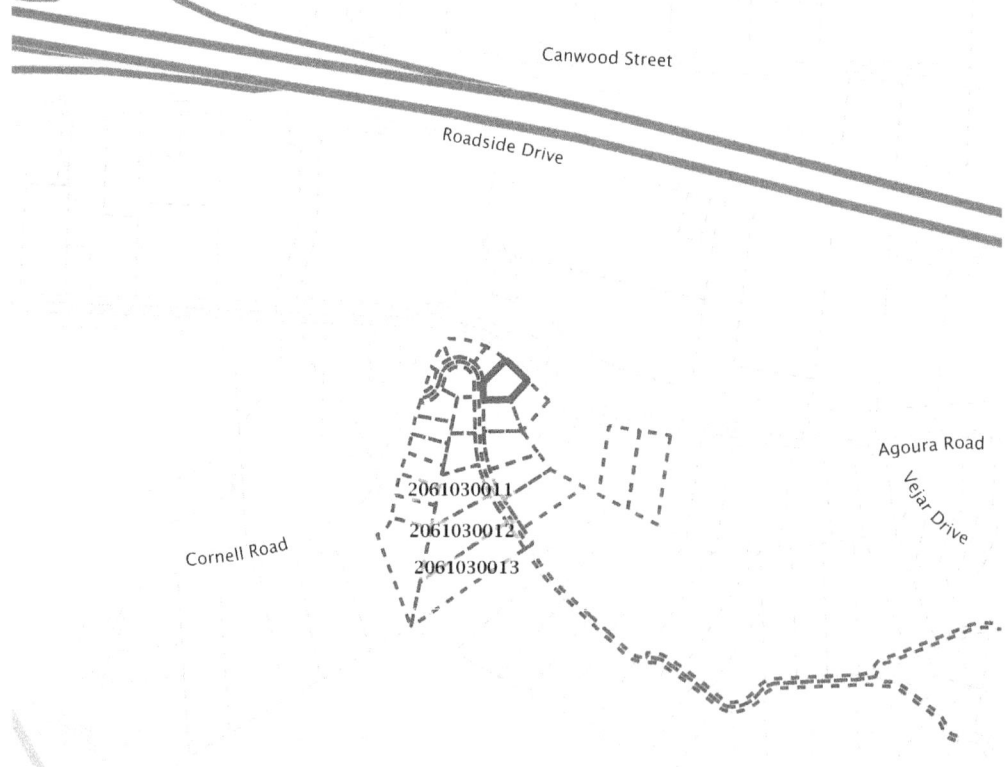

Figure 2.131: Property 96, AIN 2061029009, neighborhood view

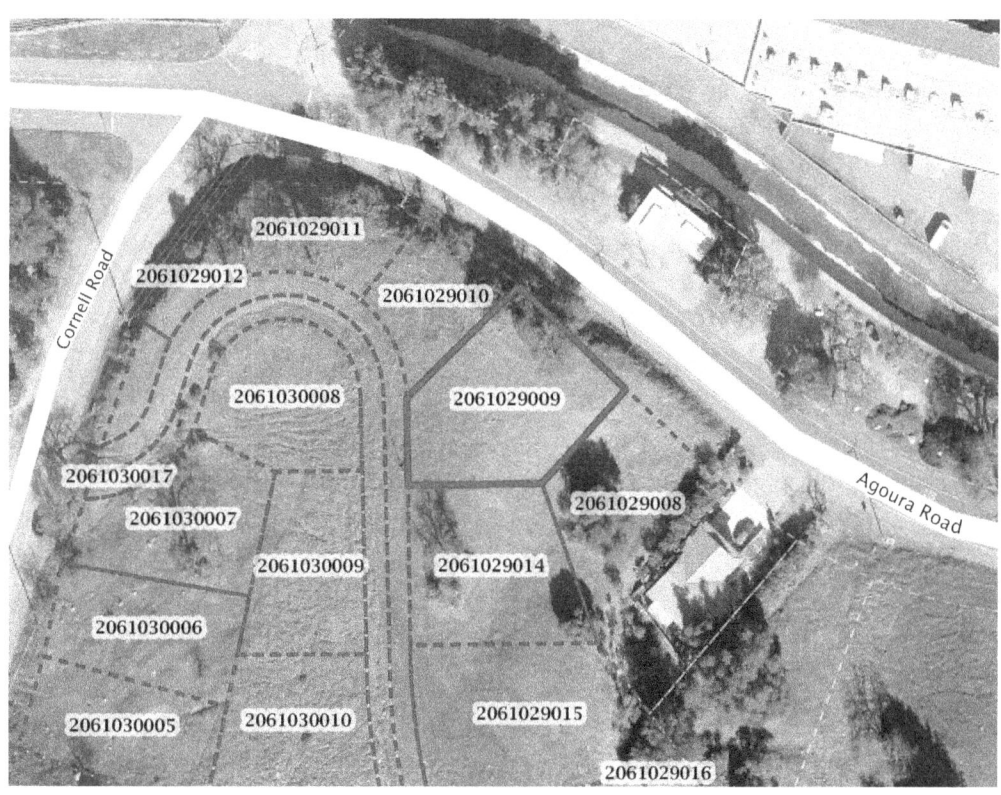

Figure 2.132: Property 96, AIN 2061029009, detailed view

2.45 Auction ID 74

The Los Angeles County Auction Book describes the property as follows.

```
TRACT NO 7661 LOT 50 ASSESSED TO AGOURA AND CORNELL 0 ROADS LP LOCATION
CITY-AGOURA HILL PROPERTY ADDRESS: VACANT LOT
```

The property is located in the general vicinity of Figure 2.133. It is identified by Assessor's Identification Number (AIN) 2061029010. The starting bid is $8,776. Comparable improved properties in this area is about $292/sqft. Comparable unimproved lots in this area is about $63/sqft. This parcel is approximately 5428 sqft. Note, however, that the parcel may be larger than the property under consideration. In case of condominiums, for example, the parcel may encompass other units of the development - those unrelated to the property to be auctioned.

The property is in a parcel zoned Specific Plan in Agoura Hills, for 0 to 15 dwelling units.

Figures 2.134 and 2.135 show street map and corresponding detailed aerial view, respectively. In both cases, the map is centered on the property with the containing parcel marked in heavy blue. If surrounding nearby properties are also part of this auction, the street and aerial maps highlights these in heavy, dashed blue outline.

This assessed entity may have other properties that are also in this auction:

1. AIN 2061029008 (auction ID 72): TRACT NO 7661 LOT 48 . . . ASSESSED TO AGOURA AND CORNELL 0 ROADS LP LOCATION CITY-AGOURA HILL PROPERTY ADDRESS: VACANT LOT. See page 200.

2. AIN 2061029009 (auction ID 73): TRACT NO 7661 LOT 49 . . . ASSESSED TO AGOURA AND CORNELL 0 ROADS LP LOCATION CITY-AGOURA HILL PROPERTY ADDRESS: VACANT LOT. See page 204.

3. AIN 2061029011 (auction ID 75): TRACT NO 7661 EX OF ST LOT 51 . . . ASSESSED TO AGOURA AND 0 CORNELL ROADS LP LOCATION CITY-AGOURA HILL PROPERTY ADDRESS: VACANT LOT. See page 212.

4. AIN 2061029012 (auction ID 76): TRACT NO 7661 EX OF ST LOT 52 . . . ASSESSED TO AGOURA AND 0 CORNELL ROADS LP LOCATION CITY-AGOURA HILL PROPERTY ADDRESS: VACANT LOT. See page 216.

5. AIN 2061029013 (auction ID 77): TRACT NO 7661 EX OF ST LOT 53 . . . ASSESSED TO AGOURA AND 0 CORNELL ROADS LP LOCATION CITY-AGOURA HILL PROPERTY ADDRESS: VACANT LOT. See page 220.

6. AIN 2061029014 (auction ID 78): TRACT NO 7661 LOT 54 . . . ASSESSED TO AGOURA AND CORNELL 0 ROADS LP LOCATION CITY-AGOURA HILL PROPERTY ADDRESS: VACANT LOT. See page 224.

7. AIN 2061029015 (auction ID 79): TRACT NO 7661 LOT 55 . . . ASSESSED TO AGOURA AND CORNELL 0 ROADS LP LOCATION CITY-AGOURA HILL PROPERTY ADDRESS: VACANT LOT. See page 228.

8. AIN 2061029016 (auction ID 80): TRACT NO 7661 LOT 56 . . . ASSESSED TO AGOURA AND CORNELL 0 ROADS LP LOCATION CITY-AGOURA HILL PROPERTY ADDRESS: VACANT LOT. See page 232.

9. AIN 2061029017 (auction ID 81): TRACT NO 7661 LOT 57 . . . ASSESSED TO AGOURA AND CORNELL 0 ROADS LP LOCATION CITY-AGOURA HILL PROPERTY ADDRESS: VACANT LOT. See page 236.

10. AIN 2061029023 (auction ID 82): VAC ST ADJ LOTS 49 THRU 58 TR NO 7661 ON SW 0 . . . ASSESSED TO AGOURA AND CORNELL ROADS LP LOCATION CITY-AGOURA HILL PROPERTY ADDRESS: VACANT LOT. See page 240.

11. AIN 2061030001 (auction ID 83): TRACT NO 7661 LOT 103 . . . ASSESSED TO AGOURA AND CORNELL 0 ROADS LP LOCATION CITY-AGOURA HILL PROPERTY ADDRESS: VACANT LOT. See page 244.

12. AIN 2061030002 (auction ID 84): TRACT NO 7661 LOT 104 . . . ASSESSED TO AGOURA AND CORNELL - 0 ROADS LP LOCATION CITY-AGOURA HILL PROPERTY ADDRESS: VACANT LOT. See page 248.

13. AIN 2061030003 (auction ID 85): TRACT NO 7661 LOT 105 . . . ASSESSED TO AGOURA AND CORNELL 0 ROADS LP LOCATION CITY-AGOURA HILL PROPERTY ADDRESS: VACANT LOT. See page 252.

14. AIN 2061030004 (auction ID 86): TRACT NO 7661 LOT 106 . . . ASSESSED TO AGOURA AND CORNELL 0 ROADS LP LOCATION CITY-AGOURA HILL PROPERTY ADDRESS: VACANT LOT. See page 256.

15. AIN 2061030005 (auction ID 87): TRACT NO 7661 LOT 107 . . . ASSESSED TO AGOURA AND CORNELL 0 ROADS LP LOCATION CITY-AGOURA HILL PROPERTY ADDRESS: VACANT LOT. See page 260.

16. AIN 2061030006 (auction ID 88): TRACT NO 7661 EX OF ST LOT 108 . . . ASSESSED TO AGOURA AND 0 CORNELL ROADS LP LOCATION CITY-AGOURA HILL PROPERTY ADDRESS: VACANT LOT. See page 264.

17. AIN 2061030007 (auction ID 89): TRACT NO 7661 EX OF ST LOT 109 . . . ASSESSED TO AGOURA AND 0 CORNELL ROADS LP LOCATION CITY-AGOURA HILL PROPERTY ADDRESS: VACANT LOT. See page 268.

18. AIN 2061030008 (auction ID 90): TRACT NO 7661 LOT 110 . . . ASSESSED TO AGOURA AND CORNELL 0 ROADS LP LOCATION CITY-AGOURA HILL PROPERTY ADDRESS: VACANT LOT. See page 272.

19. AIN 2061030009 (auction ID 91): TRACT NO 7661 LOT 111 . . . ASSESSED TO AGOURA AND CORNELL 0 ROADS LP LOCATION CITY-AGOURA HILL PROPERTY ADDRESS: VACANT LOT. See page 276.

20. AIN 2061030010 (auction ID 92): TRACT NO 7661 LOT 112 . . . ASSESSED TO AGOURA AND CORNELL 0 ROADS LP LOCATION CITY-AGOURA HILL PROPERTY ADDRESS: VACANT LOT. See page 280.

21. AIN 2061030011 (auction ID 93): TRACT NO 7661 LOT 113 . . . ASSESSED TO AGOURA AND CORNELL 0 ROADS LP LOCATION CITY-AGOURA HILL PROPERTY ADDRESS: VACANT LOT. See page 284.

22. AIN 2061030012 (auction ID 94): TRACT NO 7661 LOT 114 . . . ASSESSED TO AGOURA AND CORNELL 0 ROADS LP LOCATION CITY-AGOURA HILL PROPERTY ADDRESS: VACANT LOT. See page 288.

23. AIN 2061030013 (auction ID 95): TRACT NO 7661 LOT 115 . . . ASSESSED TO AGOURA AND CORNELL 0 ROADS LP LOCATION CITY-AGOURA HILL PROPERTY ADDRESS: VACANT LOT. See page 292.

24. AIN 2061030017 (auction ID 96): VAC ST ADJ LOTS 109 THRU 115 TR NO 7661 ON NW AND NE 0 . . . ASSESSED TO AGOURA AND CORNELL ROADS LP LOCATION CITY-AGOURA HILL PROPERTY ADDRESS: . . . . See page 296.

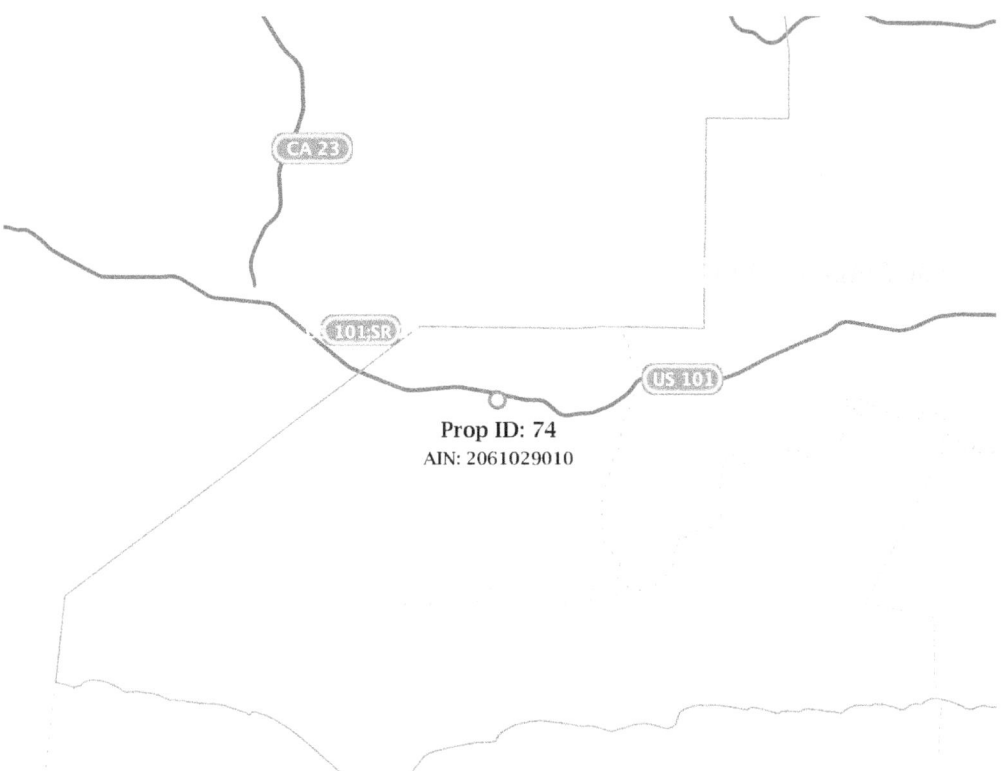

Figure 2.133: Property 96, AIN 2061029010, overview map

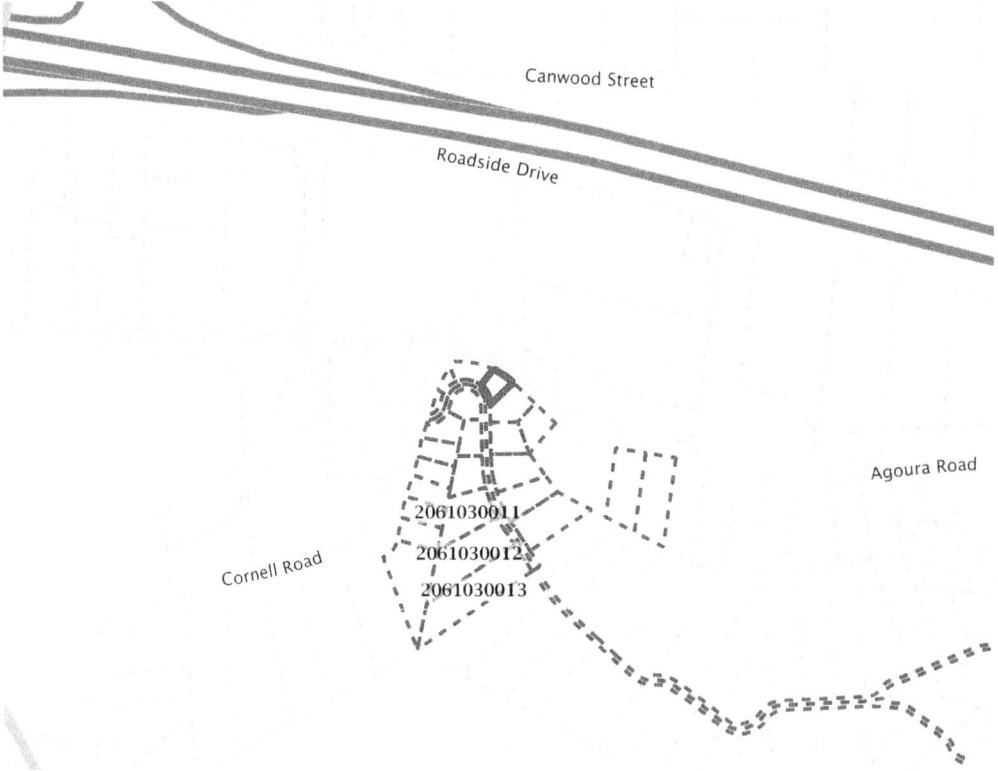

Figure 2.134: Property 96, AIN 2061029010, neighborhood view

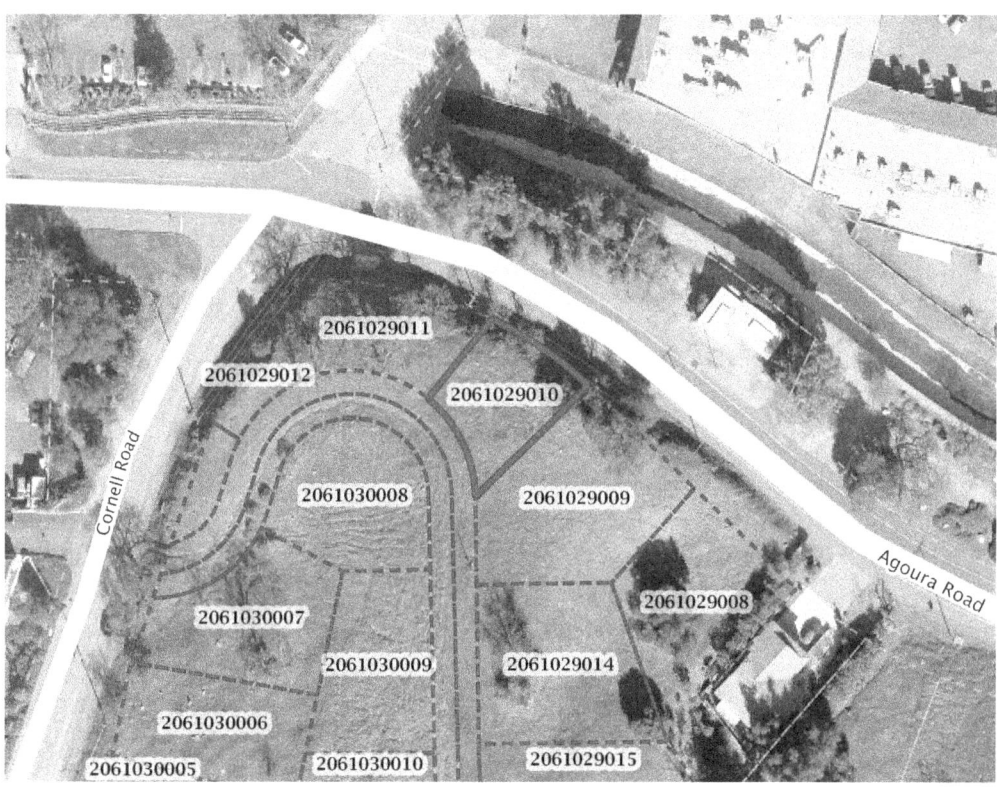

Figure 2.135: Property 96, AIN 2061029010, detailed view

2.46 Auction ID 75

The Los Angeles County Auction Book describes the property as follows.

```
TRACT NO 7661 EX OF ST LOT 51 ASSESSED TO AGOURA AND 0 CORNELL ROADS
LP LOCATION CITY-AGOURA HILL PROPERTY ADDRESS: VACANT LOT
```

The property is located in the general vicinity of Figure 2.136. It is identified by Assessor's Identification Number (AIN) 2061029011. The starting bid is $9,554. Comparable improved properties in this area is about $296/sqft. Comparable unimproved lots in this area is about $64/sqft. This parcel is approximately 6709 sqft. Note, however, that the parcel may be larger than the property under consideration. In case of condominiums, for example, the parcel may encompass other units of the development - those unrelated to the property to be auctioned.

The property is in a parcel zoned Specific Plan in Agoura Hills, for 0 to 15 dwelling units.

Figures 2.137 and 2.138 show street map and corresponding detailed aerial view, respectively. In both cases, the map is centered on the property with the containing parcel marked in heavy blue. If surrounding nearby properties are also part of this auction, the street and aerial maps highlights these in heavy, dashed blue outline.

This assessed entity may have other properties that are also in this auction:

1. AIN 2061029008 (auction ID 72): TRACT NO 7661 LOT 48 ... ASSESSED TO AGOURA AND CORNELL 0 ROADS LP LOCATION CITY-AGOURA HILL PROPERTY ADDRESS: VACANT LOT. See page 200.

2. AIN 2061029009 (auction ID 73): TRACT NO 7661 LOT 49 ... ASSESSED TO AGOURA AND CORNELL 0 ROADS LP LOCATION CITY-AGOURA HILL PROPERTY ADDRESS: VACANT LOT. See page 204.

3. AIN 2061029010 (auction ID 74): TRACT NO 7661 LOT 50 ... ASSESSED TO AGOURA AND CORNELL 0 ROADS LP LOCATION CITY-AGOURA HILL PROPERTY ADDRESS: VACANT LOT. See page 208.

4. AIN 2061029012 (auction ID 76): TRACT NO 7661 EX OF ST LOT 52 ... ASSESSED TO AGOURA AND 0 CORNELL ROADS LP LOCATION CITY-AGOURA HILL PROPERTY ADDRESS: VACANT LOT. See page 216.

5. AIN 2061029013 (auction ID 77): TRACT NO 7661 EX OF ST LOT 53 ... ASSESSED TO AGOURA AND 0 CORNELL ROADS LP LOCATION CITY-AGOURA HILL PROPERTY ADDRESS: VACANT LOT. See page 220.

6. AIN 2061029014 (auction ID 78): TRACT NO 7661 LOT 54 ... ASSESSED TO AGOURA AND CORNELL 0 ROADS LP LOCATION CITY-AGOURA HILL PROPERTY ADDRESS: VACANT LOT. See page 224.

7. AIN 2061029015 (auction ID 79): TRACT NO 7661 LOT 55 ... ASSESSED TO AGOURA AND CORNELL 0 ROADS LP LOCATION CITY-AGOURA HILL PROPERTY ADDRESS: VACANT LOT. See page 228.

8. AIN 2061029016 (auction ID 80): TRACT NO 7661 LOT 56 ... ASSESSED TO AGOURA AND CORNELL 0 ROADS LP LOCATION CITY-AGOURA HILL PROPERTY ADDRESS: VACANT LOT. See page 232.

9. AIN 2061029017 (auction ID 81): TRACT NO 7661 LOT 57 ... ASSESSED TO AGOURA AND CORNELL 0 ROADS LP LOCATION CITY-AGOURA HILL PROPERTY ADDRESS: VACANT LOT. See page 236.

10. AIN 2061029023 (auction ID 82): VAC ST ADJ LOTS 49 THRU 58 TR NO 7661 ON SW 0 . . . ASSESSED TO AGOURA AND CORNELL ROADS LP LOCATION CITY-AGOURA HILL PROPERTY ADDRESS: VACANT LOT. See page 240.

11. AIN 2061030001 (auction ID 83): TRACT NO 7661 LOT 103 . . . ASSESSED TO AGOURA AND CORNELL 0 ROADS LP LOCATION CITY-AGOURA HILL PROPERTY ADDRESS: VACANT LOT. See page 244.

12. AIN 2061030002 (auction ID 84): TRACT NO 7661 LOT 104 . . . ASSESSED TO AGOURA AND CORNELL - 0 ROADS LP LOCATION CITY-AGOURA HILL PROPERTY ADDRESS: VACANT LOT. See page 248.

13. AIN 2061030003 (auction ID 85): TRACT NO 7661 LOT 105 . . . ASSESSED TO AGOURA AND CORNELL 0 ROADS LP LOCATION CITY-AGOURA HILL PROPERTY ADDRESS: VACANT LOT. See page 252.

14. AIN 2061030004 (auction ID 86): TRACT NO 7661 LOT 106 . . . ASSESSED TO AGOURA AND CORNELL 0 ROADS LP LOCATION CITY-AGOURA HILL PROPERTY ADDRESS: VACANT LOT. See page 256.

15. AIN 2061030005 (auction ID 87): TRACT NO 7661 LOT 107 . . . ASSESSED TO AGOURA AND CORNELL 0 ROADS LP LOCATION CITY-AGOURA HILL PROPERTY ADDRESS: VACANT LOT. See page 260.

16. AIN 2061030006 (auction ID 88): TRACT NO 7661 EX OF ST LOT 108 . . . ASSESSED TO AGOURA AND 0 CORNELL ROADS LP LOCATION CITY-AGOURA HILL PROPERTY ADDRESS: VACANT LOT. See page 264.

17. AIN 2061030007 (auction ID 89): TRACT NO 7661 EX OF ST LOT 109 . . . ASSESSED TO AGOURA AND 0 CORNELL ROADS LP LOCATION CITY-AGOURA HILL PROPERTY ADDRESS: VACANT LOT. See page 268.

18. AIN 2061030008 (auction ID 90): TRACT NO 7661 LOT 110 . . . ASSESSED TO AGOURA AND CORNELL 0 ROADS LP LOCATION CITY-AGOURA HILL PROPERTY ADDRESS: VACANT LOT. See page 272.

19. AIN 2061030009 (auction ID 91): TRACT NO 7661 LOT 111 . . . ASSESSED TO AGOURA AND CORNELL 0 ROADS LP LOCATION CITY-AGOURA HILL PROPERTY ADDRESS: VACANT LOT. See page 276.

20. AIN 2061030010 (auction ID 92): TRACT NO 7661 LOT 112 . . . ASSESSED TO AGOURA AND CORNELL 0 ROADS LP LOCATION CITY-AGOURA HILL PROPERTY ADDRESS: VACANT LOT. See page 280.

21. AIN 2061030011 (auction ID 93): TRACT NO 7661 LOT 113 . . . ASSESSED TO AGOURA AND CORNELL 0 ROADS LP LOCATION CITY-AGOURA HILL PROPERTY ADDRESS: VACANT LOT. See page 284.

22. AIN 2061030012 (auction ID 94): TRACT NO 7661 LOT 114 . . . ASSESSED TO AGOURA AND CORNELL 0 ROADS LP LOCATION CITY-AGOURA HILL PROPERTY ADDRESS: VACANT LOT. See page 288.

23. AIN 2061030013 (auction ID 95): TRACT NO 7661 LOT 115 . . . ASSESSED TO AGOURA AND CORNELL 0 ROADS LP LOCATION CITY-AGOURA HILL PROPERTY ADDRESS: VACANT LOT. See page 292.

24. AIN 2061030017 (auction ID 96): VAC ST ADJ LOTS 109 THRU 115 TR NO 7661 ON NW AND NE 0 . . . ASSESSED TO AGOURA AND CORNELL ROADS LP LOCATION CITY-AGOURA HILL PROPERTY ADDRESS: . . . . See page 296.

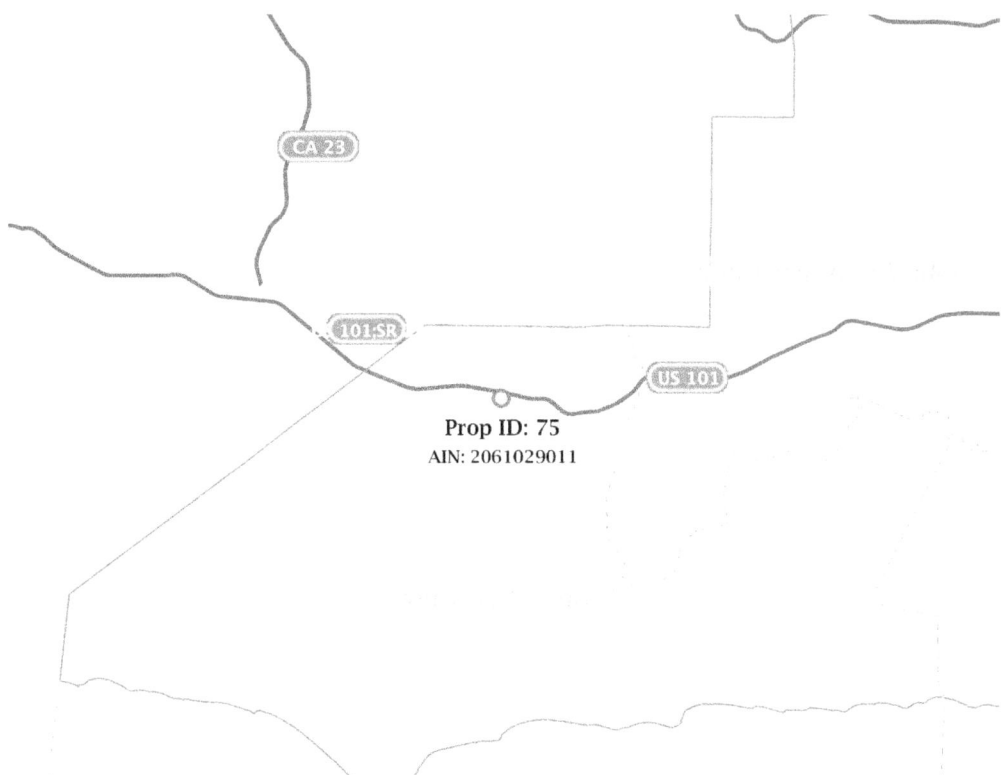

Figure 2.136: Property 96, AIN 2061029011, overview map

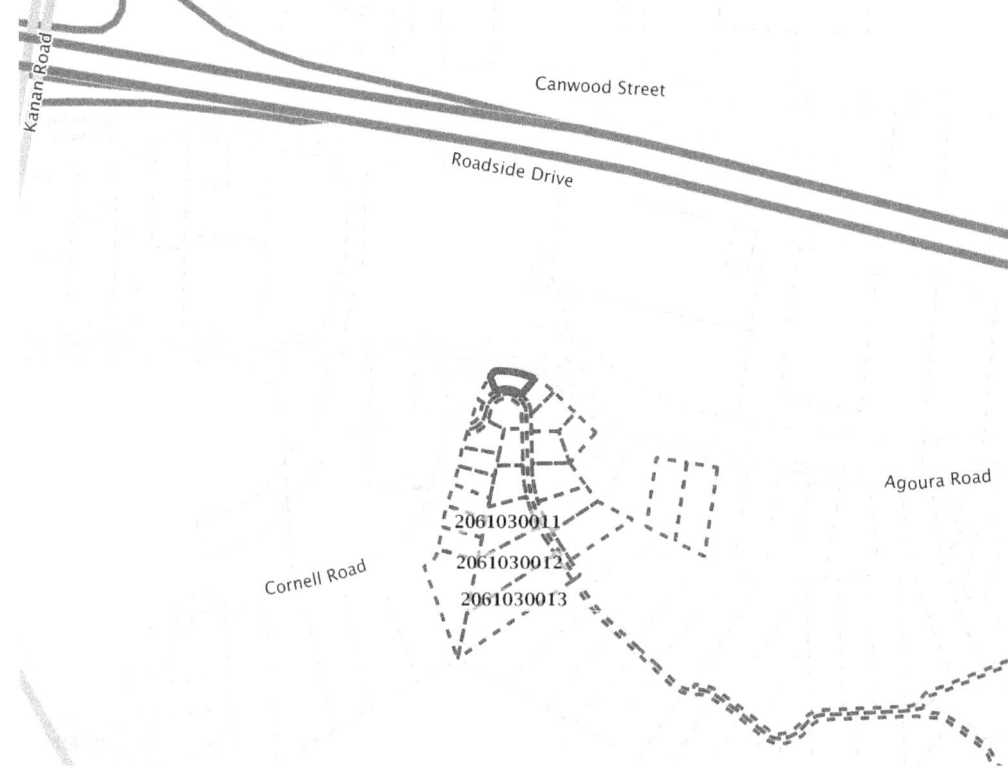

Figure 2.137: Property 96, AIN 2061029011, neighborhood view

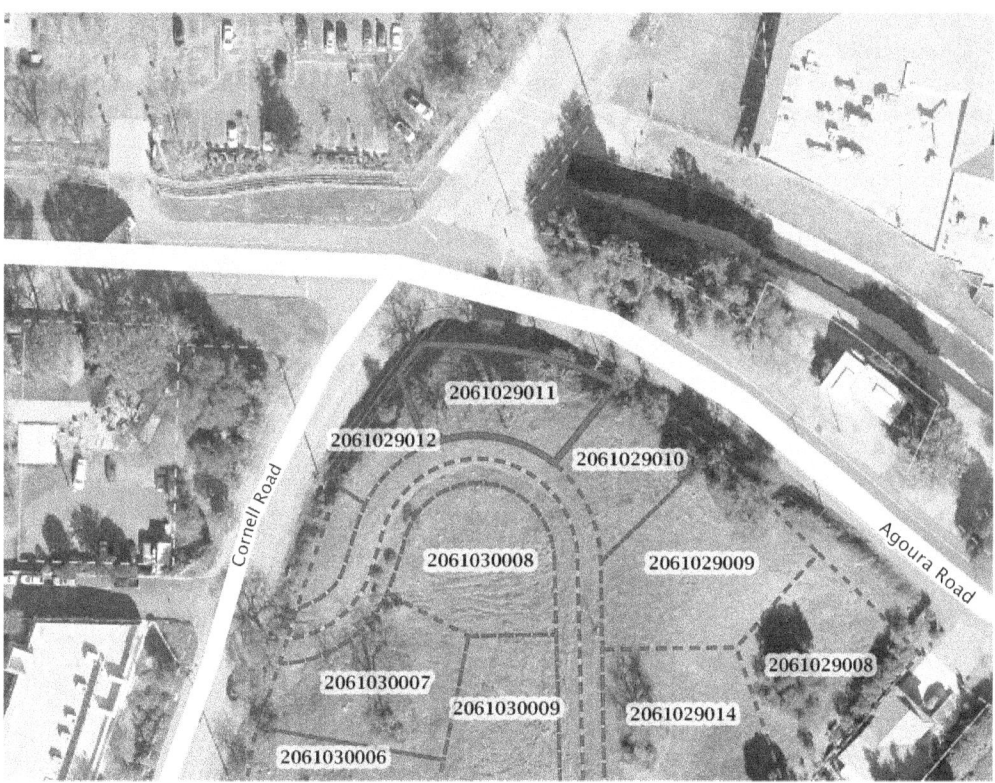

Figure 2.138: Property 96, AIN 2061029011, detailed view

2.47   Auction ID 76

The Los Angeles County Auction Book describes the property as follows.

```
TRACT NO 7661 EX OF ST LOT 52 ASSESSED TO AGOURA AND 0 CORNELL ROADS
LP LOCATION CITY-AGOURA HILL PROPERTY ADDRESS: VACANT LOT
```

The property is located in the general vicinity of Figure 2.139. It is identified by Assessor's Identification Number (AIN) 2061029012. The starting bid is $5,823. Comparable improved properties in this area is about $296/sqft. Comparable unimproved lots in this area is about $64/sqft. This parcel is approximately 2061 sqft. Note, however, that the parcel may be larger than the property under consideration. In case of condominiums, for example, the parcel may encompass other units of the development - those unrelated to the property to be auctioned.

The property is in a parcel zoned Specific Plan in Agoura Hills, for 0 to 15 dwelling units.

Figures 2.140 and 2.141 show street map and corresponding detailed aerial view, respectively. In both cases, the map is centered on the property with the containing parcel marked in heavy blue. If surrounding nearby properties are also part of this auction, the street and aerial maps highlights these in heavy, dashed blue outline.

This assessed entity may have other properties that are also in this auction:

1. AIN 2061029008 (auction ID 72): TRACT NO 7661 LOT 48 . . . ASSESSED TO AGOURA AND COR-NELL 0 ROADS LP LOCATION CITY-AGOURA HILL PROPERTY ADDRESS: VACANT LOT. See page 200.

2. AIN 2061029009 (auction ID 73): TRACT NO 7661 LOT 49 . . . ASSESSED TO AGOURA AND COR-NELL 0 ROADS LP LOCATION CITY-AGOURA HILL PROPERTY ADDRESS: VACANT LOT. See page 204.

3. AIN 2061029010 (auction ID 74): TRACT NO 7661 LOT 50 . . . ASSESSED TO AGOURA AND COR-NELL 0 ROADS LP LOCATION CITY-AGOURA HILL PROPERTY ADDRESS: VACANT LOT. See page 208.

4. AIN 2061029011 (auction ID 75): TRACT NO 7661 EX OF ST LOT 51 . . . ASSESSED TO AGOURA AND 0 CORNELL ROADS LP LOCATION CITY-AGOURA HILL PROPERTY ADDRESS: VACANT LOT. See page 212.

5. AIN 2061029013 (auction ID 77): TRACT NO 7661 EX OF ST LOT 53 . . . ASSESSED TO AGOURA AND 0 CORNELL ROADS LP LOCATION CITY-AGOURA HILL PROPERTY ADDRESS: VACANT LOT. See page 220.

6. AIN 2061029014 (auction ID 78): TRACT NO 7661 LOT 54 . . . ASSESSED TO AGOURA AND COR-NELL 0 ROADS LP LOCATION CITY-AGOURA HILL PROPERTY ADDRESS: VACANT LOT. See page 224.

7. AIN 2061029015 (auction ID 79): TRACT NO 7661 LOT 55 . . . ASSESSED TO AGOURA AND COR-NELL 0 ROADS LP LOCATION CITY-AGOURA HILL PROPERTY ADDRESS: VACANT LOT. See page 228.

8. AIN 2061029016 (auction ID 80): TRACT NO 7661 LOT 56 . . . ASSESSED TO AGOURA AND COR-NELL 0 ROADS LP LOCATION CITY-AGOURA HILL PROPERTY ADDRESS: VACANT LOT. See page 232.

9. AIN 2061029017 (auction ID 81): TRACT NO 7661 LOT 57 . . . ASSESSED TO AGOURA AND COR-NELL 0 ROADS LP LOCATION CITY-AGOURA HILL PROPERTY ADDRESS: VACANT LOT. See page 236.

10. AIN 2061029023 (auction ID 82): VAC ST ADJ LOTS 49 THRU 58 TR NO 7661 ON SW 0 . . . ASSESSED TO AGOURA AND CORNELL ROADS LP LOCATION CITY-AGOURA HILL PROPERTY ADDRESS: VACANT LOT. See page 240.

11. AIN 2061030001 (auction ID 83): TRACT NO 7661 LOT 103 . . . ASSESSED TO AGOURA AND CORNELL 0 ROADS LP LOCATION CITY-AGOURA HILL PROPERTY ADDRESS: VACANT LOT. See page 244.

12. AIN 2061030002 (auction ID 84): TRACT NO 7661 LOT 104 . . . ASSESSED TO AGOURA AND CORNELL - 0 ROADS LP LOCATION CITY-AGOURA HILL PROPERTY ADDRESS: VACANT LOT. See page 248.

13. AIN 2061030003 (auction ID 85): TRACT NO 7661 LOT 105 . . . ASSESSED TO AGOURA AND CORNELL 0 ROADS LP LOCATION CITY-AGOURA HILL PROPERTY ADDRESS: VACANT LOT. See page 252.

14. AIN 2061030004 (auction ID 86): TRACT NO 7661 LOT 106 . . . ASSESSED TO AGOURA AND CORNELL 0 ROADS LP LOCATION CITY-AGOURA HILL PROPERTY ADDRESS: VACANT LOT. See page 256.

15. AIN 2061030005 (auction ID 87): TRACT NO 7661 LOT 107 . . . ASSESSED TO AGOURA AND CORNELL 0 ROADS LP LOCATION CITY-AGOURA HILL PROPERTY ADDRESS: VACANT LOT. See page 260.

16. AIN 2061030006 (auction ID 88): TRACT NO 7661 EX OF ST LOT 108 . . . ASSESSED TO AGOURA AND 0 CORNELL ROADS LP LOCATION CITY-AGOURA HILL PROPERTY ADDRESS: VACANT LOT. See page 264.

17. AIN 2061030007 (auction ID 89): TRACT NO 7661 EX OF ST LOT 109 . . . ASSESSED TO AGOURA AND 0 CORNELL ROADS LP LOCATION CITY-AGOURA HILL PROPERTY ADDRESS: VACANT LOT. See page 268.

18. AIN 2061030008 (auction ID 90): TRACT NO 7661 LOT 110 . . . ASSESSED TO AGOURA AND CORNELL 0 ROADS LP LOCATION CITY-AGOURA HILL PROPERTY ADDRESS: VACANT LOT. See page 272.

19. AIN 2061030009 (auction ID 91): TRACT NO 7661 LOT 111 . . . ASSESSED TO AGOURA AND CORNELL 0 ROADS LP LOCATION CITY-AGOURA HILL PROPERTY ADDRESS: VACANT LOT. See page 276.

20. AIN 2061030010 (auction ID 92): TRACT NO 7661 LOT 112 . . . ASSESSED TO AGOURA AND CORNELL 0 ROADS LP LOCATION CITY-AGOURA HILL PROPERTY ADDRESS: VACANT LOT. See page 280.

21. AIN 2061030011 (auction ID 93): TRACT NO 7661 LOT 113 . . . ASSESSED TO AGOURA AND CORNELL 0 ROADS LP LOCATION CITY-AGOURA HILL PROPERTY ADDRESS: VACANT LOT. See page 284.

22. AIN 2061030012 (auction ID 94): TRACT NO 7661 LOT 114 . . . ASSESSED TO AGOURA AND CORNELL 0 ROADS LP LOCATION CITY-AGOURA HILL PROPERTY ADDRESS: VACANT LOT. See page 288.

23. AIN 2061030013 (auction ID 95): TRACT NO 7661 LOT 115 . . . ASSESSED TO AGOURA AND CORNELL 0 ROADS LP LOCATION CITY-AGOURA HILL PROPERTY ADDRESS: VACANT LOT. See page 292.

24. AIN 2061030017 (auction ID 96): VAC ST ADJ LOTS 109 THRU 115 TR NO 7661 ON NW AND NE 0 . . . ASSESSED TO AGOURA AND CORNELL ROADS LP LOCATION CITY-AGOURA HILL PROPERTY ADDRESS: . . . . See page 296.

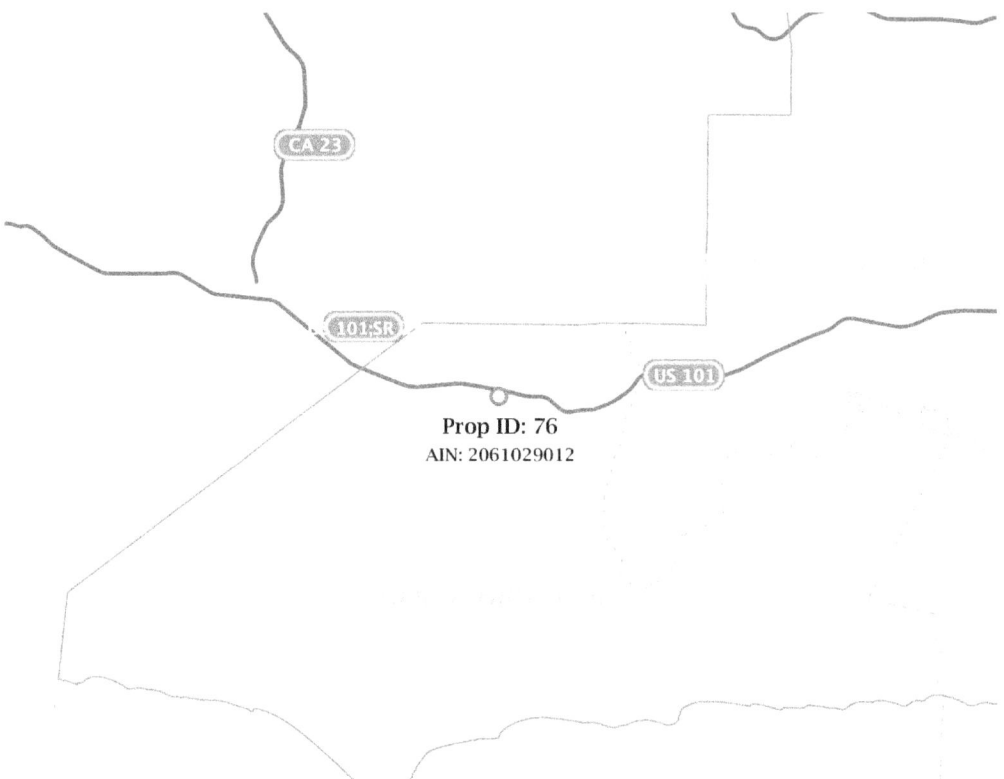

Figure 2.139: Property 96, AIN 2061029012, overview map

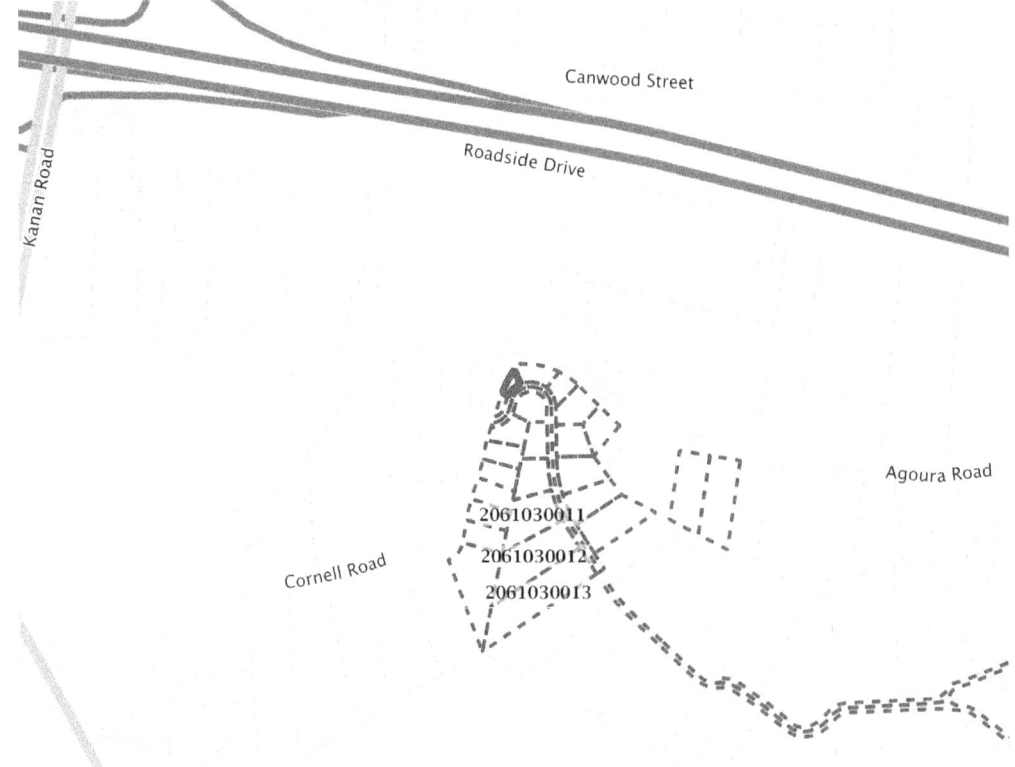

Figure 2.140: Property 96, AIN 2061029012, neighborhood view

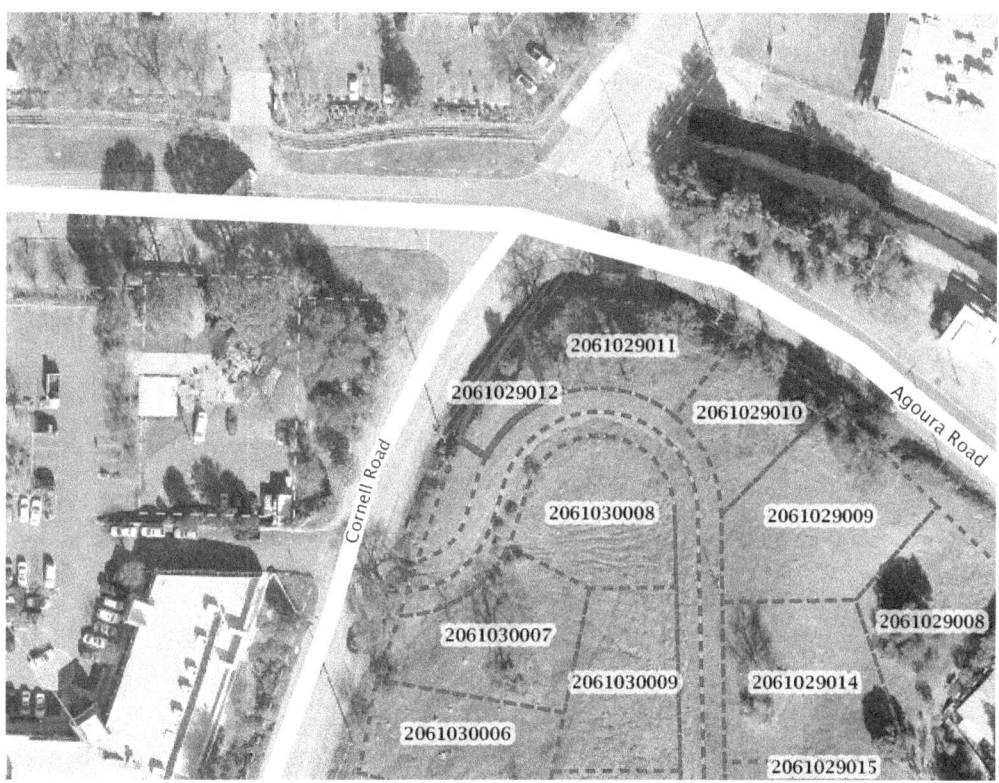

Figure 2.141: Property 96, AIN 2061029012, detailed view

2.48   Auction ID 77

The Los Angeles County Auction Book describes the property as follows.

```
TRACT NO 7661 EX OF ST LOT 53 ASSESSED TO AGOURA AND 0 CORNELL ROADS
LP LOCATION CITY-AGOURA HILL PROPERTY ADDRESS: VACANT LOT
```

The property is located in the general vicinity of Figure 2.142. It is identified by Assessor's Identification Number (AIN) 2061029013. The starting bid is $4,880. Comparable improved properties in this area is about $296/sqft. Comparable unimproved lots in this area is about $64/sqft. This parcel is approximately 1367 sqft. Note, however, that the parcel may be larger than the property under consideration. In case of condominiums, for example, the parcel may encompass other units of the development - those unrelated to the property to be auctioned.

The property is in a parcel zoned Specific Plan in Agoura Hills, for 0 to 15 dwelling units.

Figures 2.143 and 2.144 show street map and corresponding detailed aerial view, respectively. In both cases, the map is centered on the property with the containing parcel marked in heavy blue. If surrounding nearby properties are also part of this auction, the street and aerial maps highlights these in heavy, dashed blue outline.

This assessed entity may have other properties that are also in this auction:

1. AIN 2061029008 (auction ID 72): TRACT NO 7661 LOT 48 . . . ASSESSED TO AGOURA AND CORNELL 0 ROADS LP LOCATION CITY-AGOURA HILL PROPERTY ADDRESS: VACANT LOT. See page 200.

2. AIN 2061029009 (auction ID 73): TRACT NO 7661 LOT 49 . . . ASSESSED TO AGOURA AND CORNELL 0 ROADS LP LOCATION CITY-AGOURA HILL PROPERTY ADDRESS: VACANT LOT. See page 204.

3. AIN 2061029010 (auction ID 74): TRACT NO 7661 LOT 50 . . . ASSESSED TO AGOURA AND CORNELL 0 ROADS LP LOCATION CITY-AGOURA HILL PROPERTY ADDRESS: VACANT LOT. See page 208.

4. AIN 2061029011 (auction ID 75): TRACT NO 7661 EX OF ST LOT 51 . . . ASSESSED TO AGOURA AND 0 CORNELL ROADS LP LOCATION CITY-AGOURA HILL PROPERTY ADDRESS: VACANT LOT. See page 212.

5. AIN 2061029012 (auction ID 76): TRACT NO 7661 EX OF ST LOT 52 . . . ASSESSED TO AGOURA AND 0 CORNELL ROADS LP LOCATION CITY-AGOURA HILL PROPERTY ADDRESS: VACANT LOT. See page 216.

6. AIN 2061029014 (auction ID 78): TRACT NO 7661 LOT 54 . . . ASSESSED TO AGOURA AND CORNELL 0 ROADS LP LOCATION CITY-AGOURA HILL PROPERTY ADDRESS: VACANT LOT. See page 224.

7. AIN 2061029015 (auction ID 79): TRACT NO 7661 LOT 55 . . . ASSESSED TO AGOURA AND CORNELL 0 ROADS LP LOCATION CITY-AGOURA HILL PROPERTY ADDRESS: VACANT LOT. See page 228.

8. AIN 2061029016 (auction ID 80): TRACT NO 7661 LOT 56 . . . ASSESSED TO AGOURA AND CORNELL 0 ROADS LP LOCATION CITY-AGOURA HILL PROPERTY ADDRESS: VACANT LOT. See page 232.

9. AIN 2061029017 (auction ID 81): TRACT NO 7661 LOT 57 . . . ASSESSED TO AGOURA AND CORNELL 0 ROADS LP LOCATION CITY-AGOURA HILL PROPERTY ADDRESS: VACANT LOT. See page 236.

10. AIN 2061029023 (auction ID 82): VAC ST ADJ LOTS 49 THRU 58 TR NO 7661 ON SW 0 . . . ASSESSED TO AGOURA AND CORNELL ROADS LP LOCATION CITY-AGOURA HILL PROPERTY ADDRESS: VACANT LOT. See page 240.

11. AIN 2061030001 (auction ID 83): TRACT NO 7661 LOT 103 . . . ASSESSED TO AGOURA AND CORNELL 0 ROADS LP LOCATION CITY-AGOURA HILL PROPERTY ADDRESS: VACANT LOT. See page 244.

12. AIN 2061030002 (auction ID 84): TRACT NO 7661 LOT 104 . . . ASSESSED TO AGOURA AND CORNELL - 0 ROADS LP LOCATION CITY-AGOURA HILL PROPERTY ADDRESS: VACANT LOT. See page 248.

13. AIN 2061030003 (auction ID 85): TRACT NO 7661 LOT 105 . . . ASSESSED TO AGOURA AND CORNELL 0 ROADS LP LOCATION CITY-AGOURA HILL PROPERTY ADDRESS: VACANT LOT. See page 252.

14. AIN 2061030004 (auction ID 86): TRACT NO 7661 LOT 106 . . . ASSESSED TO AGOURA AND CORNELL 0 ROADS LP LOCATION CITY-AGOURA HILL PROPERTY ADDRESS: VACANT LOT. See page 256.

15. AIN 2061030005 (auction ID 87): TRACT NO 7661 LOT 107 . . . ASSESSED TO AGOURA AND CORNELL 0 ROADS LP LOCATION CITY-AGOURA HILL PROPERTY ADDRESS: VACANT LOT. See page 260.

16. AIN 2061030006 (auction ID 88): TRACT NO 7661 EX OF ST LOT 108 . . . ASSESSED TO AGOURA AND 0 CORNELL ROADS LP LOCATION CITY-AGOURA HILL PROPERTY ADDRESS: VACANT LOT. See page 264.

17. AIN 2061030007 (auction ID 89): TRACT NO 7661 EX OF ST LOT 109 . . . ASSESSED TO AGOURA AND 0 CORNELL ROADS LP LOCATION CITY-AGOURA HILL PROPERTY ADDRESS: VACANT LOT. See page 268.

18. AIN 2061030008 (auction ID 90): TRACT NO 7661 LOT 110 . . . ASSESSED TO AGOURA AND CORNELL 0 ROADS LP LOCATION CITY-AGOURA HILL PROPERTY ADDRESS: VACANT LOT. See page 272.

19. AIN 2061030009 (auction ID 91): TRACT NO 7661 LOT 111 . . . ASSESSED TO AGOURA AND CORNELL 0 ROADS LP LOCATION CITY-AGOURA HILL PROPERTY ADDRESS: VACANT LOT. See page 276.

20. AIN 2061030010 (auction ID 92): TRACT NO 7661 LOT 112 . . . ASSESSED TO AGOURA AND CORNELL 0 ROADS LP LOCATION CITY-AGOURA HILL PROPERTY ADDRESS: VACANT LOT. See page 280.

21. AIN 2061030011 (auction ID 93): TRACT NO 7661 LOT 113 . . . ASSESSED TO AGOURA AND CORNELL 0 ROADS LP LOCATION CITY-AGOURA HILL PROPERTY ADDRESS: VACANT LOT. See page 284.

22. AIN 2061030012 (auction ID 94): TRACT NO 7661 LOT 114 . . . ASSESSED TO AGOURA AND CORNELL 0 ROADS LP LOCATION CITY-AGOURA HILL PROPERTY ADDRESS: VACANT LOT. See page 288.

23. AIN 2061030013 (auction ID 95): TRACT NO 7661 LOT 115 . . . ASSESSED TO AGOURA AND CORNELL 0 ROADS LP LOCATION CITY-AGOURA HILL PROPERTY ADDRESS: VACANT LOT. See page 292.

24. AIN 2061030017 (auction ID 96): VAC ST ADJ LOTS 109 THRU 115 TR NO 7661 ON NW AND NE 0 . . . ASSESSED TO AGOURA AND CORNELL ROADS LP LOCATION CITY-AGOURA HILL PROPERTY ADDRESS: . . . . See page 296.

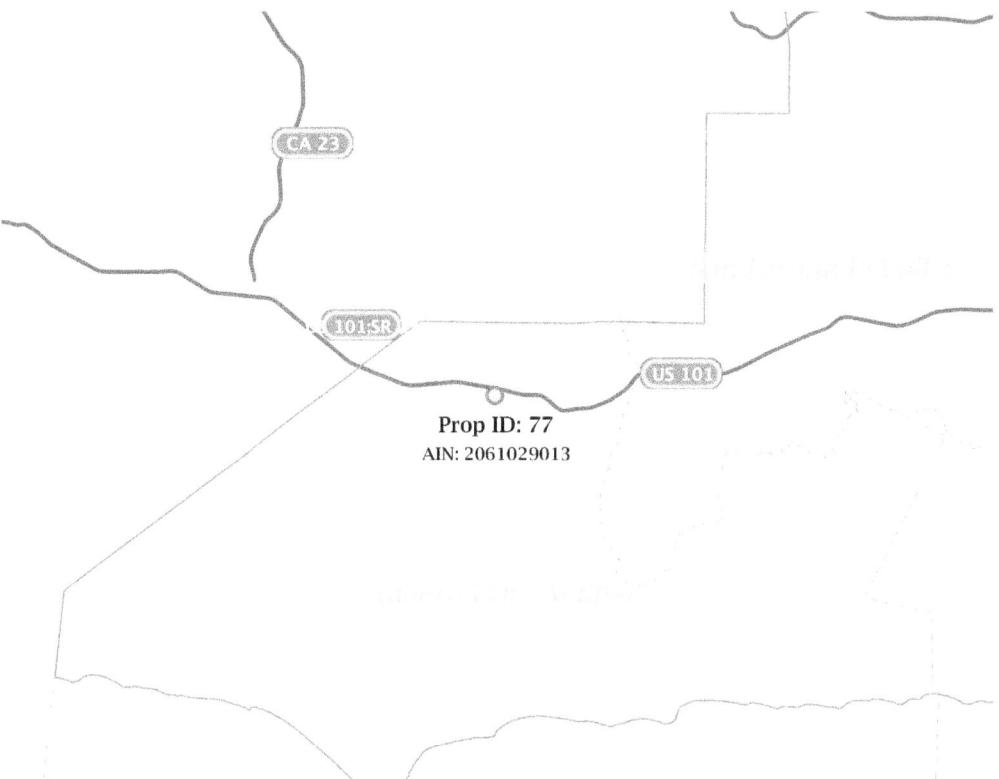

Figure 2.142: Property 96, AIN 2061029013, overview map

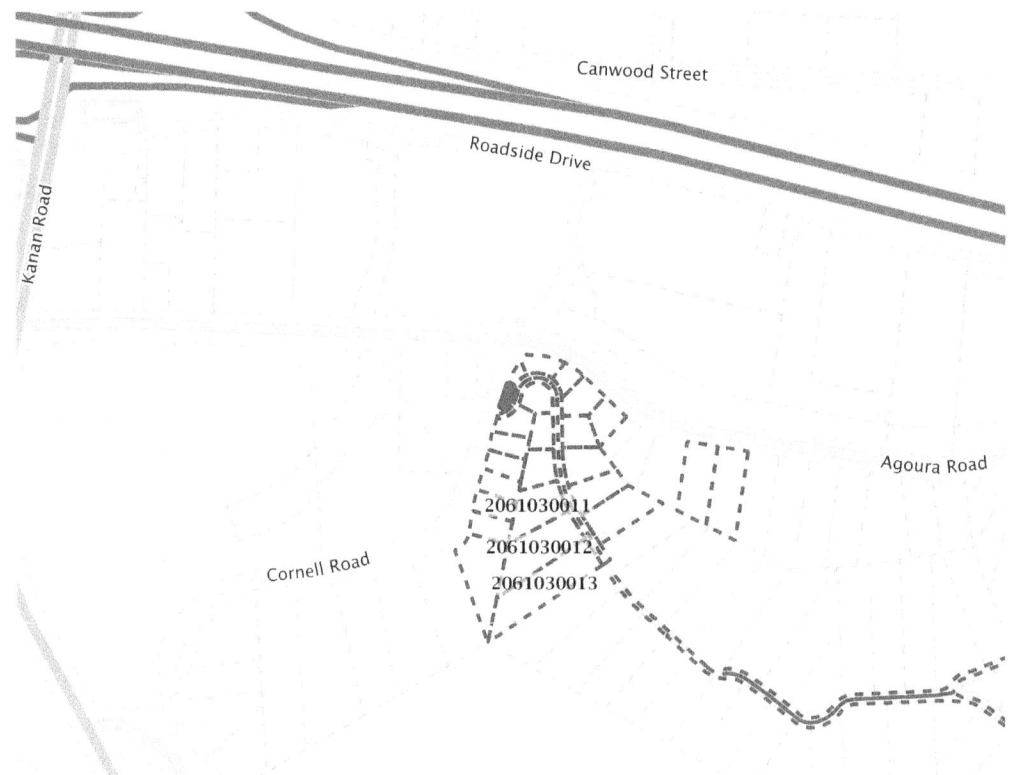

Figure 2.143: Property 96, AIN 2061029013, neighborhood view

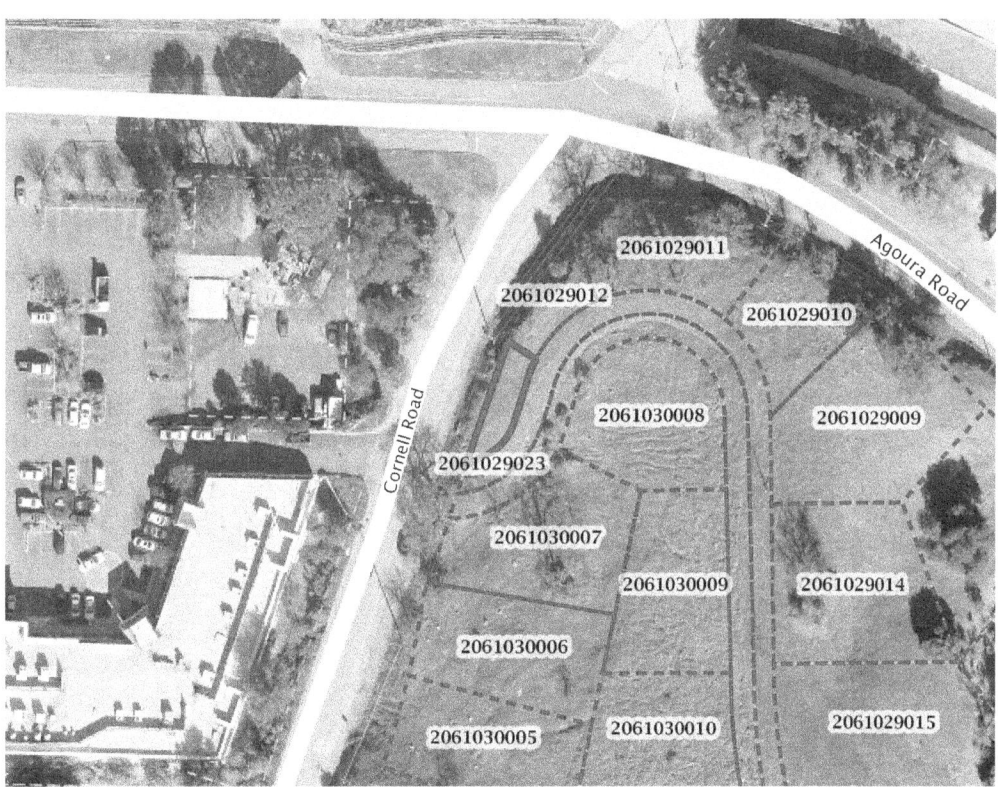

Figure 2.144: Property 96, AIN 2061029013, detailed view

2.49   Auction ID 78

The Los Angeles County Auction Book describes the property as follows.

```
TRACT NO 7661 LOT 54 ASSESSED TO AGOURA AND CORNELL 0 ROADS LP LOCATION
CITY-AGOURA HILL PROPERTY ADDRESS: VACANT LOT
```

The property is located in the general vicinity of Figure 2.145. It is identified by Assessor's Identification Number (AIN) 2061029014. The starting bid is \$12,734. Comparable improved properties in this area is about \$295/sqft. Comparable unimproved lots in this area is about \$64/sqft. This parcel is approximately 10337 sqft. Note, however, that the parcel may be larger than the property under consideration. In case of condominiums, for example, the parcel may encompass other units of the development - those unrelated to the property to be auctioned.

The property is in a parcel zoned Specific Plan in Agoura Hills, for 0 to 15 dwelling units.

Figures 2.146 and 2.147 show street map and corresponding detailed aerial view, respectively. In both cases, the map is centered on the property with the containing parcel marked in heavy blue. If surrounding nearby properties are also part of this auction, the street and aerial maps highlights these in heavy, dashed blue outline.

This assessed entity may have other properties that are also in this auction:

1. AIN 2061029008 (auction ID 72): TRACT NO 7661 LOT 48 ...ASSESSED TO AGOURA AND COR-NELL 0 ROADS LP LOCATION CITY-AGOURA HILL PROPERTY ADDRESS: VACANT LOT. See page 200.

2. AIN 2061029009 (auction ID 73): TRACT NO 7661 LOT 49 ...ASSESSED TO AGOURA AND COR-NELL 0 ROADS LP LOCATION CITY-AGOURA HILL PROPERTY ADDRESS: VACANT LOT. See page 204.

3. AIN 2061029010 (auction ID 74): TRACT NO 7661 LOT 50 ...ASSESSED TO AGOURA AND COR-NELL 0 ROADS LP LOCATION CITY-AGOURA HILL PROPERTY ADDRESS: VACANT LOT. See page 208.

4. AIN 2061029011 (auction ID 75): TRACT NO 7661 EX OF ST LOT 51 ...ASSESSED TO AGOURA AND 0 CORNELL ROADS LP LOCATION CITY-AGOURA HILL PROPERTY ADDRESS: VACANT LOT. See page 212.

5. AIN 2061029012 (auction ID 76): TRACT NO 7661 EX OF ST LOT 52 ...ASSESSED TO AGOURA AND 0 CORNELL ROADS LP LOCATION CITY-AGOURA HILL PROPERTY ADDRESS: VACANT LOT. See page 216.

6. AIN 2061029013 (auction ID 77): TRACT NO 7661 EX OF ST LOT 53 ...ASSESSED TO AGOURA AND 0 CORNELL ROADS LP LOCATION CITY-AGOURA HILL PROPERTY ADDRESS: VACANT LOT. See page 220.

7. AIN 2061029015 (auction ID 79): TRACT NO 7661 LOT 55 ...ASSESSED TO AGOURA AND COR-NELL 0 ROADS LP LOCATION CITY-AGOURA HILL PROPERTY ADDRESS: VACANT LOT. See page 228.

8. AIN 2061029016 (auction ID 80): TRACT NO 7661 LOT 56 ...ASSESSED TO AGOURA AND COR-NELL 0 ROADS LP LOCATION CITY-AGOURA HILL PROPERTY ADDRESS: VACANT LOT. See page 232.

9. AIN 2061029017 (auction ID 81): TRACT NO 7661 LOT 57 ...ASSESSED TO AGOURA AND COR-NELL 0 ROADS LP LOCATION CITY-AGOURA HILL PROPERTY ADDRESS: VACANT LOT. See page 236.

10. AIN 2061029023 (auction ID 82): VAC ST ADJ LOTS 49 THRU 58 TR NO 7661 ON SW 0 . . . ASSESSED TO AGOURA AND CORNELL ROADS LP LOCATION CITY-AGOURA HILL PROPERTY ADDRESS: VACANT LOT. See page 240.

11. AIN 2061030001 (auction ID 83): TRACT NO 7661 LOT 103 . . . ASSESSED TO AGOURA AND CORNELL 0 ROADS LP LOCATION CITY-AGOURA HILL PROPERTY ADDRESS: VACANT LOT. See page 244.

12. AIN 2061030002 (auction ID 84): TRACT NO 7661 LOT 104 . . . ASSESSED TO AGOURA AND CORNELL - 0 ROADS LP LOCATION CITY-AGOURA HILL PROPERTY ADDRESS: VACANT LOT. See page 248.

13. AIN 2061030003 (auction ID 85): TRACT NO 7661 LOT 105 . . . ASSESSED TO AGOURA AND CORNELL 0 ROADS LP LOCATION CITY-AGOURA HILL PROPERTY ADDRESS: VACANT LOT. See page 252.

14. AIN 2061030004 (auction ID 86): TRACT NO 7661 LOT 106 . . . ASSESSED TO AGOURA AND CORNELL 0 ROADS LP LOCATION CITY-AGOURA HILL PROPERTY ADDRESS: VACANT LOT. See page 256.

15. AIN 2061030005 (auction ID 87): TRACT NO 7661 LOT 107 . . . ASSESSED TO AGOURA AND CORNELL 0 ROADS LP LOCATION CITY-AGOURA HILL PROPERTY ADDRESS: VACANT LOT. See page 260.

16. AIN 2061030006 (auction ID 88): TRACT NO 7661 EX OF ST LOT 108 . . . ASSESSED TO AGOURA AND 0 CORNELL ROADS LP LOCATION CITY-AGOURA HILL PROPERTY ADDRESS: VACANT LOT. See page 264.

17. AIN 2061030007 (auction ID 89): TRACT NO 7661 EX OF ST LOT 109 . . . ASSESSED TO AGOURA AND 0 CORNELL ROADS LP LOCATION CITY-AGOURA HILL PROPERTY ADDRESS: VACANT LOT. See page 268.

18. AIN 2061030008 (auction ID 90): TRACT NO 7661 LOT 110 . . . ASSESSED TO AGOURA AND CORNELL 0 ROADS LP LOCATION CITY-AGOURA HILL PROPERTY ADDRESS: VACANT LOT. See page 272.

19. AIN 2061030009 (auction ID 91): TRACT NO 7661 LOT 111 . . . ASSESSED TO AGOURA AND CORNELL 0 ROADS LP LOCATION CITY-AGOURA HILL PROPERTY ADDRESS: VACANT LOT. See page 276.

20. AIN 2061030010 (auction ID 92): TRACT NO 7661 LOT 112 . . . ASSESSED TO AGOURA AND CORNELL 0 ROADS LP LOCATION CITY-AGOURA HILL PROPERTY ADDRESS: VACANT LOT. See page 280.

21. AIN 2061030011 (auction ID 93): TRACT NO 7661 LOT 113 . . . ASSESSED TO AGOURA AND CORNELL 0 ROADS LP LOCATION CITY-AGOURA HILL PROPERTY ADDRESS: VACANT LOT. See page 284.

22. AIN 2061030012 (auction ID 94): TRACT NO 7661 LOT 114 . . . ASSESSED TO AGOURA AND CORNELL 0 ROADS LP LOCATION CITY-AGOURA HILL PROPERTY ADDRESS: VACANT LOT. See page 288.

23. AIN 2061030013 (auction ID 95): TRACT NO 7661 LOT 115 . . . ASSESSED TO AGOURA AND CORNELL 0 ROADS LP LOCATION CITY-AGOURA HILL PROPERTY ADDRESS: VACANT LOT. See page 292.

24. AIN 2061030017 (auction ID 96): VAC ST ADJ LOTS 109 THRU 115 TR NO 7661 ON NW AND NE 0 . . . ASSESSED TO AGOURA AND CORNELL ROADS LP LOCATION CITY-AGOURA HILL PROPERTY ADDRESS: . . . . See page 296.

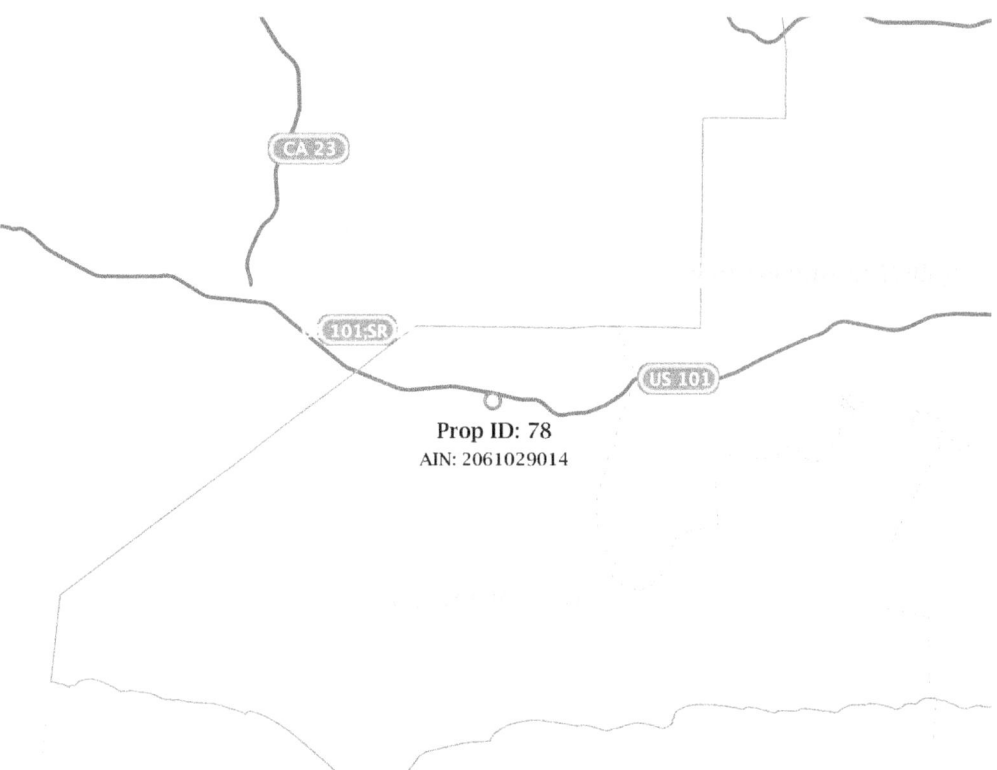

Figure 2.145: Property 96, AIN 2061029014, overview map

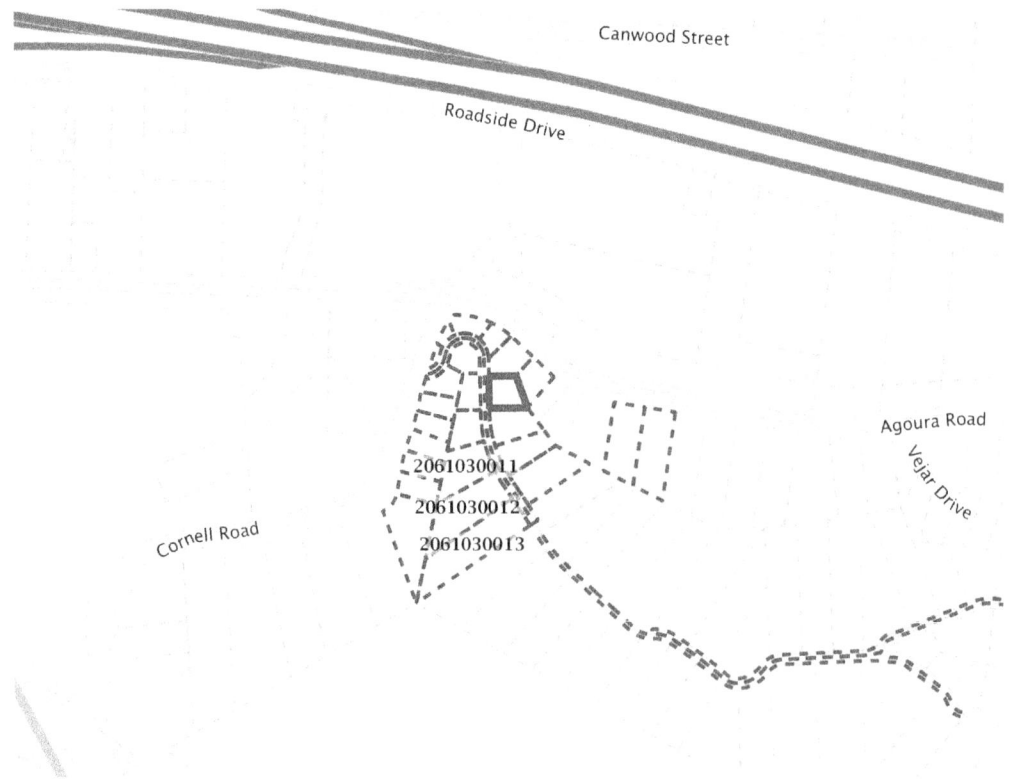

Figure 2.146: Property 96, AIN 2061029014, neighborhood view

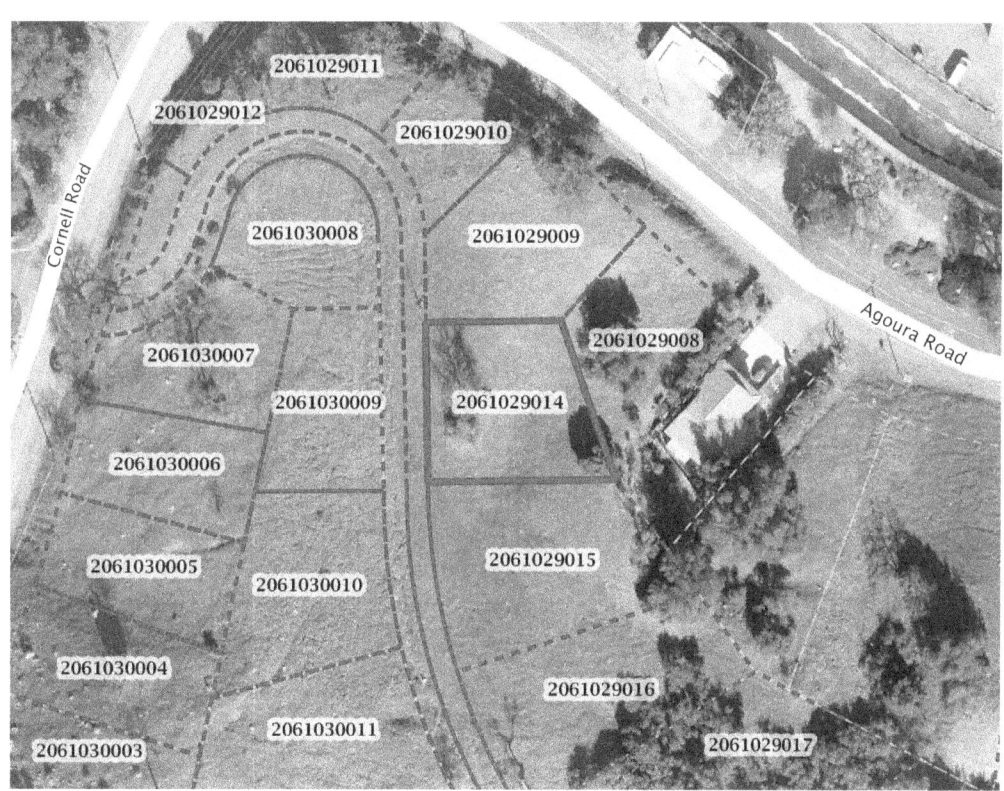

Figure 2.147: Property 96, AIN 2061029014, detailed view

2.50 Auction ID 79

The Los Angeles County Auction Book describes the property as follows.

```
TRACT NO 7661 LOT 55 ASSESSED TO AGOURA AND CORNELL 0 ROADS LP LOCATION
CITY-AGOURA HILL PROPERTY ADDRESS: VACANT LOT
```

The property is located in the general vicinity of Figure 2.148. It is identified by Assessor's Identification Number (AIN) 2061029015. The starting bid is $15,113. Comparable improved properties in this area is about $295/sqft. Comparable unimproved lots in this area is about $64/sqft. This parcel is approximately 14319 sqft. Note, however, that the parcel may be larger than the property under consideration. In case of condominiums, for example, the parcel may encompass other units of the development - those unrelated to the property to be auctioned.

The property is in a parcel zoned Specific Plan in Agoura Hills, for 0 to 15 dwelling units.

Figures 2.149 and 2.150 show street map and corresponding detailed aerial view, respectively. In both cases, the map is centered on the property with the containing parcel marked in heavy blue. If surrounding nearby properties are also part of this auction, the street and aerial maps highlights these in heavy, dashed blue outline.

This assessed entity may have other properties that are also in this auction:

1. AIN 2061029008 (auction ID 72): TRACT NO 7661 LOT 48 ... ASSESSED TO AGOURA AND CORNELL 0 ROADS LP LOCATION CITY-AGOURA HILL PROPERTY ADDRESS: VACANT LOT. See page 200.

2. AIN 2061029009 (auction ID 73): TRACT NO 7661 LOT 49 ... ASSESSED TO AGOURA AND CORNELL 0 ROADS LP LOCATION CITY-AGOURA HILL PROPERTY ADDRESS: VACANT LOT. See page 204.

3. AIN 2061029010 (auction ID 74): TRACT NO 7661 LOT 50 ... ASSESSED TO AGOURA AND CORNELL 0 ROADS LP LOCATION CITY-AGOURA HILL PROPERTY ADDRESS: VACANT LOT. See page 208.

4. AIN 2061029011 (auction ID 75): TRACT NO 7661 EX OF ST LOT 51 ... ASSESSED TO AGOURA AND 0 CORNELL ROADS LP LOCATION CITY-AGOURA HILL PROPERTY ADDRESS: VACANT LOT. See page 212.

5. AIN 2061029012 (auction ID 76): TRACT NO 7661 EX OF ST LOT 52 ... ASSESSED TO AGOURA AND 0 CORNELL ROADS LP LOCATION CITY-AGOURA HILL PROPERTY ADDRESS: VACANT LOT. See page 216.

6. AIN 2061029013 (auction ID 77): TRACT NO 7661 EX OF ST LOT 53 ... ASSESSED TO AGOURA AND 0 CORNELL ROADS LP LOCATION CITY-AGOURA HILL PROPERTY ADDRESS: VACANT LOT. See page 220.

7. AIN 2061029014 (auction ID 78): TRACT NO 7661 LOT 54 ... ASSESSED TO AGOURA AND CORNELL 0 ROADS LP LOCATION CITY-AGOURA HILL PROPERTY ADDRESS: VACANT LOT. See page 224.

8. AIN 2061029016 (auction ID 80): TRACT NO 7661 LOT 56 ... ASSESSED TO AGOURA AND CORNELL 0 ROADS LP LOCATION CITY-AGOURA HILL PROPERTY ADDRESS: VACANT LOT. See page 232.

9. AIN 2061029017 (auction ID 81): TRACT NO 7661 LOT 57 ... ASSESSED TO AGOURA AND CORNELL 0 ROADS LP LOCATION CITY-AGOURA HILL PROPERTY ADDRESS: VACANT LOT. See page 236.

10. AIN 2061029023 (auction ID 82): VAC ST ADJ LOTS 49 THRU 58 TR NO 7661 ON SW 0 . . . ASSESSED TO AGOURA AND CORNELL ROADS LP LOCATION CITY-AGOURA HILL PROPERTY ADDRESS: VACANT LOT. See page 240.

11. AIN 2061030001 (auction ID 83): TRACT NO 7661 LOT 103 . . . ASSESSED TO AGOURA AND CORNELL 0 ROADS LP LOCATION CITY-AGOURA HILL PROPERTY ADDRESS: VACANT LOT. See page 244.

12. AIN 2061030002 (auction ID 84): TRACT NO 7661 LOT 104 . . . ASSESSED TO AGOURA AND CORNELL - 0 ROADS LP LOCATION CITY-AGOURA HILL PROPERTY ADDRESS: VACANT LOT. See page 248.

13. AIN 2061030003 (auction ID 85): TRACT NO 7661 LOT 105 . . . ASSESSED TO AGOURA AND CORNELL 0 ROADS LP LOCATION CITY-AGOURA HILL PROPERTY ADDRESS: VACANT LOT. See page 252.

14. AIN 2061030004 (auction ID 86): TRACT NO 7661 LOT 106 . . . ASSESSED TO AGOURA AND CORNELL 0 ROADS LP LOCATION CITY-AGOURA HILL PROPERTY ADDRESS: VACANT LOT. See page 256.

15. AIN 2061030005 (auction ID 87): TRACT NO 7661 LOT 107 . . . ASSESSED TO AGOURA AND CORNELL 0 ROADS LP LOCATION CITY-AGOURA HILL PROPERTY ADDRESS: VACANT LOT. See page 260.

16. AIN 2061030006 (auction ID 88): TRACT NO 7661 EX OF ST LOT 108 . . . ASSESSED TO AGOURA AND 0 CORNELL ROADS LP LOCATION CITY-AGOURA HILL PROPERTY ADDRESS: VACANT LOT. See page 264.

17. AIN 2061030007 (auction ID 89): TRACT NO 7661 EX OF ST LOT 109 . . . ASSESSED TO AGOURA AND 0 CORNELL ROADS LP LOCATION CITY-AGOURA HILL PROPERTY ADDRESS: VACANT LOT. See page 268.

18. AIN 2061030008 (auction ID 90): TRACT NO 7661 LOT 110 . . . ASSESSED TO AGOURA AND CORNELL 0 ROADS LP LOCATION CITY-AGOURA HILL PROPERTY ADDRESS: VACANT LOT. See page 272.

19. AIN 2061030009 (auction ID 91): TRACT NO 7661 LOT 111 . . . ASSESSED TO AGOURA AND CORNELL 0 ROADS LP LOCATION CITY-AGOURA HILL PROPERTY ADDRESS: VACANT LOT. See page 276.

20. AIN 2061030010 (auction ID 92): TRACT NO 7661 LOT 112 . . . ASSESSED TO AGOURA AND CORNELL 0 ROADS LP LOCATION CITY-AGOURA HILL PROPERTY ADDRESS: VACANT LOT. See page 280.

21. AIN 2061030011 (auction ID 93): TRACT NO 7661 LOT 113 . . . ASSESSED TO AGOURA AND CORNELL 0 ROADS LP LOCATION CITY-AGOURA HILL PROPERTY ADDRESS: VACANT LOT. See page 284.

22. AIN 2061030012 (auction ID 94): TRACT NO 7661 LOT 114 . . . ASSESSED TO AGOURA AND CORNELL 0 ROADS LP LOCATION CITY-AGOURA HILL PROPERTY ADDRESS: VACANT LOT. See page 288.

23. AIN 2061030013 (auction ID 95): TRACT NO 7661 LOT 115 . . . ASSESSED TO AGOURA AND CORNELL 0 ROADS LP LOCATION CITY-AGOURA HILL PROPERTY ADDRESS: VACANT LOT. See page 292.

24. AIN 2061030017 (auction ID 96): VAC ST ADJ LOTS 109 THRU 115 TR NO 7661 ON NW AND NE 0 . . . ASSESSED TO AGOURA AND CORNELL ROADS LP LOCATION CITY-AGOURA HILL PROPERTY ADDRESS: . . . . See page 296.

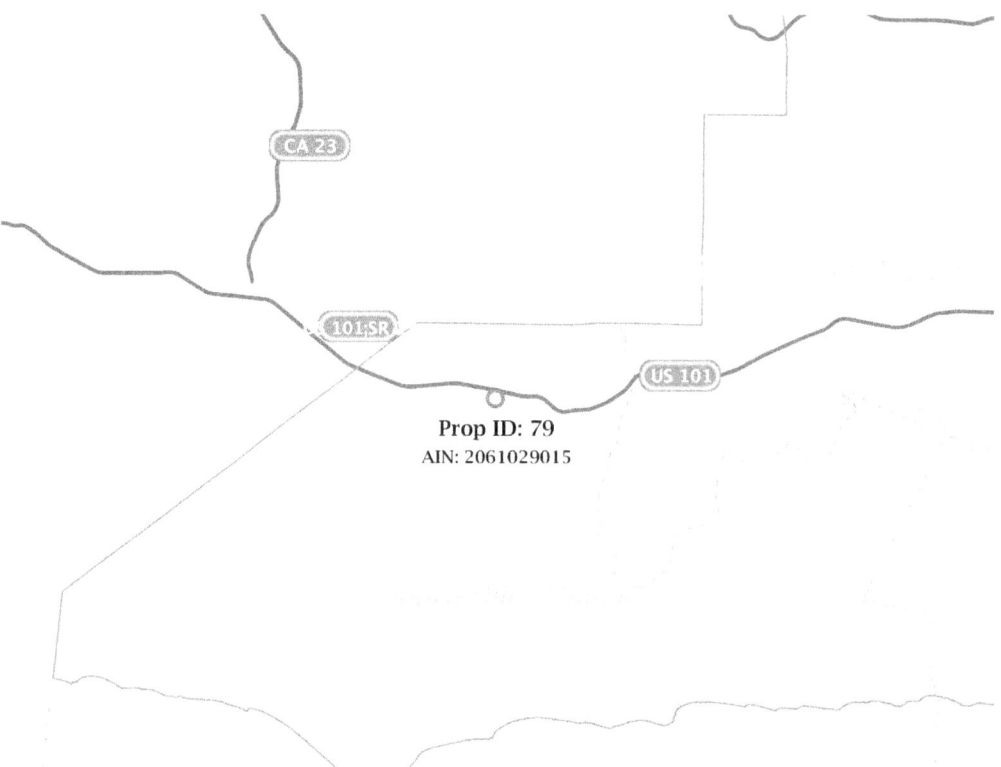

Figure 2.148: Property 96, AIN 2061029015, overview map

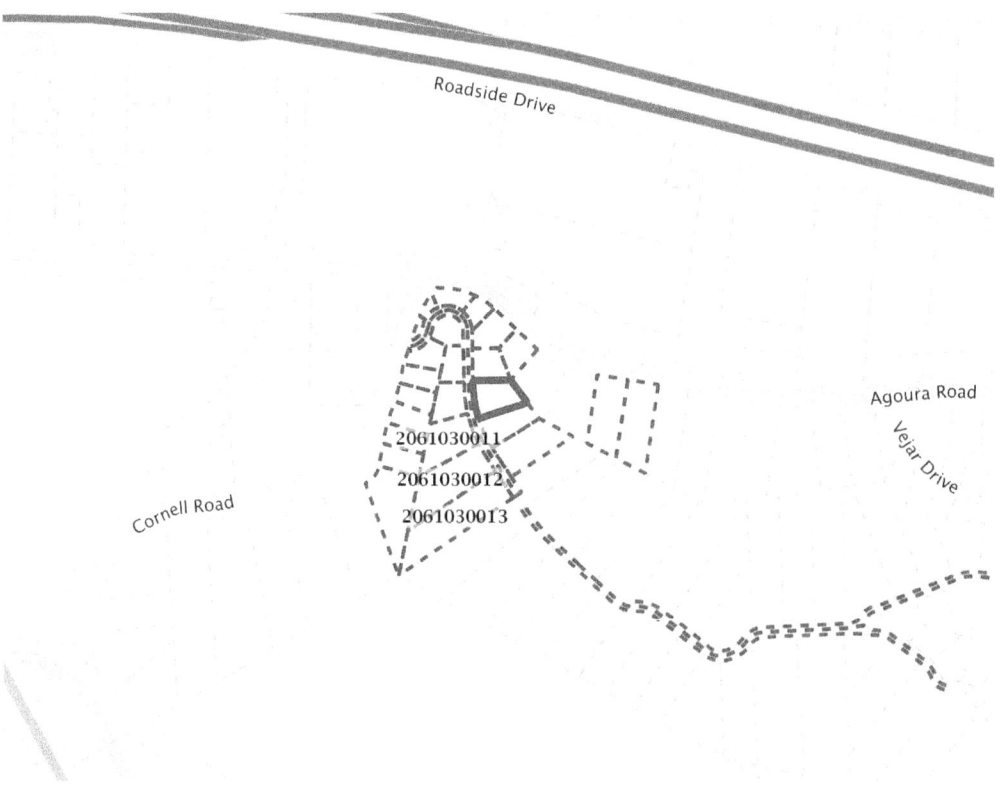

Figure 2.149: Property 96, AIN 2061029015, neighborhood view

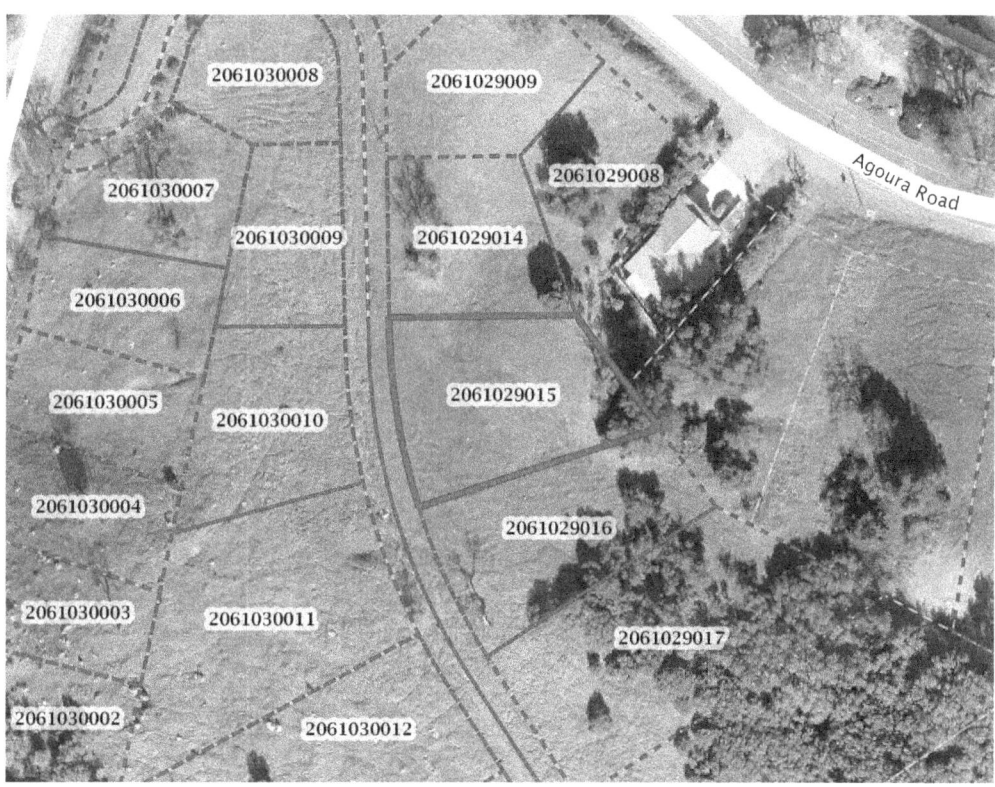

Figure 2.150: Property 96, AIN 2061029015, detailed view

2.51 Auction ID 80

The Los Angeles County Auction Book describes the property as follows.

```
TRACT NO 7661 LOT 56 ASSESSED TO AGOURA AND CORNELL 0 ROADS LP LOCATION
CITY-AGOURA HILL PROPERTY ADDRESS: VACANT LOT
```

The property is located in the general vicinity of Figure 2.151. It is identified by Assessor's Identification Number (AIN) 2061029016. The starting bid is $19,601. Comparable improved properties in this area is about $295/sqft. Comparable unimproved lots in this area is about $64/sqft. This parcel is approximately 13890 sqft. Note, however, that the parcel may be larger than the property under consideration. In case of condominiums, for example, the parcel may encompass other units of the development - those unrelated to the property to be auctioned.

The property is in a parcel zoned Specific Plan in Agoura Hills, for 0 to 15 dwelling units.

Figures 2.152 and 2.153 show street map and corresponding detailed aerial view, respectively. In both cases, the map is centered on the property with the containing parcel marked in heavy blue. If surrounding nearby properties are also part of this auction, the street and aerial maps highlights these in heavy, dashed blue outline.

This assessed entity may have other properties that are also in this auction:

1. AIN 2061029008 (auction ID 72): TRACT NO 7661 LOT 48 ... ASSESSED TO AGOURA AND CORNELL 0 ROADS LP LOCATION CITY-AGOURA HILL PROPERTY ADDRESS: VACANT LOT. See page 200.

2. AIN 2061029009 (auction ID 73): TRACT NO 7661 LOT 49 ... ASSESSED TO AGOURA AND CORNELL 0 ROADS LP LOCATION CITY-AGOURA HILL PROPERTY ADDRESS: VACANT LOT. See page 204.

3. AIN 2061029010 (auction ID 74): TRACT NO 7661 LOT 50 ... ASSESSED TO AGOURA AND CORNELL 0 ROADS LP LOCATION CITY-AGOURA HILL PROPERTY ADDRESS: VACANT LOT. See page 208.

4. AIN 2061029011 (auction ID 75): TRACT NO 7661 EX OF ST LOT 51 ... ASSESSED TO AGOURA AND 0 CORNELL ROADS LP LOCATION CITY-AGOURA HILL PROPERTY ADDRESS: VACANT LOT. See page 212.

5. AIN 2061029012 (auction ID 76): TRACT NO 7661 EX OF ST LOT 52 ... ASSESSED TO AGOURA AND 0 CORNELL ROADS LP LOCATION CITY-AGOURA HILL PROPERTY ADDRESS: VACANT LOT. See page 216.

6. AIN 2061029013 (auction ID 77): TRACT NO 7661 EX OF ST LOT 53 ... ASSESSED TO AGOURA AND 0 CORNELL ROADS LP LOCATION CITY-AGOURA HILL PROPERTY ADDRESS: VACANT LOT. See page 220.

7. AIN 2061029014 (auction ID 78): TRACT NO 7661 LOT 54 ... ASSESSED TO AGOURA AND CORNELL 0 ROADS LP LOCATION CITY-AGOURA HILL PROPERTY ADDRESS: VACANT LOT. See page 224.

8. AIN 2061029015 (auction ID 79): TRACT NO 7661 LOT 55 ... ASSESSED TO AGOURA AND CORNELL 0 ROADS LP LOCATION CITY-AGOURA HILL PROPERTY ADDRESS: VACANT LOT. See page 228.

9. AIN 2061029017 (auction ID 81): TRACT NO 7661 LOT 57 ... ASSESSED TO AGOURA AND CORNELL 0 ROADS LP LOCATION CITY-AGOURA HILL PROPERTY ADDRESS: VACANT LOT. See page 236.

10. AIN 2061029023 (auction ID 82): VAC ST ADJ LOTS 49 THRU 58 TR NO 7661 ON SW 0 . . . ASSESSED TO AGOURA AND CORNELL ROADS LP LOCATION CITY-AGOURA HILL PROPERTY ADDRESS: VACANT LOT. See page 240.

11. AIN 2061030001 (auction ID 83): TRACT NO 7661 LOT 103 . . . ASSESSED TO AGOURA AND CORNELL 0 ROADS LP LOCATION CITY-AGOURA HILL PROPERTY ADDRESS: VACANT LOT. See page 244.

12. AIN 2061030002 (auction ID 84): TRACT NO 7661 LOT 104 . . . ASSESSED TO AGOURA AND CORNELL - 0 ROADS LP LOCATION CITY-AGOURA HILL PROPERTY ADDRESS: VACANT LOT. See page 248.

13. AIN 2061030003 (auction ID 85): TRACT NO 7661 LOT 105 . . . ASSESSED TO AGOURA AND CORNELL 0 ROADS LP LOCATION CITY-AGOURA HILL PROPERTY ADDRESS: VACANT LOT. See page 252.

14. AIN 2061030004 (auction ID 86): TRACT NO 7661 LOT 106 . . . ASSESSED TO AGOURA AND CORNELL 0 ROADS LP LOCATION CITY-AGOURA HILL PROPERTY ADDRESS: VACANT LOT. See page 256.

15. AIN 2061030005 (auction ID 87): TRACT NO 7661 LOT 107 . . . ASSESSED TO AGOURA AND CORNELL 0 ROADS LP LOCATION CITY-AGOURA HILL PROPERTY ADDRESS: VACANT LOT. See page 260.

16. AIN 2061030006 (auction ID 88): TRACT NO 7661 EX OF ST LOT 108 . . . ASSESSED TO AGOURA AND 0 CORNELL ROADS LP LOCATION CITY-AGOURA HILL PROPERTY ADDRESS: VACANT LOT. See page 264.

17. AIN 2061030007 (auction ID 89): TRACT NO 7661 EX OF ST LOT 109 . . . ASSESSED TO AGOURA AND 0 CORNELL ROADS LP LOCATION CITY-AGOURA HILL PROPERTY ADDRESS: VACANT LOT. See page 268.

18. AIN 2061030008 (auction ID 90): TRACT NO 7661 LOT 110 . . . ASSESSED TO AGOURA AND CORNELL 0 ROADS LP LOCATION CITY-AGOURA HILL PROPERTY ADDRESS: VACANT LOT. See page 272.

19. AIN 2061030009 (auction ID 91): TRACT NO 7661 LOT 111 . . . ASSESSED TO AGOURA AND CORNELL 0 ROADS LP LOCATION CITY-AGOURA HILL PROPERTY ADDRESS: VACANT LOT. See page 276.

20. AIN 2061030010 (auction ID 92): TRACT NO 7661 LOT 112 . . . ASSESSED TO AGOURA AND CORNELL 0 ROADS LP LOCATION CITY-AGOURA HILL PROPERTY ADDRESS: VACANT LOT. See page 280.

21. AIN 2061030011 (auction ID 93): TRACT NO 7661 LOT 113 . . . ASSESSED TO AGOURA AND CORNELL 0 ROADS LP LOCATION CITY-AGOURA HILL PROPERTY ADDRESS: VACANT LOT. See page 284.

22. AIN 2061030012 (auction ID 94): TRACT NO 7661 LOT 114 . . . ASSESSED TO AGOURA AND CORNELL 0 ROADS LP LOCATION CITY-AGOURA HILL PROPERTY ADDRESS: VACANT LOT. See page 288.

23. AIN 2061030013 (auction ID 95): TRACT NO 7661 LOT 115 . . . ASSESSED TO AGOURA AND CORNELL 0 ROADS LP LOCATION CITY-AGOURA HILL PROPERTY ADDRESS: VACANT LOT. See page 292.

24. AIN 2061030017 (auction ID 96): VAC ST ADJ LOTS 109 THRU 115 TR NO 7661 ON NW AND NE 0 . . . ASSESSED TO AGOURA AND CORNELL ROADS LP LOCATION CITY-AGOURA HILL PROPERTY ADDRESS: . . . . See page 296.

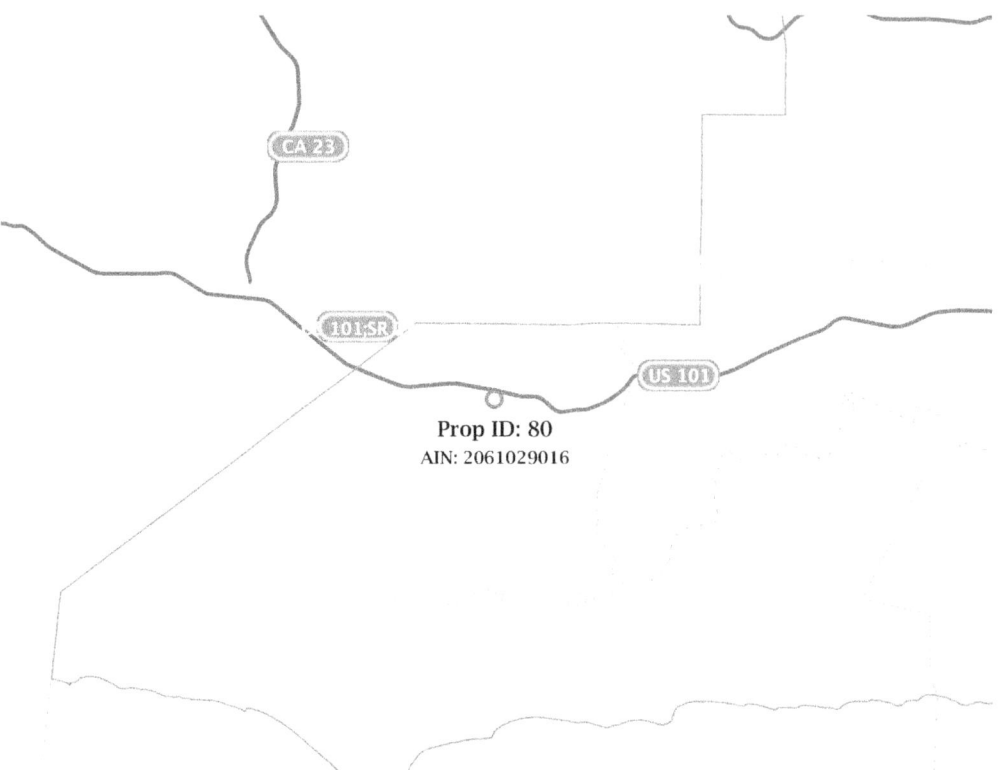

Figure 2.151: Property 96, AIN 2061029016, overview map

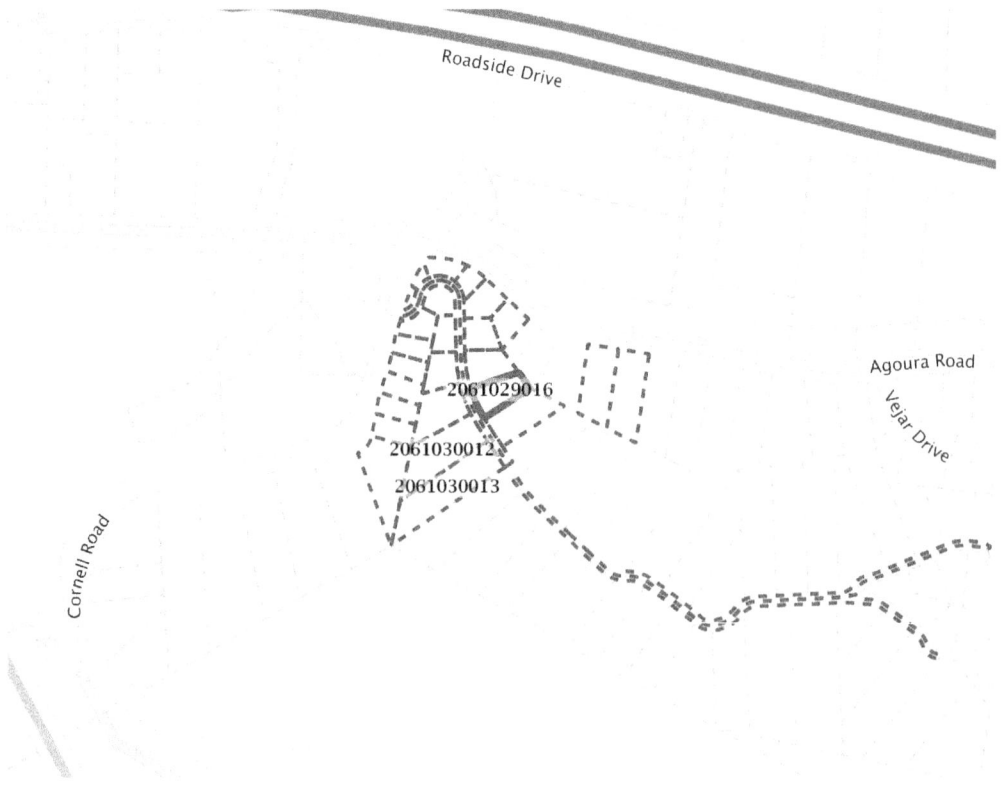

Figure 2.152: Property 96, AIN 2061029016, neighborhood view

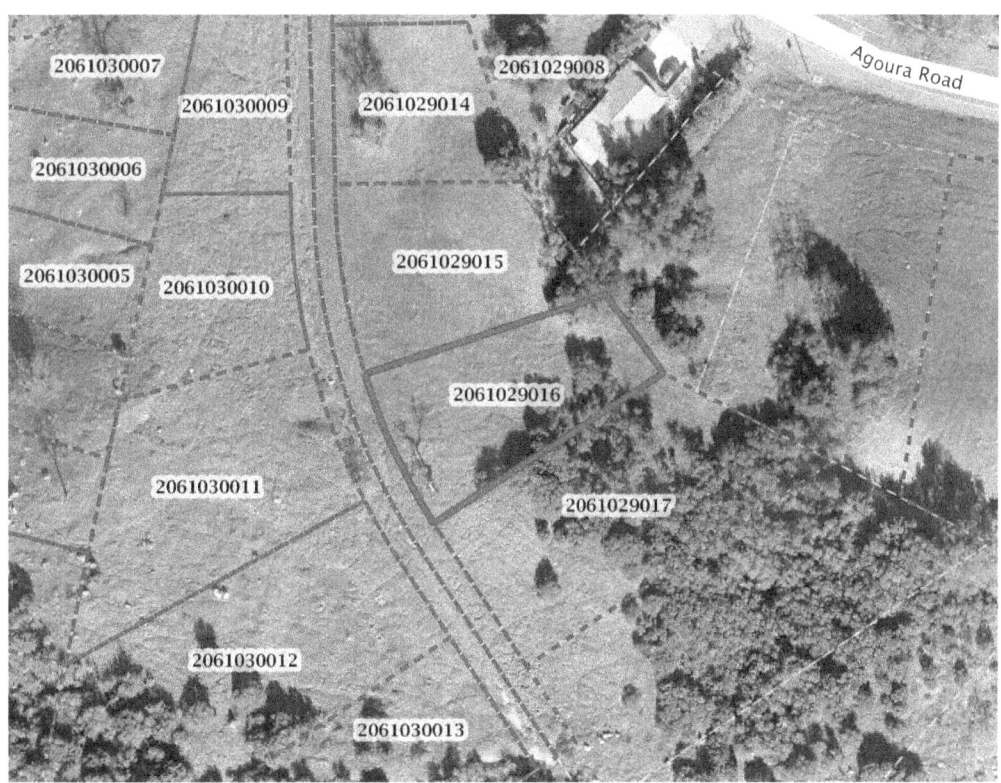

Figure 2.153: Property 96, AIN 2061029016, detailed view

2.52   Auction ID 81

The Los Angeles County Auction Book describes the property as follows.

```
TRACT NO 7661 LOT 57 ASSESSED TO AGOURA AND CORNELL O ROADS LP LOCATION
CITY-AGOURA HILL PROPERTY ADDRESS: VACANT LOT
```

The property is located in the general vicinity of Figure 2.154. It is identified by Assessor's Identification Number (AIN) 2061029017. The starting bid is $23,022. Comparable improved properties in this area is about $296/sqft. Comparable unimproved lots in this area is about $65/sqft. This parcel is approximately 21938 sqft. Note, however, that the parcel may be larger than the property under consideration. In case of condominiums, for example, the parcel may encompass other units of the development - those unrelated to the property to be auctioned.

The property is in a parcel zoned Restricted Open Space in Agoura Hills, for 0 to 0 dwelling units.

Figures 2.155 and 2.156 show street map and corresponding detailed aerial view, respectively. In both cases, the map is centered on the property with the containing parcel marked in heavy blue. If surrounding nearby properties are also part of this auction, the street and aerial maps highlights these in heavy, dashed blue outline.

This assessed entity may have other properties that are also in this auction:

1. AIN 2061029008 (auction ID 72): TRACT NO 7661 LOT 48 ... ASSESSED TO AGOURA AND COR-NELL 0 ROADS LP LOCATION CITY-AGOURA HILL PROPERTY ADDRESS: VACANT LOT. See page 200.

2. AIN 2061029009 (auction ID 73): TRACT NO 7661 LOT 49 ... ASSESSED TO AGOURA AND COR-NELL 0 ROADS LP LOCATION CITY-AGOURA HILL PROPERTY ADDRESS: VACANT LOT. See page 204.

3. AIN 2061029010 (auction ID 74): TRACT NO 7661 LOT 50 ... ASSESSED TO AGOURA AND COR-NELL 0 ROADS LP LOCATION CITY-AGOURA HILL PROPERTY ADDRESS: VACANT LOT. See page 208.

4. AIN 2061029011 (auction ID 75): TRACT NO 7661 EX OF ST LOT 51 ... ASSESSED TO AGOURA AND 0 CORNELL ROADS LP LOCATION CITY-AGOURA HILL PROPERTY ADDRESS: VACANT LOT. See page 212.

5. AIN 2061029012 (auction ID 76): TRACT NO 7661 EX OF ST LOT 52 ... ASSESSED TO AGOURA AND 0 CORNELL ROADS LP LOCATION CITY-AGOURA HILL PROPERTY ADDRESS: VACANT LOT. See page 216.

6. AIN 2061029013 (auction ID 77): TRACT NO 7661 EX OF ST LOT 53 ... ASSESSED TO AGOURA AND 0 CORNELL ROADS LP LOCATION CITY-AGOURA HILL PROPERTY ADDRESS: VACANT LOT. See page 220.

7. AIN 2061029014 (auction ID 78): TRACT NO 7661 LOT 54 ... ASSESSED TO AGOURA AND COR-NELL 0 ROADS LP LOCATION CITY-AGOURA HILL PROPERTY ADDRESS: VACANT LOT. See page 224.

8. AIN 2061029015 (auction ID 79): TRACT NO 7661 LOT 55 ... ASSESSED TO AGOURA AND COR-NELL 0 ROADS LP LOCATION CITY-AGOURA HILL PROPERTY ADDRESS: VACANT LOT. See page 228.

9. AIN 2061029016 (auction ID 80): TRACT NO 7661 LOT 56 ... ASSESSED TO AGOURA AND COR-NELL 0 ROADS LP LOCATION CITY-AGOURA HILL PROPERTY ADDRESS: VACANT LOT. See page 232.

10. AIN 2061029023 (auction ID 82): VAC ST ADJ LOTS 49 THRU 58 TR NO 7661 ON SW 0 . . . ASSESSED TO AGOURA AND CORNELL ROADS LP LOCATION CITY-AGOURA HILL PROPERTY ADDRESS: VACANT LOT. See page 240.

11. AIN 2061030001 (auction ID 83): TRACT NO 7661 LOT 103 . . . ASSESSED TO AGOURA AND CORNELL 0 ROADS LP LOCATION CITY-AGOURA HILL PROPERTY ADDRESS: VACANT LOT. See page 244.

12. AIN 2061030002 (auction ID 84): TRACT NO 7661 LOT 104 . . . ASSESSED TO AGOURA AND CORNELL - 0 ROADS LP LOCATION CITY-AGOURA HILL PROPERTY ADDRESS: VACANT LOT. See page 248.

13. AIN 2061030003 (auction ID 85): TRACT NO 7661 LOT 105 . . . ASSESSED TO AGOURA AND CORNELL 0 ROADS LP LOCATION CITY-AGOURA HILL PROPERTY ADDRESS: VACANT LOT. See page 252.

14. AIN 2061030004 (auction ID 86): TRACT NO 7661 LOT 106 . . . ASSESSED TO AGOURA AND CORNELL 0 ROADS LP LOCATION CITY-AGOURA HILL PROPERTY ADDRESS: VACANT LOT. See page 256.

15. AIN 2061030005 (auction ID 87): TRACT NO 7661 LOT 107 . . . ASSESSED TO AGOURA AND CORNELL 0 ROADS LP LOCATION CITY-AGOURA HILL PROPERTY ADDRESS: VACANT LOT. See page 260.

16. AIN 2061030006 (auction ID 88): TRACT NO 7661 EX OF ST LOT 108 . . . ASSESSED TO AGOURA AND 0 CORNELL ROADS LP LOCATION CITY-AGOURA HILL PROPERTY ADDRESS: VACANT LOT. See page 264.

17. AIN 2061030007 (auction ID 89): TRACT NO 7661 EX OF ST LOT 109 . . . ASSESSED TO AGOURA AND 0 CORNELL ROADS LP LOCATION CITY-AGOURA HILL PROPERTY ADDRESS: VACANT LOT. See page 268.

18. AIN 2061030008 (auction ID 90): TRACT NO 7661 LOT 110 . . . ASSESSED TO AGOURA AND CORNELL 0 ROADS LP LOCATION CITY-AGOURA HILL PROPERTY ADDRESS: VACANT LOT. See page 272.

19. AIN 2061030009 (auction ID 91): TRACT NO 7661 LOT 111 . . . ASSESSED TO AGOURA AND CORNELL 0 ROADS LP LOCATION CITY-AGOURA HILL PROPERTY ADDRESS: VACANT LOT. See page 276.

20. AIN 2061030010 (auction ID 92): TRACT NO 7661 LOT 112 . . . ASSESSED TO AGOURA AND CORNELL 0 ROADS LP LOCATION CITY-AGOURA HILL PROPERTY ADDRESS: VACANT LOT. See page 280.

21. AIN 2061030011 (auction ID 93): TRACT NO 7661 LOT 113 . . . ASSESSED TO AGOURA AND CORNELL 0 ROADS LP LOCATION CITY-AGOURA HILL PROPERTY ADDRESS: VACANT LOT. See page 284.

22. AIN 2061030012 (auction ID 94): TRACT NO 7661 LOT 114 . . . ASSESSED TO AGOURA AND CORNELL 0 ROADS LP LOCATION CITY-AGOURA HILL PROPERTY ADDRESS: VACANT LOT. See page 288.

23. AIN 2061030013 (auction ID 95): TRACT NO 7661 LOT 115 . . . ASSESSED TO AGOURA AND CORNELL 0 ROADS LP LOCATION CITY-AGOURA HILL PROPERTY ADDRESS: VACANT LOT. See page 292.

24. AIN 2061030017 (auction ID 96): VAC ST ADJ LOTS 109 THRU 115 TR NO 7661 ON NW AND NE 0 . . . ASSESSED TO AGOURA AND CORNELL ROADS LP LOCATION CITY-AGOURA HILL PROPERTY ADDRESS: . . . . See page 296.

Figure 2.154: Property 96, AIN 2061029017, overview map

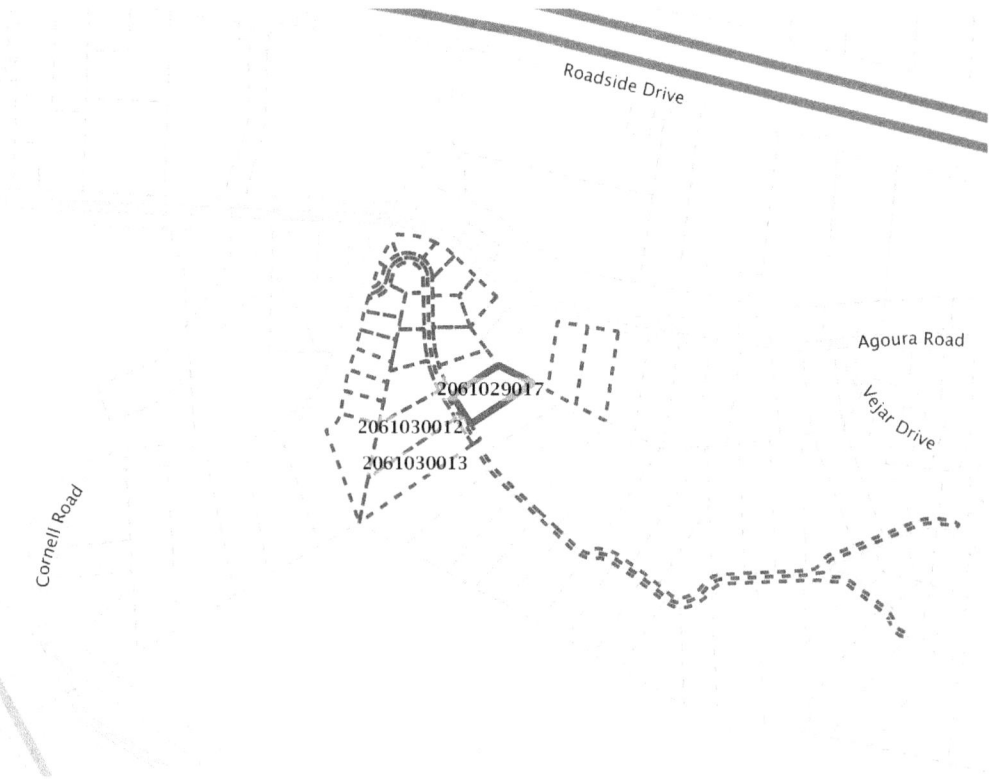

Figure 2.155: Property 96, AIN 2061029017, neighborhood view

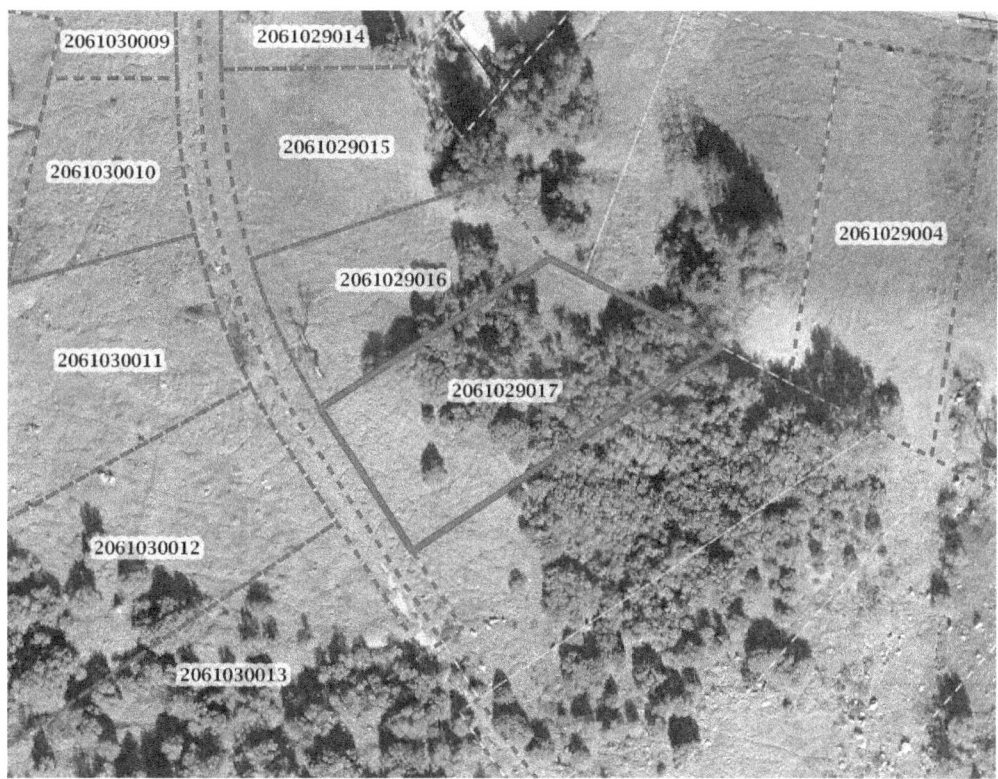

Figure 2.156: Property 96, AIN 2061029017, detailed view

2.53 Auction ID 82

The Los Angeles County Auction Book describes the property as follows.

```
VAC ST ADJ LOTS 49 THRU 58 TR NO 7661 ON SW 0 ASSESSED TO AGOURA AND
CORNELL ROADS LP LOCATION CITY-AGOURA HILL PROPERTY ADDRESS: VACANT
LOT
```

The property is located in the general vicinity of Figure 2.157. It is identified by Assessor's Identification Number (AIN) 2061029023. The starting bid is $2,011. Comparable improved properties in this area is about $292/sqft. Comparable unimproved lots in this area is about $63/sqft. This parcel is approximately 12824 sqft. Note, however, that the parcel may be larger than the property under consideration. In case of condominiums, for example, the parcel may encompass other units of the development - those unrelated to the property to be auctioned.

The property is in a parcel zoned Specific Plan in Agoura Hills, for 0 to 15 dwelling units.

Figures 2.158 and 2.159 show street map and corresponding detailed aerial view, respectively. In both cases, the map is centered on the property with the containing parcel marked in heavy blue. If surrounding nearby properties are also part of this auction, the street and aerial maps highlights these in heavy, dashed blue outline.

This assessed entity may have other properties that are also in this auction:

1. AIN 2061029008 (auction ID 72): TRACT NO 7661 LOT 48 . . . ASSESSED TO AGOURA AND COR-
   NELL 0 ROADS LP LOCATION CITY-AGOURA HILL PROPERTY ADDRESS: VACANT LOT. See
   page 200.

2. AIN 2061029009 (auction ID 73): TRACT NO 7661 LOT 49 . . . ASSESSED TO AGOURA AND COR-
   NELL 0 ROADS LP LOCATION CITY-AGOURA HILL PROPERTY ADDRESS: VACANT LOT. See
   page 204.

3. AIN 2061029010 (auction ID 74): TRACT NO 7661 LOT 50 . . . ASSESSED TO AGOURA AND COR-
   NELL 0 ROADS LP LOCATION CITY-AGOURA HILL PROPERTY ADDRESS: VACANT LOT. See
   page 208.

4. AIN 2061029011 (auction ID 75): TRACT NO 7661 EX OF ST LOT 51 . . . ASSESSED TO AGOURA
   AND 0 CORNELL ROADS LP LOCATION CITY-AGOURA HILL PROPERTY ADDRESS: VACANT
   LOT. See page 212.

5. AIN 2061029012 (auction ID 76): TRACT NO 7661 EX OF ST LOT 52 . . . ASSESSED TO AGOURA
   AND 0 CORNELL ROADS LP LOCATION CITY-AGOURA HILL PROPERTY ADDRESS: VACANT
   LOT. See page 216.

6. AIN 2061029013 (auction ID 77): TRACT NO 7661 EX OF ST LOT 53 . . . ASSESSED TO AGOURA
   AND 0 CORNELL ROADS LP LOCATION CITY-AGOURA HILL PROPERTY ADDRESS: VACANT
   LOT. See page 220.

7. AIN 2061029014 (auction ID 78): TRACT NO 7661 LOT 54 . . . ASSESSED TO AGOURA AND COR-
   NELL 0 ROADS LP LOCATION CITY-AGOURA HILL PROPERTY ADDRESS: VACANT LOT. See
   page 224.

8. AIN 2061029015 (auction ID 79): TRACT NO 7661 LOT 55 . . . ASSESSED TO AGOURA AND COR-
   NELL 0 ROADS LP LOCATION CITY-AGOURA HILL PROPERTY ADDRESS: VACANT LOT. See
   page 228.

9. AIN 2061029016 (auction ID 80): TRACT NO 7661 LOT 56 . . . ASSESSED TO AGOURA AND COR-
   NELL 0 ROADS LP LOCATION CITY-AGOURA HILL PROPERTY ADDRESS: VACANT LOT. See
   page 232.

10. AIN 2061029017 (auction ID 81): TRACT NO 7661 LOT 57 ... ASSESSED TO AGOURA AND CORNELL 0 ROADS LP LOCATION CITY-AGOURA HILL PROPERTY ADDRESS: VACANT LOT. See page 236.

11. AIN 2061030001 (auction ID 83): TRACT NO 7661 LOT 103 ... ASSESSED TO AGOURA AND CORNELL 0 ROADS LP LOCATION CITY-AGOURA HILL PROPERTY ADDRESS: VACANT LOT. See page 244.

12. AIN 2061030002 (auction ID 84): TRACT NO 7661 LOT 104 ... ASSESSED TO AGOURA AND CORNELL - 0 ROADS LP LOCATION CITY-AGOURA HILL PROPERTY ADDRESS: VACANT LOT. See page 248.

13. AIN 2061030003 (auction ID 85): TRACT NO 7661 LOT 105 ... ASSESSED TO AGOURA AND CORNELL 0 ROADS LP LOCATION CITY-AGOURA HILL PROPERTY ADDRESS: VACANT LOT. See page 252.

14. AIN 2061030004 (auction ID 86): TRACT NO 7661 LOT 106 ... ASSESSED TO AGOURA AND CORNELL 0 ROADS LP LOCATION CITY-AGOURA HILL PROPERTY ADDRESS: VACANT LOT. See page 256.

15. AIN 2061030005 (auction ID 87): TRACT NO 7661 LOT 107 ... ASSESSED TO AGOURA AND CORNELL 0 ROADS LP LOCATION CITY-AGOURA HILL PROPERTY ADDRESS: VACANT LOT. See page 260.

16. AIN 2061030006 (auction ID 88): TRACT NO 7661 EX OF ST LOT 108 ... ASSESSED TO AGOURA AND 0 CORNELL ROADS LP LOCATION CITY-AGOURA HILL PROPERTY ADDRESS: VACANT LOT. See page 264.

17. AIN 2061030007 (auction ID 89): TRACT NO 7661 EX OF ST LOT 109 ... ASSESSED TO AGOURA AND 0 CORNELL ROADS LP LOCATION CITY-AGOURA HILL PROPERTY ADDRESS: VACANT LOT. See page 268.

18. AIN 2061030008 (auction ID 90): TRACT NO 7661 LOT 110 ... ASSESSED TO AGOURA AND CORNELL 0 ROADS LP LOCATION CITY-AGOURA HILL PROPERTY ADDRESS: VACANT LOT. See page 272.

19. AIN 2061030009 (auction ID 91): TRACT NO 7661 LOT 111 ... ASSESSED TO AGOURA AND CORNELL 0 ROADS LP LOCATION CITY-AGOURA HILL PROPERTY ADDRESS: VACANT LOT. See page 276.

20. AIN 2061030010 (auction ID 92): TRACT NO 7661 LOT 112 ... ASSESSED TO AGOURA AND CORNELL 0 ROADS LP LOCATION CITY-AGOURA HILL PROPERTY ADDRESS: VACANT LOT. See page 280.

21. AIN 2061030011 (auction ID 93): TRACT NO 7661 LOT 113 ... ASSESSED TO AGOURA AND CORNELL 0 ROADS LP LOCATION CITY-AGOURA HILL PROPERTY ADDRESS: VACANT LOT. See page 284.

22. AIN 2061030012 (auction ID 94): TRACT NO 7661 LOT 114 ... ASSESSED TO AGOURA AND CORNELL 0 ROADS LP LOCATION CITY-AGOURA HILL PROPERTY ADDRESS: VACANT LOT. See page 288.

23. AIN 2061030013 (auction ID 95): TRACT NO 7661 LOT 115 ... ASSESSED TO AGOURA AND CORNELL 0 ROADS LP LOCATION CITY-AGOURA HILL PROPERTY ADDRESS: VACANT LOT. See page 292.

24. AIN 2061030017 (auction ID 96): VAC ST ADJ LOTS 109 THRU 115 TR NO 7661 ON NW AND NE 0 ... ASSESSED TO AGOURA AND CORNELL ROADS LP LOCATION CITY-AGOURA HILL PROPERTY ADDRESS: .... See page 296.

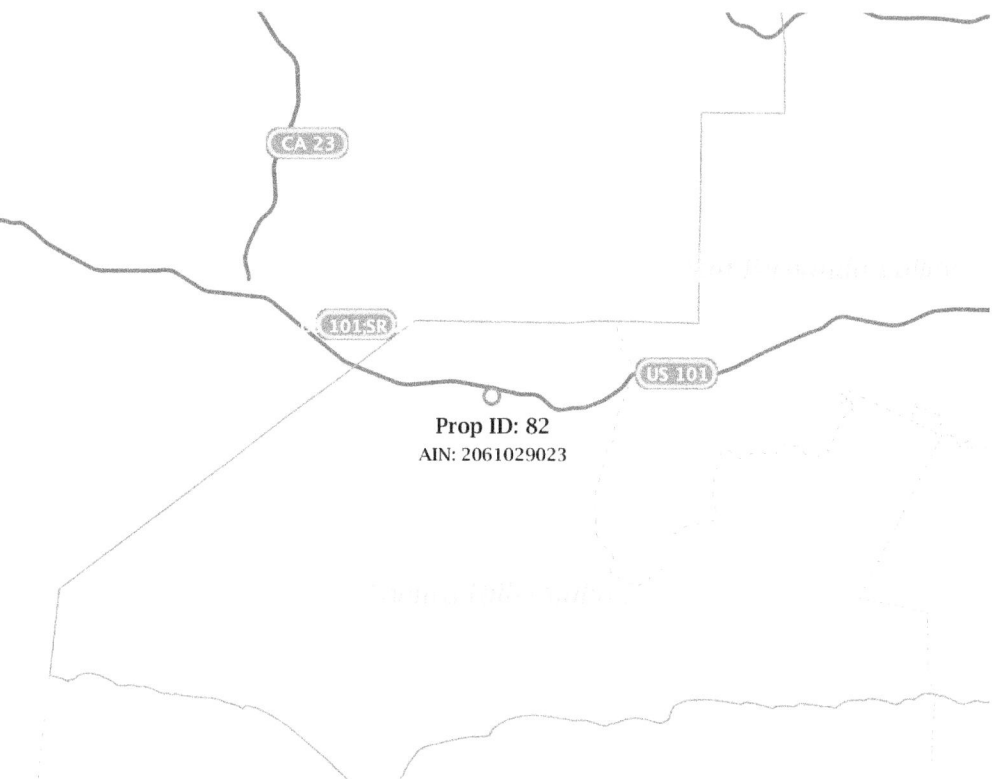

Figure 2.157: Property 96, AIN 2061029023, overview map

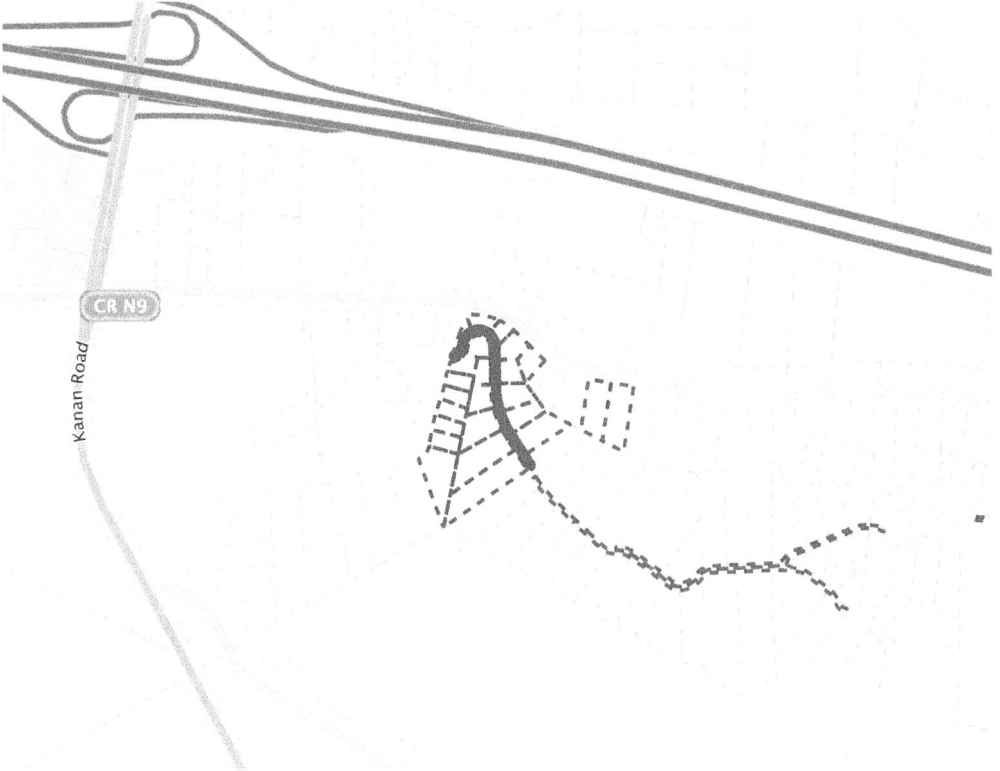

Figure 2.158: Property 96, AIN 2061029023, neighborhood view

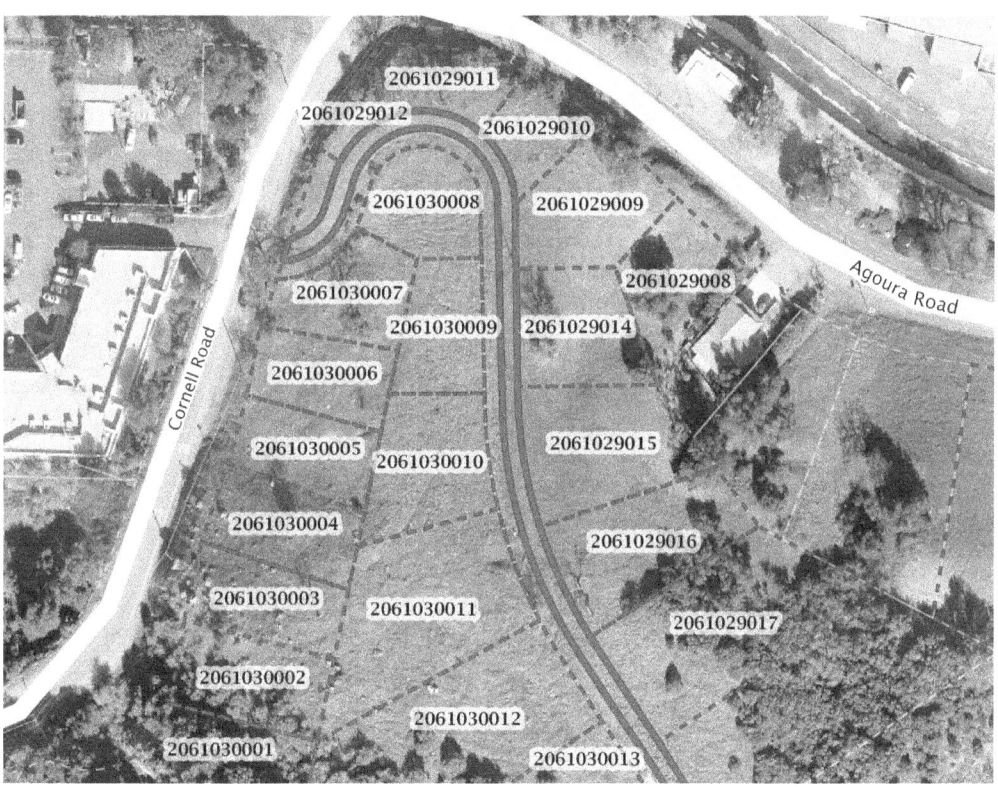

Figure 2.159: Property 96, AIN 2061029023, detailed view

2.54   Auction ID 83

The Los Angeles County Auction Book describes the property as follows.

```
TRACT NO 7661 LOT 103 ASSESSED TO AGOURA AND CORNELL 0 ROADS LP LOCATION
CITY-AGOURA HILL PROPERTY ADDRESS: VACANT LOT
```

The property is located in the general vicinity of Figure 2.160. It is identified by Assessor's Identification Number (AIN) 2061030001. The starting bid is $22,279. Comparable improved properties in this area is about $289/sqft. Comparable unimproved lots in this area is about $74/sqft. This parcel is approximately 30197 sqft. Note, however, that the parcel may be larger than the property under consideration. In case of condominiums, for example, the parcel may encompass other units of the development - those unrelated to the property to be auctioned.

The property is in a parcel zoned Specific Plan in Agoura Hills, for 0 to 15 dwelling units.

Figures 2.161 and 2.162 show street map and corresponding detailed aerial view, respectively. In both cases, the map is centered on the property with the containing parcel marked in heavy blue. If surrounding nearby properties are also part of this auction, the street and aerial maps highlights these in heavy, dashed blue outline.

This assessed entity may have other properties that are also in this auction:

1. AIN 2061029008 (auction ID 72): TRACT NO 7661 LOT 48 ... ASSESSED TO AGOURA AND CORNELL 0 ROADS LP LOCATION CITY-AGOURA HILL PROPERTY ADDRESS: VACANT LOT. See page 200.

2. AIN 2061029009 (auction ID 73): TRACT NO 7661 LOT 49 ... ASSESSED TO AGOURA AND CORNELL 0 ROADS LP LOCATION CITY-AGOURA HILL PROPERTY ADDRESS: VACANT LOT. See page 204.

3. AIN 2061029010 (auction ID 74): TRACT NO 7661 LOT 50 ... ASSESSED TO AGOURA AND CORNELL 0 ROADS LP LOCATION CITY-AGOURA HILL PROPERTY ADDRESS: VACANT LOT. See page 208.

4. AIN 2061029011 (auction ID 75): TRACT NO 7661 EX OF ST LOT 51 ... ASSESSED TO AGOURA AND 0 CORNELL ROADS LP LOCATION CITY-AGOURA HILL PROPERTY ADDRESS: VACANT LOT. See page 212.

5. AIN 2061029012 (auction ID 76): TRACT NO 7661 EX OF ST LOT 52 ... ASSESSED TO AGOURA AND 0 CORNELL ROADS LP LOCATION CITY-AGOURA HILL PROPERTY ADDRESS: VACANT LOT. See page 216.

6. AIN 2061029013 (auction ID 77): TRACT NO 7661 EX OF ST LOT 53 ... ASSESSED TO AGOURA AND 0 CORNELL ROADS LP LOCATION CITY-AGOURA HILL PROPERTY ADDRESS: VACANT LOT. See page 220.

7. AIN 2061029014 (auction ID 78): TRACT NO 7661 LOT 54 ... ASSESSED TO AGOURA AND CORNELL 0 ROADS LP LOCATION CITY-AGOURA HILL PROPERTY ADDRESS: VACANT LOT. See page 224.

8. AIN 2061029015 (auction ID 79): TRACT NO 7661 LOT 55 ... ASSESSED TO AGOURA AND CORNELL 0 ROADS LP LOCATION CITY-AGOURA HILL PROPERTY ADDRESS: VACANT LOT. See page 228.

9. AIN 2061029016 (auction ID 80): TRACT NO 7661 LOT 56 ... ASSESSED TO AGOURA AND CORNELL 0 ROADS LP LOCATION CITY-AGOURA HILL PROPERTY ADDRESS: VACANT LOT. See page 232.

10. AIN 2061029017 (auction ID 81): TRACT NO 7661 LOT 57 . . . ASSESSED TO AGOURA AND COR-NELL 0 ROADS LP LOCATION CITY-AGOURA HILL PROPERTY ADDRESS: VACANT LOT. See page 236.

11. AIN 2061029023 (auction ID 82): VAC ST ADJ LOTS 49 THRU 58 TR NO 7661 ON SW 0 . . . ASSESSED TO AGOURA AND CORNELL ROADS LP LOCATION CITY-AGOURA HILL PROPERTY ADDRESS: VACANT LOT. See page 240.

12. AIN 2061030002 (auction ID 84): TRACT NO 7661 LOT 104 . . . ASSESSED TO AGOURA AND CORNELL - 0 ROADS LP LOCATION CITY-AGOURA HILL PROPERTY ADDRESS: VACANT LOT. See page 248.

13. AIN 2061030003 (auction ID 85): TRACT NO 7661 LOT 105 . . . ASSESSED TO AGOURA AND CORNELL 0 ROADS LP LOCATION CITY-AGOURA HILL PROPERTY ADDRESS: VACANT LOT. See page 252.

14. AIN 2061030004 (auction ID 86): TRACT NO 7661 LOT 106 . . . ASSESSED TO AGOURA AND CORNELL 0 ROADS LP LOCATION CITY-AGOURA HILL PROPERTY ADDRESS: VACANT LOT. See page 256.

15. AIN 2061030005 (auction ID 87): TRACT NO 7661 LOT 107 . . . ASSESSED TO AGOURA AND CORNELL 0 ROADS LP LOCATION CITY-AGOURA HILL PROPERTY ADDRESS: VACANT LOT. See page 260.

16. AIN 2061030006 (auction ID 88): TRACT NO 7661 EX OF ST LOT 108 . . . ASSESSED TO AGOURA AND 0 CORNELL ROADS LP LOCATION CITY-AGOURA HILL PROPERTY ADDRESS: VACANT LOT. See page 264.

17. AIN 2061030007 (auction ID 89): TRACT NO 7661 EX OF ST LOT 109 . . . ASSESSED TO AGOURA AND 0 CORNELL ROADS LP LOCATION CITY-AGOURA HILL PROPERTY ADDRESS: VACANT LOT. See page 268.

18. AIN 2061030008 (auction ID 90): TRACT NO 7661 LOT 110 . . . ASSESSED TO AGOURA AND CORNELL 0 ROADS LP LOCATION CITY-AGOURA HILL PROPERTY ADDRESS: VACANT LOT. See page 272.

19. AIN 2061030009 (auction ID 91): TRACT NO 7661 LOT 111 . . . ASSESSED TO AGOURA AND CORNELL 0 ROADS LP LOCATION CITY-AGOURA HILL PROPERTY ADDRESS: VACANT LOT. See page 276.

20. AIN 2061030010 (auction ID 92): TRACT NO 7661 LOT 112 . . . ASSESSED TO AGOURA AND CORNELL 0 ROADS LP LOCATION CITY-AGOURA HILL PROPERTY ADDRESS: VACANT LOT. See page 280.

21. AIN 2061030011 (auction ID 93): TRACT NO 7661 LOT 113 . . . ASSESSED TO AGOURA AND CORNELL 0 ROADS LP LOCATION CITY-AGOURA HILL PROPERTY ADDRESS: VACANT LOT. See page 284.

22. AIN 2061030012 (auction ID 94): TRACT NO 7661 LOT 114 . . . ASSESSED TO AGOURA AND CORNELL 0 ROADS LP LOCATION CITY-AGOURA HILL PROPERTY ADDRESS: VACANT LOT. See page 288.

23. AIN 2061030013 (auction ID 95): TRACT NO 7661 LOT 115 . . . ASSESSED TO AGOURA AND CORNELL 0 ROADS LP LOCATION CITY-AGOURA HILL PROPERTY ADDRESS: VACANT LOT. See page 292.

24. AIN 2061030017 (auction ID 96): VAC ST ADJ LOTS 109 THRU 115 TR NO 7661 ON NW AND NE 0 . . . ASSESSED TO AGOURA AND CORNELL ROADS LP LOCATION CITY-AGOURA HILL PROPERTY ADDRESS: . . . . See page 296.

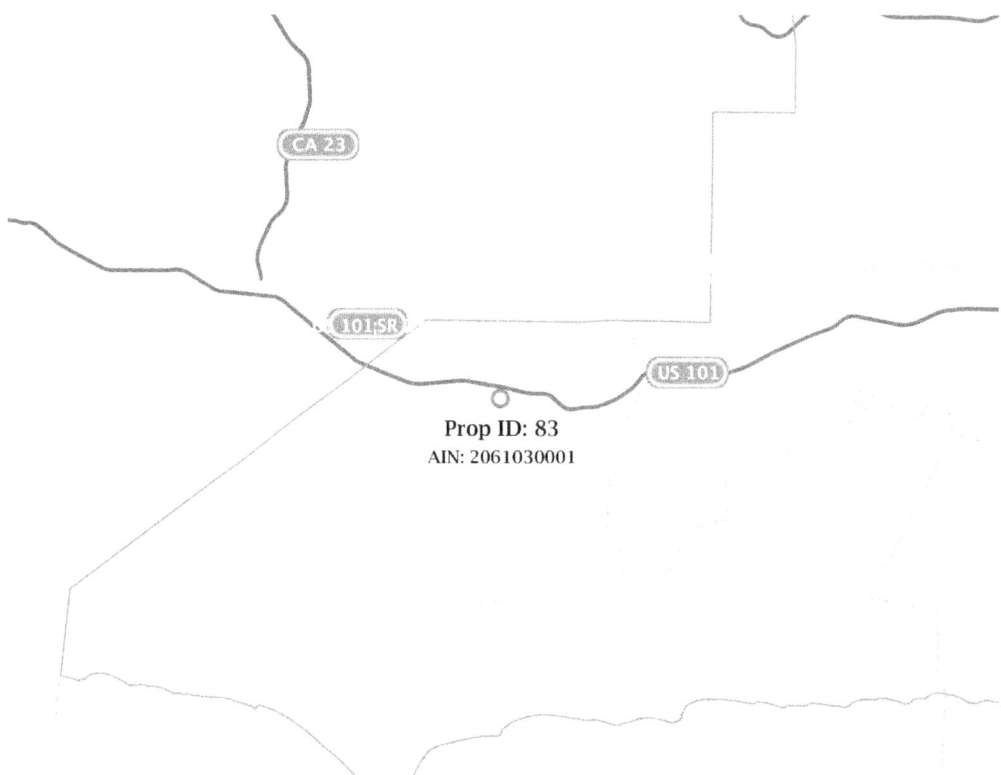

Figure 2.160: Property 96, AIN 2061030001, overview map

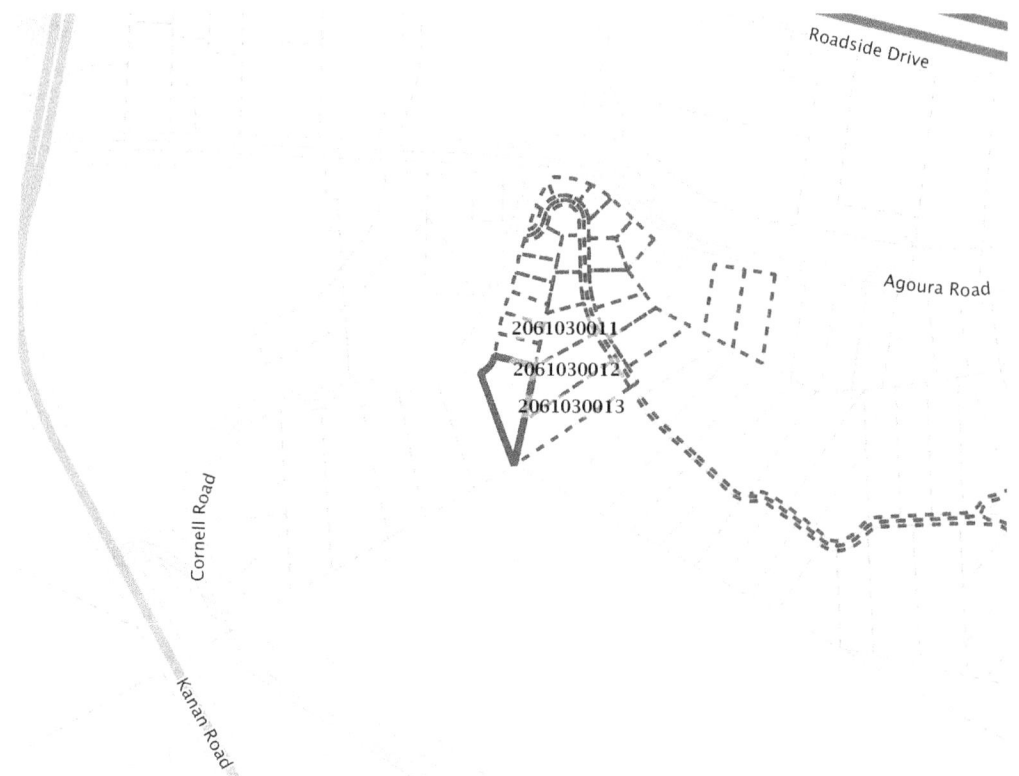

Figure 2.161: Property 96, AIN 2061030001, neighborhood view

Figure 2.162: Property 96, AIN 2061030001, detailed view

2.55   Auction ID 84

The Los Angeles County Auction Book describes the property as follows.

```
TRACT NO 7661 LOT 104 ASSESSED TO AGOURA AND CORNELL - 0 ROADS LP
LOCATION CITY-AGOURA HILL PROPERTY ADDRESS: VACANT LOT
```

The property is located in the general vicinity of Figure 2.163. It is identified by Assessor's Identification Number (AIN) 2061030002. The starting bid is $9,633. Comparable improved properties in this area is about $289/sqft. Comparable unimproved lots in this area is about $74/sqft. This parcel is approximately 9560 sqft. Note, however, that the parcel may be larger than the property under consideration. In case of condominiums, for example, the parcel may encompass other units of the development - those unrelated to the property to be auctioned.

The property is in a parcel zoned Specific Plan in Agoura Hills, for 0 to 15 dwelling units.

Figures 2.164 and 2.165 show street map and corresponding detailed aerial view, respectively. In both cases, the map is centered on the property with the containing parcel marked in heavy blue. If surrounding nearby properties are also part of this auction, the street and aerial maps highlights these in heavy, dashed blue outline.

This assessed entity may have other properties that are also in this auction:

1. AIN 2061029008 (auction ID 72): TRACT NO 7661 LOT 48 ... ASSESSED TO AGOURA AND CORNELL 0 ROADS LP LOCATION CITY-AGOURA HILL PROPERTY ADDRESS: VACANT LOT. See page 200.

2. AIN 2061029009 (auction ID 73): TRACT NO 7661 LOT 49 ... ASSESSED TO AGOURA AND CORNELL 0 ROADS LP LOCATION CITY-AGOURA HILL PROPERTY ADDRESS: VACANT LOT. See page 204.

3. AIN 2061029010 (auction ID 74): TRACT NO 7661 LOT 50 ... ASSESSED TO AGOURA AND CORNELL 0 ROADS LP LOCATION CITY-AGOURA HILL PROPERTY ADDRESS: VACANT LOT. See page 208.

4. AIN 2061029011 (auction ID 75): TRACT NO 7661 EX OF ST LOT 51 ... ASSESSED TO AGOURA AND 0 CORNELL ROADS LP LOCATION CITY-AGOURA HILL PROPERTY ADDRESS: VACANT LOT. See page 212.

5. AIN 2061029012 (auction ID 76): TRACT NO 7661 EX OF ST LOT 52 ... ASSESSED TO AGOURA AND 0 CORNELL ROADS LP LOCATION CITY-AGOURA HILL PROPERTY ADDRESS: VACANT LOT. See page 216.

6. AIN 2061029013 (auction ID 77): TRACT NO 7661 EX OF ST LOT 53 ... ASSESSED TO AGOURA AND 0 CORNELL ROADS LP LOCATION CITY-AGOURA HILL PROPERTY ADDRESS: VACANT LOT. See page 220.

7. AIN 2061029014 (auction ID 78): TRACT NO 7661 LOT 54 ... ASSESSED TO AGOURA AND CORNELL 0 ROADS LP LOCATION CITY-AGOURA HILL PROPERTY ADDRESS: VACANT LOT. See page 224.

8. AIN 2061029015 (auction ID 79): TRACT NO 7661 LOT 55 ... ASSESSED TO AGOURA AND CORNELL 0 ROADS LP LOCATION CITY-AGOURA HILL PROPERTY ADDRESS: VACANT LOT. See page 228.

9. AIN 2061029016 (auction ID 80): TRACT NO 7661 LOT 56 ... ASSESSED TO AGOURA AND CORNELL 0 ROADS LP LOCATION CITY-AGOURA HILL PROPERTY ADDRESS: VACANT LOT. See page 232.

10. AIN 2061029017 (auction ID 81): TRACT NO 7661 LOT 57 ... ASSESSED TO AGOURA AND COR-NELL 0 ROADS LP LOCATION CITY-AGOURA HILL PROPERTY ADDRESS: VACANT LOT. See page 236.

11. AIN 2061029023 (auction ID 82): VAC ST ADJ LOTS 49 THRU 58 TR NO 7661 ON SW 0 ... ASSESSED TO AGOURA AND CORNELL ROADS LP LOCATION CITY-AGOURA HILL PROPERTY ADDRESS: VACANT LOT. See page 240.

12. AIN 2061030001 (auction ID 83): TRACT NO 7661 LOT 103 ... ASSESSED TO AGOURA AND CORNELL 0 ROADS LP LOCATION CITY-AGOURA HILL PROPERTY ADDRESS: VACANT LOT. See page 244.

13. AIN 2061030003 (auction ID 85): TRACT NO 7661 LOT 105 ... ASSESSED TO AGOURA AND CORNELL 0 ROADS LP LOCATION CITY-AGOURA HILL PROPERTY ADDRESS: VACANT LOT. See page 252.

14. AIN 2061030004 (auction ID 86): TRACT NO 7661 LOT 106 ... ASSESSED TO AGOURA AND CORNELL 0 ROADS LP LOCATION CITY-AGOURA HILL PROPERTY ADDRESS: VACANT LOT. See page 256.

15. AIN 2061030005 (auction ID 87): TRACT NO 7661 LOT 107 ... ASSESSED TO AGOURA AND CORNELL 0 ROADS LP LOCATION CITY-AGOURA HILL PROPERTY ADDRESS: VACANT LOT. See page 260.

16. AIN 2061030006 (auction ID 88): TRACT NO 7661 EX OF ST LOT 108 ... ASSESSED TO AGOURA AND 0 CORNELL ROADS LP LOCATION CITY-AGOURA HILL PROPERTY ADDRESS: VACANT LOT. See page 264.

17. AIN 2061030007 (auction ID 89): TRACT NO 7661 EX OF ST LOT 109 ... ASSESSED TO AGOURA AND 0 CORNELL ROADS LP LOCATION CITY-AGOURA HILL PROPERTY ADDRESS: VACANT LOT. See page 268.

18. AIN 2061030008 (auction ID 90): TRACT NO 7661 LOT 110 ... ASSESSED TO AGOURA AND CORNELL 0 ROADS LP LOCATION CITY-AGOURA HILL PROPERTY ADDRESS: VACANT LOT. See page 272.

19. AIN 2061030009 (auction ID 91): TRACT NO 7661 LOT 111 ... ASSESSED TO AGOURA AND CORNELL 0 ROADS LP LOCATION CITY-AGOURA HILL PROPERTY ADDRESS: VACANT LOT. See page 276.

20. AIN 2061030010 (auction ID 92): TRACT NO 7661 LOT 112 ... ASSESSED TO AGOURA AND CORNELL 0 ROADS LP LOCATION CITY-AGOURA HILL PROPERTY ADDRESS: VACANT LOT. See page 280.

21. AIN 2061030011 (auction ID 93): TRACT NO 7661 LOT 113 ... ASSESSED TO AGOURA AND CORNELL 0 ROADS LP LOCATION CITY-AGOURA HILL PROPERTY ADDRESS: VACANT LOT. See page 284.

22. AIN 2061030012 (auction ID 94): TRACT NO 7661 LOT 114 ... ASSESSED TO AGOURA AND CORNELL 0 ROADS LP LOCATION CITY-AGOURA HILL PROPERTY ADDRESS: VACANT LOT. See page 288.

23. AIN 2061030013 (auction ID 95): TRACT NO 7661 LOT 115 ... ASSESSED TO AGOURA AND CORNELL 0 ROADS LP LOCATION CITY-AGOURA HILL PROPERTY ADDRESS: VACANT LOT. See page 292.

24. AIN 2061030017 (auction ID 96): VAC ST ADJ LOTS 109 THRU 115 TR NO 7661 ON NW AND NE 0 ... ASSESSED TO AGOURA AND CORNELL ROADS LP LOCATION CITY-AGOURA HILL PROPERTY ADDRESS: .... See page 296.

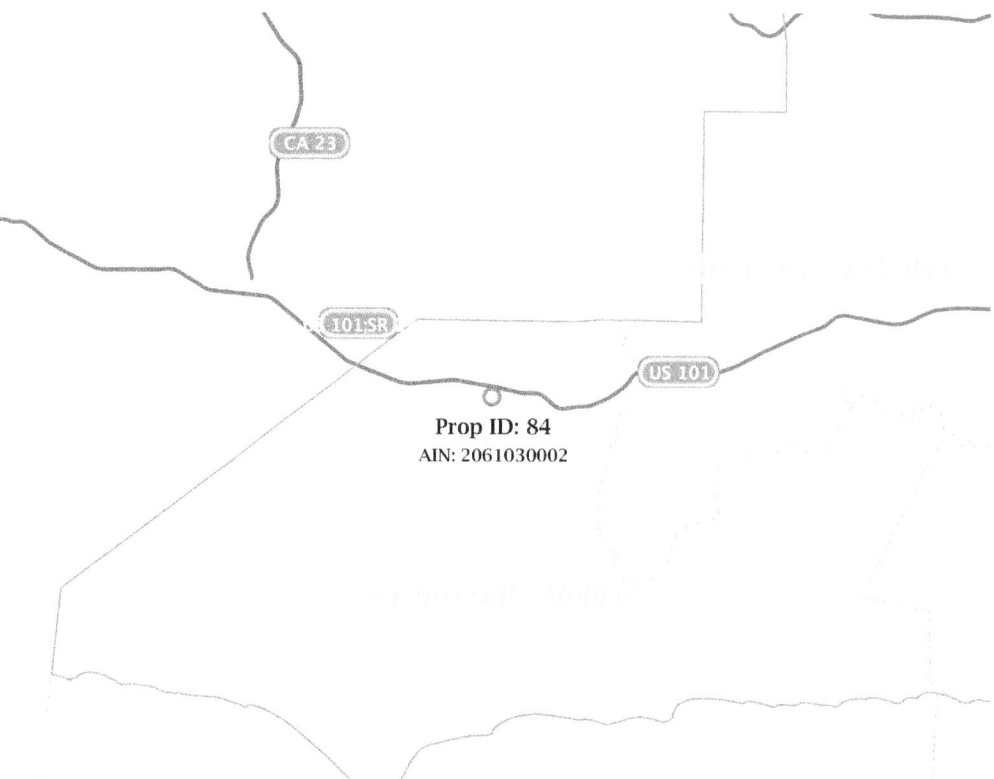

Figure 2.163: Property 96, AIN 2061030002, overview map

Figure 2.164: Property 96, AIN 2061030002, neighborhood view

Figure 2.165: Property 96, AIN 2061030002, detailed view

2.56   Auction ID 85

The Los Angeles County Auction Book describes the property as follows.

```
TRACT NO 7661 LOT 105 ASSESSED TO AGOURA AND CORNELL 0 ROADS LP LOCATION
CITY-AGOURA HILL PROPERTY ADDRESS: VACANT LOT
```

The property is located in the general vicinity of Figure 2.166. It is identified by Assessor's Identification Number (AIN) 2061030003. The starting bid is \$11,922. Comparable improved properties in this area is about \$289/sqft. Comparable unimproved lots in this area is about \$74/sqft. This parcel is approximately 8646 sqft. Note, however, that the parcel may be larger than the property under consideration. In case of condominiums, for example, the parcel may encompass other units of the development - those unrelated to the property to be auctioned.

The property is in a parcel zoned Specific Plan in Agoura Hills, for 0 to 15 dwelling units.

Figures 2.167 and 2.168 show street map and corresponding detailed aerial view, respectively. In both cases, the map is centered on the property with the containing parcel marked in heavy blue. If surrounding nearby properties are also part of this auction, the street and aerial maps highlights these in heavy, dashed blue outline.

This assessed entity may have other properties that are also in this auction:

1. AIN 2061029008 (auction ID 72): TRACT NO 7661 LOT 48 ... ASSESSED TO AGOURA AND COR-NELL 0 ROADS LP LOCATION CITY-AGOURA HILL PROPERTY ADDRESS: VACANT LOT. See page 200.

2. AIN 2061029009 (auction ID 73): TRACT NO 7661 LOT 49 ... ASSESSED TO AGOURA AND COR-NELL 0 ROADS LP LOCATION CITY-AGOURA HILL PROPERTY ADDRESS: VACANT LOT. See page 204.

3. AIN 2061029010 (auction ID 74): TRACT NO 7661 LOT 50 ... ASSESSED TO AGOURA AND COR-NELL 0 ROADS LP LOCATION CITY-AGOURA HILL PROPERTY ADDRESS: VACANT LOT. See page 208.

4. AIN 2061029011 (auction ID 75): TRACT NO 7661 EX OF ST LOT 51 ... ASSESSED TO AGOURA AND 0 CORNELL ROADS LP LOCATION CITY-AGOURA HILL PROPERTY ADDRESS: VACANT LOT. See page 212.

5. AIN 2061029012 (auction ID 76): TRACT NO 7661 EX OF ST LOT 52 ... ASSESSED TO AGOURA AND 0 CORNELL ROADS LP LOCATION CITY-AGOURA HILL PROPERTY ADDRESS: VACANT LOT. See page 216.

6. AIN 2061029013 (auction ID 77): TRACT NO 7661 EX OF ST LOT 53 ... ASSESSED TO AGOURA AND 0 CORNELL ROADS LP LOCATION CITY-AGOURA HILL PROPERTY ADDRESS: VACANT LOT. See page 220.

7. AIN 2061029014 (auction ID 78): TRACT NO 7661 LOT 54 ... ASSESSED TO AGOURA AND COR-NELL 0 ROADS LP LOCATION CITY-AGOURA HILL PROPERTY ADDRESS: VACANT LOT. See page 224.

8. AIN 2061029015 (auction ID 79): TRACT NO 7661 LOT 55 ... ASSESSED TO AGOURA AND COR-NELL 0 ROADS LP LOCATION CITY-AGOURA HILL PROPERTY ADDRESS: VACANT LOT. See page 228.

9. AIN 2061029016 (auction ID 80): TRACT NO 7661 LOT 56 ... ASSESSED TO AGOURA AND COR-NELL 0 ROADS LP LOCATION CITY-AGOURA HILL PROPERTY ADDRESS: VACANT LOT. See page 232.

10. AIN 2061029017 (auction ID 81): TRACT NO 7661 LOT 57 ... ASSESSED TO AGOURA AND CORNELL 0 ROADS LP LOCATION CITY-AGOURA HILL PROPERTY ADDRESS: VACANT LOT. See page 236.

11. AIN 2061029023 (auction ID 82): VAC ST ADJ LOTS 49 THRU 58 TR NO 7661 ON SW 0 ... ASSESSED TO AGOURA AND CORNELL ROADS LP LOCATION CITY-AGOURA HILL PROPERTY ADDRESS: VACANT LOT. See page 240.

12. AIN 2061030001 (auction ID 83): TRACT NO 7661 LOT 103 ... ASSESSED TO AGOURA AND CORNELL 0 ROADS LP LOCATION CITY-AGOURA HILL PROPERTY ADDRESS: VACANT LOT. See page 244.

13. AIN 2061030002 (auction ID 84): TRACT NO 7661 LOT 104 ... ASSESSED TO AGOURA AND CORNELL - 0 ROADS LP LOCATION CITY-AGOURA HILL PROPERTY ADDRESS: VACANT LOT. See page 248.

14. AIN 2061030004 (auction ID 86): TRACT NO 7661 LOT 106 ... ASSESSED TO AGOURA AND CORNELL 0 ROADS LP LOCATION CITY-AGOURA HILL PROPERTY ADDRESS: VACANT LOT. See page 256.

15. AIN 2061030005 (auction ID 87): TRACT NO 7661 LOT 107 ... ASSESSED TO AGOURA AND CORNELL 0 ROADS LP LOCATION CITY-AGOURA HILL PROPERTY ADDRESS: VACANT LOT. See page 260.

16. AIN 2061030006 (auction ID 88): TRACT NO 7661 EX OF ST LOT 108 ... ASSESSED TO AGOURA AND 0 CORNELL ROADS LP LOCATION CITY-AGOURA HILL PROPERTY ADDRESS: VACANT LOT. See page 264.

17. AIN 2061030007 (auction ID 89): TRACT NO 7661 EX OF ST LOT 109 ... ASSESSED TO AGOURA AND 0 CORNELL ROADS LP LOCATION CITY-AGOURA HILL PROPERTY ADDRESS: VACANT LOT. See page 268.

18. AIN 2061030008 (auction ID 90): TRACT NO 7661 LOT 110 ... ASSESSED TO AGOURA AND CORNELL 0 ROADS LP LOCATION CITY-AGOURA HILL PROPERTY ADDRESS: VACANT LOT. See page 272.

19. AIN 2061030009 (auction ID 91): TRACT NO 7661 LOT 111 ... ASSESSED TO AGOURA AND CORNELL 0 ROADS LP LOCATION CITY-AGOURA HILL PROPERTY ADDRESS: VACANT LOT. See page 276.

20. AIN 2061030010 (auction ID 92): TRACT NO 7661 LOT 112 ... ASSESSED TO AGOURA AND CORNELL 0 ROADS LP LOCATION CITY-AGOURA HILL PROPERTY ADDRESS: VACANT LOT. See page 280.

21. AIN 2061030011 (auction ID 93): TRACT NO 7661 LOT 113 ... ASSESSED TO AGOURA AND CORNELL 0 ROADS LP LOCATION CITY-AGOURA HILL PROPERTY ADDRESS: VACANT LOT. See page 284.

22. AIN 2061030012 (auction ID 94): TRACT NO 7661 LOT 114 ... ASSESSED TO AGOURA AND CORNELL 0 ROADS LP LOCATION CITY-AGOURA HILL PROPERTY ADDRESS: VACANT LOT. See page 288.

23. AIN 2061030013 (auction ID 95): TRACT NO 7661 LOT 115 ... ASSESSED TO AGOURA AND CORNELL 0 ROADS LP LOCATION CITY-AGOURA HILL PROPERTY ADDRESS: VACANT LOT. See page 292.

24. AIN 2061030017 (auction ID 96): VAC ST ADJ LOTS 109 THRU 115 TR NO 7661 ON NW AND NE 0 ... ASSESSED TO AGOURA AND CORNELL ROADS LP LOCATION CITY-AGOURA HILL PROPERTY ADDRESS: .... See page 296.

Figure 2.166: Property 96, AIN 2061030003, overview map

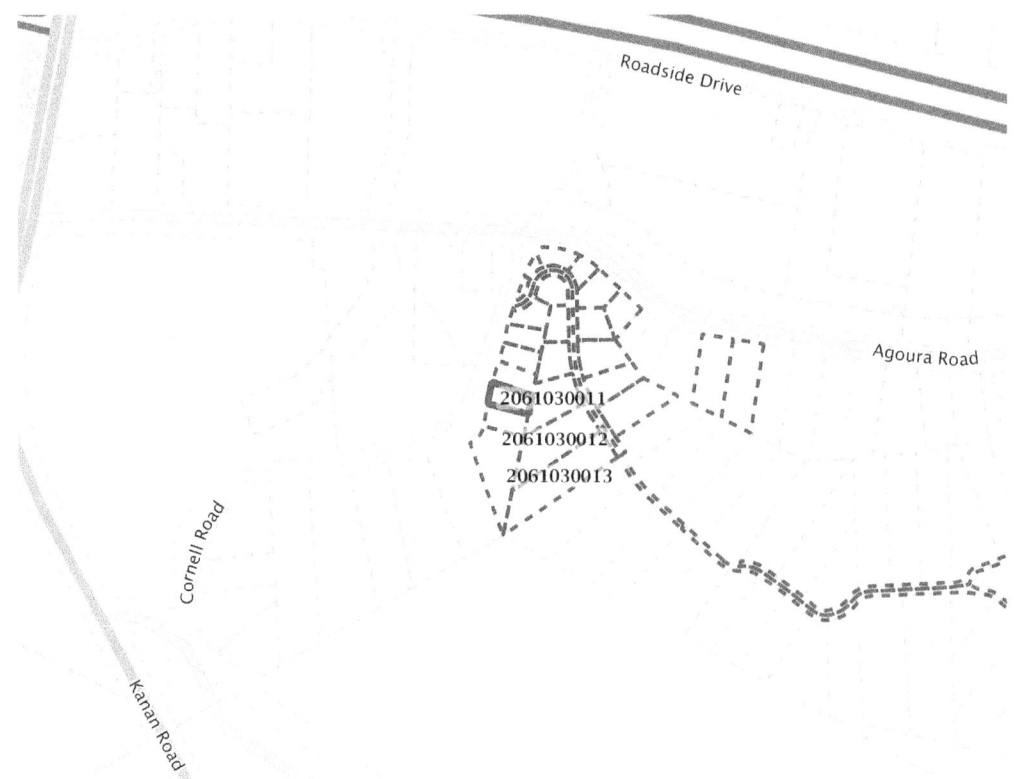

Figure 2.167: Property 96, AIN 2061030003, neighborhood view

Figure 2.168: Property 96, AIN 2061030003, detailed view

2.57 Auction ID 86

The Los Angeles County Auction Book describes the property as follows.

```
TRACT NO 7661 LOT 106 ASSESSED TO AGOURA AND CORNELL 0 ROADS LP LOCATION
CITY-AGOURA HILL PROPERTY ADDRESS: VACANT LOT
```

The property is located in the general vicinity of Figure 2.169. It is identified by Assessor's Identification Number (AIN) 2061030004. The starting bid is $14,744. Comparable improved properties in this area is about $291/sqft. Comparable unimproved lots in this area is about $71/sqft. This parcel is approximately 8860 sqft. Note, however, that the parcel may be larger than the property under consideration. In case of condominiums, for example, the parcel may encompass other units of the development - those unrelated to the property to be auctioned.

The property is in a parcel zoned Specific Plan in Agoura Hills, for 0 to 15 dwelling units.

Figures 2.170 and 2.171 show street map and corresponding detailed aerial view, respectively. In both cases, the map is centered on the property with the containing parcel marked in heavy blue. If surrounding nearby properties are also part of this auction, the street and aerial maps highlights these in heavy, dashed blue outline.

This assessed entity may have other properties that are also in this auction:

1. AIN 2061029008 (auction ID 72): TRACT NO 7661 LOT 48 ... ASSESSED TO AGOURA AND CORNELL 0 ROADS LP LOCATION CITY-AGOURA HILL PROPERTY ADDRESS: VACANT LOT. See page 200.

2. AIN 2061029009 (auction ID 73): TRACT NO 7661 LOT 49 ... ASSESSED TO AGOURA AND CORNELL 0 ROADS LP LOCATION CITY-AGOURA HILL PROPERTY ADDRESS: VACANT LOT. See page 204.

3. AIN 2061029010 (auction ID 74): TRACT NO 7661 LOT 50 ... ASSESSED TO AGOURA AND CORNELL 0 ROADS LP LOCATION CITY-AGOURA HILL PROPERTY ADDRESS: VACANT LOT. See page 208.

4. AIN 2061029011 (auction ID 75): TRACT NO 7661 EX OF ST LOT 51 ... ASSESSED TO AGOURA AND 0 CORNELL ROADS LP LOCATION CITY-AGOURA HILL PROPERTY ADDRESS: VACANT LOT. See page 212.

5. AIN 2061029012 (auction ID 76): TRACT NO 7661 EX OF ST LOT 52 ... ASSESSED TO AGOURA AND 0 CORNELL ROADS LP LOCATION CITY-AGOURA HILL PROPERTY ADDRESS: VACANT LOT. See page 216.

6. AIN 2061029013 (auction ID 77): TRACT NO 7661 EX OF ST LOT 53 ... ASSESSED TO AGOURA AND 0 CORNELL ROADS LP LOCATION CITY-AGOURA HILL PROPERTY ADDRESS: VACANT LOT. See page 220.

7. AIN 2061029014 (auction ID 78): TRACT NO 7661 LOT 54 ... ASSESSED TO AGOURA AND CORNELL 0 ROADS LP LOCATION CITY-AGOURA HILL PROPERTY ADDRESS: VACANT LOT. See page 224.

8. AIN 2061029015 (auction ID 79): TRACT NO 7661 LOT 55 ... ASSESSED TO AGOURA AND CORNELL 0 ROADS LP LOCATION CITY-AGOURA HILL PROPERTY ADDRESS: VACANT LOT. See page 228.

9. AIN 2061029016 (auction ID 80): TRACT NO 7661 LOT 56 ... ASSESSED TO AGOURA AND CORNELL 0 ROADS LP LOCATION CITY-AGOURA HILL PROPERTY ADDRESS: VACANT LOT. See page 232.

10. AIN 2061029017 (auction ID 81): TRACT NO 7661 LOT 57 ... ASSESSED TO AGOURA AND COR-NELL 0 ROADS LP LOCATION CITY-AGOURA HILL PROPERTY ADDRESS: VACANT LOT. See page 236.

11. AIN 2061029023 (auction ID 82): VAC ST ADJ LOTS 49 THRU 58 TR NO 7661 ON SW 0 ... ASSESSED TO AGOURA AND CORNELL ROADS LP LOCATION CITY-AGOURA HILL PROPERTY ADDRESS: VACANT LOT. See page 240.

12. AIN 2061030001 (auction ID 83): TRACT NO 7661 LOT 103 ... ASSESSED TO AGOURA AND CORNELL 0 ROADS LP LOCATION CITY-AGOURA HILL PROPERTY ADDRESS: VACANT LOT. See page 244.

13. AIN 2061030002 (auction ID 84): TRACT NO 7661 LOT 104 ... ASSESSED TO AGOURA AND CORNELL - 0 ROADS LP LOCATION CITY-AGOURA HILL PROPERTY ADDRESS: VACANT LOT. See page 248.

14. AIN 2061030003 (auction ID 85): TRACT NO 7661 LOT 105 ... ASSESSED TO AGOURA AND CORNELL 0 ROADS LP LOCATION CITY-AGOURA HILL PROPERTY ADDRESS: VACANT LOT. See page 252.

15. AIN 2061030005 (auction ID 87): TRACT NO 7661 LOT 107 ... ASSESSED TO AGOURA AND CORNELL 0 ROADS LP LOCATION CITY-AGOURA HILL PROPERTY ADDRESS: VACANT LOT. See page 260.

16. AIN 2061030006 (auction ID 88): TRACT NO 7661 EX OF ST LOT 108 ... ASSESSED TO AGOURA AND 0 CORNELL ROADS LP LOCATION CITY-AGOURA HILL PROPERTY ADDRESS: VACANT LOT. See page 264.

17. AIN 2061030007 (auction ID 89): TRACT NO 7661 EX OF ST LOT 109 ... ASSESSED TO AGOURA AND 0 CORNELL ROADS LP LOCATION CITY-AGOURA HILL PROPERTY ADDRESS: VACANT LOT. See page 268.

18. AIN 2061030008 (auction ID 90): TRACT NO 7661 LOT 110 ... ASSESSED TO AGOURA AND CORNELL 0 ROADS LP LOCATION CITY-AGOURA HILL PROPERTY ADDRESS: VACANT LOT. See page 272.

19. AIN 2061030009 (auction ID 91): TRACT NO 7661 LOT 111 ... ASSESSED TO AGOURA AND CORNELL 0 ROADS LP LOCATION CITY-AGOURA HILL PROPERTY ADDRESS: VACANT LOT. See page 276.

20. AIN 2061030010 (auction ID 92): TRACT NO 7661 LOT 112 ... ASSESSED TO AGOURA AND CORNELL 0 ROADS LP LOCATION CITY-AGOURA HILL PROPERTY ADDRESS: VACANT LOT. See page 280.

21. AIN 2061030011 (auction ID 93): TRACT NO 7661 LOT 113 ... ASSESSED TO AGOURA AND CORNELL 0 ROADS LP LOCATION CITY-AGOURA HILL PROPERTY ADDRESS: VACANT LOT. See page 284.

22. AIN 2061030012 (auction ID 94): TRACT NO 7661 LOT 114 ... ASSESSED TO AGOURA AND CORNELL 0 ROADS LP LOCATION CITY-AGOURA HILL PROPERTY ADDRESS: VACANT LOT. See page 288.

23. AIN 2061030013 (auction ID 95): TRACT NO 7661 LOT 115 ... ASSESSED TO AGOURA AND CORNELL 0 ROADS LP LOCATION CITY-AGOURA HILL PROPERTY ADDRESS: VACANT LOT. See page 292.

24. AIN 2061030017 (auction ID 96): VAC ST ADJ LOTS 109 THRU 115 TR NO 7661 ON NW AND NE 0 ... ASSESSED TO AGOURA AND CORNELL ROADS LP LOCATION CITY-AGOURA HILL PROPERTY ADDRESS: .... See page 296.

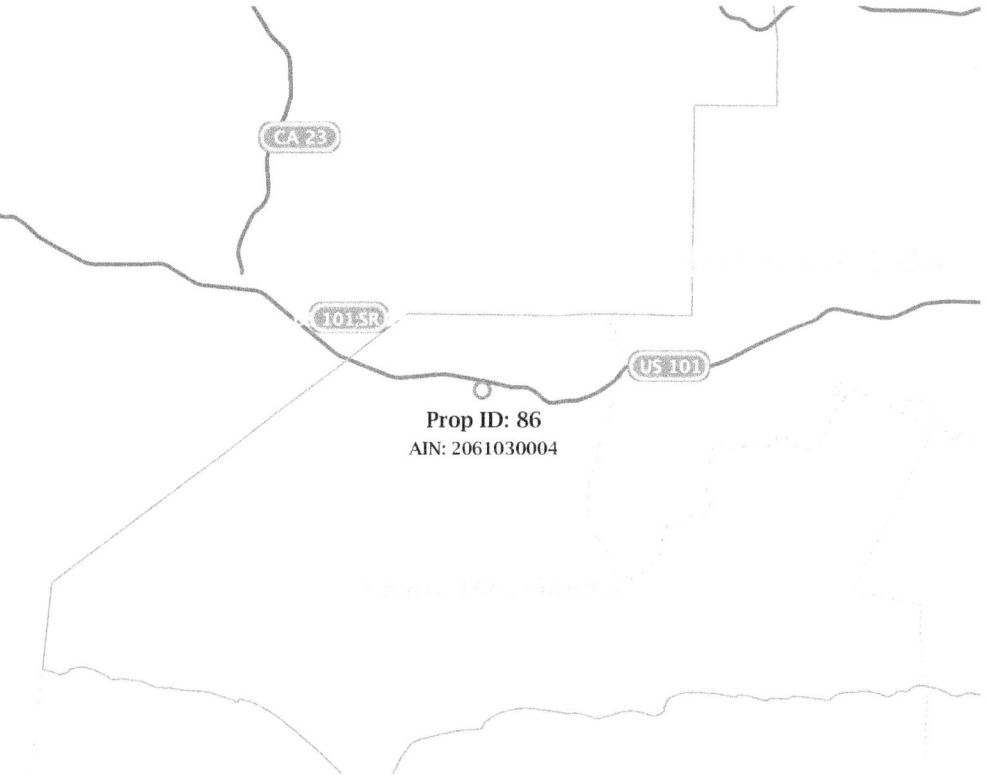

Figure 2.169: Property 96, AIN 2061030004, overview map

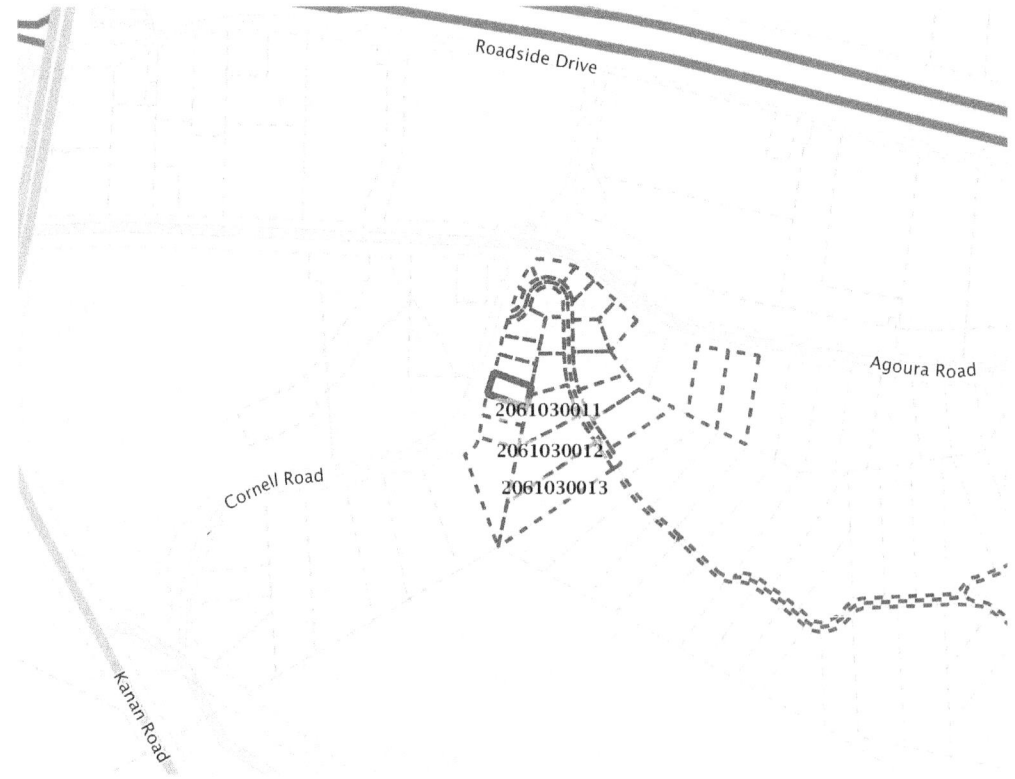

Figure 2.170: Property 96, AIN 2061030004, neighborhood view

Figure 2.171: Property 96, AIN 2061030004, detailed view

2.58   Auction ID 87

The Los Angeles County Auction Book describes the property as follows.

```
TRACT NO 7661 LOT 107 ASSESSED TO AGOURA AND CORNELL 0 ROADS LP LOCATION
CITY-AGOURA HILL PROPERTY ADDRESS: VACANT LOT
```

The property is located in the general vicinity of Figure 2.172. It is identified by Assessor's Identification Number (AIN) 2061030005. The starting bid is $13,076. Comparable improved properties in this area is about $300/sqft. Comparable unimproved lots in this area is about $66/sqft. This parcel is approximately 8071 sqft. Note, however, that the parcel may be larger than the property under consideration. In case of condominiums, for example, the parcel may encompass other units of the development - those unrelated to the property to be auctioned.

The property is in a parcel zoned Specific Plan in Agoura Hills, for 0 to 15 dwelling units.

Figures 2.173 and 2.174 show street map and corresponding detailed aerial view, respectively. In both cases, the map is centered on the property with the containing parcel marked in heavy blue. If surrounding nearby properties are also part of this auction, the street and aerial maps highlights these in heavy, dashed blue outline.

This assessed entity may have other properties that are also in this auction:

1. AIN 2061029008 (auction ID 72): TRACT NO 7661 LOT 48 ... ASSESSED TO AGOURA AND CORNELL 0 ROADS LP LOCATION CITY-AGOURA HILL PROPERTY ADDRESS: VACANT LOT. See page 200.

2. AIN 2061029009 (auction ID 73): TRACT NO 7661 LOT 49 ... ASSESSED TO AGOURA AND CORNELL 0 ROADS LP LOCATION CITY-AGOURA HILL PROPERTY ADDRESS: VACANT LOT. See page 204.

3. AIN 2061029010 (auction ID 74): TRACT NO 7661 LOT 50 ... ASSESSED TO AGOURA AND CORNELL 0 ROADS LP LOCATION CITY-AGOURA HILL PROPERTY ADDRESS: VACANT LOT. See page 208.

4. AIN 2061029011 (auction ID 75): TRACT NO 7661 EX OF ST LOT 51 ... ASSESSED TO AGOURA AND 0 CORNELL ROADS LP LOCATION CITY-AGOURA HILL PROPERTY ADDRESS: VACANT LOT. See page 212.

5. AIN 2061029012 (auction ID 76): TRACT NO 7661 EX OF ST LOT 52 ... ASSESSED TO AGOURA AND 0 CORNELL ROADS LP LOCATION CITY-AGOURA HILL PROPERTY ADDRESS: VACANT LOT. See page 216.

6. AIN 2061029013 (auction ID 77): TRACT NO 7661 EX OF ST LOT 53 ... ASSESSED TO AGOURA AND 0 CORNELL ROADS LP LOCATION CITY-AGOURA HILL PROPERTY ADDRESS: VACANT LOT. See page 220.

7. AIN 2061029014 (auction ID 78): TRACT NO 7661 LOT 54 ... ASSESSED TO AGOURA AND CORNELL 0 ROADS LP LOCATION CITY-AGOURA HILL PROPERTY ADDRESS: VACANT LOT. See page 224.

8. AIN 2061029015 (auction ID 79): TRACT NO 7661 LOT 55 ... ASSESSED TO AGOURA AND CORNELL 0 ROADS LP LOCATION CITY-AGOURA HILL PROPERTY ADDRESS: VACANT LOT. See page 228.

9. AIN 2061029016 (auction ID 80): TRACT NO 7661 LOT 56 ... ASSESSED TO AGOURA AND CORNELL 0 ROADS LP LOCATION CITY-AGOURA HILL PROPERTY ADDRESS: VACANT LOT. See page 232.

10. AIN 2061029017 (auction ID 81): TRACT NO 7661 LOT 57 . . . ASSESSED TO AGOURA AND COR-NELL 0 ROADS LP LOCATION CITY-AGOURA HILL PROPERTY ADDRESS: VACANT LOT. See page 236.

11. AIN 2061029023 (auction ID 82): VAC ST ADJ LOTS 49 THRU 58 TR NO 7661 ON SW 0 . . . ASSESSED TO AGOURA AND CORNELL ROADS LP LOCATION CITY-AGOURA HILL PROPERTY ADDRESS: VACANT LOT. See page 240.

12. AIN 2061030001 (auction ID 83): TRACT NO 7661 LOT 103 . . . ASSESSED TO AGOURA AND CORNELL 0 ROADS LP LOCATION CITY-AGOURA HILL PROPERTY ADDRESS: VACANT LOT. See page 244.

13. AIN 2061030002 (auction ID 84): TRACT NO 7661 LOT 104 . . . ASSESSED TO AGOURA AND CORNELL - 0 ROADS LP LOCATION CITY-AGOURA HILL PROPERTY ADDRESS: VACANT LOT. See page 248.

14. AIN 2061030003 (auction ID 85): TRACT NO 7661 LOT 105 . . . ASSESSED TO AGOURA AND CORNELL 0 ROADS LP LOCATION CITY-AGOURA HILL PROPERTY ADDRESS: VACANT LOT. See page 252.

15. AIN 2061030004 (auction ID 86): TRACT NO 7661 LOT 106 . . . ASSESSED TO AGOURA AND CORNELL 0 ROADS LP LOCATION CITY-AGOURA HILL PROPERTY ADDRESS: VACANT LOT. See page 256.

16. AIN 2061030006 (auction ID 88): TRACT NO 7661 EX OF ST LOT 108 . . . ASSESSED TO AGOURA AND 0 CORNELL ROADS LP LOCATION CITY-AGOURA HILL PROPERTY ADDRESS: VACANT LOT. See page 264.

17. AIN 2061030007 (auction ID 89): TRACT NO 7661 EX OF ST LOT 109 . . . ASSESSED TO AGOURA AND 0 CORNELL ROADS LP LOCATION CITY-AGOURA HILL PROPERTY ADDRESS: VACANT LOT. See page 268.

18. AIN 2061030008 (auction ID 90): TRACT NO 7661 LOT 110 . . . ASSESSED TO AGOURA AND CORNELL 0 ROADS LP LOCATION CITY-AGOURA HILL PROPERTY ADDRESS: VACANT LOT. See page 272.

19. AIN 2061030009 (auction ID 91): TRACT NO 7661 LOT 111 . . . ASSESSED TO AGOURA AND CORNELL 0 ROADS LP LOCATION CITY-AGOURA HILL PROPERTY ADDRESS: VACANT LOT. See page 276.

20. AIN 2061030010 (auction ID 92): TRACT NO 7661 LOT 112 . . . ASSESSED TO AGOURA AND CORNELL 0 ROADS LP LOCATION CITY-AGOURA HILL PROPERTY ADDRESS: VACANT LOT. See page 280.

21. AIN 2061030011 (auction ID 93): TRACT NO 7661 LOT 113 . . . ASSESSED TO AGOURA AND CORNELL 0 ROADS LP LOCATION CITY-AGOURA HILL PROPERTY ADDRESS: VACANT LOT. See page 284.

22. AIN 2061030012 (auction ID 94): TRACT NO 7661 LOT 114 . . . ASSESSED TO AGOURA AND CORNELL 0 ROADS LP LOCATION CITY-AGOURA HILL PROPERTY ADDRESS: VACANT LOT. See page 288.

23. AIN 2061030013 (auction ID 95): TRACT NO 7661 LOT 115 . . . ASSESSED TO AGOURA AND CORNELL 0 ROADS LP LOCATION CITY-AGOURA HILL PROPERTY ADDRESS: VACANT LOT. See page 292.

24. AIN 2061030017 (auction ID 96): VAC ST ADJ LOTS 109 THRU 115 TR NO 7661 ON NW AND NE 0 . . . ASSESSED TO AGOURA AND CORNELL ROADS LP LOCATION CITY-AGOURA HILL PROPERTY ADDRESS: . . . . See page 296.

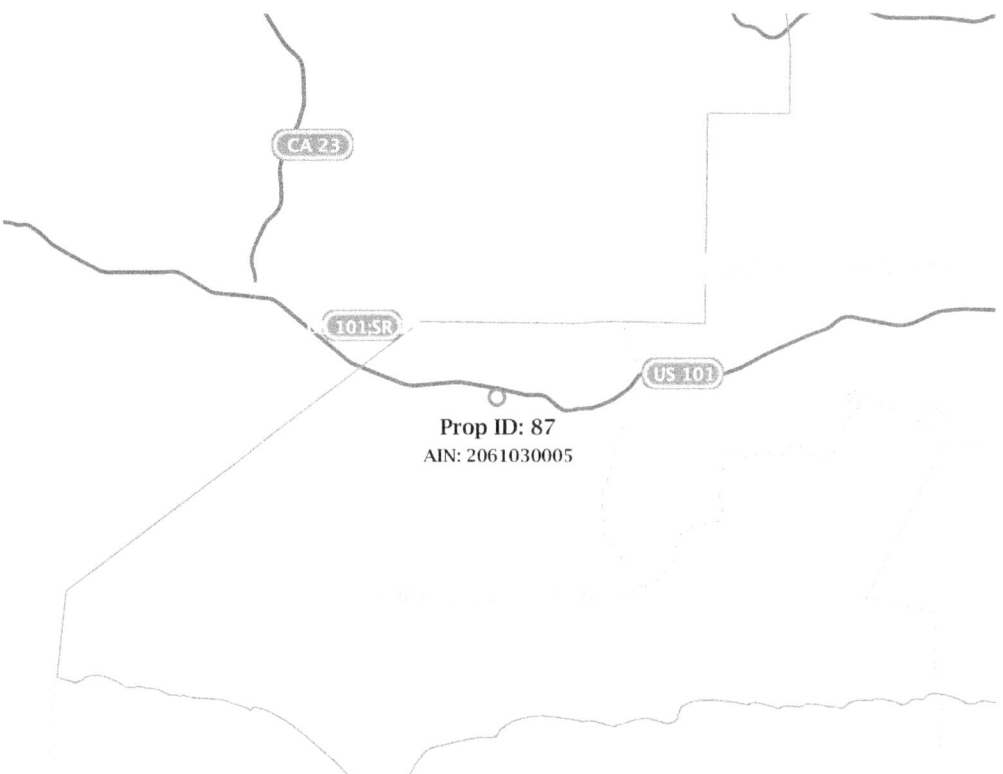

Figure 2.172: Property 96, AIN 2061030005, overview map

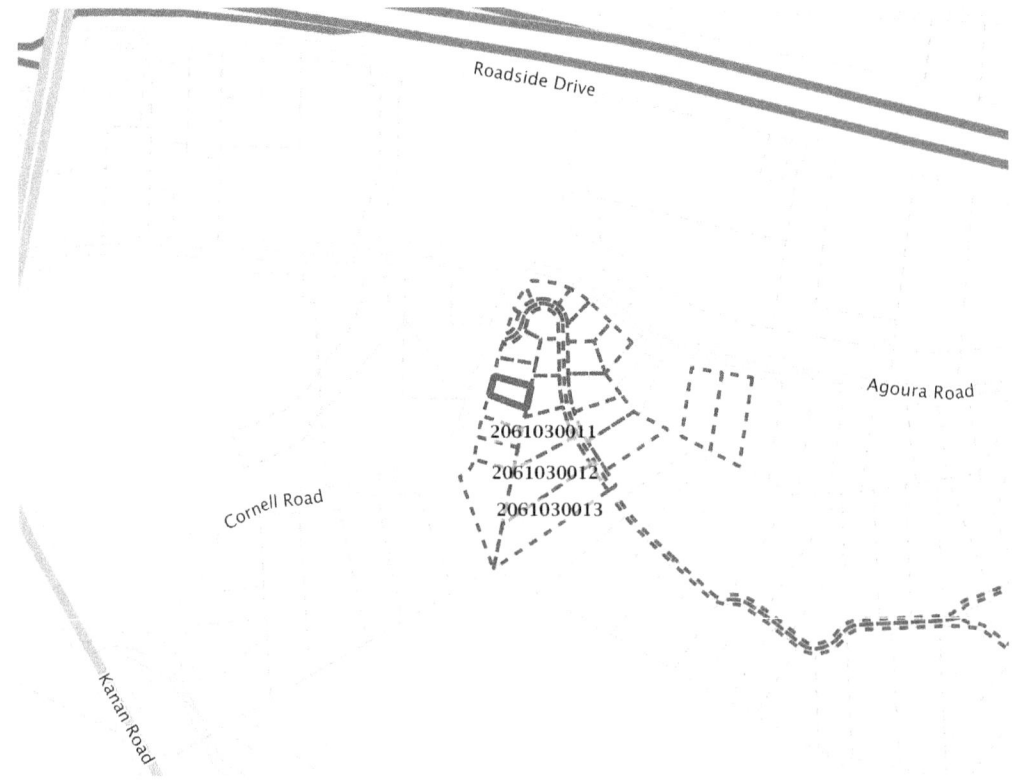

Figure 2.173: Property 96, AIN 2061030005, neighborhood view

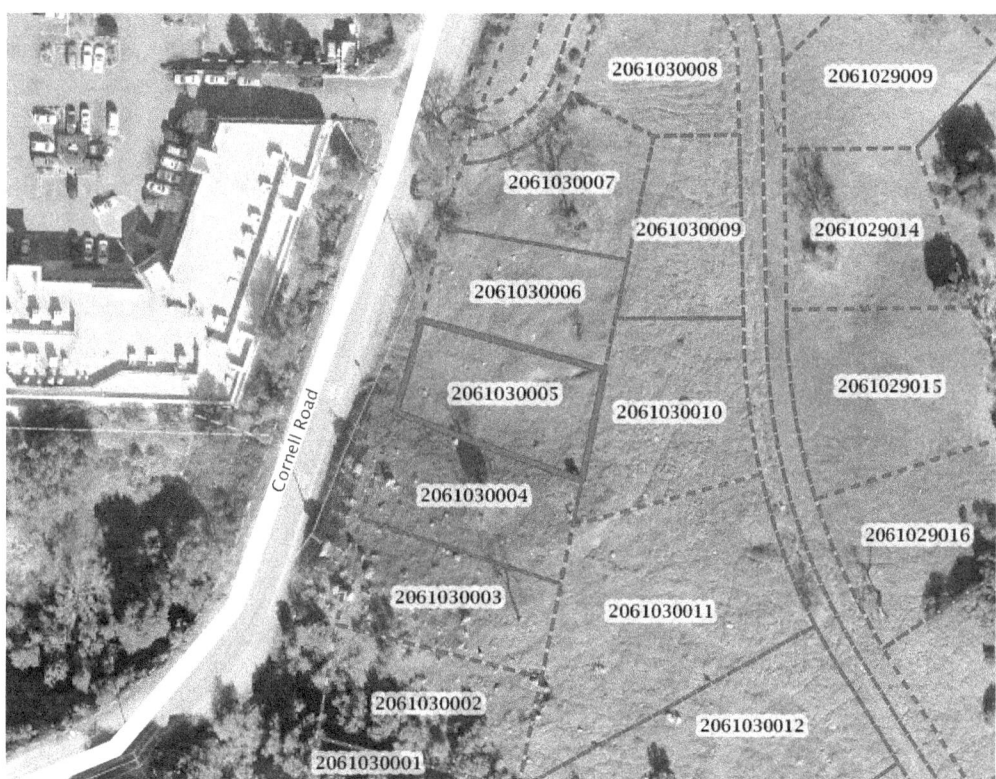

Figure 2.174: Property 96, AIN 2061030005, detailed view

2.59 Auction ID 88

The Los Angeles County Auction Book describes the property as follows.

```
TRACT NO 7661 EX OF ST LOT 108 ASSESSED TO AGOURA AND 0 CORNELL ROADS
LP LOCATION CITY-AGOURA HILL PROPERTY ADDRESS: VACANT LOT
```

The property is located in the general vicinity of Figure 2.175. It is identified by Assessor's Identification Number (AIN) 2061030006. The starting bid is $13,074. Comparable improved properties in this area is about $298/sqft. Comparable unimproved lots in this area is about $65/sqft. This parcel is approximately 7885 sqft. Note, however, that the parcel may be larger than the property under consideration. In case of condominiums, for example, the parcel may encompass other units of the development - those unrelated to the property to be auctioned.

The property is in a parcel zoned Specific Plan in Agoura Hills, for 0 to 15 dwelling units.

Figures 2.176 and 2.177 show street map and corresponding detailed aerial view, respectively. In both cases, the map is centered on the property with the containing parcel marked in heavy blue. If surrounding nearby properties are also part of this auction, the street and aerial maps highlights these in heavy, dashed blue outline.

This assessed entity may have other properties that are also in this auction:

1. AIN 2061029008 (auction ID 72): TRACT NO 7661 LOT 48 . . . ASSESSED TO AGOURA AND CORNELL 0 ROADS LP LOCATION CITY-AGOURA HILL PROPERTY ADDRESS: VACANT LOT. See page 200.

2. AIN 2061029009 (auction ID 73): TRACT NO 7661 LOT 49 . . . ASSESSED TO AGOURA AND CORNELL 0 ROADS LP LOCATION CITY-AGOURA HILL PROPERTY ADDRESS: VACANT LOT. See page 204.

3. AIN 2061029010 (auction ID 74): TRACT NO 7661 LOT 50 . . . ASSESSED TO AGOURA AND CORNELL 0 ROADS LP LOCATION CITY-AGOURA HILL PROPERTY ADDRESS: VACANT LOT. See page 208.

4. AIN 2061029011 (auction ID 75): TRACT NO 7661 EX OF ST LOT 51 . . . ASSESSED TO AGOURA AND 0 CORNELL ROADS LP LOCATION CITY-AGOURA HILL PROPERTY ADDRESS: VACANT LOT. See page 212.

5. AIN 2061029012 (auction ID 76): TRACT NO 7661 EX OF ST LOT 52 . . . ASSESSED TO AGOURA AND 0 CORNELL ROADS LP LOCATION CITY-AGOURA HILL PROPERTY ADDRESS: VACANT LOT. See page 216.

6. AIN 2061029013 (auction ID 77): TRACT NO 7661 EX OF ST LOT 53 . . . ASSESSED TO AGOURA AND 0 CORNELL ROADS LP LOCATION CITY-AGOURA HILL PROPERTY ADDRESS: VACANT LOT. See page 220.

7. AIN 2061029014 (auction ID 78): TRACT NO 7661 LOT 54 . . . ASSESSED TO AGOURA AND CORNELL 0 ROADS LP LOCATION CITY-AGOURA HILL PROPERTY ADDRESS: VACANT LOT. See page 224.

8. AIN 2061029015 (auction ID 79): TRACT NO 7661 LOT 55 . . . ASSESSED TO AGOURA AND CORNELL 0 ROADS LP LOCATION CITY-AGOURA HILL PROPERTY ADDRESS: VACANT LOT. See page 228.

9. AIN 2061029016 (auction ID 80): TRACT NO 7661 LOT 56 . . . ASSESSED TO AGOURA AND CORNELL 0 ROADS LP LOCATION CITY-AGOURA HILL PROPERTY ADDRESS: VACANT LOT. See page 232.

10. AIN 2061029017 (auction ID 81): TRACT NO 7661 LOT 57 ... ASSESSED TO AGOURA AND COR-NELL 0 ROADS LP LOCATION CITY-AGOURA HILL PROPERTY ADDRESS: VACANT LOT. See page 236.

11. AIN 2061029023 (auction ID 82): VAC ST ADJ LOTS 49 THRU 58 TR NO 7661 ON SW 0 ... ASSESSED TO AGOURA AND CORNELL ROADS LP LOCATION CITY-AGOURA HILL PROPERTY ADDRESS: VACANT LOT. See page 240.

12. AIN 2061030001 (auction ID 83): TRACT NO 7661 LOT 103 ... ASSESSED TO AGOURA AND CORNELL 0 ROADS LP LOCATION CITY-AGOURA HILL PROPERTY ADDRESS: VACANT LOT. See page 244.

13. AIN 2061030002 (auction ID 84): TRACT NO 7661 LOT 104 ... ASSESSED TO AGOURA AND CORNELL - 0 ROADS LP LOCATION CITY-AGOURA HILL PROPERTY ADDRESS: VACANT LOT. See page 248.

14. AIN 2061030003 (auction ID 85): TRACT NO 7661 LOT 105 ... ASSESSED TO AGOURA AND CORNELL 0 ROADS LP LOCATION CITY-AGOURA HILL PROPERTY ADDRESS: VACANT LOT. See page 252.

15. AIN 2061030004 (auction ID 86): TRACT NO 7661 LOT 106 ... ASSESSED TO AGOURA AND CORNELL 0 ROADS LP LOCATION CITY-AGOURA HILL PROPERTY ADDRESS: VACANT LOT. See page 256.

16. AIN 2061030005 (auction ID 87): TRACT NO 7661 LOT 107 ... ASSESSED TO AGOURA AND CORNELL 0 ROADS LP LOCATION CITY-AGOURA HILL PROPERTY ADDRESS: VACANT LOT. See page 260.

17. AIN 2061030007 (auction ID 89): TRACT NO 7661 EX OF ST LOT 109 ... ASSESSED TO AGOURA AND 0 CORNELL ROADS LP LOCATION CITY-AGOURA HILL PROPERTY ADDRESS: VACANT LOT. See page 268.

18. AIN 2061030008 (auction ID 90): TRACT NO 7661 LOT 110 ... ASSESSED TO AGOURA AND CORNELL 0 ROADS LP LOCATION CITY-AGOURA HILL PROPERTY ADDRESS: VACANT LOT. See page 272.

19. AIN 2061030009 (auction ID 91): TRACT NO 7661 LOT 111 ... ASSESSED TO AGOURA AND CORNELL 0 ROADS LP LOCATION CITY-AGOURA HILL PROPERTY ADDRESS: VACANT LOT. See page 276.

20. AIN 2061030010 (auction ID 92): TRACT NO 7661 LOT 112 ... ASSESSED TO AGOURA AND CORNELL 0 ROADS LP LOCATION CITY-AGOURA HILL PROPERTY ADDRESS: VACANT LOT. See page 280.

21. AIN 2061030011 (auction ID 93): TRACT NO 7661 LOT 113 ... ASSESSED TO AGOURA AND CORNELL 0 ROADS LP LOCATION CITY-AGOURA HILL PROPERTY ADDRESS: VACANT LOT. See page 284.

22. AIN 2061030012 (auction ID 94): TRACT NO 7661 LOT 114 ... ASSESSED TO AGOURA AND CORNELL 0 ROADS LP LOCATION CITY-AGOURA HILL PROPERTY ADDRESS: VACANT LOT. See page 288.

23. AIN 2061030013 (auction ID 95): TRACT NO 7661 LOT 115 ... ASSESSED TO AGOURA AND CORNELL 0 ROADS LP LOCATION CITY-AGOURA HILL PROPERTY ADDRESS: VACANT LOT. See page 292.

24. AIN 2061030017 (auction ID 96): VAC ST ADJ LOTS 109 THRU 115 TR NO 7661 ON NW AND NE 0 ... ASSESSED TO AGOURA AND CORNELL ROADS LP LOCATION CITY-AGOURA HILL PROPERTY ADDRESS: .... See page 296.

Figure 2.175: Property 96, AIN 2061030006, overview map

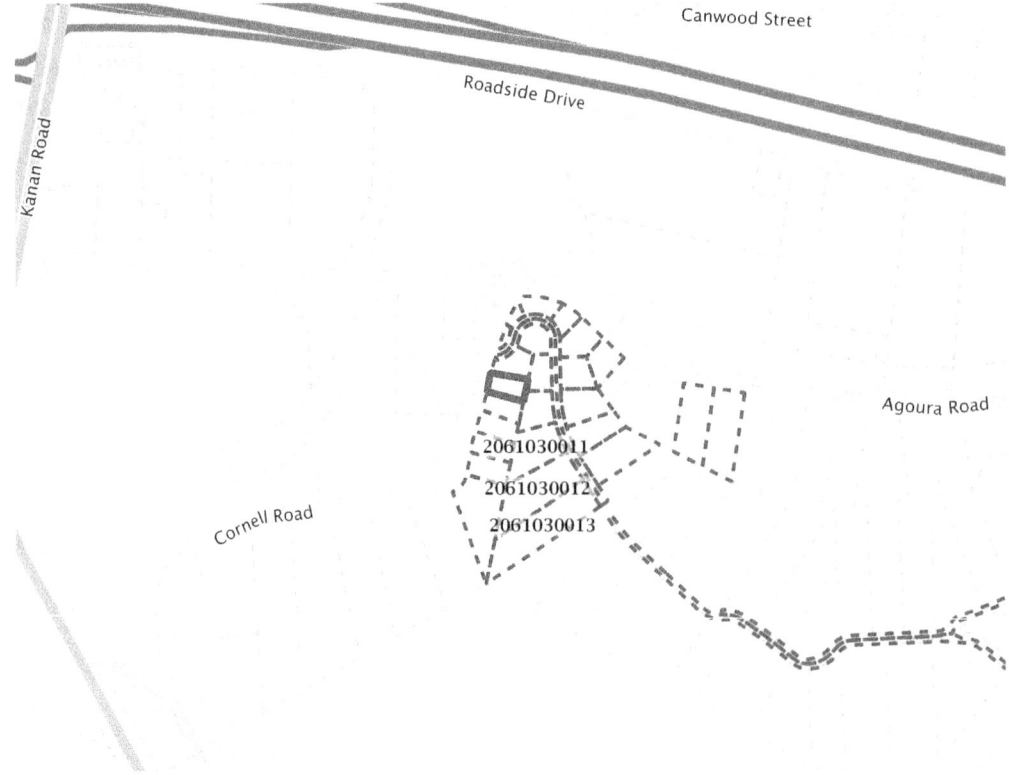

Figure 2.176: Property 96, AIN 2061030006, neighborhood view

Figure 2.177: Property 96, AIN 2061030006, detailed view

2.60   Auction ID 89

The Los Angeles County Auction Book describes the property as follows.

```
TRACT NO 7661 EX OF ST LOT 109 ASSESSED TO AGOURA AND 0 CORNELL ROADS
LP LOCATION CITY-AGOURA HILL PROPERTY ADDRESS: VACANT LOT
```

The property is located in the general vicinity of Figure 2.178. It is identified by Assessor's Identification Number (AIN) 2061030007. The starting bid is $11,976. Comparable improved properties in this area is about $298/sqft. Comparable unimproved lots in this area is about $65/sqft. This parcel is approximately 8558 sqft. Note, however, that the parcel may be larger than the property under consideration. In case of condominiums, for example, the parcel may encompass other units of the development - those unrelated to the property to be auctioned.

The property is in a parcel zoned Specific Plan in Agoura Hills, for 0 to 15 dwelling units.

Figures 2.179 and 2.180 show street map and corresponding detailed aerial view, respectively. In both cases, the map is centered on the property with the containing parcel marked in heavy blue. If surrounding nearby properties are also part of this auction, the street and aerial maps highlights these in heavy, dashed blue outline.

This assessed entity may have other properties that are also in this auction:

1. AIN 2061029008 (auction ID 72): TRACT NO 7661 LOT 48 . . . ASSESSED TO AGOURA AND COR-
   NELL 0 ROADS LP LOCATION CITY-AGOURA HILL PROPERTY ADDRESS: VACANT LOT. See
   page 200.

2. AIN 2061029009 (auction ID 73): TRACT NO 7661 LOT 49 . . . ASSESSED TO AGOURA AND COR-
   NELL 0 ROADS LP LOCATION CITY-AGOURA HILL PROPERTY ADDRESS: VACANT LOT. See
   page 204.

3. AIN 2061029010 (auction ID 74): TRACT NO 7661 LOT 50 . . . ASSESSED TO AGOURA AND COR-
   NELL 0 ROADS LP LOCATION CITY-AGOURA HILL PROPERTY ADDRESS: VACANT LOT. See
   page 208.

4. AIN 2061029011 (auction ID 75): TRACT NO 7661 EX OF ST LOT 51 . . . ASSESSED TO AGOURA
   AND 0 CORNELL ROADS LP LOCATION CITY-AGOURA HILL PROPERTY ADDRESS: VACANT
   LOT. See page 212.

5. AIN 2061029012 (auction ID 76): TRACT NO 7661 EX OF ST LOT 52 . . . ASSESSED TO AGOURA
   AND 0 CORNELL ROADS LP LOCATION CITY-AGOURA HILL PROPERTY ADDRESS: VACANT
   LOT. See page 216.

6. AIN 2061029013 (auction ID 77): TRACT NO 7661 EX OF ST LOT 53 . . . ASSESSED TO AGOURA
   AND 0 CORNELL ROADS LP LOCATION CITY-AGOURA HILL PROPERTY ADDRESS: VACANT
   LOT. See page 220.

7. AIN 2061029014 (auction ID 78): TRACT NO 7661 LOT 54 . . . ASSESSED TO AGOURA AND COR-
   NELL 0 ROADS LP LOCATION CITY-AGOURA HILL PROPERTY ADDRESS: VACANT LOT. See
   page 224.

8. AIN 2061029015 (auction ID 79): TRACT NO 7661 LOT 55 . . . ASSESSED TO AGOURA AND COR-
   NELL 0 ROADS LP LOCATION CITY-AGOURA HILL PROPERTY ADDRESS: VACANT LOT. See
   page 228.

9. AIN 2061029016 (auction ID 80): TRACT NO 7661 LOT 56 . . . ASSESSED TO AGOURA AND COR-
   NELL 0 ROADS LP LOCATION CITY-AGOURA HILL PROPERTY ADDRESS: VACANT LOT. See
   page 232.

10. AIN 2061029017 (auction ID 81): TRACT NO 7661 LOT 57 ... ASSESSED TO AGOURA AND COR-
    NELL 0 ROADS LP LOCATION CITY-AGOURA HILL PROPERTY ADDRESS: VACANT LOT. See
    page 236.

11. AIN 2061029023 (auction ID 82): VAC ST ADJ LOTS 49 THRU 58 TR NO 7661 ON SW 0 ... ASSESSED
    TO AGOURA AND CORNELL ROADS LP LOCATION CITY-AGOURA HILL PROPERTY ADDRESS:
    VACANT LOT. See page 240.

12. AIN 2061030001 (auction ID 83): TRACT NO 7661 LOT 103 ... ASSESSED TO AGOURA AND
    CORNELL 0 ROADS LP LOCATION CITY-AGOURA HILL PROPERTY ADDRESS: VACANT LOT.
    See page 244.

13. AIN 2061030002 (auction ID 84): TRACT NO 7661 LOT 104 ... ASSESSED TO AGOURA AND
    CORNELL - 0 ROADS LP LOCATION CITY-AGOURA HILL PROPERTY ADDRESS: VACANT LOT.
    See page 248.

14. AIN 2061030003 (auction ID 85): TRACT NO 7661 LOT 105 ... ASSESSED TO AGOURA AND
    CORNELL 0 ROADS LP LOCATION CITY-AGOURA HILL PROPERTY ADDRESS: VACANT LOT.
    See page 252.

15. AIN 2061030004 (auction ID 86): TRACT NO 7661 LOT 106 ... ASSESSED TO AGOURA AND
    CORNELL 0 ROADS LP LOCATION CITY-AGOURA HILL PROPERTY ADDRESS: VACANT LOT.
    See page 256.

16. AIN 2061030005 (auction ID 87): TRACT NO 7661 LOT 107 ... ASSESSED TO AGOURA AND
    CORNELL 0 ROADS LP LOCATION CITY-AGOURA HILL PROPERTY ADDRESS: VACANT LOT.
    See page 260.

17. AIN 2061030006 (auction ID 88): TRACT NO 7661 EX OF ST LOT 108 ... ASSESSED TO AGOURA
    AND 0 CORNELL ROADS LP LOCATION CITY-AGOURA HILL PROPERTY ADDRESS: VACANT
    LOT. See page 264.

18. AIN 2061030008 (auction ID 90): TRACT NO 7661 LOT 110 ... ASSESSED TO AGOURA AND
    CORNELL 0 ROADS LP LOCATION CITY-AGOURA HILL PROPERTY ADDRESS: VACANT LOT.
    See page 272.

19. AIN 2061030009 (auction ID 91): TRACT NO 7661 LOT 111 ... ASSESSED TO AGOURA AND
    CORNELL 0 ROADS LP LOCATION CITY-AGOURA HILL PROPERTY ADDRESS: VACANT LOT.
    See page 276.

20. AIN 2061030010 (auction ID 92): TRACT NO 7661 LOT 112 ... ASSESSED TO AGOURA AND
    CORNELL 0 ROADS LP LOCATION CITY-AGOURA HILL PROPERTY ADDRESS: VACANT LOT.
    See page 280.

21. AIN 2061030011 (auction ID 93): TRACT NO 7661 LOT 113 ... ASSESSED TO AGOURA AND
    CORNELL 0 ROADS LP LOCATION CITY-AGOURA HILL PROPERTY ADDRESS: VACANT LOT.
    See page 284.

22. AIN 2061030012 (auction ID 94): TRACT NO 7661 LOT 114 ... ASSESSED TO AGOURA AND
    CORNELL 0 ROADS LP LOCATION CITY-AGOURA HILL PROPERTY ADDRESS: VACANT LOT.
    See page 288.

23. AIN 2061030013 (auction ID 95): TRACT NO 7661 LOT 115 ... ASSESSED TO AGOURA AND
    CORNELL 0 ROADS LP LOCATION CITY-AGOURA HILL PROPERTY ADDRESS: VACANT LOT.
    See page 292.

24. AIN 2061030017 (auction ID 96): VAC ST ADJ LOTS 109 THRU 115 TR NO 7661 ON NW AND
    NE 0 ... ASSESSED TO AGOURA AND CORNELL ROADS LP LOCATION CITY-AGOURA HILL
    PROPERTY ADDRESS: .... See page 296.

Figure 2.178: Property 96, AIN 2061030007, overview map

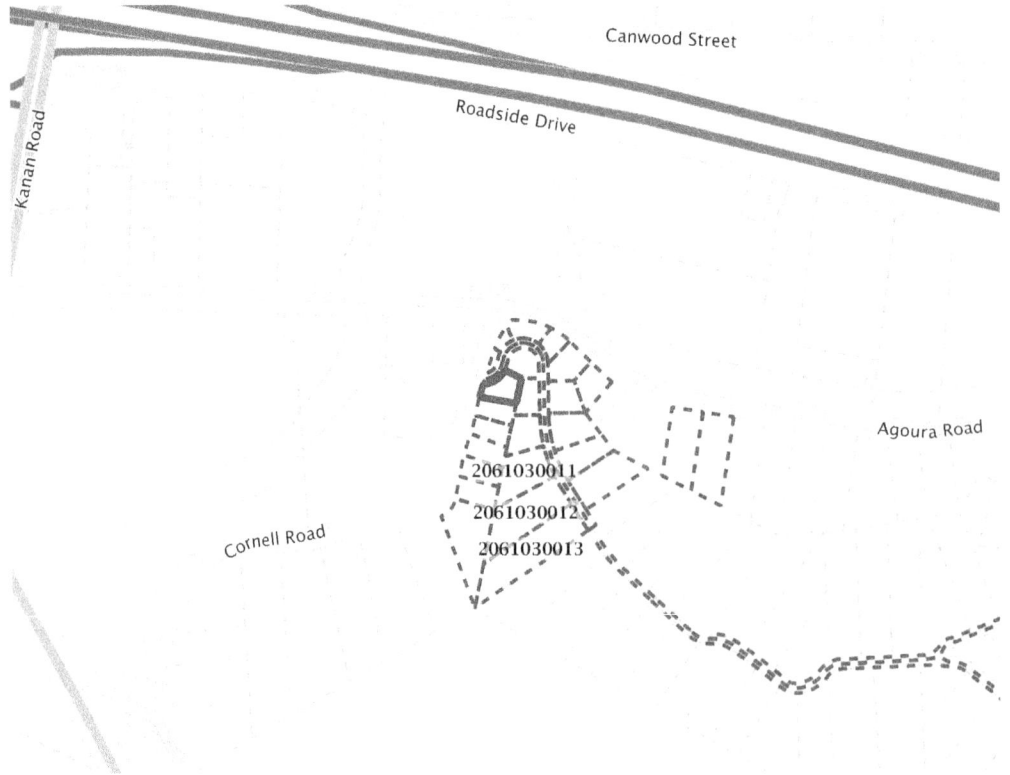

Figure 2.179: Property 96, AIN 2061030007, neighborhood view

Figure 2.180: Property 96, AIN 2061030007, detailed view

2.61 Auction ID 90

The Los Angeles County Auction Book describes the property as follows.

```
TRACT NO 7661 LOT 110 ASSESSED TO AGOURA AND CORNELL 0 ROADS LP LOCATION
CITY-AGOURA HILL PROPERTY ADDRESS: VACANT LOT
```

The property is located in the general vicinity of Figure 2.181. It is identified by Assessor's Identification Number (AIN) 2061030008. The starting bid is $10,954. Comparable improved properties in this area is about $296/sqft. Comparable unimproved lots in this area is about $64/sqft. This parcel is approximately 8041 sqft. Note, however, that the parcel may be larger than the property under consideration. In case of condominiums, for example, the parcel may encompass other units of the development - those unrelated to the property to be auctioned.

The property is in a parcel zoned Specific Plan in Agoura Hills, for 0 to 15 dwelling units.

Figures 2.182 and 2.183 show street map and corresponding detailed aerial view, respectively. In both cases, the map is centered on the property with the containing parcel marked in heavy blue. If surrounding nearby properties are also part of this auction, the street and aerial maps highlights these in heavy, dashed blue outline.

This assessed entity may have other properties that are also in this auction:

1. AIN 2061029008 (auction ID 72): TRACT NO 7661 LOT 48 ... ASSESSED TO AGOURA AND CORNELL 0 ROADS LP LOCATION CITY-AGOURA HILL PROPERTY ADDRESS: VACANT LOT. See page 200.

2. AIN 2061029009 (auction ID 73): TRACT NO 7661 LOT 49 ... ASSESSED TO AGOURA AND CORNELL 0 ROADS LP LOCATION CITY-AGOURA HILL PROPERTY ADDRESS: VACANT LOT. See page 204.

3. AIN 2061029010 (auction ID 74): TRACT NO 7661 LOT 50 ... ASSESSED TO AGOURA AND CORNELL 0 ROADS LP LOCATION CITY-AGOURA HILL PROPERTY ADDRESS: VACANT LOT. See page 208.

4. AIN 2061029011 (auction ID 75): TRACT NO 7661 EX OF ST LOT 51 ... ASSESSED TO AGOURA AND 0 CORNELL ROADS LP LOCATION CITY-AGOURA HILL PROPERTY ADDRESS: VACANT LOT. See page 212.

5. AIN 2061029012 (auction ID 76): TRACT NO 7661 EX OF ST LOT 52 ... ASSESSED TO AGOURA AND 0 CORNELL ROADS LP LOCATION CITY-AGOURA HILL PROPERTY ADDRESS: VACANT LOT. See page 216.

6. AIN 2061029013 (auction ID 77): TRACT NO 7661 EX OF ST LOT 53 ... ASSESSED TO AGOURA AND 0 CORNELL ROADS LP LOCATION CITY-AGOURA HILL PROPERTY ADDRESS: VACANT LOT. See page 220.

7. AIN 2061029014 (auction ID 78): TRACT NO 7661 LOT 54 ... ASSESSED TO AGOURA AND CORNELL 0 ROADS LP LOCATION CITY-AGOURA HILL PROPERTY ADDRESS: VACANT LOT. See page 224.

8. AIN 2061029015 (auction ID 79): TRACT NO 7661 LOT 55 ... ASSESSED TO AGOURA AND CORNELL 0 ROADS LP LOCATION CITY-AGOURA HILL PROPERTY ADDRESS: VACANT LOT. See page 228.

9. AIN 2061029016 (auction ID 80): TRACT NO 7661 LOT 56 ... ASSESSED TO AGOURA AND CORNELL 0 ROADS LP LOCATION CITY-AGOURA HILL PROPERTY ADDRESS: VACANT LOT. See page 232.

10. AIN 2061029017 (auction ID 81): TRACT NO 7661 LOT 57 . . . ASSESSED TO AGOURA AND COR-NELL 0 ROADS LP LOCATION CITY-AGOURA HILL PROPERTY ADDRESS: VACANT LOT. See page 236.

11. AIN 2061029023 (auction ID 82): VAC ST ADJ LOTS 49 THRU 58 TR NO 7661 ON SW 0 . . . ASSESSED TO AGOURA AND CORNELL ROADS LP LOCATION CITY-AGOURA HILL PROPERTY ADDRESS: VACANT LOT. See page 240.

12. AIN 2061030001 (auction ID 83): TRACT NO 7661 LOT 103 . . . ASSESSED TO AGOURA AND CORNELL 0 ROADS LP LOCATION CITY-AGOURA HILL PROPERTY ADDRESS: VACANT LOT. See page 244.

13. AIN 2061030002 (auction ID 84): TRACT NO 7661 LOT 104 . . . ASSESSED TO AGOURA AND CORNELL - 0 ROADS LP LOCATION CITY-AGOURA HILL PROPERTY ADDRESS: VACANT LOT. See page 248.

14. AIN 2061030003 (auction ID 85): TRACT NO 7661 LOT 105 . . . ASSESSED TO AGOURA AND CORNELL 0 ROADS LP LOCATION CITY-AGOURA HILL PROPERTY ADDRESS: VACANT LOT. See page 252.

15. AIN 2061030004 (auction ID 86): TRACT NO 7661 LOT 106 . . . ASSESSED TO AGOURA AND CORNELL 0 ROADS LP LOCATION CITY-AGOURA HILL PROPERTY ADDRESS: VACANT LOT. See page 256.

16. AIN 2061030005 (auction ID 87): TRACT NO 7661 LOT 107 . . . ASSESSED TO AGOURA AND CORNELL 0 ROADS LP LOCATION CITY-AGOURA HILL PROPERTY ADDRESS: VACANT LOT. See page 260.

17. AIN 2061030006 (auction ID 88): TRACT NO 7661 EX OF ST LOT 108 . . . ASSESSED TO AGOURA AND 0 CORNELL ROADS LP LOCATION CITY-AGOURA HILL PROPERTY ADDRESS: VACANT LOT. See page 264.

18. AIN 2061030007 (auction ID 89): TRACT NO 7661 EX OF ST LOT 109 . . . ASSESSED TO AGOURA AND 0 CORNELL ROADS LP LOCATION CITY-AGOURA HILL PROPERTY ADDRESS: VACANT LOT. See page 268.

19. AIN 2061030009 (auction ID 91): TRACT NO 7661 LOT 111 . . . ASSESSED TO AGOURA AND CORNELL 0 ROADS LP LOCATION CITY-AGOURA HILL PROPERTY ADDRESS: VACANT LOT. See page 276.

20. AIN 2061030010 (auction ID 92): TRACT NO 7661 LOT 112 . . . ASSESSED TO AGOURA AND CORNELL 0 ROADS LP LOCATION CITY-AGOURA HILL PROPERTY ADDRESS: VACANT LOT. See page 280.

21. AIN 2061030011 (auction ID 93): TRACT NO 7661 LOT 113 . . . ASSESSED TO AGOURA AND CORNELL 0 ROADS LP LOCATION CITY-AGOURA HILL PROPERTY ADDRESS: VACANT LOT. See page 284.

22. AIN 2061030012 (auction ID 94): TRACT NO 7661 LOT 114 . . . ASSESSED TO AGOURA AND CORNELL 0 ROADS LP LOCATION CITY-AGOURA HILL PROPERTY ADDRESS: VACANT LOT. See page 288.

23. AIN 2061030013 (auction ID 95): TRACT NO 7661 LOT 115 . . . ASSESSED TO AGOURA AND CORNELL 0 ROADS LP LOCATION CITY-AGOURA HILL PROPERTY ADDRESS: VACANT LOT. See page 292.

24. AIN 2061030017 (auction ID 96): VAC ST ADJ LOTS 109 THRU 115 TR NO 7661 ON NW AND NE 0 . . . ASSESSED TO AGOURA AND CORNELL ROADS LP LOCATION CITY-AGOURA HILL PROPERTY ADDRESS: . . . . See page 296.

Figure 2.181: Property 96, AIN 2061030008, overview map

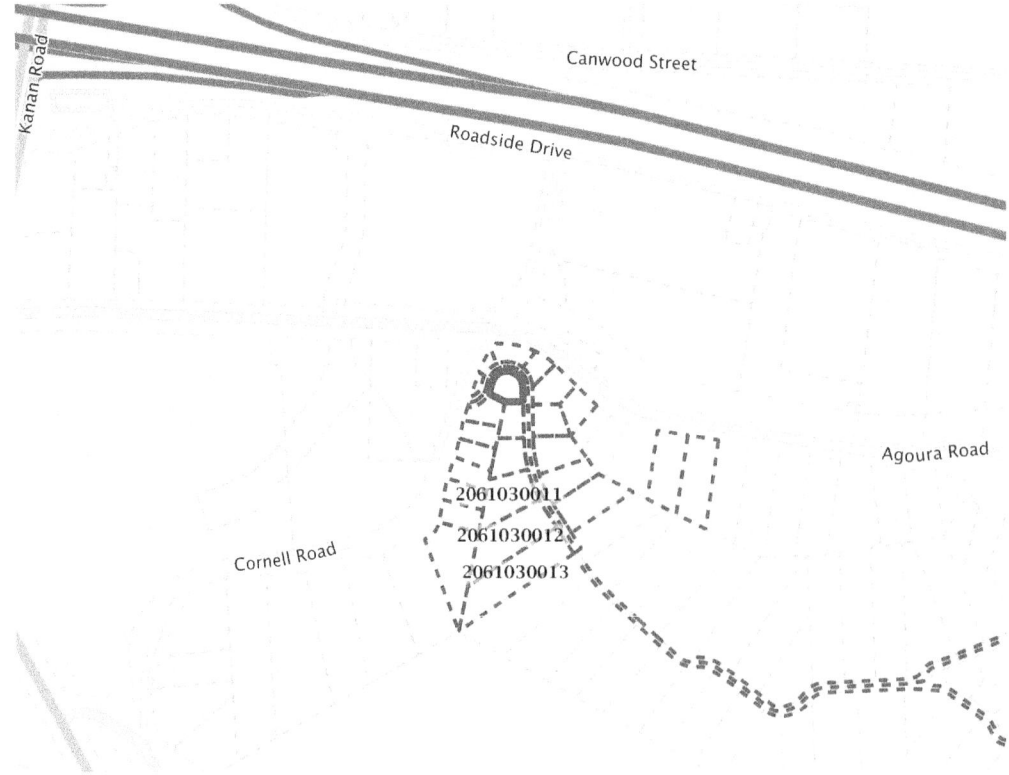

Figure 2.182: Property 96, AIN 2061030008, neighborhood view

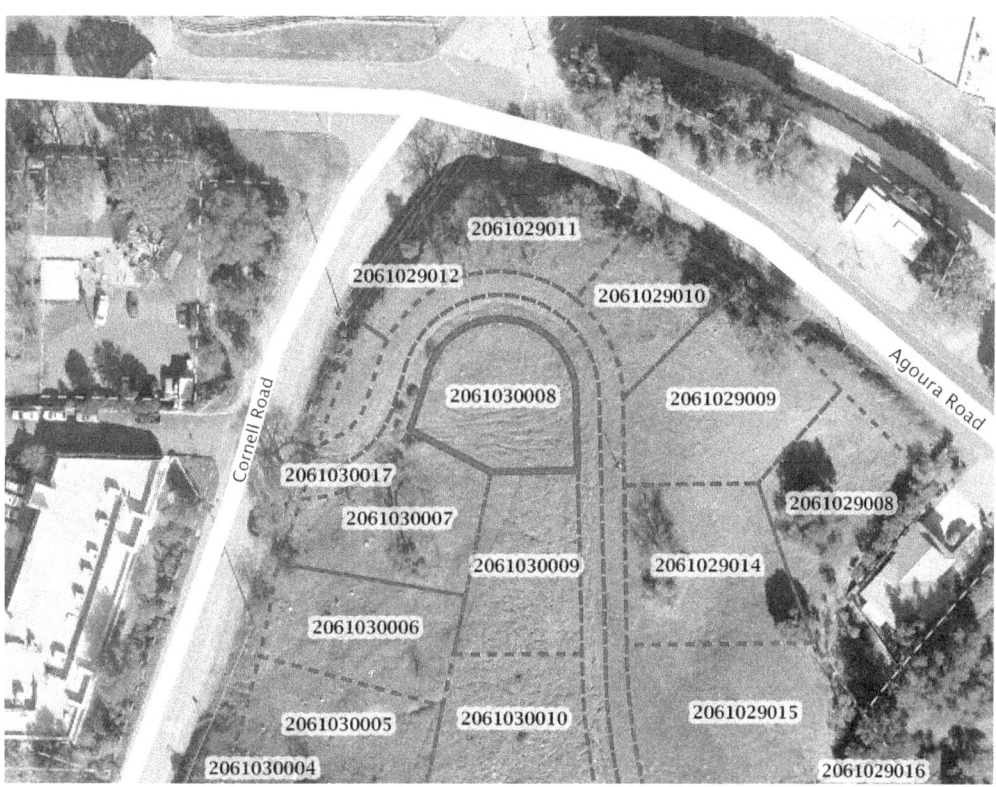

Figure 2.183: Property 96, AIN 2061030008, detailed view

2.62   Auction ID 91

The Los Angeles County Auction Book describes the property as follows.

```
TRACT NO 7661 LOT 111 ASSESSED TO AGOURA AND CORNELL O ROADS LP LOCATION
CITY-AGOURA HILL PROPERTY ADDRESS: VACANT LOT
```

The property is located in the general vicinity of Figure 2.184. It is identified by Assessor's Identification Number (AIN) 2061030009. The starting bid is $10,455. Comparable improved properties in this area is about $295/sqft. Comparable unimproved lots in this area is about $64/sqft. This parcel is approximately 7957 sqft. Note, however, that the parcel may be larger than the property under consideration. In case of condominiums, for example, the parcel may encompass other units of the development - those unrelated to the property to be auctioned.

The property is in a parcel zoned Specific Plan in Agoura Hills, for 0 to 15 dwelling units.

Figures 2.185 and 2.186 show street map and corresponding detailed aerial view, respectively. In both cases, the map is centered on the property with the containing parcel marked in heavy blue. If surrounding nearby properties are also part of this auction, the street and aerial maps highlights these in heavy, dashed blue outline.

This assessed entity may have other properties that are also in this auction:

1. AIN 2061029008 (auction ID 72): TRACT NO 7661 LOT 48 ... ASSESSED TO AGOURA AND CORNELL 0 ROADS LP LOCATION CITY-AGOURA HILL PROPERTY ADDRESS: VACANT LOT. See page 200.

2. AIN 2061029009 (auction ID 73): TRACT NO 7661 LOT 49 ... ASSESSED TO AGOURA AND CORNELL 0 ROADS LP LOCATION CITY-AGOURA HILL PROPERTY ADDRESS: VACANT LOT. See page 204.

3. AIN 2061029010 (auction ID 74): TRACT NO 7661 LOT 50 ... ASSESSED TO AGOURA AND CORNELL 0 ROADS LP LOCATION CITY-AGOURA HILL PROPERTY ADDRESS: VACANT LOT. See page 208.

4. AIN 2061029011 (auction ID 75): TRACT NO 7661 EX OF ST LOT 51 ... ASSESSED TO AGOURA AND 0 CORNELL ROADS LP LOCATION CITY-AGOURA HILL PROPERTY ADDRESS: VACANT LOT. See page 212.

5. AIN 2061029012 (auction ID 76): TRACT NO 7661 EX OF ST LOT 52 ... ASSESSED TO AGOURA AND 0 CORNELL ROADS LP LOCATION CITY-AGOURA HILL PROPERTY ADDRESS: VACANT LOT. See page 216.

6. AIN 2061029013 (auction ID 77): TRACT NO 7661 EX OF ST LOT 53 ... ASSESSED TO AGOURA AND 0 CORNELL ROADS LP LOCATION CITY-AGOURA HILL PROPERTY ADDRESS: VACANT LOT. See page 220.

7. AIN 2061029014 (auction ID 78): TRACT NO 7661 LOT 54 ... ASSESSED TO AGOURA AND CORNELL 0 ROADS LP LOCATION CITY-AGOURA HILL PROPERTY ADDRESS: VACANT LOT. See page 224.

8. AIN 2061029015 (auction ID 79): TRACT NO 7661 LOT 55 ... ASSESSED TO AGOURA AND CORNELL 0 ROADS LP LOCATION CITY-AGOURA HILL PROPERTY ADDRESS: VACANT LOT. See page 228.

9. AIN 2061029016 (auction ID 80): TRACT NO 7661 LOT 56 ... ASSESSED TO AGOURA AND CORNELL 0 ROADS LP LOCATION CITY-AGOURA HILL PROPERTY ADDRESS: VACANT LOT. See page 232.

10. AIN 2061029017 (auction ID 81): TRACT NO 7661 LOT 57 ... ASSESSED TO AGOURA AND COR-NELL 0 ROADS LP LOCATION CITY-AGOURA HILL PROPERTY ADDRESS: VACANT LOT. See page 236.

11. AIN 2061029023 (auction ID 82): VAC ST ADJ LOTS 49 THRU 58 TR NO 7661 ON SW 0 ... ASSESSED TO AGOURA AND CORNELL ROADS LP LOCATION CITY-AGOURA HILL PROPERTY ADDRESS: VACANT LOT. See page 240.

12. AIN 2061030001 (auction ID 83): TRACT NO 7661 LOT 103 ... ASSESSED TO AGOURA AND CORNELL 0 ROADS LP LOCATION CITY-AGOURA HILL PROPERTY ADDRESS: VACANT LOT. See page 244.

13. AIN 2061030002 (auction ID 84): TRACT NO 7661 LOT 104 ... ASSESSED TO AGOURA AND CORNELL - 0 ROADS LP LOCATION CITY-AGOURA HILL PROPERTY ADDRESS: VACANT LOT. See page 248.

14. AIN 2061030003 (auction ID 85): TRACT NO 7661 LOT 105 ... ASSESSED TO AGOURA AND CORNELL 0 ROADS LP LOCATION CITY-AGOURA HILL PROPERTY ADDRESS: VACANT LOT. See page 252.

15. AIN 2061030004 (auction ID 86): TRACT NO 7661 LOT 106 ... ASSESSED TO AGOURA AND CORNELL 0 ROADS LP LOCATION CITY-AGOURA HILL PROPERTY ADDRESS: VACANT LOT. See page 256.

16. AIN 2061030005 (auction ID 87): TRACT NO 7661 LOT 107 ... ASSESSED TO AGOURA AND CORNELL 0 ROADS LP LOCATION CITY-AGOURA HILL PROPERTY ADDRESS: VACANT LOT. See page 260.

17. AIN 2061030006 (auction ID 88): TRACT NO 7661 EX OF ST LOT 108 ... ASSESSED TO AGOURA AND 0 CORNELL ROADS LP LOCATION CITY-AGOURA HILL PROPERTY ADDRESS: VACANT LOT. See page 264.

18. AIN 2061030007 (auction ID 89): TRACT NO 7661 EX OF ST LOT 109 ... ASSESSED TO AGOURA AND 0 CORNELL ROADS LP LOCATION CITY-AGOURA HILL PROPERTY ADDRESS: VACANT LOT. See page 268.

19. AIN 2061030008 (auction ID 90): TRACT NO 7661 LOT 110 ... ASSESSED TO AGOURA AND CORNELL 0 ROADS LP LOCATION CITY-AGOURA HILL PROPERTY ADDRESS: VACANT LOT. See page 272.

20. AIN 2061030010 (auction ID 92): TRACT NO 7661 LOT 112 ... ASSESSED TO AGOURA AND CORNELL 0 ROADS LP LOCATION CITY-AGOURA HILL PROPERTY ADDRESS: VACANT LOT. See page 280.

21. AIN 2061030011 (auction ID 93): TRACT NO 7661 LOT 113 ... ASSESSED TO AGOURA AND CORNELL 0 ROADS LP LOCATION CITY-AGOURA HILL PROPERTY ADDRESS: VACANT LOT. See page 284.

22. AIN 2061030012 (auction ID 94): TRACT NO 7661 LOT 114 ... ASSESSED TO AGOURA AND CORNELL 0 ROADS LP LOCATION CITY-AGOURA HILL PROPERTY ADDRESS: VACANT LOT. See page 288.

23. AIN 2061030013 (auction ID 95): TRACT NO 7661 LOT 115 ... ASSESSED TO AGOURA AND CORNELL 0 ROADS LP LOCATION CITY-AGOURA HILL PROPERTY ADDRESS: VACANT LOT. See page 292.

24. AIN 2061030017 (auction ID 96): VAC ST ADJ LOTS 109 THRU 115 TR NO 7661 ON NW AND NE 0 ... ASSESSED TO AGOURA AND CORNELL ROADS LP LOCATION CITY-AGOURA HILL PROPERTY ADDRESS: .... See page 296.

Figure 2.184: Property 96, AIN 2061030009, overview map

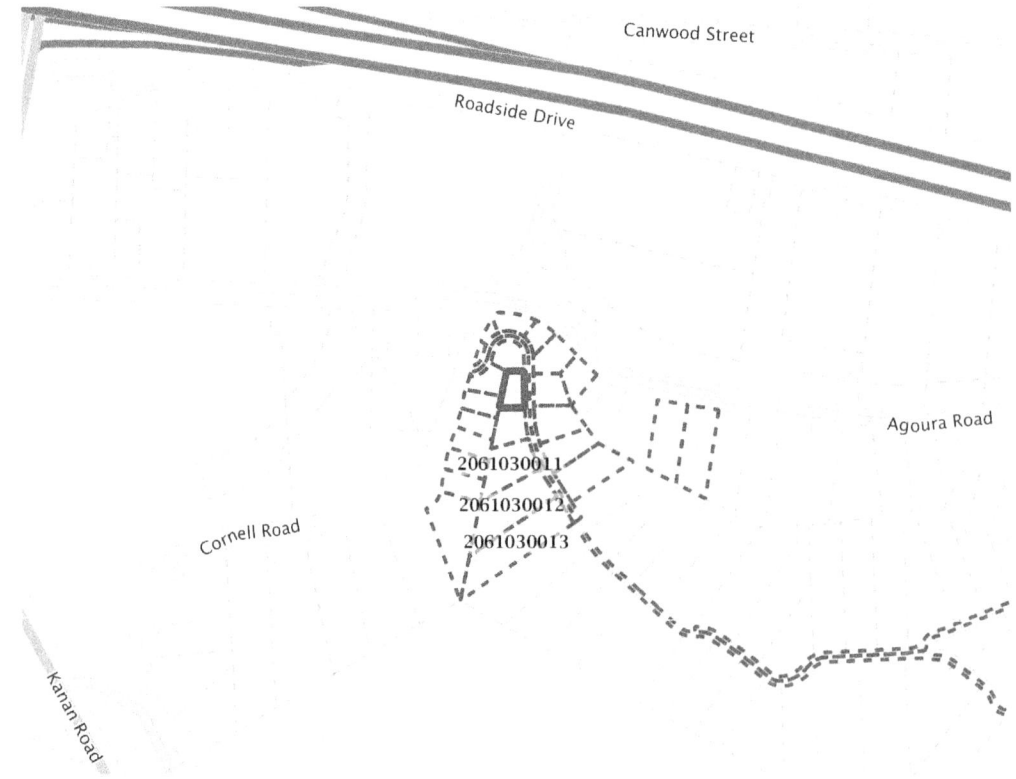

Figure 2.185: Property 96, AIN 2061030009, neighborhood view

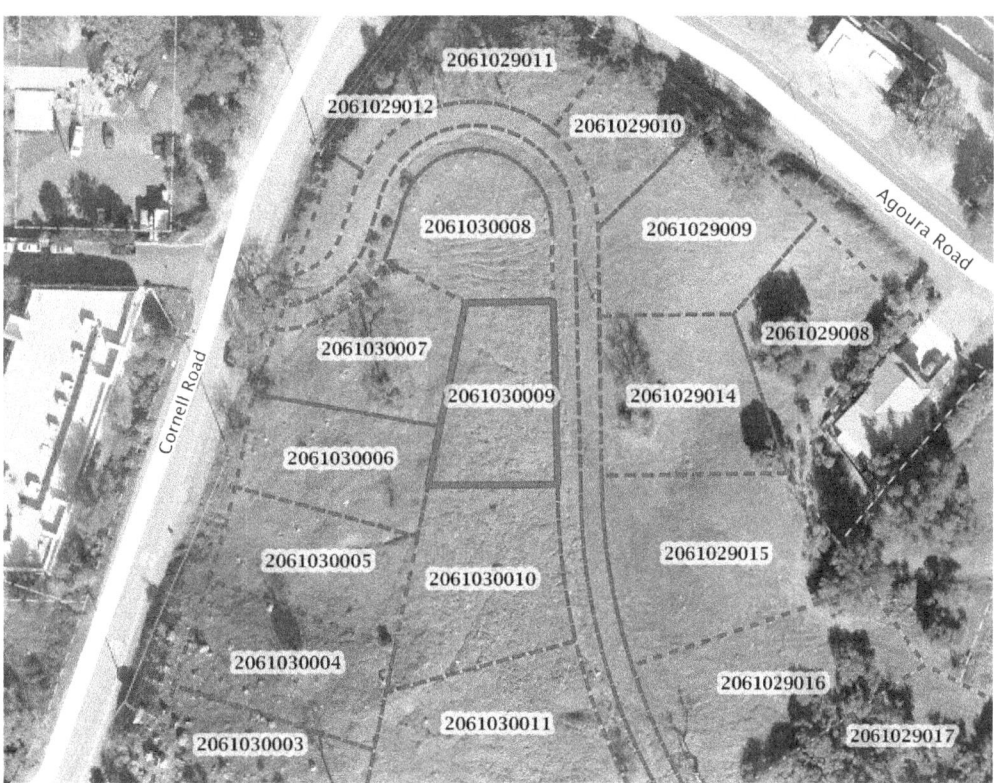

Figure 2.186: Property 96, AIN 2061030009, detailed view

2.63   Auction ID 92

The Los Angeles County Auction Book describes the property as follows.

```
TRACT NO 7661 LOT 112 ASSESSED TO AGOURA AND CORNELL 0 ROADS LP LOCATION
CITY-AGOURA HILL PROPERTY ADDRESS: VACANT LOT
```

The property is located in the general vicinity of Figure 2.187. It is identified by Assessor's Identification Number (AIN) 2061030010. The starting bid is $12,267. Comparable improved properties in this area is about $295/sqft. Comparable unimproved lots in this area is about $64/sqft. This parcel is approximately 11324 sqft. Note, however, that the parcel may be larger than the property under consideration. In case of condominiums, for example, the parcel may encompass other units of the development - those unrelated to the property to be auctioned.

The property is in a parcel zoned Specific Plan in Agoura Hills, for 0 to 15 dwelling units.

Figures 2.188 and 2.189 show street map and corresponding detailed aerial view, respectively. In both cases, the map is centered on the property with the containing parcel marked in heavy blue. If surrounding nearby properties are also part of this auction, the street and aerial maps highlights these in heavy, dashed blue outline.

This assessed entity may have other properties that are also in this auction:

1. AIN 2061029008 (auction ID 72): TRACT NO 7661 LOT 48 ... ASSESSED TO AGOURA AND COR-NELL 0 ROADS LP LOCATION CITY-AGOURA HILL PROPERTY ADDRESS: VACANT LOT. See page 200.

2. AIN 2061029009 (auction ID 73): TRACT NO 7661 LOT 49 ... ASSESSED TO AGOURA AND COR-NELL 0 ROADS LP LOCATION CITY-AGOURA HILL PROPERTY ADDRESS: VACANT LOT. See page 204.

3. AIN 2061029010 (auction ID 74): TRACT NO 7661 LOT 50 ... ASSESSED TO AGOURA AND COR-NELL 0 ROADS LP LOCATION CITY-AGOURA HILL PROPERTY ADDRESS: VACANT LOT. See page 208.

4. AIN 2061029011 (auction ID 75): TRACT NO 7661 EX OF ST LOT 51 ... ASSESSED TO AGOURA AND 0 CORNELL ROADS LP LOCATION CITY-AGOURA HILL PROPERTY ADDRESS: VACANT LOT. See page 212.

5. AIN 2061029012 (auction ID 76): TRACT NO 7661 EX OF ST LOT 52 ... ASSESSED TO AGOURA AND 0 CORNELL ROADS LP LOCATION CITY-AGOURA HILL PROPERTY ADDRESS: VACANT LOT. See page 216.

6. AIN 2061029013 (auction ID 77): TRACT NO 7661 EX OF ST LOT 53 ... ASSESSED TO AGOURA AND 0 CORNELL ROADS LP LOCATION CITY-AGOURA HILL PROPERTY ADDRESS: VACANT LOT. See page 220.

7. AIN 2061029014 (auction ID 78): TRACT NO 7661 LOT 54 ... ASSESSED TO AGOURA AND COR-NELL 0 ROADS LP LOCATION CITY-AGOURA HILL PROPERTY ADDRESS: VACANT LOT. See page 224.

8. AIN 2061029015 (auction ID 79): TRACT NO 7661 LOT 55 ... ASSESSED TO AGOURA AND COR-NELL 0 ROADS LP LOCATION CITY-AGOURA HILL PROPERTY ADDRESS: VACANT LOT. See page 228.

9. AIN 2061029016 (auction ID 80): TRACT NO 7661 LOT 56 ... ASSESSED TO AGOURA AND COR-NELL 0 ROADS LP LOCATION CITY-AGOURA HILL PROPERTY ADDRESS: VACANT LOT. See page 232.

10. AIN 2061029017 (auction ID 81): TRACT NO 7661 LOT 57 ... ASSESSED TO AGOURA AND CORNELL 0 ROADS LP LOCATION CITY-AGOURA HILL PROPERTY ADDRESS: VACANT LOT. See page 236.

11. AIN 2061029023 (auction ID 82): VAC ST ADJ LOTS 49 THRU 58 TR NO 7661 ON SW 0 ... ASSESSED TO AGOURA AND CORNELL ROADS LP LOCATION CITY-AGOURA HILL PROPERTY ADDRESS: VACANT LOT. See page 240.

12. AIN 2061030001 (auction ID 83): TRACT NO 7661 LOT 103 ... ASSESSED TO AGOURA AND CORNELL 0 ROADS LP LOCATION CITY-AGOURA HILL PROPERTY ADDRESS: VACANT LOT. See page 244.

13. AIN 2061030002 (auction ID 84): TRACT NO 7661 LOT 104 ... ASSESSED TO AGOURA AND CORNELL - 0 ROADS LP LOCATION CITY-AGOURA HILL PROPERTY ADDRESS: VACANT LOT. See page 248.

14. AIN 2061030003 (auction ID 85): TRACT NO 7661 LOT 105 ... ASSESSED TO AGOURA AND CORNELL 0 ROADS LP LOCATION CITY-AGOURA HILL PROPERTY ADDRESS: VACANT LOT. See page 252.

15. AIN 2061030004 (auction ID 86): TRACT NO 7661 LOT 106 ... ASSESSED TO AGOURA AND CORNELL 0 ROADS LP LOCATION CITY-AGOURA HILL PROPERTY ADDRESS: VACANT LOT. See page 256.

16. AIN 2061030005 (auction ID 87): TRACT NO 7661 LOT 107 ... ASSESSED TO AGOURA AND CORNELL 0 ROADS LP LOCATION CITY-AGOURA HILL PROPERTY ADDRESS: VACANT LOT. See page 260.

17. AIN 2061030006 (auction ID 88): TRACT NO 7661 EX OF ST LOT 108 ... ASSESSED TO AGOURA AND 0 CORNELL ROADS LP LOCATION CITY-AGOURA HILL PROPERTY ADDRESS: VACANT LOT. See page 264.

18. AIN 2061030007 (auction ID 89): TRACT NO 7661 EX OF ST LOT 109 ... ASSESSED TO AGOURA AND 0 CORNELL ROADS LP LOCATION CITY-AGOURA HILL PROPERTY ADDRESS: VACANT LOT. See page 268.

19. AIN 2061030008 (auction ID 90): TRACT NO 7661 LOT 110 ... ASSESSED TO AGOURA AND CORNELL 0 ROADS LP LOCATION CITY-AGOURA HILL PROPERTY ADDRESS: VACANT LOT. See page 272.

20. AIN 2061030009 (auction ID 91): TRACT NO 7661 LOT 111 ... ASSESSED TO AGOURA AND CORNELL 0 ROADS LP LOCATION CITY-AGOURA HILL PROPERTY ADDRESS: VACANT LOT. See page 276.

21. AIN 2061030011 (auction ID 93): TRACT NO 7661 LOT 113 ... ASSESSED TO AGOURA AND CORNELL 0 ROADS LP LOCATION CITY-AGOURA HILL PROPERTY ADDRESS: VACANT LOT. See page 284.

22. AIN 2061030012 (auction ID 94): TRACT NO 7661 LOT 114 ... ASSESSED TO AGOURA AND CORNELL 0 ROADS LP LOCATION CITY-AGOURA HILL PROPERTY ADDRESS: VACANT LOT. See page 288.

23. AIN 2061030013 (auction ID 95): TRACT NO 7661 LOT 115 ... ASSESSED TO AGOURA AND CORNELL 0 ROADS LP LOCATION CITY-AGOURA HILL PROPERTY ADDRESS: VACANT LOT. See page 292.

24. AIN 2061030017 (auction ID 96): VAC ST ADJ LOTS 109 THRU 115 TR NO 7661 ON NW AND NE 0 ... ASSESSED TO AGOURA AND CORNELL ROADS LP LOCATION CITY-AGOURA HILL PROPERTY ADDRESS: .... See page 296.

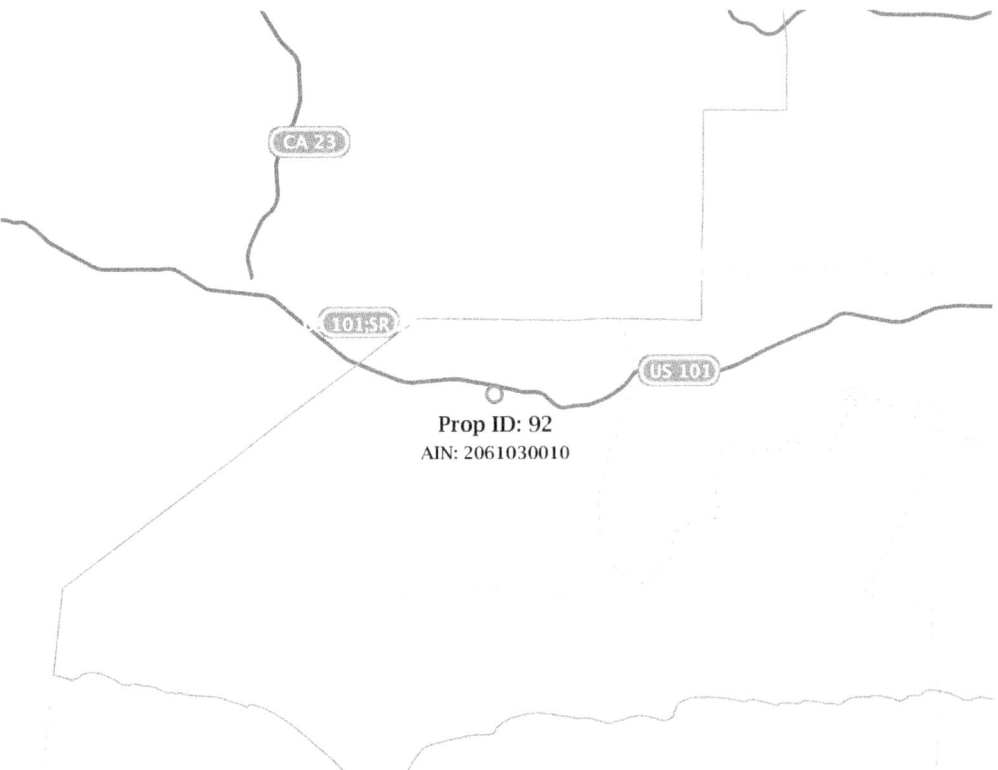

Figure 2.187: Property 96, AIN 2061030010, overview map

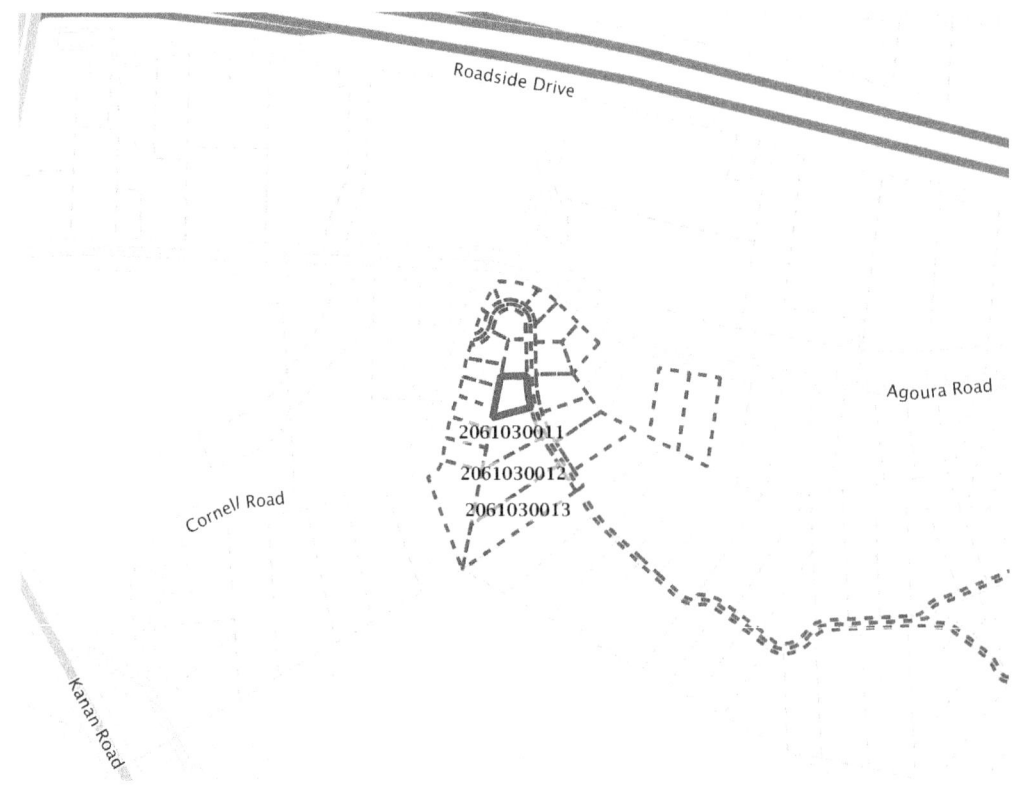

Figure 2.188: Property 96, AIN 2061030010, neighborhood view

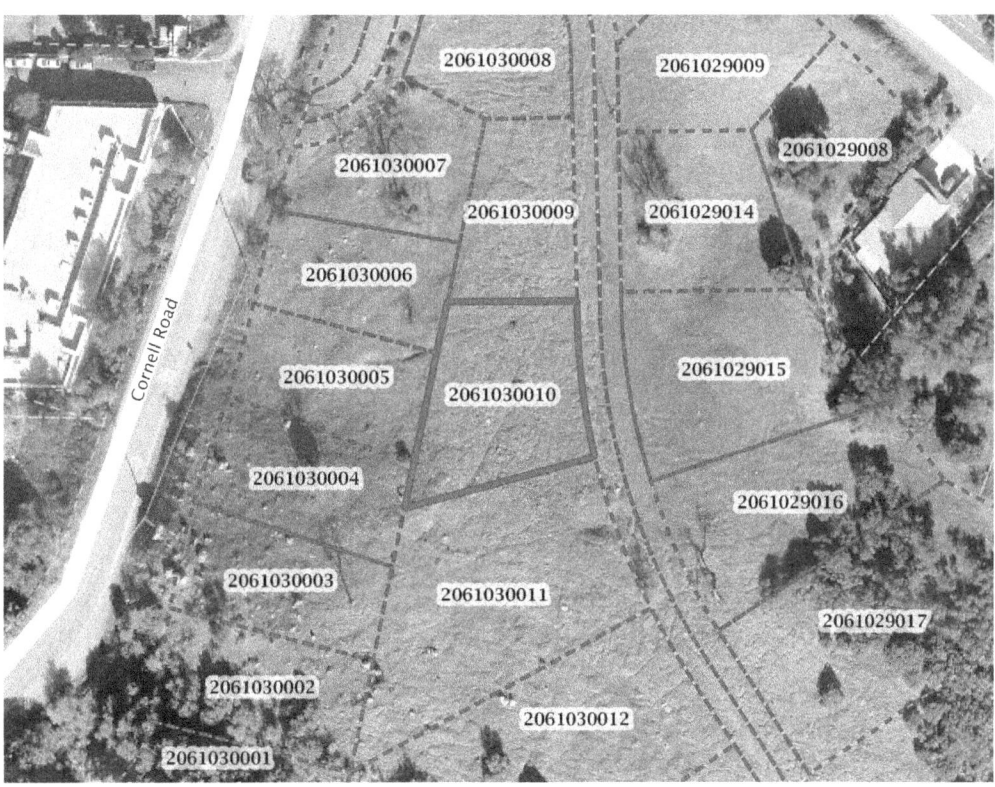

Figure 2.189: Property 96, AIN 2061030010, detailed view

2.64   Auction ID 93

The Los Angeles County Auction Book describes the property as follows.

```
TRACT NO 7661 LOT 113 ASSESSED TO AGOURA AND CORNELL 0 ROADS LP LOCATION
CITY-AGOURA HILL PROPERTY ADDRESS: VACANT LOT
```

The property is located in the general vicinity of Figure 2.190. It is identified by Assessor's Identification Number (AIN) 2061030011. The starting bid is $18,584. Comparable improved properties in this area is about $296/sqft. Comparable unimproved lots in this area is about $65/sqft. This parcel is approximately 20289 sqft. Note, however, that the parcel may be larger than the property under consideration. In case of condominiums, for example, the parcel may encompass other units of the development - those unrelated to the property to be auctioned.

The property is in a parcel zoned Specific Plan in Agoura Hills, for 0 to 15 dwelling units.

Figures 2.191 and 2.192 show street map and corresponding detailed aerial view, respectively. In both cases, the map is centered on the property with the containing parcel marked in heavy blue. If surrounding nearby properties are also part of this auction, the street and aerial maps highlights these in heavy, dashed blue outline.

This assessed entity may have other properties that are also in this auction:

1. AIN 2061029008 (auction ID 72): TRACT NO 7661 LOT 48 ... ASSESSED TO AGOURA AND COR-NELL 0 ROADS LP LOCATION CITY-AGOURA HILL PROPERTY ADDRESS: VACANT LOT. See page 200.

2. AIN 2061029009 (auction ID 73): TRACT NO 7661 LOT 49 ... ASSESSED TO AGOURA AND COR-NELL 0 ROADS LP LOCATION CITY-AGOURA HILL PROPERTY ADDRESS: VACANT LOT. See page 204.

3. AIN 2061029010 (auction ID 74): TRACT NO 7661 LOT 50 ... ASSESSED TO AGOURA AND COR-NELL 0 ROADS LP LOCATION CITY-AGOURA HILL PROPERTY ADDRESS: VACANT LOT. See page 208.

4. AIN 2061029011 (auction ID 75): TRACT NO 7661 EX OF ST LOT 51 ... ASSESSED TO AGOURA AND 0 CORNELL ROADS LP LOCATION CITY-AGOURA HILL PROPERTY ADDRESS: VACANT LOT. See page 212.

5. AIN 2061029012 (auction ID 76): TRACT NO 7661 EX OF ST LOT 52 ... ASSESSED TO AGOURA AND 0 CORNELL ROADS LP LOCATION CITY-AGOURA HILL PROPERTY ADDRESS: VACANT LOT. See page 216.

6. AIN 2061029013 (auction ID 77): TRACT NO 7661 EX OF ST LOT 53 ... ASSESSED TO AGOURA AND 0 CORNELL ROADS LP LOCATION CITY-AGOURA HILL PROPERTY ADDRESS: VACANT LOT. See page 220.

7. AIN 2061029014 (auction ID 78): TRACT NO 7661 LOT 54 ... ASSESSED TO AGOURA AND COR-NELL 0 ROADS LP LOCATION CITY-AGOURA HILL PROPERTY ADDRESS: VACANT LOT. See page 224.

8. AIN 2061029015 (auction ID 79): TRACT NO 7661 LOT 55 ... ASSESSED TO AGOURA AND COR-NELL 0 ROADS LP LOCATION CITY-AGOURA HILL PROPERTY ADDRESS: VACANT LOT. See page 228.

9. AIN 2061029016 (auction ID 80): TRACT NO 7661 LOT 56 ... ASSESSED TO AGOURA AND COR-NELL 0 ROADS LP LOCATION CITY-AGOURA HILL PROPERTY ADDRESS: VACANT LOT. See page 232.

10. AIN 2061029017 (auction ID 81): TRACT NO 7661 LOT 57 . . . ASSESSED TO AGOURA AND COR-NELL 0 ROADS LP LOCATION CITY-AGOURA HILL PROPERTY ADDRESS: VACANT LOT. See page 236.

11. AIN 2061029023 (auction ID 82): VAC ST ADJ LOTS 49 THRU 58 TR NO 7661 ON SW 0 . . . ASSESSED TO AGOURA AND CORNELL ROADS LP LOCATION CITY-AGOURA HILL PROPERTY ADDRESS: VACANT LOT. See page 240.

12. AIN 2061030001 (auction ID 83): TRACT NO 7661 LOT 103 . . . ASSESSED TO AGOURA AND CORNELL 0 ROADS LP LOCATION CITY-AGOURA HILL PROPERTY ADDRESS: VACANT LOT. See page 244.

13. AIN 2061030002 (auction ID 84): TRACT NO 7661 LOT 104 . . . ASSESSED TO AGOURA AND CORNELL - 0 ROADS LP LOCATION CITY-AGOURA HILL PROPERTY ADDRESS: VACANT LOT. See page 248.

14. AIN 2061030003 (auction ID 85): TRACT NO 7661 LOT 105 . . . ASSESSED TO AGOURA AND CORNELL 0 ROADS LP LOCATION CITY-AGOURA HILL PROPERTY ADDRESS: VACANT LOT. See page 252.

15. AIN 2061030004 (auction ID 86): TRACT NO 7661 LOT 106 . . . ASSESSED TO AGOURA AND CORNELL 0 ROADS LP LOCATION CITY-AGOURA HILL PROPERTY ADDRESS: VACANT LOT. See page 256.

16. AIN 2061030005 (auction ID 87): TRACT NO 7661 LOT 107 . . . ASSESSED TO AGOURA AND CORNELL 0 ROADS LP LOCATION CITY-AGOURA HILL PROPERTY ADDRESS: VACANT LOT. See page 260.

17. AIN 2061030006 (auction ID 88): TRACT NO 7661 EX OF ST LOT 108 . . . ASSESSED TO AGOURA AND 0 CORNELL ROADS LP LOCATION CITY-AGOURA HILL PROPERTY ADDRESS: VACANT LOT. See page 264.

18. AIN 2061030007 (auction ID 89): TRACT NO 7661 EX OF ST LOT 109 . . . ASSESSED TO AGOURA AND 0 CORNELL ROADS LP LOCATION CITY-AGOURA HILL PROPERTY ADDRESS: VACANT LOT. See page 268.

19. AIN 2061030008 (auction ID 90): TRACT NO 7661 LOT 110 . . . ASSESSED TO AGOURA AND CORNELL 0 ROADS LP LOCATION CITY-AGOURA HILL PROPERTY ADDRESS: VACANT LOT. See page 272.

20. AIN 2061030009 (auction ID 91): TRACT NO 7661 LOT 111 . . . ASSESSED TO AGOURA AND CORNELL 0 ROADS LP LOCATION CITY-AGOURA HILL PROPERTY ADDRESS: VACANT LOT. See page 276.

21. AIN 2061030010 (auction ID 92): TRACT NO 7661 LOT 112 . . . ASSESSED TO AGOURA AND CORNELL 0 ROADS LP LOCATION CITY-AGOURA HILL PROPERTY ADDRESS: VACANT LOT. See page 280.

22. AIN 2061030012 (auction ID 94): TRACT NO 7661 LOT 114 . . . ASSESSED TO AGOURA AND CORNELL 0 ROADS LP LOCATION CITY-AGOURA HILL PROPERTY ADDRESS: VACANT LOT. See page 288.

23. AIN 2061030013 (auction ID 95): TRACT NO 7661 LOT 115 . . . ASSESSED TO AGOURA AND CORNELL 0 ROADS LP LOCATION CITY-AGOURA HILL PROPERTY ADDRESS: VACANT LOT. See page 292.

24. AIN 2061030017 (auction ID 96): VAC ST ADJ LOTS 109 THRU 115 TR NO 7661 ON NW AND NE 0 . . . ASSESSED TO AGOURA AND CORNELL ROADS LP LOCATION CITY-AGOURA HILL PROPERTY ADDRESS: . . . . See page 296.

Figure 2.190: Property 96, AIN 2061030011, overview map

Figure 2.191: Property 96, AIN 2061030011, neighborhood view

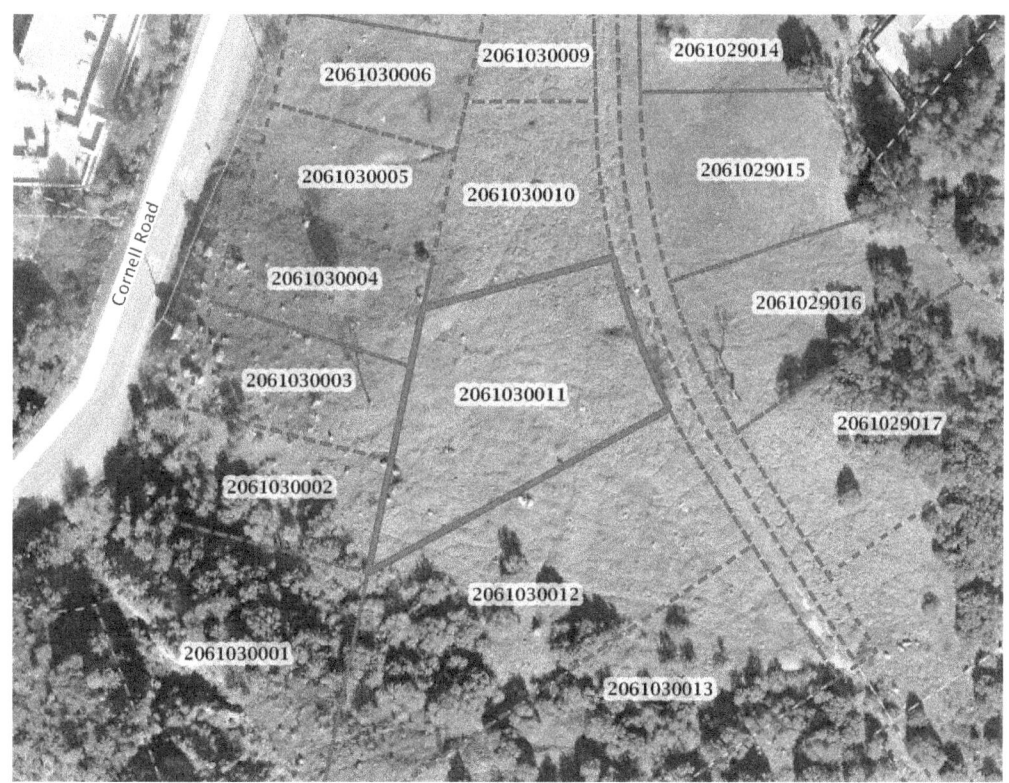

Figure 2.192: Property 96, AIN 2061030011, detailed view

2.65   Auction ID 94

The Los Angeles County Auction Book describes the property as follows.

```
TRACT NO 7661 LOT 114 ASSESSED TO AGOURA AND CORNELL 0 ROADS LP LOCATION
CITY-AGOURA HILL PROPERTY ADDRESS: VACANT LOT
```

The property is located in the general vicinity of Figure 2.193. It is identified by Assessor's Identification Number (AIN) 2061030012. The starting bid is $25,244. Comparable improved properties in this area is about $296/sqft. Comparable unimproved lots in this area is about $65/sqft. This parcel is approximately 31746 sqft. Note, however, that the parcel may be larger than the property under consideration. In case of condominiums, for example, the parcel may encompass other units of the development - those unrelated to the property to be auctioned.

The property is in a parcel zoned Specific Plan in Agoura Hills, for 0 to 15 dwelling units.

Figures 2.194 and 2.195 show street map and corresponding detailed aerial view, respectively. In both cases, the map is centered on the property with the containing parcel marked in heavy blue. If surrounding nearby properties are also part of this auction, the street and aerial maps highlights these in heavy, dashed blue outline.

This assessed entity may have other properties that are also in this auction:

1. AIN 2061029008 (auction ID 72): TRACT NO 7661 LOT 48 ... ASSESSED TO AGOURA AND CORNELL 0 ROADS LP LOCATION CITY-AGOURA HILL PROPERTY ADDRESS: VACANT LOT. See page 200.

2. AIN 2061029009 (auction ID 73): TRACT NO 7661 LOT 49 ... ASSESSED TO AGOURA AND CORNELL 0 ROADS LP LOCATION CITY-AGOURA HILL PROPERTY ADDRESS: VACANT LOT. See page 204.

3. AIN 2061029010 (auction ID 74): TRACT NO 7661 LOT 50 ... ASSESSED TO AGOURA AND CORNELL 0 ROADS LP LOCATION CITY-AGOURA HILL PROPERTY ADDRESS: VACANT LOT. See page 208.

4. AIN 2061029011 (auction ID 75): TRACT NO 7661 EX OF ST LOT 51 ... ASSESSED TO AGOURA AND 0 CORNELL ROADS LP LOCATION CITY-AGOURA HILL PROPERTY ADDRESS: VACANT LOT. See page 212.

5. AIN 2061029012 (auction ID 76): TRACT NO 7661 EX OF ST LOT 52 ... ASSESSED TO AGOURA AND 0 CORNELL ROADS LP LOCATION CITY-AGOURA HILL PROPERTY ADDRESS: VACANT LOT. See page 216.

6. AIN 2061029013 (auction ID 77): TRACT NO 7661 EX OF ST LOT 53 ... ASSESSED TO AGOURA AND 0 CORNELL ROADS LP LOCATION CITY-AGOURA HILL PROPERTY ADDRESS: VACANT LOT. See page 220.

7. AIN 2061029014 (auction ID 78): TRACT NO 7661 LOT 54 ... ASSESSED TO AGOURA AND CORNELL 0 ROADS LP LOCATION CITY-AGOURA HILL PROPERTY ADDRESS: VACANT LOT. See page 224.

8. AIN 2061029015 (auction ID 79): TRACT NO 7661 LOT 55 ... ASSESSED TO AGOURA AND CORNELL 0 ROADS LP LOCATION CITY-AGOURA HILL PROPERTY ADDRESS: VACANT LOT. See page 228.

9. AIN 2061029016 (auction ID 80): TRACT NO 7661 LOT 56 ... ASSESSED TO AGOURA AND CORNELL 0 ROADS LP LOCATION CITY-AGOURA HILL PROPERTY ADDRESS: VACANT LOT. See page 232.

10. AIN 2061029017 (auction ID 81): TRACT NO 7661 LOT 57 . . . ASSESSED TO AGOURA AND COR-NELL 0 ROADS LP LOCATION CITY-AGOURA HILL PROPERTY ADDRESS: VACANT LOT. See page 236.

11. AIN 2061029023 (auction ID 82): VAC ST ADJ LOTS 49 THRU 58 TR NO 7661 ON SW 0 . . . ASSESSED TO AGOURA AND CORNELL ROADS LP LOCATION CITY-AGOURA HILL PROPERTY ADDRESS: VACANT LOT. See page 240.

12. AIN 2061030001 (auction ID 83): TRACT NO 7661 LOT 103 . . . ASSESSED TO AGOURA AND CORNELL 0 ROADS LP LOCATION CITY-AGOURA HILL PROPERTY ADDRESS: VACANT LOT. See page 244.

13. AIN 2061030002 (auction ID 84): TRACT NO 7661 LOT 104 . . . ASSESSED TO AGOURA AND CORNELL - 0 ROADS LP LOCATION CITY-AGOURA HILL PROPERTY ADDRESS: VACANT LOT. See page 248.

14. AIN 2061030003 (auction ID 85): TRACT NO 7661 LOT 105 . . . ASSESSED TO AGOURA AND CORNELL 0 ROADS LP LOCATION CITY-AGOURA HILL PROPERTY ADDRESS: VACANT LOT. See page 252.

15. AIN 2061030004 (auction ID 86): TRACT NO 7661 LOT 106 . . . ASSESSED TO AGOURA AND CORNELL 0 ROADS LP LOCATION CITY-AGOURA HILL PROPERTY ADDRESS: VACANT LOT. See page 256.

16. AIN 2061030005 (auction ID 87): TRACT NO 7661 LOT 107 . . . ASSESSED TO AGOURA AND CORNELL 0 ROADS LP LOCATION CITY-AGOURA HILL PROPERTY ADDRESS: VACANT LOT. See page 260.

17. AIN 2061030006 (auction ID 88): TRACT NO 7661 EX OF ST LOT 108 . . . ASSESSED TO AGOURA AND 0 CORNELL ROADS LP LOCATION CITY-AGOURA HILL PROPERTY ADDRESS: VACANT LOT. See page 264.

18. AIN 2061030007 (auction ID 89): TRACT NO 7661 EX OF ST LOT 109 . . . ASSESSED TO AGOURA AND 0 CORNELL ROADS LP LOCATION CITY-AGOURA HILL PROPERTY ADDRESS: VACANT LOT. See page 268.

19. AIN 2061030008 (auction ID 90): TRACT NO 7661 LOT 110 . . . ASSESSED TO AGOURA AND CORNELL 0 ROADS LP LOCATION CITY-AGOURA HILL PROPERTY ADDRESS: VACANT LOT. See page 272.

20. AIN 2061030009 (auction ID 91): TRACT NO 7661 LOT 111 . . . ASSESSED TO AGOURA AND CORNELL 0 ROADS LP LOCATION CITY-AGOURA HILL PROPERTY ADDRESS: VACANT LOT. See page 276.

21. AIN 2061030010 (auction ID 92): TRACT NO 7661 LOT 112 . . . ASSESSED TO AGOURA AND CORNELL 0 ROADS LP LOCATION CITY-AGOURA HILL PROPERTY ADDRESS: VACANT LOT. See page 280.

22. AIN 2061030011 (auction ID 93): TRACT NO 7661 LOT 113 . . . ASSESSED TO AGOURA AND CORNELL 0 ROADS LP LOCATION CITY-AGOURA HILL PROPERTY ADDRESS: VACANT LOT. See page 284.

23. AIN 2061030013 (auction ID 95): TRACT NO 7661 LOT 115 . . . ASSESSED TO AGOURA AND CORNELL 0 ROADS LP LOCATION CITY-AGOURA HILL PROPERTY ADDRESS: VACANT LOT. See page 292.

24. AIN 2061030017 (auction ID 96): VAC ST ADJ LOTS 109 THRU 115 TR NO 7661 ON NW AND NE 0 . . . ASSESSED TO AGOURA AND CORNELL ROADS LP LOCATION CITY-AGOURA HILL PROPERTY ADDRESS: . . . . See page 296.

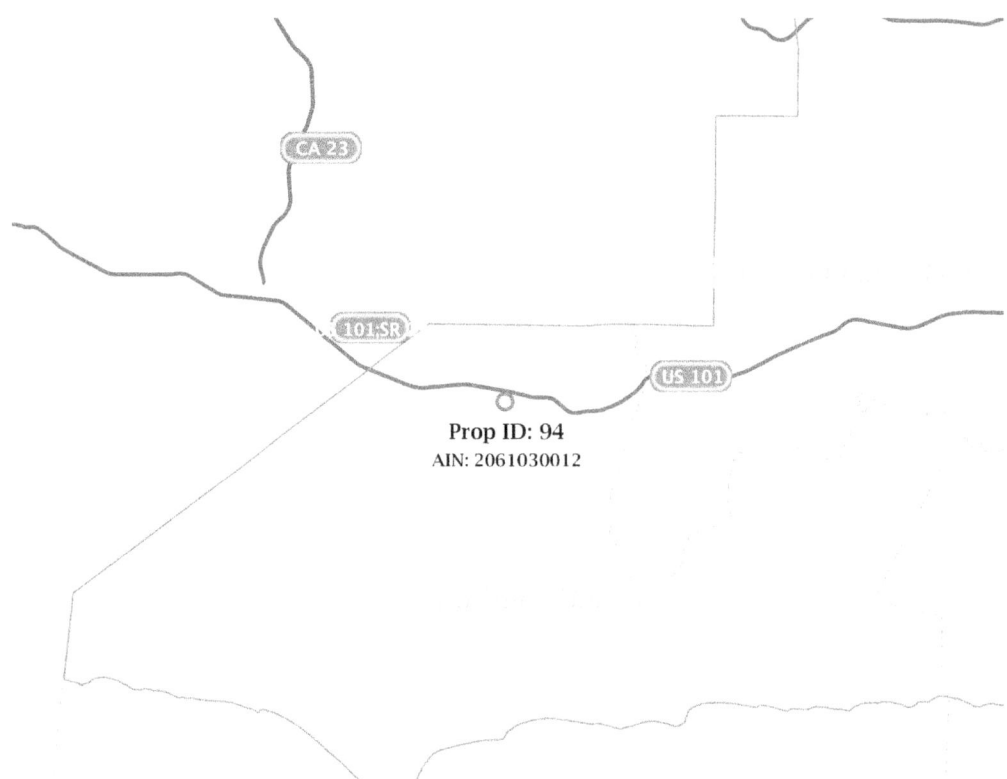

Figure 2.193: Property 96, AIN 2061030012, overview map

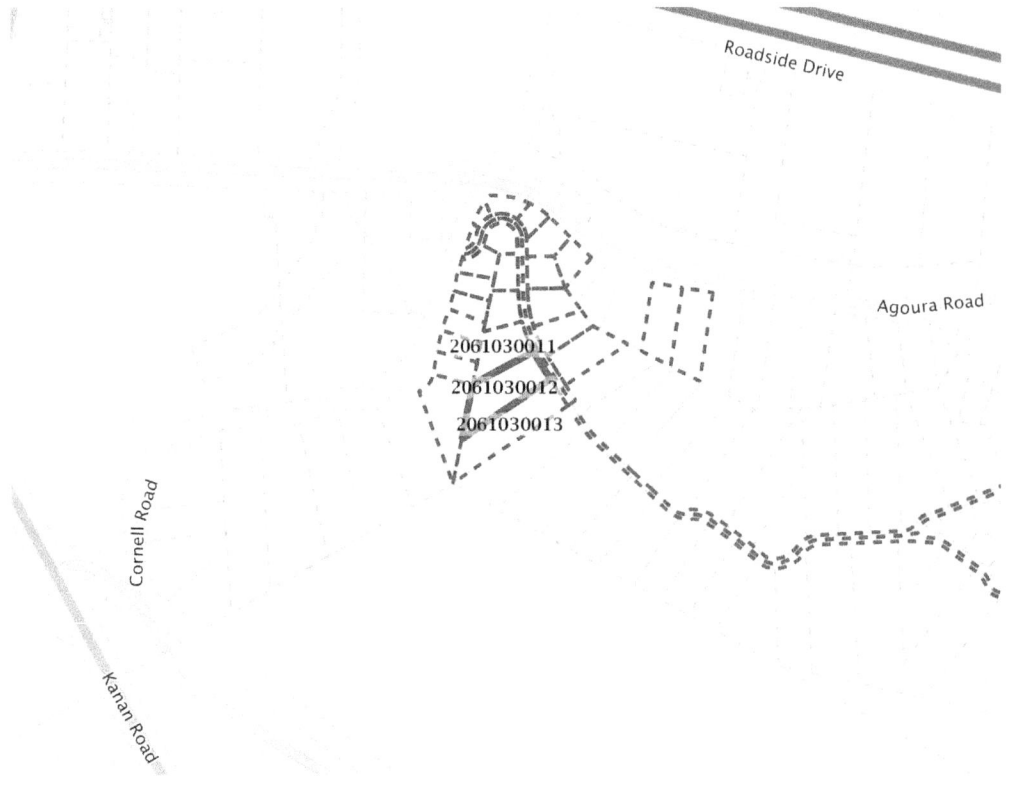

Figure 2.194: Property 96, AIN 2061030012, neighborhood view

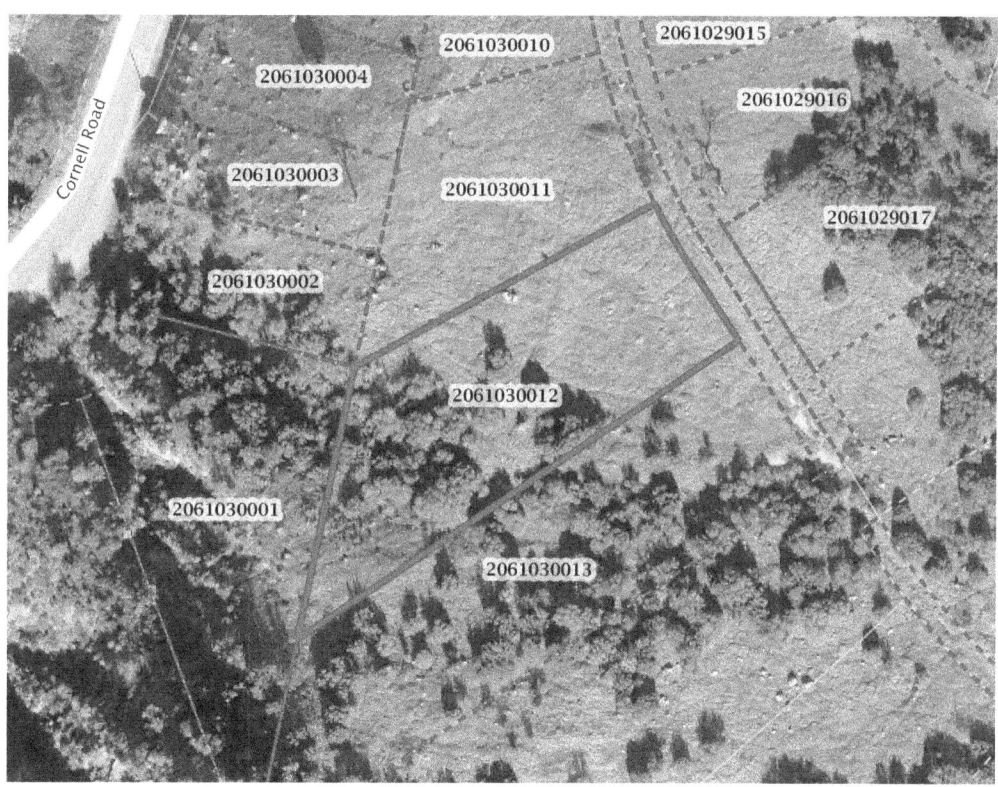

Figure 2.195: Property 96, AIN 2061030012, detailed view

2.66   Auction ID 95

The Los Angeles County Auction Book describes the property as follows.

```
TRACT NO 7661 LOT 115 ASSESSED TO AGOURA AND CORNELL 0 ROADS LP LOCATION
CITY-AGOURA HILL PROPERTY ADDRESS: VACANT LOT
```

The property is located in the general vicinity of Figure 2.196. It is identified by Assessor's Identification Number (AIN) 2061030013. The starting bid is $29,901. Comparable improved properties in this area is about $295/sqft. Comparable unimproved lots in this area is about $68/sqft. This parcel is approximately 39004 sqft. Note, however, that the parcel may be larger than the property under consideration. In case of condominiums, for example, the parcel may encompass other units of the development - those unrelated to the property to be auctioned.

The property is in a parcel zoned Specific Plan in Agoura Hills, for 0 to 15 dwelling units.

Figures 2.197 and 2.198 show street map and corresponding detailed aerial view, respectively. In both cases, the map is centered on the property with the containing parcel marked in heavy blue. If surrounding nearby properties are also part of this auction, the street and aerial maps highlights these in heavy, dashed blue outline.

This assessed entity may have other properties that are also in this auction:

1. AIN 2061029008 (auction ID 72): TRACT NO 7661 LOT 48 ... ASSESSED TO AGOURA AND CORNELL 0 ROADS LP LOCATION CITY-AGOURA HILL PROPERTY ADDRESS: VACANT LOT. See page 200.

2. AIN 2061029009 (auction ID 73): TRACT NO 7661 LOT 49 ... ASSESSED TO AGOURA AND CORNELL 0 ROADS LP LOCATION CITY-AGOURA HILL PROPERTY ADDRESS: VACANT LOT. See page 204.

3. AIN 2061029010 (auction ID 74): TRACT NO 7661 LOT 50 ... ASSESSED TO AGOURA AND CORNELL 0 ROADS LP LOCATION CITY-AGOURA HILL PROPERTY ADDRESS: VACANT LOT. See page 208.

4. AIN 2061029011 (auction ID 75): TRACT NO 7661 EX OF ST LOT 51 ... ASSESSED TO AGOURA AND 0 CORNELL ROADS LP LOCATION CITY-AGOURA HILL PROPERTY ADDRESS: VACANT LOT. See page 212.

5. AIN 2061029012 (auction ID 76): TRACT NO 7661 EX OF ST LOT 52 ... ASSESSED TO AGOURA AND 0 CORNELL ROADS LP LOCATION CITY-AGOURA HILL PROPERTY ADDRESS: VACANT LOT. See page 216.

6. AIN 2061029013 (auction ID 77): TRACT NO 7661 EX OF ST LOT 53 ... ASSESSED TO AGOURA AND 0 CORNELL ROADS LP LOCATION CITY-AGOURA HILL PROPERTY ADDRESS: VACANT LOT. See page 220.

7. AIN 2061029014 (auction ID 78): TRACT NO 7661 LOT 54 ... ASSESSED TO AGOURA AND CORNELL 0 ROADS LP LOCATION CITY-AGOURA HILL PROPERTY ADDRESS: VACANT LOT. See page 224.

8. AIN 2061029015 (auction ID 79): TRACT NO 7661 LOT 55 ... ASSESSED TO AGOURA AND CORNELL 0 ROADS LP LOCATION CITY-AGOURA HILL PROPERTY ADDRESS: VACANT LOT. See page 228.

9. AIN 2061029016 (auction ID 80): TRACT NO 7661 LOT 56 ... ASSESSED TO AGOURA AND CORNELL 0 ROADS LP LOCATION CITY-AGOURA HILL PROPERTY ADDRESS: VACANT LOT. See page 232.

10. AIN 2061029017 (auction ID 81): TRACT NO 7661 LOT 57 ...ASSESSED TO AGOURA AND COR-NELL 0 ROADS LP LOCATION CITY-AGOURA HILL PROPERTY ADDRESS: VACANT LOT. See page 236.

11. AIN 2061029023 (auction ID 82): VAC ST ADJ LOTS 49 THRU 58 TR NO 7661 ON SW 0 ...ASSESSED TO AGOURA AND CORNELL ROADS LP LOCATION CITY-AGOURA HILL PROPERTY ADDRESS: VACANT LOT. See page 240.

12. AIN 2061030001 (auction ID 83): TRACT NO 7661 LOT 103 ...ASSESSED TO AGOURA AND CORNELL 0 ROADS LP LOCATION CITY-AGOURA HILL PROPERTY ADDRESS: VACANT LOT. See page 244.

13. AIN 2061030002 (auction ID 84): TRACT NO 7661 LOT 104 ...ASSESSED TO AGOURA AND CORNELL - 0 ROADS LP LOCATION CITY-AGOURA HILL PROPERTY ADDRESS: VACANT LOT. See page 248.

14. AIN 2061030003 (auction ID 85): TRACT NO 7661 LOT 105 ...ASSESSED TO AGOURA AND CORNELL 0 ROADS LP LOCATION CITY-AGOURA HILL PROPERTY ADDRESS: VACANT LOT. See page 252.

15. AIN 2061030004 (auction ID 86): TRACT NO 7661 LOT 106 ...ASSESSED TO AGOURA AND CORNELL 0 ROADS LP LOCATION CITY-AGOURA HILL PROPERTY ADDRESS: VACANT LOT. See page 256.

16. AIN 2061030005 (auction ID 87): TRACT NO 7661 LOT 107 ...ASSESSED TO AGOURA AND CORNELL 0 ROADS LP LOCATION CITY-AGOURA HILL PROPERTY ADDRESS: VACANT LOT. See page 260.

17. AIN 2061030006 (auction ID 88): TRACT NO 7661 EX OF ST LOT 108 ...ASSESSED TO AGOURA AND 0 CORNELL ROADS LP LOCATION CITY-AGOURA HILL PROPERTY ADDRESS: VACANT LOT. See page 264.

18. AIN 2061030007 (auction ID 89): TRACT NO 7661 EX OF ST LOT 109 ...ASSESSED TO AGOURA AND 0 CORNELL ROADS LP LOCATION CITY-AGOURA HILL PROPERTY ADDRESS: VACANT LOT. See page 268.

19. AIN 2061030008 (auction ID 90): TRACT NO 7661 LOT 110 ...ASSESSED TO AGOURA AND CORNELL 0 ROADS LP LOCATION CITY-AGOURA HILL PROPERTY ADDRESS: VACANT LOT. See page 272.

20. AIN 2061030009 (auction ID 91): TRACT NO 7661 LOT 111 ...ASSESSED TO AGOURA AND CORNELL 0 ROADS LP LOCATION CITY-AGOURA HILL PROPERTY ADDRESS: VACANT LOT. See page 276.

21. AIN 2061030010 (auction ID 92): TRACT NO 7661 LOT 112 ...ASSESSED TO AGOURA AND CORNELL 0 ROADS LP LOCATION CITY-AGOURA HILL PROPERTY ADDRESS: VACANT LOT. See page 280.

22. AIN 2061030011 (auction ID 93): TRACT NO 7661 LOT 113 ...ASSESSED TO AGOURA AND CORNELL 0 ROADS LP LOCATION CITY-AGOURA HILL PROPERTY ADDRESS: VACANT LOT. See page 284.

23. AIN 2061030012 (auction ID 94): TRACT NO 7661 LOT 114 ...ASSESSED TO AGOURA AND CORNELL 0 ROADS LP LOCATION CITY-AGOURA HILL PROPERTY ADDRESS: VACANT LOT. See page 288.

24. AIN 2061030017 (auction ID 96): VAC ST ADJ LOTS 109 THRU 115 TR NO 7661 ON NW AND NE 0 ...ASSESSED TO AGOURA AND CORNELL ROADS LP LOCATION CITY-AGOURA HILL PROPERTY ADDRESS: .... See page 296.

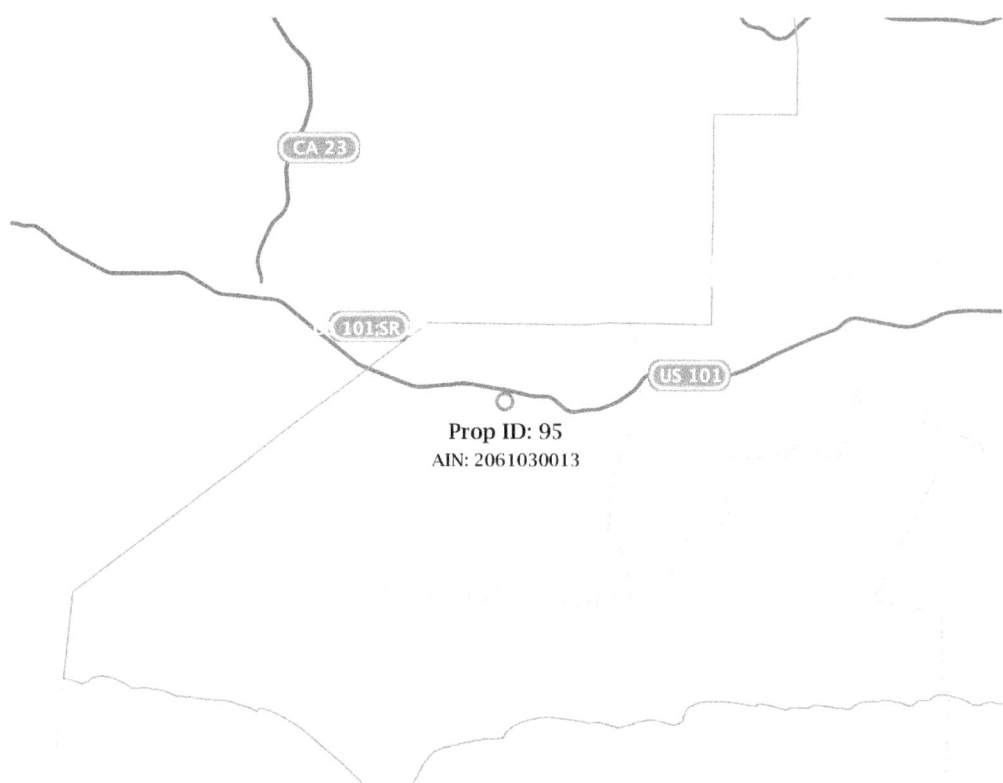

Figure 2.196: Property 96, AIN 2061030013, overview map

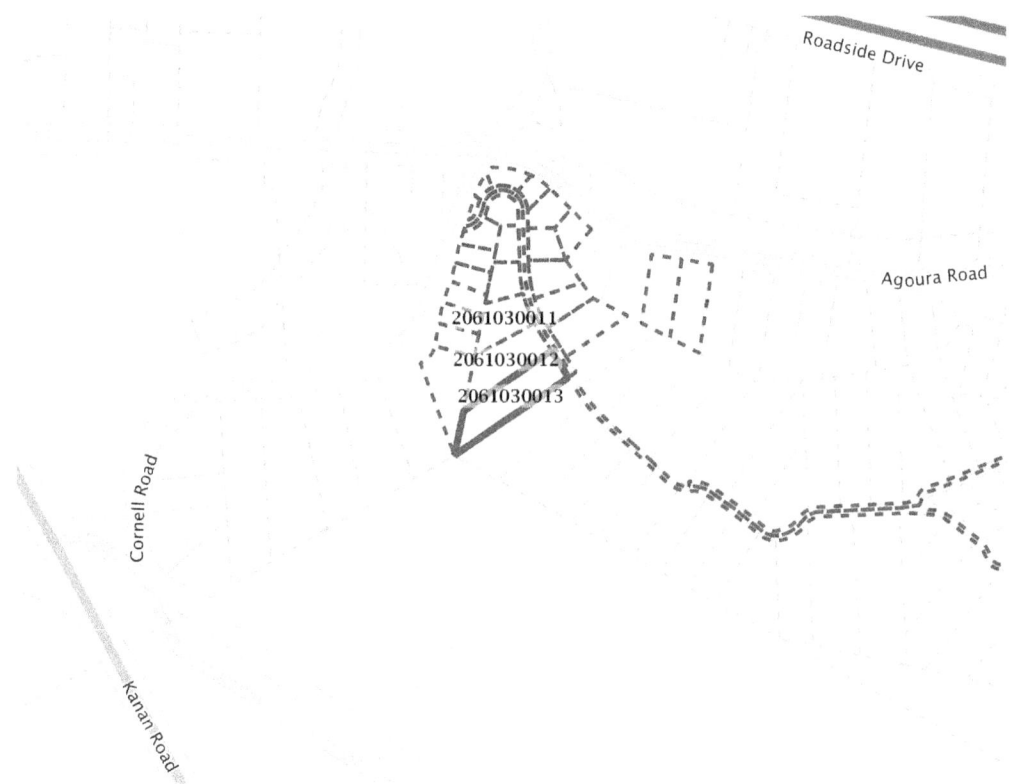

Figure 2.197: Property 96, AIN 2061030013, neighborhood view

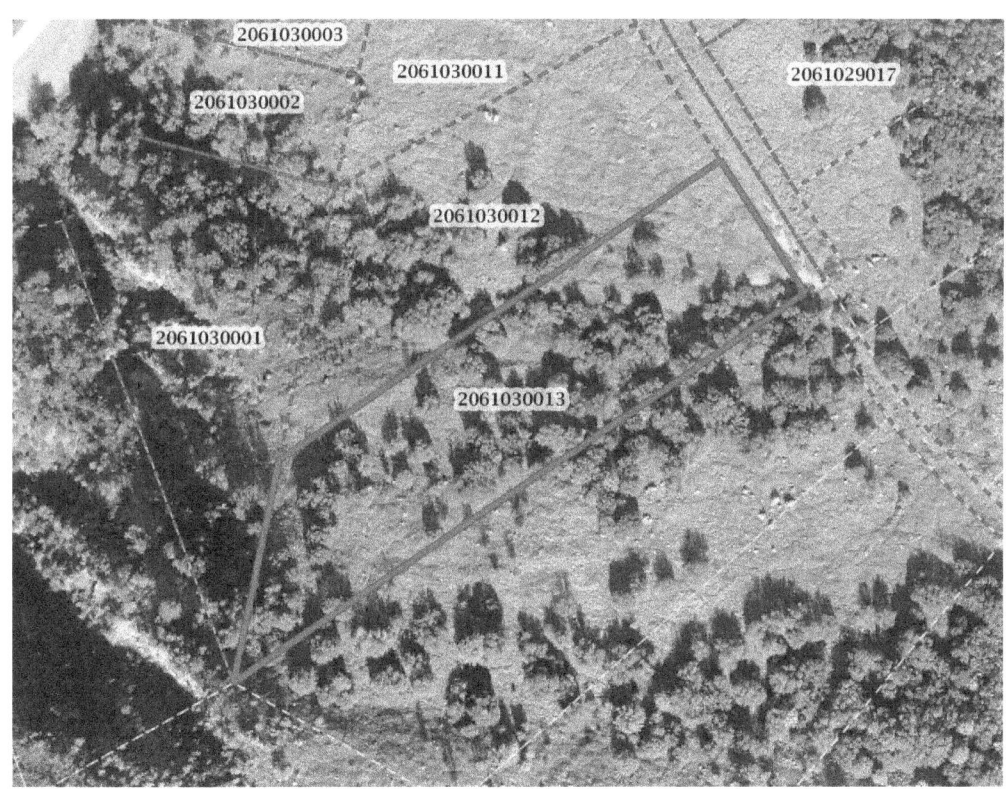

Figure 2.198: Property 96, AIN 2061030013, detailed view

2.67   Auction ID 96

The Los Angeles County Auction Book describes the property as follows.

```
VAC ST ADJ LOTS 109 THRU 115 TR NO 7661 ON NW AND NE 0 ASSESSED TO
AGOURA AND CORNELL ROADS LP LOCATION CITY-AGOURA HILL PROPERTY ADDRESS:
VACANT LOT
```

The property is located in the general vicinity of Figure 2.199. It is identified by Assessor's Identification Number (AIN) 2061030017. The starting bid is $2,009. Comparable improved properties in this area is about $292/sqft. Comparable unimproved lots in this area is about $63/sqft. This parcel is approximately 12424 sqft. Note, however, that the parcel may be larger than the property under consideration. In case of condominiums, for example, the parcel may encompass other units of the development - those unrelated to the property to be auctioned.

The property is in a parcel zoned Specific Plan in Agoura Hills, for 0 to 15 dwelling units.

Figures 2.200 and 2.201 show street map and corresponding detailed aerial view, respectively. In both cases, the map is centered on the property with the containing parcel marked in heavy blue. If surrounding nearby properties are also part of this auction, the street and aerial maps highlights these in heavy, dashed blue outline.

This assessed entity may have other properties that are also in this auction:

1. AIN 2061029008 (auction ID 72): TRACT NO 7661 LOT 48 ... ASSESSED TO AGOURA AND COR-NELL 0 ROADS LP LOCATION CITY-AGOURA HILL PROPERTY ADDRESS: VACANT LOT. See page 200.

2. AIN 2061029009 (auction ID 73): TRACT NO 7661 LOT 49 ... ASSESSED TO AGOURA AND COR-NELL 0 ROADS LP LOCATION CITY-AGOURA HILL PROPERTY ADDRESS: VACANT LOT. See page 204.

3. AIN 2061029010 (auction ID 74): TRACT NO 7661 LOT 50 ... ASSESSED TO AGOURA AND COR-NELL 0 ROADS LP LOCATION CITY-AGOURA HILL PROPERTY ADDRESS: VACANT LOT. See page 208.

4. AIN 2061029011 (auction ID 75): TRACT NO 7661 EX OF ST LOT 51 ... ASSESSED TO AGOURA AND 0 CORNELL ROADS LP LOCATION CITY-AGOURA HILL PROPERTY ADDRESS: VACANT LOT. See page 212.

5. AIN 2061029012 (auction ID 76): TRACT NO 7661 EX OF ST LOT 52 ... ASSESSED TO AGOURA AND 0 CORNELL ROADS LP LOCATION CITY-AGOURA HILL PROPERTY ADDRESS: VACANT LOT. See page 216.

6. AIN 2061029013 (auction ID 77): TRACT NO 7661 EX OF ST LOT 53 ... ASSESSED TO AGOURA AND 0 CORNELL ROADS LP LOCATION CITY-AGOURA HILL PROPERTY ADDRESS: VACANT LOT. See page 220.

7. AIN 2061029014 (auction ID 78): TRACT NO 7661 LOT 54 ... ASSESSED TO AGOURA AND COR-NELL 0 ROADS LP LOCATION CITY-AGOURA HILL PROPERTY ADDRESS: VACANT LOT. See page 224.

8. AIN 2061029015 (auction ID 79): TRACT NO 7661 LOT 55 ... ASSESSED TO AGOURA AND COR-NELL 0 ROADS LP LOCATION CITY-AGOURA HILL PROPERTY ADDRESS: VACANT LOT. See page 228.

9. AIN 2061029016 (auction ID 80): TRACT NO 7661 LOT 56 ... ASSESSED TO AGOURA AND COR-NELL 0 ROADS LP LOCATION CITY-AGOURA HILL PROPERTY ADDRESS: VACANT LOT. See page 232.

10. AIN 2061029017 (auction ID 81): TRACT NO 7661 LOT 57 . . . ASSESSED TO AGOURA AND CORNELL 0 ROADS LP LOCATION CITY-AGOURA HILL PROPERTY ADDRESS: VACANT LOT. See page 236.

11. AIN 2061029023 (auction ID 82): VAC ST ADJ LOTS 49 THRU 58 TR NO 7661 ON SW 0 . . . ASSESSED TO AGOURA AND CORNELL ROADS LP LOCATION CITY-AGOURA HILL PROPERTY ADDRESS: VACANT LOT. See page 240.

12. AIN 2061030001 (auction ID 83): TRACT NO 7661 LOT 103 . . . ASSESSED TO AGOURA AND CORNELL 0 ROADS LP LOCATION CITY-AGOURA HILL PROPERTY ADDRESS: VACANT LOT. See page 244.

13. AIN 2061030002 (auction ID 84): TRACT NO 7661 LOT 104 . . . ASSESSED TO AGOURA AND CORNELL - 0 ROADS LP LOCATION CITY-AGOURA HILL PROPERTY ADDRESS: VACANT LOT. See page 248.

14. AIN 2061030003 (auction ID 85): TRACT NO 7661 LOT 105 . . . ASSESSED TO AGOURA AND CORNELL 0 ROADS LP LOCATION CITY-AGOURA HILL PROPERTY ADDRESS: VACANT LOT. See page 252.

15. AIN 2061030004 (auction ID 86): TRACT NO 7661 LOT 106 . . . ASSESSED TO AGOURA AND CORNELL 0 ROADS LP LOCATION CITY-AGOURA HILL PROPERTY ADDRESS: VACANT LOT. See page 256.

16. AIN 2061030005 (auction ID 87): TRACT NO 7661 LOT 107 . . . ASSESSED TO AGOURA AND CORNELL 0 ROADS LP LOCATION CITY-AGOURA HILL PROPERTY ADDRESS: VACANT LOT. See page 260.

17. AIN 2061030006 (auction ID 88): TRACT NO 7661 EX OF ST LOT 108 . . . ASSESSED TO AGOURA AND 0 CORNELL ROADS LP LOCATION CITY-AGOURA HILL PROPERTY ADDRESS: VACANT LOT. See page 264.

18. AIN 2061030007 (auction ID 89): TRACT NO 7661 EX OF ST LOT 109 . . . ASSESSED TO AGOURA AND 0 CORNELL ROADS LP LOCATION CITY-AGOURA HILL PROPERTY ADDRESS: VACANT LOT. See page 268.

19. AIN 2061030008 (auction ID 90): TRACT NO 7661 LOT 110 . . . ASSESSED TO AGOURA AND CORNELL 0 ROADS LP LOCATION CITY-AGOURA HILL PROPERTY ADDRESS: VACANT LOT. See page 272.

20. AIN 2061030009 (auction ID 91): TRACT NO 7661 LOT 111 . . . ASSESSED TO AGOURA AND CORNELL 0 ROADS LP LOCATION CITY-AGOURA HILL PROPERTY ADDRESS: VACANT LOT. See page 276.

21. AIN 2061030010 (auction ID 92): TRACT NO 7661 LOT 112 . . . ASSESSED TO AGOURA AND CORNELL 0 ROADS LP LOCATION CITY-AGOURA HILL PROPERTY ADDRESS: VACANT LOT. See page 280.

22. AIN 2061030011 (auction ID 93): TRACT NO 7661 LOT 113 . . . ASSESSED TO AGOURA AND CORNELL 0 ROADS LP LOCATION CITY-AGOURA HILL PROPERTY ADDRESS: VACANT LOT. See page 284.

23. AIN 2061030012 (auction ID 94): TRACT NO 7661 LOT 114 . . . ASSESSED TO AGOURA AND CORNELL 0 ROADS LP LOCATION CITY-AGOURA HILL PROPERTY ADDRESS: VACANT LOT. See page 288.

24. AIN 2061030013 (auction ID 95): TRACT NO 7661 LOT 115 . . . ASSESSED TO AGOURA AND CORNELL 0 ROADS LP LOCATION CITY-AGOURA HILL PROPERTY ADDRESS: VACANT LOT. See page 292.

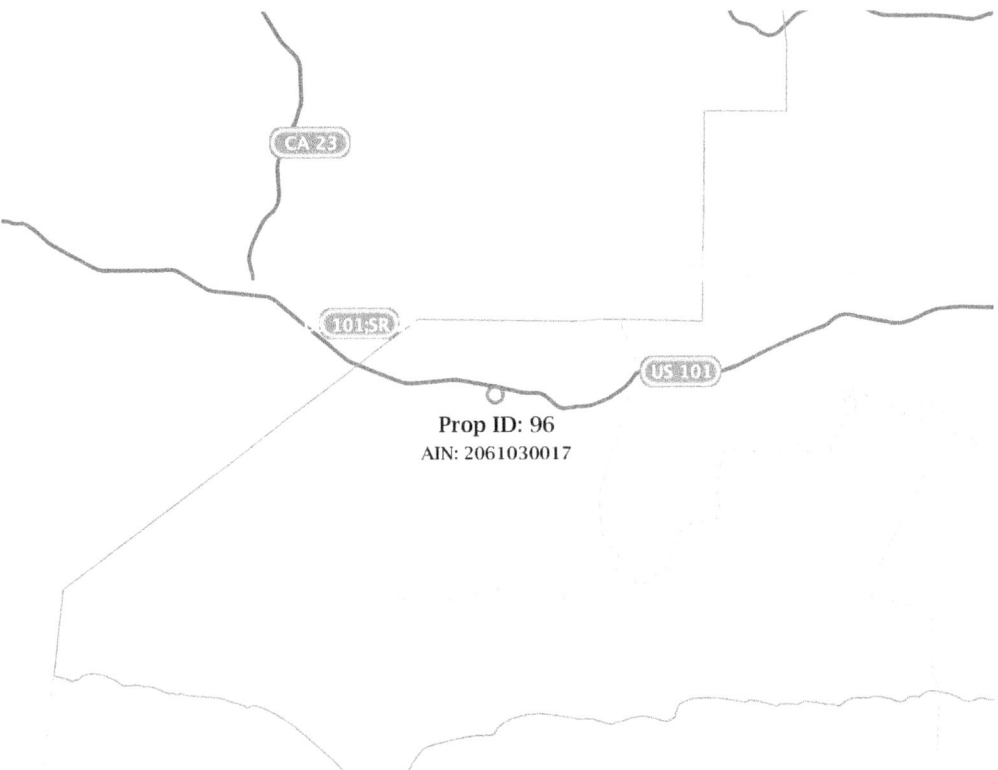

Figure 2.199: Property 95, AIN 2061030017, overview map

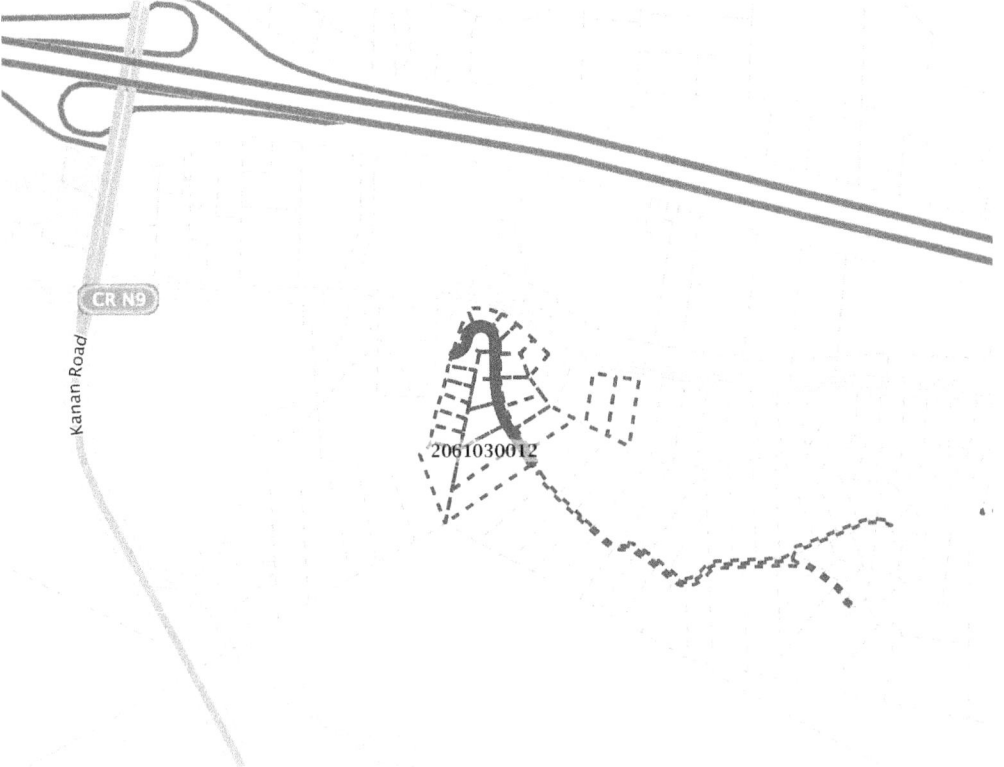

Figure 2.200: Property 95, AIN 2061030017, neighborhood view

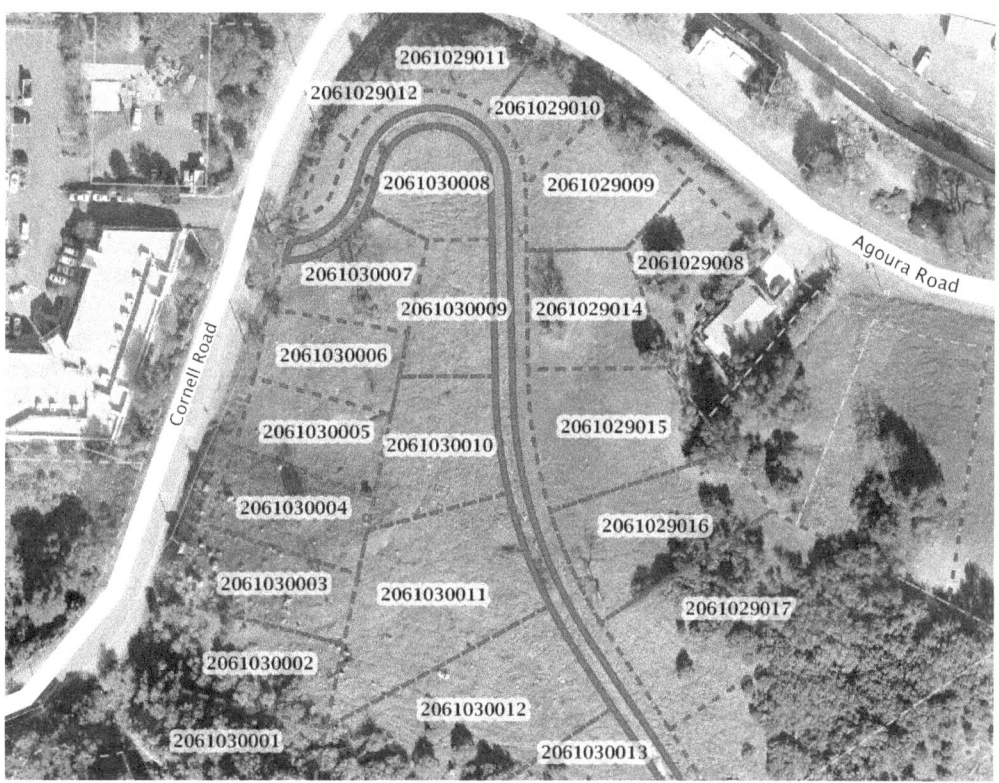

Figure 2.201: Property 95, AIN 2061030017, detailed view

2.68   Auction ID 97

The Los Angeles County Auction Book describes the property as follows.

```
VAC ST ADJ LOTS 116,117 AND 118 TR NO 7661 ON NE 0 ASSESSED TO STROUD,ROBERT
C CO TR ET AL STROUD FAMILY TRUST AND GERTLER,CO TR GERTLER TRUST
LOCATION CITY-AGOURA HILL PROPERTY ADDRESS: VACANT LOT
```

The property is located in the general vicinity of Figure 2.202. It is identified by Assessor's Identification Number (AIN) 2061030019. The starting bid is $1,517. Comparable improved properties in this area is about $298/sqft. Comparable unimproved lots in this area is about $60/sqft. This parcel is approximately 3896 sqft. Note, however, that the parcel may be larger than the property under consideration. In case of condominiums, for example, the parcel may encompass other units of the development - those unrelated to the property to be auctioned.

The property is in a parcel zoned Restricted Open Space in Agoura Hills, for 0 to 0 dwelling units.

Figures 2.203 and 2.204 show street map and corresponding detailed aerial view, respectively. In both cases, the map is centered on the property with the containing parcel marked in heavy blue. If surrounding nearby properties are also part of this auction, the street and aerial maps highlights these in heavy, dashed blue outline.

This assessed entity may have other properties that are also in this auction:

1. AIN 2061024005 (auction ID 65): VAC ST ADJ LOTS 146, 147, 148 AND 149 TRACT NO 0 7661 ON N . . . ASSESSED TO STROUD, ROBERT C CO TR ET AL STROUD FAMILY TRUST . . . . See page 187.

2. AIN 2061027013 (auction ID 66): VAC STS ADJ LOTS119 THRU 130 TR NO 7661 ON NE AND NW 0 . . . ASSESSED TO STROUD, ROBERT C CO TR ET AL STROUD FAMILY TRUST AND . . . . See page 190.

3. AIN 2061028040 (auction ID 67): VAC ST ADJ LOTS 63 THRU 73 TR NO 7661 ON SW AND SE 0 . . . ASSESSED TO STROUD, ROBERT C CO TR ET AL STROUD FAMILY TRUST . . . . See page 193.

Figure 2.202: Property 67, AIN 2061030019, overview map

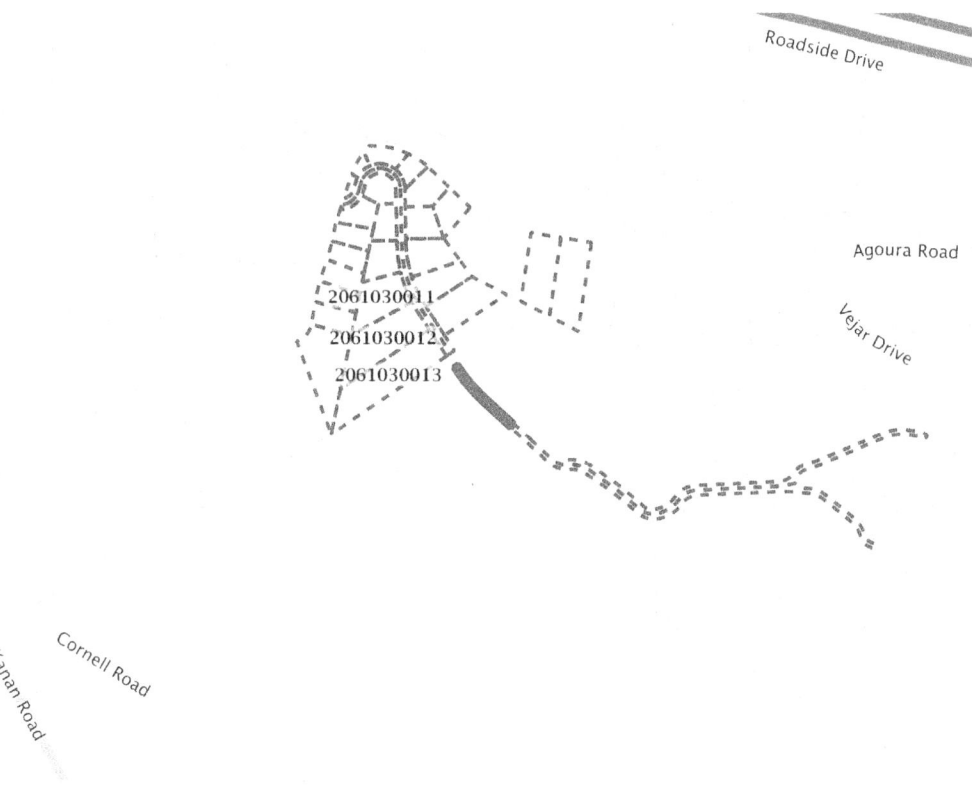

Figure 2.203: Property 67, AIN 2061030019, neighborhood view

Figure 2.204: Property 67, AIN 2061030019, detailed view

2.69 Auction ID 5137

The Los Angeles County Auction Book describes the property as follows.

```
VAC ST ADJ LOT 13 TRACT NO 7661 ON W ASSESSED TO 0 HALZLE,CORWIN J
LOCATION CITY-AGOURA HILL PROPERTY ADDRESS: VACANT LOT
```

The property is located in the general vicinity of Figure 2.205. It is identified by Assessor's Identification Number (AIN) 2061025045. The starting bid is $2,621. Comparable improved properties in this area is about $297/sqft. Comparable unimproved lots in this area is about $45/sqft. This parcel is approximately 2523 sqft. Note, however, that the parcel may be larger than the property under consideration. In case of condominiums, for example, the parcel may encompass other units of the development - those unrelated to the property to be auctioned.

The property is in a parcel zoned Single Family-Residential in Agoura Hills, for 2 to 6 dwelling units.

Figures 2.206 and 2.207 show street map and corresponding detailed aerial view, respectively. In both cases, the map is centered on the property with the containing parcel marked in heavy blue. If surrounding nearby properties are also part of this auction, the street and aerial maps highlights these in heavy, dashed blue outline.

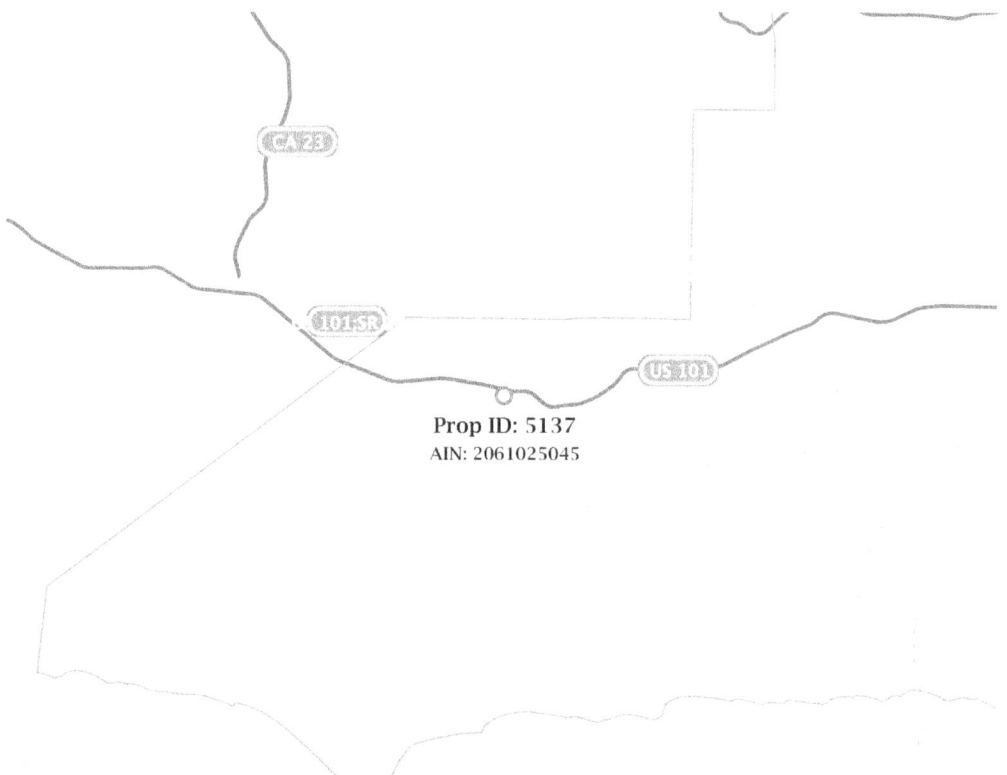

Figure 2.205: Property 5137, AIN 2061025045, overview map

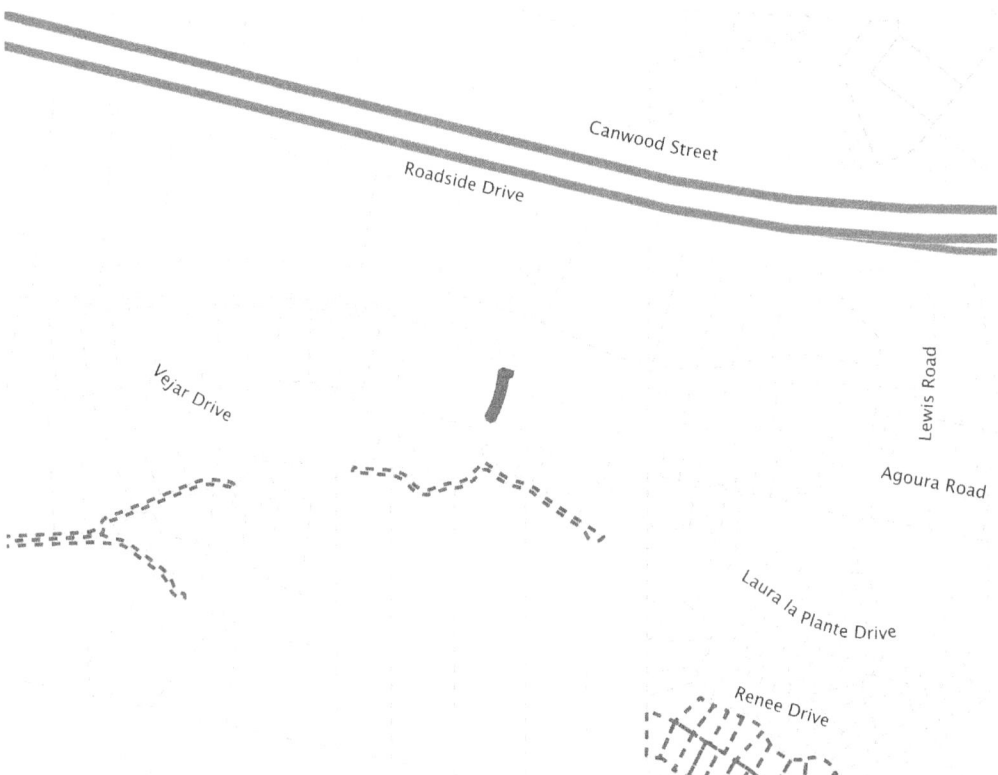

Figure 2.206: Property 5137, AIN 2061025045, neighborhood view

Figure 2.207: Property 5137, AIN 2061025045, detailed view

Calabasas

A total of 5 properties are listed for auction in the Calabasas community. Table 3.1 lists the improved properties by lowest starting bid; Table 3.2 show the non-improved properties in the same fashion. In both cases, estimated comparable pricing is indicated as well.

Table 3.3 presents the properties in Calabasas ordered by auction ID.

Table 3.1: Improved properties for auction in Calabasas sorted by starting bid price

PROPERTY ID	AIN	STARTING BID	COMPARABLE FINISHED $/SQFT	COMPARABLE LOT $/SQFT	PROPERTY DETAILS
2382	4455057051	$85,016	$371	$130	See page 310

Table 3.2: Non-improved properties for auction in Calabasas sorted by starting bid price

PROPERTY ID	AIN	STARTING BID	COMPARABLE FINISHED $/SQFT	COMPARABLE LOT $/SQFT	PROPERTY DETAILS
2410	4464013028	$6,149	No information	No information	See page 314
111	2080027025	$8,238	$337	$76	See page 306
2407	4462016018	$11,150	No information	No information	See page 312
2380	4455018010	$88,818	$409	$13	See page 308

Table 3.3: Properties for auction in Calabasas sorted by auction property ID

AUCTION ID	AIN	STARTING BID	PROPERTY DETAILS
111	2080027025	$8,238	See page 306
2380	4455018010	$88,818	See page 308
2382	4455057051	$85,016	See page 310
2407	4462016018	$11,150	See page 312
2410	4464013028	$6,149	See page 314

3.1   Auction ID 111

The Los Angeles County Auction Book describes the property as follows.

```
TR=40932 THAT POR INTRA 10900 OF LOT 32 ASSESSED TO 0 LANDECKER,RONALD
S AND MARTHA J LOCATION CITY-CALABASAS T PROPERTY ADDRESS: VACANT
LOT
```

The property is located in the general vicinity of Figure 3.1. It is identified by Assessor's Identification Number (AIN) 2080027025. The starting bid is $8,238. Comparable improved properties in this area is about $337/sqft. Comparable unimproved lots in this area is about $76/sqft. This parcel is approximately 6277 sqft. Note, however, that the parcel may be larger than the property under consideration. In case of condominiums, for example, the parcel may encompass other units of the development - those unrelated to the property to be auctioned.

The property is in a parcel zoned RS in Calabasas, for 2 to 6 dwelling units.

Figures 3.2 and 3.3 show street map and corresponding detailed aerial view, respectively. In both cases, the map is centered on the property with the containing parcel marked in heavy blue. If surrounding nearby properties are also part of this auction, the street and aerial maps highlights these in heavy, dashed blue outline.

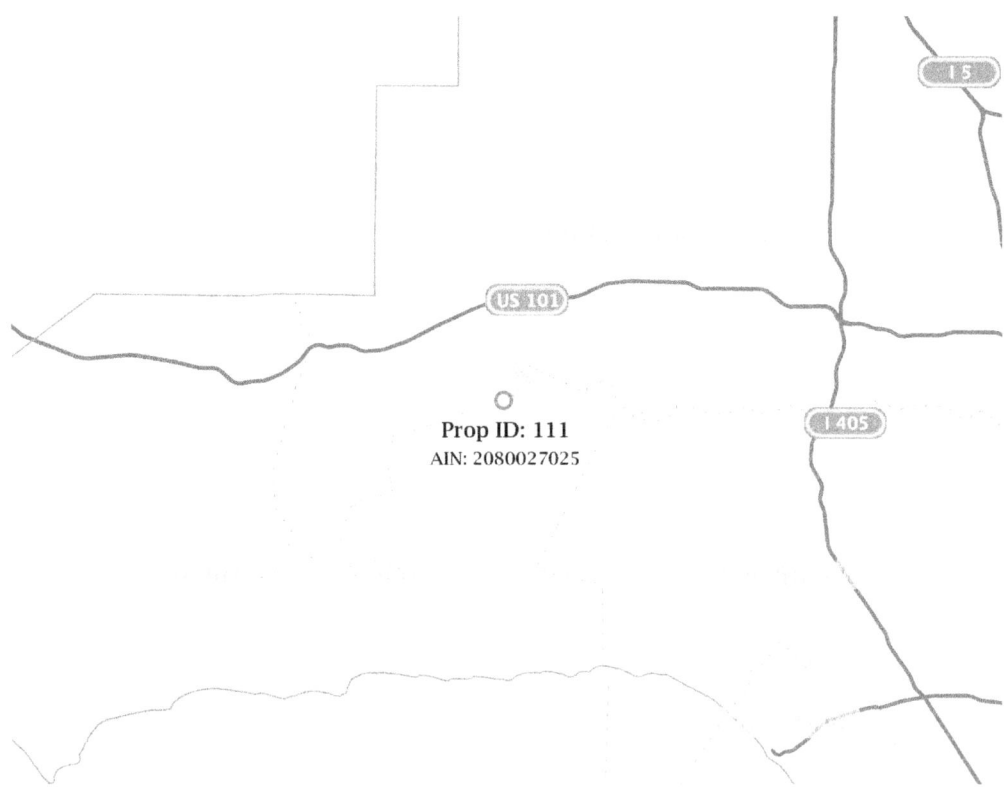

Figure 3.1: Property 111, AIN 2080027025, overview map

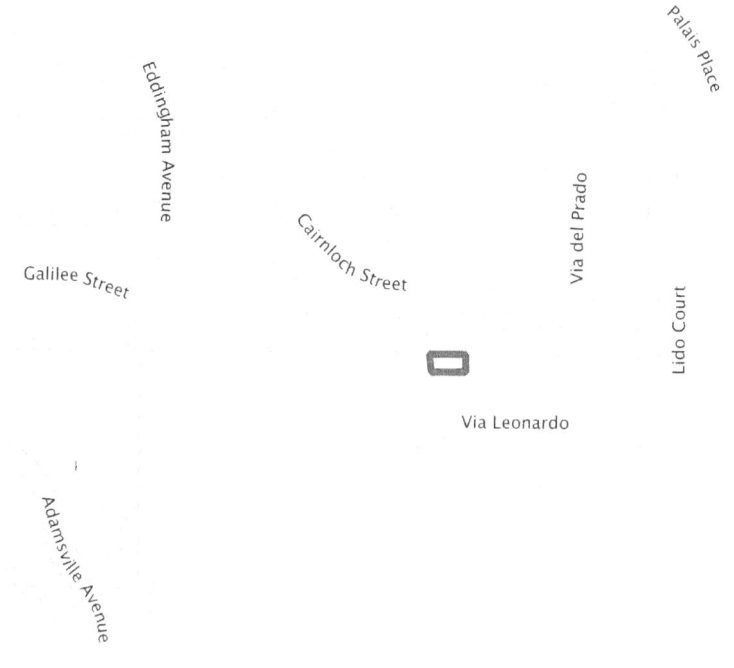

Figure 3.2: Property 111, AIN 2080027025, neighborhood view

Figure 3.3: Property 111, AIN 2080027025, detailed view

3.2   Auction ID 2380

The Los Angeles County Auction Book describes the property as follows.

```
MORE OR LESS ACS COM SW ON NW LINE OF MULHOLLAND O HWY PER CSB2336-2
378 FT AND N 27*04'24" E 127.7 FT FROM INTER- SECTION OF SD NW LINE
WITH A LINE PARALLEL WITH AND DIST W AT R/A 405 FT FROM E LINE OF
S 1/2 OF NW 1/4 OF SEC 9 T 1S R 17W TH S 78*37' 05" W 198 FT TH N
11*19'50" W 90 FT TH S 77*53'01" W TO SE LINE OF COLD CANYON RD TH
NE ON SD SE LINE TO N LINE OF SD S 1/2 OF NW 1/4 TH E THEREON TO SW
LINE OF SD COLD CANYON RD TH SE THEREON TO A PT N 27*04' 24" E FROM
BEG TH S 27*04'24" W TO BEG PART OF S 1/2 OF NW 1/4 OF LOT 9 DIV 1
REG 17 ASSESSED TO CANDOFF,LUCKI R AND JENNIFER LOCATION COUNTY OF
LOS ANGELES PROPERTY ADDRESS: VACANT LOT
```

The property is located in the general vicinity of Figure 3.4. It is identified by Assessor's Identification Number (AIN) 4455018010. The starting bid is $88,818. Comparable improved properties in this area is about $409/sqft. Comparable unimproved lots in this area is about $13/sqft. This parcel is approximately 77644 sqft. Note, however, that the parcel may be larger than the property under consideration. In case of condominiums, for example, the parcel may encompass other units of the development - those unrelated to the property to be auctioned.

The property is in a parcel zoned A-1-1 in Unincorporated Las Virge*, for 0 to 0 dwelling units.

Figures 3.5 and 3.6 show street map and corresponding detailed aerial view, respectively. In both cases, the map is centered on the property with the containing parcel marked in heavy blue. If surrounding nearby properties are also part of this auction, the street and aerial maps highlights these in heavy, dashed blue outline.

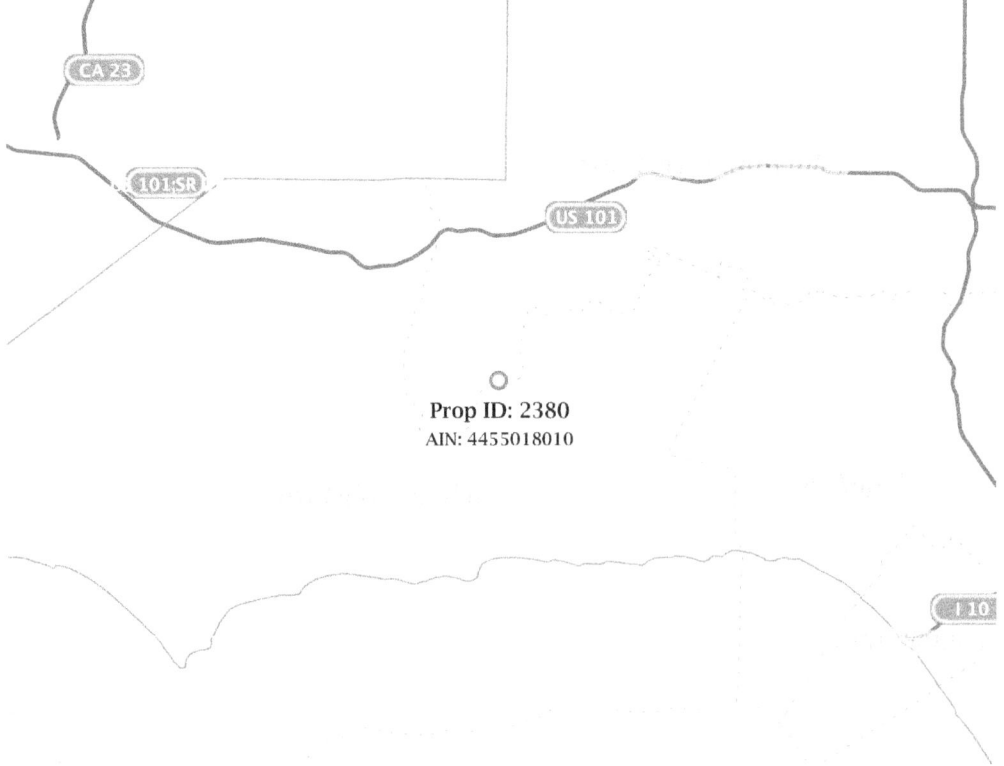

Figure 3.4: Property 2380, AIN 4455018010, overview map

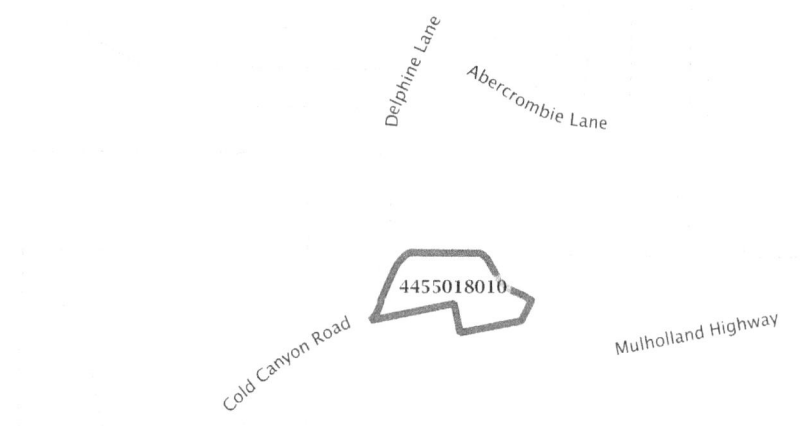

Figure 3.5: Property 2380, AIN 4455018010, neighborhood view

Figure 3.6: Property 2380, AIN 4455018010, detailed view

3.3   Auction ID 2382

The Los Angeles County Auction Book describes the property as follows.

```
TR=49594 LOT 21 ASSESSED TO KAPLAN,STEVEN AND O KIMBERLY TRS BABY
BIRD TRUST LOCATION CITY-CALABASAS T PROPERTY ADDRESS: 3339 PASEO
DEL SOL CALABASAS CA 91302-3013
```

The property is located in the general vicinity of Figure 3.7. It is identified by Assessor's Identification Number (AIN) 4455057051. The starting bid is \$85,016. Comparable improved properties in this area is about \$371/sqft. Comparable unimproved lots in this area is about \$130/sqft. This parcel is approximately 14887 sqft. Note, however, that the parcel may be larger than the property under consideration. In case of condominiums, for example, the parcel may encompass other units of the development - those unrelated to the property to be auctioned.

The property is in a parcel zoned RS in Calabasas, for 2 to 6 dwelling units.

Figures 3.8 and 3.9 show street map and corresponding detailed aerial view, respectively. In both cases, the map is centered on the property with the containing parcel marked in heavy blue. If surrounding nearby properties are also part of this auction, the street and aerial maps highlights these in heavy, dashed blue outline.

A parcel may encompass multiple street addresses. The following address(es) are at this parcel:

- 3339 PASEO DEL SOL , 91302

Figure 3.7: Property 2382, AIN 4455057051, overview map

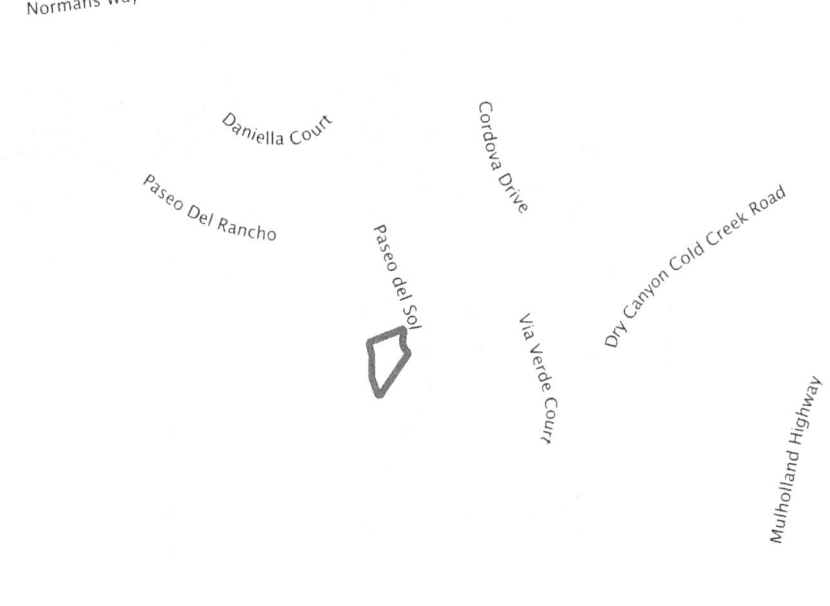

Figure 3.8: Property 2382, AIN 4455057051, neighborhood view

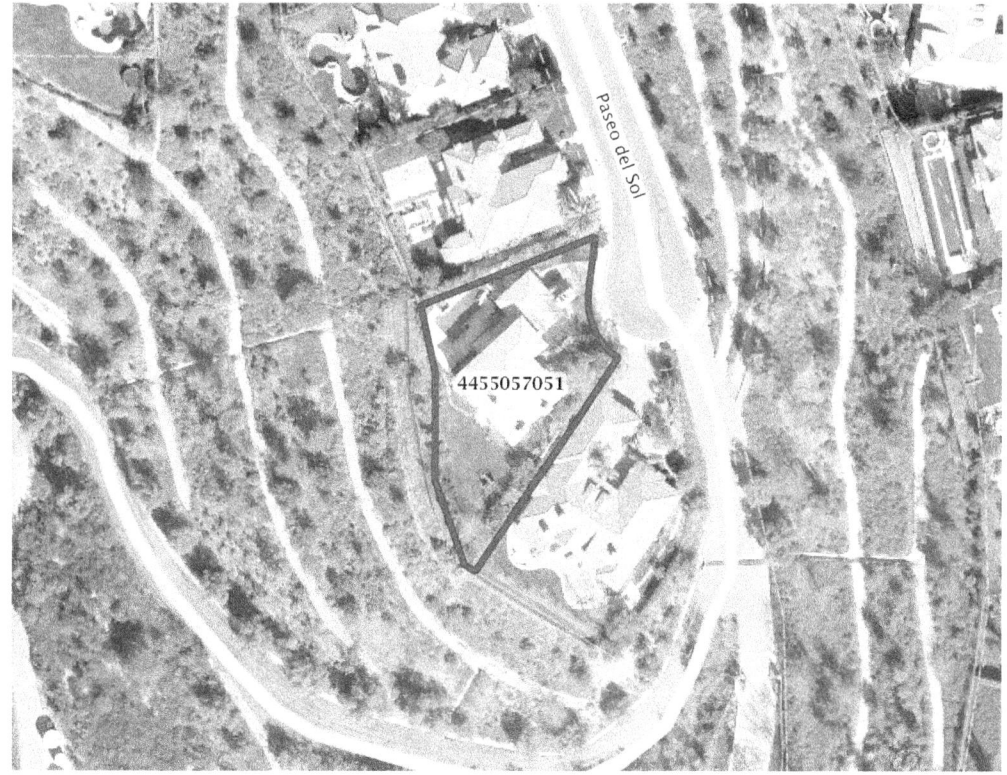

Figure 3.9: Property 2382, AIN 4455057051, detailed view

3.4   Auction ID 2407

The Los Angeles County Auction Book describes the property as follows.

> TRACT # 8228 LOT 130 ASSESSED TO TRAVIS,CINDY O LOCATION COUNTY OF
> LOS ANGELES PROPERTY ADDRESS: VACANT LOT

The property is located in the general vicinity of Figure 3.10. It is identified by Assessor's Identification Number (AIN) 4462016018. The starting bid is $11,150. No improved property comparable price information is available for this property. No comparable price information is available for nearby unimproved lots. This parcel is approximately 6416 sqft. Note, however, that the parcel may be larger than the property under consideration. In case of condominiums, for example, the parcel may encompass other units of the development - those unrelated to the property to be auctioned.

The property is in a parcel zoned R-1-1 in Unincorporated Las Virge*, for 0 to 0 dwelling units.

Figures 3.11 and 3.12 show street map and corresponding detailed aerial view, respectively. In both cases, the map is centered on the property with the containing parcel marked in heavy blue. If surrounding nearby properties are also part of this auction, the street and aerial maps highlights these in heavy, dashed blue outline.

A parcel may encompass multiple street addresses. The following address(es) are at this parcel:

- 1906 LOOKOUT DRIVE , 91301

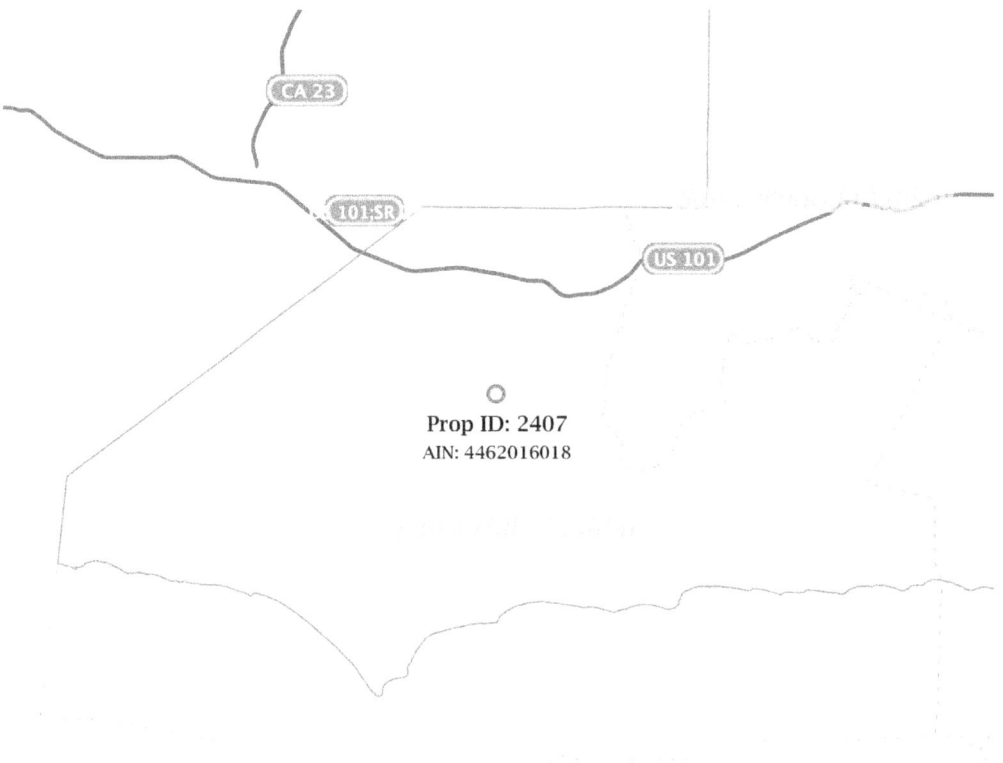

Figure 3.10: Property 2407, AIN 4462016018, overview map

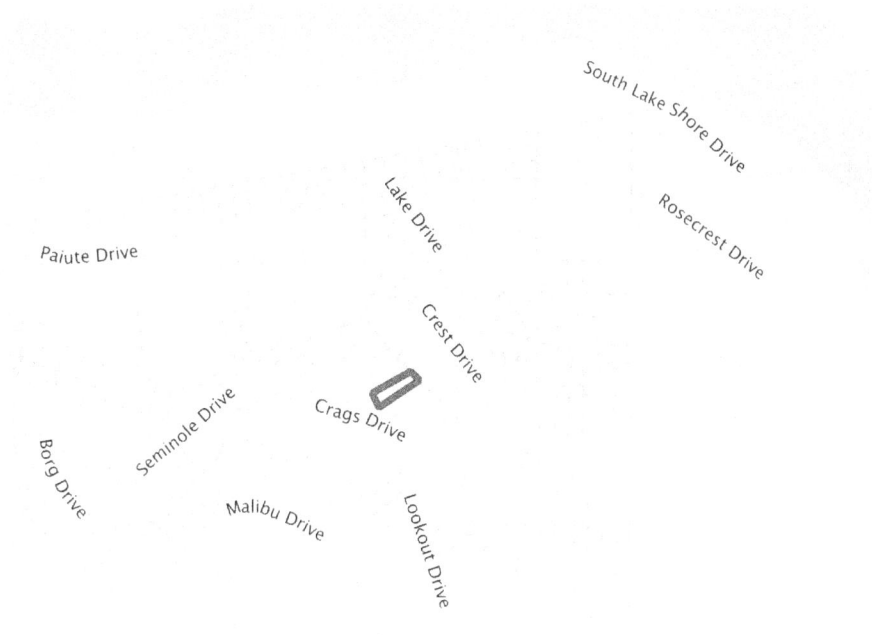

Figure 3.11: Property 2407, AIN 4462016018, neighborhood view

Figure 3.12: Property 2407, AIN 4462016018, detailed view

3.5   Auction ID 2410

The Los Angeles County Auction Book describes the property as follows.

```
TR=10596 FOR DESC SEE ASSESSOR'S MAPS POR OF LOTS 35 0 AND 36 ASSESSED
TO JORDANOU,MARIE H LOCATION COUNTY OF LOS ANGELES PROPERTY ADDRESS:
VACANT LOT
```

The property is located in the general vicinity of Figure 3.13. It is identified by Assessor's Identification Number (AIN) 4464013028. The starting bid is $6,149. No improved property comparable price information is available for this property. No comparable price information is available for nearby unimproved lots. This parcel is approximately 8980 sqft. Note, however, that the parcel may be larger than the property under consideration. In case of condominiums, for example, the parcel may encompass other units of the development - those unrelated to the property to be auctioned.

The property is in a parcel zoned A-1-5 in Unincorporated Las Virge*, for 0 to 0 dwelling units.

Figures 3.14 and 3.15 show street map and corresponding detailed aerial view, respectively. In both cases, the map is centered on the property with the containing parcel marked in heavy blue. If surrounding nearby properties are also part of this auction, the street and aerial maps highlights these in heavy, dashed blue outline.

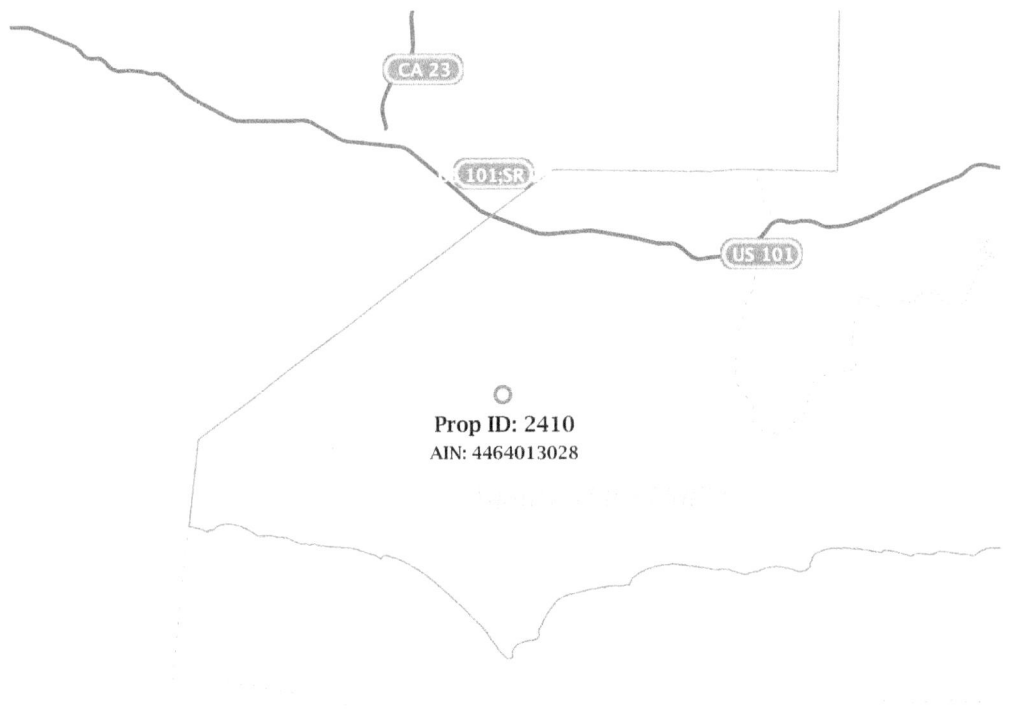

Figure 3.13: Property 2410, AIN 4464013028, overview map

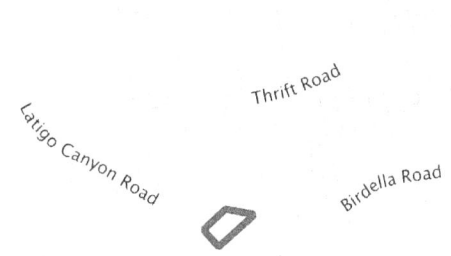

Figure 3.14: Property 2410, AIN 4464013028, neighborhood view

Figure 3.15: Property 2410, AIN 4464013028, detailed view

www.ingramcontent.com/pod-product-compliance
Lightning Source LLC
Chambersburg PA
CBHW081431170526
45166CB00008B/2171